CHILD PSYCHOLOGY

BY

ARTHUR T. JERSILD, Ph.D.

PROFESSOR OF EDUCATION
TEACHERS COLLEGE, COLUMBIA UNIVERSITY

THIRD EDITION

New York
PRENTICE-HALL, INC.

PRENTICE-HALL PSYCHOLOGY SERIES

Copyright, 1933, 1940, 1947, by
PRENTICE-HALL, INC.
70 Fifth Avenue, New York

ALL RIGHTS RESERVED. NO PART OF THIS BOOK MAY BE REPRODUCED IN ANY FORM, BY MIMEOGRAPH OR ANY OTHER MEANS, WITHOUT PERMISSION IN WRITING FROM THE PUBLISHERS.

Third Edition

First printing .... June, 1947
Second printing .... November, 1947
Third printing .... September, 1948
Fourth printing .... March, 1949
Fifth printing .... January, 1950

PRINTED IN THE UNITED STATES OF AMERICA

TO C. L. J.

PREFACE TO THE THIRD EDITION

In this edition I have tried to bring the 1940 version up to date, and I have tried also to remedy certain shortcomings in the old text while preserving qualities that were well received.

The present text takes more adequate account of the interplay between forces in the growing organism and the impact of various aspects of development upon each other. The present edition also draws more attention than did its predecessor to the question as to what a child's overt behavior reveals about his private thoughts and feelings. More consideration is also given to the influence of the cultural environment and the attitudes of others on a child's behavior and adjustment.

More prominence has been given to principles and generalizations, but in this edition, as in the preceding ones, I have cited freely from the research literature in presenting generalizations as well as supporting details. As I mentioned in the preface to the second edition, I do not assume that the students will be required necessarily to memorize the authorship of each bit of evidence that is reported.

The formal organization of the book, although changed in some ways, is much the same as before. As in the earlier editions, the order in which some of the chapters appear is somewhat arbitrary, and it will be feasible, if so desired, to modify this order in reading or assigning the various chapters.

Acknowledgment is due to the psychologists upon whose published works I have drawn, to teachers and parents who have lent me some of their wisdom, to children whom I have had the privilege of knowing and who have responded so generously in connection with my own investigations, and to my son and daughters who have held out to me more knowledge than I have had the capacity to receive. I am deeply indebted to Mrs. Margaret F.

PREFACE TO THE THIRD EDITION

Meigs for help in all the operations connected with the writing of this book, to Dr. Charlotte Del Solar for criticizing portions of the book, to Mrs. Elizabeth Penn for help with the bibliographies, and to Mrs. Muriel M. Dalton for bringing her mind as well as her fingers to bear on the manuscript. I am most grateful to my wife who has shared the author's labor pains for the third time in connection with this book.

A. T. J.

CONTENTS

CHAPTER		PAGE
I.	BEGINNINGS OF BEHAVIOR	1
	The First Great Hurdle	1
	The World Surrounding the Newborn Child	2
	Early Behavior Manifestations	4
	Direction of Early Development	5
	Activity before Birth	6
	Organization of Behavior	7
	Behavior at Birth	10
	Special Senses	13
	Differences in Degree of Maturity at Birth	16
	The Emotions of the Newborn Child	19
	The Beginnings of "Personality"	25
	Learning during the First Days and Weeks of Life	27
II.	SOME GENERAL CHARACTERISTICS OF DEVELOPMENT	39
	Development as a Product of Learning and Growth	39
	Growth Factors in Establishment of Basic Coördinations	41
	Experimental Studies of Effects of Training in Relation to Maturity	43
	Nature or Quality of Learning in Relation to Maturity Level	46
	Varying Timeliness in Relation to Maturity	48
	Other Principles of Development	50
III.	SOME ASPECTS OF LIVING AND LEARNING IN INFANCY AND EARLY CHILDHOOD	60
	Feeding and Behavior Associated with Feeding	61
	Spontaneous Food Demands	66
	Self-Help in Eating	73
	Food Preferences	76
	"Feeding Problems"	77
	Sleeping	80
	Elimination	88

CONTENTS

CHAPTER		PAGE
IV.	**MOTOR DEVELOPMENT**	101
	Trends in Physical Growth	101
	Locomotion	102
	Impact of Walking	104
	Use of Arms, Hands, and Fingers	104
	Later Features of Motor Development	108
	Interrelations in Motor Development	116
	Relation of Physical and Mental Ability	120
	Handedness	121
V.	**DEVELOPMENT OF SOCIAL BEHAVIOR**	131
	Sequences in Social Behavior	132
	Later Trends in Group Behavior	137
	Resistant Behavior	141
	Children's Fights and Quarrels	146
	Sympathy	157
	Competition and Coöperation	160
VI.	**DEVELOPMENT OF SOCIAL BEHAVIOR (*Continued*)**	173
	Children's Friendships	173
	Factors in Friendship and Choices of Companions among Older Children	175
	Popularity	176
	Leadership	182
	The Desire to Belong	185
	Social Hierarchies	188
	Boy-Girl Relationships	189
	The Impact of Adult Social Stratification on the Child	192
	Effects of Nursery School Experience	198
	Influence of Skills on Social Behavior and Adjustment	204
	Influence of Play Equipment and Adult Patterns of Behavior	208
	Influence of Adult Direction and Management	209
VII.	**FEELING AND EMOTION**	225
	Early Emotional Reactions	225
	The Role of Needs, Drives, Motives, Goals	226
	Developmental Changes in Susceptibility to Emotion	230
	Affection	231
	Pleasure and Boredom in Child Life	240
	Sympathy	244
	Crying, Laughter, and Humor	245
	Sex	251

CONTENTS

CHAPTER		PAGE
VIII.	FEELING AND EMOTION (*Continued*)	260
	Fear	260
	The Role of Maturation	261
	The Role of Learning	263
	Changes with Age in the Expression of Fear	263
	Age Trends	266
	Children's Fears as Compared with "Worst Happenings"	272
	Persisting Fears	273
	Factors Contributing to Susceptibility to Fear	275
	Values of Fear	278
	Overcoming Fear	279
	Anger, Hostility, and Aggressive Behavior	287
	The Prevention of Anger	297
	Jealousy	302
	Other Emotional Aspects of Parent-Child Relationships	309
IX.	LANGUAGE DEVELOPMENT	321
	Early Vocalizations	321
	Later Language Development	330
	Mental and Social Orientation of the Young Child as Revealed by His Language	333
	Factors in the Development and Acquisition of Language	336
	Academic Aspects of Language Development	343
X.	THE GROWTH OF UNDERSTANDING	349
	Early Mental Development	349
	Signs of Increasing Awareness and Alertness	349
	Memory	351
	Perception	355
	Capacity for Attention and Concentration	357
	Children's Questions	360
XI.	GROWTH OF UNDERSTANDING (*Continued*)	371
	Mental Development in Later Childhood	371
	Expansion of Intellectual Horizons	372
	Children's Reasoning	379
	Children's Information and Concepts	389
	Cultural Influences on the Learning of Concepts	409
	Emotional and Intellectual Elements in Children's Thinking	410

CHAPTER		PAGE
XII.	CHILDREN'S MAKE-BELIEVE, DREAMS, AND OTHER IMAGINATIVE ACTIVITIES	417
	Early Manifestations	417
	Functions of Make-Believe	419
	Functions of Make-Believe in Social Development	424
	Daydreams and Fantasies	427
	Imaginary Companions	429
	Other Forms of Vivid Imagery and Association of Images	432
	Children's Dreams	432
	Projective Methods	437
XIII.	CHILDREN'S IDEALS, MORALS, AND RELIGION	443
	Factors in the Moral Training of Children	443
	Honesty	451
	Generosity	454
	Children's Heroes and Ideals	456
	Religion	459
	Altruism	466
	Prejudices	467
XIV.	CHILDREN'S INTERESTS	475
	Disparity between Expressed and Potential Interests	476
	Limiting Factors in Children's Interests	478
	Interest as Related to Skill	479
	Areas of Interest	479
	Children's Preferences in Games	480
	Reading Interests	490
	Radio Interests	496
	Motion-Picture Interests	505
	Comics	508
	Interests and Incentives as Related to Learning	511
XV.	THE GROWTH AND PREDICTION OF INTELLIGENCE	521
	Limits of Intellectual Growth	536
	The Influence of Nature and Nurture on Individual Differences in Mental Ability	538
	Effect of Schooling on Intellectual Development	545
	Gifted Children	555
	Mental Deficiency	561
	Family and Socio-Economic Status and Intelligence	564

CHAPTER		PAGE
XVI.	PERSONALITY AND PROBLEMS OF ADJUSTMENT	575
	Approaches to the Study of Personality	575
	"External" Aspects of Personality	576
	"Internal" Aspects of Personality	577
	Consistency and Change	580
	Impact of the Environment	584
	Problems of Adjustment	591
	AUTHOR INDEX	607
	SUBJECT INDEX	617

Chapter I

BEGINNINGS OF BEHAVIOR

Birth means the coming of a new human being who only forty weeks earlier consisted of a single cell. He looks helpless, yet he is capable of the processes necessary for maintaining life. Many of his movements are aimless and undefined, but changes in his behavior come rapidly, even within the first few hours. In the near future his movements will be fashioned into countless skills; he will master the intricacies of language; his mental world will include memories of the past and plans for the future; as a social creature he will be deeply involved in the fortunes of his fellows. Increasingly the characteristics that mark him as a distinct and unique personality will be established.

The contrast between the infant's limitations at birth and his characteristics within only a few months thereafter is striking. But quite as spectacular are the developments shown at birth by the child who forty weeks earlier was a single-celled organism. The following discussion will deal with some of the characteristics of the child before he is born and during the first few days of life.

THE FIRST GREAT HURDLE

Much as we should like to, we cannot peer into the mental life of the newborn child. We can only guess at what his experience of the world might be by watching how he behaves. Although there is a high degree of continuity between development before and after birth, the event of being born obviously calls for many new adjustments. During prenatal life, the infant received nourishment through the umbilical cord; now he must suck and swallow. Before he was born he did not even have to breathe; now he must depend upon his own equipment for respiration as well as for the regulation of bodily temperature and the elimination of waste. He now is exposed to countless lights and sounds and contacts, whereas earlier he was insulated from the outside world.

No episode in the life span represents a more drastic change than that of being delivered from the womb into the world of men. If an infant were sensitive to all that this change involves, the business of being born would be quite an ordeal. It has been conjectured that the birth process may be so overwhelming to the child that it can produce a profound "psychic" injury. It has also been conjectured that there may persist, long after, an unconscious desire to return to the peace and protection of the mother's womb. It goes without saying that such claims must be taken with a good deal of salt. The person who is being born is, after all, not an imaginative and sensitive adult but an immature child, with an immature nervous system and with immature capacities for sensing and feeling.

THE WORLD SURROUNDING THE NEWBORN CHILD

The event of birth does not mean simply that a new bundle of life in human form has arrived. Back of the child are his ancestors. The roots of his inheritance extend into past generations. What we now see, and much that we cannot foresee in his later development, are determined by his heredity. Within the child himself resides also a powerful impulse to grow. Surrounding him are the forces of the culture into which he has been born and the immediate environment in which he is to live. From the moment of his coming this environment will influence the shaping of his habits and the molding of his character.

In the environment that surrounds him is much that is obvious to the eye but also much that cannot be seen. There is the visible cradle in which he lies. There is also an invisible environment consisting of the thoughts and feelings, the attitudes, desires, hopes, and expectations of members of his family. If all is well, this composite of thoughts and feelings will offer the child a comfortable berth. His mother will be drawn to him with feelings of pride in her role as one who has brought forth a child, and she will feel a strong impulse to protect him. His father will be drawn to him with sentiments that no man can know until he has had the experience of being a father. Also, if all is well, older brothers and sisters will be prepared to welcome him, even though they may be somewhat disturbed by the events surrounding his birth and perplexed as to what it will mean in their own lives to have a new member in the household.

On the other hand, this environment may not be so hospitable. For one cause or another, the child may be unwanted by one or both parents. He may come as an intruder in the relations between his father and mother or in the relations between his parents and other children in the family. He may be born into a whirlpool of conflicting emotions. If so, the impact of such conflicting emotions will sooner or later be felt in his own life.

The attitudes of his elders may quickly be translated into practical acts. These attitudes may determine whether they adopt, for example, a policy of picking him up when he frets and cries or of leaving him to "cry it out" for long periods at a time.

Apart from the question as to whether the child's coming is completely welcome or viewed with some misgivings, there will be tremendous variations between one family situation and another in the feelings and motives that come into play. The child may be accepted for what he is, for his own sake, or he may serve an ulterior purpose, such as gratifying parental ambition, or serving as a means of continuing the family name, or fulfilling a sense of duty, and the like. Again, there will be wide differences even between adoring mothers. Simply in the practical details of everyday care of the child, one mother may be motherly, self-assured, another may be uncertain of her own skills and judgment; one may handle the youngster in a relaxed and smooth way, another may be more tense and abrupt.

Although there are differences such as the foregoing, and countless others, in the setting into which the child is born, the child is not entirely at the mercy of conditions as they are. From the beginning he is not merely a creature of his environment; he helps to create his environment. In his very weakness there is strength, for his helplessness draws others to him. Through his appearance and all his ways he commands attention, makes impressions, and, without so intending, influences the attitudes of his elders whatever they may have thought or felt beforehand. So, a father who was secretly convinced that he could not love a second child as much as the first may discover that it is quite a different story when the new youngster begins to put in his licks. A woman who vowed that she could never become "crazy" about a baby may find when the baby comes that he has completely taken her over. The tide may, of course, run in the other direction if a parent has nurtured a glorified image of a baby-to-be and then finds that the real baby is quite somebody else, or if the parents have looked forward to the child's coming through a haze of sentimentality and are not ready to make all the practical readjustments that the presence of a new baby demands.

EARLY BEHAVIOR MANIFESTATIONS

Behavior begins long before the child is born, well in advance of the time when the mother first detects movements of the child at about four and a half months after conception. By the end of the second month of fetal life the child can be recognized as human in form. Well before this, bodily activity has begun.[1] By the end of the third week the heart has begun to beat. By the end of the twenty-fifth week the child "is equipped with practically all the activities basic to postnatal existence, though most, if not all, require further maturation" (29, p. 27).

Movements involving muscles other than those of the internal organs also appear quite early in the life of the fetus. In a study by Hooker (29) it was observed that a fetus at about eight and a

---
[1] For a review of studies dealing with fetal behavior see L. Carmichael (12).

half weeks reacted when stroked with a hair in the region of the mouth.

During the third month of fetal life, and increasingly thereafter, responses that involve the transmission of nerve impulses from one part of the body to another have been observed.

The developments that take place before birth illustrate strikingly what might be called "the forehandedness of development." The capacity for many functions is established well in advance of the time when normally there is a need to use these functions. The mechanisms for sucking and for breathing, for example, are relatively well developed several months before a full-term baby would be called upon to suck or to breathe. One result of this forehandedness is that even though babies normally are born about 280 days after conception, it is possible for a child to survive after having spent only about 180 days in the mother's body. Claims have even been made that younger fetuses have survived.

This tendency to anticipate future activities and future needs appears also in developments that occur after birth.

DIRECTION OF EARLY DEVELOPMENT

It has been noted that development before birth tends to proceed in a *cephalo-caudal* direction (60)—that is, growth and differentiation progress from the head to the tail region. During the earlier stages of growth, development in the head region is far in advance of development in the posterior part of the body. This does not mean, of course, that development is complete at one end before it begins at the other. Illustrating this trend in development on the physical side is the fact that the head is well developed before the legs assume their final form and that the arms are budding before leg buds appear. Analogous to this, after the child is born, is the fact that a child can make good use of his arms and hands in reaching and grasping before he can use his legs in standing and walking.

In the development of segments of the body, there is a parallel to this cephalo-caudal trend in the body as a whole. Development is in a *proximo-distal* direction: the structures that lie nearest the main axis of the body mature earlier than those that are more remote. Again, after birth, we see a behavior trend analogous to this in the fact, for example, that control of gross movements of the arm and forearm comes earlier than control of the wrist and fingers.

ACTIVITY BEFORE BIRTH

Activity of the unborn child rises to a peak at about the eighth to the ninth month (59). Much of the movement of the unborn child seems to be in response to internal conditions, but it is possible also sometimes to provoke movement by external means. One observer noted, for example, that a kick and other movements were exhibited by a child thirty-one days before birth when the sides of the bathtub in which the mother was lying were struck with a metal rod (19). During late stages of pregnancy, mothers have also reported that a musical concert may lead to increased fetal activity.

In one study (71, 72), apparatus consisting of rubber sacs was attached to the mother's abdomen and connected with tambours that activated recording pens. Various sounds—such as those made by a bell, a buzzer, and a wooden knocker with a sound block placed over the location of the fetal head—were produced. Response to stimulation of this sort was noted (that is, movement in excess of what normally occurred) at about the thirty-first week of intra-uterine life.

Conditions in the daily life of the mother may likewise precipitate greater than normal amounts of fetal activity (70). In the case of two mothers, for example, more fetal movement occurred during periods of severe emotion than during moments of calm. Many mothers who were questioned reported that they experienced more feeling of fetal activity when they were fatigued than when they were rested (although, as is pointed out in the study, this may be due to greater sensitivity on the mother's part). Changes were also noted in the fetal heart rate. In some instances, the rate was found to be higher after the mother had climbed a flight of stairs than some minutes later, and higher after she had smoked a cigarette than just before or some time later; however, such an increase did not appear in all cases, and there were large individual variations.[2]

Individual differences in amount of fetal activity and in the changes in activity occur as pregnancy advances. The fact that fetal movements have been found to vary under different circumstances and that they perhaps may be influenced, to some extent, both by the general condition of the mother and by the mother's response to external stimuli, opens quite a field for speculation and research concerning the possible influence of the prenatal environment on the later behavior and personality of the child. In view of all the factors that influence behavior before and after birth, and in view of the protection with which nature surrounds the unborn child, it no doubt would be difficult to find conclusive evidence in such a line of study.

In an investigation of twelve infants who were under observation both before and after birth, preliminary findings (58) suggested that the amount of activity exhibited by the child before he is born might foreshadow, to some degree, the rate of his development as compared with that of other children during the first few months of postnatal life. However, the likelihood that the amount of prenatal activity might give a prediction of later rate of growth was not borne out by further study (57), (47).

ORGANIZATION OF BEHAVIOR

Apart from the question as to the observable characteristics of the behavior of the child at birth, there is the question as to the process or sequence through which the behavior comes into being

---

[2] Studies have also been made to find whether the unborn child is able to "learn" (54, 71), but results have been inconclusive.

and the general nature of the process by which new forms of behavior emerge as development goes on after birth.

In theory, we might assume that organized behavior takes form through the knitting together of separate movements and bits of behavior through a process of combining parts into larger wholes. As against this, we might assume that the course is precisely the opposite: that activities involving the entire organism come first and that it is only in the further course of development that behavior limited to any segment or separate group of muscles appears. On this assumption, development proceeds from the whole to the part, rather than from part to whole.

Actually, as we shall see, the development of behavior takes both courses.

Discussions of this subject have been based in large part upon observations of the development of behavior in lower animals because of the practical difficulties involved in obtaining systematic observations of human beings at various known stages of prenatal growth. On the basis of observations of *amblystoma* (a salamander), Coghill (15), (16) several years ago took issue with the notion that behavior represents a knitting together of many independent movements. Rather, he maintained, reactions of the total organism precede separate movements of parts of the body. The primary state is one of integration, and partial movements become individuated out of this preceding total. Swimming movements in the salamander begin, for example, before mobile limbs and appendages have developed. As development proceeds, the gills can be observed to move, then the forelimbs, then the hind limbs; but these appendages are not, at the start, capable of independent movement. Movements of the individual limbs are tied in with, and are an integral feature of, movement of the body as a whole before separate or independent movements of the limbs are possible.

In like manner, Coghill describes the first visual responses of *amblystoma* as total reactions, involving coördination of various parts of the body in one integrated movement. As an object moves from left to right through the animal's field of vision, the animal does not sit like a sphinx with roving eyes that can follow the object while the rest of the body stays put. Instead, the whole organism of the young salamander, according to Coghill's account, participates in the act. As the object moves toward the right, there is flexion of the trunk to the right, movements of head and eyes, of upper and lower limbs, all integral features of this larger activity. It is not until a later stage of development that these parts can move more or less independently.

Coghill implies that these and similar observations of the salamander and other lower animals (16) hold true for animals in general as well as for man. On this point, however, investigators do not agree. In experiments by Carmichael and others with the fetuses of mammals, it has not been found that all observed movements conform to the concept of a gradually expanding total pattern, completely integrated from the beginning (9, 12, 13, 77, 78). While a process of individuation of specific movements out of previously larger activities accounts for much that occurs in the development of behavior, a full description would have to go many steps further (12).[3] Various activities are differentiated at different times. Different aspects of development proceed at different rates. New relationships between some specific responses are established before specialization has gone far in other activities.

The full story would also have to take account of the development of behavior as it finally takes form after birth, when various movements and muscle groups are organized in countless ways in the thousand-and-one skills that the child eventually acquires. The development of behavior after birth occurs through both a refinement and increasing specialization of movements that already exist as well as a tying together of movement systems that were not integrated at the start.

---

[3] For an account of changes in activity as related to the prenatal environment, see also Kuo (37).

BEHAVIOR AT BIRTH

Much of the infant's activity is related to the state of his stomach. He requires frequent feedings (10, 25, 55) and, when hunger contractions occur, he is likely to squirm, cry, kick, and thrash, and he cannot easily be diverted by other stimuli.[4]

Generalized movement. Although it is possible to distinguish a large number of more or less clearly defined acts in the flow of the newborn infant's activity, an outstanding characteristic of his early behavior is the occurrence of a vast amount of diffuse and seemingly uncoördinated movement. Such movements (30, 31, 67) may at times, during waking moments, be so rapid and varied that an observer is unable to give a detailed account of them. The infant thrashes about with his arms and legs, and sometimes every part of his body seems to be active at once, with little or no coördination between the various members.

In these activities the infant displays considerably less specialization of movement than will appear in time. Even in connection with apparently simple reflex activities, or in response to external stimuli applied to a limited area of the body, there may be a variety of associated movements in other parts of the body. For example, when an object is brought into contact with the infant's mouth, he is likely to begin to suck; but in response to the same stimulus, he may show many apparently unrelated additional movements in other parts of his body. Some activities may be elicited by happenings that seemingly should have little bearing on the act that is produced. Thus one investigator (34) found that infants made sucking movements when their hair was pulled, when they were dropped, and when someone pinched their big toes.

Other investigators (51) have reported that stimulation of almost any group of receptors by almost any kind of stimulus will lead to a response in almost any part of the organism. But move-

---
[4] For a review of studies dealing with the newborn child, see Pratt (50).

ments are likely to be more generalized in connection with some activities than others. The state of affairs thus described does not mean, however, that the infant's responses are so unorganized that no adaptive movements are possible. Even though a pinch of the toe may produce sucking movements, and even though sucking in response to a stimulus applied to the mouth may be accompanied by movements of the leg, there still is a good deal of method in this seeming madness. Offer the healthy child a nipple when he is hungry and he will do a fine job of sucking, regardless of other activities that may accompany it. Pinch his toe, and his response is likely to be more pronounced in the limb that is pinched than in more remote areas of the body. In other words, even though the child exhibits a great deal of generalized movement, there is a degree of specialization of behavior from the beginning.

It is possible to detect quite a repertory of accomplishments in the general flow of his activity. He sucks, swallows, excretes, defecates, vomits, salivates, hiccoughs, sneezes, yawns, stretches, kicks, waves arms and legs, trembles, shivers, turns his head, grimaces, moves his eyes, blinks, cries, grunts, and sighs. He can meet the world more than halfway in his ability to make his presence known. He exhibits also a large array of additional reflexes.

Reflex action. The term "reflex" has been used to designate an involuntary reaction that is not learned but occurs by virtue of an inborn stimulus-response connection. The term also implies a rather specific and fixed reaction. Actually, however, some responses that are labeled as reflexes are somewhat less fixed and specific when they are first exhibited by the newborn child than they are with the passage of time.[5] Sucking, for example, is a response that is ready for business when the child is born. Even so, as noted above, sucking may be elicited by happenings that have nothing to do with the process of feeding. Moreover, even the act of sucking, as such, changes and becomes more efficient during the days following birth (25). Changes also occur in the plantar re-

---
[5] For a general discussion of studies dealing with this topic, see J. E. Anderson (3).

flex, which may roughly be described as flexion of the toes following scratching or tickling of the soles of the feet (49, 56).

In the course of development some reflex activities wane or are displaced by other forms of behavior. As the child's nervous system matures it becomes possible for him to check or inhibit some reflex actions. One reflex that shows an interesting course is the Moro *Umklammerungs,* or clasping or embrace reflex (21, 45). This reflex may be elicited by striking a sharp blow on the surface on which a child is lying on his back. The infant throws out his arms and then brings them together as if in an embrace. At the same time, the legs are thrown out and then flexed. This reaction was believed by its discoverer to be an atavistic or primitive fright reaction in response to the jarring of the body (45). In a primate, such movements of the limbs possibly might serve to grab hold of the mother's body or the trunk of a tree. One investigator (Schaltenbrand, 61) terms it a "readiness-to-jump reaction, ensuring a safe landing." This reflex undergoes changes during the first months of life. In a study of the Moro reflex in a number of infants (39) it was found that at about three or four months the gross movements had diminished considerably. At about seven months, overt movements have further waned, so that practically all that was exhibited was a weak body jerk accompanied by blinking. The changes from the more massive to the more refined and subdued response, according to the investigator (McGraw), parallels certain developments in the infant's nervous system. According to this account, the cerebral cortex is not functioning in the first phase of the response. As the cortex develops and comes into play, the response becomes more restrained, so to speak.

The grasp reflex, which occurs when an object is brought into contact with the palms of the hands of a young infant, also changes with time. Often this grasp is so powerful at first that the infant can cling to a bar as it is lifted into the air and support his own weight for many seconds. The strength of the reflex seems to be greatest when the infant is excited or crying, least when asleep (64). The "involuntary" grasping of the young infant recedes as the child matures and becomes increasingly capable of voluntary control of the movements of his hands.

Reflexes suggestive of locomotion also prevail for a time and then seem to wane. If placed prone on a hard surface, or if stimulated on the sole of the foot, the newborn infant will sometimes make crawling or swimming movements, in an apparent effort to propel himself forward (46, 67). He will make swimming movements if placed in a tank of water. If held upright, with feet touching a table or hard surface, he will make "stepping" or "dancing" movements (14, 67). These reflexes of locomotion wane within a few weeks after birth and seem to bear no immediate relationship to the later progressive stages of learning to crawl, creep, stand, and walk.[6]

SPECIAL SENSES

The question as to whether, what, and how well the newborn child can see, hear, smell, and taste is a difficult one to answer. The infant's response must be judged by his overt behavior and such behavior will be influenced by many conditions, such as being wet or dry, hungry or sated, asleep or awake. Generalized activities such as have been described above further complicate matters. Further difficulties are involved in applying, timing, and grading the stimuli that are to be used.

There also is the problem of how to adjust observations of the child to his own ways. The immature infant is unable to do much to coöperate, so that it becomes the observer's job to coöperate with the infant. Suggestive in this connection is a study dealing with infants' ability to fix their gaze upon an object and follow it with their eyes as it moves about (4). One procedure might be to make conditions constant by approaching all children,

---

[6] A full catalog of the reflexes and characteristic movements would run to great length. For a summary of findings in studies of behavior in early infancy from 1920 to 1934, see Dewey (18).

at all times, in the same manner, holding the light at a given distance and at a given angle, and then moving it around in the field of vision always over the same path, at the same speed, and so on. Another approach, used in the study here in question, would be to try to meet the infant at least halfway. The investigator first moved his stimulus (a light, or a small cylinder, or the experimenter's fingers) into the child's line of vision until he found the point at which the child's eyes seemed to be fixed upon it. The point at which fixation was thus secured varied considerably with different infants. Only after fixation had thus been procured did the experimenter proceed with the next step of finding how far and how long the infant would continue to keep his eyes on the object as it was moved about in the field of vision. The results indicate that during the first few days of life children were more capable of following a visual stimulus than would have been the case if more arbitrary experimental procedures had been used.

Sight. As already suggested, the average infant, almost from the time of birth, is capable of a variety of movements that normally are associated with proper use of the eyes (38). When an infant is able to fixate an object and to pursue it briefly, it seems reasonable to infer that he is seeing or obtaining glimpses of one sort or another, although we have no way of knowing what kind of visual impression he obtains. Infants vary considerably in their apparent ability to fixate, and in some children movements of the eyes are uncoördinated for a time after birth. Not until many weeks after birth are eye coördinations in fixating and pursuing an object that moves up and down or from side to side in the field of vision fully established.

The average infant likewise can open and shut his eyes and blink. However, some infants who blink when someone blows on their eyelids or touches them may fail to blink if an object is moved rapidly toward their eyes (74). Enlargement and contraction of the pupils have also been observed during the first days of life, although the response may be less prompt and uniform than at a later age (32). In studies of the infant's bodily reactions to light, it has been found that the amount of activity does not always vary directly with the intensity of the light (31). It was observed in one study that a bright, intense flash of light may produce a bodily reaction, accompanied by changes in breathing and circulation, as though the infant were startled (48).

Hearing. As stated above, a child even before birth may be responsive to the physical vibrations that produce sound. It cannot be surmised from this, however, just what the child actually hears. In a review of studies on this subject, Pratt points out that some investigators have claimed that infants are deaf at birth; but in numerous studies it has been found that a majority of subjects observed respond in one manner or another to sounds within the first days of life. There are wide variations between individual children. When an infant does seem to be insensitive to auditory stimuli, this condition may in some cases be associated with obstructions or physical imperfections in the organs of hearing at the time of birth.

Other sensory responses. As indicated by the amount of sucking and the facial and bodily reactions of various types, it appears that although the average baby reacts the same to mother's milk as to cow's milk, he responds positively to milk *per se* and to sweet solutions, and gives a negative response to solutions that are strongly salt, sour, or bitter (51).

In carefully conducted studies of the infant's sense of smell, it has been found that odors such as ammonia and acetic acid, which are powerful enough to cause discomfort to adults (perhaps by virtue of pain rather than olfactory stimulation), also produce reactions in newborn infants, while milder odors, which adults are able to detect, appear to have little effect (51). Infants react to temperatures that are hotter or colder than the normal temperature of the body, and they appear to react more to extremes of cold than to extremes of heat (51). Incidentally, it may be noted that the matter of temperature regulation at birth is complicated by the fact that the surface area is larger per unit of total bodily weight in the infant than in the adult.

From the time of birth infants are responsive to the stimulus of pressure or contact. During the first days of life infants also show a variety of responses to changes in their bodily positions. Righting responses of a sort that are eventually involved in maintaining an upright posture can be observed during the first days of life.

DIFFERENCES IN DEGREE OF MATURITY AT BIRTH

While the average child is born approximately 280 days after conception, there are wide individual variations around this average, especially in the direction of shorter periods of gestation. It is difficult to obtain precise records as to the "age" of children at birth, but the age can be determined at least approximately. In addition, it is possible to apply an objective criterion, such as weight at birth; it can be assumed that a child weighing less than five and a half pounds at birth has been born before the full normal term of forty weeks (60).

Children at birth vary considerably in "maturity." One writer has estimated that the range in age of newborn babies who are viable, or capable of living, is as wide as from twenty-six to forty-six weeks (24). Although the average birth weight is a little above seven pounds for girls, and a little under seven and a half for boys, babies have survived who weighed as little as one and a half pounds or even less (27). However, according to findings reviewed by Benton, it is unlikely that a child weighing less than about two and a half pounds will survive, and the chances of survival increase with added weight up to four or five pounds (5).

Children who clearly are born well before full term are popularly known as "premature" babies. This label is a useful one, but it is somewhat lacking in precision. Actually, two children may be born at exactly the same fetal age, yet one may be more "mature"—more fully developed—than the other (7). Again, a child may be "premature" in the sense that he has been born in advance of the average of forty weeks and yet be more "mature" in the sense that he is more advanced in his development than another child who has been born at "full term" (5, 24). Differences in rate of growth, which are so conspicuous after birth, appear also in growth before birth.

The "premature" child has the characteristics of an "immature" child in that he has not had time to complete the developments that occur between the period of his untimely delivery and the period when babies normally are born. Accordingly, the younger he is, the less fully is he equipped to carry on the business of living an independent life. The more poorly equipped he is, the more help he needs: care must be taken to keep him warm (partly because he lacks the deposits of fat that normally accumulate during the later stages of fetal growth); it may be necessary to aid his respiration by feeding him oxygen; he may need help in taking nourishment by reason of weak sucking or swallowing reflexes, or inadequacies in his digestive processes.

The fact of being born prematurely does not enable the child to "skip a grade" in his development. If he is born at six months he has the characteristics of a six-months fetus. As Gesell puts it, "He remains faithful to his fetality, even when birth has made him an infant."[7] However, even though he does not leap into a later phase of development, he is likely to set a faster pace in many aspects of his development from the time of his birth until the time when he normally would have been born than is set by the child who is spending this same period in his mother's womb. A child who was born at six months after conception is likely three months later to be more competent and alert to his environment than a full-term baby who similarly is nine months old (from time of conception) but who has newly been born. However, the full-term baby, three months from the time of his birth (or almost twelve months from the time of conception), is likely to be quite

---

[7] A. Gesell, *The Embryology of Behavior* (New York: Harper and Brothers, 1945), p. 143.

advanced in his development as compared with a premature child born at the same date as he.

When age is calculated from time of birth, the average premature child is definitely, at the start, backward in his development as compared with full-term children. However, the difference between them tends to diminish as time passes. The premature child tends to "catch up" (although there are exceptions, of course, especially if the child also suffers from organic defects). Investigators differ in their estimate as to when the premature child is likely to have caught up; indeed, the estimates have varied from a matter of months to a matter of several years (5, 42, 66). The process of reducing the gap between the premature and the full-term child may vary with respect to different mental and physical qualities and characteristics.

Prematurely born children eventually show much the same range of individual differences in mental and physical characteristics, in temperament and personality traits, as do children born at full term. However, some investigators have maintained that certain mannerisms and characteristics are peculiar to prematurely born youngsters during the first years of life and perhaps even later. Some investigators (44, 66) report that prematurely born children are relatively more advanced in "personal-social" behavior (smiling, noticing people, and so on) than in motor ability. Again, investigators report that prematurely born children are relatively more on the alert in their sensory than in their motor behavior; they tend, according to these investigators, to be quite sensitive to sights, colors, moving objects, and noises and sounds, while remaining somewhat backward in motor performances such as sitting upright or manipulating objects with their hands (42, 65).

Apart from factors in his own make-up, special factors in the environment may have a bearing on the development of the premature child: He begins life even more helpless than the normal child; he must have extra care and attention; his parents may look anxiously for signs of normal development and may greet his advances with special acclaim. At first, his parents may be rather self-conscious, gingerly protective and anxiously conscientious about him. At a later time, according to Shirley, parents may shift from a policy of shielding him to a policy of trying to urge him on, to push or accelerate his development (66). This is one illustration of what might happen to make the lot of the premature child less easy-going and "natural" than the lot of a robust baby born at full term. In keeping with this, Shirley reports that the premature children in her study showed more nervous mannerisms (such as nail-biting) and more irascibility than did full-term babies. However, it has not been demonstrated that factors such as these, associated with prematurity, will necessarily have a lasting effect on a child's disposition or temperament (6).

THE EMOTIONS OF THE NEWBORN CHILD

It is easy for adults to read their own emotions into the behavior of an infant. Cries, starts, and squirms can readily be interpreted as signs of pain, of anger, or of fear, such as an adult probably might be experiencing if he were showing the same amount of physical agitation. Adults may be mistaken, however, when they thus interpret the infant's behavior in terms of their own experiences (64).[8]

Hunger. In the life of the newborn child certain happenings loom relatively larger than they will at a later time. Much of the child's daily activity revolves around his digestive tract. He shows his hunger by means of cries and restless movements. When fed, he tends to quiet down, and then, within a relatively short period, he again demands food, throughout the night as well

---

[8] The view that the young infant is subject to profound emotional experiences has been set forth by Freud and his followers (20, 33, 36, 53, 62). Freud speaks, among other matters, of the infant's helplessness as a factor that brings into being the first situation of danger and creates a need to be loved which the human being is destined never to renounce. Isaacs maintains that wants and wishes, fears and angers, love and hate are there from the beginning

as the day. Healthy babies demand food about every three hours, on the average. There is wide variation from child to child, however, and the periods between demands for food may fluctuate widely also in the case of an individual child.

If the child is not fed when he announces his hunger, his crying and activity are likely to increase. Similarly, if a youngster has been fed on a regular schedule for several days after birth and then, on occasion, his feeding is delayed well beyond the customary time, there likewise is likely to be a distinct increase in crying, fussing, and general activity.

Just what are the feelings associated with this cycle of hunger and satiety? We have no direct way of knowing. There are times when a baby will cry as though his innermost being were in torment. Is he perhaps swept by vague fear of annihilation because his need for food is not satisfied? Is he perhaps consumed with rage because his desires are not being met? Do the softer notes that appear among his more strident outcries mean that his terror and rage are blended with feelings of gloom—the gloom of one neglected by elders whose withholding of food means also the withholding of love? It would give a dramatic quality to the young infant if we could answer yes to these questions. Actually, we cannot confidently answer either yes or no. Obviously the infant exhibits some kind of excitement. But we go beyond our knowledge of the make-up of the infant if we assume that his outward signs of frustration denote overwhelming emotional experiences such as we would assume if an older person behaved with similar violence.

We must consider the child's reaction in the light of the immaturity of the "higher" centers of his nervous system, his lack of ability to interpret the present in the light of associations from the past, his probable inability to translate the immediate happenings into forebodings with regard to the future such as are so prominent in the anxieties of adults. But this does not mean that we write off the infant's signs of distress as unimportant. Certainly the infant's agitation, when he is throwing his whole being into demands for food, must be supremely important to him within the limits of his capacity to experience.

Experiences involved in bodily contacts. The experiences involved in being hungry and being fed, then, seem to have a relatively greater prominence in the life of the young infant than they will have later on, and the same seems to be true of the contacts with other persons that occur when his bodily wants are being cared for. These contacts are intimately interwoven with his well-being and his survival from day to day. Within a few days after birth, he will cease his crying, at least for a time, if only he is held in someone's arms, whereas earlier it required not holding alone but food to pacify him. Within a short time, likewise, he will cease fussing simply in response to sights or sounds that betoken that another person is near. Later comes a time when he solicits the presence of someone else even though he is comfortably warm and dry and well fed, as though he desired company for its own sake. The question as to whether this desire for contact with others, this apparent desire for being "mothered," is derived from the association of other persons with the gratification of hunger and other needs, or whether it is a primary motive, a need in its own right, does not have to deter us here. Whatever may be the source of this desire, it appears early and it is strong. From his crib in early infancy the baby seeks to confirm the injunction that it is not good for man to be alone.

Again, in connection with this matter, as in connection with hunger, we cannot tell just what is the nature of the emotional experience involved. We can only recognize that all the signs seem to indicate that contact with another person, and, failing that, at least the presence of another, early becomes a matter of great importance to the infant. With the passage of time, the child welcomes contact with a friendly parent not only as a source of apparent satisfaction in itself but also as a help in bearing the hurts and bruises of everyday life. Pain from a burned finger, fright from a fall, anger from the loss of a toy, rage from having been struck by another child subside as he is held in a parent's arms. He continues after birth to derive psychological support from such contacts just as he derived life and physical well-being from the body of his mother before the time of his birth.

Pain. The infant seems relatively insensitive to certain forms of pain stimulation. It is not possible to tell how soon or how deeply the infant feels pains as they are experienced by adults, but it is undoubtedly true that many of the pains of adults are more intense by reason of past experiences. If pain stimulation could be stripped of previous associations of tensions and fears that grow out of past experience, many agonies experienced by older people would, no doubt, be less severe.

It is interesting to observe how the infant's apparent insensibility to certain pains is reflected in medical practice. Circumcisions performed upon a child under two weeks of age without the use of an anaesthetic, and other forms of surgical treatment, do not customarily produce signs of suffering as acute as one would expect if an older person received similar treatment. However, we cannot be certain that absence of outward signs denotes a similar absence of feeling.

Absence of clearly defined emotional responses. As we have seen, there are periods when the child during the first two or three weeks of life shows general excitement by way of crying and diffuse bodily activity. Such behavior does not show clear-cut patterns, now of anger, now of fear. Even in an older person these patterns are none too clearly differentiated, but as a person grows older there are times when his expressions have unmistakable earmarks of anger, fear, or joy.

The question as to what emotions can be aroused at birth, and how, has been the subject of many careful research studies. Various stimuli calculated to produce anger have been used, such as compressing the child's nostrils, restraining the use of his arms by pinning them to the sides of his body, interfering with the child's head movements by pressure against his chin. In a majority of instances, infants who have been subjected to such treatment for brief periods during the first two or three weeks after birth have not shown anything resembling the classic picture of rage. Indeed, many infants bear treatment of this sort as though it were a neutral incident rather than an affront.

Before many months have passed it will be a different story, of course. Physical restraint and thwarting of movement become quite effective in eliciting anger. But even when the child has become able to put on a show of anger, what constitutes restraint or interference will not depend solely on what another person does to him. If he is quiescent, or if he is in the mood, so to speak, for a little horseplay, he will allow his arms to be held to his sides for a time and he will even patiently accept the indignity of having his head pushed back by pressure on his chin. On the other hand, anger is likely to ensue if the thwarting is real from the standpoint of the child—if, for example, his arms are forcibly restrained just as he is busy in the act of using them, or if his feeding is delayed after he has seen the bottle and is all set to take his milk. Similarly, the act of placing him in his crib may elicit anger in a child who has reached the creeping stage and wants to be on the go, whereas the same act has no such effect at an earlier stage.

In one study, Dennis (17) concludes that at birth the infant reacts with crying and restlessness to any form of intense and enduring stimulation, of which rough restraint may be one form. The infants were subjected to stimuli such as holding of the head between the experimenter's hands or pressing the nose with the experimenter's forefinger. These experiments began when the infants were about two months old. It was noted that the responses of the children varied considerably from time to time; but in approximately two-thirds of the instances of stimulation the movie records showed behavior which could be characterized as struggling, thrashing about, or crying. However, much the same reactions of the limbs appeared in response to certain strong taste stimuli—a saturated salt solution, a very bitter quinine solution, and a diluted citric acid solution. Restraint of movement achieved without the use of intense stimulation does not necessarily cause negative reactions in the newborn. At a later age the infant will react also with crying and restlessness when his accustomed ways of behaving are interfered with.

A sharp, shrill, or loud noise may cause an infant during the first days of life to start, kick, squirm, and perhaps cry. Such behavior has the appearance of fear. But other forms of stimulation, which a sympathetic adult would not regard as particularly fear-inspiring, may produce similar bodily movements and similar cries. Moreover, infants often seem undisturbed by rather drastic treatment. In one study (31), each of twenty-four infants under one month of age was raised in a supine position above the experimenter's head, was dropped, and was caught after he had fallen a distance of two feet. In eighty-five trials of this sort, crying resulted only twice. In twelve per cent of the trials the infant made no detectable overt response. In half the number of instances in which the children did react to this treatment, their movements were confined to the arms alone.

From the viewpoint of emotional expression, the child's reactions during the first weeks of life group themselves roughly on the one hand as reactions of apparent withdrawal or rejection, such as squirms, twists, tension, movements of the trunk and the arms and extremities, turning of the head, and crying. On the other hand, there are reactions of apparent acceptance, quiescence, passivity, and a rudimentary form of pursuit, such as is found when the child turns his head and opens his mouth to suckle when an object is moved toward his lips. His overt behavior during the early days of his life does not show organized responses to which a particular label, such as anger, fear, or joy, can confidently be attached.

THE BEGINNINGS OF "PERSONALITY"

Almost from the moment of birth, infants seem to exhibit differences in personality. Some are decidedly more mobile, active, and on the go than others. During ensuing hours and days, some babies tend to be more or less restless, irritable, fussy, whereas others are more placid and serene.

In a study of newborn infants, hospital nurses who bathed, fed, and dressed the infants recorded items of behavior, such as whether the infant was asleep or awake, restless, irritable and crying, or placid (64). These records, in turn, were compared with records obtained in studies of the reflexes and sensory responses of the same infants. There was a high degree of agreement between nurses as to who were the "good" babies. It was found that the "good" babies exhibited many of the characteristics of sleeping babies; the pupils of their eyes were smaller and their pupillary reactions to light were slower, and they were less responsive to pain stimulation. On the other hand, they compared favorably with other babies in their grasp reflexes, defense reactions, and general coördination.

Owing to the many factors that may influence a child's behavior during the first days of life—including, among other matters, the "age" of the child when delivered (whether "premature" or full term) and the circumstances of his delivery—it is hardly to be expected that the infant's behavior soon after birth will give a reliable prediction of the distinctive personality traits which the same child will show as he grows older. In one study, infants were rated on such items as restlessness, fussing when not promptly fed, and frequency of crying while in a maternity hospital (8), and then, two years later, the same children were scored in terms of a rating scale. There proved to be little resemblance between the earlier and the later ratings. In another study (22), the investigator followed the development of several babies from before birth to the age of three years. Babies at birth were classified into three groups as "active," "moderately active," and "quiet" —all within the normal range. The investigator reports that the "activity pattern" tends to remain "fairly constant," but it can be modified by the physical and psychological environment and by changes in the child himself that may be caused, for example, by illness.

Parents frequently are struck by the difference between a new baby and previous babies born to the family. Likewise, observers who are not intimately associated with the family can begin to note, by the time children are only a few weeks old, characteristics which seem to distinguish one child from another as a distinct personality. In an investigation (69) in which twenty-five babies were observed repeatedly from the time of birth to the age of three years, the investigator describes numerous characteristics that distinguished babies from one another from the time of birth, such as irritability, tone and timbre of cries, motility and tonicity of muscles. The investigator also noted that distinctive patterns of behavior could be observed that characterized a baby's reactions in a variety of situations. Similar observations are reported by another investigator in an earlier study of a pair of twins (23). Although both children shared the same home, the same mother, and similar physical health, the children showed consistent differences in such matters as "placidity, length of crying, vigor of protest, tolerance of physical discomfort, readiness of smiling, social responsiveness," and so forth. Such observations suggest that there are inborn differences, but both investigators cited above emphasize the difficulty of evaluating the relative roles of inborn and environmental factors. The interaction of hereditary and environmental factors in a child's development is so complex that it would be difficult to isolate either in pure form.

Apart from the question of whether, or to what extent, early differences in personality are inborn, it is obvious that differences in behavior can also be traced to conditions in the environment. Crying in infants exemplifies this. The infant is likely to cry more if the adult is preoccupied with other things (2), or if, as noted earlier, he is used to a fixed schedule of feeding and is not fed when he is hungry. The very fact that there are vast individual differences among adults who are caring for infants means differences in the environments to which infants are exposed. The personality of the adult is bound to influence his general attitude toward the child. The adult's personality is likely also, in one way or another, to be reflected in the specific practices he uses with the child.

LEARNING DURING THE FIRST DAYS AND WEEKS OF LIFE

As soon as a child is born the stage is set for him to begin his career as a learner. In due time his behavior becomes modified as a consequence of impact with the external environment and changes within himself that take place in the process of growth. How early does this process of learning begin? Probably from the time of birth, if not before.

Mothers sometimes report signs of learning within a week or so after birth when a hungry, crying baby ceases his crying as soon as he is picked up and held in his mother's arms. Previous to this he became quiet only when actually fed. Now the preparatory step, being picked up and held, produces quiet. It is as though the child accepts the picking up and holding as a signal of feeding. If the child thus responds to a signal, where previously he actually had to have a sip, we can properly say that he has "learned." However, observations such as these do not necessarily prove that learning has taken place. It is possible that the experience of being picked up and held would at the later age have a quieting effect in itself, even if not previously associated with the experience of being fed. The evidence of learning becomes more convincing if the child resumes his crying more vigorously than ever if there is a longer than usual delay between the time when he is picked up and the moment he is fed.

Many interesting studies have dealt with the subject of learning in early infancy. Some of these have raised the question of whether it is possible for a child during the first days of life to acquire a "conditioned" response. In one such experiment (40), eight infants were bottle-fed from the time of birth and at each feeding a buzzer was sounded. After three to six days, seven of the eight infants exhibited many responses related to feeding, such as an increase in sucking and mouth-opening, a lessening of general activity, and crying in response to the buzzer alone. Since, as noted earlier, an infant's response to any sort of stimulus may be quite generalized, some of these effects might possibly have occurred even if feeding had not been used as a "conditioning" stimulus. In another study (1), an apparently "conditioned" response to sound was produced in an infant who did not, when the experiment began, respond to the usual tests of hearing. The baby's foot was scratched with a pin and, at the same time, a bell was rung, out of sight of the baby. After this procedure had been repeated at intervals for several hours, the infant withdrew his leg when nothing was done to his foot and only the bell was rung.

In some other studies, using various methods, the findings have been negative or equivocal (75, 76). In one investigation an electric shock, applied to the sole of the foot and eliciting withdrawal of the foot, was the "unconditioned" stimulus. The "conditioned" stimulus was the sound of a muffled buzzer. The buzzer was sounded for a moment before the shock occurred and for a moment thereafter. Nine of twelve infants in the experimental group gave conditioned responses to the buzzer alone on the third day. However, these results were clouded by the fact that many of the infants in a control group also showed withdrawal in response to a buzzer even though they had not been exposed to the shock and the buzzer at the same time. In other words, the investigation did not find unequivocal evidence of the establishment of conditioned responses.

A clearer picture emerges in a study (35) of sixteen infants whose ages when the experiment first began ranged from one month and fourteen days to three months and twenty-seven days. In this study a buzzer was sounded for five seconds and then continued to sound during fifteen additional seconds as the nipple of a milk bottle was inserted in the infant's mouth and the infant proceeded to feed. Here it was found that sucking in response to the buzzer alone was established in from three to nine feedings (during the course of which the buzzer and the bottle had been presented together from sixteen to fifty-three times).

An interesting feature of the findings, however, was that the infants would give the sucking response to the buzzer when they were hungry but not when they were sated. In other words, even though a connection had been established between sucking and the buzzer, it required the motive of hunger to call it forth. In a sense we might say that the infants used what they had learned only when there was good use for it. In addition, it was found that the conditioned response to the buzzer disappeared or was extinguished when, in a second part of the experiment, the buzzer was sounded repeatedly without the accompaniment of feeding after the infants were partially sated. In other words, these young infants on the one hand learned to respond to significant signals (buzzing as a signal of food) and they, on the other hand, also came to discard false signals (buzzing that no longer betokened food). While still less than four months old, these infants were thus demonstrating "intelligent" behavior.

Another approach to this problem was made in an investigation which raised this question: "Do infants adapt to (that is, 'learn') a feeding schedule within the first ten days of life?" (41). A record was obtained of the general bodily activity of sixteen babies who were fed on a three-hour schedule until they were eight days old and then, on the ninth day, changed to a four-hour schedule. A record was also made of the activity of another group of newborns who were on a four-hour schedule and of another group fed on a self-demand schedule, that is, fed whenever they seemed hungry. Activity was recorded mechanically by a device that supported the bassinets in which the infants lay. For convenience in measuring activity, the time between feedings was divided into successive ten-minute periods and a tally was made of each half-minute interval during which an infant made movements sufficient to activate the recording device. From this it was possible to compute the percentage of half-minute intervals of activity per ten minutes.

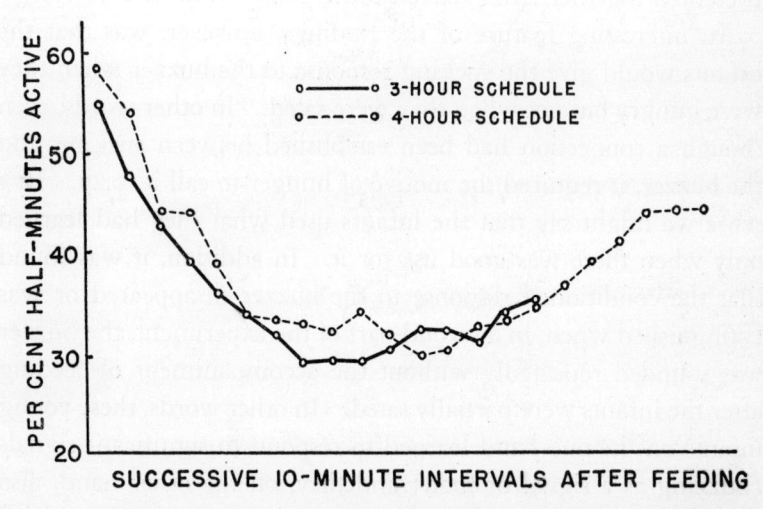

Fig. 1. Comparison of activity between feedings of babies fed on a three-hour and a four-hour schedule. Average of all subjects, days 2-8. Adapted from Marquis, D. P., "Learning in the Neonate: The Modification of Behavior Under Three Feeding Schedules." *Journal of Experimental Psychology*, 1941, 29, 270. Used by permission.

Figure I gives a picture of the activity of the three-hour and four-hour groups during selected between-feeding periods from the second through the eighth day. Both groups show a falling off in activity after a feeding, as though the infants were gradually settling down. At the end of three hours, the three-hour group is relatively quiet, while the four-hour infants thereafter show a rising rate of activity. Contrast this with the curves in Figure II. This shows what happened when the three-hour group was put on a four-hour schedule. At the end of the third hour, when they usually had been fed, the activity of these infants increased abruptly and by the end of the fourth hour it reached a level higher than at any previous time. It also quite exceeded the level shown by the children who had been fed on a four-hour schedule from the beginning.

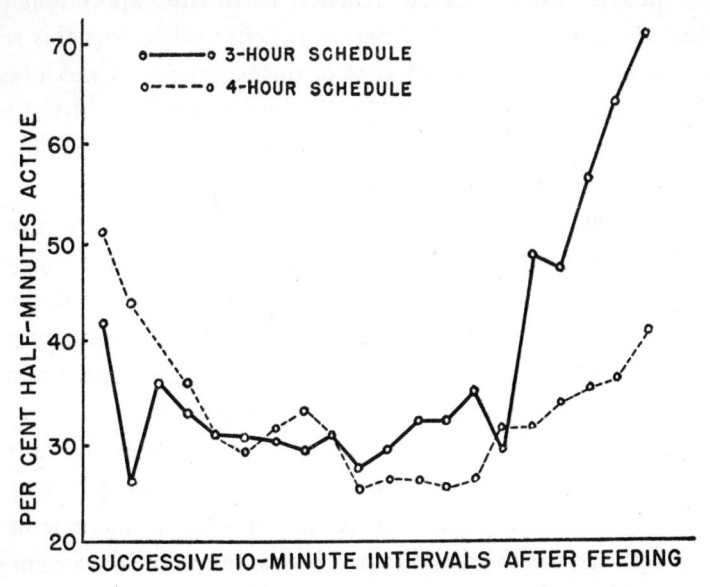

Fig. 2. Comparison of activity between feedings of babies on a four-hour schedule and babies previously fed on a three-hour schedule but now changed to a four-hour schedule. Average of forenoon and afternoon periods for all subjects on Day 9. Adapted from Marquis, D. P., "Learning in the Neonate: The Modification of Behavior Under Three Feeding Schedules." *Journal of Experimental Psychology*, 1941, 29, p. 273. Used by permission.

This high level of activity was frequently accompanied by crying. Moreover, an increased rate of activity continued even after the infants had been fed. It might have been expected that the infants, when changed from a three-hour to a four-hour schedule, would have become so fatigued by the excess of activity during the extra hour's wait that they would settle down after at last having been fed and would go to sleep sooner than before. Instead, the opposite occurred. During the periods following the shift to a four-hour schedule the infants continued to be more active than usual and again, at the end of three hours, there was an abrupt rise in activity.

These observations indicate that the infants on the three-hour schedule had "learned" to expect food, so to speak, at the end of three hours. Their vigorous reaction when this expectation was defeated is vividly shown in Figure II. Just what does this reaction mean from the point of view of the experience of the infant? Are the infant's reactions accompanied by awareness and feeling? Does this treatment represent a kind of frustration, and do the infant's crying and thrashing about have an aggressive quality, an element of anger? We can only conjecture as to what the answer might be. However, it does not require a stretch of the imagination to conceive that many such disruptions and uncertainties in feeding and other aspects of everyday care might eventually have an important bearing upon the child's mood and temperament and on the shaping of what we call his "personality."

In this same study, there also was evidence, although not unmistakable, that the infants on a four-hour schedule were "learning" to wait four hours. As indicated, they showed an increase in activity between the third and fourth hours; but as the days went on, this activity tended to lessen rather than to increase.

During the period of the study the infants who were on a self-demand schedule appeared to be hungry and were fed approximately every three hours on the average. In other words, while other infants of the same age sought food about every three hours, the four-hour babies seemed to be on the way toward accepting the four-hour schedule. Already the "four-hour" babies were adapting themselves to a mode of life (as far as feeding was concerned), even though this did not conform to what many of them would have chosen for themselves. Thus during the first days of life does a child reveal a resiliency, a capacity to adapt to what the environment demands or affords. As time goes on he will continue to show this capacity as he adapts to countless demands, whether these be arbitrary or inevitable, wise or foolish. However, as we shall see in later chapters, there are limits beyond which a child cannot be pushed and there are demands he is unable to sustain.

BIBLIOGRAPHY

1. Aldrich, C. A.: "A New Test for Hearing in the Newborn: The Conditioned Reflex," *American Journal of Diseases of Children* (1928), 35:36-37.
2. Aldrich, C. A., Sung, C., and Knop, C.: "The Crying of Newly Born Babies: I. Community Phase," *Journal of Pediatrics* (1945), 26:313-326.
3. Anderson, J. E.: "Child Development and the Interpretation of Behavior," *Science* (1936), 83:245-252.
4. Beasley, W. C.: "Visual Pursuit in 109 White and 142 Negro Newborn Infants," *Child Development* (1933), 4:106-120.
5. Benton, A. L.: "A Study of the Development of Intelligence in Prematurely Born Children," *Psychological Bulletin* (1938), 35:714.
6. ———: "Mental Development of Prematurely Born Children," *American Journal of Orthopsychiatry* (1940), 10:719-747.
7. Blatz, W. C. and Millichamp, D. A.: "The Mental Growth of the Dionne Quintuplets," in Blatz, W. C. *et al: Collected Studies of the Dionne Quintuplets* (Toronto, Canada: University of Toronto Press, 1937).
8. Bonham, M. A. and Sargent, M.: *A Study of the Development of Personality Traits in Children Twenty-Four and Thirty Months of Age*, Master's Thesis (Washington, D. C.: Catholic University of America, 1928), 40 pp. Reviewed by Murphy, G. and Murphy, L.: *Experimental Social Psychology* (New York: Harper, 1931), pp. 209-213.
9. Bridgman, C. S. and Carmichael, L.: "An Experimental Study of the Onset of Behavior in the Fetal Guinea-Pig," *Journal of Genetic Psychology* (1935), 47:247-267.
10. Carlson, A. J. and Ginsburg, H.: "The Tonus and Hunger Contractions of the Stomach of the Newborn," *American Journal of Physiology* (1915), 38:29-32.
11. Carmichael, L.: "The Experimental Embryology of Mind," *Psychological Bulletin* (1941), 38:1-28.
12. ———: "The Onset and Early Development of Behavior," *Manual of Child Psychology,* edited by L. Carmichael (New York: Wiley, 1946), Ch. II, pp. 43-166.

13. ———: "A Re-Evaluation of the Concepts of Maturation and Learning as Applied to the Early Development of Behavior," *Psychological Review* (1936), 43:450-470.
14. Chaney, L. B. and McGraw, M. B.: "Reflexes and Other Motor Activities in Newborn Infants: A Report of 125 Cases as a Preliminary Study of Infant Behavior," *Bulletin of the Neurological Institute* (1932), 2:1-56.
15. Coghill, G. E.: *Anatomy and the Problem of Behavior* (New York: Macmillan, 1929), 113 pp.
16. ———: "Integration and Motivation of Behavior as Problems of Growth," *Journal of Genetic Psychology* (1936), 48:3-19.
17. Dennis, W.: "Infant Reactions to Restraint: An Evaluation of Watson's Theory," *Transactions of the New York Academy of Science* (1942), Ser. II, Vol. 2, No. 7.
18. Dewey, E.: *Behavior Development in Infants* (New York: Columbia University Press, 1935), 321 pp.
19. Forbes, H. S. and Forbes, H. B.: "Fetal Sense Reaction: Hearing," *Journal of Comparative Psychology* (1927), 7:353-355.
20. Freud, S.: *The Problem of Anxiety* (New York: Norton, 1936), 165 pp.
21. Freudenberg, E.: "Der Morosche Umklammerungsreflex und das Brudzinkische Nackenzeichen als Reflexe des Sauglingsalters," *München med. Wchnschr.* (1921), 68:1646-1647.
22. Fries, M. E. and Lewi, B.: "Interrelated Factors in Development. A Study of Pregnancy, Labor, Delivery, Lying-in Period and Childhood," *American Journal of Orthopsychiatry* (1938), 8:726-752.
23. Gesell, A.: *Infancy and Human Growth* (New York: Macmillan, 1928), 418 pp.
24. Gesell, A. and Amatruda, C. S.: *The Embryology of Behavior* (New York: Harper, 1945), 289 pp.
25. Gesell, A. and Ilg, F. L.: *Feeding Behavior of Infants* (Philadelphia: Lippincott, 1937), 201 pp.
26. Guernesy, M.: "A Quantitative Study of the Eye Reflexes in Infants," *Psychological Bulletin* (1929), 26:160-161.
27. Hoffman, S. J., Greenhill, J. P., and Lundeen, E. C.: "A Premature Infant Weighing 735 Grams and Surviving," *Journal of the American Medical Association* (1937), 110:283-285.
28. Hooker, D.: "Fetal Behavior," *1938 Proceedings of the Association for Research in Nervous and Mental Diseases* (1939), 19:237-243.
29. ———: "Reflex Activities in the Human Fetus," *Child Behavior and Development,* edited by R. G. Barker, J. S. Kounin, and H. F. Wright (New York: McGraw-Hill, 1943), Ch. II, pp. 17-28.
30. Irwin, O. C.: *The Amount and Nature of Activities of Newborn In-*

fants Under Constant External Stimulation Conditions During the First Ten Days of Life, Genetic Psychology Monographs (1930), 8:1-92.
31. ———: "Infant Responses to Vertical Movements," *Child Development* (1932), 3:167-169.
32. Irwin, O. C., Weiss, L. A., and Stubbs, E. M.: *Studies in Infant Behavior,* I, University of Iowa Studies in Child Welfare (1934), 9, No. 4:175 pp.
33. Isaacs, S.: *The Nursery Years* (New York: Vanguard Press, 1936), 138 pp.
34. Jensen, K.: *Differential Reactions to Taste and Temperature Stimuli in Newborn Infants,* Genetic Psychology Monographs (1932), 12:361-479.
35. Kantrow, R. W.: *An Investigation of Conditioned Feeding Responses and Concomitant Adaptive Behavior in Young Infants,* University of Iowa Studies in Child Welfare (Iowa City, 1937), 13, No. 3, 64 pp.
36. Klein, M.: *The Psycho-Analysis of Children* (New York: Norton, 1932), 393 pp.
37. Kuo, Z. Y.: "Ontogeny of Embryonic Behavior in Aves: V. The Reflex Concept in the Light of Embryonic Behavior in Birds," *Psychological Review* (1932), 39:499-515.
38. McGinnis, J. M.: *Eye-Movements and Optic Nystagmus in Early Infancy,* Genetic Psychology Monographs (1930), 8:321-430.
39. McGraw, M. B.: "The Moro Reflex," *American Journal of Diseases of Children* (1937), 54:240-251.
40. Marquis, D. P.: "Can Conditioned Responses Be Established in the Newborn Infant?" *Journal of Genetic Psychology* (1931), 39:479-492.
41. ———: "Learning in the Neonate: The Modification of Behavior Under Three Feeding Schedules," *Journal of Experimental Psychology* (1941), 29:263-282.
42. Melcher, R.: "Development within the First Two Years of Infants Prematurely Born," *Child Development* (1937), 8:1-14.
43. Minkowski, M.: "Sur les Mouvements, les Reflexes, et les Reactions Musculaires du Foetus Humain de 2 a 5 Mois et leurs Relations avec le Systeme Nerveux Foetal," *Rev. Neur.* (1921), 37:1105-1118; 1235-1250.
44. Mohr, G. J. and Bartelme, P. F.: "Mental and Physical Development of Prematurely Born," *American Journal of Diseases of Children* (1930), 40:1000-1015.
45. Moro, E.: "Das erste Trimenon," *Munchen med. Wchnschr.* (1918), 65:1147-1150.

46. Myers, G. C.: "Infants' Inhibition: A Genetic Study," *Pedagogical Seminary* (1922), 29:288-301.
47. Nelson, V. L. and Richards, T. W.: "Studies in Mental Development: I. Performance on Gesell Items at Six Months and Its Predictive Value for Performance on Mental Tests at Two and Three Years," *Journal of Genetic Psychology* (1938), 52:303-325.
48. Peiper, A.: "Sinnesreaktionen des Neugebornen," *Zeitschr. f. Psych.* (1930), 114:363-370.
49. Pratt, K. C.: "Generalization and Specificity of the Plantar Response in Newborn Infants. The Reflexogenous Zone: II. Segmental Patterning of Responses," *Journal of Genetic Psychology* (1934), 45:22-38.
50. ———: "The Neonate," *Manual of Child Psychology,* edited by L. Carmichael (New York: Wiley, 1946), Ch. IV, pp. 190-254.
51. Pratt, K. C., Nelson, A. K., and Sun, K. H.: *The Behavior of the Newborn Infant* (Columbus: Ohio State University Press, 1930), 237 pp.
52. Preyer, W.: *Embryonic Motility and Sensitivity,* Monograph of the Society for Research in Child Development (1937), Vol. II, No. 6, Ser. 13, 115 pp.
53. Rank, O.: *Modern Education: A Critique of Its Fundamental Ideas* (New York: Knopf, 1932), 243 pp.
54. Ray, W. S.: "A Preliminary Report on a Study of Fetal Conditioning," *Child Development* (1932), 3:175-177.
55. Richards, T. W.: "The Importance of Hunger in the Bodily Activity of the Neonate," *Psychological Bulletin* (1936), 33:817-835.
56. Richards, T. W. and Irwin, O. C.: *Plantar Responses of Infants and Young Children: An Examination of the Literature and Reports of New Experiments,* University of Iowa Studies in Child Welfare (1935), 11, No. 1:1-146.
57. Richards, T. W. and Nelson, V. L.: "Abilities of Infants During the First Eighteen Months," *Journal of Genetic Psychology* (1939), 55:299-318.
58. Richards, T. W. and Newbery, H.: "Studies in Fetal Behavior: III. Can Performance on Test Items at Six Months Postnatally Be Predicted on the Basis of Fetal Activity?" *Child Development* (1938), 9:79-86.
59. Richards, T. W., Newbery, H., and Fallgatter, R.: "Studies in Fetal Behavior: II. Activity of the Human Fetus *in Utero* and Its Relation to Other Prenatal Conditions, Particularly the Mother's Basal Metabolic Rate," *Child Development* (1938), 9:69-78.
60. Scammon, R. E. and Calkins, L. A.: *The Development and Growth of the External Dimensions of the Human Body in the Fetal Period* (Minneapolis: University of Minnesota Press, 1929), 367 pp.

61. Schaltenbrand, G.: "Normale Bewegungs- und Lage-Reaktionen bei Kindern," *Deutsch. Ztschr. f. Nervenh.* (1925), 87:23-59.
62. Sharpe, E. F.: "Planning for Stability," *On the Bringing Up of Children*, edited by J. Richman (London: Kegan Paul, Trench, Trubner, 1938), pp. 1-30.
63. Sherman, M. and Sherman, I. C.: "Sensori-Motor Responses in Infants," *Journal of Comparative Psychology* (1925), 5:53-68.
64. Sherman, M., Sherman, I. C., and Flory, C. D.: *Infant Behavior*, Comparative Psychology Monographs (1936), 12, No. 59, 107 pp.
65. Shirley, M. M.: "Behavior Syndrome Characterizing Prematurely Born Children," *Child Development* (1939), 10:115
66. ———: "Development of Immature Babies During the First Two Years," *Child Development* (1938), 9:347-360.
67. ———: *The First Two Years: A Study of Twenty-Five Babies*, Vol. I: *Postural and Locomotor Development*, Institute of Child Welfare Monograph Series (Minneapolis: University of Minnesota, 1931), No. 6, 227 pp.
68. ———: *The First Two Years: A Study of Twenty-Five Babies*, Vol. II: *Intellectual Development*, Institute of Child Welfare Monograph Series (Minneapolis: University of Minnesota, 1933), No. 7, 513 pp.
69. ———: *The First Two Years: A Study of Twenty-Five Babies*, Vol. III: *Personality Manifestations*, Institute of Child Welfare Monograph Series (Minneapolis: University of Minnesota Press, 1933), No. 8, 228 pp.
70. Sontag, L. W. and Richards, T. W.: *Studies in Fetal Behavior: I. Fetal Heart Rate as a Behavioral Indicator*, Monographs of the Society for Research in Child Development (1938), III, No. 4, 72 pp.
71. Sontag, L. W. and Wallace, R. F.: "Preliminary Report of the Fels Fund: Study of Fetal Activity," *American Journal of Diseases of Children* (1934), 48:1050-1057.
72. Sontag, L. W. and Wallace, R. F.: "The Movement Response of the Human Fetus to Sound Stimuli," *Child Development* (1935), 6:253-258.
73. Tuge, H.: "The Development of Behavior in Avian Embryos," *Journal of Comparative Neurology* (1937), 66:157-179.
74. Valentine, C. W.: "Reflexes in Early Childhood: Their Development, Variability, Evanescence, Inhibition and Relation to Instincts," *British Journal of Medical Psychology* (1927), 7:1-35.
75. Wenger, M. A.: *An Investigation of Conditioned Responses in Human Infants*, University of Iowa Studies in Child Welfare (1936), 12, No. 318:7-90.
76. Wickens, D. D. and Wickens, C.: "A Study of Conditioning in the Neonate," *Journal of Experimental Psychology* (1940), 26:94-102.

77. Windle, W. F.: "Correlation Between the Development of Local Reflexes and Reflex Arcs in the Spinal Cord of Cat Embryos," *Journal of Comparative Neurology* (1934), 59:487-505.
78. Windle, W. F., O'Donnell, J. E., and Glasshagle, E. E.· "The Early Development of Spontaneous and Reflex Behavior in Cat Embryos and Fetuses," *Physiological Zoology* (1933), 6:521-541.

Chapter II

SOME GENERAL CHARACTERISTICS OF DEVELOPMENT

In the preceding chapter we noted certain broad trends in the development of the infant before and immediately following birth. The present chapter will deal with certain additional general characteristics that can be observed in development from birth onward. By reason of their importance for the understanding of development, these general characteristics are here set forth in a separate chapter, although there will be occasion in later chapters to refer to them again.

DEVELOPMENT AS A PRODUCT OF LEARNING AND GROWTH

Throughout the period of a child's development two factors are at work—growth and learning. These factors are interdependent; they cannot be isolated in pure form, yet they can be separated for purposes of discussion. In everyday speech we continually make such a distinction. We note that a child has *grown* two inches in height since we saw him last and that he has *learned* to recite "Jack and Jill."

When we say a child has "grown," we are describing certain physical and physiological changes that normally occur in a healthy child with the passage of time and that have results such as an increase in height, weight, length of bones, changes in bone structure, changes in the structure of parts of the nervous system, and the like. As against this, "learning" represents a modification of behavior that has come about by virtue of experience, use, or exercise. The term "maturation" is also prominently used in discussion of development. This term, which has many general as well as special meanings, denotes, in a developmental setting, the process of ripening, of moving toward complete, or *mature,* development. The foregoing statements indicate that growth and maturation have a meaning in common. However, as sometimes used, and as used in this book, the term "maturation" denotes not solely change in physical characteristics but also the changes in *function, in capacity to perform or behave,* that become possible through changes in the physical characteristics of any part of the organism.

These distinctions, like the illustration above, oversimplify matters somewhat, for growth and maturation do not normally take place in a vacuum devoid of experiences or opportunities for learning. If we looked into the matter of "Jack and Jill," for example, we would find that the four-year-old who now is able to memorize this verse could not possibly have done so at six months. He might have succeeded at two years, but it was considerably easier at four. Back of the ability to pronounce the words and to memorize the lines of "Jack and Jill" there has been growth which corresponds in some respects to the growth underlying the increase in stature and in number of teeth, even though it would be impossible to isolate this growth as a separate factor.[1]

A practical distinction between changes effected by learning and by growth and maturation is important from both the viewpoint of understanding the child and that of practical issues in the rearing of children at home and their education at school. The child's education begins at birth, if not before. Much of this education takes place through countless contacts with his daily environment that are not definitely planned; but from the very

---

[1] An example of the fact that internal changes that will have an influence on behavior may be going on apart from "learning" or exercise or use or practice as a result of external stimulation is offered in a study by Carmichael (4) of embryo salamanders and frogs. An experimental group was placed in a chemical solution which anaesthetized the animals sufficiently to prevent movement in response to external stimulation without causing impairment of growth. When transferred to ordinary tap water at a time when animals in a control group were just beginning to make swimming movements, the experimental animals also soon proceeded to make swimming movements and within half an hour it was difficult to distinguish them from the controls.

beginning much in his environment and many experiences calculated to promote his development are controlled by his elders. The huge budgets involved in the formal schooling of children represent only a small fraction of the total outlay of time and means devoted to the training of children from early infancy. To make this investment yield the best returns for all concerned, to prevent the discouraging effects of failure, and to make the best use of the stimulus of success, it is important to try to adapt the child's training to his growing abilities.

If, within broad limits, we could find at what stage in the child's development various activities and performances might best be cultivated, it would be a decided boon to both the child and his teachers. Such information would enable us to avoid efforts to force the child's development or to impose tasks or obstacles that are beyond his powers and that may produce irritation and resistance, whereas at a later time they might be undertaken with interest. It would also enable us to avoid the condition of supplying less opportunity and less stimulation than is needed to challenge the child's powers. Obviously, a definitive schedule for introducing various opportunities and requirements into the child's training could never be obtained. The child does not become "ready" for a given activity at one particular day or hour, and his behavior is influenced by many variables that are difficult to weigh or define. Even so, anything that research findings can offer in this area is of value.[2]

GROWTH FACTORS IN ESTABLISHMENT OF BASIC COÖRDINATIONS

Studies of children during the first two years of life indicate that the growth factor plays a predominant role in the development of the basic coördinations involved in locomotion (such as creeping, standing, and walking) and in prehension (such as reaching,

---

[2] More extended treatments of the topic of maturation are offered by Gesell (13) and McGraw (29).

grasping, and apposition of thumb and fingers in handling an object). This does not mean that these accomplishments simply thrust themselves upon a passive organism, for the healthy child spends much of his waking time in exercising and in trying out his powers. It does mean, however, that the impetus for these early developments springs largely from within. There is not much that an ambitious adult can do to hasten them.

Children's rate of progress toward the ability to walk alone cannot be speeded materially by special coaching and encouragement (36). Much the same seems to hold true also in the development of some of the basic coördinations underlying the use of the arm, wrist, and fingers (1, 12, 13, 17). In one study (1), in which the movements and manipulations of infants were recorded by a motion-picture camera, it was concluded: "The fact that in such various fields of behavior new and often complex behavior patterns can appear for the first time in a form so complete that several weeks, often several months, of exercise do not appreciably change either their form or speed, strongly suggests that such patterns are determined by internal maturational rather than experiential factors."

The importance of changes that occur as a child matures with the passage of time, as distinguished from the influence of training or exercise, appears also in studies of infants who have less opportunity for exercise than does the usual child. In one study (7) two girls were kept in a very restricted environment until they were seven months old. They spent their time in separate individual enclosures; they received no toys; no one played with them; and they received little or no attention beyond what was necessary to take care of their routine wants. Yet the progress of these children did not differ substantially from the progress made by other children in a normal environment. Their progress fell within the normal range in the following: ability to hold the head up while lying in a prone position, hand-to-mouth reactions, ability to hold chest up while lying prone, ability to play with the hands, and ability to follow a moving object with head and eyes. In certain activities (sitting alone, standing with help, creeping, standing alone) that usually do not reach their full development until after the age of seven months (when the rigid schedule was relaxed), they lagged somewhat behind the norm, but not to a degree which the investigator regarded as significant.

The retarding effects of deprivation would no doubt become increasingly apparent, at least in a number of performances, if the regimen according to which these infants were reared had been continued well beyond the age of seven months. But as far as they go, the findings indicate that the small infant is not a creature who is entirely at the mercy of what his environment affords as long as he is well fed and housed, free from disease, and has some freedom to exercise in his own way. The impulse to grow is strong, behavior mechanisms mature, and in spite of lack of encouragement the child finds means of exercising his growing talents to some degree.

In another study (8) it was found that the infants of Hopi Indian mothers who followed the practice of using cradle boards—a rigid structure to which the infant was bound and on which he spent many of his waking hours—during much of the first year of life did not differ substantially in their early motor development from infants whose mothers did not use the cradle board.

EXPERIMENTAL STUDIES OF EFFECTS OF TRAINING IN
RELATION TO MATURITY

In many studies it has been found that the effects of an opportunity to practice, use, or exercise a performance are relative to the level of maturity that a child has reached when the opportunity is provided. It is not possible to get a child to skip a grade in his development by giving him extra or unusual opportunities.

In a number of performances, a relatively short period of practice when a child is somewhat older will yield as much competence as a longer period of practice begun when the child was younger.

In one study (16), involving a pair of twins, beginning at the age of forty-six weeks one twin was encouraged daily for a six-week period to manipulate and use cubes. In the meantime, the other twin, who served as a control, was denied this experience. At fifty-two weeks the behavior of the two children in reaching for, manipulating, and exploiting the objects was highly similar. <u>Efforts to promote skill in the manipulation of cubes in the one case and the withholding of such opportunities in the other did not alter the course of development.</u> The same twins were similarly used in a study of stair-climbing, beginning when the children were forty-six weeks old. Again it appeared that the ability involved in stair-climbing was influenced more by factors attending normal growth than by special stimulation such as was provided in the study. At the age of fifty-three weeks the control twin, without previous training, climbed the stairs unaided and rapidly reached as high a level of achievement as the twin who had received special attention daily for six weeks.

Similar results have been found in certain other studies of a number of other performances at varying maturity levels (11, 18, 19). In one such study (20) a group of children at an average age of twenty-eight months received training in buttoning, cutting with scissors, and climbing. During this period the experimenter tried in every way to help the child to learn the right movements, to eliminate wrong movement, to improve upon the speed and quality of his performance. Various devices were used to stimulate the children's interest and to motivate their efforts.

The children who had received practice were superior to control subjects at the end of the training period, but the control subjects rapidly overcame this advantage. During a week of practice at the end of the twelve-week experimental period the children in the control group achieved almost as high a level of performance as was achieved by children in the experimental group who had had twelve weeks of practice.

The fact that added maturity brings an increased capacity to profit from practice has been noted also in connection with studies of certain intellectual operations. One study (38) deals with language. Beginning at the age of eighty-four weeks, one twin was kept in a nonverbal environment—no words were spoken in her presence—while the other received daily drills in naming objects and in the use of words for five weeks. After five weeks of this, the "untrained" twin was given special training for a period of four weeks, during which time little language was used with the previously trained child. Three months later, both twins were tested again. The twin who had first received training had a definite advantage at the end of the first five weeks of the experiment, but when given an opportunity, her sister speedily began to reduce the difference. At the later period, the latter learned new words at a faster pace than had her twin at an earlier time. The child who received earlier training continued for some time to be superior in her pronunciation and her use of two-word sequences, but after three months the differences between the children were disappearing.

In a pioneer study by Gates (10) it was similarly found that children aged four to six who practiced the memorizing of numbers showed some advantage at the end of the period of practice over control subjects, but that this difference soon was overcome when the control subjects, now somewhat older, similarly received practice. Results similar to this have been found in other studies involving tests of performances such as naming colors.

In a study of the development of children's time concepts (35) it was found that sixth-grade pupils who had been exposed to a good deal of systematic training in chronology during a school year did not score higher on tests of time concepts than did a control group. The children in the control group had received no systematic training in history and chronology and had had the advantage only of an increase in chronological and mental age plus such knowledge as a child gains by way of reading, motion pictures, listening to the radio, and other everyday experiences.

In a study by Benezet (3) it was found that children whose formal training in arithmetic was postponed to the sixth grade rapidly gained as much competence as children who had struggled with formal arithmetic in earlier grades.

Other studies dealing directly or indirectly with the effects of special training or with the effects of varying amounts of time spent in training have dealt with spelling (6, 39) and the social studies (9).

The studies cited above indicate that an opportunity for concentrated practice of a performance is not a substitute for the changes that come with growth and such practice as a child receives incidentally in the course of his everyday life.

The effects of maturing, as distinguished simply from an opportunity to practice or to learn, appear also in the development of social and emotional behavior. Studies dealing with these topics are mentioned in later chapters.

NATURE OR QUALITY OF LEARNING IN RELATION TO MATURITY LEVEL

The influence of the child's level of maturity is revealed not only by the fact that he can or cannot profit from practice or can learn much or little at a particular time; the influence is seen also in the nature or quality of what he learns. Before a child can walk, he can learn to play ball—but only the kind of ball play of which a child at that level of development is capable. A child who is still in the creeping stage can learn to climb, but his climbing is the climbing of a creeper (27); that is, he tends to push himself upward and forward by gripping with his toes. When, at a later level, this same child is able to walk, his climbing takes on the walking pattern; and where earlier he depended a good deal upon his toes for gripping and pushing, he now has to depend more upon his arms for pulling himself upward.

The extent to which a performance learned at one level of maturity will carry over, or will need to be readapted, to a later level of maturity appears in a follow-up study of a pair of twins who took part in a study of roller skating, tricycling, and other activities before the age of two years. A further study was made of the children at the age of six years, about four years after the termination of the main experiment (28). Both children maintained their proficiency in riding a tricycle. As neither had a tricycle at home, this suggests that this type of skill does not deteriorate materially with disuse, although it could not be determined how much practice the children might have had on borrowed wheels; moreover, a normal six-year-old masters a tricycle quickly, even if he has never ridden one before. In contrast, proficiency in roller skating deteriorated after the practice period. Partly by reason of changes in bodily proportions as they grew older (including relatively longer length of legs and a shift in the center of gravity), the children had difficulty in maintaining their balance on roller skates. It appeared that a gross motor skill adapted to the bodily structure of a toddler did not carry over entire to a later stage when bodily proportions were different, and that intervening practice (which these children did not receive, except on brief occasions) was necessary to adapt the performance to progressive bodily changes and to maintain it at a high level. In climbing up a steep slope the child whose training began earlier remained superior to his brother, but as the children grew older, both had difficulty in managing their longer legs. On the other hand, there was not a similar loss in proficiency in getting off a pedestal and in descending a slide; in these activities, structural changes in the body apparently did not require substantial readjustments in mode of performance.

We shall have occasion throughout many later sections of this book to give other illustrations and to point out implications of this matter of readiness. It will come into the picture when we consider the development of routine habits such as bladder control, self-help in eating, dressing, and the like. It will appear also in connection with the discussion of development of social behavior, the growth of understanding, personality development, and in connection with all other aspects of development.

VARYING TIMELINESS IN RELATION TO MATURITY

Findings dealing with the subject of readiness to learn in relation to maturity have indicated, as one would expect, that a youngster at a certain level may be unready for the learning of one form of activity and ripe and ready for the learning of another activity. In one study (27) it was found, for example, that a child was able to make phenomenal progress in learning how to roller skate, beginning when he was little more than a year old; but it was not until many months later that he was able to make progress in learning to propel a tricycle. Two studies (22, 40) have shown that children of preschool age are able to make spectacular gains in the singing of tones, intervals, and phrases, while on the other hand, at the same age level, children have been found to make little or no gain in keeping exact time to music while walking or beating time with their hands (5, 23).

These modest examples of learnings that can be undertaken with profit at an early age are limited, yet they are very suggestive. The idea back of an inquiry into the timeliness of learning in relation to maturity is definitely not to encourage a policy of simply standing by on the theory that anything children might learn now could be learned much better if we waited until they were more mature. Actually, a child is occupied with the business of learning during most of his waking life. If he is not being compelled to learn one thing, he is likely, on his own accord, to be busy with something else. But there are many forms of learning that he cannot undertake unless equipment, facilities, and some encouragement, as, for instance, the example set by another person, are provided.

Unfortunately, the data in the study of children do not begin to provide a complete answer to what are the most timely learning situations at different maturity levels. Ordinary observation suggests that tremendous potentialities for learning and tremendous resources for achievement and enjoyment are being neglected and wasted. Nearly all human beings have voices and are able to sing, yet only a small proportion use and cultivate their voices in such a way as to get full use and enjoyment out of singing during childhood or adult years. Large numbers of persons could learn to obtain enjoyment in various other arts, such as the playing of musical instruments, dancing, painting, sculpture, and so forth; but in a large proportion of cases resources and potentialities of this sort are not cultivated. It appears also from ordinary observation that many persons, during childhood and adult years, are unable to execute or enjoy a variety of performances—such as skating, swimming, operations involved in the use of machines and tools, performances involved in various kinds of play and recreation that are suitable for all maturity levels—because they did not have the opportunity or incentive to learn when they were children. In order to provide opportunity and incentive, it is not necessary simply to supply equipment and facilities such as skates and musical instruments. It is quite as important to release time and energy that may be spent inefficiently in learning other things

Findings such as those reviewed in this chapter do not, of course, show that opportunities to practice or to learn have little or no effect on a child's development. Actually, of course, some learning and some practice are required in connection with practically everything that a child does. The lesson is rather that practice or the opportunity to use or to learn may have relatively little influence on a given performance at a given level of maturity, whereas rapid and large gains may be achieved through less practice or opportunity at a somewhat later level of maturity.

Findings such as these have tremendous implications for the child's training at home and at school. At home there is no point in trying to "teach" a child to walk or to climb or to handle a fork or to do a hundred and one other things until he is ready. Similarly, in school it is a waste of effort and resources to devote a great deal of time to the teaching of academic skills to a young child if the same amount of proficiency could be achieved through a very short period of teaching when the child is somewhat more mature.

Unfortunately, studies dealing with the question of the maturity level at which it would be most timely and strategic for a child to learn the countless things that he eventually must learn at home or at school are too limited to make it possible to outline all the details of the educational program of a normal child if this program were scaled to the child's maturing capacities. However, such data as are available indicate that very important changes in what we expect of a child at home and in school, and very great improvements in the range of accomplishments that children could learn to master and enjoy, would occur if the entire educational program were examined from this point of view.

OTHER PRINCIPLES OF DEVELOPMENT [3]

Certain other broad principles or general characteristics of development may be mentioned briefly.

Spontaneous use as a feature of growing ability. As a child develops he has an impulse to put his growing powers into use. Development involves both mechanical and dynamic changes. When the mechanics involved in creeping, for example, have been established, a child will creep of his own accord even if there is nothing external, such as a toy, to lure him from one spot to another. When his equipment is such that he can stand, he repeatedly tries to stand, even if there are obstacles and despite unpleasant falls. In his language development he industriously coos, babbles, and prattles, and in time he will practice words and phrases over and over again.[4] As he becomes able to imagine, he plunges of his own accord into make-believe. As his intellectual abilities develop, he exhibits avid curiosity: he asks questions, he

---

[3] The principles here set forth are adapted from an article by the writer and Fehlman (25) and a later statement by the writer and others (24).

[4] Numerous examples of apparently self-initiated practice are given by Shirley (37).

explores, he experiments, he seeks to know. Similarly in other aspects of his behavior. From early infancy onward, in all aspects of his development, a child will set himself tasks and he will practice and drill of his own accord.

These examples illustrate a principle of development—*the principle of indigenous motivation:* an integral feature of the development of a capacity or power is a tendency to use that capacity or power. The machinery of development is equipped with a self-starter, so to speak.

There is a strong positive motivation in childhood behavior. It is true, of course, that negative motives also come into play as the child meets with thwartings and frustrations and encounters conditions that frighten him, or arouse his anger, or bore him. Moreover, the impulse to put growing powers to work may be thwarted, discouraged, or diverted. Also, as a child matures and his abilities expand, increasing competition between different interests will arise. Along with the expansion of what he is able to do as he becomes older, a youngster's interests will also be increasingly influenced by what his environment offers or denies. Interests in one area may be stimulated by a taste of successful achievement, and potential interests in another area may go sour if the child is pushed beyond his depth. There is the further fact, of course, that interest in any performance may lag when it is fully mastered and no longer serves as a challenge or as a means toward further accomplishment. These factors make it more difficult to detect the principle of indigenous motivation as a child grows older.

"Wholeheartedness and gradation." [5] The tendency to put a growing power to use frequently means that a child will be intensely absorbed for a time by any new mode of behavior or phase of development. In trying out a new-found performance or experience, the child may seem to an observer to exaggerate or overdo. He may be so engrossed that other things are neglected. When the child, for example, first tastes the thrill of walking, he

---
[5] The wording is from H. L. Hollingworth (21).

may throw himself into the act even when he is tired or hungry. He may demand to be fed on his feet or he may find it almost impossible to sit down long enough to finish a meal.

Examples of this tendency may be seen in other aspects of a child's development during infancy as well as in later periods. Now in this experience, now in that, the child tends to go "all out" in his enthusiasm. Then, as time passes, what was new and absorbing tends to lose its separate fascination and become a feature of the large context of behavior.

The child's wholeheartedness in new ventures sometimes becomes trying to an adult, especially if the adult has forgotten the thrill he himself derived as a child from trying new forms of experience.

Every hurdle a hazard, every gain at a price. While each new advance in development usually increases a child's powers, it also is true that each advance may expose a child to new forms of danger and failure. When he is able to walk, he is able to walk not only into new interests but also into new troubles. In social development, as he becomes capable of tasting the experience of being an accepted member of a team, he also faces the possibility of being rejected by his fellows. When, in his mental development, he becomes able, through his imagination, to anticipate a future pleasure, he also becomes able to worry about what the future will bring. A gain in power does not mean a gain in composure. In addition, the more a child can do for himself, the more there is for him to do. Gain in ability usually brings increases in responsibility. Such is the price of development.

Developmental revision of habits. At every level of maturity children show forms of behavior which they will change or abandon in their own good time. At a given level of his development a child may use a certain way of behavior over and over again, but this does not necessarily mean that he will carry this way of behavior into a later stage of his growth. Repetition of behavior that is suited to a certain level of maturity does not necessarily establish a habit that will carry over to a later level. This is in keeping with other principles that we have noted above, including the observation that a child tends to do the best with what he has. The young infant sucks; later he bites and chews. Exercise of the grasp reflex, over and over again, does not fix the reflex forever. The child creeps, but later he walks and runs. The fact that he has practiced creeping assiduously does not mean that he will creep his way through life.[6]

Similarly, in his early language development the child has difficulty in articulating or pronouncing many words, but "muvver," even though repeated again and again, becomes "mother," and "dat" becomes "that." The child who at nine years was addicted to certain radio programs may at twelve years be very disapproving of these. The fact that a child misspells a word in the third grade and does so frequently does not mean that he has acquired the habit for good. Without special teaching, children through their own discovery revise their spelling of a large number of words (6, 39). Again, the fact that a young child flits from one activity to another does not mean that he is acquiring a habit that will bar him from being able to give sustained effort to a project when he is ten, fifteen, or twenty years old.

As a child's abilities mature, and as he becomes capable of new and different interests, he will not only revise, but completely reverse, many of his earlier forms of behavior. The youngster who awoke at an ungodly hour in the morning at three years may be hard to rout out of bed at ten. The child who was unkempt at ten years may become, if anything, too much of a dandy at eighteen years.

This process of revision of behavior does not, of course, always work in the direction of greater virtue or conformity. The child who is quite confiding at six years is likely to be relatively uncom-

---

[6] Examples of changes in reflex behavior are given in Chapter I.

municative at the age of ten or fifteen years if his development has been normal. The four-year-old who begs to wash the dishes may vigorously protest against this chore when he is older.

This phenomenon, which we have here called *the developmental revision of habits,* not only deserves an important place in the psychology of learning but it also has important practical implications in the rearing of children. Parents would be spared much worry and children much bother if it were more generally realized that many forms of behavior will be abandoned by the child himself in his own good time. While this is true, it also unfortunately is true that we do not precisely know all the forms of behavior that fall in this category or just when it might be well to help to push the process of revision.

Although the process of development involves a revision of behavior, it sometimes happens also that the youngster, instead of changing, retains an older way of behaving even though a newer way would be more appropriate. When this occurs we have the phenomenon of *persistence of archaic behavior tendencies.* These may range from mildly bad habits to complex behavior patterns that disturb the child's entire personality. A child at the age of six or eight, for example, may show many forms of dependence on others that were quite appropriate at the age of three or four. By virtue of overprotection or some other misfortune, he may retain not only a habit but also an attitude of dependency, and he may shrink even from an effort to strike out for himself. Again, a child who lives for a time in an environment in which he is mistreated may continue, even when his lot improves, to react to others with a certain amount of defensiveness and suspicion. In his dealings with his siblings or peers, he may acquire very strong competitive tendencies which he will carry into situations that do not call for competitive behavior. A child may also put on a show of courage when other children taunt him and call him "fraidy cat," and this effort to put on a brave front may be carried into later dealings with people who would not disparage him if he occasionally did reveal that he was afraid.

When behavior thus persists beyond its proper season, it sometimes creates trouble. The child who shows immature dependency on others may build up an elaborate system of wiles, ruses, and rationalizations to support his dependency. In an older person such behavior may even be rationalized to such an extent that the individual refuses or is unable to see his weakness. The process of supporting such a behavior tendency may go so far that a person who is actually very dependent may in some situations make a conspicuous display of independence.

Anticipation. Much that we see in a child at a particular time represents not only something that has utility for the present but something that prepares for things to come. This fact has already been mentioned in Chapter I, where we called attention to the "forehandedness of development." Development at any particular phase or stage of growth has an eye to the future.

Recognition of this fact makes it easier to understand and to accept much that we see in a child at any given time. Viewed in this light, for example, the two-year-old's efforts to be independent and to assert himself become something more than wanton stubbornness. Already at two the child is working toward the day when he, as an adult, will have to stand on his own feet and pull his own load.

Apart from behavior which anticipates developments that will be a long time in the making, the child sometimes shows little flashes of what is soon to be. He may walk a step or two, for example, or say a word or two, and then days or weeks may go by before he repeats or enlarges upon the performance.

It does not follow, however, that everything a child manifests at a given time is pointed toward developments that lie ahead. He also, in various ways, shows vestiges of the past. For many months after birth the infant's posture, notably during sleep, reflects the position of a child in the womb. In his behavior throughout childhood he may not only retain an infantile form of behavior, as noted above, but he may revert to behavior which he earlier had abandoned for a time. Such recurrence of "infantile" behavior may be a temporary lapse, as when a child who has had good bladder control wets himself under the stress of an exciting happening. It may also take a more serious form, as when a child over a long period is babyish and demands attention such as he actually required at an earlier time.

Interaction between aspects of development. Different aspects of development interact in countless ways. This holds true even as between aspects of development each of which may have a course of its own. There are features of motor development, including, for example, the development of ability to walk, that take place quite independently of the social setting in which a child lives, yet the ability to walk has important ramifications in the child's social behavior. When able to walk, the child can not only make more social contacts, but he also is better able to get in other people's way. Likewise, developments in the child's social behavior may profoundly influence aspects of his motor development. The example set by others and all that is involved in the child's social setting influence to an important degree his learning of motor skills, such as ball play, swimming, dancing, and the like. In a great variety of ways there is similar interaction among various other aspects of motor, mental, social and emotional development.[7]

BIBLIOGRAPHY

1. Ames, L. B.: "The Constancy of Psycho-Motor Tempo in Individual Infants," *Journal of Genetic Psychology* (1940), 57:445-450.
2. Bayley, N.: *The Development of Motor Abilities During the First Three Years,* Society for Research in Child Development Monographs (1935), No. 1, 26 pp.

---

[7] The concept of "organismic age," taking into account the interplay of many features of a person's make-up, has been developed and put to empirical test by Olsen and Hughes (32, 33, 34).

3. Benezet, L. P.: "The Story of an Experiment," *Journal of the National Education Association* (1935), 24:241-244; 301-303.
4. Carmichael, L.: "The Development of Behavior in Vertebrates Experimentally Removed from the Influence of External Stimulation," *Psychological Review* (1926), 33:51-58.
5. Christiansen, H.: *Bodily Rhythmic Movements of Children in Relation to Rhythm in Music,* Teachers College Contributions to Education, No. 736 (New York: Teachers College, Columbia University, 1938), 196 pp.
6. Courtis, A.: "Maturation as a Factor in Diagnosis," *Educational Diagnosis,* 34th Yearbook of the National Society for Study of Education (1935), 169-187.
7. Dennis, W.: "Infant Development Under Conditions of Restricted Practice and of Minimum Social Stimulation: A Preliminary Report," *Journal of Genetic Psychology* (1938), 53:149-157.
8. Dennis, W. and Dennis, M. G.: "The Effect of Cradling Practices Upon the Onset of Walking in Hopi Children," *Journal of Genetic Psychology* (1940), 56:77-86.
9. Eaton, M. T.: *A Survey of the Achievement in Social Studies of 10,220 Sixth Grade Pupils in 464 Schools in Indiana,* Bulletin, School of Education, University of Indiana (1944), 20: 64 pp.
10. Gates, A. I.: "The Nature and Limit of Improvement Due to Training," *Twenty-Seventh Yearbook of the National Society for the Study of Education* (1928), Pt. I, pp. 441-460.
11. Gates, A. I. and Taylor, G. A.: "An Experimental Study of the Nature of Improvement Resulting from Practice in a Motor Function," *Journal of Educational Psychology* (1926), 17:226-236.
12. Gesell, A.: *Infancy and Human Growth* (New York: Macmillan, 1928), 418 pp.
13. ———: "Maturation and the Patterning of Behavior," *A Handbook of Child Psychology,* revised edition, edited by C. Murchison (Worcester: Clark University Press, 1933), Ch. IV, pp. 209-235.
14. ———: *The Mental Growth of the Preschool Child* (New York: Macmillan, 1925), 447 pp.
15. Gesell, A. and Thompson, H.: *Infant Behavior* (New York: McGraw-Hill, 1934), 343 pp.
16. ———: *Learning and Growth in Identical Infant Twins:* An Experimental Study by the Method of Co-twin Control, Genetic Psychology Monographs (1929), 6:1-124.
17. Halverson, H. M.: *An Experimental Study of Prehension in Infants by Means of Systematic Cinema Records,* Genetic Psychology Monographs (1931), 10:107-286.
18. Hicks, J. A.: "The Acquisition of Motor Skill in Young Children: A

Study of the Effects of Practice in Throwing at a Moving Target," *Child Development* (1930), 1:90-105.
19. Hilgard, J. R.: *The Effect of Early and Delayed Practice on Memory and Motor Performances Studied by the Method of Co-Twin Control,* Genetic Psychology Monographs (1933), 14:493-567.
20. ———: "Learning and Maturation in Preschool Children," *Journal of Genetic Psychology* (1932), 41:36-56.
21. Hollingworth, H. L.: *Mental Growth and Decline* (New York: Appleton-Century, 1927), 396 pp.
22. Jersild, A. T.: *Training and Growth in the Development of Children,* Child Development Monographs (New York, Teachers College, Columbia University, 1932), No. 10, 73 pp.
23. Jersild, A. T. and Bienstock, S. F.: *Development of Rhythm in Young Children,* Child Development Monographs (New York: Teachers College, Columbia University, 1935), No. 22, 97 pp.
24. Jersild, A. T., Chayer, M., Fehlman, C., Hildreth, G., and Young, M.: *Child Development and the Curriculum* (New York: Teachers College Bureau of Publications, 1946), 274 pp.
25. Jersild, A. T. and Fehlman, C.: "Child Development and the Curriculum: Some General Principles," *Journal of Experimental Education* (1943), 12:130-142.
26. Jones, H. E. and Jones, M. C.: "Fear," *Childhood Education* (1928), 5:136-143.
27. McGraw, M. B.: *Growth: A Study of Johnny and Jimmy* (New York: Appleton-Century, 1935), 319 pp.
28. ———: "Later Development of Children Specially Trained During Infancy: Jimmy and Johnny at School Age," *Child Development* (1939), X, 1:1-19.
29. ———: "Maturation of Behavior," *Manual of Child Psychology,* edited by L. Carmichael (New York: Wiley, 1946), Ch. VII, pp. 332-369.
30. ———: "The Moro Reflex," *American Journal of Diseases of Children* (1937), 54:240-251.
31. Mattson, M. L.: *The Relation Between the Complexity of the Habit to Be Acquired and the Form of the Learning Curve in Young Children,* Genetic Psychology Monographs (1933), 13:298-299.
32. Olson, W. C.: "The Meaning of Growth," *Child Growth in an Era of Conflict, Fifteenth Yearbook of the National Education Association,* Department of Elementary School Principals (1944), pp. 1-9.
33. Olson, W. C. and Hughes, B. C.: "Concepts of Growth—Their Significance to Teachers," *Childhood Education* (1944), 21:2-12.
34. ———: "Growth of the Child as a Whole," *Child Behavior and Development,* edited by R. G. Barker, J. S. Kounin, and H. F. Wright (New York: McGraw-Hill, 1943), Ch. II, pp. 199-208.

35. Pistor, F.: "How Time Concepts Are Acquired by Children," *Educational Method* (1940), 20:107-112.
36. Shirley, M. M.: *The First Two Years: A Study of Twenty-Five Babies,* Vol. I: *Postural and Locomotor Development,* Institute of Child Welfare Monograph Series (Minneapolis: University of Minnesota Press, 1931), 227 pp.
37. ———: *The First Two Years: A Study of Twenty-Five Babies,* Vol. II: *Intellectual Development,* Institute of Child Welfare Monograph Series (Minneapolis: University of Minnesota, 1933), No. 7, 513 pp.
38. Strayer, L. C.: *Language and Growth: The Relative Efficacy of Early and Deferred Vocabulary Training Studied by the Method of Co-Twin Control,* Genetic Psychology Monographs (1930), 8:209-319.
39. Tyler, I. K.: *Spelling as a Secondary Learning,* Teachers College Contributions to Education, No. 701 (New York: Teachers College, Columbia University, 1939), 116 pp.
40. Updegraff, R., Heiliger, L., and Learned, J.: "Part III: The Effect of Training Upon Singing Ability and Musical Interest of Three-, Four-, and Five-Year-Old Children," *Studies in Preschool Education,* University of Iowa Studies in Child Welfare, New Series (1938), No. 346, Vol. I, 14:83-131.

CHAPTER III

SOME ASPECTS OF LIVING AND LEARNING IN INFANCY AND EARLY CHILDHOOD

The activities involved in obtaining food and rest and in the elimination of waste are of vital importance to the physical welfare of the infant, and they are a matter of considerable concern to his elders. These activities continue, of course, to be important concerns throughout life. The present chapter will deal with these worthy occupations.

The young infant spends a large part of his time in sleep. By the time he reaches school age he still sleeps about half of every twenty-four hours. By the time he is eighteen and from then on until death, he devotes about one-third of his time to sleep. In the meantime, his sleeping habits have received a good deal of attention, first from his parents and later from himself.

Even more demanding of attention during early infancy are the functions involved in getting nourishment and eliminating waste. The infant's cycle of quiescence and activity is largely governed by periodic demands for food. He also periodically voids his bladder and his bowels. In due time, this natural flow of events is drastically changed. Where before the child need only suck for a living, he now has to chew and take a more active part in the feeding process, and even when he is very young his eating becomes regimented in countless ways. The processes of elimination, which at the start were completely involuntary, are also brought under control, usually with considerable prompting from the child's diligent mother. Much of the child's earliest education revolves around activities connected with feeding, sleeping, and other "routine" details of his everyday care. It is by way of these

INFANCY AND EARLY CHILDHOOD

activities that he is first introduced to many of the demands and taboos of the society in which he lives.

FEEDING AND BEHAVIOR ASSOCIATED WITH FEEDING

One might expect that the establishment of good feeding habits would be the easiest feature of a child's training, for the drive to obtain nourishment is perhaps the strongest drive in living creatures. As one can observe in everyday life, however, children's feeding behavior often gives a good deal of trouble. The more a child's diet and eating routines can be based upon natural wants rather than upon a conglomeration of rules and formulas, the smoother the road should be (29, 35, 39). Likewise, the more nearly changing demands, such as the introduction of solids, weaning, the use of motor skills involved in handling cups and other utensils, and the niceties of eating behavior, can be scaled to the child's growing capacities, the better the outcome is likely to be.

To find what is natural as regards wants and appetites and the abilities underlying the skills involved in eating, unfortunately, is no simple task. There are differences between individual children with respect to needs, tempo, and rate of progress. Quite as important a complication is the fact that the child's natural tendencies, whatever they may be, often come into conflict with customs, parental attitudes, and habits, which are associated not only with feeding as such, but also with all other aspects of the child's daily relationships with his parents.

Suckling. In the average newborn child the impulse to suckle is strong enough to enable the child to take food if he is given the breast or the bottle. Some babies, however, need help to initiate the process of sucking. Moreover, there are modifications in the sucking mechanism and in the sucking behavior after the child is born, but in most infants sucking is pre-eminently something the infant can do very well. Furthermore, as Feldman has pointed out (16), the mechanism involved in sucking is highly protected against physical damage. The composition of the pad of fat in each cheek, the so-called suction cushion, is such that it is not readily absorbed. Feldman reports that it is present even in very emaciated babies when fat has disappeared from every other part of the body. It is also rich in blood supply.

Although the sucking mechanism is comparatively well developed and is highly protected, there are changes after birth in the structures involved, and there is an increase also in the nerve supply of the lips (18). The newborn child often drools and leaks at the corners of his mouth by reason of imperfect coördination between lips and tongue and the fact that the angles of the lips are not as completely supplied with nerve endings or as completely under control as are the median portions of the lips. Likewise, the newborn's suckling and swallowing movements are closely merged, so that unswallowed milk runs out of his mouth when he releases the nipple. During the act of nursing, he also swallows a good deal of air, and feeding must sometimes be interrupted so that he may belch. This ritual, in some parts, is called "burping the baby," and it seems that adults differ considerably in their ability to hold a child in just the right position for achieving an optimum burp. As the child grows older and becomes more proficient at nursing, less air is swallowed and the need for belching diminishes.

Sucking activities apart from food-getting. Although sucking and mouthing serve primarily the purpose of food-getting, the impulse to suck may become relatively independent of the process of feeding. Sucking frequently becomes an activity which seems to be undertaken for its own sake; the baby sucks even though his appetite for food is sated. Many babies do a certain amount of sucking, apart from nursing, from the time of birth. The act may be most prominent when the child is hungry and may continue immediately after he has been fed. A case has even been reported of an infant who, to all appearances, had sucked his

INFANCY AND EARLY CHILDHOOD

thumb before he was born (18). The baby's thumb was swollen on delivery, and soon after the birth cry he placed the swollen thumb in his mouth.

Although there are differences in time of onset and in amount of finger-sucking, all babies are likely to suck their fists, fingers, or thumbs at some time or other during infancy. In the period preceding the eruption of the first tooth and throughout the period of teething, the hand is brought to the mouth a good deal, and there is much mouthing of the fist.

In many young children, there are recurrent periods of finger-sucking. A child may cease to suck for a time and then do so again more vigorously than before. Many children, as is well known, continue the finger- or thumb-sucking habit for several years.

The fact that practically all babies at some time or another suck their fingers is a matter of importance because it is a feature of child behavior and also because adults so often are disturbed by it. The reasons for adult disapproval seem to vary from the notion that there is something unbecoming about finger-sucking to the belief that such sucking, if it continues, will cause malformation of the jaw.[1] By reason of the importance attached by adults to the habit, some extra space is devoted to it here.

There have been many explanations or theories to account for finger-sucking. One theory is that the child sucks his thumb or fingers because the need for exercise of the sucking mechanism is not satisfied in the process of sucking to obtain food. Levy has reported observations in support of this explanation (25). Apparently a bottle-fed child is more likely to continue to suck if the

---

[1] The question as to what are the chances that thumb-sucking will cause malformation of the jaw cannot be answered on the basis of available data. Apparently the chances are greater if the practice is continued vigorously after the child has his secondary teeth (28). Many children who suck persistently for extended periods of time and who then drop the habit do not show any dental effects. Moreover, it appears that in some cases where malformation has taken place, the deformity is corrected in the process of growth if the sucking habit is stopped.

aperture of the nipple is large, permitting the free flow of milk, than if the aperture is small and the child must give more time and effort to obtain the same amount of milk.

By way of analogy, Levy gives the example, familiar to everyone who has been raised on a farm, of the behavior of young calves. A dairy calf which is not allowed to suckle its mother but is taught from the start to feed from a pail is likely, for some time after its first feedings, to suck an accommodating finger or the ear or tail of another calf or any other object that is handy. To be sure, such sucking may be due to the fact that the pail-fed calf probably gets a smaller ration of milk than a suckling calf, but at any rate the sucking will continue when even the calf must realize that there is not much nourishment in it. Such sucking by the calf seems to correspond, at least in some respects, to thumb-sucking in the child, although in the child's case the sucking is likely to be more persistent and the habit will be influenced by many factors which do not bother the average calf.

If finger-sucking is brought about by lack of sufficient exercise of sucking apparatus, one might expect that some babies would take to finger-sucking when they are being transferred from bottle feeding to feeding out of a cup. Levy gives such an example of a child who took to sucking his thumb when one bottle feeding was dropped from his daily schedule; the child stopped thumb-sucking when this bottle feeding was resumed. However, while such deprivation of sucking at the bottle may bring about sucking of the thumb, it does not appear that all instances of thumb-sucking can thus be accounted for.

Whatever may be the immediate causes, certain obvious conditions encourage a child to suck his thumb. For one thing, the thumb is about the most convenient thing in the world for him to suck. It is always with him. It is the handiest device for setting off a mechanism that is primed for action from the time of birth and that from an early age is a feature of what must be a rather satisfying experience.

The context in which sucking occurs—the alleviation of hunger—is one of the earliest and most profound satisfactions in a child's life. The getting of food, of which sucking is the most active part, from an early age has a pervasively quieting and comforting effect. There was a gnawing at his vitals, now it is being relieved; he was restless, now he is relaxed; he was troubled, now he is at peace. The act of sucking is entrenched in a larger context of satisfaction and comfort. That the child should discover ways of partly re-establishing at least a feature of this context, namely, sucking, is not to be wondered at. Moreover, adults who have their own pet pleasures, as most adults do, should think twice before they regard this habit as objectionable *per se* or proceed to try to stamp it out.[2]

Sensory functions of mouth and lips. Many of the child's first active contacts with his environment come by way of his mouth and lips. Even after he has become alert to sights and sounds he continues for a long time to make considerable use of mouth and lips in exploring the world about him. When he has acquired the ability to bring objects to his mouth with his hands, there is a period during which he tries to carry to his mouth practically everything he can grasp. The mouth is a sensory avenue to the environment much as are the eyes and the ears. It is almost as though the lips and tongue serve the infant in a manner analogous to the way in which cutaneous impressions from the fingers serve the blind adult. As soon as he is able to bring things to his mouth, the infant explores contours of surfaces, tests the hardness and softness of things with his lips and teeth, and also apparently explores the temperature of objects and appears to be active in exploring the taste of things. Although this exploration of the taste of things may even be secondary, it becomes quite prominent; and so the child will cram a block into his mouth, insert balls of lint,

---

[2] The extent to which the sucking of a thumb may be regarded by a child as a source of comfort is illustrated by the behavior of a two-year-old who, on observing her father sink into a chair with a groan of fatigue, came to him and offered to let him have her "fumb" to suck.

bits of earth, crayons, and morsels of food that he discovers on the floor after he has refused what remains on his own plate and has had his fill. It is as though the child yet was hungry and every new object had the lure of a delicious steak.

Chewing. The newborn child is structurally better equipped for sucking than for chewing, not merely by virtue of his lack of teeth, but also because of the formation of his jaws. His lower jaw is poorly developed. Biting is usually not prominent until about the fourth month, although it may appear considerably earlier. Gesell and Ilg (18) observe that occasionally children even at the time of birth show "surprising strength of bite," and they add that "this strength is not only unseasonable but unsuitable to normal suckling" (18, p. 28). Chewing movements likewise may appear even before a child has any teeth and may precede by a considerable time the actual chewing of food. In Buhler's inventory of the behavior development of infants (6), chewing is noted at the sixth month; the ability to chew well, in connection with feeding, is placed at forty-four weeks, but at that age the child is not able to masticate all foods; the ability to chew unground meat well is placed at eighteen months.

Many children go through the motions of chewing before chewing functions as a necessary feature of feeding. They "chew" on milk, applesauce, puréed vegetables, and the like. It is as though they were practicing the performance in preparation for future use. In this they provide another illustration of the developmental principle of anticipation as set forth in Chapter II.

SPONTANEOUS FOOD DEMANDS

To what extent can a healthy child's own demands be trusted as a guide for determining when, what, and how much he should be fed? This is a rather vital question both from a practical and a theoretical point of view. If a child's appetite for food is trustworthy, both he and his parents could be spared much trouble (if their larder were stocked with the right things). The question also has theoretical importance, for what is found true of demands for food might also, on investigation, prove to be true of certain other demands. The more it can be shown that a child's wants or desires provide a good indication of his needs, the less necessary it becomes to restrict and restrain him and to push him around.

The evidence bearing on this question is limited but provocative. In studies of babies during the first few months of life, preceding and following the weaning period, it has been found that the spontaneous food demands of young children tend to be rather wise.

The findings that have been obtained in studies of infants who have been on a "self-demand" feeding schedule from the time of birth or soon thereafter go counter to some practices and conventions in child care that have, until recently, been applied quite generally. One finding, already noted in Chapter I, is that a schedule of feeding the child approximately every three hours is more in keeping with the child's own demands than is the frequently adopted policy of feeding him every four hours. This statement should be qualified by a word to the effect that there are such wide variations between children that any fixed schedule, whether it provides long or short intervals between feedings, would frequently be out of step with the needs of individual children. Even so, it would be a good thing, apparently, if hospitals that accept "lying in" cases and homes to which newborn babies go would expand their charity or increase their budget to accommodate a more flexible schedule of feeding.

In one study (37) it was found that in the interval between the second and the tenth day of life there was one day on which a child on a self-demand schedule demanded to be fed only six times and another day on which the same child demanded eleven feedings. In spite of such fluctuations, this child and others who have been observed tend to show a certain amount of consistency in the number of feedings demanded per day. In the study just cited there were five days out of nine during which this newborn demanded nine feedings.

A further observation has been that as the infant grows older he spontaneously reduces the number of feedings demanded per day. Still another observation is that the amount of food intake varies widely from day to day and from feeding to feeding. The systematic findings bearing upon this problem in early infancy are limited partly because only recently has anyone undertaken to do systematic research on this subject, and partly because research of this kind is very time-consuming. It is interesting to note, however, that the studies reported so far are in agreement on main points such as those mentioned above.[3]

The findings in self-demand studies at the early infancy level also indicate that infants seem to be well nourished when on a feeding schedule geared to their own demands. There has been no evidence that any of the infants who were fed according to their own demands suffered any ill effects from this policy. In addition, some mothers will maintain that the experience is, if anything, psychologically more satisfying both to the infant and to the mother than is a fixed schedule.

Although the findings obtained in studies of the responses of young infants to a self-demand schedule are generally favorable as far as they go, they leave certain questions unanswered. The children with whom this program has been followed systematically from a research point of view are few in number, and it is by no means certain that they are from families representing a normal sampling of the population. Moreover, there are many practical difficulties. Where there are several members in the household, many things happen unavoidably that interfere with freedom to give prompt attention to the infant's demands for food. The demands of the child may interfere with other de-

---

[3] Studies of infants on self-demand schedules have been reported by Gesell and Ilg (18) and by Trainham *et al.* (40).

mands. Moreover, there no doubt are mothers who would find it difficult to relax and to be at ease by reason of the uncertainty and unpredictability of a self-demand schedule; this difficulty might, in turn, have an unfavorable effect on the way in which the mother deals with the infant and other members of the family.[4]

Reservations such as these do not detract from the importance of the findings. It may also be said that the findings that have been obtained square pretty well with common sense. Certainly it seems to be good judgment to feed a hungry child rather than to have him wait until the clock strikes a certain hour. Similarly, it is only reasonable to accept the fact that a child is more hungry at some times than at other times. It is a curious fact that it has been necessary for the benefit of both doctors and laymen to reaffirm ordinary wisdom such as this.

Self-selection of formulas in early infancy. Infants have shown a wisdom and logic of their own, not only when given a choice as to when and how much they should eat, but also when given some choice as to what food to take.

In one experiment (10), three infants, beginning at or before the tenth day of life, were offered, in rotated order, four different formulas at each feeding and were permitted to take as much of each as they wished. Apart from variations and vagaries in amount consumed, the children showed unmistakable preferences almost from the beginning. As the children grew older (the experiment was continued until they were about eight months old), they would sometimes reject the bottle with the unfavored formula without even tasting it, thus indicating that they apparently also were responding to odor, appearance, or some other cue. There were found to be large differences among the babies in the patterns of choice.

At the end of the experiment the nutritional status of the infants was reported to be "excellent in every way."

---

[4] E. B. Jackson (22) discusses difficulties encountered by a mother on attempting to continue at home a self-demand regimen successfully followed while she and her baby were in the hospital.

Spontaneous food selection and consumption in later infancy. When a child's diet includes solids, his feeding increasingly involves questions of what to eat as well as when and how much. To what extent can a child now be trusted to make good choices?

Findings bearing on this point have been reported by Davis (11, 12), who observed children when they were free to select their own diets. The children had several choices at each meal, but all of the items in the total menu were not presented at any single meal.

Following is a sample tray in one series of experiments with three newly weaned babies: lactic milk, whole milk, cooked marrow, raw beef, cooked beef, chicken, sea salt, ordinary salt (no foods were salted, but the child was free to take salt as he pleased), raw carrots, cooked turnips, cauliflower, crisp rye crackers. The twelve items represent a selection from a larger list of over thirty items which were variously combined at different meals. The children were free to choose; food was not offered to them or suggested; the nurse simply sat by and helped the child to get what he wanted, as he indicated his wants by pointing, reaching, opening his mouth to receive food previously pointed out, and in other ways. As far as they desired or were able, the children were permitted to feed themselves by means of their fingers and to wield their own spoons.

It was found that there were wide variations in the self-selected menus of the same child from time to time and in the menus selected by different children. The selections often were thoroughly unorthodox and sometimes startling from the point of view of an adult. But physical examinations and measurements seemed to show that the children made wholesome choices and thrived. Some illustrative findings and observations are reviewed below. The reader is referred to the original studies for more complete details.

When the experiment was begun—with three newly weaned infants who had had no experience with solid foods—each infant at first chose some foods which he spat out. The factors that determined initial choices could not readily be determined. After the first few meals, however, the infants chose foods promptly without regard to their position on the tray, and there was not the subsequent spitting out which had occurred at the start. At a given meal, a youngster would often select a bizarre diet, including as many as seven eggs at a single sitting (in another series of observations, a two-and-a-half-year-old child ate ten eggs at one meal!) or as many as four bananas. Salt was taken only occasionally, and often when taken the infant would splutter, choke, and even cry, but he would refrain from spitting it out and would later repeat the performance with the same spluttering.

The infants tended to eat certain foods in waves: after eating given articles—such as fruits, eggs, or cereal—in moderate amounts, there would follow a period when larger and sometimes "astonishingly large" amounts were taken, followed in turn by a decline to the previous level. Symptoms of overeating did not appear in connection with such "jags"; nor were they followed by periods of disgust. The children were omnivorous, and their preferences were unpredictable. They showed no consistent preferences for cooked or raw food, but some items were definitely preferred cooked and others raw. Spontaneous dunking of hard crackers in milk or water was observed, especially at periods when a new tooth was erupting. The infants tended to take their foods "straight" rather than to mix foods or even to pour milk over cereals. One infant who had active rickets when the study began spontaneously consumed large quantities of cod-liver oil, and then later left it untouched when this active condition had been overcome, as revealed by blood tests and X-ray examinations.

In a later study (13), Davis reports observations made of fourteen children in a hospital ward, each of whom selected his own diet from the various foods prepared for the day. The findings in this series of observations conformed to those noted above, and the children, for all the vagaries of their appetites and occasionally grotesque choices, seemed to be wise in their choices as far as could be determined by records of their digestive balance, health, energy, and growth. There was also less waste than under the usual system, as measured by the weights of garbage from this and other wards.

The evidence in Davis' study, as well as in other observations, indicates that a young child has more sense about eating what is good for him than he often is credited with, granted that he has wholesome articles of diet from which to choose. Among the many significant observations in these studies is that a nutritionally balanced diet is not something that need be supplied by an arbitrary package of so much of this and so much of that every day. The balance can be achieved over longer periods of time. Recognition of this fact alone can spare parents a good deal of anxiety and children a good deal of nagging.

Interesting as the above findings may be, their applicability in the case of a given child is not so simple. In the home, where means and time are limited, the provision of a variety of articles of food would be difficult, although many different alternative items that add up to a complete diet need not be presented at every meal.

A self-selection program in the average home would involve many complications and, to be properly safeguarded, would require much knowledge about nutrition (33). Another serious consideration is the fact that a child's appetite, his eating, and his "feeding problems" do not occupy a little compartment of their own but are influenced by attitudes and habits that are determined not only by what happens in the eating situation but by all that is involved in the relationship between the child and other members of the household.

There are many other complications. A child's demands for certain foods may vary if his mother happens to be a good or a poor cook. Available evidence does not solve other practical problems. The evidence does not adequately answer, for example, the problem as to what to do with the large number of children who demand, or at least would accept, what seems to be an excessive amount of sweets.

SELF-HELP IN EATING

The development of self-help in eating obviously depends to a large degree upon the child's motor development, since it involves postural control, the ability to reach, grasp, and convey objects to the mouth.

In studies of the sequence of development involved in the ability to handle a cup, Gesell and Ilg (18) note changes such as these: At twelve weeks, the average child will notice the cup but is unable to grasp it; his movements are jerky, gross, and lacking in direction. At sixteen weeks the normal infant makes contact with the cup; at twenty weeks he makes a "corralling" approach upon the sides of the cup; at twenty-eight weeks he grasps and lifts it, usually with both hands; at thirty-two weeks he grasps the handle; but it is not until thirty-six weeks that his manner of lifting the cup in an upturned position, grasping the handle, and mouthing the rim approximates the true raising of a cup to the lips for drinking purposes. Although he thus manipulates the cup, at thirty-six weeks his "concept of the cup as a utensil and as a receptacle is still in a very rudimentary state. . . ." (18, p. 44).

Sequences can also be observed in a child's handling of a spoon, beginning with regard for the spoon at sixteen to twenty weeks. Although the child exhibits much activity both with spoon and cup for a long period, it was not until fifty-two weeks that the average child in a study by Gesell and Ilg brought the two into combination and definitely began to treat the cup as a receptacle and the spoon as a tool to be inserted into the cup. Well-defined self-management of the cup was not observed in the typical child until about sixty-five weeks. He now tilted the cup as it emptied, but by means of his palms; not until later did his fingers assume the main role in tilting. An indication of the complexity of the act of drinking from a cup can be gathered from the fact that the act calls not only for skillful manual control but also coördination of hand and finger movements with respiratory movements and rhythmic action of the tongue.

The child is likely to do a good deal of finger-feeding during the second year, while the development of ability to use cup and spoon is going on and, unless he is curbed, his hands and fingers will come into play a good deal for a long time thereafter. Use of a blunt fork may be expected at about two to three years, of a blunt knife between the ages of three and five, and of the knife for cutting at about five to six (42), although here, as in other matters, there are wide variations among children.

In the process of acquiring skill in self-help, there will obviously be a good deal of awkwardness, spilling, messing, dropping of utensils, and the like. In order to practice eating skills, the child must necessarily be given a chance to make mistakes. Moreover, in these skills as in other developments, a child may not follow an invariable course of constant improvement; he may show a momentary advance, only to revert for a time to an earlier form of behavior. Such fluctuations are a feature of normal development.

The period during which a child is learning to handle feeding utensils is often a trying period to a parent. Even if a parent is not finicky or squeamish, he is likely to become impatient at times with the spilling and messing, the clumsy tipping of containers of food, the child's insistence on doing some things for himself when it is obvious that he cannot succeed. The child, on his part, also has quite a job, for not only must he cope with new skills but he also often must put up a struggle for permission to try his hand.

The following summary illustrates an aspect of one of the many skills related to self-help in feeding. It is based upon observations of nursery-school children in the act of pouring water from a pitcher into a small glass. The performances of the children were roughly classified according to four levels, as indicated in the summary, which is adapted from Slater (38).

TABLE I

LEVEL OF PERFORMANCE AT VARIOUS AGE LEVELS IN POURING FROM A PITCHER[5]

Level of Performance	Number of Children at Each Level of Performance at Each Age						
	2 yrs.	2½ yrs.	3 yrs.	3½ yrs.	4 yrs.	4½ yrs.	Total
Water goes all over the table.........	3	5	3				11
It goes into the cup, but overflows it..		8	7	2	1		18
Wobbly control, some spilling, stop before overflow..................		6	12	6	5		29
Firm, easy control; little spilling....		1	8	7	7	4	27

The summary in Table I indicates that in this particular group of nursery-school children it was not until the age of three and a half that the median child had achieved good control, with little spilling, in pouring water from a pitcher into a glass. At the age of four years, there still were several children whose performance was somewhat unsteady. Before the age of three, a majority of the children were unskilled in the performance, but this did not deter them from trying. It is characteristic of the young child that, with the motor skills involved in eating, as with many other operations, he will try his hand before he has the necessary neuromuscular control to master the performances involved. Unless he is restrained, he practices the operations, and this practice goes on apace with the maturation of the underlying mechanism. Both the learning and the growth process must receive due recognition. Attempts to force his progress and demands for a degree of skill that is beyond his power are undesirable, just as are undue efforts to prevent him from trying his hand for fear that he will spill and drop things.

---

[5] Adapted from Slater, E.: *II. Types, Levels, and Irregularities of Response to a Nursery School Situation of Forty Children Observed With Special Reference to the Home Environment,* Studies from the Center for Research in Child Health and Development, School of Public Health, Harvard University. Monographs of the Society for Research in Child Development (1939), IV, No. 2, 148 pp. Reproduced by permission.

FOOD PREFERENCES

As we have indicated, children are likely to exhibit food preferences at an early age. Various factors play a part in such preferences, including taste, texture, and consistency, the appearance of the food, the way it is served, and so on. In some cases there may be an organic aversion, as in allergic conditions. Some articles may be generally disliked as compared with others (4), but there are pronounced individual differences. When a child shows aversion to a food, it obviously would be well to know the cause, especially if the item represents a convenient means of supplying an important feature of his diet. As noted earlier, a child will show shifts in his preferences from time to time. It also has been observed that a child may show dislike for a new article of diet when it is first introduced and then spontaneously acquire a liking for it if it is made available from time to time and no effort is made to coerce him.

Parental influences on food preferences. As children grow older and observe the example set by others, their food preferences are influenced to some degree by the attitudes and idiosyncrasies of their parents. In a study by McCarthy (30) of forty-eight children aged two to seven and a half years, inquiries were made concerning the eating habits and food aversions of children and their parents. It was found that the parents' food dislikes were sometimes reflected in the behavior of children, but to a larger extent of children who were "problems" than of those who were regarded as normal.

The effect of family influences on food habits is further brought out in a study by Campbell (8) in which the later food habits of children who had attended nursery school, where efforts usually are made to reduce finicalness in food choices, were compared with those of a control group who had not had the benefit of such nursery-school training. Little difference was found between the two groups, and the food habits of children from the same home

INFANCY AND EARLY CHILDHOOD

were found to be similar, even if one child had attended nursery school and the other had not.

"FEEDING PROBLEMS"

Many of the so-called "behavior problems" that arise in connection with the rearing of children represent problems of feeding, sleeping, and elimination (29). In one study (23), in which five hundred parents reported pleasures and problems connected with the having and upbringing of children, it was found that difficulties with "routine care" constituted the second largest group of problems reported by the parents.[6] When all the various problems reported by the parents were classified according to age level of the children, it was found, as might be expected, that the problems relating to "routines" were relatively more prominent in infancy and early childhood than in later childhood years. However, even up to the age of twelve there was a relatively high incidence of problems in this category.

Most frequent among the problems under the heading of "routines," as reported by parents in this study, were problems of feeding. Second in frequency were problems of sleep; "dress, grooming, personal adornment" stood third in frequency; this was followed by a category containing problems of elimination (most of these had reference to bladder control).

Nearly all children present their parents with a feeding problem at one time or another. The problem may range from behavior that is only mildly perplexing to behavior that produces severe annoyance or anxiety in the parent and that represents serious trouble for the child. Very often the feeding problem is a problem because the parent regards it as such and not because the child actually is getting too little food or is demanding the wrong kind of food. Often the feeding problem is not primarily a problem of feeding but a symptom or consequence of other difficulties in the child's life.

---
[6] For further details see Table XXI, pages 310-312.

Whatever may be the circumstance, however, difficulties connected with feeding are among the most prominent problems that occur in the upbringing of children. There are, of course, several reasons for this. Food in proper amount and kind is so necessary for health and growth that parents quite understandably are much concerned about it. The child, on his part, quite understandably rebels against the prodding and prompting and occasionally resists the rules, standards, and restraints that surround any human being who is bent on getting some food into his stomach. Many children also learn at an early age that the feeding situation is the Achilles' heel in the parent-child relationship. They learn that the feeding situation provides an effective means of gaining attention, of showing rebellion or resistance, of asserting themselves as independent persons.

A list of the forms that feeding problems may take would fill a heavy volume. The following items represent only a few of the more common everyday complaints: The child is a light eater; he takes too much of one kind of food, too little of another; he refuses to take his quart or pint of milk a day; he will not take milk unless it is mixed with coffee and sugar or unless he can have coffee as a chaser; he will eat dry cereal but not cooked cereal; he will eat hardly any breakfast; he eats lightly at mealtime and then wants to nibble between meals; he scarcely touches his own meal and then cadges the food of others; he refuses a bit of food, then demands it, then rejects it when it is brought; he asks for food which takes time to prepare and then when it is ready he does not want it; he instigates mutiny and disaffection among younger siblings by voicing his dislike of food that is being served; he wants to eat with a big fork, then demands a small one; he fills his mouth too full; he retains food in his mouth at length without chewing or swallowing; he bolts his food; he dawdles; when food is passed he fingers several pieces before making a choice; and so forth.

Many of these examples are relatively trivial in character. The problem becomes more serious from the parent's point of view if the child, in the judgment of the parent, is not regularly obtaining an adequate and balanced diet over a period of time.

In many cases parental concern over a child's feeding behavior is complicated by the fact that some children who had voracious appetites at the age of one or two seem to want too little food at the age of three or four. Some children around the age of four seem to require less food, even though they are now bigger, than they required at an earlier age when their rate of growth was more rapid. Moreover, as a child grows older he may revise the timing of his food intake. A child who is just beginning to go to school, for example, may take very little breakfast but eat heartily at lunch and suppertime. Another youngster may distribute his food intake more evenly among the three meals.

The factors that produce a "feeding problem," whether the problem represents a genuine difficulty or is a problem because the parents so regard it, are as varied as are the problems themselves. There is space only to indicate a few of these factors. The difficulty may reside in the child himself: his health may be poor or he may be suffering from allergies and the like. The difficulty may be influenced largely by the child's emotional condition: his feeding behavior may be adversely affected by conditions within or outside the feeding situation that have led him to be anxious, hostile, or resistant. The difficulty, on the other hand, may occur largely as a result of the emotional condition of the parents: they, on their part, may be anxious or hostile, ready to take offense, impatient, overly insistent that the child be obedient and good. The difficulty may be due in part to the fact that parents expect too much of the child and, as a result, become impatient if the child is clumsy or takes extra time or seems to be slow in learning the niceties of table manners and the like. Again, the difficulty may be due in part to the fact that parents have stereotyped or mistaken notions as to how much a child should eat.

The problem may be influenced by local stereotyped prejudices or rules which the parent may never have thought out from a nutritional point of view. Rules of this sort may vary from one locality and even from one moment to another. Thus, there may be the rule that a child should not eat meat unless he also eats potatoes; there may be the notion that cheese, peanut butter, and jam are never to be eaten and enjoyed by themselves but must always be spread on a piece of bread; dessert is conceived of as a reward and not as a part of the meal; the child is allowed to have no second helpings of anything until he has finished everything that was set before him; there are certain things meant only for adults (so it is claimed) and it is morally wrong for a child short of college age to touch or taste them.

While children's food-getting often is complicated by such arbitrary rules and prejudices, it does not follow, of course, that good management of children's feeding always requires that the parent give in to the child. For practical reasons, if on no other grounds, it becomes necessary to insist upon a certain amount of regularity in eating hours, to limit between-meal snacks, and to see to it that the child, as he grows older, does not use table manners that are discomforting to other members of his household and that would make him an unwelcome guest in other homes.

SLEEPING

In the newborn child, periods of complete wakefulness tend to be briefer, and periods during which the child is fully asleep seem also to be considerably briefer than is the case later on. As time passes, periods of wakefulness increase in length, especially during the daytime hours, and periods of uninterrupted sleep likewise increase. The total amount of time spent in sleep also diminishes, although with many fluctuations. If placed on an arbitrary schedule of feedings which does not correspond to his own spontaneous demands, the child often must be awakened to be fed, and sometimes such a child will refuse to nurse or take the bottle, or will do so while remaining in a rather sleepy state.

INFANCY AND EARLY CHILDHOOD

Table II shows the approximate average amount of time spent in sleep at various age levels from one month to eight years. The averages are based on results for all seasons combined and are therefore approximate, since the amount of sleep varies with the seasons, being greater in winter and smaller in summer. The table is based on studies by Foster, Goodenough, and Anderson, who, through the coöperation of parents, obtained about a thousand records of children's sleep for each day of a week during each

TABLE II

AVERAGE AMOUNT OF SLEEP PER DAY AT VARIOUS AGE LEVELS[7]
(The values represent averages for all seasons combined.)

Age	Hours	Minutes
1–6 months	15	3
6–12 months	14	9
12–18 months	13	23
1½–2 years	13	6
2–3 years	12	42
3–4 years	12	7
4–5 years	11	43
5–6 years	11	19
6–7 years	11	4
7–8 years	10	58

TABLE III

AVERAGE AMOUNT OF TIME SPENT IN BED FROM 8 TO 18 YEARS, AS REPORTED BY CHILDREN THEMSELVES[8]

Age in Years	Hours	Minutes
8–9	10	42
9–10	10	13
10–11	9	56
11–12	10	00
12–13	9	36
13–14	9	31
14–15	9	06
15–16	8	54
16–17	8	30
17–18	8	46

---

[7] From *The Sleep of Young Children* (Minneapolis: University of Minnesota, Institute of Child Welfare, 1930), Circular No. 4, 11 pp. Reproduced by permission. See also Foster, Goodenough, and Anderson (17).

[8] From Terman, L. M. and Hocking, A.: "The Sleep of School Children," in *Journal of Educational Psychology* (1913), 4:138-147, 199-208, 269-282. Reproduced by permission.

of the four seasons of the year. Table III shows the average amount of time children aged eight to eighteen spend in bed, as reported by themselves.

The records on which Table II is based showed large individual variations at all age levels. Below the age of one year, there was a difference of more than three hours between the ten per cent of children who slept most and the ten per cent who slept least. Up to the age of four years, the corresponding difference was more than two hours; and from four to eight years, the difference was more than an hour. The differences between individual children at the two extremes were decidedly larger.

In dealing with young children it is well to remember that children show wide differences in the amount of sleep they seem to require. Translated into practical terms, a difference of two hours in the sleep needs of two children who get up at the same time in the morning, and who have similar naps, would mean that if one child is put to bed at seven in the evening, the other might properly stay up until nine. Again, it may mean that a two-year-old who happens to require less sleep than the average may get along with less sleep than is required by a four-year-old who happens to require more than the average. Actually, of course, it would be hard to judge just what a child *requires* and just what would be optimum, but the practical importance of recognizing individual differences still remains.

Many difficulties are involved in obtaining measurements of time spent in sleep as a basis for practical recommendations. Even a careful observer will have difficulty in telling whether a child whose eyes are closed actually is asleep.

Apart from this difficulty of determining the time actually spent in sleep, there is the difficulty of determining the "natural" sleep needs. A healthy infant, left free to sleep whenever he wants to, without interruption, does not present a problem on this score; but the problem arises as a child grows older. For one thing, the amount of time an older child spends in bed is governed to a large extent by conventions. It is possible that some children are prevailed upon to stay in bed longer than is necessary, but it is no simple matter to let the runabout child control his sleep schedule according to his own "natural" demands, for many happenings in his environment may conspire to keep him awake when he normally would become drowsy (such as boisterous play and excitement) and to keep him from becoming "slept out" (such as the bustle of the household or the demands of the home and school schedule). The difficulty in this connection is exemplified by the fact that as children grow older they desire more and more to stay up late in the evening, and, at the same time, more and more of them have to be called in the morning. The difficulties of "natural self-regulation" of sleep are even greater in the case of children whose equilibrium is disturbed by malnutrition, illness, digestive difficulties, or other bodily disorders. Such disturbances may make a child wakeful when he is much in need of sleep.[9]

Lacking full information as to a given child's natural sleep needs, conscientious parents generally lean toward the view that the more sleep a child can conveniently get the better it is for him, and they try to govern his routines accordingly. They are likely to be all the more inclined toward this by reason of the fact that once the child is asleep, he is no longer underfoot and the parents' hard day's work will soon be done. However, in trying to make sure that the child gets plenty of sleep, parents sometimes invite needless trouble. By insisting that the child go to bed early they may simply be depriving themselves of sleep, for the child may become wakeful and awaken them early in the morning.

Studies of children's sleep demands have yielded certain findings that parallel some findings with respect to children's spontaneous food demands. Reynolds and Mallay (32) studied the sleep of thirty-four children who, for several weeks during the summer, spent the twenty-four hours of the day in a nursery school. Note was made of when the children went to bed, when

---

[9] Sleep disturbances because of unpleasant dreams are discussed in Chapter XII.

they fell asleep (as far as could be determined by close observation), and when they awakened.

The respective number of hours spent in sleep, including naptimes, by two-, three-, and four-year-old children was twelve and a half hours, eleven hours and twenty-three minutes, and ten hours and fifty-seven minutes. These averages parallel but are somewhat lower than the averages found for the same ages on the basis of mothers' reports, during the summer season, in the study represented in Table II. The average child spent an hour in bed before falling asleep. (This item should be considered against the fact that the time was summer and that there were many other children sleeping in the same building.)

The children showed wide variations in amount of sleep from day to day. However, when results were computed in terms of longer periods, such as two or three weeks, it was found that there was a high degree of constancy in the amount of sleep taken. This phenomenon, it may be noted, corresponds to what has been found with regard to children's eating—a child may show wide short-term fluctuations in the times when he is hungry and in the amount of food intake, and yet show a high degree of stability when trends are measured in terms of weeks rather than hours or days. It was likewise observed that if for one reason or another a child lost a good deal of sleep during one day, he did not promptly counterbalance this by sleeping that much more the following day; rather, he made it up over several ensuing days.

Daytime naps. The reduction in total amount of sleep during the twenty-four hours is brought about, even during the first weeks after birth, mainly by a decline in amount of time spent in sleep during the daytime hours. The reduction is linked with increases in the duration of uninterrupted sleep at night. In the case of many children, the previous early morning nap, following a feeding early in the morning, and the late evening nap are merged with night-time sleep. Along with this trend, periods of wakefulness during the day lengthen and become more clearly demarcated from periods of sleep, leaving a late morning and an afternoon nap. In the second year, the afternoon nap usually gains ascendancy, although individual children vary in this. After the second year, inroads are likewise made on the afternoon nap, again with individual variations.

An afternoon sleep period is usually a part of the child's conventional routine at about the age of two. Many children continue for some time to sleep during this period; others tend more and more to remain wakeful during part or all of it. As described by Sherman, "The child learns to stay in bed a certain amount of time" (36). In the study by Reynolds and Mallay, it was found that in the case of many children the daytime nap drops out on an all-or-none basis; instead of gradually tapering off, some children either continue to sleep during the nap period or at a certain point discontinue naptime sleep altogether.

The findings with regard to children's own daytime sleep behavior do not support a policy of fixed standards, similar for all children. The problem of managing sleep and rest periods remains a puzzling one during preschool years and on into adult life. It may be much to the child's advantage to get him to acquire the habit of taking rest periods during the day, whether or not he falls asleep during those periods. One thing that is much needed by many older children, as well as by many adults, is the ability to relax completely during the course of the day's activities.

Studies of fatigue and rest have shown that brief rest periods may have more recuperative value than the equivalent amount of time spent in one long rest period. The ability to relax, and even to doze off during free moments between strenuous activity, would be a boon alike to older children and adults. It does not appear that this happy faculty is fostered by a sleep regime which, from preschool years and onward, is governed more by conventions and the clock than by the child's own varying needs from day to day and even from hour to hour. One obvious difficulty is that practical arrangements, both at home and at school, require a certain amount of regularity of schedule; the competition of other demands makes it difficult, first, to gauge a child's natural demands and, second, to adapt his schedule to such demands.

Some problems connected with sleep. Problems connected with children's sleep range from problems of practical management to those of a complicated psychological nature. The problem of children's sleep is intertwined also with the problem of adequate rest and sleep for the entire family. If the child is a poor sleeper, or if he is faced with conditions that disturb his sleep, other members of the household are likely to suffer along with him.

Children's sleep is, of course, affected by anything in their everyday lives that disposes them to be excited or relaxed, tranquil or disturbed. Children's sleep may be much affected by their fears. Again, a child's willingness to go to bed and to slough off his daytime preoccupations may be affected by the extent to which he is friendly and at peace with other members of the household and the extent to which he is resistant and hostile. It is not only the painful or hostile emotions that may make inroads on sleep. An alert, interested child, happy in his surroundings, may also try to remain awake as long as he can.

Many children establish quite a bed-going ritual. There may be a series of songs that must be sung, verses that must be said; the child may need not one but several drinks of water; the shade must be adjusted just so; dolls or other possessions must be settled in the right place; for good measure, the child may demand an extra bit of "scratching." When all this has been done, the parent may be called back again for another round on the plea that a detail has been forgotten or that the youngster has a new bit of information to convey or a new question to ask.

Tactics such as these, which are found at the preschool level considerably more than in older children, and which have the effect of delaying the last goodnight, serve many functions in the child's life. For some children, bedtime may be the time of day when the child and parent are most warmly and comfortably responsive to each other. If a child is afraid, this ritual may serve the purpose of staving off the moment when he will be left to himself. It may be a period during which he assures himself of the companionship and friendliness of his parent. Again, in the course of bedtime activities, the child often takes occasion to practice and to rehearse operations that are important features of his development. He practices his language and powers of conversation; at the period when he is becoming able to memorize and to sing songs, the bedtime ritual may be a time of rehearsal. The activities connected with going to bed may serve different motives at different times for the same child.

As a child grows older, especially after he has learned to read, has become interested in radio programs, or has acquired other persisting interests of his own, he may try to establish a bed-going routine that is quite different from the foregoing. Instead of seeking to prolong the attention he is receiving from his parent, he may try to get rid of it.

More serious from the point of view of the parents in many ways than the maneuvers of a child who is trying to delay his bed-going is the problem of the child who falls asleep and then becomes wakeful during the night. Such a child may demand that the ritual of bed-going be repeated, or he may ask to get into bed with one of his parents. He may complain of noises that scare him or of aches and pains that bother him. The simplest explanation of such wakefulness may be that the child is being kept in bed longer than is necessary: he may be wakeful at night because of a long daytime nap or because he has been asleep since early in the evening. However, such wakefulness is more serious if it is due to a physical disorder or to emotional distress, such as fear. It is better, in such a case, to try to deal with the physical condition, or to try to overcome the fear, than to deal with the problem as primarily a problem of sleep.

An account of the practical considerations involved in the management of sleep would involve lengthy treatment of such topics as the relation of sleep habits to health, nutrition, exhaustion, excitement before bedtime, various forms of negative conditioning, bladder and bowel control, emotional insecurity, anger, fear, and physical factors such as temperature, crowding, noise, illumination, and so forth. For a discussion of these practical aspects of the subject, the reader is advised to consult books dealing with the general subject of child care and with the subject of sleep. Suggested references are given in the bibliography under numbers (1, 3, 5, 15).

ELIMINATION

Children and parents alike would be spared much trouble if infants were housebroken at birth. As it is, the development of bladder and bowel control is a relatively slow, often laborious process, entailing much labor on the parent's part and frequently a good deal of emotional complication as far as the child is concerned. Control of elimination requires the ability to inhibit processes that are completely involuntary at the start and it involves the control of muscle groups that are obscure and unseen. As in other aspects of the child's development, it is important to scale the child's training to his growth. At the start, the child lacks the nervous mechanism for voluntary control and would be unable to control his elimination even if, by some freak of nature, he had a desire to do so.

Progress in the control of elimination. Many features of the child's progress in gaining voluntary control have been described by Gesell and Ilg (18). In discussing the problem of voluntary control, these investigators draw an interesting analogy between the eliminative processes and the development of voluntary control of movement. For example, when a child releases an object at will it means that his grasp reflex has yielded to a mechanism of inhibition and control. The investigators point out that the power deliberately to release an object is acquired rather slowly; that it is not until the end of the first year that a majority of infants

INFANCY AND EARLY CHILDHOOD

consistently are able to let go when in the act of trying to drop a small block into a container. They further point out that an equivalent control of the tonus of the bladder sphincter may in some respects be more difficult. Accordingly, a child's failure to respond well to training may be due to the immaturity of the sensorimotor mechanism, rather than to perversity and resistance. "Here is a field where the demands of culture may be brought to bear too heavily on an immature nervous system" (p. 18, 125).

In their discussion of developmental aspects of bladder control, Gesell and Ilg point out that for some time after birth many infants will wake up and cry when wet, but the same infants, at about the age of three or four months, may tolerate wetness and fail to fuss or complain until about the age of a year.

For a considerable time, the infant's "bladder control" is largely a control exercised by the vigilant parent who anticipates voidance of the bladder before it occurs.

During the first part of the second year, while the mechanism for control of the bladder is being perfected, the child is also undergoing the process perfecting his postural control. Gesell and Ilg describe how complications may arise in coördinating the two. Placement on the toilet seat may produce tensions that result in the withholding of urine, and then the child may promptly urinate when removed from the seat.

The fact that progress in bladder control is tied to the process of maturation is indicated in an interesting study by McGraw (31). Observations were made of two pairs of identical male twins. The observations began when the twins were about a month old and continued for well over a year. One twin of each pair was given systematic "training" on four days each week by being placed on the toilet receptacle every hour.[11] Records were kept of the number of times the bladder was emptied in the receptacle or elsewhere and the measure of achievement was the percentage of

---

[11] It would require further study to determine whether training might have been more effective if a more flexible schedule had been used.

times it occurred in the receptacle. The other twin in each set was not allowed to use the toilet facilities until, respectively, at about the age of 14½ and 24 months.

The effort spent in training the one member of each pair did not yield corresponding achievement. One of the untrained twins, when introduced to the laboratory pot at 430 days, came to within ten percentage points of the success ratio of his brother who had had hourly access to the chamber four days each week since he was twenty-three days old. The untrained twin in the other pair was first introduced to the laboratory pot at the age of two years. At this time his achievement was about the same as that of his brother who had had the pot as a daily companion. Indeed, this "untrained" boy, who had not been allowed by his mother (in coöperation with the investigator) to use a toilet chamber at home, earned nearly a perfect score from the time when, at the ripe old age of two years, he first had a chance to use the toilet.

The two twins who received "training" did not show steady improvement. Instead, their performance showed interesting ups and downs.[12] Both began with fairly high initial success,[13] followed by slumps and rises which reached their lowest level in the period when both babies were about six to ten or eleven months old. Following this, around the first birthday, there occurred an increase in successes, followed, in turn, by declines. This gain in control, according to McGraw, marks the time when intelligent participation in the process is becoming possible. The fact that the child is acquiring this power to control what originally was an involuntary act may be marked not only by the fact that he uses the toilet chamber successfully but also by other signs. Signs of awareness appear when the child apparently notices the tinkle, appears to realize that the sound effects originate with him, shows

---

[12] Records of intervals between urination, kept during one day each week with all four children, did not reveal any consistent "rhythms" such as parents have frequently been advised to capitalize on.

[13] This initial success was explained on the ground that the reflex mechanism governing micturition is quite sensitive to stimulation during the first couple of months.

interest in puddles, and is responsive to the use of a word or sound to designate the act of urination. "Even a glint in his eye may reveal his awareness of the act" (although the happy event is perhaps even more likely to be greeted with a glint in the eyes of his parents).

However, the first flush of success in control does not necessarily mean that the child will go on from victory to victory or even that he will maintain his level of success. There may be regressions, arising from many circumstances. One child may stay dry consistently, another may fluctuate. Not only will the child's consistency of control be influenced by factors pertaining to bladder control as such but also by other events in his life. He may become so absorbed in play that he chooses not to be diverted. Even if he heeds the call of nature he may wet himself because he does not give himself enough time. The development of locomotion and the other motor performances and the development of speech may bring competing interests, and so forth.

Definitive statements as to when the child may be expected to assume full responsibility in these matters cannot be made because of individual differences in children and because of differences in the circumstances in which their training occurs (5, 34, 42). In an investigation by Scoe (34) it was found that most of the children who were studied had established control by the time they reached their second birthday, but that many children who turn out to be fine citizens do not achieve control as a regular habit until the age of three or even four or five. The "norms" for bladder control, as reported by different investigators, show much variation. Moreover, a child may achieve rather consistent control and still occasionally wet himself, or wet his bed at night, for several years thereafter.

Daytime control usually (but not at all invariably) precedes nighttime control. A large proportion of children have pretty well acquired the "dry habit" during the day by about the age of two and a half. However, some have not. It may be another year before the two-and-a-half-year-old who keeps dry during the day is equally in control at night.

After the child has established control, much time may still have to elapse before he is capable of self-help in going to the toilet and in managing his clothes. This is especially true if the fixtures and his clothing are unsuited to his limited motor powers.

The foregoing statements deal mainly with bladder control. Control of the bowel usually is established more readily. In the healthy child, bowel movements are more regular and considerably less frequent; they can be anticipated more accurately and at an earlier age than can voidance of the bladder, thereby facilitating the learning process of associating a movement with being placed on the toilet. In this function, however, there are again large individual differences. Bowel control, and attitudes associated with defecation, may be complicated by parental attitudes and practices such as disgust, a policy of compelling the child to sit on the pot for long periods, a policy of making excessive use of suppositories and laxatives, and other practices.

Lapses, hindrances, and later progress. Even after the habit of letting needs be known has been fairly well established, there are likely to be many lapses, reversions to earlier forms of behavior, or fluctuations in the consistency with which control is exercised. Moreover, a boy is likely from time to time to experiment with his aim and trajectory. A girl may also experiment, may try to perform in the manner of a boy when she has taken notice of such sex differences. Such experimentation, the trying out of new or different ways of doing things, occurs also, of course, in connection with other activities.

Occasionally the child who seems well on the way to complete control of the eliminative functions will backslide. When accidents occur, he may resort to furtiveness and falsehood, may even disclaim responsibility for the mess he has made, blaming it on others. Such digressions are so common that they should probably be regarded as normal features of the child's advance. The child's performance is likely also to be affected variously by many other factors, such as teething, illness, temperature, consumption of liquids. Even after several years of consistent control a child may relapse under trying conditions. Some children, for example, again wet their beds when they begin to go to school, apparently as a symptom of strain or fatigue. The fact that stresses in a child's life may produce a greater than usual amount of incontinence has been reported in investigations of British children who were evacuated from city to country places during World War II (7).

In time, many children learn to exploit the processes of elimination as a means of gaining attention from adults. In a study by the writer and an associate, a young nursery-school child, who much preferred the company of adults to that of children, quickly discovered that he could gain his ends by asking to go to the toilet. During one fifteen-minute period, he slyly managed to go to the toilet four times, once with each of the four teachers and assistants who were in charge of the group. Apparently as a device for gaining attention, a child will sometimes revert to incontinence when a new baby arrives in the family.

Attitudes with regard to elimination and the genital organs. In due time, in our culture, the process and the organs of elimination tend to become enveloped in an atmosphere of furtiveness, secrecy, and shame. The factors that cause this, including associations between elimination, nakedness, and sex, obviously are many. The attitudes that are established often extend far beyond the practical requirements of privacy and circumspection that would be justified simply on sanitary, aesthetic, and moral grounds.

Changes with age in children's attitudes toward elimination and the genital organs are shown in an interesting fashion in a study by Dillon of two groups of nursery-school children (14). One group included twenty-two children aged twenty-seven to forty-eight months; the other included sixteen children aged forty-two to sixty-two months. The younger group had an average age of about thirty-five months; the older, fifty-one months.

In the younger group, there was relatively little self-consciousness or furtiveness with regard to elimination, nakedness, or the sex organs; in the older group, many signs of awareness were revealed by attempts at concealment, secretiveness, use of "bad words," and so forth.

Tabooed language was more manifest with the older children. For example, some of them would whisper "bad words" (terms having to do with elimination) to each other or giggle and snicker. It was noted, incidentally, that children whose parents had taught them accurate terms for designating elimination and the genitals would adopt the baby terms used by other children and use them in preference. Other observers have similarly noted that young children sometimes learn from one another to use words that seem to be especially charged with feeling from the child's point of view, even if adults see nothing objectionable in the words. One child of four who had learned to regard the expression "Do do sissy pants" as something especially forbidden and obscene was scandalized when her father repeated these words quite nonchalantly.

A difference between the attitudes of the younger and older children was observed in the study cited above in connection with a game of taking rectal temperature. When a teacher tried to discourage this make-believe game, the children of the younger group went to secluded places and showed increased interest in it. But when it was suggested that they play the game openly, they readily complied; and after a few weeks without interference, interest in it disappeared. This game, which was generally out of keeping with the nonchalance showed by the younger children toward elimination, illustrated the manner in which the excretory organs can take on a tabooed lure, even at an early age. The older group took over this game from the younger ones, but their attitude toward it appeared to be distinctly different; from the start they were more furtive, and their interest in the game lasted longer.

The difficulty adults encounter in being thoroughly matter-of-fact was exemplified in this study by the fact that, during the periods of observation, the teachers did not once refer to the organs of elimination by name (such as penis), even though they tended to assume a matter-of-fact attitude toward the process of elimination and toward the genital organs.

Attitudes toward genital organs. Note was also made, in the study cited above, of children's behavior with respect to the genital organs. In the younger group, handling of the genital organs was less frequent than in the older group; it was shown by fewer children, took place more openly, and in most cases was more fleeting than in the older group. Such play was observed in the case of seven of the twenty-two younger children and eight of the sixteen children in the older group. The children who gave more than passing attention to this play tended to show more tenseness in other aspects of their behavior than did the other children. The behavior did not seem to be stimulated materially by nakedness, the presence of both sexes, or elimination; rather, it appeared to be related to a state of emotional tension. At no time was a child observed to try to conceal such activity or to show guilt or shame. Several children were observed to show an interest in the genitalia, the anus, breasts, navel, and other organs, much as they might show an exploratory interest in other events that caught their attention; but a few children showed an interest in the opposite sex that did not seem to arise simply from curiosity as to physical appearance.

The children in the group aged twenty-seven to forty-two months gave little evidence of a clear differentiation between the sexes, but children in the older group all showed some consciousness of sex differences. Not all of the older children, however, had a clear recognition of physical differences. Some would recognize differences in clothing and costumes, never fail to apply the words "boy" and "girl" correctly, and yet apparently regard the male sex organ as an incidental possession which girls did not have rather than as an essential distinguishing characteristic.

Practices associated with the genital organs in early childhood. A large number of children at an early age show through their behavior that the genital organs are more than just passive appendages associated with the process of elimination. Infant boys have the experience of tumescence (resulting in erection of the penis) and detumescence. In one study of nine male infants aged three to twenty weeks (19) it was found that tumescence occurred at least once daily in at least seven of the nine and that, in individual children, it might occur from four to over thirty times during an eight-hour period. Moreover, tumescence was accompanied by restlessness while detumescence was associated with a more relaxed state.

This phenomenon does not, of course, necessarily mean that the young boy has sensations or feelings of an erotic or sexual nature; it does mean, however, as stated above, that the genital organ comes to the young child's attention. In addition, parents will report the fact that a large proportion both of boys and girls during the first year or two manipulate or stimulate their genital organs. Again it may be said that such manipulation should not necessarily be regarded as an experience equivalent to masturbation; but it does represent an active experience involving the genital organs. Such behavior at the infancy level, and similar behavior, sometimes accompanied by other signs of interest in sex, at the preschool level (21, 24, 26), may be transitory, or it may persist for an extended period of time; it may occupy a child many times during a day, or it may occur at widespread intervals. In this behavior, as in all other aspects of development, there are, of course, wide individual differences among normal children.

The sex organs are likely to come to a child's attention in other ways. Sooner or later he will notice anatomical differences between the male and the female. Many youngsters, once they have noticed the difference, are quite interested. Moreover, if the child is interested but is hindered through the prudery of his parents, he may even at the early age of two or three become quite furtive in his efforts to satisfy his curiosity by peeking or trying by stealth to obtain a view of the naked human body.[14] Facts such as these have obvious practical implications. Through failure to recognize that phenomena such as the foregoing are common and are a normal feature of development, some parents become unduly alarmed. If parents apply severe restraint or punishment, or obviously show an attitude of squeamishness or revulsion, they may have a very unwholesome effect on the attitudes which the child acquires. This aspect of development should neither be treated more roughly nor as something requiring more extreme delicacy than other aspects of development. By a display of their own irrational attitudes, parents may stimulate the child's interest or induce unwholesome feelings of anxiety, and impulses and behavior tendencies of the child which the parents deplore may become stronger rather than weaker.

Actually, a large proportion of children who stimulate themselves abandon the practice of their own accord or after a few matter-of-fact promptings, just as a large proportion of children suck their thumbs for a time and then stop. Many children appear to have an active interest in matters relating to sex for a time, then seem to lose interest, and, later, show a renewed interest.

Apart from the foregoing, the early appearance of certain forms of behavior relating to sex is an interesting illustration of the developmental principle of anticipation which was noted in Chapter I. Developments relating to sex are so forehanded that even as an infant in his crib, more than a dozen years in advance of the

---

[14] Some have maintained that the child's discovery of the differences between the genital organs of the two sexes produces a severe emotional shock and leads to feelings of anxiety or hostility or a mixture of both (27). However, ordinary observation, as well as systematic study of normal children, indicates that such reactions are not typical (9).

time when he will be able to procreate, the child first begins to manifest forms of behavior and interests that anticipate his role as one destined by nature to reproduce his kind.

BIBLIOGRAPHY

1. Aldrich, C. A. and Aldrich, M. M.: *Babies Are Human Beings; An Interpretation of Growth* (New York: Macmillan, 1938), 128 pp.
2. ———: *Feeding Our Old-Fashioned Children* (New York: Macmillan, 1941), 112 pp.
3. Blatz, W. E.: "The Physiological Appetites," *A Handbook of Child Psychology,* revised edition, edited by C. Murchison (Worcester: Clark University Press, 1933), pp. 723-770.
4. Borgeson, G. M.: *Techniques Used by the Teacher During the Nursery School Luncheon Period,* Child Development Monographs (New York: Teachers College Bureau of Publications, 1938), No. 24, 214 pp.
5. Bott, E. A., Blatz, W. E., Chant, N., and Bott, H.: *Observation and Training of Fundamental Habits in Young Children,* Genetic Psychology Monographs (1928), 4, No. 1:1-161.
6. Bühler, C.: *The First Year of Life* (New York: John Day, 1930), 281 pp.
7. Burt, C.: "The Incidence of Neurotic Symptoms Among Evacuated School Children," *British Journal of Educational Psychology* (1940), 10:8-15.
8. Campbell, E. H.: "The Effect of Nursery School Training Upon the Later Food Habits of the Child," *Child Development* (1933), 4:329-345.
9. Conn, J. H.: "Children's Reactions to the Discovery of Genital Differences," *American Journal of Orthopsychiatry* (1940), 10:747-755.
10. Davis, C. M.: "Choice of Formulas Made by Three Infants Throughout the Nursing Period," *American Journal of Diseases of Children* (1935), 50:385-394.
11. ———: "A Practical Application of Some Lessons of the Self-Selection of Diet Study to the Feeding of Children in Hospitals," *American Journal of Diseases of Children* (1933), 46:743-750.
12. ———: "Self-Selection of Diet by Newly Weaned Infants," *American Journal of Diseases of Children* (1928), 36:651-679.
13. ———: "Self-Selection of Diets: An Experiment with Infants," *The Trained Nurse and Hospital Review* (1931), 86:5.
14. Dillon, M. S.: "Attitudes of Children Toward Their Own Bodies and

Those of Other Children," *Child Development* (1934), 5, No. 2:165-176.
15. Faegre, M. L. and Anderson, J. E.: *Child Care and Training*, fourth edition (Minneapolis: University of Minnesota Press, 1937), 327 pp.
16. Feldman, W. M.: *The Principles of Ante-Natal and Post-Natal Child Physiology; Pure and Applied* (New York: Longmans, Green and Co., 1920), 694 pp.
17. Foster, J. C., Goodenough, F. L., and Anderson, J. E.: "The Sleep of Young Children," *Pedagogical Seminary and Journal of Genetic Psychology* (1928), 35:201-218.
18. Gesell, A. and Ilg, F. L.: *Feeding Behavior of Infants* (Philadelphia: J. B. Lippincott, 1937), 201 pp.
19. Halverson, H. M.: "Genital and Sphincter Behavior of the Male Infant," *Journal of Genetic Psychology* (1940), 56:95-136.
20. Institute of Child Welfare: *The Sleep of Young Children* (Minneapolis: University of Minnesota, 1930), Circular No. 4, 11 pp.
21. Isaacs, S.: *Social Development in Young Children: A Study of Beginnings* (New York: Harcourt, Brace, 1933), 480 pp.
22. Jackson, E. B.: "Prophylactic Consideration for the Neonatal Period. Development of a Home Visiting Plan for Pediatric Internees," *American Journal of Orthopsychiatry* (1945), 15:98.
23. Jersild, A. T., Woodyard, E., and Fehlman, C., *et al.: Joys and Problems of Child Rearing*, unpublished (New York: Teachers College, Columbia University).
24. Koch, H. L.: "An Analysis of Certain Forms of So-Called 'Nervous Habits' in Young Children," *Journal of Genetic Psychology* (1935), 46:139-170.
25. Levy, David M.: "Thumb or Finger Sucking from the Psychiatric Angle," *Child Development* (1937), 8:99-101.
26. ———: "Fingersucking and Accessory Movements in Early Infancy," *American Journal of Psychiatry* (1928), 7:881-918.
27. ———: " 'Control-Situation' Studies of Children's Responses to the Difference in Genitalia," *American Journal of Orthopsychiatry* (1940), 10:755-763.
28. Lewis, S. J.: "The Effect of Thumb and Finger Sucking on the Primary Teeth and Dental Arches," *Child Development* (1937), 8:93-98.
29. Louttit, C. K.: *Clinical Psychology* (New York: Harper, 1936), 695 pp.
30. McCarthy, D.: "Children's Feeding Problems in Relation to the Food Aversions in the Family," *Child Development* (1935), 6:277-284.
31. McGraw, M. B.: "Neural Maturation as Exemplified in Achievement of Bladder Control," *Journal of Pediatrics* (1940), 16:580-590.
32. Reynolds, M. M. and Mallay, H.: "Sleep of Young Children," *Peda-

gogical Seminary and Journal of Genetic Psychology (1933), 43:322-351.
33. Roberts, L. J.: *Nutrition Work with Children,* second edition (Chicago: University of Chicago Press, 1935), 555 pp.
34. Scoe, H. F.: *Bladder Control in Infancy and Early Childhood,* University of Iowa Studies in Child Welfare (1933), 5: No. 4, 83 pp.
35. Senn, M. J.: *All About Feeding Children* (New York: Doubleday, Doran, 1944).
36. Sherman, M.: "Afternoon Sleep of Young Children: Some Influencing Factors," *Pedagogical Seminary* (1930), 38:114-126.
37. Simsarian, F. P. and McLendon, P. A.: "Feeding Behavior of an Infant During the First Twelve Weeks of Life on a Self-Demand Schedule," *Journal of Pediatrics* (1942), 20:93-103.
38. Slater, E.: II. *Types, Levels, and Irregularities of Response to a Nursery School Situation of Forty Children Observed With Special Reference to the Home Environment,* Studies from The Center for Research in Child Health and Development, School of Public Health, Harvard University, Society for Research in Child Development Monographs (1939), Vol. IV, No. 2, 148 pp.
39. Spock, B.: *The Common Sense Book of Baby and Child Care* (New York: Duell, Sloan and Pearce, 1945), 527 pp.
40. Terman, L. M. and Hocking, A.: "The Sleep of School Children," *Journal of Educational Psychology* (1913), 4:138-147; 199-208; 269-282.
41. Trainham, G., Pilafian, G. J., and Kraft, R. M.: "A Case History of Twins Breast-Fed on a Self-Demand Regime," *Journal of Pediatrics* (1945), 27:97-108.
42. Wooley, H. T.: "Eating, Sleeping, and Elimination," *A Handbook of Child Psychology,* edited by C. Murchison (Worcester: Clark University Press, 1931), pp. 28-70.

Chapter IV

MOTOR DEVELOPMENT

In this chapter we shall deal with some general characteristics of the child's motor development and shall single out certain achievements for special examination. Developments such as those that enable a child to walk and to perform complicated movements with his hands have an interesting story of their own and they also have an important bearing upon other aspects of behavior. It is to a large extent by virtue of his motor development that a child moves from the helplessness of early infancy toward self-help and independence. Motor activities also play a large role in his intellectual enterprises and his social contacts.

TRENDS IN PHYSICAL GROWTH

The development of motor activities is closely related to changes in gross bodily size, in the size of various parts of the body, and in bodily mechanics.[1] The average newborn child is about twenty and a half inches long. During the first year, his length increases by over a third, and by the age of five years he will be about twice as tall as he was at birth. During the period of physical growth, continuing changes in the proportions of the body take place. The young child's head, for example, is relatively large at birth and does not increase as rapidly or as much in size as does his total stature. There is a considerably larger increase in the length of the trunk, an even greater increase in the length of the arms, and, by the time full stature is attained, a still greater increase in the length of the legs. These trends are generally in keeping with

---

[1] An adequate treatment of anatomical and physiological growth would constitute a volume in itself. For a more extended treatment of this subject, the reader is referred to references listed under the following numbers: 2, 3, 8, 38, 48, 49, 51.

the cephalo-caudal direction of development noted earlier in the discussion of prenatal growth.

Different parts of the body grow at different rates and reach their approximate maximum at different times during the period from early childhood to maturity. The same is true also of the various internal organs of the body. Not only is there a differential course of growth for different parts of the body, but the pattern varies from individual to individual.

LOCOMOTION

The child's first step comes as the climax of a long series of developments. The groundwork for the ability to walk is being laid long before the infant is able to stand by himself or to sit alone, or even to raise his chest from the crib in which he is lying. The first "steps" in locomotion, so to speak, are not taken with the legs but with the muscles in the upper trunk and arms.

Many achievements which mean that a child is able more and more to carry the load of his body can be noted from birth until he attains the ability to creep. After birth, a child will continue for some time to assume the curled-up posture of a fetus. Within the first three weeks or so the average child will be able to lift his head and raise his chin clear of the table on which he is lying. A further advance appears as he raises his head higher, holds it up longer, and, in time, raises his chest as well as his head. In one study (47), the ability to raise head and chest, while supporting the weight on elbows and forearms, appeared at an average age of about nine weeks. Such activities represent an important advance even though they may seem to have no immediate connection with creeping or walking. At twenty-five weeks, the median child of Shirley's study was able to sit alone momentarily, and at sixty-four weeks he was able to walk alone. The order in which various achievements appeared in this study is shown in Table IV.

Although there is a high degree of similarity between different children in the sequence or order of various developments, there

TABLE IV

THE MEDIANS AND QUARTILES FOR STAGES IN THE DEVELOPMENT OF LOCOMOTION[2]

Description of Stage	Number of Cases	Age in Weeks Q_1	Median	Q_3
First-Order Skills:				
On stomach, chin up	22	2.0	3.0	7.0
On stomach, chest up	22	5.0	9.0	10.0
Held erect, stepping	19	11.0	13.0	15.0
On back, tense for lifting	19	14.0	15.0	18.0
Held erect, knees straight	18	13.0	15.0	19.0
Sit on lap, support at lower ribs and complete head control	22	15.0	18.5	19.5
Second-Order Skills:				
Sit alone momentarily	22	20.5	25.0	26.0
On stomach, knee push or swim	22	22.0	25.0	27.0
On back, rolling	19	25.0	29.0	32.0
Held erect, stand firmly with help	20	29.0	29.5	33.0
Sit alone one minute	20	27.0	31.0	34.0
Third-Order Skills:				
On stomach, some progress	17	32.5	37.0	41.0
On stomach, scoot backward	16	34.0	39.5	45.5
Fourth-Order Skills:				
Stand holding to furniture	22	41.0	42.0	45.0
Creep	22	41.0	44.5	45.0
Walk when led	21	37.5	45.0	45.5
Pull to stand by furniture	17	42.0	47.0	49.5
Fifth-Order Skills:				
Stand alone	21	56.0	62.0	66.0
Walk alone	21	59.0	64.0	67.0

are differences in the manner of the first movements. Some children in the study by Shirley were able to move while lying in a prone position even before creeping developed. Some could creep backward before they were able to make progress in a forward direction. A few could make progress by "hitching" while lying on their backs.

[2] Each median value represents the age at which fifty per cent of the children achieved the performance in question; Q_1 represents the age at which the most accelerated one fourth of the group reached the performance; and Q_3 the age at which seventy-five per cent of the children reached a given stage. Adapted from Shirley, M. M.: *The First Two Years: A Study of Twenty-Five Babies, Vol. I. Postural and Locomotor Development* (Minneapolis: University of Minnesota Press, 1931), p. 99. Reproduced by permission.

The child's first steps obviously do not mark the end of developments involved in the ability to walk, for with time come changes in the length of the child's stride and the angle of his steps, as well as improvements in his equilibrium, in the regularity of his gait, and in speed and precision.

The acquisition of ability to walk alone is only a part of a larger, continuing process of motor development. As soon as the child is able to walk, he launches upon other activities that incorporate elements of walking into larger patterns of activity, such as jumping, hopping, dodging, and dancing.

IMPACT OF WALKING

The fact that a child now can walk represents an important milestone. The ability to cover ground, first by creeping and then by walking, has an important impact on all other aspects of his development. He is able now to increase his contacts with other people; but while able to walk into new areas of interest, exploration, and adventure, he is also able to walk into mischief and danger. It becomes more of a trial for his parents to keep an eye on him. The beginning of walking ushers in a period lasting roughly from the age of a little over a year to about the age of four, a period that is strenuous indeed from the point of view of the parent. The child is on the go, and often his ability to get about and to get into things exceeds his judgment and awareness of danger. As a result, this is a time when many parents become anxious for the child's safety as well as a time of increasing opportunity to enjoy the child as a companion on walks and in other undertakings.

USE OF ARMS, HANDS, AND FINGERS

When an adult at dinner picks up and devours the kernel of a small peanut, no one at table with him is likely to remark or to wonder at the consummate act of skill that has just been performed. It is likely that the peanut eater himself is only half-aware of his performance, so sure is his aim, so expert is his use of thumb and forefinger in grasping the peanut, so smooth is his act of conveying it to his mouth. But back of this seemingly automatic act lies quite a story of development, beginning when the infant is unskilled not only in the finer movements but also in the grosser coördinations between eye and hand.

Following are some of the steps in the development of reaching and grasping after the third month, as described by Halverson from a study of infants by means of motion pictures (19).

At sixteen weeks, the typical child, as represented by Halverson's subjects, will follow the hand of the experimenter as he places a small cube within reaching distance on the table at which the infant is seated. The infant slides his hand about on the table and keeps one or both hands on the table for a period; but he will not, as a rule, reach the cube. At about twenty weeks, the child stretches out both hands simultaneously, scratches the table, and attempts to get both hands about the cube, and if he succeeds in touching the object, he is likely to push it out of reach or simply to hold it. At twenty-four and twenty-eight weeks, he approaches the cube with a scooping motion and surrounds or "corrals" it. Even at this age he often uses both hands, and he may still clumsily push the object out of reach. If he succeeds in getting hold of the cube, he will carry it to his mouth, inspect it briefly, and perhaps release and procure it again.

At first the child's reaching consists of crude shoulder and elbow movements, illustrating the proximo-distal direction of development noted in an earlier chapter. His aim is poor and his approach clumsy. In time, he becomes able to make selective movements with his wrist, to aim more accurately, and to rotate his hands. In his first attempts at grasping, he makes practically no use of his thumb, but closes in upon the object with a mass movement of the palm and fingers. This, in time, yields to a deft and well-aimed grasping with the thumb and the tip of the forefinger. Up to the age of about twenty-four weeks, the infant's approach seems to consist of three distinct acts, including the raising of the hand, a circuitous and forward thrust of the hand, and then a lowering of the hand. Finally, at about forty weeks, the act is coordinated into a single performance, with little remaining trace of separate acts.

These observations illustrate only a few of the steps involved in the development of the seemingly simple act of reaching, grasping, and handling an object. The age at which children achieve the performances described above will vary, of course, with different individuals.

The summary in Table V gives the median age at which various performances with arms, wrists, and fingers were achieved by infants who were the subjects in a study by Bayley (6). The items that are listed have been selected from a larger list of motor items, some of which are reproduced elsewhere in this chapter. It will be noted, among other things, that Bayley distinguishes between

TABLE V

ADVANCES IN PREHENSION[3]

Motor Performance	Age Placement in Months
Retains red ring (retains a ring, designed for the test, when placed in his hand)	0.7
Arm thrusts in play (when lying in a dorsal position, makes vertical arm thrusts in random play)	1.7
Hands predominantly open (hands predominantly open even though not grasping an object)	3.6
Beginning thumb opposition (beginning evidence of use of thumb in opposed manner in grasping a cube)	4.1
Partial thumb opposition (opposes thumb to fingers in a partial, but not complete, manner, using the palm of the hand, as well as thumb and fingers in picking up the cube)	5.1
Unilateral reaching (tends to reach and manipulate with one hand more often than bimanually)	6.4
Rotates wrist (rotates wrist in manipulating toys)	6.7
Complete thumb opposition (picks up the cube with thumb and fingers completely opposed, and without the use of the palm)	7.6
Partial finger prehension (picks up a small pellet with several fingers opposed to thumb and not with a scooping into the palm with the fingers)	7.8
Fine prehension with pellet (picks up a small pellet precisely with thumb and forefinger)	9.3

[3] Adapted from Bayley, N.: *The Development of Motor Abilities During the First Three Years,* Monographs of the Society for Research in Child Development (1935), No. 1, 26 pp. Reproduced by permission.

"beginning," "partial," and "complete" thumb opposition; and that separate ages are given for prehension involving thumb opposition in the grasping of a cube, as distinguished from "partial" and "fine" prehension in picking up a small pellet.

Developmental changes in interest and attitude with reference to a motor performance. All aspects of motor development during early childhood illustrate the principle, set forth in Chapter II, that a child seeks spontaneously to make use of his growing powers.[4] This tendency may, however, show itself in different ways and with varying intensity at different stages in the development of ability. An illustration of this fact appears in a study of the responses of a child to an opportunity to climb an inclined board (11). The first observations were made at eight months when the youngster had just begun to creep. At this time the opportunity to climb was not, in itself, a strong attraction, apparently, for the child was lured on by means of a toy. But the child's attention span was short; he was easily distracted, and so he would pause to examine a knot in the wood, a speck of dust, or a scratch in the varnish. At a later phase the lure, instead of helping, sometimes interfered, for in his eagerness to secure the toy the child would, for example, slip back when he raised his head and shoulders to see the prize and thus shift his center of gravity. At a later phase the performance of climbing the board became satisfying in itself. At this time the youngster frequently went up and down the slide several times even though there was no lure. At a still later phase the motor task of climbing the inclined board had been mastered and seemed no longer to offer a challenge in itself. Now, again, the child was distracted, not because he was overstimulated by the lure, but apparently because he was bored. In order to make things more interesting, he would try variations in his usual methods of climbing.

---

[4] Studies dealing with motor activities that are reviewed in Chapter II in the discussion of the role of learning and growth in development are not reintroduced in the present chapter.

LATER FEATURES OF MOTOR DEVELOPMENT

After the child has reached the ability to walk alone, his motor progress and the specific skills he acquires depend to a larger degree upon special environmental opportunities than was the case at an earlier time. This does not mean that each child's progress becomes a law unto itself. Children reared in similar environments exhibit, within broad limits, a good deal of uniformity in the manner in which they progress from one level of performance to the next or progressively add new skills to their repertory. Moreover, in some studies it has been observed that children whose opportunity to acquire a certain skill has been delayed will tend to pass through stages similar to those exhibited by children who had opportunities for practice at an earlier age. However, the older child, when he does get an opportunity, is likely to pass through the preliminary stages more rapidly.

TABLE VI

ADVANCES IN LOCOMOTION [5]

Motor Performance	Age Placement in Months
Walks sideways	16.5
Walks backward	16.9
Stands on one foot with help	19.9
Walks upstairs with help	20.3
Walks downstairs with help	20.5
Walks upstairs alone, marks time	24.3
Walks downstairs alone, marks time	24.5
Jumps off floor; both feet	28.0
Stands on left foot alone	29.2
Stands on right foot alone	29.3
Walks on tiptoe	30.1
Stands on walking board with both feet	31.0
Walks on line; general direction	31.3
Jumps from chair	32.1
Walks upstairs, alternating forward foot	35.5
Walks tiptoe three meters	36.2
Jumps from height of 30 cm.	37.1
Distance jump—36 to 60 cm.	39.7
Jump over rope less than 20 cm. high	41.5
Distance jump—60 to 85 cm.	48.4
Hops on right foot less than 2 meters	49.3
Walks downstairs—alternating forward foot	50.0

[5] Adapted from Bayley, N.: *The Development of Motor Abilities During the First Three Years,* Society for Research in Child Development Monographs (1935), No. 1, 26 pp. Reproduced by permission.

MOTOR DEVELOPMENT

TABLE VII

MEASUREMENTS OF SELECTED MOTOR ACHIEVEMENTS DURING PRESCHOOL YEARS[6]

Activity	Motor Age in Months	
Hopping:	Both feet	One foot
1 to 3 steps	38	43
4 to 6 steps	40	46
7 to 9 steps	41	55
10 or more steps	42	60
Skipping:		
Shuffle		38
Skip on one foot		43
Alternate feet		60
	Straight	Circular
	(10 feet)	(4½ feet diameter)
Walking on One-Inch Path; No Steps off	37	45
	3-step stair	11-step stair
Ascending Steps:		
Mark time, without support	27	29
Alternate feet, with support	29	31
Alternate feet, without support	31	41
	3-step stair	11-step stair
Descending Steps:		
Mark time, without support	28	34
Alternate feet, with support	48	48
Alternate feet, without support	49	55

	12 inches	18 inches	28 inches
Jumping:			
With help		27	36
Alone, with one foot ahead	27	31	43
Alone, feet together	34	37	46

Walking, running, jumping. Tables VI and VII present summaries that indicate children's progress in certain motor skills after the age of learning to walk. The first summary, which is adapted from Bayley's study, shows the rate of advance in certain aspects of

---

[6] Adapted from Wellman, B. L.: "Motor Achievements of Preschool Children," *Childhood Education* (1937), 13:311-316. Reproduced by permission. "Motor Age" represents the age at which fifty per cent of the children showed the accomplishment that is indicated.

locomotion. A number of motor performances are represented in Table VII, which is based upon studies by Wellman (54), McCaskill (33), and McCann (32).

Use of wheel toys. An account by Jones of the development of children's uses of a number of wheel toys (doll carriage, wagon, dump truck, kiddie car, and tricycle) offers many insights into changing motor reactions as children become older. The study involved observation of twenty-four children from the age of twenty-one to forty-eight months (29). The following account illustrates a change in the uses made of vehicles, and shifts in interests as the child's ability increases.

At ten months, David crept to a small doll carriage which was in the room. He looked inside it, then held on to the side as he raised himself a little, and ran his finger along the rough surface. He started to creep away, but turned and gave the carriage a small push. His interest span was thirty-five seconds.

At twelve months, Barbara, who could walk only a few steps alone, saw her older brother, aged thirty months, climb into a large doll carriage. She rose to her feet and pushed the carriage with her brother in it across the floor. At other times she was unable to push it because it slipped away from her. (This item illustrates the fact that small children will often, at first, try to make use of a carriage as a support in walking; a relatively heavy, sturdy carriage, which has a low center of gravity and which does not move at a light touch, is more congenial to the child's purposes at this age than is a flimsy or easily pushed vehicle.)

At later ages, as would be expected, the children became more adept at using the doll carriage for pulling and pushing on the level floor or up an incline or under an arch. At twenty-one months, fifteen per cent of the children used the carriage as a conveyance for other materials; at thirty-six months, fifty-five per cent of them did this. In time, the doll carriage provided less interesting usage than did certain other wheel toys, except as a conveyance.

The following statements offer further descriptive accounts of the use made of the wagon by the same child at successive age levels; the records are much abridged:

Twenty-one months: Starts to climb in; walks away; returns and looks at wagon; pushes it forward from behind; leaves; examines other material in the room; manipulates a light fixture on the wagon; pushes wagon back and forth; plays with other material in the room, etc. (During ten minutes, he has gone to the wagon and left it again three times.)

Twenty-four months: Gets into wagon with right knee in and left foot on floor; leans over and examines light; sits and shakes handle (note that there is no propelling, although he is in a position to propel); touches trademark on side; he examines wheels, touches various parts, etc.; gets out, examines parts; pulls wagon to the incline and makes one attempt to pull it up, lays the handle down and says: "I want to go home and see Charlie" (this after five minutes spent entirely in or with wagon); observer suggests that he use the wagon; he makes a few passes at wagon, pulls it briefly, then wanders about.

Thirty months: Gets into wagon with right knee, with left foot on floor, and propels the wagon, first forward and then backward; gets out and asks for doll carriage (apparently desires to combine other materials with wagon, for when asked to continue to use wagon, he gets a small wagon and puts it into the larger one); pushes and pulls; sits astride and tries to propel with both feet, but cannot reach the floor, then propels with one leg as before; continues pushing, pulling, etc.

Thirty-six months: Propelling with one foot now established; a new performance is to pull wagon empty to the top of an incline and coast down; the child also hauls dirt with the wagon.

Forty-eight months: Pulling, pushing, propelling, coasting, and use of wagon to haul things continues, with two notable additions: (1) uses in make-believe game ("I'm playing moving van"); and (2) stands up in wagon, steering it by means of the handle, as his sister pushes him on request, saying, "Look everybody, I'm standin' up riding," and later telling another boy: "Did you ever stand . . . ? It's lots of fun. . . . Can you hold your balance?"

In this study it was noted that unskilled repetition of activities, manipulative in nature, was characteristic of the children from approximately twenty-one to twenty-four months. From twenty-four to twenty-six months, abilities involving muscular control increased, followed by the practice of skills from twenty-six to thirty-six months.

Merging of activities that previously took place as separate performances seemed to begin as soon as each activity had reached a stage at which the child's entire attention was not required in its performance.

At forty-eight months, the behavior of the median child was usually influenced by a predominating idea which he was attempting to put into practice. As a result, the performance of a certain skill was usually secondary to the project as a whole.

Increase in speed and strength. As the child advances in age, there is an increase in expertness and versatility in his skills, and there is a change also in the underlying strength and speed of his movements. An indication of increases with age in speed of motor response appears in Table VIII. This table shows median scores obtained by individuals at various age levels in a test of the speed with which the individual can execute a voluntary motor response on hearing a sound.

TABLE VIII

MEDIAN REACTION TIME BY AGE AND SEX IN SIGMA UNITS (0.001 SECOND), AS MEASURED BY THE MILES REACTION-TIME BOARD[7]

Age in Years	Boys	Girls
$3\frac{1}{2}$	492	518
$4\frac{1}{2}$	356	424
$5\frac{1}{2}$	311	356
$6\frac{1}{2}$	259	286
$7\frac{1}{2}$	260	250
$8\frac{1}{2}$	223	249
$9\frac{1}{2}$	218	202
$10\frac{1}{2}$	229[a]	229[a]
$11\frac{1}{2}$	192[a]	192[a]
College students	171	172

[a] Scores for boys and girls combined.

---

[7] Adapted from Goodenough, F. L.: "The Development of the Reactive Process from Early Childhood to Maturity," *Journal of Experimental Psychology* (1935), 18:431-450. Reproduced by permission.

Further indications of changes in speed, accuracy, and power in certain athletic performances is shown in Table IX. This table is based upon findings obtained by Jenkins (22) in measurements of fifty boys and fifty girls at each age level from five to seven years. The original study should be consulted for information concerning the children who were tested and concerning the spread of scores at each age level. A study by Baldwin (3) of strength of grip, as measured by a dynamometer which a child squeezes in his hand, portrays increases that come from seven years onward. Seventeen-year-old boys had more than three times as strong a grip as seven-year-olds, and in girls the strength of grip more than doubled during this period. Differences between the sexes in strength of grip was evident at all ages.

TABLE IX

AVERAGE SCORES OBTAINED BY FIVE-, SIX-, AND SEVEN-YEAR-OLD CHILDREN IN VARIOUS MOTOR PERFORMANCES[8]

Activity and Measure Used in Scoring	5 Years Boys	5 Years Girls	6 Years Boys	6 Years Girls	7 Years Boys	7 Years Girls
35-yard dash—timed in seconds	9.30	9.70	8.52	8.84	7.92	8.02
Hop 50 feet without error—timed in seconds	10.82	10.33	9.20	8.89	8.81	7.59
Baseball throw at target—10-foot distance —error in inches	8.87	16.90	5.40	13.17	4.20	8.50
Baseball throw—distance in feet	23.60	14.50	32.80	17.80	41.40	24.40
Soccer kick—distance in feet	11.50	8.00	18.40	10.10	25.40	15.00
Standing broad jump—distance in inches	33.70	31.60	39.30	38.00	42.20	41.00
Running broad jump—distance in inches	34.40	28.60	45.20	40.00	58.80	50.80
Jump and reach—vertical distance in inches	2.52	2.22	4.02	3.48	4.98	4.28

Integration of skills into complex activities. As motor skills become established, they tend more and more to be incorporated into larger projects and enterprises. In her study of the development of children's uses of wheel toys, Jones found that children

---

[8] Adapted from Jenkins, L. M.: *A Comparative Study of Motor Achievements of Children at Five, Six, and Seven Years of Age,* Contributions to Education (New York: Teachers College, Columbia University, 1930), No. 414, 54 pp.

would concentrate all their attention on a certain motor performance as a project sufficient in itself while they were still in the process of mastering the performance (29). But once the children had mastered the basic operations (such as riding the tricycle, propelling the kiddie kar with good control of direction), she found that they tended to spend less time on the activity as an occupation in itself and merged it with a more extensive enterprise, such as a make-believe game of transportation.

The mere fact that a child has achieved substantial mastery of a skill does not mean, however, that the performance no longer has any appeal in its own right, for the child may go on to perfect and enlarge his skill, to add hazards and "embroideries" to his performance, as when he takes his tricycle over the bumps or rides it along ledges or down steep grades, or when he goes down the slide backward, or endeavors to make a one-hand or running catch after he has become adept at catching a ball with both hands while standing still. Some skills that can be used satisfactorily even by a small child still afford almost limitless opportunity for further refinement and improvement as he grows older. Examples are such activities as playing marbles, roller skating, swimming, bicycling, and ball play of various sorts. However, when a child spends time in devising new stunts and hazards in his use of a given skill, it is not always because he is deeply interested in this activity. He may be lacking in opportunity to try his hand at something else. In a study of nursery-school and kindergarten children, Gutteridge (18) found that by the age of three or four years many children have mastered a number of the elementary activities afforded by the conventional equipment in a nursery school or kindergarten, and they continue to repeat the old performances or try to make elaborations upon old skills for lack of anything else to do.[9]

---

[9] The subject of motor activities is touched upon again in later chapters. Some considerations in adjusting educational opportunities to children's motor development, including a brief discussion of sex differences, are presented by the writer in another connection (23).

Motor and artistic activities. One area, among many others, in which motor operations play an important role is in the field of the arts. Such activities as drawing and constructing models or designs with clay or blocks, æsthetic dancing, and the playing of musical instruments, require manual skill as well as the ability to conceive and plan. An interesting account of children's progress in block-building is offered by Johnson and her associates (24). According to this account, the child at first simply handles and carries the blocks and piles them into irregular masses. This is followed by the beginning stages of construction, between two and three years, including simple designs such as are achieved by placing the blocks in a row, one on top of the other, to form a tower, and experimentation with a plan, such as spacing alternating sizes, or attempts to make a structure, such as a bridge or an enclosure. These activities are followed by further development of attempts to devise patterns and by improvement of technique in handling the blocks. By the ages of four and five years, the children are described as using the blocks for dramatic representation; and at five or six years, attempts are made to reproduce actual structures. Individual children vary considerably with respect to timing and sequence. It was noted, however, that children who had had no previous experience with blocks at the age of four or five years tended to repeat the stages exhibited by children who began their block play at the age of two, but the older children passed through the various stages at a more rapid rate.

Table X, based upon results obtained by Slater (50) in observations of nursery-school children's spontaneous uses of blocks for building purposes, shows the frequency of various structures at different age levels. The children's handiwork was graded according to a four-point scale, as indicated in the summary.

In children's attempts to draw, likewise, a general pattern of progress has been noted. According to observations made by Biber (7), the child passes through a stage of exploration, followed first by acquisition of some manual control, then by efforts to

Table X

BLOCK-BUILDING ACTIVITIES[10]

Levels of Performance in Block-Building	Number of Children Showing the Various Levels of Performance						
	2 years	2½ years	3 years	3½ years	4 years	4½ years	Total
Crude, unsteady towers (which toppled over on their own accord or were "joyously demolished by their maker,")	3	9	4				16
Towers, carefully done (primitive, but blocks fitted so they would stand with some apparent joy in workmanship)	1	5	7	9	3		25
Some imaginative elaboration (a definite plan, such as a train or house, somewhat recognizable)		1	6	1	4	2	14
Careful, symmetrical construction (houses with windows, trains on tracks, etc.)		2	2	1	2	2	9

make designs, and finally by the beginnings of representative drawing at about the age of three and a half and four years. In their first attempts to draw, many children make vertical lines before they are able to make horizontal lines; they also find it easier to imitate a drawing made by another as they watch than to imitate a finished copy.

INTERRELATIONS IN MOTOR DEVELOPMENT

From early childhood into adult years, motor achievement represents an interrelation of many factors, among the more obvious being strength and speed, size, and anatomical build. Among the more elusive factors that influence motor performance are such factors as interest, self-confidence, the tendency to be intrepid or fearful, willingness to take a chance, self-consciousness and its opposite, and so forth. The interplay of what might be called "personality" factors, as distinguished from "motor" abilities, has

[10] Adapted from Slater, E.: II. *Types, Levels, and Irregularities of Response to a Nursery School Situation of Forty Children Observed With Special Reference to the Home Environment.* Studies from the Center for Research in Child Health and Development, School of Public Health, Harvard University, Monographs of the Society for Research in Child Development (1939), IV, 2, 148 pp. Reproduced by permission.

not been probed systematically, although it represents an important subject from the standpoint of an individual's personal and social adjustment.

A few comments may be added to those already set forth with respect to the importance of motor development in the life and adjustment of the total person. We have already noted how motor activities come into play in the child's intellectual and artistic enterprises, and we have commented on the role of motor activities in the development of social behavior. Motor ability also has an obvious bearing upon emotional behavior and adjustment: through his motor competence a child can overcome many obstructions that otherwise would cause anger; he can cope with many conditions that otherwise would cause fear; and by pursuing interests that involve motor skill, he will be able to gain many satisfactions and he may be spared a good deal of boredom.

The fact that motor abilities tend to be rather specific, so that a child who excels in one performance will not necessarily excel in others, and a child who is poor in one performance need not be poor in others, implies that opportunities for motor learning should be as varied as is practical, in order that all children may have a chance to come into their own. One child who takes to the sidelines when only baseball is available might be an active participant if there were an opportunity to swim, and another sideliner might join enthusiastically if tools and equipment for shopwork were available. It may also be noted that if children, in their group activities, are left entirely to their own devices, the interests of a few may dominate the situation in such a manner that individual children do not have the incentive or opportunity to exercise their own special interests and talents.

The importance of variety in the opportunities offered to children in the motor sphere also emerges as a practical implication of the fact that there is a rather low correlation, in general, between mental and motor abilities. The child who has a hard time in an intellectual task such as arithmetic may be able to do very well in various practical arts and crafts. The more the school program calls for only one kind of ability the more likely it is that there will be children whose main experience in school is failure or humiliation or boredom. The more the program calls for, and honors, the varied abilities of children, the more children there will be who have a chance to achieve something. The personal satisfaction and the social recognition that can be derived from being able to do something well are important factors in emotional and social adjustment. In other words, motor development deserves important consideration from the point of view of good mental hygiene. In the opinion of the writer, the people in the school and in the community at large who determine how schools are to be equipped and what the curriculum shall be have tended grievously to underrate the importance of motor development.

The importance of opportunities for motor learning is further emphasized by findings in a recent study (41) which indicate that the motor activities undertaken by adults are influenced to a large degree by what the adult learned or failed to learn as a child. It appears to be rather seldom that a person chooses to take up an entirely new motor skill after he has reached the adult level. It does not follow, of course, that each motor skill that a person learns as a child will be used with profit at the adult level. But even though all that is learned during childhood may not necessarily stand in good stead during adult years, it still is apparent that the provision of opportunities for motor learning in childhood not only may contribute in important ways to the child's welfare at the time but also may be an investment that yields fine dividends in the future. In passing it may be noted that of the skills that had been carried on into adult years in the study most had been acquired outside of school hours.

Factors that may inhibit a person's disposition to plunge into motor activities are obviously many. A previous tumble or an especially harrowing or humiliating experience may have a restraining effect. Overprotection from parents and others, and constant reminders against danger and overexertion, may likewise have an inhibiting influence. Highly important are the many factors that influence a child's own habitual use of and attitude toward his physical powers. Although all normal children are born with a disposition to exercise their limbs and to use their bodies, this inner urge alone may not suffice to carry the child over all the hurdles he meets after his basic coördinations are established. During preschool and later years, motor interests thrive on successful accomplishment. Motor interests that lead the child to new ventures and further improvement of ability are reinforced and augmented by success in earlier ventures. Proper facilities and opportunities, with judicious instruction where warranted, therefore not only can help to give the child more skill and mastery over his physical environment at a given time but may also provide the impetus for further ventures on his part.

Apart from a child's own initial interest in using his body and his limbs, an important factor is the social influence of other children. The example and incentive provided by other children may lead the child into endeavors that he would not undertake if left to himself or exclusively in the company of older persons. Under some circumstances, however, a child may be barred from the benefits of this influence if, for one reason or another, he lags far behind his peers and is unable to follow them and share their activities. Again—and this is more likely to occur at the elementary school age and later, rather than during early childhood—his sensitivity concerning his lack of competence may be a hindrance. Rather than risk embarrassment through lack of proficiency, he may withdraw entirely from the games of his fellows. Sometimes a vicious circle may be started when a child for one reason or another falls behind his group; he becomes reluctant to join in group games, and the more he stays away, the greater becomes the difference between his skill and that of the other children, for they continue to practice and to learn.

A child may be quite unskilled at one performance and still do well in others. In studies that have been made to date, it appears that there is relatively little correlation between ability in various specific motor performances (14, 18, 28, 54). Low correlations,[11] usually ranging below 0.30, have been found between scores in separate activities, such as throwing, climbing, and jumping. Whereas correlations between various tests of strength tend to be considerably higher (ranging from 0.40 above 0.80), there may be relatively little relationship between strength and speed. In commenting on this fact, Wellman, in a study cited previously, states that, by virtue of this lack of interrelation, one should be hesitant in speaking about "the motor ability" of the child. Rather, on the basis of present information, it is safer to talk about "motor abilities" as a series of skills that are not closely related. Further study would be necessary to determine the extent to which this lack of interrelation is due to chance factors in the environment and to determine to what extent general factors of ability might be found.

A problem that also needs further study in this connection is the extent to which competence in one skill may help a child to undertake another skill with more confidence, even though, for the time being, he may stand high in one and be quite low in the other. In McGraw's study, cited earlier (35), it was observed that the twin who received special training seemed to show more courage than did his brother in venturing into new activities.

RELATION OF PHYSICAL AND MENTAL ABILITY

The general finding has also been that there is a low positive correlation between the mental and physical status of children. In a study dealing with the relationship between mental growth and physical growth, Abernethy (1) investigated a large number of children and college men and women. The physical data included measures of standing and sitting height, weight, carpal de-

---

[11] For a brief account of what is meant by a correlation coefficient and an illustrative computation, see page 526.

velopment, chest girth, lung capacity, and records of pubescence. The data with regard to mental development were obtained from systematic mental tests. Abernethy found, as have other investigators, that there was a positive correlation between mental and physical status, but that this correlation was relatively low. The highest correlation was between intelligence and standing height for boys. The coefficients between mental and physical measurements tended to decrease after the age of fourteen or fifteen years. Changes in rate of mental and physical development were unrelated. At the adult level, the correlations between mental and physical measurements were practically negligible. An incidental finding indicated that the age of onset of puberty had no relation to the mental test ratings of young women.

In her study of young children, Bayley (5) found that during the first fifteen months there was a relatively high degree of relationship (a correlation of 0.50) between "motor" and "mental" abilities, as far as these could be differentiated and separately measured. Success in one sphere seemed to be associated with success in the other. However, after the age of fifteen months the correlations were low although positive. This suggests that possibly the operations labeled as mental and motor during early infancy were not well differentiated. Shirley found a correlation of 0.28 between precocity in walking and intelligence (as measured at eighteen months). In studies of older children and adults, relatively low relationships have been found between intellectual ability and motor ability or physique (14, 34, 44). In cases of extreme mental deficiency, however, children are likely to be also below normal in their physical and motor development.

HANDEDNESS

In the theories set forth to account for handedness it has been variously assumed that handedness is inherited; that it is due to anatomical differences between the two sides of the body; that it is due to the fact that one hemisphere of the brain is dominant; that it is due to dominance of one eye over the other; that it arises through chance; that it is due to direct or indirect training imposed by others who have grown up in a traditionally right-handed world.[12]

Although a majority of children eventually become predominantly right-handed, it is not usually until several months after birth that a definite hand preference is established. Even when apparently well established, hand preference may be less clear-cut than appears at first glance. A person may use the right hand in writing, throwing, and eating with knife and fork and yet, on further examination, it may be found that he uses his left hand for some performances and that there may be many additional acts which he can perform equally well with both hands. Again, a person may do better with one hand when fine movements are involved and do about equally well with both hands in a grosser form of the same movements, as when a person writes better with his right hand on paper but does almost as well with his left as with his right in writing on the blackboard. However, most persons do exhibit so distinct a preference for one hand or the other in the ordinary acts of everyday life that, for practical purposes, we may call them right- or left-handed.

The degree to which the right hand is preferred in certain acts of common use is indicated in a study by Hicks (21), who found that ninety-six per cent of a group of sixty children aged two to six years used the right hand in throwing a ball at a moving target, and by Jenkins (22), who found that from eighty-five to ninety per cent of three hundred children aged five to seven years used their right hands exclusively in tossing a beanbag, throwing a baseball, and in reaching while jumping.

Early manifestations. The age at which hand preference appears has variously been set at from four to seven months by different investigators. Children have sometimes been observed to

---

[12] For accounts of the development of hand preference, in addition to the studies mentioned below, see references 10, 20, 27, 30, 36, 42, 46, and 52.

show a slight preference for the left hand during early months and then to shift to the right. Children who were observed in one investigation (31) used right and left hands about equally often when accepting an object at four and a half months, but thereafter use of the right hand increased. At twelve months, about seventy per cent accepted objects with the right hand. Even when it seems that the baby definitely shows a preference for the right hand, he may continue to show a good deal of ambidexterity for several months.

Differentiation of the use of the hands during the period from two weeks to eight months is shown in a study by Giesecke (15) of seven infants who were observed from the time they were two weeks old until they were from four to eight months old (supplemental observations were also made of other children). Records were made of the infants' spontaneous use of their hands, and test situations were provided to precipitate hand movements. Interestingly enough, in four cases the differentiation favored the right hand and in three cases, the left. Even though the trend was toward preference for one hand over the other, this trend did not proceed regularly from the age of two weeks to the age of six months; rather, there were shifts in preference during this period.

Hand preference does not appear as an isolated event but is accompanied by lateral dominance of the same side of the body, according to Giesecke's study; she points out that there is evidence that lateral dominance concerns the body as a whole rather than merely the hands. In other words, handedness may be an aspect of "sidedness." Likewise, the head is more often turned toward the side of the preferred hand, and the eyes tend to turn toward the hand that is used; this suggests that eye dominance may be influenced by hand dominance (rather than the reverse), or, what is perhaps just as likely, that both the eye dominance and hand dominance may be aspects of general lateral dominance.

One of the prominent uses of the nondominant hand is for support while the other hand is active. Giesecke found that if no support was needed, the nonpreferred hand did not remain entirely motionless, but it was not actively used like the other. It can be seen from this that even though it might be a physiological factor that initially disposes the child to use one side more than the other, his "sidedness" will be further confirmed by habit as one hand repeatedly receives more practice than the other.

The number of left-dominant children found in Giesecke's study (six in a total of seventeen in the study as a whole) was relatively larger than one would expect from the proportions found among older children and adults. This suggests that there might be a relatively larger percentage of southpaws in the population at large than now are found if the tradition of right-handedness were not so firmly established. The evidence in the study was not conclusive as to hereditary factors in handedness.

In studies by Johnson and his associates (25, 26) it was found that hand preference tends to be quite stable after the age of six years. A battery of tests including thirty-two items was administered to six- and seven-year-old children and to high-school pupils. Among the performances included in the test were the following: pulling down a curtain; tearing paper from a tablet; picking up a card; drawing a picture; writing with a pen; filling a pen. It was noted in connection with each item whether the child used the right hand, or the left, or both. It was found that the median "dextrality-quotient" or degree of right-handedness for high-school pupils, as measured in terms of these specific performances, was 0.79. The dextrality-quotient for six- and seven-year-olds was almost the same, 0.82 and 0.83. In the period of approximately ten years, from the age of six to the high-school age, there was little shift in the extent to which one hand is preferred over the other in specific performances covered by the study. It was noted that a child of six or seven is likely to be highly consistent in his inconsistencies—that is, he may use the "other" hand for certain performances, but in connection with a given performance he does not waver from one hand to the other; rather, he tends to be one hundred per cent right-handed in certain performances and one hundred per cent left-handed in others.

Practical considerations in connection with handedness. That children who have been compelled to change from the left to the right hand may show a tendency to stutter, at least for some time, has been observed in some cases, but the cause-and-effect relationship here is not entirely clear. It is difficult to determine whether the stuttering is directly due to the change in handedness or whether it is due primarily to the methods that are used and the atmosphere that prevails when the child is being forced into using his right hand. The stuttering, in other words, may be a symptom of the tension and confusion produced by the pressures that are brought to bear rather than a direct result of the change itself. Furthermore, while stuttering sometimes occurs, it by no means occurs in all cases in which a child is prevailed upon to change to the right hand; in addition, stuttering appears in cases in which there is no clear evidence of any difficulties with regard to hand preference. The important fact still remains that a change in hand preference as the result of pressure from others may, in individual cases, have unwholesome consequences. The risk of such consequences is certainly not worth while, and even if there are no unwholesome effects, it can hardly be said that the change from left- to right-handedness is worth the trouble.

Considerably more frequent than efforts to change an established preference for the left hand are the efforts parents exert while hand preference is still in its formative stages. In a great many cases, youngsters seem spontaneously to develop a preference for the right hand, without parental intervention. But with many children parents take a good deal of pains to cultivate the right hand—as when they always make it a point to favor the child's right side in placing toys and tools within his reach; always place the spoon, cup, or pencil in his right hand; and gently transfer operations to the right hand if the child seems in a random way to have started with the left. There are numerous little steps that parents can take to encourage the use of the right hand, and in most cases the child turns out to be the fine little right-hander that his parents intended him to be, with no ill effect.

As long as no harm is done, there certainly can be no objection to such maneuvers, but the question can be raised as to whether, from the child's point of view, all this fuss is worth while. A left-handed person may be handicapped in some ways but not many (unless he is hounded by persons who look upon handedness as a matter of principle rather than as a practical issue). As far as the writer knows, no systematic study has been made of the inconveniences involved in being left-handed. That there are some inconveniences is obvious. A left-hander usually has some trouble, for example, in learning to write gracefully from left to right across a page, especially with ink, which smears; and some left-handers find it difficult to learn shorthand. Many tools and utensils are made for right-handers—such as certain types of fishing reels and kettles with lips on one side only. A left-hander usually is handicapped when he tries to borrow a baseball glove or a golf club (but then he profits at the lending end).

Because of the lay of the land in a right-handed world, the left-hander is lured into some habits which are inconvenient, as when he habitually lifts the telephone receiver with his left hand and then is called upon to write a message. Many other examples might be given. Whatever the various inconveniences may be, it is possible in many cases that they are offset by the greater degree of ambidexterity which some left-handers seem to acquire. There is room for more systematic study in this area, but certainly it could be argued that the importance of handedness is often overestimated, and, what with all the other restraints that adults must impose upon young children, they could at least let the child be free to lead with his left hand or his right, as he squares off for the battle of life.

BIBLIOGRAPHY

1. Abernethy, E. M.: *Relationships Between Mental and Physical Growth,* Society for Research in Child Development Monographs (1936), Vol. I, 7; 80 pp.
2. Ames, V. C.: "Physical Growth from Birth to Maturity," *Review of Educational Research* (1944), 14:427-437.
3. Baldwin, B. T.: *The Physical Growth of Children from Birth to Maturity,* University of Iowa Studies in Child Welfare, First Series (1921), I, No. 1, 411 pp.
4. Baldwin, B. T., Busby, L. M., and Garside, H.: *Anatomic Growth of Children,* University of Iowa Studies in Child Welfare (1928), IV, No. 1, 88 pp.
5. Bayley, N.: *The California First Year Mental Scale,* University of California Syllabus Series (1933), No. 243, 24 pp.
6. ———: *The Development of Motor Abilities During the First Three Years,* Society for Research in Child Development Monographs (1935), No. 1, 26 pp.
7. Biber, B.: *Children's Drawings; from Lines to Pictures,* New York: Bureau of Educational Experiments; 1934, 43 pp.
8. Boyd, E.: *Outline of Physical Growth and Development* (Minneapolis: Burgess, 1941), 43 pp.
9. Carpenter, A.: "The Measurement of General Motor Capacity and General Motor Ability in the First Three Grades," *Research Quarterly of the American Association for Health, Physical Education, and Recreation* (1942), 13:444-465.
10. Cromwell, H. and Rife, D. C.: "Dermatoglyphics in Relation to Functional Handedness," *Human Biology* (1942), 14:516-526.
11. Damann, V. T.: "Developmental Changes in Attitude as One Factor Determining Energy Output in a Motor Performance," *Child Development* (1941), 12:241-246.
12. Dawson, H. L. and Stoddard, G. D.: "Physical Growth from Birth to Puberty," *Review of Educational Research* (1933), 3:130-149.
13. Fenton, J. C.: *A Practical Psychology of Babyhood* (New York: Houghton Mifflin, 1925), 348 pp.
14. Gates, A. I. and Scott, A. W.: "Characteristics and Relations of Motor Speed and Dexterity Among Young Children," *Pedagogical Seminary and Journal of Genetic Psychology* (1931), 39:423-454.
15. Giesecke, M.: *The Genesis of Hand Preference,* Society for Research in Child Development Monographs (1936), 1, 5, 102 pp.
16. Goodenough, F. L.: "The Development of the Reactive Process from Early Childhood to Maturity," *Journal of Experimental Psychology* (1935), 18:431-450.

17. Goodenough, F. L. and Smart, R. C.: "Inter-relationships of Motor Abilities in Young Children," *Child Development* (1935), 6:141-153.
18. Gutteridge, M. V.: *A Study of Motor Achievements of Young Children,* Archives of Psychology (1939), No. 244, 178 pp.
19. Halverson, H. M.: *An Experimental Study of Prehension in Infants by Means of Systematic Cinema Records,* Genetic Psychology Monographs (1931), 10:107-286.
20. Heinlein, J. H.: "A Study of Dextrality in Children," *Pedagogical Seminary and Journal of Genetic Psychology* (1929), 36:91-119.
21. Hicks, J. A.: *The Acquisition of Motor Skill in Young Children: An Experimental Study of the Effects of Practice in Throwing at a Moving Target,* University of Iowa Studies in Child Welfare (1931), IV, No. 5, 80 pp.
22. Jenkins, L. M.: *A Comparative Study of Motor Achievements of Children at Five, Six, and Seven Years of Age,* Teachers College Contributions to Education (New York: Teachers College, Columbia University, 1930), No. 414, 54 pp.
23. Jersild, A. T.: "Education in Motor Activities," *Child Development and the Curriculum, Thirty-Eighth Yearbook of the National Society for the Study of Education* (1939), Pt. I, Ch. II: 57-83.
24. Johnson, H. M.: *The Art of Block Building* (New York: John Day, 1933), 47 pp.
25. Johnson, W. and Bissell, V.: "Iowa Hand Usage Dextrality Quotients of One Hundred High School Students," *Journal of Educational Psychology* (1940), 31:148-151.
26. Johnson, W. and Duke, D.: "Revised Iowa Hand Usage Dextrality Quotients of Six-Year-Olds," *Journal of Educational Psychology* (1940), 31:45-52.
27. Jones, H. E.: "Dextrality as a Function of Age," *Journal of Experimental Psychology* (1931), 14:125-143.
28. Jones, H. E., et al.: *Inter-relationships Among Motor Abilities,* Institute of Child Welfare Monograph, unpublished (Berkeley: University of California).
29. Jones, T. D.: *The Development of Certain Motor Skills and Play Activities in Young Children,* Child Development Monographs (New York: Teachers College, Columbia University, 1939), No. 26, 180 pp.
30. Lederer, R. K.: "An Exploratory Investigation of Handed Status in the First Two Years of Life," *Studies in Infant Behavior V,* University of Iowa Studies in Child Welfare (1939), XVI, No. 2, 103 pp.
31. Lippman, H. S.: "Certain Behavior Responses in Early Infancy," *Peda-

gogical Seminary and Journal of Genetic Psychology (1927), 34:424-440.
32. McCann, K.: *A Seriatum Study of Motor Achievements of Preschool Children,* unpublished Master's thesis (Iowa City: University of Iowa, 1936), 94 pp.
33. McCaskill, C. L.: *A Study of Common Motor Achievements at the Preschool Ages,* unpublished Master's thesis (Iowa City: University of Iowa, 1936), 112 pp.
34. McElwee, E. W.: "Standardization of the Stenquist Mechanical Assemblying Test: Series III," *Journal of Educational Psychology* (1932), 23:451-454.
35. McGraw, M. B.: *Growth: A Study of Johnny and Jimmy* (New York: Appleton-Century, 1935), 319 pp.
36. Major, D. R.: *First Steps in Mental Growth* (New York: Macmillan, 1906).
37. Mead, C. D.: "The Age of Walking and Talking in Relation to General Intelligence," *Pedagogical Seminary* (1913), 20:460-484.
38. Meek, L. H.: *Your Child's Development and Guidance* (Philadelphia: Lippincott, 1940), 166 pp.
39. Meredith, H. V. and Stoddard, G. D.: "Physical Growth from Birth to Maturity," *Review of Educational Research* (1936), 6:54-84.
40. Miles, W. R.: "Correlation of Reaction and Coordination Speed with Age in Adults," *American Journal of Psychology* (1931), 43:377-391.
41. Nestrick, W. V.: *Constructional Activities of Adult Males,* Contributions to Education (New York: Teachers College, Columbia University, 1939), No. 780, 128 pp.
42. Ojemann, R. H.: "Studies in Handedness: I. A Technique for Testing Unimanual Handedness," *Journal of Educational Psychology* (1930), 21:597-611.
43. ———: "Studies in Handedness: II. Testing Bimanual Handedness," *Journal of Educational Psychology* (1930), 21:695-702.
44. Paterson, D. G.: *Physique and Intellect* (New York: Appleton-Century, 1930), 304 pp.
45. Peatman, J. G. and Higgins, R. A.: "Relation of Infant Weight and Body Build to Locomotor Development," *American Journal of Orthopsychiatry* (1942), 12:234-240.
46. Shinn, M. W.: *Notes on the Development of a Child* (Berkeley: University of California, 1909), 424 pp.
47. Shirley, M. M.: *The First Two Years: A Study of Twenty-Five Babies,* Vol. I. Postural and Locomotor Development Institute (Minneapolis: University of Minnesota Press, 1931), 227 pp.

48. Shock, N.: "Physiological Aspects of Development," *Review of Educational Research* (1944), 14:413-426.
49. Shuttleworth, F. K.: *Sexual Maturation and the Physical Growth of Girls Age Six to Nineteen,* Society for Research in Child Development Monographs (1937), II, 5, Serial No. 12, 253 pp.
50. Slater, E.: *II. Types, Levels, and Irregularities of Response to a Nursery School Situation of Forty Children Observed With Special Reference to the Home Environment,* Studies from the Center for Research in Child Health and Development, School of Public Health, Harvard University, Society for Research in Child Development Monographs (1939), IV, 2, Serial No. 21, 148 pp.
51. Todd, T. W.: "Growth and Development of the Skeleton," *Growth and Development of the Child* (New York: Appleton-Century, 1933), pp. 26-31.
52. Updegraff, R.: "Preferential Handedness in Young Children," *Journal of Experimental Education* (1932), 1:134-139.
53. Vickers, V., Poyntz, L., and Baum, M.: "The Brace Scale Used with Young Children," *Research Quarterly of the American Association for Health, Physical Education, and Recreation* (1942), 13:299-308.
54. Wellman, B. L.: "Motor Achievements of Preschool Children," *Childhood Education* (1937), 13:311-316.

Chapter V

DEVELOPMENT OF SOCIAL BEHAVIOR

From the time when his life begins, each child is very much a social being, although at the start he plays the passive role of one who receives much and gives little. Even before birth he has a profound influence upon those about him. Once he is born, his social influence becomes even more marked. From the time of birth, even while he himself is quite passive, strong ties are being established between him and other human beings. Interwoven with the child's earliest experiences and expectations, and intimately connected with his survival from day to day, are associations with other human beings and their activities. These associations accumulate as he emerges from the somnolence of the first few days of life, and they multiply during the ensuing weeks and months as he grows more alert to what is happening about him.

These ties, born of a child's complete dependence upon others, perhaps only dimly defined in his earliest experiences, and taken quite for granted at a later time, remain powerful influences as long as he lives. As time passes, he becomes more independent and as his individual powers increase, he becomes more self-assertive. His self-assertion may reach the point of apparent defiance of society and all its ways and works. But whatever front he may assume, he is never completely weaned from his dependence upon others; he never becomes so self-sufficient that he is immune to the approval or disapproval of his fellows or free from a desire for affection and security in his relations with his fellow men.

The story of social development is also a story of the child's struggle to be an individual in his own right, to assert and express himself as an independent creature. In the normal course of events he becomes more "social" as he grows older, forms ties with other persons, and acquires values and aspirations that have a social orientation. But, along with this development he also learns to become more "individual," to assert himself, to be independent, and to have a voice in the management of his own affairs.

In adult parlance, we sometimes speak of the "individual" and the "social" as though they represent tendencies that are mutually exclusive and inimical. If we look to the growing child, however, we find that this is not the case. The run-about child is highly individualistic but, at the same time, highly sociable. On the individualistic side we may note at various stages his readiness to protect his own interests and to rebuff invaders, and his personal ambitions. On the "social" side, we may note his early impulse to smile and laugh in the company of others, to solicit their company, to join when he is old enough to do so in common projects with others; his occasional displays of sympathy when he is small and of compassion when he is older; his evident desire for social approval, for belonging; his eventual loyalty to his group; his patriotism and readiness even to die for a common cause.

SEQUENCES IN SOCIAL BEHAVIOR

The child's social life at first revolves mainly around persons older than himself. The usual child is quite sophisticated in his relations with older persons before he has much dealing with children of his own age. Even after he is able to run about in the company of his peers he is likely to continue frequently to come to the parent or the one who substitutes for the parent, as though in need of the kind of attention or assurance that an older person can provide.

However, from an early age, well before he is able to walk or talk, a child takes notice of other young children, and by the age of two or three years, if he has a chance, he becomes more and more involved in the society of his peers. From an early age he begins to throw in his lot with his own generation. It is, of course, with this generation that he eventually will share the responsibilities of adult life.

Early social responses. Occasionally an infant as young as two or three weeks will fix his eyes upon his mother's face and smile in response to her smile, but it is difficult to tell whether such apparent social communication is more than a chance happening.

By about the age of three months, most children will show many signs of social awareness, such as ceasing their crying when a person comes, turning their gaze upon a person, giving heed to another's voice, whimpering or crying when a person leaves their presence, making searching movements to locate an approaching adult, smiling in response to another's gaze. Until the age of five months smiles in response to the gaze or the voice of another person are likely to appear whether the voice is friendly or angry in tone or whether the gaze is accompanied by an angry or friendly expression. But at about five months and thereafter, infants begin to show more discrimination of tone and expression (6). At about the fifth month, the infant likewise becomes more active in his advances toward others by way of vocalizations and attempts to grasp and to touch.

A further development, which appears during the first half-year of life, is the ability to distinguish one person from another. Signs that the child recognizes his mother may appear at three months or even earlier, but the ability to distinguish between persons whom he sees less frequently usually comes somewhat later. By the end of the fifth month, and increasingly thereafter, this ability to discriminate becomes more evident.

The development of this ability to discriminate may be accompanied by other forms of behavior which hitherto have not been exhibited, such as the first signs of timidity and shyness (46). Coincident with such signs of timidity may also appear the first signs of fear of strangers. In a study by Shirley, six of a group of twenty-five babies, whom the investigator had visited time and again from the first week of life, showed fear of the investigator for the first time during the latter part of the fourth month or at the age of five or six months. Similar instances of fear of people, coinciding with the development of signs of ability to discriminate among different persons, have been noted in other studies of children's fears (28), thus illustrating the manner in which the mental, social, and emotional aspects of a child's development are interwoven with one another.

Timidity or fear of strangers does not invariably accompany the development of increased discrimination among other persons, and when such symptoms occur they may wane within a short time. Voices and faces that were unfamiliar tend in time, if they recur, to recede into the realm of the familiar. During a child's entire career many phenomena of this kind are likely to occur. Through the combined effects of growth and learning, he comes to the threshold of a new discovery or a new experience, or reaches a stage of understanding at which he can appreciate new or different meanings in the circumstances that surround him. Each such new experience may give the child pause. If the event or discovery comes upon him suddenly or overwhelms him, he may exhibit fear. But in the normal course of things, more and more events lose their arresting qualities and are "laid by" as part of the accumulating total of familiar experience.

After the first half-year of life there is, as one would expect, an increase in the number and complexity of social reactions. Between the ages of six and ten months, babies learn to participate in social interplay in such activities as peek-a-boo, rock-a-bye, waving a bye-bye, yelling at adults, and begging for attention by means of squeals and grunts (46). In such activities, the child gives as well as takes.

Response to other children. By the age of six months a child is likely to begin to take notice of another child of his own age, and during coming months his interest in other children becomes more active. Before the age of one year, many children will exhibit reactions such as giving heed when another child cries, making active attempts to exclude another child from their sphere of activity, or babbling to other children to gain attention (6). It usually is not until considerably later that coöperative play with another child occurs.

A "baby-party" technique has been used to investigate young children's reactions to one another. Two or more children are placed together in a more or less standardized situation, and their behavior is observed. In a study by Maudry and Nekula (36), in which pairs of children similar in age were placed together for periods of a few minutes at a time, it was found that up to the age of nine months children showed relatively little social interchange or response to one another; from nine to fourteen months, the children continued to give more attention to their surroundings and to play materials than to one another, and their social interchanges included many negative responses, such as trying to push the other child aside; from fourteen to eighteen months, the children's behavior showed a gradual transition in the direction of more social response of a positive sort; and by the age of twenty-five months, their social responses and interest in play materials became more closely integrated, and responses of a friendly and coöperative nature predominated over negative responses. At this age some children likewise seem to be sensitive to being excluded from a group, and they may show distinct preferences for particular children.

At the age of two, instances of coöperative give-and-take between two or more children are not likely to be of long duration. When several children of this age occupy the same play space, they will, to be sure, take notice of one another, tend to congregate in the same locality a good deal of the time, and make contacts with one another. A good part of the time, however, the children's activities will be parallel and adjacent—with occasional interchanges—rather than merged into a joint, continuing activity (41). It should be noted in passing that, at this age, a child's "occupation span"—the length of uninterrupted time he spends at an activity—is likely to be brief, whether he plays with other children or alone (see Chapter IX).

Group activities during preschool years. After the age of three an increase in coöperative play occurs and group activities become longer in duration. With increasing age, there is an increase both in the size of the group with which a child will be in mutual contact and in the duration of group projects. By the age of five or six years, children will sometimes play in groups as large as five or six members or more, but groups limited to about three members are preferred at the later nursery-school and kindergarten age (7, 13, 47, 50).

Increase with age in duration of play with several children is shown in the following results from a study by Green (22): five-year-old children played with three or more children eighteen per cent of the time and with two children twenty-two per cent of the time. Two-year-old children played with three or more children only two per cent of the time and with two children nine per cent of the time. Two-year-olds played alone sixty-two per cent of the time, while five-year-olds played alone thirty per cent of the time.

Although this progress from relatively little social interchange to participation with more and more children can be noted, these developments do not constitute clearly demarcated stages. A child may revert to earlier forms of nonparticipation as a result of problems that arise in his own private adjustment or his relationship to the group. He may be a participator in one group and an onlooker in another; he may return to solitary or hermitlike behavior if, as sometimes happens, he matures more rapidly than his associates or acquires special interests of his own, so that the activities of his former playmates no longer interest or challenge him. Furthermore, at any stage of growth, when a child encounters a new social situation, his first tentative approaches may roughly reproduce the sequence noted in his early behavior before he feels at home with his new associates.

LATER TRENDS IN GROUP BEHAVIOR

The foregoing brief sketch has omitted many forms of behavior that will be considered separately in ensuing pages. It should also be noted that at all stages of development a child's social behavior is interwoven with other aspects of his development. An increase in ability to discriminate and to undertake more complex activities, an increase with age in the child's "occupation span," an increase in his intellectual grasp of group values and of the opinions and customs of others, and improvements in his motor abilities parallel and form an integral part of the picture.

At the age of six, a child's capacity for group formation is still quite limited.[1] He is beginning to show an interest in games that require the participation of several children, but the games in which he joins are likely to be loosely organized games—such as tag (16)—and much of his play will involve make-believe dramatic themes that allow for a good deal of individual freedom. In their free activities in class or on the playground, first-grade children are not likely to operate as an organized group involving all members of a class of twenty or thirty children (unless their play is directed by an adult).

At the first-grade level, the children who are leaders are likely to lead small groups rather than the entire class (42). It is not until about the fourth grade or later that a class is likely to act as a whole, united under a common leader, on a common project, originated and directed by the children themselves. However, it is not possible to set an exact time when children will reach this level of development, since their behavior will be influenced by many variables, such as past training and opportunity, the urgency or interest value of the project on which they are engaged, the pres-

---

[1] C. Bühler, who, together with her students, has contributed many studies of the development of social behavior in infancy, has also given considerable attention to the social behavior of elementary-school children and adolescents. See her account of "The Social Behavior of Children," in *A Handbook of Child Psychology*, Ch. IX. See also Murphy, Murphy, and Newcomb (38).

ence of resourceful leaders, and the characteristics of the individual children who happen to be the members of a given group.

Gains with age in capacity for group action and teamwork are shown in children's out-of-school play activities. As children grow older, they are increasingly able to identify themselves with the fortunes of a team or club and they show increased interest and ability in following complex rules of action. In their own activities, children come in time to establish quite complicated regulations as to procedure, the function and role of individual members, precedent in "taking turns," and the like. When children of a wide age range play together, they frequently will adapt their procedures to the varying degrees of capacity for teamwork exhibited; thus, while the ten-year-old boys in a ball game are expected to take regular positions on the field and to follow a definite order in batting, a six-year-old who may be playing with them is given a roving commission as backstop for both teams, with freedom to drop in and out of the game, and he may even be indulged with an occasional irregular turn at bat. In a game of cops and robbers, the older child is expected to stay "dead" when he is shot until the rules of the game permit him to revive, while a younger child may be permitted to "peek" when he is supposed to be dead, and to interchange roles as the spirit moves him.

Recognition of own status and the characteristics of others. Along with the development of the child's ability to participate actively in more complex social enterprises, there is an increase with age also in his perception of social relationships and in his awareness of his own status as compared with that of others. As will be noted in more detail at a later point, by the time a child reaches school age, he is likely to understand the meaning of competition and to appreciate, at least in some fields of his activity, how he compares with others. Many children of this age are capable also of a certain amount of self-criticism in the light of their own aspirations and on the basis of their appreciation of the standards set by others, and many of them are sensitive also to the possibility of ridicule, failure, and loss of prestige. As one result of this a child may become shy and self-conscious in connection with performances that earlier were quite spontaneous (such as singing in the presence of others or exhibiting his drawings).

Social perception. An important aspect of social behavior is the development of ability to be cognizant of others, to achieve some degree of awareness of the other fellow's feelings. This aspect of social development is difficult to study, since the child is likely to have difficulty in formulating in so many words his concept of the other fellow; and his ideas and perceptions cannot be fully understood simply by noting isolated acts in his overt dealings with others.

One feature of awareness of the other person's feelings consists in the ability to interpret expressions of emotion by others. The ability to discriminate between different facial expressions improves as the child grows older. In a study by Gates (18, 19), children ranging in age from three to fourteen years were shown photographs of an actress whose facial expressions were designed to show joy, anger, surprise, fear, scorn, and pain. Adults are usually able to identify the expressions which these pictures are intended to show. At the kindergarten level, laughter was correctly named by over seventy per cent of the children; but pain, anger, and fear were recognized by less than half. None of the children of kindergarten age understood the pictures of surprise and scorn. More than half of the children could identify anger at the age of seven, fear at ten, and surprise at eleven. In daily life, with familiar, living faces before them, most of these children undoubtedly recognized the expressions a good deal earlier than they were able to recognize the expression in a photograph of a stranger, but it is nonetheless instructive to note how far the child lags behind the adult in recognizing conventional signs.

During the elementary-school years, children also become increasingly able to formulate in words the traits and characteristics of others which they like or dislike. In a study in which children were asked, among other things, to describe what they disliked in the world about them, an increasing percentage of children from the age of five and upward named people or undesirable traits in people. Six per cent of the answers at five to six years, and twenty-two per cent at eleven to twelve, fell into this category (30).

"Natural" and acquired aspects of social behavior. One question deserves brief consideration: To what extent are changes in social behavior such as those described above due to learning and to what extent are they governed by factors within the child himself that become operative as a result of maturation?

It is impossible at best, in analyzing human behavior, to isolate what is due to original nature and what is due to learning and experience; but some observations reported by investigators are interesting. As noted above, Bühler reports that the babies in her study began, at about the age of six weeks, to respond differently to the human voice and gaze than to other noises and visible objects. The babies smiled. Bühler recognizes that this smile may possibly be a "conditioned reflex transferred from the situation of satiety to the human being present at the moment"; but she also points out that adults are present in many other situations, comforting as well as painful, in which satiety is not a factor. She considers it more likely that the smile is an "original and primary reaction to the human voice and look" (7, p. 377). Observations made by Dennis (12) in an experiment with a pair of infant twins are interesting in this connection. As mentioned in an earlier chapter, these twins were kept in a very restricted environment until the age of seven months. Among other things no one smiled at them or cuddled, fondled, or played with them. But when they reached the age when babies usually begin to smile to adults, these babies smiled. When they reached the age when babies usually laugh, they laughed, and they also gave signs of affection for their stolid attendants. Such observations do not, of course, prove that this behavior is instinctive, but they do indicate that responses of this kind can come to the fore with a minimum of stimulation from other persons.

On the basis of continuing observations and tests of infants during the first two years of life, Shirley is of the opinion that social behavior, in all likelihood, has its own sequence just as truly as does motor development. She reports, for example, that certain manifestations of shyness and self-consciousness during the second year of life appeared so consistently as to suggest that they did not spring from environmental influences alone but represented also a normal manifestation of growth (46).

Observations such as these do not, of course, imply that various types of social response spring forth full-fledged, apart from environmental influences. Without a social environment, there obviously could be no social behavior.

In his dealings with other persons the child, like the adult, shows many different forms of contrasting behavior: he may be hostile or friendly; he may coöperate or compete; he may be timid or brash; and so on. The remaining sections of this chapter will give separate attention to some of these forms of behavior. A later chapter will deal with certain other aspects of social behavior and with a consideration of the impact of varying cultural and social pressures on the developing child.

RESISTANT BEHAVIOR

"Resistant" or "negative" behavior occurs so commonly in children that it may be regarded as a normal feature of the child's social development. Signs of resistance, such as the stiffening of the limbs, averting of the head, firm closure of the lips, can be observed when a child is only a few months old. As usually employed, "resistance" denotes opposition to adult authority and wishes or aggressions against adults or anyone who is vested with authority or is trying to influence or direct a child's conduct. Actually, much of a child's "resistance" is a feature of his effort to achieve self-help and independence and is only incidentally a form of opposition to others. Resistance to other children also occurs, of course. Such resistance will be considered in a later section.

In many children, resistance begins to become most noticeable, roughly, at about eighteen months, with a peak at about the age of three and decline in overt manifestations at about the age of four (43). In the young child, resistance frequently takes the form of failure to comply with apparently understood requests, of apparent stubbornness in matters of eating and the daily routine, and of countless little acts of self-assertion. Children sometimes carry their resistance to the extreme of refusing to urinate until they no longer can retain themselves, forced vomiting, refusal to take food or to swallow, efforts to hold the breath until blue in the face.

Resistance may also take the form of bickering and argumentativeness and continuous questioning after an answer has been given. An example of this appeared in the case of a two-and-a-half-year-old child who, for some reason, had become extremely disputatious. At one time, his father was telling this boy and two other children about a chicken farm once owned by the boy's grandfather. Some of the chickens on this farm, the father related, were black and some were white. The boy interrupted to say: "Naw, they were not black and white, they were blue." This form of bickering, after a short time, disappeared almost as suddenly as it had come. In a case such as this there undoubtedly were many factors contributing to the resistant behavior, but it appeared that the child's behavior represented in part, at least, a form of experimentation which coincided with a newly acquired ability to question others and to voice his own opinions.

Resistance may also take the form of refusal to accept reality or refusal to bow to the inevitable. Thus, a child still hungry for pudding may refuse to accept the fact that there is no pudding even though the empty dish is there for him to see.

In a study by Reynolds (43), "negativism" in children was approached from several angles. Children were rated by their parents and by nursery-school teachers and were also observed under experimental conditions. Negativism was defined as refusal to comply with understood requests. Records were taken of the child's response when asked to repeat numbers, when commanded to stop playing with blocks, when lifted into the experimenter's lap, when neglected, and at other times. The experimental situations afforded thirteen opportunities to be resistant (such as refusing to repeat numbers, continuing to play with blocks when asked not to). Wide differences between children were observed. The resistance scores ranged from 0 to 12, with an average of 4.38.

This study brought out the fact that what is called "negativism" may appear in one situation and not in another. There was no significant resemblance between the negativism scores in the experimental situations and the parents' and teachers' ratings of the same children.

In everyday observations one sometimes can verify this finding. A child who is stubborn and headstrong at home may be quite compliant and coöperative at school or when visiting a neighbor. Accordingly, a parent and a teacher might have quite different ideas with respect to a child's tendency to be resistant.

Older children in the study cited above were less resistant than younger, although there were many exceptions to the rule. The decline in resistance with age takes place partly because the older child understands better what is expected of him, is better able to comply, and has learned that he will be more comfortable if he complies with the wishes of others, and also because he has learned to express himself better by means of words and has acquired other more subtle means of asserting his independence. A decline in resistance may also be due to the fact that a child's elders have been learning how to handle issues that are likely to provoke resistance.

Resistance is frequently encountered when intelligence tests are being administered to young children. A child's resistance may mean that he is unable to do what is requested of him, but often lack of ability is not the cause. This appeared in a study by Rust (44) of resistance during mental tests. One hundred three-year-old children were tested on two standard scales (Kuhlmann-Binet and Merrill-Palmer). On the first day, approximately half of each scale was administered, and on a following day the next half was given. On the third and fourth days this procedure was repeated, so that each child was tested twice on both scales. Instances of resistance (as distinguished from failure in efforts to perform) were noted. On the first tests, eighty-four of the one hundred children in the study resisted one or more test items (by spoken refusal, physical protests, silence, and so forth), but there remained only *four* children who continued to resist one or more items of the test at the end of the experiment. This decline in resistance, as the children and the examiner became better acquainted, is in itself of interest. However, this degree of success in overcoming resistance cannot be regarded as standard, since adults differ in their ability to establish rapport and to gain a young child's coöperation.

This study showed that a child would frequently resist because he was unable to do what was asked. One would expect this. But the interesting fact is that about fifty-eight per cent of the test items initially refused by the children were passed successfully on subsequent presentations, even though the children received no further help. The chief cause of resistance in the test situation, accordingly, was not the difficulty of what the child was asked to do but rather that the items of the test did not fully enlist the child's interest and effort.

Some contributing factors. Many conditions impel a child to become resistant. He is likely to resist in time if he is often needlessly interfered with, if he is jerked or forced abruptly while already trying to obey a command, if he is frequently caressed and fondled against his wishes, or if he is frequently teased or given contradictory commands. His efforts to protest or to protect himself in specific instances are likely to become habitual if he is often provoked. Moreover, if he meets the same person or similar advances in many situations, he may come to resist this person and such advances in other situations as well. Resistant behavior is sometimes an outgrowth of the fact that people who associate with young children do not take proper account of the child's limited capacity for concentration. In playing with a child, adults often are tempted to overdo their attentions. If a child is just beginning to talk, for example, it is fascinating to try to coax him to repeat words or to speak new words. Such attentions may soon become quite tedious to the youngster. Sometimes, too, resistance is a bid for attention, as when a child who is left to care for himself while his mother is attending to a younger brother or sister dawdles, procrastinates, or demands help in what he actually is able to do for himself.

The fact that children show resistance is, of course, not remarkable when one considers how much they are pushed around, even by parents who are patient and wise. The parents themselves are subject to many rules and restraints which they take for granted. The culture into which the child is being reared is full of countless regulations. In the matter of eating alone there are many rules that an adult accepts as a matter of course but that must strike the child as rather arbitrary. He must sit down, not stand, when eating. He may be pleasantly settled with a toy, and then the words "Dinner is ready" may come like a mandate from on high. In like manner many safety regulations must strike him as arbitrary (until he has learned through painful experience). He must not play with pins or touch a hot iron; he must stay away from the oven and not come near when hot fat is on the stove. These are small details, but there are many such.

Even in the best home the young child is subject to numberless noes and don'ts, many of them spoken, many of them expressed through restraining gestures and other techniques that keep a child from forbidden ground. If these could be tallied, it no doubt would be found that the noes and don'ts to which a child is exposed are much more frequent than the noes and I wants with which he retorts. The fact that a great many rules and restraints are not only inevitable but reasonable from an adult point of view means little to the child.

Later symptoms. Although overt resistance usually declines after the fourth year, it persists in one form or another throughout later years. As the child grows older, his methods of resisting become more subtle. The child may pretend that he does not hear or understand, may stubbornly refuse to see the point, persist in referring to a topic that has been closed, make repeated complaints, assume a careless manner in executing commands, tease, resort to indirect recriminations, or employ a number of other devices.

Resistant tendencies resembling those of children sometimes can be found even in otherwise normal adults, as when an adult chronically "rises" against suggestions, goes out of his way to eat or to wear what he has been advised against, or persists in mannerisms for no apparent reason other than the fact that he has been urged not to.

CHILDREN'S FIGHTS AND QUARRELS

As soon as children are old enough to fraternize with one another, bickerings and altercations are common in their group behavior.[2]

Varying causes, motives, and functions. As a child makes his way among his peers, entering now into this activity, now into that, his desires may clash with those of others; he may bump into another, get into another's way, interfere, or enter where he is not wanted, and brief arguments or more vigorous physical encounters ensue.

Studies of children's conflicts indicate that the number of such

---

[2] For detailed studies of children's conflicts with one another, see Burk (8), Caille (9), Dawe (11), Fite (15), Green (21), Isaacs (26), Jersild and Fite (27), and Jersild and Markey (29).

altercations is correlated, to a high degree, with a child's general activity; the more a child "gets around" and the more contacts he makes, the more he is likely to enter into a number of altercations.

The fact that many conflicts arise in connection with the general flow of his activity is set forth by Green, who observed that quarrels are likely to be more frequent among children who are close companions (21). Green found that "mutual friends are more quarrelsome, and mutual quarrelers are more friendly than the average," and that "quarreling is a part of friendly, social intercourse at these ages." In other studies, likewise, it has been found that there is a positive correlation between aggressive and sympathetic behavior, although, of course, there are notable exceptions to this trend (29), (39).

Combativeness is not, however, a function only of the general flow of a child's activity, for his aggressions against another child may serve many purposes. Not only may the motive be different in different children, but it may differ within the same child from time to time; and sometimes a child's contact with another will combine both an aggressive and a friendly act, as when he pushes a child down and then helps him to his feet. In the conflicts of children of preschool age, especially before ideas of property rights and inhibitions clustering around these have been fully formed, many of the conflicts involve an effort to procure or protect play material. Thirty-six per cent of the conflicts of nursery-school children, according to a study by Appel (5), centered around possession of property. Aggressive behavior may also serve the child as a means of winning his way into a group, of bringing himself to the attention of another child, or of rebuffing the advances of another.

In Appel's study it was found that about twenty-three per cent of nursery-school children's conflicts fell in these categories: "intrusion or rejection of companionship," teasing, and cross purposes.

A child will sometimes block another, interfere with his activities, and even take a tentative poke at him not, as far as can be ascertained, because of any animus or ulterior desire for conquest or possession, but more in the interest of experimenting to see what will happen. Again, children will sometimes blunder into a fracas with no initial intention, as far as can be ascertained, either of stirring up a fight or of gaining anything in particular by it.

A child's aggressiveness may also be an expression of jealousy, as when he goes out of his way to irritate, tease, or hit another child who has received attentions from adults or other children. Further, even though most of the altercations between young children are brief in duration, a child may return again and again to attack another, as though moved by a lingering resentment; sometimes, one will repeatedly do something that irritates another, as though seeking to provoke an attack so that he, in turn, may "defend" himself by a strong counterattack. Sometimes it is the child who is least sure of himself in his relations with his group who is the most belligerent.

The fact that combativeness may function in different ways is illustrated by the records of two nursery-school children who showed a notable increase in the frequency of their conflicts during the course of the school year (27). In one case it appeared that combativeness was a feature of poor social adjustment, and in the other case it appeared that it was a feature of improved social adjustment. One of the children was a boy who, at the beginning of the school year, spent much of his time with a companion whom he dominated; but with the help of the teachers, the dominated child established ties with other children. When the boy found that his hold over his companion had been broken, he tried to establish other contacts. But partly because of his aggressive techniques and small size, he met rebuffs from other children whom he tried to join. They would tell him to go away; he would then tell them to shut up, and they would tell him to shut up; he would hit and they would hit; and thus there was an increase in the frequency of his conflicts. This increase was, in effect, a symptom of maladjustment in the child's social relations.

The other child who also showed a conspicuous increase in frequency of conflicts was a girl, who, at the beginning of the year, was dominated to a large extent by a playmate of about her own age. As the weeks went by, this girl became more and more sociable in her relations with other children on the playground, but as this happened, she had to fight off her dominating companion. In this case, an increase in conflicts was, in effect, associated with an improvement in the child's social adjustment within the group as a whole.

One factor, among many, which no doubt helps to accentuate a child's aggressiveness, is the example set by other children and adults. An adult's treatment of a child may strike him as a form of aggression, even though the adult is not conscious of being aggressive. For example, when an older child refuses to yield his toy to a younger sibling and is then compelled to yield by his mother, the mother's intervention, as far as the older child is concerned, may not differ materially from the child's own behavior when he, in his own way, snatches another child's material.

It appears that there are factors in the personality of the child as well as factors in the external situation that dispose a child to be aggressive in his social dealings. According to studies by H. H. Anderson (1, 2, 3) a child's combativeness may be a feature of a more inclusive behavior tendency. Anderson distinguishes between two broad categories of behavior which he calls "dominative" and "integrative." The "dominative" person not only expends energy against others but he also tends, according to Anderson's account, to be rigid and static. He is not one who seeks better understanding and to solve differences. He does not seek change but the status quo. "Integrative" behavior, in contrast, as described by Anderson, is more flexible, yielding, spontaneous, and receptive to change. In investigations in which Anderson studied the behavior of young children from the point of view of these broad concepts he found that children tend to respond in kind: if a child is "dominative" in his behavior, he incites a dominative response, whereas "integrative" behavior induces integrative behavior in a companion.

Age, sex, and group differences in the conflicts of nursery-school children. In one study of children's conflicts with one another (29), children in three nursery schools were observed during the course of the year, and a number of them were reobserved the following year in nursery schools and kindergartens. The conflicts that were noted ranged from brief verbal disputes to fights of a more violent character, involving biting, hitting, pushing, scratching, and the like. The fifty-four two- to four-year-old children who were observed exhibited an average of one conflict per child every five minutes, but most of these conflicts were very brief (lasting less than half a minute). A conflict was defined as "any instance in which one child attacks another's person or materials or by word or deed interferes with the person, activities, or possessions of another, or threatens by word or gesture to do so, or endeavors by force or verbal demands to possess another's belongings, or to direct another's activities in opposition to the apparent desires of the other child."

At one extreme was a child who engaged in 141 conflicts during the course of the observations, while at the other extreme was a child who took part in only 17; one child made a personal attack on another (hitting, pushing, throwing things at, holding, threatening gestures, and so forth) 87 times, while there was another child who did not lay hands on another, or threaten to do so, a single time.

The frequency of conflicts tended to decline with age (from two to four years), but this trend was not conclusive. The most notable change that occurred at this age was in the techniques used during conflicts. From the age of two to four years, there was a decline in screaming, weeping, and cries for help. There was a decline also in hitting and other forms of physical attack and an increase in the use of language during conflicts.

As children grow older their conflicts with one another tend to last longer, and aggressors and victims alike tend to become more versatile and competent in their methods of combat. In the study by Appel (5) it was found that when two-year-olds fought with one another, only forty per cent of their conflicts extended beyond one stage or "round," while sixty-seven per cent of conflicts between four-year-olds went to two rounds or more.

In the study mentioned above, it was found that the younger the child, the more similar boys and girls were likely to be. At two years, for example, boys and girls were quite similar in the frequency of their screaming and crying. But with added age, the girls did not exhibit so large a decrease in screaming and weeping as did the boys. Boys tended to hit more frequently than did the girls and also tended to be aggressive more often than girls.

Large group differences also appeared. Children in a day nursery, representing a somewhat unprivileged economic and educational background, exhibited more conflicts than did children in a nursery school that enrolled children who came from homes of higher socio-economic status. Group differences were noted also in the study by Appel cited above. Children representing homes of relatively low socio-economic status showed more conflicts over possession of material objects than did children of higher socio-economic status.

Adult responses to children's combativeness. Adults show a great variety of reactions to children's fights and quarrels. In about a third of the children's conflicts in one of the studies cited above, the teachers took steps to stop or settle the disputes. In a majority of such instances the teachers decided the issue against the children who were most aggressive and who "won" a high proportion of their conflicts when left to themselves (29). Frequently this seemed justified, but such favoritism toward the less aggressive child sometimes went so far as to leave him the winner in a dispute where the aggressor might well feel an injustice had been done. It has also been noted that an adult, coming abruptly upon a fracas between children, may fail to take proper account of the underlying issue (15). Two children may, for example, be engaged in a tug of war over a small box. On the surface, it seems that only the box is at stake and that a reasonable solution can readily be found; actually, however, the struggle for the box may be only incidental to an effort by one of the combatants to rebuff the other. Teachers differ considerably in the techniques they commonly use when dealing with children's fracases. Some teachers seemed much more intent than others simply on putting a stop to the fighting, whereas other teachers made more of an effort to make use of the occasion to help children to learn friendly ways of getting along together (5).

Children's learning of socially approved ways of getting along with one another is not necessarily hastened by an adult policy of preventing fights and quarrels. In one of the groups included in the study mentioned above, there was not only more active and frequent interference by the teachers than in another group, but there also was more passive interference, by virtue of the fact that there usually were three or four teachers in charge, as compared with only one or two in the other group. During the year, when these conditions prevailed, the much-interfered-with children fought less often than did the children who had more freedom. But the following year, when children from both groups moved on to two respective kindergartens, in both of which the teachers interfered relatively little with the children, a different turn of events appeared. The previously little-fighting and much-interfered-with children doubled the frequency of their conflicts. On the other hand, the previously little-interfered-with and much-fighting children, instead of fighting even more when allowed a greater degree of freedom, actually did slightly less fighting than during the preceding year.

A finding such as this does not mean that a child of three or four has within him a certain amount of fight which he must get out of his system; rather it suggests that children must practice and have experience in order to work out their techniques of dealing with one another. The fact that such learning of more peaceable techniques can be expedited with adult help is shown in an interesting study by Chittenden (10). The children who were selected for training were youngsters who tended to be very domineering, who were inclined to use force, threats, commands, and criticism in dealings with other children and refusal to follow the suggestions of other children. Play situations in which dolls, in the role of preschool children, took part in social situations such as those a preschool child himself faces, were used in an effort to help the children to understand and interpret social situations and to learn coöperative techniques. The training schedule included eleven sessions of about fifteen minutes each. The children who had received this training showed a marked decline in "dominating" behavior as compared with a control group. This decline was not accompanied by a decline in social activity, but there was not an increase in "coöperative" behavior corresponding to the decline in dominating behavior. Training, within the bounds of the experiment, seemed to be more effective in teaching children to inhibit dominating techniques than to acquire coöperative techniques.

Conflicts of older children. As noted above, overt fighting and squabbling tend to occur less frequently from the preschool period into the elementary-school years, although most children continue to have occasional battles and some children maintain continuing feuds with siblings or neighbors. Many factors, both in the child and in the environment, contribute to a decline in bickering. The child's increased understanding of property rights obviates many conflicts on that score. One investigator (14) found that most children at the age of six had a workable knowledge of property rights that are involved in the ordinary social dealings of children at that age. The child has more understanding also of other children, what he can expect from them, what they will tolerate from him, what might happen in his relations with them if he is combative. Increasingly, also, the child understands and accepts the unwritten rules and codes of group behavior which children impose upon one another.

The decline in combativeness is perhaps more apparent than real, for there may not be a corresponding decline in feelings of hostility. The youngster learns to conceal or disguise his feelings. He learns many subtle techniques for avoiding or repelling persons who offend him and for seeking out persons who are congenial. Moreover, while there is a decline in provocations of some kinds, there may be an increase in other kinds, notably in connection with various forms of competition in games, in classwork, and the like.

Toward the end of preschool years, and more especially during the school-age period, many children show an interest in fighting as a sport. Some boys will even assert with pride and with a smile that they "like to fight," and one of the things many boys will claim when asked how boys differ from girls is that "boys fight, but girls don't fight much." In many seemingly playful combats, there is likely to be more than a sheer sporting interest. A certain amount of animus and a good deal of self-assertiveness frequently enter in. Anger may rapidly mount on both sides, even if the bout began on a rather friendly basis. Fighting of this sort may spring from many motives, including underlying maladjustments, but it also is part of a child's experimentation in social living; too, it is a means whereby he tests his powers and explores his status within his group.

In school, unless conditions are exceptional, there usually will be fewer physical altercations in the elementary grades than in nursery school or kindergarten, partly by reason of the fact that older children are usually working on supervised projects while school is in session. Where enough freedom prevails, children will, however, attack each other in the classroom on occasion, sometimes in a spirit of mischief or fun, sometimes in a spirit of genuine hostility. Hostility often finds expression in the criticisms children make of one another's work at school.

It frequently happens that critical comments and hostile reactions will be directed especially toward one or two members of a class whose behavior is annoying. As noted elsewhere, in observations of small groups of children, Lewin, Lippitt, and White (32) found that aggressiveness in the relations of children may be intensified by the restraints imposed by adults who supervise them.

Aggressions may become quite cruel, especially when several children band together against a single child or a minority group. Sometimes children's cruelty and intolerance may arise through lack of understanding. An elementary-school class, at Christmas, presented a corsage to the teacher with a note: "From all of the class, except Bill." It was discovered that poor Bill, who was thus pointedly condemned, had the will but not the pennies to contribute; some of the other pupils, similarly poor, had borrowed money from the very teacher to whom the gift was presented, but Bill refused to do this. Most adults would regard his stand as quite admirable, but it is unlikely that this fact would remove the sting of being censured by his own classmates.

Frequently, in groups of children who have known each other for some time, the members of the group come to recognize a more or less clearly established hierarchy of dominance, with a child at one extreme whom all of the children, by mutual consent or through bitter experience, look upon as the best fighter and who had better be left alone, and at the other extreme a noncombative child whom no one fears, while other youngsters occupy positions between these extremes.

In their own way, children frequently build up many unwritten rules of combat. Certain methods of attack, such as throwing stones or using icy snowballs, are frowned upon; a child should "pick on" someone his own size; certain tactics are permitted in fights between boys but may not be used when a boy fights a girl (although this rule frequently breaks down at home in fights between brothers and sisters); hostilities between members of a group must be buried when the group is attacked by another gang; and so forth.

Teasing, bullying, and disguised hostility. Beginning early in preschool years and extending throughout childhood, children use a large variety of aggressive techniques that fall short of physical combat. Teasing often occurs in the relations of children in the same family who goad each other to anger but dare not openly hit. At school, children devise many techniques of teasing. Teasing and opprobrious nicknames are much used in children's efforts to discipline one another.

Occasionally a child will join others in teasing someone, even though he bears him no ill will but is simply following the crowd. Frequently, however, there is bad feeling behind teasing, and the child who is inclined to tease is expressing tensions and problems in his own life. An interesting sequence in behavior of this kind in a summer camp is described by Osborne (40). When first introduced into the camp, a child was the butt of much teasing and bullying, partly because of certain "babyish" traits. As he continued in camp, he mended his ways, but during the transition, as he was in the process of becoming adjusted to the group, he went through a stage when he in turn teased and bullied other children. As time went on and as the child's poise and adjustment in the group improved, he abandoned teasing and bullying. In observations of preschool children, Murphy (39) has also noted that teasing may be an expression of insecurity.

As a child becomes older and more clever he may be able to express deep hostility even though he never lifts his voice or raises his hand to strike. He may use the technique of eloquent silence or pointedly ignore others or persist in argumentation of an apparently disinterested and very tolerant sort. A skillful antagonist may even use a crusade of apparent good will as a means of attack upon individuals or groups.[3]

---

[3] The subject of aggressiveness in social relationships is discussed also under the headings of prejudice and anger in other sections of this book.

SYMPATHY

Expressions of sympathy in young children can be observed in acts such as helping, removing or attempting to remove causes of distress, comforting, punishing the cause of distress, protecting and defending the distressed person, warning, telling an adult or some other child about another's distress, questioning to discover the cause of distress, suggesting or effecting a solution, and anxious or disorganized responses, such as staring with an anxious expression, evidences of worry, head shaking, frowning, compression of lips, and crying and whimpering (39).

It has been observed that children of two and three years of age do not tend, in general, to respond sympathetically to stimuli such as black and blue wounds, swellings, lumps, and other minor distortions of flesh which to an adult would suggest discomfort or illness, or to the account of Red Riding Hood being eaten by the wolf, or pictures of accidents, of funerals, of someone crippled or carrying crutches, and the like (39). Younger children apparently have not, in general, acquired the level of discrimination and perception to recognize these phenomena as signs of distress. A child of this age might, for example, recognize conspicuous bandages or the flow of blood as a sign of distress, but fail so to recognize a blue bruise or swelling. Murphy observed that many three-year-olds, but not all, would respond to distress as indicated by bandages, blindness, bruises colored with iodine, red swellings, scars, scratches; by deprivation of toys, food, or of mother; by physical confinement such as being caught in a pen; by interference of activity suffered by a child who has to stay in bed or is not able to run or play; by frustration of activity; by being attacked by another person; by evidences of an accident, such as falling; and by crying.

In direct observation of two groups of nursery-school children, Murphy found the following incidence of expressions of sympathy:

	Hours of Observation	Number of Sympathetic Responses	Number of Unsympathetic Responses
Group *A*	188	318	195
Group *B*	234	398	60

The children in Group *B* represented a wider age range and higher average age and had a larger playground than the children in Group *A*. The ratio of sympathetic to unsympathetic responses, initiated and received, varied considerably from child to child.

Older children in the study cited above tended to show sympathy more frequently than did younger children. Older children responded to a wider range of distress situations and, as noted above, they were more likely than the younger ones to exhibit active responses of comfort, help, and defense, as distinguished from more passive responses such as anxiously staring or asking about the distress of another. However, within a given age group, factors in the personality of the individual children were more important than the factor of age alone. Likewise, although the factor of intelligence appeared to contribute to the quality of sympathetic responses and to the insight which a child might have into the distress of another, the factor of intelligence was less influential than were other factors, such as a child's social interests and responsiveness to other children.

When the children in Murphy's study were rated with respect to sympathy and aggressiveness, the scores showed a positive relationship; in other words, the children who most often sympathized tended also most often to be aggressive. There were notable exceptions to this trend, however; one child, for example, stood near the bottom in his tendency to be sympathetic and near the top in his tendency to be aggressive.

Influence of varying motives on sympathetic behavior. Sympathetic or unsympathetic responses may vary considerably within the same child from time to time. A child might be quick with his sympathies when he comes upon a situation in which another child is in distress, but show just the opposite response if the distress and wishes of the other child are in conflict with his own desires. Again, if a child's initial effort to be sympathetic is rebuffed, he may become aggressive and change from a friendly to a hostile response, just as in everyday life a child may show anger toward a wounded or hungry animal which at first aroused his compassion but ran away from the child's proffer of food or help. Furthermore, one child may be most sympathetic when he himself is somewhat afraid and insecure, and then grow less sympathetic as he gains in confidence; while another child may show the reverse tendency. Also, as a child becomes more at ease in the group, there may be an increase both in his aggressiveness and in his readiness to show sympathy. One child, while in the position of trying to win favor with his fellows, may be more sensitive to their needs, not only because of his wish to please them, but also because of his tendency to see his own apprehensions reflected in others. Another child, also insecure in his relations with the group, may be so wrapped up in his own problems that he is unable to perceive the distress of others.

Variations in response were noted in Murphy's study in connection with experimental situations that were used to precipitate a sympathetic response. In one such situation, the procedure was to leave the child alone at the side of a play pen in which a two-year-old baby girl was confined. If the subject did nothing, the experimenter would ask questions such as: "She hasn't got any of her things, has she?" "What do you think she wants?" The experimenter later started to pull out the child, behaved as though she had difficulty in doing so, waited ten seconds for help, and then asked for help. The responses of different children to this situation varied from complete inaction to immediate and wholehearted responses that indicated concern over the predicament of the little child. There was little relationship, however, between the children's responses in this situation and the responses of the same children in their contacts with one another on the playground.

When eighteen children were presented with a variety of situations designed, like the foregoing, to elicit sympathy, five of them were quite consistently unsympathetic. Seven were quite consistently sympathetic, and six children fluctuated.

In observations of pairs of sisters, McFarland (33) noted that a child's tendency to sympathize with another child depended not simply upon the degree of distress shown by a sufferer, but upon the child's relation to this distress. For example, if one child's distress jeopardized the security or interests of another, the sympathetic response was frequently inhibited. Likewise, a child would sympathize with her sister when the sister herself had got into trouble or when her distress was caused by someone else, but would fail to sympathize when she herself was the cause of distress. McFarland noted also that children who were very responsive to the distress of their sisters tended also to be sympathetic toward others who were in distress. This observation suggests that cultivation of sympathy, like charity, might best begin at home.

A many-sided systematic study, such as is represented by Murphy's investigation, has not been made of sympathetic behavior in older children and adults, but some material on the subject appears in treatments of other topics, such as children's friendships, coöperation, and affectionate behavior.

COMPETITION AND COÖPERATION

Coöperation and competition have many elements in common, and activities which outwardly appear to be competitive or coöperative may have different and quite mixed motives behind them. Competition usually denotes a struggle or contest in which one individual seeks to equal or excel another, or to obtain objects, recognition, prestige, attainments, or honors also sought by others.

Coöperation, on the other hand, involves joint action with others on a common enterprise toward a common goal. Although the one form of behavior is often regarded as the antithesis of the other, it frequently happens that both forms appear as parts of a larger project. Many competitive games involve more coöperation than competition, just as many coöperative ventures entail a good deal of competition between individuals who are joined in a common interest.

In the everyday life of children, it frequently is very difficult to judge what forms of such behavior are being displayed. In connection with a class project, for example, one pupil may make a contribution primarily to promote the work at hand, while another child, or the same child at another time, may make a similar contribution primarily to be heard or to receive recognition. Frequently the underlying motive is difficult, if not impossible, to appraise, although the pattern of a child's behavior from day to day is likely to provide some clews. In passing we might note that the child who is not actively competing may in actuality be highly competitive in his attitude: his own standing may mean so much to him that he will not join in group activity for fear that he won't make a good showing.

It is difficult not only to make an absolute distinction between competition and coöperation but also to estimate the relative value of the two forms of behavior. As a competitor, the individual asserts his own immediate interests; as a coöperator, he promotes the immediate interests of his group. In the end, the promotion of self-interest may be much to the disadvantage of the group, but it may also be of great value. Similarly, the promotion of group interests will usually be of value to the individual, but it may also be damaging if the interests of the group are evil or misguided.

Rivalry. During the first few weeks of life, the child's behavior cannot be described either as competitive or coöperative. During the first two years, however, many children exhibit signs of rivalry for the affection and attention of others.

Signs of rivalry in matters of prestige and accomplishment usually are later in appearance than symptoms of jealousy for the affections of parents, but many children at the age of two, and more thereafter, are likely to show some awareness of what the other child is doing and to be sensitive to their own showing as compared with that of other youngsters. Expressions such as: "I am older," "I am bigger," "Mine's nicer" are among the milder forms. One child, on learning that today was the birthday of a playmate, proceeded not only to claim that today was *his* birthday too, but also went the rounds to individual children inviting them to his birthday party.

In such verbal "I-am-better-than-you" battles, the child with the superior vocabulary may have quite an advantage, as illustrated in the following encounter between two five-year-old children:

John: I can count up to 100.
Frank: I can count to 1,000.
John: I can count up to a million.
Frank: I can count up to a billion.
John: I can count up to a trillion.
Frank: I can count to infinity.

It is not until after the third year that a large proportion of children exhibit evidences of rivalry concerning accomplishment, such as are displayed by children in the elementary grades. In a study by Leuba (31), children aged two to six years were brought into an experimental room singly and then in pairs. The children were given an opportunity to play with a peg board, and their conversation and behavior were recorded. In the two-year-old group, the presence of another child did not seem to have much influence on what a child did or said. The children exhibited little competition but showed an interest mainly in the materials before them. Three-year-old children showed some competition; they were interested in the social situation but showed awareness of what the other child was doing. At four to six years, a majority of children manifested a desire to excel, and they exhibited an increased degree of understanding of the idea of excelling. At six years, some of the children also showed an increase in critical judgment of their own work.

A similar increase in competitions was observed in a study by Greenberg of children aged two to seven years (23). Children were brought in pairs into a small room where there was a table and a pile of building blocks. They were encouraged to build whatever they wanted with the blocks. The behavior of the children showed notable change with age in many respects. Older children were likely to go to work and to build something with the blocks, while the younger ones were likely to play in a more desultory fashion. Children aged two to four tended to pick up blocks as they needed them, but four- to seven-year-old children more often cornered a supply. There was an increase with age in children's favorable remarks about their own work and a steady increase from one year to the next in the percentage of children who exhibited various signs of competition (the percentages at the successive age levels of three, four, five, and six years were, respectively, 42.6, 69.2, 75.4, 86.5).

The fact that competition is an influential factor in the behavior of children of kindergarten age was noted also in a study by Wolf (51) which dealt with the ability of children to persist in a task. The children stayed longer with a task on the average when competing than when working alone. However, some children responded much less to competition than did others.

Many instances of rivalry were noted in a study by McFarland of twenty pairs of sisters (33). Individual children were aroused to rivalry by different types of situation, and pairs of sisters who showed rivalry most frequently were about as companionable as those who showed signs of rivalry relatively seldom.

Competition at later age levels. At the elementary-school age it has been found that a majority of children will exert themselves more and accomplish more when working for themselves or for individual honors or rewards than when working for the group (35). Yet, if the flavor of a group versus group contest can be injected, many children are likely to exert themselves more than when this element of competition is lacking (25). Maller found this especially true when the group is one of the children's own choosing (35).

One thing much needed is more research that deals with competition and coöperation in realistic settings. In the case of young children, it is possible to devise quite realistic experimental play situations; but with older children this seems to be more difficult. The experimental situation used with older children may simply touch off specific habits of competition that have already been established, so that the dice are already loaded in favor of competition. For example, after children have struggled individually to master problems in addition, it is only reasonable to expect that they will apply themselves more energetically when competing with other individual performers than when they are asked to work hard to raise the general average of the class. A real test of coöperativeness would require situations about which children actually feel some concern.

Motives and values. Many factors in both the situation and the individual influence the conditions under which competition is likely to arise, the effects of competition, and the merits or shortcomings of competition. The issues over which children compete vary from child to child. A child may be highly competitive in one group and not in another. A child may applaud and feel delighted when some of his associates equal or surpass him but react in quite the opposite manner when others, with whom he does not feel as closely identified, succeed under similar circumstances. A child may find satisfaction in the success of a youngster who is not especially his friend but who defeats a rival of the child. Behavior that appears highly coöperative or even self-sacrificing may spring, indirectly, from competitive motives, and, contrariwise, a person may show his coöperativeness by plunging zestfully into a competitive enterprise. Among adults, one group of individuals may coöperate zealously to foster or protect a competitive mode of life, while others enter into spirited competition to promote a coöperative society.

In general, competitive enterprises among children are likely to be most zestful when the competitors are about evenly matched, although there are many exceptions to this. Often, when an older and a younger child are competing in a foot race, the abler child will voluntarily assume a handicap or give the other a "head start," in order that there may be a semblance of a contest (however, such sporting tactics are less likely to appear if there are spoils for the victor at the end of the race).

Even in a one-sided contest, the effects of competition may sometimes be salutary. A boy who was husking corn with his own wagon and team and who did about thirty-five to forty bushels a day when left to himself, rose to fifty bushels per day for a few days when a man who regularly husked eighty-five bushels a day came into the field. After a few days, however, he gave up the contest with the superior worker and slumped back to forty. When this man left and the boy was alone again, he slumped still further to about thirty-five and sometimes as low as twenty-five. Shortly thereafter he kept a pace of slightly above fifty bushels a day when a man who habitually did about that number joined him in the field; on odd days, when a neighbor who did between sixty and sixty-five bushels a day joined in the work, the boy's output rose to about sixty and reached a peak of sixty-five. This high point was reached partly by virtue of preceding practice, but much of it was accomplished through the spur of competition, for he again reverted to an output of fifty to fifty-five bushels when the fifty-bushel man was the only other person in the field.

Another person can provide a visible standard of achievement, and the opportunity to compete with this standard can give zest to an otherwise tiresome job. In countless practical situations, the presence of a pacemaker and competitor may be of value, not only in the doing of a specific job, but also in the larger sphere of habit formation and social conduct. This is even more true of children than of adults, for the child's performance is more fluid and variable than is an adult's, and the opportunity to appraise his own performance in the light of the performance of his peers can bring home to him many lessons that cannot be impressed upon him by adult exhortations. Under the spur of competition with a visitor or camp mate the child may discover that he can put on his shoes in half the time it used to take, stub his toe without crying, jump into the water without cringing, endure a slight without running to mother to complain, exhibit a modicum of sportsmanship, or do homely chores without feeling abused.

In such behavior there are many of the elements that are involved in competition, namely, recognizing a level of achievement as exhibited by another and striving to close the gap between this standard and one's accustomed performance, or to surpass the standard.

Competitive enterprises of one sort or another are likely to arise in any enterprising society, but the competitive situations will differ in different cultures and even in different localities within the same culture. The competition that occurs may be inevitable and spontaneous or it may be forced and manufactured. Again, the rewards may flow naturally from the enterprise itself, or, in contrast, the rewards may be highly artificial. On the subjective side, one competitor may strive with zest and a light heart and take his successes and reverses in stride, while another driven by inner distress, uses the enterprise only as a means toward a more remote objective, and is troubled with a sense of inferiority or with feelings of spite and vengefulness.

While some values can be derived from competition, it has its bad side, too. Bad effects are especially likely to arise if children are under strong pressure from home and from school to compete in a narrow range of activities. The narrower the range of interests and activities the environment affords the more likely it is that a few children will always come out on top while others fail. There are children who can never hope to excel in arithmetic, for example (even though these same children in a noncompetitive situation might derive satisfaction from numbers and mastering arithmetical problems). But some of the children who cannot hope to be very successful in arithmetic might get satisfaction in music, or in other arts, or in certain crafts, or in certain athletic sports. Human abilities are so varied and uneven that the environment must offer a variety of opportunities for achievement if each person is to have a chance to realize and enjoy his abilities and potentialities.

Competition becomes burdensome when it goes beyond contests that give zest to life and that have a quality of freedom and spontaneity and becomes instead a chronic, compulsive form of behavior. A highly competitive attitude may be a sign of underlying fear and insecurity (25a). It may also be a sign of hostility. It may mean not only that the individual feels hostile toward others but also that he expects them to feel hostile toward him. Often it appears that a person's competitiveness bars him from winning the very approval he is seeking so hard to gain. Competitive attitudes acquired in childhood frequently make life harder at the adult level. A person may be so driven that he is unable to enjoy his work or his play but is compelled instead with each new success to expend new effort in protecting his reputation and in increasing his power. He may go to great lengths to oppose or to evade criticism; he may strive to avoid contact with others whose work rivals his own; he may reject new ideas, largely because he did not originate them himself. In these and other ways he may be barred from easy and friendly relationships with his fellow men. The more his competitiveness thus takes the form of self-protection, the more of a burden it becomes to him and the more of a liability it becomes to society at large.

Apart from the foregoing there is the more or less obvious point that artificial or forced competition should not be used as a means of motivating children's learning. In everyday life people do not read, for example, in order to excel someone else in reading: they read to get practical information, or to enjoy a story, and the like. To conduct a reading class in the manner of a contest, with each child trying to outdo the other as a reader, may be stimulating to some children, but it is an artificial procedure, out of line with the genuine functions and usages of reading. Much the same can be said with respect to all other specialized forms of learning.

Coöperation. As noted earlier, conflict and competition are likely to attract more attention than are friendliness and coöperation, with the result that the former types of behavior are often overemphasized while a large number of coöperative acts come to be taken for granted. Actually a child is likely to be more coöperative and friendly than competitive and hostile.

The findings in a study by Mengert (37) are instructive in this connection. Two-year-old children were observed when brought into a small playroom in pairs during twenty-minute periods. Each child in the study was paired with each of the other children. When responses were tallied, those which could be classed as overtly friendly outnumbered the overtly unfriendly responses by more than four to one (the respective average scores were 89.5 and 20.5).

The exact proportions between friendly and unfriendly responses will vary considerably with different children and in different situations, but it is significant that in both of the above studies the balance runs so strongly in favor of the friendly forms of behavior. Indeed, even in the case of children who exhibit relatively much aggressive or hostile behavior, such behavior may still be outweighed by nonhostile contacts. In a study by Jersild and Fite (27), it was noted that two children were outstanding with respect to the relative frequency of their conflicts; in both cases, however, social contacts that did not involve conflict outnumbered those in which aggressions occurred. The fact that a child tends to be friendly rather than hostile in his initial response to a newcomer appears from a study by Wright (52). Children in this study gave desirable toys more frequently to strangers who were introduced into the experiment than to their own established friends. According to this study, a child does not subscribe to a philosophy of *bellum omnes contra omnium*.

Findings such as the foregoing suggest that the potentialities for friendly, coöperative behavior are as strong as, or perhaps stronger than the potentialities for behavior that involves self-assertion at the expense of or in opposition to others. When one considers that friendly relations with others usually are comfortable and rewarding and the fact, as noted above, that competitive attitudes toward others may become very painful and burdensome, it is remarkable that so little systematic effort has been made in psychological and educational research to discover how best to help children to cultivate their potentialities for friendly dealings with their fellows.

BIBLIOGRAPHY

1. Anderson, Harold H.: "An Experimental Study of Dominative and Integrative Behavior in Children of Preschool Age," *Journal of Social Psychology* (1937), 8:335-345.
2. ———: "Domination and Integration in the Social Behavior of Young Children in an Experimental Play Situation," *Genetic Psychology Monograph* (1937), 19, No. 3, 341-408.
3. ———: "Domination and Social Integration in the Behavior of Kindergarten Children in an Experimental Play Situation," *Journal of Experimental Education* (1939-1940), 8:123-131.
4. Anderson, H. H. and Brewer, H. M.: "Studies of Teachers' Classroom Personalities, II, Dominative and Socially Integrative Behavior of Kindergarten Teachers," *Applied Psychology Monograph* (1945), No. 6, p. 157.
5. Appel, M. H.: "Aggressive Behavior of Nursery School Children and Adult Procedures in Dealing with Such Behavior," *Journal of Experimental Education* (1942), 11:185-199.
6. Bühler, C.: *The First Year of Life* (New York: John Day, 1930), 281 pp.

7. ———: "The Social Behavior of Children," *A Handbook of Child Psychology,* second revised edition, edited by C. Murchison (Worcester: Clark University Press, 1933), Ch. IX, pp. 374-416.
8. Burk, F. L.: "Teasing and Bullying," *Pedagogical Seminary* (1897), 4:336-371.
9. Caille, R. K.: *Resistant Behavior of Preschool Children,* Child Development Monographs (New York: Teachers College, Columbia University, 1933), No. 11, 142 pp.
10. Chittenden, G. E.: "An Experimental Study in Measuring and Modifying Assertive Behavior in Young Children," *Monograph of Society for Research in Child Development* (1942), 7, 87 pp.
11. Dawe, H. C.: "An Analysis of Two Hundred Quarrels of Preschool Children," *Child Development* (1934), Vol. 5, 2:139-157.
12. Dennis, W.: "Infant Development Under Conditions of Restricted Practice and of Minimum Social Stimulation: A Preliminary Report," *Journal of Genetic Psychology* (1938), 53:149-157.
13. Doroschenko, O.: "Der Einfluss des Milieus auf den Inhalt und den Aufbau frei entstehender Kallektive im vor schulpflichtigen Alter," *Zsch. f. angew. Psychol.* (1928), 30:150-167.
14. Eberhart, J. C.: "Attitudes Toward Property: A Genetic Study by the Paired-Comparisons Rating of Offenses," *Journal of Genetic Psychology* (1942), 60:3-35.
15. Fite, M. D.: *Aggressive Behavior in Young Children and Children's Attitudes Toward Aggression,* Genetic Psychology Monographs (1940), 22:151-319.
16. Furfey, P. H.: *The Growing Boy* (New York: Macmillan, 1930), 192 pp.
17. ———: "Some Factors Influencing the Selection of Boys' Chums," *Journal of Applied Psychology* (1927), 11:47-51.
18. Gates, G. S.: "An Experimental Study of the Growth of Social Perception," *Journal of Educational Psychology* (1923), 14:449-462.
19. ———: "A Preliminary Study of a Test for Social Perception," *Journal of Educational Psychology* (1925), 16:452-457.
20. Gesell, A.: *The Mental Growth of the Preschool Child* (New York: Macmillan, 1925), 447 pp.
21. Green, E. H.: "Friendships and Quarrels Among Preschool Children," *Child Development* (1933), 4:237-252.
22. ———: "Group Play and Quarreling Among Preschool Children," *Child Development* (1933), 4:302-307.
23. Greenberg, P. J.: "Competition in Children: An Experimental Study," *American Journal of Psychology* (1932), 44:221-248.
24. Hollingworth, L. S.: *Gifted Children, Their Nature and Nurture* (New York: Macmillan, 1926), 374 pp.

25. Hurlock, E. B.: "The Use of Group Rivalry as an Incentive," *Journal of Abnormal and Social Psychology* (1927), 22:278-290.
25a. Horney, K.: *The Neurotic Personality of Our Time* (New York: W. W. Norton, 1937), 299 pp.
26. Isaacs, Susan: *Social Development in Young Children: A Study of Beginnings* (New York: Harcourt Brace, 1933), 480 pp.
27. Jersild, A. T. and Fite, M. D.: *The Influence of Nursery School Experience on Children's Social Adjustments,* Child Development Monographs (New York: Teachers College, Columbia University, 1939), No. 25, 112 pp.
28. Jersild, A. T. and Holmes, F. B.: *Children's Fears,* Child Development Monographs (New York: Teachers College, Columbia University, 1935), No. 20, 356 pp.
29. Jersild, A. T. and Markey, F. V.: *Conflicts Between Preschool Children,* Child Development Monographs (New York: Teachers College, Columbia University, 1935), No. 21, 181 pp.
30. Jersild, A. T., Markey, F. V., and Jersild, C. L.: *Children's Fears, Dreams, Wishes, Daydreams, Likes, Dislikes, Pleasant and Unpleasant Memories,* Child Development Monographs (New York: Teachers College, Columbia University, 1933), No. 12, 172 pp.
31. Leuba, C.: "An Experimental Study of Rivalry in Young Children," *Journal of Comparative Psychology* (1933), 16:367-378.
32. Lewin, K., Lippitt, R., and White, R.: "Patterns of Aggressive Behavior in Experimentally Created 'Social Climates,'" *Journal of Social Psychology* (1939), 10:271-299.
33. McFarland, M. B.: *Relationships Between Young Sisters as Revealed in Their Overt Responses,* Child Development Monographs (New York: Teachers College, Columbia University, 1938), No. 24, 230 pp.
34. McKinnon, Kathryn: *Consistency and Change in Personality and Behavior Manifestations—as Observed in a Group of 16 Children During a Five Year Period* (New York: Teachers College, Columbia University, 1942), 144 pp.
35. Maller, J. B.: *Cooperation and Competition: An Experimental Study in Motivation,* Teachers College Contributions to Education (New York: Teachers College, Columbia University, 1929), No. 384, 176 pp.
36. Maudry, M. and Nekula, M.: "Social Relation Between Children of the Same Age During the First Two Years of Life," *Journal of Genetic Psychology* (1939), 54:193-215.
37. Mengert, I. G.: "A Preliminary Study of the Reactions of Two-Year-Old Children to Each Other When Paired in a Semi-Controlled Situation," *Journal of Genetic Psychology* (1931), 39:393-398.
38. Murphy, G., Murphy, L. B., and Newcomb, T. M.: *Experimental*

Social Psychology, revised edition (New York: Harper and Brothers, 1937), 1121 pp.
39. Murphy, L. B.: Social Behavior and Child Personality (New York: Columbia University Press, 1937), 344 pp.
40. Osborne, Ernest G.: Camping and Guidance (New York: Association Press, 1937), 260 pp.
41. Parten, M. B.: "Social Participation Among Preschool Children," Journal of Abnormal and Social Psychology (1932), 27:243-269.
42. Reininger, K.: "Das soziale Verhalten von Schulneulingen" (Vienna: Deutscher Verlag für Jugend und Volk, 1929), 84 pp.
43. Reynolds, M. M.: Negativism of Preschool Children, Teachers College Contributions to Education (New York: Teachers College, Columbia University, 1928), No. 288, 126 pp.
44. Rust, M. M.: The Effect of Resistance on Intelligence Test Scores of Young Children, Child Development Monographs (New York: Teachers College, Columbia University, 1931), No. 6, 80 pp.
45. Salusky, A. S.: "Collective Behavior of Children at a Preschool Age," Journal of Social Psychology (1930), 1:367-378.
46. Shirley, M. M.: The First Two Years: A Study of Twenty-Five Babies, Vol. II: Intellectual Development (Minneapolis: University of Minnesota Press, 1933), 513 pp.
47. Thomas, D. S. and associates: Some New Techniques for Studying Social Behavior, Child Development Monographs (New York: Teachers College, Columbia University, 1929), No. 1, 203 pp.
48. Updegraff, R. and Herbst, E. K.: "An Experimental Study of the Social Behavior Stimulated in Young Children by Certain Play Materials," Journal of Genetic Psychology (1933), 42:372-391.
49. Wellman, B. L.: "The School Child's Choice of Companions," Journal of Educational Research (1926), 14:126-132.
50. Wislitzky, S.: "Beobachtungen über das soziale Verhalten im Kindergarten," Zsch. f. Psych. (1928), 107:179-188.
51. Wolf, T. H.: The Effect of Praise and Competition on the Persisting Behavior of Kindergarten Children, University of Minnesota Institute of Child Welfare Monograph Series (Minneapolis: University of Minnesota Press, 1938), 138 pp.
52. Wright, B. A.: "Altruism in Children and the Perceived Conduct of Others," Journal of Abnormal and Social Psychology (1942), 37:218-233.

CHAPTER VI

DEVELOPMENT OF SOCIAL BEHAVIOR
(Continued)

CHILDREN'S FRIENDSHIPS

Before the age of two, some children show preferences among other children, and at the age of three or four years strong attachments between two children may occur.[1] Such attachments may last only a few days or weeks, but sometimes they persist over a period of months and even years, even though in the meantime each child may have become acquainted with many others.

Companionships between children as young as three may become so engrossing as to limit a child's sphere of activities, as when the dominant member pre-empts all of a companion's time and attention and prevents him from widening his social contacts.

Even at the nursery-school age two or more children may establish a little fraternity among themselves from which others are excluded (4). In such friendships as well as in less closely knit companionships, it has been observed that one member often tends to dominate the relationship. Sometimes one child may take the lead in certain situations, while another child dominates other situations.

Factors that influence the formation of friendships in young children include those of similarity in age, intelligence, or sociability, similarity of interest, resemblance to a previous companion or a sibling, resourcefulness in enlisting coöperation, and so forth. But each such friendship has peculiar characteristics of its own. Frequently when a child first comes into a group, he will attach himself to another youngster who shows himself to be friendly

---
[1] For discussions of friendships between young children, see Beaver (4), Challman (15), Fite (28), Green (30) (31), Hagman (33), Koch (50), and Lippitt (58).

and helpful. As the new child begins to find his way around and feels more sure of himself, he may break away and seek other friends. Sometimes children in a nursery school can be observed to make what seems to be a deliberate effort to win the loyalty of a newcomer or of a timid child, by such techniques as hovering near the child, smiling, patting, giving invitations, and suggestions as to games that might be undertaken. As noted elsewhere, the efforts of a child to hold a companion who is trying to break away may produce many struggles.

A child's effort to win the friendship of this or that youngster may be a feature of an effort to gain prestige or to hold an important position in a group.

Among young children, one can frequently observe a child who seems to have no particular friends among the other children. Such a child may be one whose behavior is such that others reject him; he may be one who is ill at ease with other children and seeks rather to associate with adults who might happen to be around; or he may be a child who seems interested for the time being in following his own solitary pursuits.

One such rather solitary child, who was observed in one study, was unusually precocious in his language development; he used words that other children could not understand, and, when he approached them, they did not actively rebuff him but merely gave him an uncomprehending look and went on with their own affairs.

Sometimes a child may be friendless by reason of characteristics which other children find unpleasant. A conspicuous example of this was a boy who spent two years in a nursery school but never, as far as could be ascertained, was warmly received by any other member of the group. This boy had a habit of poking about, edging up now to one group, now to another, and always letting his presence be known by asking, in a somewhat whining tone, such questions as: "What's that you are making?" "Why do you do that?" "What's that for?"

FACTORS IN FRIENDSHIP AND CHOICES OF COMPANIONS AMONG OLDER CHILDREN

A child's choice of friends and close associates naturally must depend to a large degree upon who is available. When children name their friends, the persons they name are likely to be children who live near them, who use the same playground, who attend the same school and the same class (73, 77). This same factor operates, of course, to a large degree also in determining friendships among adults. Moreover, propinquity is not entirely a chance factor, since, in the case of adults at least, such matters as similarity in education, economic status, profession, group loyalties, and the like will carry a good deal of weight in deciding where one is going to reside.

Apart from this factor of nearness, children are more likely to choose as friends those who are similar to them in various characteristics—such as intelligence, height, and age—than children who are dissimilar. Although general similarities may be found when the average scores of friends are compared, close friends may differ considerably with respect to any of these characteristics. Differences which enable friends to complement one another or which enable one to occupy an ascendant or nonascendant role play an important part.[2]

Children of elementary-school age are likely to name as their best friends children of the same sex, as will be noted later.

The feelings and motives that come into play in associations between children vary greatly in quality and intensity. Two children may be companions largely because it is convenient; two others may be companions through fervent choice. The child with whom a youngster associates in his immediate community may be less favored than the one whom he seeks out as a com-

---

[2] Comparisons between friends among children beyond the preschool age have been made in studies by Furfey (29), Jenkins (40), Seagoe (77), and Wellman (91). A study by Neugarten (67) shows parallels between friendship and socio-economic status.

panion at school. In the home neighborhood or at school or in camp one child may have as his companion someone whom he really wants, another's companion may be a second or a third choice. A child who fails to win the friendship of his own age or grade group may seek the companionship of someone outside this group. Thus a dull boy may make friends with a smaller, younger child, or, if he is good at boyish things outside the classroom he may have a friend in a higher grade. A girl who is rejected by her own classmates may try to join in the play of the boys and go to great lengths to win their attention and good will.

The child's role and his prestige also may vary from one group or companionship to another. A child of eight years may be the most respected member of a group of children of about his own age but he may be the tolerated and not particularly welcome follower when he joins the playmates of his older brother. On the other hand, a child may be warmly accepted by youngsters many years his senior because he is such a cute little child, but those same cute ways may not make him attractive to children of his own age.

POPULARITY

To understand a child it is important to know how he rates with other children, and why. Often a teacher is in a better position to get this information than is the parent. Indeed, it is often very difficult for a parent to get a chance to learn how his child is regarded by others.

In a group situation such as is found in the school or in a camp or recreation center there are many methods that an adult can use to study the extent to which individual children are accepted or rejected by their peers. The method that comes most readily to hand is simply to observe the children. It is possible to note the order in which children are chosen when the youngsters are selecting committees or teams, to note who is nominated and elected for office, and by whom.

An observant adult can gain much simply by being alert to such happenings, but additional and sometimes unexpected information can be obtained if children's reactions are not merely noted in a chance fashion but are systematically studied. When children report their likes and preferences, for example, they sometimes reveal things that could not be gained from observation alone.

Among the various methods that can be used to study children's acceptance of one another are a number of so-called "sociometric techniques." [3] These are relatively simple, and in many situations it is possible to apply them to obtain information that an investigator might put to practical use. In school, children might be asked, for example, to name one or two or three pupils whom they would like most to have as seat mates or neighbors. In institutions where children spend all their time sociometric techniques have been used to find out whom the inmates would prefer as table mates or as cottage mates, and the like. It is possible also to ask a variety of other questions, such as whom the youngster wishes to play with, go to a picnic with, or whom he would prefer to have as his best friend.

It is also possible to get negative information by asking youngsters to name persons whom they would not especially care to have as friends, or as seat mates, or as study companions, and so on. This negative approach has not been used as commonly as the positive approach, since invidious information of this sort may be less reliable and, in many circumstances, there will be children who will be embarrassed and reluctant to speak ill of their associates. Some negative information can be inferred from the positive approach. For example, if a child is not named by anyone when children choose their seat mates, it is quite evident that he is not especially popular. It does not follow, however, that he is actively disliked, for the fact that he is not mentioned may mean that he is just being ignored.

---

[3] Research in this area received a great impetus from studies published in 1934 by Moreno (64).

FIGURE 3
DISTRIBUTION OF CHOICES AND REJECTIONS AMONG BOYS—MADE BY FOURTEEN BOYS IN A FOURTH-GRADE CLASS

Name and Number	Sex	Age	Chooses	Chosen by:	Rejects	Rejected by:	Mutual Choices	M R*	C-R†	R-C‡
1. Don	B	10	2, 12, 8	—	4	5	—	—	—	—
2. Duval	B	9	5, 6, 8, 12, 13	1, 3, 5, 6, 8, 12	—	—	5, 6, 8, 12	—	—	—
3. Henry	B	10	2, 8, 12	2, 5	10	—	—	—	—	—
4. Harper	B	9	—	—	—	1, 6, 7, 8, 10	—	—	—	—
5. James	B	10	2, 3, 11, 12	2, 11	1, 7	—	2, 11	—	—	—
6. Jasper	B	9	2, 8, 13	2, 11, 12	4	—	2	—	—	—
7. Jacob	B	9	10, 11	11	4	5, 9	11	—	—	—
8. Luke	B	8	2	1, 2, 3, 6	4	—	2	—	—	—
9. Matthew	B	9	14	11	7	—	—	—	—	—
10. Porter	B	9	12	7, 11	4	3	—	—	—	—
11. Philip	B	9	5, 6, 7, 9, 10	5, 7	12	—	5, 7	—	—	—
12. Ramos	B	9	2, 6, 13	1, 2, 3, 5, 10	—	11	2	—	—	—
13. Tom§	B	—	—	2, 6, 12	—	—	—	—	—	—
14. Fritz§	B	—	—	9	—	11	—	—	—	—

* M R—Mutual rejections. No items here. † C-R—Choice-rejection. In this group there was no instance of a child choosing another who actively rejected him.
‡ R-C—Rejection-choice. No instance in this group of the reverse of C-R. § Absent but either chosen or rejected.

178

An example of results obtained by means of a sociometric method applied in a fourth-grade group is shown in Figures 3 and 4. The children were asked to name the person or persons in their class whom they would like best to have as a friend. They were also asked to name the person or persons in the class whom

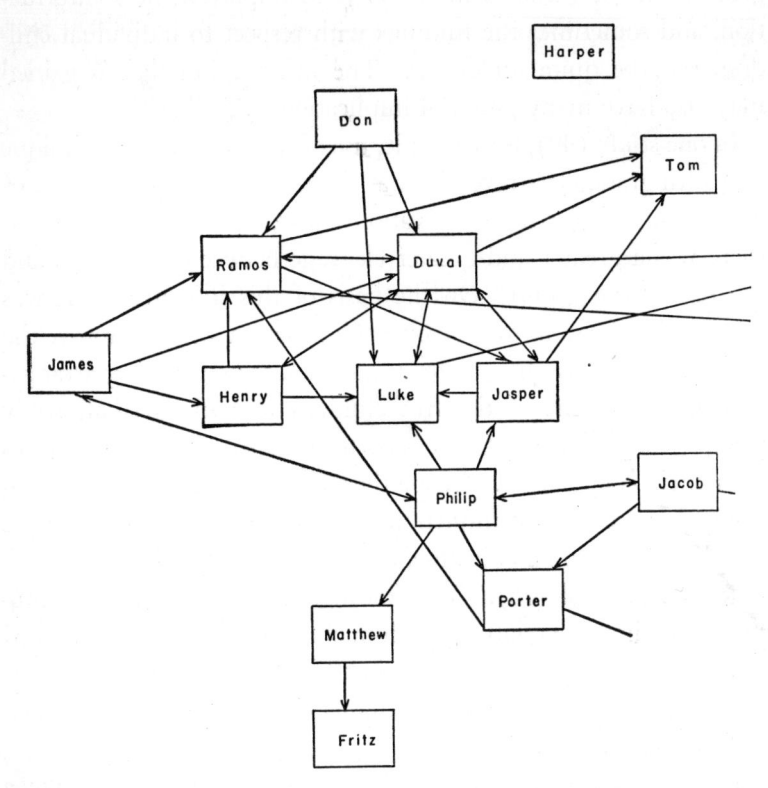

Fig. 4. Sociogram showing choices (but not rejections) by boys represented in Figure 3.

they did not especially care to be friends with. Figure 4 presents what is known as a sociogram. The illustration shows only the positive responses represented in Figure 3.

The information so obtained may be used to answer a variety of questions, such as, who is chosen most? Who is chosen least or not at all? Who is chosen by whom, but does not reciprocate? To what extent are choices associated with certain factors such as age, sex, socio-economic status, nationality, race, and so on? Some of the findings obtained by means of this technique may simply confirm what a person already has discovered by observing the group; but the findings may also yield important new information, and sometimes the findings with respect to individual children may be quite surprising. The information that is gained may also have many practical implications (45, 48, 49).

In one study (49), for example, use of the sociometric technique in a fifth-grade class revealed that there was an isolated clique of five boys, and further observation showed that as time passed there was a greater and greater cleavage between these boys and the rest of the group. On the basis of this information it was possible to take steps to overcome this isolation and to improve the attitudes of the five boys by methods such as new seating arrangements, assignment of the five children to various small study groups, coupled with other efforts to understand the boys and to gain their coöperation. In another study, the sociometric techniques were used in conjunction with other methods to study the social and emotional adjustments of children who were repeating a grade in school (76). The findings showed that the nonpromoted pupils were relatively seldom chosen by regularly promoted pupils and that the nonpromoted children, more often than their classmates, named children in higher grades when they named their choice of friends.[4]

Factors associated with popularity. The factors that make a child appealing in the eyes of one or more of his fellows are numerous, but certain qualities have been found in several studies to be more characteristic of children who are popular than of children who are not popular (5, 6, 27, 34, 52, 68, 69). Popular children, to a greater extent than children in general, have been de-

---

[4] A variety of methods of studying the behavior of pupils have been described by Prescott and his associates (72), Driscoll (25), and Wrightstone and others (44, 95).

scribed by their associates as active and alert (but not restless or obviously out to get attention), good looking, cheerful, and friendly. Popular children tend, if anything, to be above average in intelligence, scholastic standing, and health; there are, however, notable individual exceptions. In one study it was found that a large proportion of elementary-school children who are rated as popular by other children are also rated as popular by teachers (8). On the other hand, in a study of older boys in a correctional institution it was found that teachers and house parents designated as leaders among the boys less than fifty per cent of youngsters whom the boys themselves named as leaders (27).

Whether or not a child will be popular in a given group depends not solely upon his own qualities but also upon the tastes and intents of the group. A notable illustration of this fact is given by L. S. Hollingworth (37) in an account of a very bright boy who was transferred from an average class to a special class consisting of bright children. In the class that consisted mainly of children of average intelligence, the boy had been practically isolated from the social life of the group, but in the special class the other bright children noticed and warmly appreciated his unusual abilities.

The factors associated with unpopularity are quite varied. In a study by Northway (68, 69) it was found that among the children who stood low in popularity there were some who seemed to have no apparent interest in the general environment, there were some who seemed to lack interest in other persons and who tended to be quiet and shy, and there were some who were "socially ineffective," tending to be noisy, rebellious, and boastful.

Descriptions of characteristics such as the foregoing do not give the full flavor of the variety of qualities that make a child popular or unpopular with his group. Although qualities in a child that appeal to others may vary as he grows older, it appears that popularity tends to be persistent. The child who is popular at one age level is more likely than not to continue to be popular as he grows older, at least within the elementary-school period. In a study by

Bonney of groups of children over a period of three years (8, 9), it was found that children's "social acceptance" scores remained almost as constant from year to year as did their scores on intelligence tests and on academic achievement tests. This constancy, as measured by the correlation between "social acceptance" scores one year and the next, was notably marked (with a correlation of .90) in one group in which the membership remained much the same from year to year. But children also showed a strong tendency to maintain their position of popularity when there was a large turnover in the membership of the group to which they belonged. It would require further study of the same group to determine the extent to which popularity at the elementary-school level also tends to carry over into adolescent years. In one study it was found that there were certain changes from age twelve to age fifteen, notably in girls, in the qualities which children most admired in one another (84).

LEADERSHIP

From the time when children are of nursery-school age a child's leadership of others may take many forms and his position may be won in a variety of ways. The techniques and characteristics of two children who are leaders may differ decidedly. One child may be a leader partly by reason of the fact that he is very voluble and mobile and covers much ground. Another child may take an upper hand by selecting and dominating the play activities of a group by virtue of aggressive methods and various forms of coercion. Still another child may lead by reason of his resourcefulness in seeing new and original possibilities and in establishing friendly relations with other children.

Perhaps the most warmly accepted leader is the one who makes it pleasant to be a follower. An example of resourcefulness of this sort follows: Kirk was a child who had a knack for making the other fellow feel important, while he himself was running things. On one occasion, he initiated a make-believe game of running a boat. He approached another child, asked him to be the captain (saying, "The captain is the big boss, you be the captain. I'll be the engineer."), and then, when the "captain" was installed in all his glory on the deck of the boat (a big box), the humble engineer, from below, ran both the captain and the ship.

The apparent differences between children in their ability to exercise leadership may be deceptive. The child who makes quite a splash and who seems to be directing others may actually be having less influence than a child who is mild and quiet in his ways but who suggests ideas which a more aggressive child proceeds to exploit.

The characteristics of the leader among children who are older are likely to vary somewhat with the nature of the situation in which he takes the lead. Athletic leaders, for example, are likely to stand high in physical achievement; leaders in intellectual activities in the classroom are likely to be those who stand high in scholarship. In a study by Caldwell and Wellman (11), children who were leaders in school were found to be above average in scholarship. The difference was not so large in the case of athletic leaders, but even these exceeded the average of their class.

The leader is likely to be somewhat above the average of his group in intelligence and, as a rule, he is likely to be somewhat larger, better dressed, more fluent of speech, better looking, more self-controlled, and more daring. In a study by Terman (81a) it was found that leaders tended to be conspicuous, even though they might not be conspicuously good; they tended to rate either very high or very low, rather than merely average, in such matters as size, dress, and schoolwork. However, it appears that a child may fail to achieve leadership if he is too far above his associates in ability. In many situations, the leader is one who also can be a good follower when occasion so demands.

In the study by Jennings (41), sociometric techniques were applied at intervals during a period of two years and seven months to study affinities between members of a group and evidences of leadership. The subjects were girls, aged twelve to eighteen years, in a training school. From an earlier study it appeared that the choosing of table associates, "eating at the same table," provided a significant basis for study of the role occupied by the individual members. Among the findings were the following: In a group structure that already is highly evolved and quite firmly established, it may be very difficult for a child who is on the fringe to enter and participate. Leadership appears to be a process of choosing as well as of being chosen—it was observed that incipient leadership was indicated by the fact that children on their way to a leading position would choose individuals who already occupied a position of leadership, even though such choices at first met with no reciprocation or encouragement. Children who suddenly moved into a prominent position were more likely just as suddenly to lose their prominence than were the individuals who pushed steadily and gradually to the fore. Once a child had acquired a prominent position through persistent effort, she was not easily displaced.

Practical considerations. Although superior ability and skill may not suffice to make a child a leader, yet the fact that the more able are most likely to lead has obvious implications for education. But leadership need not be viewed as an all-or-none or absolute matter. When children make their own selections, the choice may fall upon different children in different activities and projects. This fact alone allows several children to experience a measure of prominence within a given group. Apart from this, it is not so important to see that every child becomes a leader—since this would be nearly impossible; it is more important to see that he is not always at the other end of the procession, always distinctly in the back seat, always overwhelmed by the prestige and authority of others, and never given a chance to assert himself as an individual. The fact that there is a leader at one end does not imply that there must be a browbeaten nonentity at the other.

THE DESIRE TO BELONG

In time, through a combination of many factors, one of the strongest motives in a child's life is the desire to be accepted, to belong, and, eventually, to achieve some measure of recognition and prestige in his relations with his fellow men. This expresses itself first in a child's desire for security in his relations with his parents. When he moves into a larger world, a similar desire goes with him.

Young children sometimes go to almost any length in order to be noticed. Many children become angrier if they are completely ignored than if they are crossed and punished; but whether their bid for attention takes the form of humility or perversity, or merely follows a middle road, underneath it there is a wish to be noticed and appreciated.

In his home relations, a child's underlying security counts for a good deal more than this or that practice which his parents may use. By virtue of this, many specific rules with regard to how children should be reared may be more of a hindrance than a help, especially if such rules inhibit natural and common-sense reactions and cause parents to indulge or restrain the child in ways that eventually bring trouble to all concerned. The value of any particular technique for disciplining the child depends not so much on the method itself as the attitude of the parent and the total setting in which it is used. There are children who are occasionally spanked, for example, who are more serene and spontaneous in their relations with their parents than children who are never spanked but are rejected or intimidated in more subtle and pervasive ways.

In his relationships with adults outside the home, the child has a similar need for an emotional anchorage. Adults who are in a position of authority, such as the teacher at school or his playground director, are, to a large degree, reacted to as substitute or temporary parents. However much the child's behavior sometimes may gainsay it, he still greatly desires the approval and affection of these substitute parents. For this reason, the attitude of the teacher toward the child may be profoundly important to the child even though he may try not to reveal it. It is likely that even the most incorrigible child, who may seem to be endowed by the devil himself, usually would like very much to be liked by his teacher. If he is a spoiled child from the start, has poor techniques that rub the teacher the wrong way and produce a negative response, he may, from the very beginning, get the impression that the teacher is against him. His answer may be further obstinacy, rebelliousness, and all manner of behavior that plagues the teacher. Frequently the child who gets a bad start when he begins school develops habits and acquires a reputation that follows him from class to class and from teacher to teacher. The behavior of such a child may be very irritating and discomforting to the teacher, but the child himself is likely to be even more miserable. To break through the crust of hostile habits and attitudes which a child in this plight has acquired is one of the most difficult tasks that confront a teacher.

The child's desire for status appears also in his relations with other children, and in order to win a place for himself he will go to great lengths. Sometimes behavior that is puzzling to adults may be motivated by the child's desire to please his peers or to gain their attention. Most children also learn eagerly to accept the symbols and forms that betoken kinship with the group, such as sharing secrets and confidences, entering into partnerships, or joining clubs and societies which may last for days or years.

The child who is striving to be accepted by others is also sensitive to rebuffs and rejection. His feelings when scorned or ridiculed by his peers may range from grief to intense rage. Children are loath to express such feelings, and the reasons for them, to adults. It is difficult for a child to admit to himself, or to others, the bitter fact that persons whose good will he desires actually do not like him. He may, to be sure, show that his feelings are aroused by reactions such as finding fault, fighting back, complaining, and other responses of the "sour-grapes" variety. But in so doing he is not likely to reveal the true cause of his feelings. Accordingly, his elders may not realize that when he is telling how much he detests certain children he actually may be expressing how much he would like to be liked by these same children.

The following account shows how one child reacted to rejection by her peers. She was six years old and in the first grade. On two occasions the parents, while driving past the school during recess, happened to notice that the girl stood by herself while the other children were playing. This seemed unusual, for the child was quite gregarious, but they did not realize that there was more to the story. At a later time the girl happened to mention that she had played that day with some "big boys from the third grade." Some days later she again mentioned that she had played with one of the big boys and had pulled his shirttails out of his pants. That evening, as though troubled, the girl asked her mother at bedtime, "Have I been a good girl today?" In answer to this unusual question the mother said yes, and then added rather lightly that she thought it would be better if the girl did not pull shirttails out of boys' pants. At this the child burst into tears. She sobbingly asked, "Then who shall I play with? When I eat lunch I sit alone, and out on the playground the other girls don't play with me." It appeared that most of the other girls in the class had been playmates before coming to school and were playing in a closed group, which this girl, a newcomer, had been unable to enter.

In this case, the child happened to reveal her feelings, but only after she apparently had been troubled for several weeks. It was possible now for the parents to consider whether they should take a hand or let the child try to win her own battle. As it happened, two schoolmates of the girl's choosing were invited home by the mother the next day and this may or may not have been partly responsible for the fact that the girl soon seemed to be happily adjusted.

When children have troubles of this sort and do not reveal them, it is difficult, of course, for adults to understand or to try to help. Through lack of understanding the adult may even make things harder for the child. In the instance above, for example, it might have made matters worse if the mother through ignorance of the real state of affairs had scolded the child for rough play with an older boy when actually this play, from the child's point of view, was only a poor substitute for play with girls of her own age.

In the normal course of social development the child may receive many rebuffs and slights from his peers without necessarily needing adult help. Such rebuffs may help him to learn ways of behaving that are agreeable to others. Often, however, he cannot cope with the circumstances. Through misfortunes or lacks in his past experience, he may have acquired deeply entrenched habits and attitudes that cause offense or elicit ridicule. Moreover, regardless of his own merit, he may face rejection by reason of belonging to a religion, nationality, or race against which there is a prejudice. Certainly no child can change the color of his skin or change his parentage. To be sure, neither can such a change be made for him by a helpful adult. But the adult can still help by being a buffer, or by being a friend, or by trying to mitigate prejudices or their effects. The adult is all the more obligated to do this because it is adult society which fosters many of the prejudices that children bring to bear against each other.

SOCIAL HIERARCHIES

The child's desire to be accepted by other children will not always be satisfied simply if he is well received by random members of his group. He may seek to be accepted by certain individual children in the group who represent a select clique.

In a heterogeneous group of children from the first grade onward one can sometimes observe several cliques, varying in prestige. There may be a small cluster which all the most enterprising children would like to join, but failing in this, some of them must seek companions at another level, so that sometimes the cronies with whom a child regularly associates represent second or third choices, with whom he shares a moderately happy companionship.

While the average child may learn to find his place in the childhood social milieu and contentedly take whatever place he can win, there are some children who are more deeply affected if they do not succeed in joining the "right" company. A child who is rejected by his fellows may develop resentments and compensatory drives that influence his behavior for years to come.

BOY-GIRL RELATIONSHIPS

Interesting age trends appear in social relationships between boys and girls. When the child is first old enough to enter into social relations with other children, distinctions between boys and girls are not likely to appear. Boys and girls play together and enjoy much the same activities. Even at the preschool level, however, some distinctions and differences appear. Boys tend on the average to be somewhat more active in their play, although differences within each sex group are larger than the differences between the two sexes. At the ages of three and four boys enter into a larger number of conflicts than do girls and are more likely to resort to hitting. In a mixed group, it also appears that boy-boy and girl-girl conflicts are likely to be more frequent than boy-girl conflicts, but there are large individual differences. At the preschool level, likewise, especially after the age of two years, boy-boy and girl-girl friendships are likely to be more numerous than friendships between a boy and a girl.[5] However, even though children prefer playmates of their own sex, there is a good deal of interplay, and at this early age a child is not likely to be disturbed if he is in a group in which all members are of the opposite sex.

[5] See Challman (15) and Hagman (33).

"Social distance" between the sexes which can be noted as early as the age of two or three (50, 58) becomes more conspicuous at the elementary-school level. Social distance between the sexes was studied by Koch (50) in an investigation that included children from nursery school to high school. One of the methods employed was to have a pupil name his preference when each child in his class was paired with each of the others. At the preschool, elementary-school, and even at the high-school level boys showed a higher preference for boys and girls for girls. This preference for members of the same sex increased up to high-school level and then decreased. The tendency to cleave to one's own sex was shown more pronouncedly at the elementary-school level by the girls than by the boys. However, this was reversed at the high-school level where boys showed a higher preference for boys than girls for girls.

Other changes associated with age in the social-sex relations of children have been reported by Campbell (12). In the age range from five to eight years, it was found that the average boy would play contentedly when he found himself in a group composed entirely of girls; that he was not likely to show protective habits toward girls; that he was not self-conscious with regard to posture, gesture, and clothing in the presence of girls, or with regard to physical contacts with them; that he was not concerned with girls as attractive creatures and would fight them or would choose one for his "side" if the game did not involve physical skill. In general, he preferred women to girls, especially women who would play with him.

A greater tendency for boys to prefer boys on their "side" was shown after the age of nine. At this time also boys showed more self-consciousness with respect to physical contacts and to being alone in a group of girls.

The youngest girls likewise showed little embarrassment about posture, clothes, physical contacts, or being alone with a group of boys. At age eight and onward, more self-consciousness appeared;

there was a greater tendency to avoid groups consisting entirely of boys and to avoid physical contacts, and there was more awareness of games that are "boy" games and "girl" games. In approaching the teens, the girls exhibited a "whispering period"; they became more "modest" and conscious about their clothes and about exposing their bodies. With the development of adolescent interests boys and girls changed their earlier tendency to draw apart and paid increasing attention to each other. In this study as in several others it was found that boys tend to lag somewhat behind girls in certain manifestations of heterosexual interests. It was also noted, among other things, that whereas boys as they grew older lost interest in displays of adult affection, a similar loss of interest was not shown by the girls.

The cleavage between the sexes can be observed in almost any situation where boys and girls gather together for free, unsupervised play. However, it can also be observed that under the leadership of an adult girls and boys seem to enjoy many activities in common, even though, when left to themselves, they tend to segregate. Moreover, in a given neighborhood there may be a good deal of interplay between boys and girls who, when gathered in larger groups, as on the school playground, play only with members of their own sex. In other words, the tendency of children to prefer members of their own sex is by no means an invariable or universal phenomenon.

There are from an early age certain differences in the interests of boys and girls which lead a child to seek out members of his own sex. As indicated above, boys tend from an early age to show somewhat more interest than girls in robust forms of physical activity; they also tend to be relatively more interested in *things* while girls tend to be relatively more interested in *people*.

In many families, also, boys have more freedom to plunge into physical activities and more freedom to roam about in the community than do girls.

Whether and to what extent factors inherent in children themselves tend to produce differences such as the above would be difficult to determine. It is easy to see that those differences, whatever may be their origin, can be prompted and encouraged by the culture in which a child lives. By the same token the social cleavage between the sexes during elementary-school years may to a large degree be a consequence of cultural pressures.

THE IMPACT OF ADULT SOCIAL STRATIFICATION ON THE CHILD

Sooner or later the child's social behavior will be influenced by the fact that people in the adult society in which he lives differ in social rank, position, or prestige.[6] Labels such as "upper," "middle," and "lower" class have been used to denote such differences and distinctions. There are objections, however, to the use of the term "class," since the term connotes a rather rigid form of stratification. Actually, a person with certain qualities and characteristics might belong to the "upper crust" of society in one community, but a person with similar qualities might stand several rungs lower on the social ladder in another community that has different standards as to what constitutes wealth, or good family connections, or superior manners and breeding, and so on. However·this may be, it is apparent that in most communities, if not in all, there will be differences in rank and position of individual members, whether these fall into clearly defined "classes" or not.

The manners, customs, and privileges of the social group to which a child's family belongs will have a bearing on his everyday

---

[6] For illustrative discussions of status or rank systems see: Warner, W. L. *et al.* (87, 88, 89), West (92), Davis (21, 22), Dollard (24), and Warner, Havighurst, and Loeb (90). Warner and his associates distinguished not simply the conventional "upper," "middle," and "lower" groups, but within each of these groups they made a further distinction between an "upper" and "lower" subgroup, yielding six groups in all: "upper-upper," "lower-upper," "upper-middle," "lower-middle," "upper-lower," "lower-lower." Cattell (14) has proposed a metric scale of social status with "social grades" ranging from I, including the highest eminence in what has been called the upper class, to Social Grade X, representing casual laborers, unemployed, and institution inmates.

life at an early age. Different social groups have differing practices, for example, with reference to breast feeding or bottle feeding, time of weaning, time when training in bladder control is begun. Again, the family's socio-economic status may make a difference in the amount of play space a child has or determine whether he will have to share a room with others.[7]

Partly by virtue of the fact that families in the "lower" groups tend to be larger, with less adult attention available per child, children may be given practical responsibilities for their own care and safety to a greater extent and at an earlier age than children in higher socio-economic groups. So, too, parents in higher socio-economic groups may be more on the alert than parents in the "lower" groups to discourage fighting and aggressiveness and "bad" language. Indeed, in certain "lower" groups a child may be encouraged to be a fighter, although subject to certain rules (21). Again, there are status-related differences with respect to other manners, etiquette, sex behavior, attitudes toward property, and the like. These do not, of course, necessarily take the form of greater modesty or more rigorous standards in the "upper" groups.

There also are factors related to social position that might, *in a very subtle way,* affect a child's evaluation of himself, his confidence in facing new or different social situations, or his assurance or lack of assurance as to whether other people are likely to receive him well. On the other hand, an environment that is less privileged may also be less demanding, with the result that the child may be spared some tensions that befall more affluent youngsters. In a brief review of a series of studies, still in progress, on the subject of social class, Havighurst (36) reports that in one community it was found that middle-class parents were more rigorous than lower-class parents in their training of children for feeding and cleanliness habits. They also expected children to take responsi-

---

[7] A study by J. E. Anderson (2) shows a great range of practical ramifications associated with differences in socio-economic status.

bility for themselves in these matters earlier than did lower-class parents. Also, according to this study, middle-class parents placed their children under a stricter regime, with more frustration of their impulses. In passing it is interesting to note that the same types of differences were found to exist between middle- and lower-class Negroes and between middle- and lower-class whites.

In another study mentioned by Havighurst it was found that the school environment is essentially middle class in its values, teaching, and staff and, as such, it reinforces the attitudes and habits taught to children in middle-class homes. The lower-class child, on the other hand, may find that what the school teaches is not entirely in accord with ways of behaving and believing that he has been taught at home, and while some lower-class children, with the encouragement of their parents, seek to learn at school what they have not been taught at home, there are others who turn against the school and reject the precepts it teaches.

Certainly the burden of proof would fall upon anyone who argues that poverty is an aid to the development of good character traits. According to a study by Stagner (78), those who have grown up in poor circumstances are more likely than others to show traits such as "nervousness," "social passivity," and feelings of inferiority.

A number of differences between parents of high and of low socio-economic status in attitudes toward children appeared in a study of the joys and problems of child-rearing represented in Table XXI in Chapter VIII. Parents in poor economic circumstances gave relatively more emphasis to the physical aspects of child-rearing (such as the comforts or discomforts of the family living quarters, adequacy or inadequacy of financial means), while parents of higher status gave relatively more emphasis to the psychological aspects (such as children's personality traits).

Differences in the moral concepts and attitudes of children of different socio-economic groups provide one indication of the differences in social pressures that are brought to bear upon children in different status groups.[8] Some studies indicate that children of lower status tend to accept a more arbitrary or authoritarian position as to what is right and wrong, and tend also to condone punishment more than do children of higher status. In a study by Harrower, cited in Chapter XIII, it was found that a larger proportion of children in the former than in the latter group regarded cheating, for example, as something bad or naughty in itself, as distinguished from something that is wrong because it is unfair to the other fellow or as something wrong because cheating does not help a person to learn how to get the answers by himself. Again, when asked how to deal with a wrongdoer (for example, a boy who had broken another boy's toy), children in the "lower" group tended to say that the wrongdoer should be smacked, while children in the "upper" group tended much more to advise that the wrongdoer should try to make amends.

This tendency toward a more authoritarian and punitive attitude toward misbehavior in the "lower" socio-economic groups was noted in a study which compared children from a very formal public school in a rather poor section of a large city with children of the same age and grade in a private school representing relatively "high" social status (23). In writing a composition about what should be done to Jimmy, a rather obnoxious boy in a story who was always interfering with his older brother, the children in the "lower" group twice as often recommended a "nonconstructive" approach, such as scolding and punishment. In answer to a question as to what to do with Fred, who had stolen marbles from Bob, the "lower" group showed a decidedly greater tendency to condemn and punish rather than to excuse or to help Fred to find an acceptable solution to his desire for marbles. A decidedly larger percentage of children in the "lower" than in the "higher" group also maintained unconditionally that a child should not talk

---

[8] One difficulty with findings on this subject is that they are not entirely "pure." Children of lower socio-economic status tend also to have a lower average intelligence and their concept formation will be influenced by this factor as well as by the example and instruction of their associates.

back to his parents (seventy-one and fifteen per cent) or to his teacher (eighty-one and twenty-nine per cent).

In another study (by Stendler, 79), the removing of plants from a public park, even though there were signs forbidding it, was not deemed to be as serious an offense by children of a lower socio-economic group as by children of a higher socio-economic group. Likewise, the former did not regard the taking of gum that had spilled out of an overturned truck as a form of stealing, comparable to stealing from another child, to the same extent as did children in the latter group. On the other hand, children in this particular "lower" group had learned to look upon reference to the sex organs as something obscene while boys and girls in the "higher" group were able, during a class discussion, to refer to these organs in quite a matter-of-fact manner.

The fact that there are differences such as those described above between children at different socio-economic levels is not, of course, surprising. The children reflect the values, ideas, and practices of the adults who surround them. It should be noted that there were differences within the groups as well as between the groups, so that in a given comparison a child at one socio-economic level may be more like a child at a higher or lower level than like his own group.

Awareness of symbols of social position. In addition to reflecting the distinctive manners and values of his own group, the normal child in time becomes aware of differences between groups. He becomes aware also, in time, of symbols that betoken socio-economic status, such as the silk hat of the man in the limousine as distinguished from the chauffeur's cap. Preliminary findings in the study by Stendler mentioned above give information with respect to this. First graders in this study tended to describe their families as rich to a greater extent than did fourth graders; sixth graders were more conservative than fourth graders on this score; and at the eighth grade there not only was no child who described his family as being rich but many of the children were reluctant to answer the question. The older children quite generally ascribed to themselves a middle position between poverty and wealth. The children from wealthier homes, by saying they were "in-between," tended to understate their financial circumstances, and the children from poorer homes by similarly saying they were "in-between" tended, at least in relative terms, to overstate their condition. This tendency by children to put themselves in the middle group is in keeping with a finding by Cantril (13) in a study of adults: adults at all economic levels tend to identify themselves as belonging somewhere in the middle social class.

Children in the first grade were not only inclined to rate themselves as rich but they also rated a large proportion of their classmates as rich. In their naming of children who had "lots of money" they showed little agreement with adults. At the fourth-grade level, and even more at the sixth- and eighth-grade levels, the children were much less naïve and, at the two upper levels, they could rate with high accuracy (as measured against the judgment of well-informed adults) the financial status of any ten classmates named at random.

A developmental trend in the direction of clearer and more realistic perception of signs of wealth appeared also when children in this study were asked how one can tell whether a person is rich or poor. First-grade children used chiefly criteria such as whether the person is clean or dirty; whether he does what is forbidden or what is right; what he has to play with and to wear. Only one child in the first grade mentioned the part of town from which a child came as a sign or evidence of poverty or wealth. At the fourth grade, more mention was made of the section of town in which the person lived, and some of the children seemed to be aware of the higher status value of certain occupations, such as being a doctor or banker. At the sixth- and eighth-grade levels, each of the children tended to name several criteria such as an adult would name, including the location and sumptuousness of a person's house, his manners and clothes, his profession or job, the prestige of his family name, having a maid, and the like. Over half the comments of eighth-grade children had reference to occupation of the father, to clothes, or to manners. Mention of clothes included references to style and appropriateness, but not to cleanliness as it did at the age of six.

Findings such as the foregoing indicate that children near the end of the elementary school years or at about the beginning of the teens tend to be quite well aware of differences in socio-economic status. Children's awareness of status differences may become intensified during adolescence as the young person becomes interested in dating and the beginnings of courtship. At this time the disadvantage of living on the wrong side of the tracks, and the advantage of coming from a "good" family may be brought home to the child quite sharply.[9]

EFFECTS OF NURSERY-SCHOOL EXPERIENCE

In order to learn to live sociably with his fellows, a child must have a chance to associate with other children. Partly for the purpose of supplementing such social contacts as the young child may have with other children in his home environment, an increasing number of parents in recent years have established coöperative play groups or have used the facilities of day nurseries and nursery schools. Several studies have been made to probe some of the effects of such opportunities. In some of these studies, comparisons have been made between the behavior of children before and after nursery-school attendance; in others, children have been studied to note changes during the course of their attendance; in

---

[9] For an account of increased awareness of status differences at adolescence see Meek (62). Children's self-awareness with respect to their racial identity has been investigated in studies of Negro children by Clark and Clark (16, 17, 18) and by Horowitz (38). Clark found that Negro children in mixed groups (Negro and white) tended to identify themselves as being colored at a later age than did Negro children in segregated groups. In both kinds of grouping, however, a larger proportion of four-year-olds than three-year-olds correctly identified themselves (from among several pictures, the Negro child chose a picture of a Negro child as being most like himself).

still others, children have been compared at a later time with other youngsters of similar age who have not attended nursery school. In studies of this kind, it is important to take account of the factor of maturation, among other things; for, in the normal course of development, there are changes in the character of a child's social activities, whether or not he happens to be a member of an organized group.

Group trends. Among the trends indicated more or less conclusively by studies[10] in this area are the following: nursery-school children have shown an increase in participation in group activities and in number and variety of social contacts, and a diminution of "onlooker" forms of behavior; they have shown an increase in poise and spontaneity in social participation and a decrease in the tendency to show fear of other people, to shrink from notice, and to hover near adults. In several studies, it has been noted that the average nursery-school child has improved in his routine habits —competence in self-help in eating, dressing, toileting, and so forth —with resulting increases in freedom of action, diminished dependence upon adults, and diminished occasion for resisting adults.

Nursery-school attendance seems to help to dilute tensions between a child and others in the home environment. Indeed, one very important, although little publicized, function of the nursery school is to free the mother for a little while from the necessity of meeting the child's continuing demands. Even the fondest mother will report that a two-or-three-year-old child "gets in her hair" at times. Although no study has been made of the extent to which the respite helps the mother to put more verve and patience into her dealings with the child during the rest of the day, it seems reasonable to believe the effects might be good.

---

[10] Representative studies that deal directly or indirectly, in whole or in part, with this problem include investigations by Caille (10), Cushing (20), Ezekiel (26), Greene (32), Hattwick (35), Jersild and Fite (42), Kawin and Hoefer (47), Mallay (60), Murphy (65), Taylor and Frank (80), Tedsten (81), Thompson (82), Walsh (86), and Wellman (91).

Gains have also been noted, as one might properly expect, in skill and resourcefulness in using the play materials and equipment provided by the nursery school. Some of these gains may be only temporary, to be sure, or restricted largely to the nursery-school environment, especially if different habits are cultivated at home.

It is noteworthy that the children's gains in sociability in the nursery school do not mean that the individual children are being submerged more and more by the group. Rather, along with an increase in sociability, it has also been found that there is an increase in the child's tendency to exercise independence, to assert himself as an individual, to stand up for his interests and his rights as he sees them. In observations of nursery-school children it has been found, for example, that children's scores in resistance (the number of times they refused, by word or deed, to carry out the demands of others, to yield ground to another, and so on) was somewhat more closely related to the length of time the children had spent in nursery school than to the factor of chronological age (10). Again, it was observed in one group that children who, at the beginning of the school year, were rather unaggressive showed an increase in their tendency to attempt to make themselves the center of an activity; on the other hand, those who showed this tendency more strongly when the school term first began continued to retain this characteristic with the passage of time (Ezekiel, 26).

Individual variations. The foregoing statements are based upon general trends or averages for entire groups and relate primarily to effects noted during nursery-school attendance or within a short period thereafter. Actually, many children fail to conform to the general trend. In one study of twenty-one children it was found that while there was a large average increase in frequency of successful social contacts made by the children as the year progressed, there were a few children who showed a loss rather than a gain (60). In another study (42) it was observed that, while the groups as a whole showed a sharp increase in frequency of social contacts, some children showed relatively little change, and two children showed a loss when records of behavior in the spring were compared with records of behavior after the school year began in the fall. Indeed, even in the case of children who do not go counter to the trend, the adjustments that are made and the changes that may be exhibited are likely to vary considerably from child to child. To gauge the effect of nursery-school experience and fully to appraise its value would require intensive study of the individual child; but although this is recognized, the general drift of findings based upon surveys of groups, rather than intensive study of each individual, are still significant and have practical implications.

Table XI illustrates the extent to which individual children may change during the course of a year. In the study on which this table is based, a group of children was observed in the fall, soon after the beginning of the school term, and again in the spring, near the end of the school year. Each child was observed systematically a number of times (ten fifteen-minute periods in the fall; eight five-minute periods in the spring). Among other things, a count was made of "social contacts"; the child received a tally of one for each half-minute period during part or all of which he engaged in social interchanges with other children. The table shows results in terms of percentages; a value of fifty per cent means that the child was in social contact with one or more of his schoolmates during half of the intervals during which he was observed.

It can be noted that the "old" children represented in Table XI exhibited more than twice as many social contacts, on the average, at the beginning of the school year as did "new" children who had never before attended nursery school. But by spring, the two groups were practically equal. Indeed, computations not shown

TABLE XI

PERCENTAGE OF INTERVALS DURING WHICH
SOCIAL CONTACTS OCCURRED[11]

(Chronological ages in years and months, in the fall, are shown in parentheses.)

"New" Children (without previous nursery-school experience)			"Old" Children (with one or more preceding years of nursery-school experience)		
Name	Fall	Spring	Name	Fall	Spring
Alice (3–6).......	42.0	82.5	Holden (2–11).....	67.3	45.0
Thelma (3–8).....	25.7	58.8	Dennison (3–0)....	64.0	81.3
Dick (3–9)........	25.7	64.5	Nancy (3–6).......	58.3	83.8
Sally (2–10)......	25.7	43.8	Evan (3–6)........	53.3	71.3
Morris (3–10).....	14.0	47.5	Kirk (3–5)........	46.3	71.3
Nell (3–1)........	10.0	61.3	Joyce (2–10)......	21.7	42.5
Sammy (2–10)....	6.0	21.3	Bernard (3–8).....	19.3	12.5
Average......	21.3	54.2	Average......	47.2	58.2

Children "new" to the group but with one year of previous experience in other, separate, schools:

Jerry (2–10)......	50.3	73.8
Carter (3–6)......	36.7	71.3

in Table XI indicated that the "new" children began to gain rapidly on the "old" ones during the first few weeks of school.[12]

An analysis of the behavior of individual children showed that a large proportion of the social contacts exhibited by the "old" children in the fall consisted of interchanges between pairs of children who had become close friends during the preceding year; but even when such contacts were discounted, it did appear that the veteran nursery-school children surpassed the new recruits in readiness to enter into social enterprises when the school year began. However, as noted, the new children had not sustained a

---

[11] Adapted from Jersild, A. T. and Fite, M. D.: *The Influence of Nursery School Experience on Children's Social Adjustments,* Child Development Monographs (New York: Teachers College, Columbia University, 1939), No. 25, 112 pp. Reproduced by permission.

[12] It is not here taken for granted that the more "social contacts" a child exhibits the better off he is. Although an increase in sociability, as measured by the present techniques, usually represents a wholesome trend, his social adjustment cannot be determined simply by a tally of his social contacts, without regard for the nature of his contacts and the larger pattern of his behavior.

permanent disadvantage by virtue of not having had one or two previous years of experience; even while not attending nursery school, they were maturing and gaining such experiences as children may encounter outside of school, and, when given a chance, they quickly made up for lost time. This does not mean, of course, that by delaying a year a child can gain as much from nursery school as he would gain had he attended that year as well as the year before. To measure the values that are gained from earlier attendance would require a comprehensive investigation. It would be necessary also to have information as to whether the same facility in making up for lost time would appear as children grow older.

The effect of nursery-school experience or of any provision that enables a child to be with other children will depend, of course, upon what the school or the play group offers. A school that has clearly formulated educational objectives may have quite a different impact on the child's behavior than a school which has no well-defined policies. This is brought out impressively in a study by Thompson (82) in which a comparison is made between children in two nursery-school groups with differing policies with respect to the role of the teacher. In both schools (designated *A* and *B*) the teachers were instructed to be responsive to the children, but in school *A* the teacher was instructed to make a minimum of contacts with the children on her own initiative and to let the children work out their own plans and activities, assisting only when asked. In school *B* the teacher was instructed to participate more actively, to try to become a warm friend of each child, to guide the children's thinking and activities into productive channels *not* by telling the children what to do but by her own interested participation and willingness to supply information, to coöperate, to supply and arrange materials in the most constructive manner. At the beginning of the experiment the children in groups *A* and *B* were equivalent; at the end of the experiment (eight months later) they differed in many ways (as measured by quantitative records of their behavior). As a group, the children who received teacher guidance excelled the group with little teacher guidance in *constructiveness* when faced with possible failure, in *ascendant behavior,* in *social participation,* and in *leadership*. The group with a carefully planned guidance policy also showed fewer *nervous habits,* but the difference in this particular was not statistically significant, and there was no significant difference between the two groups in IQ.

While a study such as the foregoing indicates that the educational policy of a nursery school may have quite pronounced effects on the behavior of children, it does not presume to show to what extent these outcomes within the nursery school also influenced the child's life outside of school or his behavior and adjustments at a later age. It seems likely that the effects would not be entirely limited in time and place, but further study would be needed to throw light on this point. Apart from the general educational policy of a school, it is likely, also, that the benefits children derive will be influenced to a large degree by the personality and competence of the teacher. As noted in an earlier section, some nursery-school teachers in one study tended to make a constructive approach when dealing with children's conflicts with one another, while other teachers tended to take a more disciplinary approach by more or less arbitrarily ending the fracas.[13]

INFLUENCE OF SKILLS ON SOCIAL BEHAVIOR AND ADJUSTMENT

Whether a child be young or old, lack of competence in the activities normally engaged in by his group is likely to affect his social adjustments.

One can repeatedly observe evidences of the ways in which a child who lacks motor skill may be barred from social participa-

---

[13] Differences in the attitudes and practices of different teachers are shown in several studies (54, 66, 74).

tion. When his playmates dash across the playground on tricycles or down the street on roller skates he either is left behind or must follow on foot; when they climb, he is left watching on the ground. In countless ways, he is "out of it." Sometimes, to be sure, a child who is inept in the use of his limbs will make extra use of his wits in directing the play into channels where he can hold his own. Furthermore, lack of motor skill will have varying effects in the case of different children; some seem to get along quite well either by contentedly taking the role of an onlooker or by devising substitute activities that seem to satisfy them.

Skill in everyday games and occupations is important, but this does not mean that every child, in order to be well adjusted, must be an athlete or a jack-of-all-trades. It can be noted, however, that children who lose their stride in activities and skills which are important in the social life of their peers may react in ways that are not particularly advantageous. They may exhibit timidities and fears where other children are well at ease; they may seek the companionship of younger and less stimulating companions; they may stay away from club meetings, parties, or other get-togethers that happen to call for a display of skills in which they are deficient; or they may become the butt of teasing and ridicule.

Changes in social behavior. The way in which a gain in proficiency in handling a situation may influence a child's role in social dealings with others is provided in an investigation by Jack (39). A number of children were first studied to note their tendency to be ascendant or nonascendant in their relations with others, the extent to which they exhibited behavior such as: verbal attempts to secure play materials; forceful attempts to secure play materials; success in procuring play materials; efforts to defend or retrieve possessions; attempts to direct the behavior of a companion; directing or supplying a pattern of behavior for the companion to imitate; and criticisms, reproofs, and interdictions directed against companions.

Five children who were found to be least ascendant were chosen for special study. These children were helped to achieve competence in certain performances. One performance involved the construction of designs in fitting mosaic blocks into a cardboard frame; in another, the child learned to fit together the parts of a picture puzzle; in a third, the experimenter read a story to the children, and after the story had been told three or four times, the child was invited to join with the experimenter in telling the story until he could tell it alone. After the children had become competent in these activities, each of the five children was observed when paired with other children while dealing with these materials. The five children showed a distinct change in their relations with their companions following the period of training. They now more often showed a tendency to lead, to assert themselves, to direct the other child, and to exhibit "ascendant" behavior than in the initial series of observations. In other words, the competence which the children had acquired not only increased their success in the skills which they had mastered, but also modified their relationships with other children, at least within the setting in which the skills could be applied.

In everyday life, situations frequently arise in which an adaptation of the techniques used by Jack (39) in the study cited above might be used in practical ways. The value of special coaching, help in acquiring skills that are useful in social intercourse, and help in overcoming handicaps that have arisen through lack of opportunity or faulty procedures is frequently demonstrated in the practical experience of parents, teachers, playground supervisors, and camp counselors (70). Indeed, the practice of helping children to improve their social adjustments by means of improved competence in big or little undertakings is used extensively by many persons who come to take the techniques and the outcomes more or less for granted. It would be highly instructive, and valuable from a practical point of view, if experiences in this area could be made more articulate and if a systematic compilation could be made of techniques that have been used in different situations with varying degrees of success.

Apart from active attempts to promote skills of various sorts, another procedure which teachers often find useful is to encourage a child to exercise special abilities and talents which he already possesses. A child who habitually is on the fringe may rise and shine when an adult recognizes the light which the child hitherto has hidden under a bushel or sponsors group projects that give the child a chance to show qualities that are not called for in the group's ordinary run of activities. Again, it has been found that a child who is overwhelmed or is shy and retiring in his customary group contacts may find his stride if transferred for a time to a new group or if placed for a time in a group in which the pace is less trying. Sometimes a child becomes resigned to an unimportant role, and the group comes to take for granted that he is a shy "fringer," so that he occupies this role more from force of habit than from lack of potential ability. If given an opportunity, without being pressed or urged or without being overwhelmed, many children who are backward socially are likely to seek ways of making contacts and of getting into group play.

A study by Lowenstein and Svendsen (59) provides interesting findings concerning thirteen children (aged six to ten years) who were shy or withdrawn and who exhibited other symptoms of maladjustment. These children were sent for a period of several weeks to a small farm camp where there were no other children. It was observed that at first the children played alone; then, in time, they played in small groups; and as time went on they played in larger groups. As this change occurred, the children also became more disposed to assert themselves and to be more aggressive, and there was a decline also in other specific symptoms of maladjustment that had been associated with their shyness. From information obtained in a follow-up study it appeared that of nine children who returned to their earlier home environment, five showed distinct improvement, as compared with their former status, and one showed partial improvement. Four children who did not return to their old environment but to a new situation showed improved adjustment.

Recognition of the importance of skills does not, of course, rule out the importance of other factors. Children may be quite similar in their skills and achievements and still be quite different in their adjustments to other persons due to the play of other factors that determine their attitudes and the quality of their behavior in dealings with other persons.

INFLUENCE OF PLAY EQUIPMENT AND ADULT PATTERNS OF BEHAVIOR

As one would expect, any number of conditions in the surrounding environment may have an effect on children's social behavior. Updegraff and Herbst have shown, for example, how the amount of talking children do and the extent to which they cooperate will vary with different play materials (85).

An interesting account of the manner in which children's play may be influenced by the environment is offered in a study by Salusky (75) of two groups of kindergarten children in Russia. One of the groups was located in the center of an industrial city. The parents of these children exemplified the "new" mode of life: there was little religion in the home; revolutionary holidays were observed; and family life was unconventional, as compared with the past. The other group of children attended a kindergarten on the outskirts of the city; the parents of these children were less prosperous and conformed more to the "old" mode of life in the matter of religious observances and customs. These differences between the home backgrounds of the two groups were reflected to a marked degree in the social play of the children. The old mode of life appeared in 49 per cent of the games in the latter kindergarten, as compared with only 6.3 per cent in the former. In the more modern group, in contrast, the children played games reflecting the communal household, revolutionary modes of life, and depicting the revolution. Apparently, ways of life which the more "modern" parents had more or less consciously adopted were transferred spontaneously into the play of the children. The results here are suggestive of the manner in which habits, standards, and ways of thinking and living which adults conform to may be injected into the thought and action of young children. However, to discover the extent of the influence of the new mode of life on the play of the children, it would be necessary to study the situation more intensively to find whether their play involved rea· changes in social relationships or served merely as a general frame work for much the same forms of coöperation and competition snatching and snaring, dominance and submission, aggression and sympathy, as appeared in the play of the children who imitated the old mode of life.

INFLUENCE OF ADULT DIRECTION AND MANAGEMENT

In everyday life, it is possible repeatedly to observe the way in which children's social reactions to one another can be influenced by the kind of direction they receive from adults who are in charge of the group. One teacher, for example, manages much better than another to promote coöperation and camaraderie. The adult influences that affect children's social relations may range all the way from subtle and relatively intangible factors to concrete practices and policies. Fite has described how a teacher may betray her attitude toward a child and, in effect, give other children to understand that it would be all right for them, for example, to attack a particular child whom the teacher disapproves (28).

The tactics used by an adult have an important effect on the reaction of the child. In a study of children aged two and a half to eight and a half years, Johnson studied the relative effectiveness of a large number of types of verbal requests, remarks, and prohibitions. It was found that specific and simple instructions were more advantageous than general and verbose instructions, that requests that had a pleasant tone were more effective than scolding, that positive prohibitions were more effective than threats, and that unhurried directions brought better results than hurried directions (46). It is likely, of course, that the person who tends to use a friendly suggestion rather than a sharp command will be, in general, a more friendly person: in other words, the specific technique may represent a general attitude toward which the child is reacting in kind. Adults frequently have occasion to discover that a friendly or conciliatory approach is more effective than the opposite with some children, even if the adult is rather exasperated and has to make an effort to appear friendly.

The example set by the adult may have an important effect. Observations reported in the study by Osborne show how the attitude of camp counselors toward various activities may influence children. When the boys in this study first came to a summer camp, their indicated game preferences conformed to the conventional notions as to what a robust ten-year-old child should like to do; but within a short time, under counselors who were not bound by stereotyped ideas as to what children should do, many of the youngsters joined in forms of play that, under other circumstances, they might have regarded as "sissyish" and eventually applied a high degree of skill to such games.

The fact that children respond more favorably to an adult who identifies himself with their concerns and is pleasant in his dealings can be observed repeatedly in everyday life, as well as in research studies (1, 53). Table XII shows qualities and characteristics of teachers who were "liked best" and "liked least" as described by pupils.

In an experiment by Lippitt (57), comparisons were made between children's responses to "autocratic" and "democratic" management of small clubs with five members. It was noted that as time went on the children who were treated in rather peremptory ways exhibited considerably more aggressive domination in their relations with one another than did the children with whom techniques of a man-to-man character were used. Expressions of hos-

TABLE XII

CHARACTERISTICS MENTIONED BY CHILDREN IN DESCRIPTIONS OF TEACHERS WHOM THEY "LIKED BEST" AND "LIKED LEAST"[14]

(Values show the percentage of children naming each characteristic.)

Teachers "Liked Best"				Teachers "Liked Least"			
Age[a]	5–8	9–12	13–17	Age[a]	5–8	9–12	13–17
Grade	1–3	4–6	7–12	Grade	1–3	4–6	7–12
Number of Children	25	203	298	Number of Children	9	99	265
I. Human Qualities as a Person:				I. Human Qualities as a Person:			
1. Kind, sympathetic, considerate	16	24	16	1. Unkind, unsympathetic, ridicules	11	9	16
2. Interested in, liked, and adjusted to pupils as persons	0	1	16	2. Lacking in interest of pupils as persons	0	1	2
3. Natural, approachable, companionable, good sport	0	3	8	3. Not natural, unapproachable, prim, self-important, not good sport	0	2	7.3
4. Vivacious, cheerful, smiling	8	3	9	4. Never smiled, sour, glum, solemn	11	0	4
5. Sense of humor, joked, funny	4	1	5	5. No sense of humor	0	0	0
6. Good-tempered (not bad-tempered, cranky, etc.)	4	7	2	6. Cross, ill-tempered, "ranky"	11	19	18
7. Dignified, not "fresh" or common	4	0	.03	7. Tactless, "fresh"	0	4	1
				8. Nervous, jittery, fussy	0	1	1
				9. Flighty, silly	0	0	1
				10. Emotionally unbalanced, "queer," "talked to self"	0	0	2
				11. Dishonest, "sneaky," told lies	0	0	0
II. Physical Appearance, Grooming, Voice:				II. Physical Appearance, Grooming, Voice:			
1. Attractive, good-looking, pretty eyes, nice figure, etc.	0	6	5	1. Unattractive of feature, face, figure, "ugly face," etc.	0	3	2
2. Nice voice, nice manner of talking	0	2	2	2. Unpleasant voice, too loud, rasping, too low	0	4	4
3. Attractive clothes, well-groomed, neat, clean	0	3	2	3. Unattractive clothes and grooming, "sloppy" clothes, unattractive hair	11	2	3
4. Youthful, not elderly	0	0	.05	4. Elderly—poor health	0	4	2.3
				5. Unpleasant mannerisms	0	0	1

[a] The "age" entries represent ages of children for whom no grades were indicated; the main classification was according to grade.

[14] From Jersild, A. T. and Holmes, F. B.: "Characteristics of Teachers Who Are 'Liked Best' and 'Disliked Most,'" *Journal of Experimental Education* (1940), 9, 139–151. Reproduced by permission.

TABLE XII (*Continued*)

	Teachers "Liked Best"				Teachers "Liked Least"		
III.	Characteristics as a Disciplinarian or Class Director:			III.	Characteristics as Disciplinarian or Class Director:		
1.	Fair, just.............................	4	15	11	1. Unfair, unjust, punished all for error of one, *etc.*................................	0	13	8
2.	Impartial, no favorites or pets........	0	5	5	2. Partial, had pets.....................	0	10	11
3.	Discipline effective, respected, consistent	4	11	16	3. Discipline rigid, too strict, inconsistent, poor................................	22	26	21.3
4.	Didn't scold, yell, holler, shout.......	12	5	8	4. Constant scold, yells at you...........	56	5	9
5.	Did not use corporal punishment......	4	2	0	5. Used corporal punishment.............	0	15	3
6.	Did not treat ignorance as moral wrong..	0	0	1	6. Treated failure to learn as moral wrong, impatient with error.................	0	1	2
7.	Lenient, easygoing, let us have own way	4	4	3	7. Too lenient..........................	0	2	1
8.	Did not require hard work or "too much work".................................	16	2	9	8. Preachy, bossy, domineering..........	0	1	4
					9. Never praises........................	0	0	.3
IV.	Participation in Activities; Providing Gifts, Entertainment:			IV.	Participation in Children's Interests; Entertainment, *etc.*:		
1.	Joins in or permits games and play, tells stories, *etc.*..........................	32	7	4	1. Did not join in children's games, hobbies, interests.............................	11	2	1
2.	Special attentions: parties, food, trips, hobbies..............................	8	4	2				
V.	Performance as Teacher, Teaching:			V.	Performance as Teacher, Teaching:		
1.	Interesting, resourceful, enthusiastic as teacher..............................	4	4	13	1. Uninteresting, uninspired, dull, boring..	0	1	4
2.	Supplied interesting school projects, activities, experiments, *etc.*............	24	12	5	2. Uninteresting assignments, cut and dried, never do interesting things..........	0	0	1
3.	Taught, explained, well...............	8	26	34	3. Not a good instructor, didn't know much, not clear, *etc.*.................	0	9	10
4.	Helped individual pupils with lessons...	4	5	10	4. No help to individual pupils in lessons..	0	2	3
5.	Permitted expression of opinion, voice in class affairs........................	0	2	2	5. No judgment as to assignments........	0	2	0
					6. Allowed no expression of opinion, choice	0	0	1
					7. Standards too high in lessons..........	0	1	1
					8. Indoctrinated pupils with own beliefs...	0	0	1
					9. Used unwise forms of motivation......	0	0	0
					10. Too much homework.................	11	14	14

TABLE XII (*Continued*)

Teachers "Liked Best"				*Teachers "Liked Least"*			
VI. Miscellaneous and General:				VI. Miscellaneous and General:			
1. Miscellaneous: he's a man; intelligent, room tidy, *etc.*	0	2	1	1. He's a man, she's a woman; not intelligent, room untidy, poor order, because of subject	11	3	1.3
2. (Egocentric) She liked *me*, praised *me*, gave *me* prize, *etc.*	20	17	5	2. She disliked *me*, gave *me* bad report	11	7	5
3. Indefinite, general, no specific reason	12	4	.05	3. No reason given—indefinite	0	7	6

tility, resistance, demands for attention, hostile criticism, and competition were more than twice as frequent in the former group. In the "authoritarian" groups, the relation of the children to the leader tended to be one of submission or of frequent demands for attention, while the relations between the children and the adult leader in the "democratic" group were more free, spontaneous, and friendly.

This line of experimentation was carried further in a study reported by Lewin, Lippitt, and White (56). Three types of adult direction were used in connection with such activities as mask making, mural painting, soap carving, and model airplane construction.

The "authoritarian" leader was dictatorial; he decided everything that was to be done, one thing at a time; he was "personal" in his criticism and praise; and he remained aloof, without actively participating in the work of the group, except when demonstrating (a skillful autocrat would, of course, use more subtle techniques).

The "democratic" leader permitted group discussion and group decisions within the broad limits of the experiment, allowed more freedom, participated actively as a regular member, and was "objective" in his praise and criticism.

The "laissez-faire" leader allowed complete freedom, did not participate in the activity or discussion of plans, and made infrequent comments on the activities of the club members. The same leaders variously applied the three types of direction with different groups, so that the factor of the personality of the leader was controlled as far as possible.

Under autocratic management one of the groups showed considerably more aggressiveness than did groups with democratic management, while other children who were handled autocratically reacted by showing a good deal of apathy. However, also in an apathetic group it was found that, when the autocratic leader left the room, there was a sharp rise in the amount of aggressiveness shown by the children.

In response to interviews, nineteen of the twenty boys stated that they liked the leader in the democratic setting better than the leader in the autocratic setting; the one exception was a boy who liked the leader because he "was the strictest." According to their own accounts, in seven cases out of ten, the children preferred the laissez-faire leader to the autocratic leader.

On two occasions, following the deliberate intrusion of an adult who criticized the work of the children, fighting broke out immediately afterward between children who happened to be sharing the same room at the time in the autocratic group. Among the factors that appeared to increase the tension in the autocratic groups were the higher frequency of directions given by the leader —which, in effect, put more pressure on the children—restrictions of freedom of movement, and greater rigidity of the group structure.

In several studies it has been found that children respond favorably to "newer," more democratic practices in the classroom, such as prevail in an "activity" program or in schools that have adopted "progressive" principles (44, 55, 95). Among other matters it has been found that children in such classes tend to show more initiative, a higher quality of coöperation and leadership. In a study by R. L. Thorndike it was found that children from "activity" schools were, if anything, more courteous and more responsible in their conduct when on field trips (such as a visit to the museum) than children from control schools (83).

Variable effects of different practices. There is in this study and others cited in the present section evidence to indicate that democratic procedures with children not only are more pleasant but are more efficient than an arbitrary, autocratic, or authoritarian approach. An adult may, of course, use tactics that will cause irritation no matter what the general philosophy of his approach to a child might be. In a later interesting study, Bavelas and Lewin (3) found that adults who habitually had used rather authoritarian methods in dealing with children could be led to adopt more democratic techniques by way of lectures, demonstrations, and an opportunity to practice and to discuss. In this study it also was found that the morale of the adult leaders (in a recreation center) improved after the shift to democratic practices.

It should be noted that when an adult sets out to use democratic methods it does not mean that he drops his role as an adult and simply becomes an easy-going member of the gang. In most situations it is likely that democratic procedures will call for more rather than less ingenuity and active participation. Moreover, the adoption of democratic methods by the adult does not mean that he merely turns the leadership over to one or two children in the group. As a matter of fact, one of the problems involved in democratic procedures in the classroom is that the more a teacher tries to consult, plan, and participate rather than to ride herd the more opportunity there may be for a few alert, talkative, and enterprising children to monopolize a large proportion of the discussion and to "run things" (43).

The extent to which a few children tend to monopolize a large proportion of the time and attention of the class when pupils are allowed to express themselves freely is shown in Table XIII. In the study on which these findings are based, a record was made of the number of times individual pupils recited, spoke, or made self-initiated or spontaneous contributions during class periods and group discussions in elementary-school classrooms. Each class was observed during a total period of about six hours (omitting study periods, gym periods, and so forth). Separate results are given for schools that had officially adopted newer, "progressive" practices and schools that still, officially, used more traditional procedures (these are identified, respectively, as "activity" and as "control" groups). As it happens, there is not a great deal of difference between the two groups in the behavior of the most

TABLE XIII

DISTRIBUTION OF PARTICIPATION BY INDIVIDUAL PUPILS DURING APPROXIMATELY SIX HOURS OF CLASS SESSIONS [15]

	"Activity"	"Control"
No. of classes	8	8
A. Recitational contributions:		
Median of median contributions per child	6.85	12.4
Median per cent of contributions made by the most talkative pupil in each class	9%	9%
Median per cent of contributions made by pupils with the lowest score in each class	.7%	1.0%
Median number of children at lower end of distribution in each class whose contributions were equalled or exceeded by the pupil with the highest score	6.5	5.5
Median per cent of total contributions made by the three children with the highest scores in each class	22.5%	22%
Median per cent of contributions made by pupils in the highest quartile in each class	45.5%	39%
C. Self-initiated, supplementary, self-assertive contributions:		
Median of median contributions per child	2.95	1.5
Median per cent of contributions made by the most talkative pupil in each class	16.5%	16.5%
Median per cent of contributions made by pupils with the lowest score in each class	0%	0%
Median number of children at lower end of distribution in each class whose scores were equalled or exceeded by the pupil with the highest score	16	13
Median per cent of total contributions made by the three children with the highest scores in each class	38.5%	41%
Median per cent of contributions made by pupils in the highest quartile in each class	63%	64%
A. + C.		
Median of median contributions per child	9.85	15.0
Median per cent of contributions made by the most talkative pupil in each class	10.5%	11%
Median per cent of contributions made by pupils with the lowest score in each class	.1%	1.0%
Median number of children at lower end of distribution in each class whose scores were equalled or exceeded by the pupil with the highest score	8.5	6
Median per cent of total contributions made by the three children with the highest scores in each class	25.5%	24.5%
Median per cent of contributions made by pupils in the highest quartile in each class	50%	41.5%

loquacious and enterprising pupils when the children were free to volunteer during class discussions. In the table it can be noted

---

[15] The results show medians of the median scores obtained in each of the six classes in the two groups. Reproduced from Jersild, A. T., Goldman, B., Jersild, C. L., and Loftus, J. J.: "Studies of Elementary School Classes in Action: II. Pupil Participation and Aspects of Pupil-Teacher Relationships," *Journal of Experimental Education* (1941), 10:119-137. Reproduced by permission.

that the most talkative pupil in the median "activity" class made as many spontaneous or self-initiated contributions as were made by the sixteen least talkative children combined.[16] The three most talkative children (representing less than ten per cent of the total class population) made about forty per cent of the contributions when the children were free to talk. Participation in the discussion was more evenly divided when the teachers used the recitation method and pointedly called now upon this, now upon that child to recite.

In some classes included in the study, it was found that the tendency on the part of a few pupils to "run things" was especially marked when the class was under the leadership of a pupil chairman. In one class it was found that when a pupil chairman was in charge, the most talkative pupil talked as much as did the eighteen least talkative children combined. On the other hand, when the teacher was in charge of the class, the most talkative pupil did only as much talking as eight children combined. Findings such as these indicate that in a shift from authoritarian to democratic procedures it is necessary not only for the adult leader but also for the children to learn how to work together in a democratic manner.

BIBLIOGRAPHY

1. Anderson, H. H. and Brewer, H. M.: "Studies of Teachers' Classroom Personalities. I. Dominative and Socially Integrative Behavior of Kindergarten Teachers," *Applied Psychology Monographs* (1945), 6:157 pp.
2. Anderson, J. E.: *The Young Child in the Home,* White House Conference Series (New York: Appleton-Century, 1936), 415 pp.
3. Bavelas, A. and Lewin, K.: "Training in Democratic Leadership," *Journal of Abnormal and Social Psychology* (1942), 37:115-119.
4. Beaver, A. P.: "A Preliminary Report on a Study of a Preschool 'Gang,'" Thomas, D. S., et al.: *Some New Techniques for Studying*

---

[16] In the same study it was found that there tended to be a positive but low relationship between frequency of contributions and academic ability or achievement. It appeared that "the extent of a child's loquacity and his ability to get a hearing is primarily determined by factors other than knowledge or information such as was measured by the tests administered in the study."

Social Behavior, Child Development Monographs (New York: Teachers College, Columbia University, 1929), No. 1:99-117.
5. Bonney, M. E.: "A Sociometric Study of the Relationship of Some Factors to Mutual Friendship on the Elementary, Secondary and College Levels," *Sociometry* (1946), 9:21-47.
6. ———: "Personality Traits of Socially Successful and Socially Unsuccessful Children," *Journal of Educational Psychology* (1943), 34:449-472.
7. ———: "A Study of the Relation of Intelligence, Family Size, and Sex Differences with Mutual Friendships in the Primary Grades," *Child Development* (1942), 13:79-99.
8. ———: "The Constancy of Sociometric Scores and Their Relationship to Teacher Judgments of Social Success and to Personality Self Ratings," *Sociometry* (1943), 6:409-424.
9. ———: "The Relative Stability of Social, Intellectual, and Academic Status in Grades II to IV, and the Inter-Relationships between These Various Forms of Growth," *Journal of Educational Psychology* (1943), 34:88-102.
10. Caille, R. K.: *Resistant Behavior of Preschool Children,* Child Development Monographs (New York: Teachers College, Columbia University, 1933), No. 11, 142 pp.
11. Caldwell, O. W. and Wellman, B.: "Characteristics of School Leaders," *Journal of Educational Research* (1926), 14:1-13.
12. Campbell, E. H.: *The Social-Sex Development of Children,* Genetic Psychology Monographs (1939), 21:461-552.
13. Cantril, H.: "Identification with Social and Economic Class," in Harriman, P. L., editor, *Twentieth Century Psychology* (New York: Philosophical Library, 1946), 146-152.
14. Cattell, R. B.: "The Concept of Social Status," in Harriman, P. L., editor, *Twentieth Century Psychology* (New York: Philosophical Library, 1946), pp. 128-145.
15. Challman, R. C.: "Factors Influencing Friendships Among Preschool Children," *Child Development* (1932), 3:146-158.
16. Clark, K. B. and Clark, M. K.: "The Development of Consciousness of Self and the Emergence of Racial Identification in Negro Children," *Journal of Social Psychology* (1939), 10:591-599.
17. ———: "Skin Color as a Factor in Racial Identification of Negro Preschool Children," *Journal of Social Psychology* (1940).
18. ———: "Segregation as a Factor in the Racial Identification of Negro Preschool Children; A Preliminary Report," Journal of Experimental Education (1939), 7:161-163.
19. Criswell, J. H.: "A Sociometric Study of Race Cleavage in the Classroom," *Archives of Psychology* (1939), No. 235, 82 pp.

20. Cushing, Hazel M.: "A Tentative Report of the Influence of Nursery School Training upon Kindergarten Adjustment as Reported by Kindergarten Teachers," *Child Development* (1934), 5:304-314.
21. Davis, A.: "Socialization and Adolescent Personality," *Adolescence, 43rd Yearbook of the National Society for the Study of Education,* Part I, Chapter XI, 198-216.
22. Davis, A., Gardner, B. B., and Gardner, M. R.: *Deep South* (Chicago: University of Chicago Press, 1941), 558 pp.
23. Dolger, L. and Ginandes, J.: *Children's Attitudes Toward Discipline,* unpublished.
24. Dollard, J.: *Caste and Class in a Southern Town* (New Haven: Yale University Press, 1939), 104 pp.
25. Driscoll, G.: *How to Study the Behavior of Children* (New York: Teachers College, Columbia University, 1941), 83 pp.
26. Ezekiel, L. F.: "Changes in Egocentricity of Nursery School Children," *Child Development* (1931), 2:74-75.
27. Fauquier, W. and Gilchrist, J.: "Some Aspects of Leadership in an Institution," *Child Development* (1942), 13:55-64.
28. Fite, M. D.: *Aggressive Behavior in Young Children and Children's Attitudes Toward Aggression,* Genetic Psychology Monographs (1940), 22:151-319.
29. Furfey, P. H.: *The Growing Boy* (New York: Macmillan, 1930), 192 pp.
30. Green, E. H.: "Friendships and Quarrels Among Preschool Children," *Child Development* (1933), 4:237-252.
31. ———: "Group Play and Quarreling Among Preschool Children," *Child Development* (1933), 4:302-307.
32. Greene, K. B.: "Relations Between Kindergartens and Nursery Schools," *Childhood Education* (1931), 7:352-355.
33. Hagman, Elizabeth P.: *The Companionships of Preschool Children,* University of Iowa Studies in Child Welfare (1933), 7, 4:69 pp.
34. Hardy, M. C.: "Social Recognition at the Elementary School Age," *Journal of Social Psychology* (1937), 8:365-384.
35. Hattwick, B. W.: "The Influence of Nursery School Attendance upon the Behavior and Personality of the Preschool Child," *Journal of Experimental Education* (1936), 5:180-190.
36. Havighurst, R. J.: "Child Development in Relation to Community Social Structure," *Child Development* (1946), 17:85-90.
37. Hollingworth, L. S.: *Gifted Children, Their Nature and Nurture* (New York: Macmillan, 1926), 374 pp.
38. Horowitz, R. E.: "Racial Aspects of Self-Identification in Nursery School Children," *Journal of Psychology* (1939), 7:91-99.

38a. Isaacs, Susan: *Social Development in Young Children: A Study of Beginnings* (New York: Harcourt Brace, 1933), 480 pp.
39. Jack, L. M.: "An Experimental Study of Ascendant Behavior in Preschool Children," Jack, L. M., Manwell, E. M., Mengert, I. G., et al.: *Behavior of the Preschool Child,* University of Iowa Studies in Child Welfare (1934), 9, 3:7-65.
40. Jenkins, G. G.: "Factors Involved in Children's Friendships," *Journal of Educational Psychology* (1931), 22:440-448.
41. Jennings, H.: "Structure of Leadership—Development of Sphere of Influence," *Sociometry* (1937), 1:99-143.
42. Jersild, A. T. and Fite, M. D.: *The Influence of Nursery School Experience on Children's Social Adjustments,* Child Development Monographs (New York: Teachers College, Columbia University, 1939), No. 25, 112 pp.
43. Jersild, A. T., Goldman, B., Jersild, C. L., and Loftus, J. J.: "Studies of Elementary School Classes in Action. II. Pupil Participation and Aspects of Pupil-Teacher Relationships," *Journal of Experimental Education* (1941), 10:119-137.
44. Jersild, A. T., Thorndike, R. L., Goldman, B., and Loftus, J. J.: "An Evaluation of Aspects of the Activity Program in the New York City Public Elementary Schools," *Journal of Experimental Education* (1939), 8, 2:166-207.
45. Johnson, A. D.: "An Attempt at Change in Inter-Personal Relationships," *Sociometry* (1939), 2, 3:43-48.
46. Johnson, M. W.: *Verbal Influences on Children's Behavior,* University of Michigan Monographs in Education (Ann Arbor: University of Michigan Press, 1939), 191 pp.
47. Kawin, E. and Hoefer, C.: *A Comparative Study of a Nursery School vs. a Non-Nursery School Group* (Chicago: University of Chicago Press, 1931), 52 pp.
48. Kephart, N.: "A Method of Heightening Social Adjustment in an Institutional Group," *American Journal of Orthopsychiatry* (1938), 8:710-717.
49. Kerstetter, L. M. and Sargent, J.: "Reassignment Therapy in the Classroom," *Sociometry* (1940), 3:293-306.
50. Koch, H. L.: "A Study of Some Factors Conditioning the Social Distance Between the Sexes," *Journal of Social Psychology* (1944), 20:79-107.
51. Krout, M. H.: "Periodic Changes in Social Distance; a Study in the Shifting Bases of Perception," *Sociology and Social Research* (1943), 27:339-351.
52. Kuhlen, R. G. and Lee, B. J.: "Personality Characteristics and Social

Acceptability in Adolescence," *Journal of Educational Psychology* (1943), 34:321-340.
53. Lafore, G. G.: "Practices of Parents in Dealing with Preschool Children," *Child Development Monographs* (New York: Bureau of Publications, Teachers College, Columbia University, 1945), 150 pp.
54. Landreth, C., Gardner, G. M., Eckhardt, B. C., and Prugh, A. D.: "Teacher-Child Contacts in Nursery Schools," *Journal of Experimental Education* (1943), 12:65-91.
55. Leonard, J. P. and Eurich, A. C.: *An Evaluation of Modern Education* (New York: D. Appleton-Century Company, 1942), 299 pp.
56. Lewin, K., Lippitt, R., and White, R.: "Patterns of Aggressive Behavior in Experimentally Created 'Social Climates,'" *Journal of Social Psychology* (1939), 10:271-299.
57. Lippitt, R.: *An Experimental Study of the Effect of Democratic and Authoritarian Group Atmospheres,* University of Iowa Studies in Child Welfare (1940), 16, 3:43-195.
58. ———: "Popularity Among Preschool Children," *Child Development* (1941), 12:305-332.
59. Lowenstein, P. and Svendsen, M.: "Experimental Modification of the Behavior of a Selected Group of Shy and Withdrawn Children," *American Journal of Orthopsychiatry* (1938), 8:639-653.
60. Mallay, H.: "Growth in Social Behavior and Mental Activity After Six Months in Nursery School," *Child Development* (1935), 6:303-309.
61. McFarland, M. B.: *Relationships Between Young Sisters as Revealed in Their Overt Responses,* Child Development Monographs (New York: Teachers College, Columbia University, 1938), No. 24, 230 pp.
62. Meek, L. H.: *Personal-Social Development of Boys and Girls with Implications for Secondary Education* (New York: Committee on Workshops, Progressive Education Association, 1940), 243 pp.
63. Meyers, C. E.: *The Effect of Conflicting Authority on the Child,* University of Iowa Studies in Child Welfare (1944), 20, No. 409:31-98.
64. Moreno, J. L.: *Who Shall Survive?* (Washington, D. C.: Nervous and Mental Disease Publishing Company, 1934), 440 pp.
65. Murphy, L. B.: *Social Behavior and Child Personality* (New York: Columbia University Press, 1937), 344 pp.
66. Nesbitt, M.: "Student and Child Relationships in the Nursery School," *Child Development* (1943), 19:143-166.
67. Neugarten, B. L.: "Social Class and Friendship Among School Children," *American Journal of Sociology* (1946), 51:305-313.
68. Northway, M. L.: "Children with Few Friends," *School* (1944), 32: 380-384.
69. ———: "Outsiders; a Study of the Personality Patterns of Children

Least Acceptable to Their Age Mates," *Sociometry* (1944), 7:10-25.
70. Osborne, E. G.: *Camping and Guidance* (New York: Association Press, 1937), 260 pp.
71. ———: *Individual Adjustment Through Group Activity*, University of Iowa Child Welfare Pamphlets (1938), No. 65, 14 pp.
72. Prescott, D. and Staff of the Division on Child Development and Teacher Personnel: *Helping Teachers Understand Children* (Washington: American Council on Teacher Education, 1945), 468 pp.
73. Potashin, R.: "A Sociometric Study of Children's Friendships," *Sociometry* (1946), 9:48-70.
74. Rigney, M. G.: *Practices of Teachers in Dealing with Preschool Children*, unpublished (Teachers College, Columbia University).
75. Salusky, A. S.: "Collective Behavior of Children at a Preschool Age," *Journal of Social Psychology* (1930), 1:367-378.
76. Sandin, A. A.: *Social and Emotional Adjustments of Regularly Promoted and Non-Promoted Pupils*, Child Development Monographs (New York: Bureau of Publications, Teachers College, Columbia University, 1944), No. 32, 142 pp.
77. Seagoe, M. V.: "Factors Influencing the Selection of Associates," *Journal of Educational Research* (1933), 27:32-40.
78. Stagner, R.: "Economic Status and Personality," *School and Society* (1935), 42:551-552.
79. Stendler, C.: *A Study of Children's Awareness of Social Class*, unpublished (Teachers College, Columbia University).
80. Taylor, M. W. and Frank, G. G.: "An Experiment in Nursery School Follow-up," *Childhood Education* (1931), 7:474-481.
81. Tedsten, D. and Coy, G. L.: "A Study of Beginning First Grade Children to Determine the Effect of Kindergarten Training in Social Behavior," in Smith, P. H.: *The Practical Value of Early Childhood Education*, Bulletin of the Association for Childhood Education, Washington, D. C. (1934), 25-29.
81a. Terman, L. M.: "A Preliminary Study in the Psychology and Pedagogy of Leadership," *Pedagogical Seminary* (1904), 11:413-451.
82. Thompson, G. G.: "The Social and Emotional Development of Preschool Children Under Two Different Types of Educational Program," *Psychological Monographs* (1944), No. 258, 56.
83. Thorndike, R. L., Loftus, J. J., and Goldman, B.: "Observation of Excursions in Activity and Control Schools," *Journal of Experimental Education* (1941), 10:146-149.
84. Tryon, C. M.: "Evaluation of Adolescent Personality by Adolescents," *Monograph Soc. Res. Child Development* (Washington: National Research Council, 1939), Vol. 4, No. 4.
85. Updegraff, R. and Herbst, E. K.: "An Experimental Study of the So-

cial Behavior Stimulated in Young Children by Certain Play Materials," *Journal of Genetic Psychology* (1933), 42:372-391.
86. Walsh, M. E.: *The Nursery School and Behavior,* Studies in Child Welfare, Social Science Monographs (1929), 1, 2:43-51.
87. Warner, W. L. and Lunt, P. S.: *Yankee City Series, Vol. I, The Social Life of a Modern Community* (New Haven: Yale University Press, 1941), 460 pp.
88. ———: *Yankee City Series, Vol. II, The Status System of a Modern Community* (New Haven: Yale University Press, 1942), 246 pp.
89. Warner, W. L. and Stole, L.: *Yankee City Series, Vol. III, The Social Systems of American Ethnic Groups* (New Haven: Yale University Press, 1945), 318 pp.
90. Warner, W. L., Havighurst, R. J., and Loeb, M. B.: *Who Shall Be Educated?* (New York: Harper and Brothers, 1944), 190 pp.
91. Wellman, B. L. and Pegram, E. L.: "Binet I.Q. Changes of Orphanage Preschool Children: A Re-Analysis," *Journal of Genetic Psychology* (1944), 65:239-263.
92. West, J.: *Plainville, U.S.A.* (New York: Columbia University Press, 1945), 238 pp.
93. Wright, B. A.: "Altruism in Children and the Perceived Conduct of Others," *Journal of Abnormal and Social Psychology* (1942), 37:218-233.
94. Wright, M. E.: "The Influence of Frustration upon the Social Relations of Young Children," *Character and Personality* (1943), 12:111-122.
95. Wrightstone, J. W.: *Appraisal of Newer Elementary School Practices* (New York: Bureau of Publications, Teachers College, Columbia University, 1938), 221 pp.

CHAPTER VII

FEELING AND EMOTION

Fears and resentments, joys and sorrows, the experience of being bored, annoyed, or contented, and all other manner of emotional response are interwoven with the events of everyday life. For this reason emotion cannot be isolated in pure form, yet the subject deserves an emphasis of its own.

On the subjective side, emotion involves an experience of feeling, as when we report that we feel angry or afraid. Also on the subjective side, it involves an impulse or disposition to act in one way or another, to attack in anger, or to flee in fear. Emotion also involves physical and physiological phenomena; some of these are expressed quite obviously, as when a person grows pale with fear; some apparent to the individual himself are less obvious to others, such as a quickened heartbeat; and some can be detected only by after-effects or by precise laboratory tests.

EARLY EMOTIONAL REACTIONS

In Chapter I we noted that there is a lack of differentiation in behavior at the newborn level that seems to have an emotional quality. We noted also that the child is immune to many conditions that will arouse an emotional response as he matures.[1] In any event, as a child grows older his expressions become more clearly differentiated and distinguishable. In a study by Goodenough (25) it was found that adult judges showed more accuracy than could be expected by chance when asked to identify pictures taken of a ten-months-old child who, at different times,

---

[1] Various conjectures with regard to the emotions of the young infant are also discussed in the section of Chapter I which calls attention to the theories of Freud and his followers.

had been exposed to stimuli designed to provoke fear, astonishment, satisfaction, anger, and the like. The vocal expression of the infant's emotional behavior also becomes more definite after a time. At the age of one month, he will give different cries for hunger, pain, and discomfort, according to Gesell (21). Soon thereafter he will smile at the approach of a person and give vocal expression to apparent feelings of pleasure.[2]

THE ROLE OF NEEDS, DRIVES, MOTIVES, GOALS

Whether or not a child's feelings will be aroused by a given happening will depend, in part, upon what he, himself, has at stake. Feelings are likely to be aroused by anything that furthers or threatens his motives and plans, anything that blocks or facilitates activities which he, himself, has initiated, or anything that helps or hinders his hopes and aspirations. As a result, the same external event may have varied effects. To a child who is poised to go to a picnic, a rainstorm may be a catastrophe, while the same rain brings joy to another child whose garden is suffering from drought.

To catalog the drives that render a person emotionally vulnerable would be an almost impossible undertaking, for while some are "original," common to all persons, and quite obvious (such as the drive to obtain food when hungry), others have been influenced by learning and past experience and may be unique (such as a certain child's desire to collect the stubs of theater tickets). It is possible, however, to illustrate certain groups or classes of motives that come into play.

Some needs and drives. First there are drives associated with primary needs of the organism, such as the need for food, for drink, for air, for maintaining protection against heat or cold, for protection of bodily tissue against damage through bruises and

---

[2] For accounts of expressions of emotion in children, as well as older persons, see (16, 25, 42, 43, 58). Studies by Goodenough (24) and Thompson (64) indicate that there are many similarities between the facial expressions of blind and seeing children when emotionally aroused.

punctures, the need for rest and sleep, and the need for carrying on the various functions of the body. Connected with these needs there may be cravings of varying intensity, such as a thirsty person's craving for water.

In addition, human beings, in common with other creatures, have drives toward activity, impulses to convert the latent energies of the organism into kinetic energy. These drives are less sharply defined than the drives mentioned above, and they are more varied and subject to modification during the course of growth and as a result of experience. In this group fall such examples as the impulse to use one's legs in walking, the exercise of curiosity, the impulse to explore the environment, the impulse to be on the go and to enter into a variety of experiences.

Another category of motives that come into play sooner or later are those involved in the child's relations with other people. At an early age he desires the company of his elders.

Eventually he seeks to belong, to be accepted, to have a place and to have status with his own age group. The way these desires are expressed and the strength of the motives behind them vary with different children and will be influenced by learning and experience.

In addition to drives connected with physical survival and social relationships, there are almost countless forms and varieties of motivation of a more optional character that are described by everyday terms such as interests,[3] wishes and desires, wants and hopes. These wants and wishes are influenced to a large degree by the cultural environment. In connection with all of these it is possible for the person to meet helps and hindrances, to succeed or to fail; and all such possibilities add to the total of circumstances that may arouse emotional reactions.

Aspiration and "levels of aspiration." As the child's abilities increase in the course of growth and through the effects of practice, there are changes in the standards of achievement and con-

---
[3] Chapter XV deals separately with the subject of children's interests.

duct which the child sets for himself, and such changes also mean a change in what, from his point of view, is a threat or constitutes a thwarting or a furthering of his wishes. There are changes in what he aspires to do—as when he insists on holding the cup from which he is drinking, or insists on cutting his own meat, or, later, on buying his own clothes. There are changes also in the level of performance to which he aspires in undertakings which can be rated according to difficulty or which can be scaled according to scope or size, or according to goodness or excellence of performance.[4]

The child's "level of aspiration" may be in evidence within a quite limited and specific setting, as when he sets out to bounce a ball forty times in succession without a miss. Or it may be more inclusive, as when he aims to get a perfect mark in all his subjects at school. The standard representing the child's level of aspiration may be defined with reference to the task itself—such as in the example of bouncing forty times—or the standard may be relative to the performance of others, as when the child aspires to surpass all his companions whether this means bouncing forty times or more or fewer. Again, the standard the child aspires to attain may function in terms of a variety of contexts: one pupil's high aspirations in his art work at school may be a feature of fervent ambition to be an artist, while another's drive to maintain a high standard in the art class may spring less from devotion to art than from an ambition to stand high in all his subjects at school.

Ideas about self. As the child matures he not only becomes able thus to set goals or standards for himself in a number of specific situations, but he is also in the process of forming ideas about himself and of establishing the beginnings of a concept or image of himself as a person. Included in this image are ideas of what he looks like to himself and what he thinks he looks like in the eyes of others. The ideas he has about himself will be influenced by his own direct discoveries and also by what others say about him,

---

[4] For an account of level of aspiration, see Lewin, K. (49).

the attitudes they show toward him, and his own wish to accept, or his efforts to refute, the evaluations others make of him. The notions he has about himself, what a person such as he should be expected to like or dislike, to do or not to do, to accept or hate or fear will, in many instances, determine whether a certain happening is seen as something that threatens or thwarts him, as a temptation to be avoided or an opportunity to be grasped, as an occasion for joy or a cause for remorse.

Subjective factors in determining what constitutes success and failure. The level of a child's aspiration, and what he has personally at stake, will have an important bearing upon what constitutes success or failure from the child's point of view.[5] Success or failure cannot be defined simply in terms of the external task. Whether or not a child will feel that he has succeeded or failed will depend to a large extent upon what he expects of himself, what he hopes to attain, what is important to him. Accordingly, one pupil may feel that he has "failed," be keenly disappointed if he earns an average of 95, rather than 98, on a set of examinations, while another pupil may feel very "successful" and experience intense elation if he barely "passes" each test and earns an average of about 70. This fact that the experience of success and failure is relative to the individual's own standards also has a bearing upon what, from his own point of view, constitutes praise or reproof. Praise for being the star soccer player on Team B may have a sour taste to a youngster who fervently aspires to be a member of Team A.

Factors influencing self-set standards and aspirations. While a child's ability is an important factor in determining his level of aspiration, a vast array of other factors also comes into play. Two children may be similar in ability, but one seeks to achieve near the upper limits of his ability, while another sets a lower standard for himself. A youngster may strive to function near the summit

---

[5] An article by Lewin, Dembo, Festinger, and Sears discusses the manner in which the experience of success or failure is relative to a frame of reference (50).

of his ability in some undertakings but not in others. As a result of failure, one child may lower the goal he set for himself in an enterprise, while another may cling to the standard he first aimed to reach. After repeated success, one child may raise his level of aspiration, while another may be content to coast along. A child may raise his level of aspiration if he learns that he is performing below the standard of his group (17). Children tend to raise their self-set standards in a group setting and under the spur of competition (19).[6]

DEVELOPMENTAL CHANGES IN SUSCEPTIBILITY TO EMOTION

The development of emotions during infancy and childhood is closely interwoven with other aspects of development. As a child's senses become more acute, as his capacities for discrimination and perception mature, and as he moves forward in all aspects of his development, the range of events which arouse emotion grows wider and wider. With the growth of the child's understanding and imagination the things that affect him emotionally become increasingly involved with symbols and fancies, with abstract plans and values. The child becomes concerned not merely with the immediate and passing event but with events that have occurred in the past and with what may happen in the future.

In the expression of emotion, there likewise are changes paralleling the child's mental and emotional development. As noted earlier, a child's movements become more specialized as he grows older, and, to some degree, there is a corresponding specialization of his emotional expressions and experiences. Moreover, as the child grows older and more able to suit his actions to his impulses, he also becomes more capable of suppressing outward signs of stress.

---

[6] For other studies concerning factors influencing level of aspiration, see Challman (11), Gould (27), and P. Sears (57).

AFFECTION

As noted earlier, children at an early age display a desire to receive and an impulse to bestow affection. The topic of affection is important from the standpoint of child psychology and it is also of special interest by reason of differing viewpoints on the topic. Writings on child rearing in recent years have placed much emphasis on the child's need for affection. This is in contrast to a notion that received a good deal of attention about twenty-five years ago when John B. Watson, the behaviorist, wrote and spoke against "too much mother love" (67).

There are differences in interpretation also concerning the origins of love. There is the view that love is an original, primary emotion, inherent in the child's nature. There is the view that a child's need for affection is an outgrowth of his helplessness. Again there is the view that the child's love for a person or thing is a conditioned response.

This latter interpretation, which implies that a child's affection for other persons and things may be merely an extension of his own "selfish" concerns, seems to square with some manifestations of affection that can be observed in everyday life. But this represents only a part of the story. Although learning is involved in determining whom and what a child will be fond of, quite as important is the fact that the child has the potentiality for fondness and concern for persons and things. This potentiality is a feature of his original nature.

The child has this capacity not only for affection toward intimates who minister to his more or less self-centered desires, but also for affection of a more spontaneous character. The issue as to whether all concern for others is an extension of concern for self is not a crucial one. In the first place, a thoroughgoing distinction between self-love and altruistic love cannot be made; concern for self and concern for others are not discrete but complementary.

Second, even if affection for others did originate in concern for self, such affection can go to such lengths of devotion and the sacrifice of immediate personal ends that it is tantamount to affection of a genuinely altruistic sort.

Expressions of affection. The first expressions of affection that meet the eye after a child is born are not those which the baby displays toward others, but those which others display toward him. As noted in an earlier chapter, under normal circumstances the child's birth is likely to touch off affectionate impulses in the mother; and the father, although he is more of a bystander, is also likely to be affected. Except where illness or other disorders prevail, earlier reasons pro and con on the subject of having a baby—such as the plea of religious duty, social conformity, a desire to hold the husband or the wife, the need for someone to carry on the family name, and so forth—tend to be forgotten, at least for a time. Often a mother's previous indifference or even opposition to the child's coming is changed to devotion once the child is born and seen and held. To be sure, such a response may not necessarily denote a parental "instinct," but the important thing is the readiness with which there is displayed "responsiveness to the looks, gestures and cries" of the infant, an impulse to perform comforting acts in response to "childish signs of pain, grief and misery," and, in time, to find a delight in "childish gurglings, smiles and affectionate gestures." [7]

An infant very early in life welcomes the experience of being held and fondled, and, as noted in a previous chapter, he soon actively reciprocates human contacts by smiling or laughing at the approach of his mother and by showing affection in other playful ways. In due time, also, he becomes attached to children of his own age. As noted earlier, under normal circumstances his friendly responses to other children in time outnumber overtly

---

[7] A partial rephrasing of a description by Thorndike, in 1913, of the maternal instinct. The account includes also the following: "To a woman who has given birth to a child, a baby to see, to hold, and suckle is perhaps the most potent satisfaction that life can offer; its loss, the cause of the saddest yearning" (65).

unfriendly acts, even though he may at times display an ample amount of aggression and resistance. In time he forms attachments to many persons and things. He shows delight at the homecoming of a relative or the visit of a neighbor. He shows acute concern, sometimes a high degree of terror, when it appears that harm is befalling a member of his circle.

Likewise, after the age of a year or so, a child is likely to form a strong attachment to inanimate objects and animals—a certain blanket, a cup, a spoon, a little kit, an old sweater. He may treasure an old teddy bear, a tattered doll, or an old box with a devotion stronger than ever is won by newer and costlier possessions. His affections may embrace the family dog and cat and other animals, extending in time to equipment about the home; even the old family automobile may find a place in his heart, just as did the old oaken bucket of an earlier generation, and just as did the old gray mare before she wasn't what she used to be.

The course of the development of the normal child's affections for his brothers and sisters has not been studied systematically from the developmental point of view over a period of months and years. Generalizations concerning the development of affection between siblings are likely to be especially misleading if they are based upon the testimony of maladjusted adults or upon the study of children who are being treated for severe symptoms of jealousy or for other behavior problems. Interestingly enough, emotional factors in the relationships between siblings have been approached largely from the point of view of evidences of jealousy, discord, dominance, and aggressiveness, rather than from the point of view of ties of friendship and affection. Through focusing only upon evidences of hostility and rivalry, one can readily obtain a distorted picture of the relationships that exist and fail to notice that two siblings may be genuinely fond of each other, even though they bicker a good deal of the time.

Two children who seem to be especially contentious in their everyday relations may have more affection for each other than another pair who get along quite peaceably by holding aloof. Two children who fight vigorously at home may unite loyally against aggression by an outsider, and either one may, on occasion, go to great lengths of devotion. In healthy, alert children, friction and occasional hostility are normal phenomena. Their presence does not denote genuine incompatibility. Nor does the fact that such children at one time fight and at another time go out of their way to help each other or grieve at one another's hurts and misfortunes mean that the children are chronically torn between conflicting feelings of hatred and love. To be sure, such ambivalent attitudes may exist in some cases, just as the balance between affection and hostility may vary considerably in different sibships. The home environment may produce strong hatreds, just as it may produce strong ties of affection.

In a large family, varying degrees of affection may develop between the different members even when all get along quite amicably. Thus, an older child may "adopt" one of the younger ones as his or her special favorite, or two children near each other in age may become especially loyal to each other, share candy and other goods, and never tattle about each other. Special loyalties of this kind may persist over a period of several years and may continue into adult life; but by reason of changing interests and other factors, a complete shift in such alignments may occur in adult years.

The bearing of affection on development and adjustment. Many studies deal with the bearing that affection or the lack of affection may have on a child's development and adjustment. In a monograph dealing with infants, Ribble (56) claims that affectionate treatment is important both for the emotional and physical well-being of young children. As time passes a child's intellectual and emotional development is likely to proceed better in a home situation that can provide close companionship than in an institution where many children are in the care of a few adults and where it is not possible for children to receive as much personal attention as in the home (23). Interesting findings on this point are reported in a study by Skeels and others (60) which, though not dealing specifically with the matter of affection, shows impressively the manner in which children in an orphanage where human contacts have been limited and restricted may be more on the defensive, less free to avail themselves of the friendly attention of an adult, than children who have learned to count upon adult companionship such as is enjoyed by the normal child. A study by Brodbeck and Irwin (5) shows that even during the first six months of life infants in an orphanage made fewer and less varied speech sounds than did children of high and of low socioeconomic status who were being brought up by the parents in their own homes.

Findings in some studies also indicate that the degree of cordiality that existed between a person and his parents when he was a child may have a bearing upon a person's attitudes, his tendency, for example, to be conservative or radical as a young adult (61, 62). Psychiatric case studies contain many accounts of ways in which hidden or partly concealed attitudes of hostility toward a parent may color a person's attitudes and influence his prejudices and fears.

The importance to the child of "security" in his accustomed ties and contacts with adults has been emphasized in several studies dealing with the effects of wartime happenings, notably evacuation, upon the behavior of children (10, 13, 34, 35). It appeared that some children were emotionally more affected by the fact of leaving home and living in a new place with strange people than by being exposed to air raids at home.

The fact that children thrive best in an atmosphere of affection is not, of course, surprising. When the parent genuinely likes his child and enjoys him as a companion, there will be more give and take, more mutual participation in common activities, less unresolved friction, less need for concealment and evasion, more occasion to venture into new experiences, more protection against damaging shocks.

"Rejection and overprotection." The term "rejection" and the label "rejected child" have been used to denote the condition of a child who is not loved by a parent (or parent substitute). The term "overprotection" has been used to designate a parental attitude involving excessive contact and mothering.[8]

Among the more extreme signs or symptoms that a parent is rejecting his child, as described by one writer (18), are items such as evicting or deserting the child, putting him into an institution (reform school, military school, and so on) in order to discipline him or to avoid being bothered by him, seeing mainly the child's faults, and using very severe punishment. Other items signifying rejection, according to this account, are frequent criticism, threats to evict, locking the child up (in closet or basement), or deliberately frightening him. Still other signs of rejection, rated as somewhat less severe, include nagging, spanking, paying no attention to the child, failing to provide him with money or toys or advantages, comparing the child unfavorably with others, making no effort to seek ways of improving his condition by enlisting the services of doctors, teachers, and the like. It is not implied that each one of these items alone marks the parent as a "rejecting" parent, but it would be difficult to defend some of the practices listed as good forms of discipline, and if a parent habitually uses many of them, with no offsetting friendly ways, it seems highly probable that he not only lacks affection for his child but actually feels hostile toward him.

Behavior such as the following has been regarded as a sign of an "overprotecting" attitude, as contrasted with a "rejecting" atti-

---

[8] For studies dealing with the effects of parental attitudes, including rejection, nonrejection, and overprotection see Fitz-Simons (18), David Levy (45), Symonds (63) (maternal overprotection). A series of studies initiated by Levy has been published in several numbers of the journal *Smith College Studies in Social Work* during the years 1930 and 1931.

tude: excessive contact of mother with child (sleeping in same bed, continually keeping within sight, and so on); prolongation of infantile care; lack or excess of parental control; indulging child (cannot refuse requests); caring for child's physical needs to an unusual degree.[9]

Levy has advanced the hypothesis that a mother's tendency to reject or to overprotect may be due to factors in her life history, such as a long period of anticipation or frustration prior to having a child (due, for example, to miscarriages or death of other infants) or unsatisfactory marital relationship and hunger for affection. According to Levy, an attitude of overprotection might also be influenced by conditions in the child that threatened his life, such as severe illness.

In passing it may be pointed out that great caution should be used in applying the concepts of parental rejection and overprotection. Parents may be equally devoted to their children and yet differ in their notions as to methods of child rearing and in their ideas as to how "strict" or "lenient" a parent should be. Some parents may even use discipline that seems to be quite harsh (in dealing, for example, with thumbsucking, lying, nail biting, masturbation), not because they wish the child to suffer but because of their notions as to the seriousness of the behavior in question. Moreover, in a normal home there are times when a fond but tired parent would like nothing better than to have someone take his children off his hands for a while.[10] Apart from this, the concept should not be applied as an epithet or accusation. Actually, a parent who lacks fondness for his child is a pitiable creature. He is subject to social pressure to bear the labors and responsibilities of a parent, and when parenthood is not a labor of love it is labor indeed.

---

[9] This list combines items from a list by Levy (45) and a scale by Fitz-Simons (18).
[10] The fact that parents and children, like husbands and wives, view each other with varying degrees of enthusiasm from time to time has been brought out in a very readable book by Levy and Monroe (48).

As is only to be expected, a "rejected" child faces many problems and difficulties. Parental rejection may be a factor in the causation of behavior problems and emotional maladjustment. Moreover, once he is in difficulty, it may be much harder for him than for a child whose parents are eager to help to overcome his difficulty through aid he receives at school or from a guidance clinic. However, while the parental attitude toward the child is an important factor, it is not, of course, the only factor. In a study of delinquent children who had received treatment it was found that about the same percentage of young persons had the affection of their fathers in the group that was unreformed as in the group that was reformed after fifteen years (22).

Other practical implications. It is likely that a systematic study of affectionate behavior in children would show that children have greater capacity for affection and concern for others than usually is assumed in our present ways of dealing with them. From the point of view of larger adult affairs, it is conceivable that a different emphasis in the education of children at home and at school might utilize many resources that now are more or less ignored. In contemporary social and political strife, the rallying cry of groups working for this or that cause seems frequently to be one of hatred for those whom the group opposes and who stand in the way of the group's self-aggrandizement than one of friendly concern for those whose lot the group ostensibly is seeking to improve.

A child's experience of affection in the home environment may have an important influence upon the development and expression of his own affection for others. As the normal child grows older, he acquires many loyalties outside the home, whereas originally his attachments were almost entirely centered within the home. He will be handicapped if his attachment to one or both parents has become so strong, and involves so much dependence, as to prevent him from acquiring a wholehearted interest in other people. A child who is thus bound is likely sooner or later to encounter difficulties such as excessive jealousy, homesickness, and difficulty in winning full acceptance by others. He will also have fewer resources for meeting the shock that comes with the loss of a loved one. On the other hand, lack of experience of close ties in the home and lack of experience from an early age in expressing feelings of affection may likewise be a handicap in later life, especially when the individual reaches the age of readiness for courtship, marriage, and family life, for loving takes learning, just as does almost everything else.

When young children are questioned as to whom they love most, the mother is named more frequently than is the father, by both boys and girls, but many children will report that they love both parents equally much. In a study by Simpson (59), children aged five to nine years were questioned directly as well as indirectly (for example, a picture of a man and a woman was shown to them, and they were asked to point to the one they liked best) concerning their preferences. In response to a direct question: "Whom do you like best at home?" at the end of the interview that was held with each child, 69.6 per cent of 250 boys named their mothers, 22.4 per cent named their fathers, and the remaining children named both father and mother (with the exception of one boy who named neither). The girls likewise named their mothers most often (61 per cent), but a slightly larger number of girls than of boys named the father (28 per cent) or named both father and mother (10.4 per cent). A higher percentage of preference for the mother than for the father appeared at all age levels, with one exception (the five-year-old girls named fathers more frequently than mothers). These results in the case of the girls do not indicate that children are likely uniformly to prefer the parent of the opposite sex, as was found in a study of adults (29). Studies of older persons reveal a more nearly equal balance of affection for both parents (62).

The degree of a child's attachment to his parents and his expression of his attachment may vary in different circumstances. The youngster may, for example, prefer to romp and play with his father but demand the company of his mother when he is sick or when he awakens from a bad dream.

Among children, as among adults, one sometimes finds individuals who are very strongly attached to the parent of the opposite sex. A boy's devotion to his mother, and a girl's to her father, may be so influential that the characteristics of the favored parent serve as a standard or model when the individual, in adult life, looks for a husband or wife. Needless to say, regardless of the degree of affection that exists between child and parent, an individual's loyalties and affinities with other persons in later years will be influenced in many ways by factors in his relationships with his parents.[11]

PLEASURE AND BOREDOM IN CHILD LIFE

Some organic reactions have been found to be more or less characteristic of pleasant emotional states. When in an agreeable frame of mind, one will tend to relax rather than to grow tense, to lean forward rather than recoil; and there will be an extension and expansion rather than a flexion and contraction of the muscles (14). An example of the muscular accompaniments of satisfaction is given in an experiment by Goodenough and Brian (26) in which children threw rings upon a peg. When a child, to his joy, made a "ringer," his exuberance was such that on the next trial he was likely to overshoot the target. A somewhat similar result is given in a study in which students were asked to draw lines on paper (55). When requested to think about pleasant events, they showed an involuntary tendency to draw longer lines than what they were supposed to reproduce; when dwelling upon unpleasant thoughts, they involuntarily drew shorter lines.

This dynamogenic effect of pleasant emotional stimuli has much significance in daily life. We see these effects illustrated in the

---

[11] Other emotional aspects of parent-child relationships are presented in the following chapter in the discussions of anger, fear, and jealousy and in a section dealing specifically with the joys and problems of child raising.

FEELING AND EMOTION

finding that praise and reward tend to promote efficiency more than do reproof and punishment. Again, if the child is in a relaxed state or is already bubbling and expansive, his laughter rings louder and his smiles are freer when some new engaging stimulus is placed in his way. The organic background of joy, like the organic background of rage and fear, has indeed an important effect upon the way in which a child will respond to a new stimulus. But an observer cannot judge the tonus of his muscles or gauge the volume of glandular products circulating in his blood. Such unseen internal conditions account to a large degree for the fact that a child will sometimes be elated and at other times will be annoyed in response to the same external stimulus.

Conditions underlying pleasure. Satisfying conditions range from stimulation of specific sense organs to conditions involving the free flow of activity. Whatever may be the underlying cause, it seems, as a practical matter, that pleasure often is associated with sheer activity. The infant coos and gurgles, exercises his voice, kicks with his feet, manipulates convenient objects with his hands, ventures into creeping and crawling and walking, and, as time passes, he enters into a great variety of activities apparently through his own spontaneous impulses. Whether there is as much pleasure in his activity as his movements seem to indicate, we have no way of telling, but it would appear that, like the healthy puppy who frisks playfully even though no fleas are biting him, the child draws satisfaction from being active on his own accord.

As the child becomes older his activities increase in scope and the occasions that may produce such satisfactions increase accordingly. In time he becomes able to respond in terms of long-time ambitions and to gain satisfaction from subtle indications that his plans are being realized.

The pleasures and satisfactions involved in uninhibited and successful activity can be noted in all aspects of the child's behavior. Sometimes, as noted above, action may be accompanied by exuber ant outbursts of apparent joy; but more often the expressions are more subdued. We see signs of this "activity pleasure," not simply in connection with motor activities, but also in other connections. Indeed, the exercise of any capacity may be a source of satisfaction. A child will, for example, exercise his capacities for fear by taking chances or by seeking vicarious stimulation through stories and pictures. He likewise "plays" with anger, by entering into games that involve mild forms of hostility and conflict. He may deliberately expose himself to situations that are potentially annoying, as when he begins a fracas in a playful mood, knowing from past experience that the game may turn into a real fight, or tries, without apparent underlying rancor, to get a "rise" out of his parents or teachers, or invites thwarting by tackling a difficult project that he knows he cannot handle. In like manner, satisfactions may come from the exercise of his capacities for social activities and his intellectual abilities.

This matter of satisfaction through activity overlaps with the large topic of children's interests. This topic is treated in another chapter, but certain points may be emphasized here. First there is the fact that although a project is likely to produce dissatisfaction if it definitely is beyond a child's powers, it is likely to be most satisfying if it constitutes something of a challenge. Second, there is the matter of boredom.

Boredom. The term "boredom" covers a variety of experiences that are "negative" in the sense that the individual is marking time with nothing stimulating or challenging to absorb his attention. Boredom involves a complete absence of "activity pleasure" as described above. Although boredom in one form or another is a very common experience, it has received little attention in psychological research. In everyday speech boredom is revealed by expressions such as being "fed up"; "nothing ever happens around here." The term "tired" often denotes boredom rather than fatigue, and even the term "pain" often has this denotation.

A study of boredom would no doubt reveal that much of the

mischievousness and misbehavior of children springs from a desire for something to happen. Children will even court the danger of severe punishment in order to stir up some "excitement." Similarly, mishaps and minor tragedies may be welcomed as a break in the monotony of life, as when a child dances with delight when the family car is stuck in the snow or when he learns that a bat has got into grandma's bedroom. Many adults also, of course, go to great lengths to relieve boredom. Boredom sometimes is a precursor of anger, as when a child is not allowed simply to be inattentive or to leave but is forced to listen to long lectures, or to stay at table until others are finished, and the like.

Much of children's boredom centers in the school. Boredom can be observed in the behavior of children who have attended a nursery school or kindergarten for two or more years and have mastered most of the projects which the school affords. And especially can it be noted in the average classroom, where much of the time of a capable child is spent in idling. If the facts could be ascertained, it is likely that for every child in school who is dissatisfied because the work is too hard there are several children who are bored, if not actively dissatisfied, because the work is not sufficiently challenging. Such boredom can easily be mistaken for surliness and even for lack of social adjustment. Thus, a child who had seemed apathetic and something of a "fringer" during the latter part of her stay in nursery school and kindergarten blossomed forth with new interest and vitality when she moved on to the first grade and got her teeth into reading and other school projects.

It would be impossible, of course, to arrange matters so that everything which occupies a child's time is so scaled and varied as to continue to challenge his growing abilities, since many activities of daily life, both during childhood and adult years, consist of chores that one must learn to take in one's stride. Failure to adjust to this fact may become a source of much dissatisfaction, but the situation is even worse when everything in the day's activities becomes a matter of uninteresting routine. This problem is likely to be more acute in adult years, after the individual is pretty well established and finds that his daily round of duties no longer challenges his powers. Regardless of the importance of his duties in the larger scheme of things, he may find them boring; and there may develop, as happens with many adults, a sense of futility accompanied by a search for remedies that will either dull the senses or excite them. Much worse, of course, than the condition of boredom in an adult who has an occupation is the plight of an able-bodied person who has no occupation.

Chronic and pervasive boredom of the sort sometimes found in adults is not likely to occur in a child, for so much still lies ahead of him and he is constantly meeting new experiences. The frontiers of his world are still wide open, so to speak. But the child and his activities have a definite bearing upon the adult problem, for the resources for satisfaction through activity which an adult possesses in his thirties and beyond are much influenced by his training and experiences as a child. Many adult hobbies and avocations first began to flower early in childhood, then, perhaps, they may have been dormant for a time through adolescence and youth, only to grow again in later years. Indeed, activities and skills which a child exercised only because he had to may, in later years, be revived with enthusiasm, as when a person who worked in the garden reluctantly as a child later, as an adult, picks up his spade and hoe and goes joyfully to work.

SYMPATHY

In a literal definition of sympathy, the emphasis is on feeling—"suffering with" another, being affected by and being sensitive to another's plight or condition—as distinguished, say, from coöperation, where the literal emphasis is on doing rather than feeling.[12] As usually employed, however, sympathy denotes an expression of

---

[12] The topic of sympathy, from the point of view of its manifestations in social situations, is treated in Chapter V.

feeling ranging from meaningful silence to ostentatious condolences and from inept gestures to deeds that help to assuage another's distress. At the adult level the overt expression of sincere fellow feeling may range from acts that bear the stamp of kindness to superficial gruffness, hilarity, and apparent unconcern. In the case of children, it likewise is sometimes difficult to detect sympathetic behavior, for although young children tend to express their emotions more freely than older persons, they are less able than adults to describe in words the nuances of their feelings or to formulate their impulses in terms of appropriate action.

In the study by Murphy cited in Chapter V, it is pointed out that the more closely knit the structure of a society becomes, "the more demands are put upon individuals to respond to the needs of others." She further points out that sympathy, "when it is sensible and genuine," and not merely a "projection of the sympathizer's anxiety" for his own safety and security or "a way of dominating others, is intimately connected with all other responses of a friendly and constructive nature that are the foundation of a coöperative society" (52).

CRYING, LAUGHTER, AND HUMOR

A brief word will be said about laughter and crying because of their frequent occurrence as expressions of emotion.

Crying. Crying is usually present at birth, and most of the infant's cries are a feature of his general, undifferentiated activity. However, crying becomes more differentiated in time, as we have seen. As the child grows older, he learns to make use of crying as a means of getting his way, just as he may indulge in temper tantrums for the same purpose; some children become so accustomed to solving problems by means of tears that they often use the same solvent when they have reached adult years. But, because of social restraints, crying usually becomes more and more a private matter as one grows older.

The crying of sixty-one infants was studied by Bayley (1) in situations which included mental tests, tests of reflexes, motor tests, anthropometric measurements, and so forth over a period of several months. These tests involved many conditions and persons that were unfamiliar to the child.

The time spent in crying amounted, on the average, to fifteen per cent of the total examination time. Crying diminished somewhat after the first month, reaching its lowest point at four months, but then increased somewhat during the rest of the year. During the first months of life crying resulted mostly from internal causes, such as bodily pain and distress; during later months, the external environment, fear of the strange situation, and dislike of unusual handling became relatively more important. There was a good deal of consistency in the relative amount of crying of the individual infants from month to month, particularly during the second half-year. But Bayley indicates that the data do not tell whether this consistency is due to innate factors or to early environmental influences.

The degree to which a child will resort to tears depends to a large extent upon his surroundings. A child will often give vent to loud lamentations at home, while similar hurts may produce only a Spartan fortitude when he is out in company. This observation illustrates the degree to which the child's behavior may vary in different situations as the result of specific learning. In a study of the laughter, smiling, and crying of over fifty children between the ages of two and five years (15) only sixteen instances of crying were noted during the period of observations, while, in the meantime, there were several hundred instances of laughter. The crying occurred more frequently as a sign of anger, as when a child was pushed over or deprived of a toy by another, than as a sign of pain. If the child tumbled through his own fault and apparently hurt himself, he was less likely to cry than if an older child gave him a painless shove. Feeble-minded children in an institution where there was less disapproval of crying than in a normal environment were found in one study to cry more than normal children (4).

In time, it comes to be expected that boys will cry less than girls, and the boys more or less fall in line with this expectation, at least in adult years; but individual differences within each sex in the tendency to cry are considerably greater than are the differences between one sex and the other. A study by Juliet Bell (2) offers interesting findings concerning the crying of boys and girls when placed in a trying situation. Bell undertook the heroic job of observing and recording the behavior of dentists and their child patients during dental treatment. In observations of about a hundred treatments, involving children aged three to nine, Bell found no significant difference between boys and girls in their tendency to cry.

Laughter. In a study of infants, Washburn (66) found the first appearance of laughter at twelve weeks as a response when the experimenter bent over the child and made a chirruping sound. Among the stimuli used to provoke laughter were games of peek-a-boo, sudden reappearances from under the table, tickling, rhythmical hand clapping, and the like. Most effective in producing laughter was the "threatening-head" stimulus: while holding the child's hands, the experimenter shook her head playfully from side to side and then ducked rapidly, until her head came into contact with the center of the child's body, whence it was immediately withdrawn again. Laughter in response to this action appeared at sixteen weeks.

In the study of children aged two to five cited above (15), laughter occurred predominantly in connection with some form of motor activity. The young child seldom just sits and laughs (neither, for that matter, does an adult). Many of the conditions which have been proposed in theories of laughter in the case of adults were not confirmed by the behavior of children. It did not appear that such factors as derision, or feelings of superiority because of another's coming to grief, or vindictiveness played a prominent part in causing children's laughter.

The child learns to use laughter in his social contacts with others. He is more likely to laugh when with others than when playing alone, more when with friends than with strangers; and he is also more likely to laugh at the antics of those whom he knows than at similar behavior in strangers.

A study of Kenderdine (38) combined observations of preschool children in experimental situations with observations of the children during their free play. As has been observed in other studies, laughter occurred most frequently when the child was in the company of other children and as an accompaniment of his own movements, rather than as a response to the movements of other persons or things. Four toys which might be expected to cause some amusement were exhibited to the children, but nearly all of them showed interest and curiosity rather than amusement (the toys were a spotted dog with movable ears and tail, a spotted rubber dog that squeaked and that had a movable head and talked, a fur-covered clown hung on an elastic string, and a jumping jack). There were a hundred occasions in which the children came upon one of these toys and had an opportunity to play with them, but in only twelve instances did the children really laugh; smiles occurred in sixty per cent of the instances. At two years, laughter in response to motions made by the child himself or others was highest in frequency, followed by laughter in response to socially unacceptable situations. At three years, the latter situations led the former in frequency. Other situations that provoked laughter included noises made by the child himself or others; grimaces made by the child himself or others; pleasure in accomplishment, general well-being, word play, imitative laughter, and inferiority in others.

In an interesting study by Justin (37), children aged three through six years were exposed to a number of situations that were designed to represent each of six prominent theories as to the cause of laughter. A brief identification of each theory, together with an illustrative situation, follows:

1. *Surprise or defeated expectation.* There are three small buckets, one containing sand, one containing water, and one empty; each is covered with paper. The child reaches into the first to discover what it contains, then into the second. By this time, everything, including the experimenter's directions, has been calculated to lead the child to expect that the third bucket will also contain something; but when he reaches into that, he finds it empty.
2. *Superiority and degradation.* The experimenter, with an egg in one hand and a watch in the other, makes ready to boil the egg in a pot of water, but instead of the egg, he drops the watch into the water.
3. *Incongruity and contrast situations.* A doll is displayed, with eyes in the back of its head; a baby bonnet and a man's silk hat are displayed —the former is put on the adult experimenter's head, the latter on the child's head, and both look at themselves in the mirror; and so forth.
4. *Social smile as a stimulus.* While displaying pictures, the experimenter looks up and, with a smile and laugh, talks to the child about a happening earlier in the day.
5. *Relief from strain situation.* The child walks a chalk line, carrying a parasol in one hand and a potato in a spoon in the other.
6. *Play situation.* This includes a play on words, by means of a jingle; also physical play situations, with a jumping jack, a tower which the child builds and then knocks down, and so forth.

All of these experimental situations produced smiling and laughter in some children at all age levels. In general, there was no large shift in the effectiveness of the various situations from one age level to the next, although the incongruity, superiority, and play situations became somewhat more laughter-provoking as age increased. The major change with age consisted not so much in the appearance of laughter in response to a type of situation that previously was ineffective, as in an increased tendency to laugh at more of the specific situations used to represent a given class of laughter-provoking stimuli. Six-year-olds laughed less than did five-year-olds. Justin suggests that this decrease may be due to a toning down or subduing effect associated with school attendance. All of the six-year-olds in the study were first-graders, and most of them were studied in their own school building.

Justin found a positive relation between I.Q. and tendency to laugh, especially in response to incongruity. In the study by Kenderdine, cited above, it was also observed that the brightest children tended to laugh more than did children of average or somewhat above average I.Q.;[13] but at later age levels, it is likely that the I.Q. will be related less to total amount of laughter than to specific situations that cause laughter.

The development of humor is interrelated with other aspects of development (41, 53). When a child is able to appreciate relationships in size and space, he may notice and laugh at incongruities which he did not notice before, such as Junior's small cap on Papa's big head. When he himself is able to discriminate and to articulate speech sounds, he may find it humorous when a younger child makes mistakes such as he himself had made at an earlier age (like singing, "Me muvver and fahver were Irish"). As he gains increased understanding he may appreciate word play: (*"Question:* What did the rug say to the floor? *Answer:* Stick 'em up, I got you covered. *Question:* Why did the ram fall over the cliff? *Answer:* He didn't see the U-turn. *Question:* Mr. and Mrs. Bigger had a baby. Now, who was the biggest in the family? *Answer:* The baby, because he was a little Bigger.") When he appreciates human foibles of various kinds he may relish jokes that bear on such foibles: (*"Boy:* Dad, I want a quarter for being good. *Dad:* When I was a boy I was good for nothing." "One painter to another who is standing on the top of a stepladder, painting the ceiling: Hold on to your brush, George, I'm going to borrow your ladder.") [14]

---

[13] For a handy tabular review of earlier observations regarding situations that produce laughter in young children and descriptions of laughter situations at the preschool level, see Blatz, Allin, and Millichamp (3).

[14] These examples are from a collection of favorite jokes of a group of sixth-grade pupils. They are representative but not typical.

FEELING AND EMOTION

At the elementary school level and beyond, a good deal of children's humor, at least as represented by "favorite jokes," deals with topics and ideas that are slightly, if not entirely, on the forbidden or tabooed side (7). ("What would you do if you saw a bear?" "Run." "What! With a bear behind?") In a study by Brumbaugh of elementary school children it was found that children often waited for a signal from the teacher before they felt free to laugh at something which apparently struck them as funny (6). Brumbaugh also found that many teachers used humor sarcastically, by saying something that made other children laugh at a youngster, much more often than they used humor in a friendly spirit.

SEX

A mature person's attitudes, interests, and adjustments with respect to sex have a history extending back to early infancy.[15] Many theories concerning the development of sexuality and the role of sex in human behavior have been proposed by Freud (20) and his followers of the psychoanalytical school. These theories have not won general acceptance, since the evidence in support of many of them is quite inadequate in the judgment of many persons trained in the use of scientific methods. Yet the theories of Freud and his followers have been of great value, for, whether adequately supported or not, they have drawn attention to a highly important aspect of human life.

One important generalization about sex development has already been announced, namely, that experiences related to sex enter into the child's life from the time of infancy.[16] Evidence bearing on this point was noted in Chapter III in accounts of the occur-

---

[15] Sex can hardly be called "emotion," and a discussion of sex does not follow logically from the immediately preceding section, yet the topic seemed to be more at home in this chapter than in the ones that follow.

[16] In addition to references on the subject of sex directly cited in the present discussion the reader is referred to a discussion of evidence pertaining to psychoanalytic theories by R. R. Sears (57a) and original studies or reviews of original studies of sex interests and practices by Willoughby (68), and Landis, *et al.* (44).

rence of tumescence and detumescence (28) in early infancy and various forms of self-stimulation during infancy and preschool years (33, 39, 46).

In connection with adult reactions to behavior such as is described above many children receive their first impressions of social attitudes toward sex. The parents of one child may look upon the first signs of sex behavior as a normal manifestation. The parents of another child may regard the same behavior as something that is alarming or loathsome.

By the time children reach the age of four or five most of them have noticed and have become familiar with differences in the external genital organs of the two sexes. This discovery may stimulate interest even though there is a lack of convincing scientific evidence in support of the theory, held by some, that the normal or typical child is emotionally disturbed when he becomes aware of genital differences or that such awareness variously leads to feelings of anxiety or envy or hostility.[17] However, in this as in other aspects of sex behavior children will differ widely and their reactions are likely to be influenced by adult attitudes.

As they move into the preschool years and beyond many children tend to conceal their interest in sex from the eyes and ears of adults. A large proportion of children, if not all, are interested, however, in one way or another. All normal children sooner or later become curious about reproduction and the form of their curiosity or the kind of information they seek is likely to vary as they mature. During elementary-school years a large proportion of children also have experiences relating to sex, such as observation of the sex behavior of animals or people, or being exposed to the advances of older children or adults, undertaking sex play in private, or entering into sex play with their peers. In a study of boys by Ramsay (54), it was found that 72.6 per cent of the boys had had experience with masturbation by the age of twelve. No

---

[17] For a statement of a viewpoint diverging from this statement see Levy (47) and for a study which supports the statement see Conn (12).

physical damage was reported in connection with these experiences but boys did report many fears and much worry. In this same study about a third of the boys reported that they had attempted heterosexual intercourse before adolescence. In a study by Landis, Landis, and Bolles (44) over half of a group of normal single women aged fifteen to thirty years and almost half of a group of normal married women aged twenty-two to thirty-five years reported that they had had experience with sex aggressions, prior to puberty, ranging from exploration of the body by a boy of their own age to sexual advances by an older boy or adult.

Findings such as the foregoing should not be regarded as typical for all communities or for different sections of the population. There are large variations in sex behavior as in all other matters. In any event, findings such as these, while dealing with only a very limited aspect of sex behavior, indicate impressively that a large proportion of preadolescent children have experiences with physical aspects of sex that go beyond a passive, academic interest in the subject.

Findings in various studies show that a large proportion of children have impressions or experiences relating to sex and have discussed the topic with other children before they have received any supplementing information from their parents or from other responsible adults.[18] In view of adult attitudes, this is not, of course, surprising. No matter how wholesome and healthy an adult's attitude may be it would be difficult for him to be entirely certain as to how or when to approach the topic and even the most knowing adult could not be entirely certain as to how to deal with the subject. Moreover even when relationships are very friendly and the child feels completely free to go to the parent he may prefer to discuss some aspects of sex with his own peers. It is likely that there will be matters of interest connected with sex which a ten-year-old does not especially care to discuss with Dad, just as Dad may have interests which he does not discuss with Grandpa. Sys-

---

[18] See studies reported by Willoughby (68).

tematic, scientific findings dealing with the sex development of normal children in our culture and of children's readiness at various maturity levels to receive information and to understand the rules governing sex behavior are very much needed.

Tables XIV and XV show results obtained in a study of questions relating to sex that were asked by children in a study conducted by Hattendorf (31) by means of interviews with parents.

TABLE XIV

CLASSIFICATION OF QUESTIONS WITH RESPECT TO SEX ASKED BY 1797 BOYS AND GIRLS AGED 2 TO 13 YEARS AS REPORTED BY PARENTS[19]

Question	Number	Percentage
Origin of babies	722	40.9
Coming of another baby	256	14.5
Intra-uterine growth	42	2.4
Process of birth	183	10.4
Organs and functions of the body	209	11.9
Physical sex differences	226	12.7
Relation of the father to reproduction	92	5.2
Marriage	36	2.0

TABLE XV

RANK OF INTEREST FOR 865 QUESTIONS OF CHILDREN TWO TO FIVE, 707 QUESTIONS OF CHILDREN SIX TO NINE, AND 191 QUESTIONS OF CHILDREN TEN TO THIRTEEN YEARS CLASSIFIED IN EIGHT GROUPS[19]

Classification	Age, Years 2 to 5	6 to 9	10 to 13
Origin of babies	1	1	2
Coming of another baby	4	2	1
Intra-uterine growth	7	7	8
Process of birth	5	3	5
Organs and functions	3	4	3
Physical sex differences	2	4	6
Relation of father to reproduction	6	6	4
Marriage	8	8	7

[19] Hattendorf, K. W.: "A Study of the Questions of Young Children Concerning Sex: A Phase of an Experimental Approach to Parent Education," *Journal of Social Psychology* (1932), 3:37-65.

The child's attitudes and behavior are influenced, of course, not only by factors relating to the physical aspects of sex but also by countless other factors in the total context in which impressions of his own and of the opposite sex are recorded. His attitude toward members of the opposite sex, his concept of his responsibility and role as a member of his own sex, his capacity for affection, loyalty, and tenderness in his relations with the opposite sex will be influenced by the example set by those about him, by the evidences of affection between his parents, by examples of respect, helpfulness, and the like in relations between adult members of the opposite sex, by countless factors that go into his everyday relations with peers of the opposite sex.

The bearing of this larger context of human relationships on attitudes and behavior relating to sex has not received the attention it deserves. Scientific studies of the development of sex behavior have tended to deal with quite specific interests, attitudes, and practices. Moral precepts and conventional standards have also tended to proscribe specific practices more than to encourage attitudes and ways of behaving on the positive side.

BIBLIOGRAPHY

1. Bayley, N.: "A Study of the Crying of Infants During Mental and Physical Tests," *Journal of Genetic Psychology* (1932), 40:306-329.
2. Bell, J.: *Psychological Aspects of Dental Treatment of Children* (Madison: Journal of Experimental Education, 1943), 87 pp.
3. Blatz, W. E., Allin, K. D., and Millichamp, D. A.: *A Study of Laughter in the Nursery School Child,* University of Toronto Studies in Child Development Series (1936), No. 7, 31 pp.
4. Blatz, W. E., Chant, N. F., and Salter, M. D.: *Emotional Episodes in the Child of School Age,* University of Toronto Studies in Child Development Series (1937), No. 9, 45 pp.
5. Brodbeck, A. J. and Irwin, O. C.: "The Speech Behavior of Infants Without Families," *Child Development* (1946), 17, 145-156.
6. Brumbaugh, F. N.: "Laughter and Teachers," *Educational Method* (1940), 20:69-70.
7. ———: *Stimuli Which Cause Laughter in Children* (New York: New York University Ph.D. dissertation, 1939), 200 pp.

8. Brumbaugh, F. N. and Wilson, F. T.: "Children's Laughter," *Journal of Genetic Psychology* (1940), 57:3-29.
9. Buhler, C.: *The First Year of Life* (New York: Day, 1930), 281 pp.
10. Burt, C.: "The Billeting of Evacuated Children," *British Journal of Educational Psychology* (1940), 10:8-15.
11. Challman, R. C.: "Experiments Concerning Level of Aspiration," *Advanced School Digest* (New York: Teachers College, Columbia University, 1940), 5:61-63.
12. Conn, J. H.: "Children's Reactions to the Discovery of Genital Differences," *American Journal of Orthopsychiatry* (1940), 10:747-755.
13. Davidson, M. A. and Slade, I. M.: "Results of a Survey of Senior School Evacuees," *British Journal of Educational Psychology* (1940), 10:179-195.
14. Dearborn, G. V. N.: *The Emotion of Joy,* Psychological Review Monographs (1898), Vol. II, No. 5, 70 pp.
15. Ding, G. F. and Jersild, A. T.: "A Study of the Laughing and Smiling of Preschool Children," *Journal of Genetic Psychology* (1932), 40:452-472.
16. Dunbar, H. F.: *Emotions and Bodily Changes: A Survey of Literature on Psychosomatic Interrelationships,* second edition (New York: Columbia University Press, 1938), 601 pp.
17. Festinger, L.: "Wish, Expectation, and Group Performance as Factors Influencing Level of Aspiration," *Journal of Abnormal and Social Psychology* (1942), 37:184-200.
18. Fitz-Simons, M. J.: *Some Parent-Child Relationships as Shown in Clinical Case Studies,* Teachers College Contributions to Education (New York: Teachers College, Columbia University, 1935), No. 643, 162 pp.
19. Frank, J. D.: "Some Psychological Determinants of the 'Level of Aspiration,'" *American Journal of Psychology* (1935), 47:285-293.
20. Freud, S.: *Three Contributions to the Theory of Sex,* Nervous and Mental Diseases Monograph Series (1930), No. 7, 104 pp.
21. Gesell, A.: *Infancy and Human Growth* (New York: Macmillan, 1928), 418 pp.
22. Gluek, S. and Glucck, E.: *Juvenile Delinquents Grown Up* (New York: Commonwealth Fund, 1940), 330 pp.
23. Goldfarb, W.: "The Effects of Early Institutional Care on Adolescent Personality," *Journal of Experimental Education* (1943), 12:106-129.
24. Goodenough, F. L.: "Expression of the Emotions in a Blind-Deaf Child," *Journal of Abnormal and Social Psychology* (1932), 27, 3:328-333.
25. ———: "The Expressions of the Emotions in Infancy," *Child Development* (1931), 2, 2:96-101.

26. Goodenough, F. L. and Brian, C. R.: "Certain Factors Underlying the Acquisition of Motor Skill by Preschool Children," *Journal of Experimental Psychology* (1929), 12:127-155.
27. Gould, R.: "An Experimental Analysis of 'Level of Aspiration,'" *Genetic Psychology Monograph* (1939), 21:3-115.
28. Halverson, H. M.: "Genital and Sphincter Behavior of the Male Infant," *Journal of Genetic Psychology* (1940), 56:95-136.
29. Hamilton, G. V.: *A Research in Marriage* (New York: Albert and Charles Boni, 1929), 570 pp.
30. Harms, E.: "The Development of Humor," *Journal of Abnormal and Social Psychology* (1943), 38:351-369.
31. Hattendorf, K. W.: "A Study of the Questions of Young Children Concerning Sex: A Phase of an Experimental Approach to Parent Education," *Journal of Social Psychology* (1932), 3:37-65.
32. Isaacs, S.: *The Nursery Years* (New York: Vanguard Press, 1936), 138 pp.
33. ———: *Social Development in Young Children: A Study of Beginnings* (New York: Harcourt, Brace, 1933), 480 pp.
34. Isaacs, S., Brown, S. C., and Thouless, R. H., editors: *The Cambridge Evacuation Survey* (London: Methuen, 1941), 235 pp.
35. John, E.: "A Study of the Effects of Evacuation and Air Raids on Children of Preschool Age," *British Journal of Educational Psychology* (1941), 11:173-182.
36. Jones, H. E.: "The Galvanic Skin Reflex in Infancy," *Child Development* (1930), 1:106-110.
37. Justin, F.: "A Genetic Study of Laughter Provoking Stimuli," *Child Development* (1932), 3:114-136.
38. Kenderdine, M.: "Laughter in the Pre-School Child," *Child Development* (1931), 2:228-230.
39. Koch, H. L.: "An Analysis of Certain Forms of So-Called 'Nervous Habits' in Young Children," *Journal of Genetic Psychology* (1935), 46:139-170.
40. Krout, M. H. and Stagner, R.: "Personality Development in Radicals," *Sociometry* (1939), 2:31-46.
41. Laing, A.: "The Sense of Humor in Childhood and Adolescence," *British Journal of Educational Psychology* (1939), 9:201.
42. Landis, C.: "Expressions of Emotion," *A Handbook of General Experimental Psychology,* edited by C. Murchison (Worcester: Clark University Press, 1934), Ch. VII, pp. 312-351.
43. Landis, C. and Hunt, W.: *The Startle Pattern* (New York: Farrar and Rinehart, 1939), 168 pp.
44. Landis, C., Landis, A. T., Bolles, M. M., *et al.: Sex in Development* (New York: Hoeber, 1940), 329 pp.

45. Levy, D. M.: *Maternal Overprotection* (New York: Columbia Press, 1943), 417 pp.
46. ———: "Fingersucking and Accessory Movements in Early Infancy," *American Journal of Psychiatry* (1928), 7:881-918.
47. ———: "'Control-Situation' Studies of Children's Responses to the Difference in Genitalia," *American Journal of Orthopsychiatry* (1940), 10:755-763.
48. Levy, J. and Monroe, R.: *The Happy Family* (New York: Knopf, 1938), 319 pp.
49. Lewin, K.: "Behavior and Development as a Function of the Total Situation," *Manual of Child Psychology,* edited by L. Carmichael (New York: Wiley, 1946), Ch. XVI, pp. 791-844.
50. Lewin, K., Dembo, T., Festinger, L., and Sears, P. S.: "Level of Aspiration," *Personality and the Behavior Disorders,* edited by J. McV. Hunt (New York: Ronald Press, 1944), Vol. I, Ch. X, pp. 333-378.
51. Montagu, M. F. A.: "The Acquisition of Sexual Knowledge in Children," *American Journal of Orthopsychiatry* (1945), 15:290-300.
52. Murphy, L. B.: *Social Behavior and Child Personality* (New York: Columbia University Press, 1937), 344 pp.
53. Omwake, L.: "Factors Influencing the Sense of Humor," *Journal of Social Psychology* (1939), 10:95-104.
54. Ramsay, G. V.: "The Sexual Development of Boys," *American Journal of Psychology* (1943), 56:217-233.
55. Remmers, H. H. and Thompson, L. A., Jr.: "A Note on Motor Activity as Conditioned by Emotional States," *Journal of Applied Psychology* (1925), 9:417-423.
56. Ribble, M. A.: *The Rights of Infants, Early Psychological Needs, and Their Satisfaction* (New York: Columbia Press, 1943), 118 pp.
57. Sears, P. S.: "Levels of Aspiration in Academically Successful and Unsuccessful Children," *Journal of Abnormal and Social Psychology* (1940), 9:498-536.
57a. Sears, R. R.: *Survey of Objective Studies of Psychoanalytic Concept* (New York: Social Science Research Council, 1943), Bulletin 51, 156 pp.
58. Sherman, M.: "The Differentiation of Emotional Responses in Infants," *Journal of Comparative Psychology* (1927), 7:265-284.
59. Simpson, M. S.: *Parent Preferences of Young Children,* Contributions to Education (New York: Teachers College, Columbia University, 1935), No. 652, 83 pp.
60. Skeels, H. M., Updegraff, R., Wellman, B. L., and Williams, H. M.: *A Study of Environmental Stimulation: An Orphanage Preschool Project,* University of Iowa Studies in Child Welfare (1938), No. 4, 191 pp.

61. Stagner, R.: "Studies of Aggressive Social Attitudes: III. The Role of Personal and Family Scores," *Journal of Social Psychology* (1944), 20:129-140.
62. Stagner, R. and Drought, N.: "Measuring Children's Attitudes Toward Their Parents," *Journal of Educational Psychology* (1935), 26:169-176.
63. Symonds, P. M.: "A Study of Parental Acceptance and Rejection," *American Journal of Orthopsychiatry* (1938), 8:679-688.
64. Thompson, J.: "Development of Facial Expression of Emotion in Blind and Seeing Children," *Archives of Psychology,* No. 264.
65. Thorndike, E. L.: *Educational Psychology, Vol. II. The Original Nature of Man* (New York: Teachers College, Columbia University, 1913), 327 pp.
66. Washburn, R. W.: *A Study of the Smiling and Laughing of Infants in the First Year of Life,* Genetic Psychology Monographs (1928), 6:397-539.
67. Watson, J. B.: *Psychological Care of Infant and Child* (New York: Norton, 1928), 195 pp.
68. Willoughby, R. R.: *Sexuality in the Second Decade,* Monograph of the Society for Research in Child Development (1937), Vol. 2, No. 10, 57 pp.
69. Witmer, H. L., et al.: *The Outcome of Treatment in a Child Guidance Clinic, a Comparison and an Evaluation,* Smith College Studies in Social Work (June, 1933), 339-399.

Chapter VIII

FEELING AND EMOTION (*Continued*)

FEAR

During infancy, a child's fears arise mainly in response to happenings in his immediate environment. As he grows older, the range of his fears grows wider, for as he acquires the ability to dwell upon the past and to anticipate the future, a large proportion of his fears concern remote and distant dangers and forebodings as to what the future may bring.

There have been various theories as to what are the original or unlearned fear stimuli. In an earlier day, there were theories to the effect that we are endowed with many instinctive fears, such as fear of animals, of the occult, of death, of large bodies of water, and so forth. Later the theory was advanced that there are only two original, "natural" fear stimuli, namely, loud noises and sudden displacement or loss of support (48, 49). This account of fear has been found to be quite oversimplified. The circumstances that may give rise to so-called "unlearned" fears in the infant include not simply noises and loss of support, but any intense, sudden, unexpected, or novel stimulus for which the organism appears to be unprepared.

Moreover, the fear stimulus cannot be described as consisting of an isolated stimulus, such as a noise of a given intensity and quality. Depending upon the condition of the organism at the time —whether, for example, it is in a state of tension or relaxation—a certain noise may produce fear at one time but not at another. In like manner, a given happening may produce fear in one child and not in another. It is necessary to take account not only of the condition of the individual who is responding but also of the setting of the external stimulus. English (5), for example, describes how a loud noise that was sounded just as a fourteen-months-old child was reaching for a toy failed to arouse fear; on the other hand, a child on one occasion, for no detectable reason, suddenly showed marked fear of a familiar pair of patent-leather shoes that were standing in bright sunlight. A noise and a sudden movement, each of which alone elicits no response, may, in combination, produce signs of fear; again, a jolt or slight displacement may provoke no response when the child is being cared for by a familiar person but may elicit fear if he is being cared for by an unfamiliar person.[1]

THE ROLE OF MATURATION

The young infant is unaffected by many stimuli that will frighten him at a later time when his capacities for perception and discrimination have matured. An example of this was given in the chapter on social behavior: at about six months, many children show shyness and occasionally distinct signs of fear at the approach of a stranger, while previously they have shown no such reaction. This response depends not simply on previous "conditioning" in the realm of fear alone, but upon factors associated with added mental maturity which render the child responsive to details which he did not notice at an earlier time.

The fact that the tendency to respond to an event as actually or potentially dangerous is relative to the child's level of development has been noted in many studies (19, 28). Gesell's (11) account of the response of infants at different ages to confinement in a small pen offers a further illustration. At ten weeks, the child may be completely complaisant in this situation; at twenty weeks, he may exhibit mild apprehension, as betrayed by signs of dissatisfaction, "persistent head-turning and social seeking"; at thirty weeks, his response to the same situation "may be so vigorously expressed by

---

[1] English (5), Jersild and Holmes (19), and Valentine (47) give illustrations of the difficulty of predicting when a child will be afraid.

crying that we describe the reaction as fear or fright." As the child matures, new things affect him by reason of his keener perceptions, and fear is likely to arise when the individual knows enough to recognize the potential danger in a situation but has not "advanced to the point of a complete comprehension and control of the changing situation" (27).

Changes with age in fear responses appeared impressively in a study by Jones and Jones (27), in which a large, active, harmless snake was set free in an enclosure with persons of various ages. Children up to the age of two years showed no fear of the snake; children aged three and four tended to be cautious and hesitated to approach or touch the snake; more definite signs of fear were displayed more often after the age of four and were more pronounced in adults than in children.

Changing susceptibility to fear is interwoven with other aspects of the child's development in many ways. With the development of the child's imaginative abilities, his fears become increasingly concerned with imaginary dangers. With the development of the meaning of competition and of awareness of his status as compared with others, there frequently come fears of loss of prestige, ridicule, and failure (19). The wider the scope and range of a child's understanding the more he is able to recognize possibilities of disaster. This does not mean, fortunately, that the child becomes more and more afraid, for with a gain in understanding there also is likely to be a waning of fears due to ignorance and a gain in ability to discount dangers that are highly improbable and to cope with danger that actually might occur. The fears that arise at various stages of development depend not upon specific past experiences alone, not upon "growth" alone, but upon all the complex factors involved both in experience and in growth.

Associated with the fact that maturation plays an important role in children's fears is the fact that a child who is precocious or advanced in his development may be afraid of events which do not disturb other children of his own age. A bright two-year-old may show fear of events which do not disturb the child of average mental ability until several months later (17).

THE ROLE OF LEARNING

While a child's susceptibilities change as he matures, fears are also influenced by learning to an important degree. By virtue of a painful experience, or of having been startled or overwhelmed, he may "learn" to fear something which earlier did not disturb him.

This learning may be quite direct, specific, and restricted: a child is bowled over by a dog and later fears that dog. Again, the effects may be more general: the child may fear not only the dog that hurt him but all dogs and, perhaps, he may be on guard, as never before, whenever he sees any four-footed animal. Similarly, he may not only be afraid when he sees a dog but he may also be apprehensive when he passes the yard where he knows a dog is kept, even though no dog is in sight.

The process by which fear is acquired may also involve indirect or intermediate steps. For example, a child who had been knocked down but not seriously injured by an automobile was still quite wrought up when he went to bed and then he had a bad dream. Thereafter he was afraid of going into his bedroom when dark. Through the dream, the accident and its emotional effects had been placed, so to speak, in the setting of darkness. Once a child is frightened, his fear may thus spread to many other things and conditions, as will be noted more particularly in a later section.

CHANGES WITH AGE IN THE EXPRESSION OF FEAR

As children grow older, there tends to be a decrease in the number of occasions per day or week when they exhibit overt signs of fear, such as crying, trembling, shrinking, retreating, or clinging to an adult. However, this does not mean that there is a corresponding decline in the role of fear in the child's everyday life.

The decline in overt expression occurs, in part, as a feature of the child's general tendency toward less overt expression of emotion as he grows older. The decline is associated also, in part, with changes in the character of the dangers which the child fears: lingering fears of imaginary dangers, or of misfortunes that might occur, seldom express themselves in sudden starts, cries, or fleeing. Just as fear reactions may occur in countless varieties and degrees as a child grows older, ranging from transitory fear of a specific person or event to less clearly formulated anxieties, foreboding, feelings of guilt, and uncertainty, so also the expression of fear may take on innumerable forms and occur in countless disguises.

Many social pressures are brought to bear upon children to get them to conceal or disguise their fears. Children themselves taunt each other with epithets such as "Fraidy Cat." Adults also, in many ways, discourage the display of fear, not only by practices such as asking the child to "be big" or to "be brave," but also, sometimes quite unintentionally, by the practice of telling children that there really is nothing to fear. What an adult thus says to reassure a child may fail to dispel the child's fear and only give the child the impression that it is cowardly of him to be afraid. The pressure on a child to conceal fear comes not only from his peers and from his elders but also frequently by way of ideals that are held up to him in stories and poems that he hears or reads.

By virtue of the premium that is placed on not being afraid, or, at least, on not revealing that he is afraid, the child may be driven to the point that one of his fears is the fear of showing fear. Most children, at quite an early age, get the idea that it is shameful to be afraid.

Children use a great variety of techniques and guises to conceal their fears. Following are only a few examples.

A girl of three and a half years asked her mother to fetch a doll that had been left in a room separated by a hallway from the rest of the house, and kept insisting after the mother had suggested that she get it herself. The mother, suspecting what was the matter, said, "I'll hold the door while you get it." At this the girl ran happily to the room and got the doll. The mother knew that the child had been frightened previously by the slamming of a door in this hallway, and now, instead of admitting that she was afraid, she was trying to commandeer her mother. A person unacquainted with the circumstances would not have suspected that the child was afraid but might instead have thought that the girl was being quite unreasonable.

Another example involves a girl of seven who, two nights in succession, after having been put to bed, insisted that she had to go downstairs because she had forgotten to bring a blanket for her doll and asked her mother to go with her since she did not like to go alone. On the second night, her mother, thinking that the girl was merely trying to delay her bedtime, refused to accompany her, so finally she had to go by herself. She hurriedly went all the way to the basement where she got the blanket; then she apparently went on another quick errand on the first floor, and then returned to bed. A few minutes later she revealed that the main reason why she had gone downstairs was to make sure that the front door was locked. On some previous nights she had anxiously inquired as to whether the front door was locked. It appeared that her trip downstairs was motivated by fear and that she was using the "forgotten" doll blanket simply as a device for making sure that the door was locked.

A further example concerns a boy of ten. He had earned two passes to a circus, but on coming home from the afternoon performance he said he did not care to go again and so he gave his remaining pass to his brother. It was not until some time later that he happened to reveal that on his way out of the circus grounds during the afternoon he had been threatened and chased by two older boys who belonged to the circus, and that he did not go to the show again because he was afraid.

The foregoing items illustrate only a few of the ways in which fears may be disguised. To understand the child who is afraid, it is necessary to be alert to such disguises, although no adult can be expected to be all-knowing. What seems to happen often is that parents assume that their child is quite free from fear when actually he is afraid of many things (19). Needless to say, the concealment of fear makes it all the more difficult for adults to help the child to cope with fear.

AGE TRENDS

Table XVI and Figure 5, which are based upon information obtained from parents, show certain age trends in children's overtly expressed fears, notably a decline with age in fears in response to certain tangible and immediate situations[1] (such as specific objects, noises, falling and danger of falling, strange objects and persons, and so forth) and an increase with age in the percentage of children who show fear of imaginary creatures, of the dark, of being alone or abandoned, and so forth.

Table XVI shows findings obtained in a study by Holmes (17) in which semiexperimental situations were used to investigate children's fears. The situations included: being left alone (a concealed observer watches the child as he is left alone in the experimenting room when the experimenter leaves with the excuse that she has to get her handkerchief in another part of the building); falling boards (two inclined boards so arranged that, as the child steps from one to the other, one board suddenly tilts and gives way a distance of two inches); a dark room (the child is asked to retrieve a ball seemingly inadvertently thrown by the experimenter into a long, narrow, dark passageway); a strange person (with the child in the room, and in his path if he endeavors to reach a box of toys, is a woman rakishly dressed in a long gray coat, large black hat, and a black veil that obscures the features of her face); high

---

[1] Table XVI and Fig. 5 show results obtained when a tally of one only was given in the case of each child who exhibited *one* or *several* fears of a given category. The relative frequency of various fear categories would be different if each additional item in a given category received a new tally (such as three tallies under "Animals" if a child mentions lions, tigers, and wolves (38)).

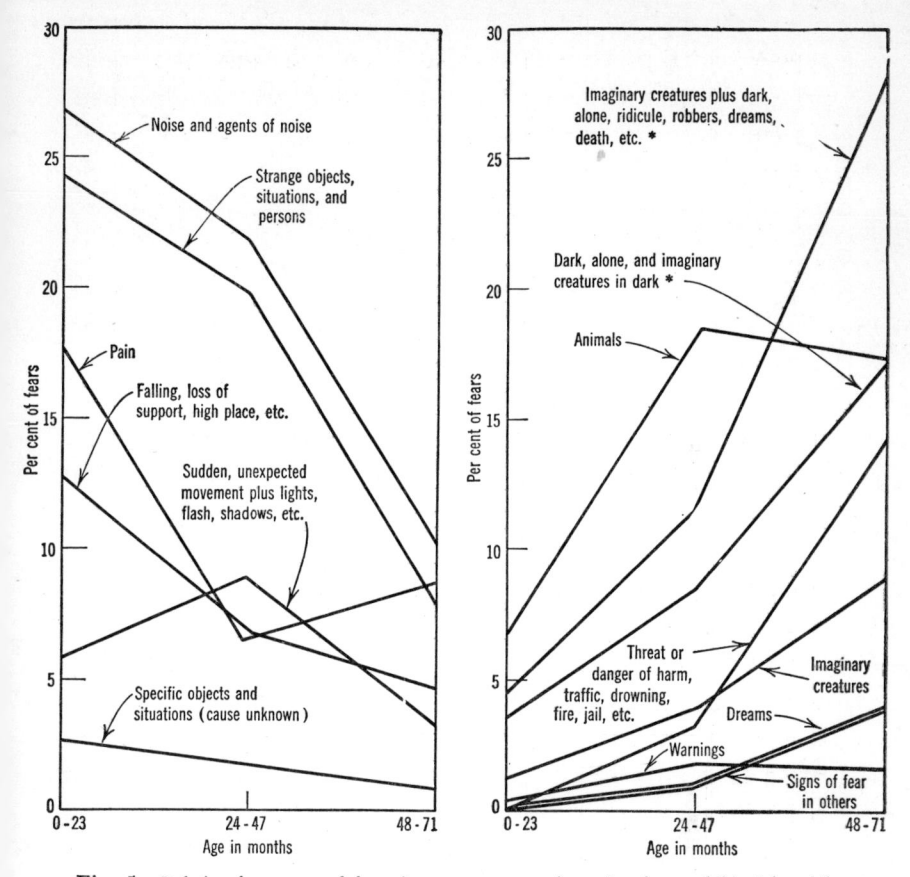

Fig. 5. Relative frequency of fears in response to various situations exhibited by children who were observed by parents or teachers. The data include 146 records of observation of children for periods of 21 days (31, 91, and 24 at the respective bi-yearly levels), combined with occasional records of 117 additional children (27, 67, and 23 at the respective levels). Adapted from *Children's Fears* by A. T. Jersild and F. B. Holmes, Child Development Monographs, 1935, No. 20, by permission of the publisher. Starred items represent the cumulative tally of two or more categories that also are depicted separately.

boards (the child is asked to walk across a plank raised at elevations of from about two to over six feet from the floor); a loud sound (produced by sharply striking an iron pipe with a hammer); a snake (the child is asked to pick a toy out of a box in which is a live snake, two feet in length); a large dog (the child

TABLE XVI

FREQUENCY AND RELATIVE FREQUENCY OF SITUATIONS IN WHICH CHILDREN WERE AFRAID DURING A PERIOD OF THREE WEEKS, AS REPORTED BY PARENTS[2]

[The first column shows total number of fears reported at all age levels combined. The second and subsequent columns show the percentage of children showing one or more fears in each classification at various yearly age levels. The third division of the table shows the percentage of children at biyearly age levels (up to 6 years) who exhibited fears in each of the categories. Separately computed percentages for several categories combined are shown in italics.]

Situation in Response to Which Fear Was Shown	Total Number of Fears Reported	\multicolumn{7}{c}{Percentage of Children Exhibiting One or More Fears in Each Category at Yearly Age Levels}	\multicolumn{3}{c}{Percentage of Children Exhibiting Fears in Each Category at Biyearly Age Levels to 6 Years}
Age in months........	3–97	0–11	12–23	24–35	36–47	48–59	60–97		0–23	24–47	48–71
Number of children....	153	8	23	45	46	21	9		31	91	24
I. Animals (not including imaginary animals)......	117	25	34.7	40	45.7	40.9	0		32.3	42.9	37.5
II. Specific objects and situations not described as strange (cause unknown)........	12	12.5	8.7	8.9	4.3	0	0		9.7	6.6	0
III. Sudden unexpected movements........	32	25	4.5	22.2	6.5	4.5	0		9.7	14.3	4.2
IV. Lights, flashes, shadows, reflections.........	11	12.5	8.7	8.9	2.2	0	0		9.7	5.5	0
V. Sudden disappearance of persons.............	2	0	0	4.4	0	0	0		0	2.2	0
VI. Rapidly approaching or passing objects (distinct from noise)............	1	0	0	0.0	2.2	0	0		0	1.1	0
VII. Sudden or rapidly approaching motion plus noise.	14	25	4.5	13.3	4.5	4.5	0		9.7	8.8	4.2
A. III–IV: *Sudden, rapid motion, lights, flashes, shadows, reflections*........	*60*	*25*	*17.4*	*37.8*	*13*	*9.1*	*0*		*19.6*	*25.3*	*8.3*
VIII. Noises and events feared by reason of previous association with noise........	157	75	60.9	55.6	37	22.7	0		64.5	46.2	20.8
B. VII–VIII: *Noises, events associated with noise, and noise plus motion*........	*171*	*75*	*60.9*	*57.8*	*41.3*	*27.3*	*0*		*64.5*	*49.5*	*25*
IX. Falling, heights, danger of falling, sudden or gradual displacement.......	58	37.5	34.8	33.3	13	13.6	0		35.5	23.1	12.5
X. Pain, persons, objects, situations inflicting or associated with pain and tactual shock........	82	25	52.2	20	15.2	13.6	55.5		45.2	17.6	16.7

[2] From Jersild, A. T. and Holmes, F. B.: *Children's Fears*, Child Development Monographs (New York, Teachers College, Columbia University, 1935). No. 20, 356 pp. Reproduced by permission.

TABLE XVI (Continued)

	Situation in Response to Which Fear Was Shown	Total Number of Fears Reported	\multicolumn{6}{c	}{Percentage of Children Exhibiting One or More Fears in Each Category at Yearly Age Levels}	\multicolumn{3}{c	}{Percentage of Children Exhibiting Fears in Each Category at Bi-yearly Age Levels to 6 Years}
			0–11	12–23	24–35	36–47	48–59	60–97	0–23	24–47	48–71
Age in months		3–97	8	23	45	46	21	9	31	91	24
Number of children		153									
XI.	Strange objects and situations and unfamiliar variations connected with familiar objects	58	25	39.1	28.9	6.5	18.2	0	35.5	17.6	16.7
XII.	Strange active or inactive persons, queer people, masked persons, unfamiliar variations connected with familiar persons	92	50	39.1	37.8	26.1	13.6	11.1	41.9	31.9	12.5
	XI–XII: *Strange objects, situations and persons*	*150*	*50*	*52.2*	*53.3*	*30.4*	*18.2*	*11.1*	*51.6*	*41.8*	*16.7*
C.											
XIII.	Bodily harm or danger or threat of injury (apart from falling or specific pain stimulation)	23	0	0	4.4	21.7	22.7	11.1	0	12.1	20.8
XIV.	Warning or previous threat	15	0	4.5	8.9	4.3	4.5	22.2	3.2	6.6	4.2
D.	*IX, XIII, XIV: Harm, danger of bodily injury, falling*	*96*	*37.5*	*34.8*	*33.3*	*34.8*	*31.8*	*33.3*	*35.5*	*33*	*29.2*
XV.	Signs of fear in others	5	0	0	4.4	2.2	9.1	0	0	3.3	8.3
XVI.	Danger of loss of property	1	0	0	0	2.2	0	0	0	1.1	0
XVII.	Fears arising during dreams	7	0	0	6.7	0	9.1	11.1	0	3.3	12.5
XVIII.	Ridicule, failure, personal inadequacy	6	0	0	0	0	0	22.2	0	0	0
XIX.	Robbers, kidnappers, etc., also death and dying (no immediate danger)	2	0	0	0	0	4.5	11.1	0	0	4.2
XX.	The dark and being alone in dark	24	0	8.7	11.1	8.7	9.1	22.2	6.5	10	12.5
XXI.	Being alone or abandoned by parent	19	0	13	8.9	8.7	9.1	11.1	9.7	8.8	12.5
XXII.	The dark or being alone plus expressed fear of imaginary creatures	13	0	0	8.9	2.2	9.1	0	0	5.5	8.3
E.	*XX, XXI, XXII: Dark, alone, and imaginary creatures when alone or in dark*	*56*	*0*	*21.7*	*24.4*	*19.6*	*18.2*	*22.2*	*16.1*	*22*	*20.8*
XXIII.	Imaginary creatures (apart from darkness or being alone)	18	0	13	8.9	2.2	13.6	11.1	9.7	5.5	16.7
F.	*XXII–XXIII: Imaginary creatures*	*31*	*0*	*13*	*15.6*	*4.3*	*22.7*	*11.1*	*9.7*	*10*	*25*
G.	*XVII–XXIII: Dreams, ridicule, death, robbers, etc., dark, alone, imaginary creatures*	*89*	*0*	*30.4*	*35.6*	*19.6*	*45.5*	*55.5*	*22.6*	*27.5*	*50*

is asked to go and pat a dog that is brought in on a leash). The experimental situations were not designed to frighten the child (except for the possibility that he might be startled by the noise and the inclined board), but rather to confront the child with a situation into which he could choose to enter and participate or from which he could withdraw and retreat. Detailed records of what the children did were made by observers, and the presence or absence of "fear" was determined according to carefully formulated definitions and criteria. The number of children at each yearly age level ranged from twelve to forty-five, with the smallest numbers at sixty to seventy-one months.

TABLE XVII

PERCENTAGE OF CHILDREN AT YEARLY AGE LEVELS FROM 24 TO 71 MONTHS WHO SHOWED FEAR IN VARIOUS EXPERIMENTAL SITUATIONS[3]

Situation	\multicolumn{4}{c}{Percentage of Children Showing Fear}
	24–35 months	36–47 months	48–59 months	60–71 months
I. Being left alone	12.1	15.6	7.0	0
II. Falling boards	24.2	8.9	0	0
III. Dark room	46.9	51.1	35.7	0
IV. Strange person	31.3	22.2	7.1	0
V. High boards	35.5	35.6	7.1	0
VI. Loud sound	22.6	20.0	14.3	0
VII. Snake	34.8	55.6	42.9	30.8
VIII. Large dog	61.9	42.9	42.9	...
Total	32.0	30.2	18.1	4.5

Results in a study of this kind do not show the extent to which a stimulus of a certain class (such as the presence of a snake) will be more or less fear-inspiring than stimuli of another class (such as loud noises), since it is not possible to equate these stimuli and since a child's response will be influenced by surrounding circumstances which may vary from time to time. But the results shown

---

[3] From Holmes, F. B.: "An Experimental Study of the Fears of Young Children," Jersild, A. T. and Holmes, F. B.: *Children's Fears,* Child Development Monographs (New York: Teachers College, Columbia University, 1935), No. 20, Pt. III, pp. 167-296. Reproduced by permission.

in Table XVII do give clear indications of some trends. There was a general trend toward a decrease with age in fear of the specific situations employed in the study. At the five-year level, only the snake elicited signs of fear. At five years, even the dark room did not produce overt symptoms of fear (but undoubtedly the presence of an adult accounted for this; for, according to their own reports, many children of this age are afraid of dark places, especially when they are alone).

Limited situations such as those that can be used in this experiment do not, of course, tap the fears of older children. On the other hand, at a given age level, an experimental situation may reveal fears that parents have failed to discern. Holmes found, for example, that the percentage of children who were afraid of the dark was considerably larger than the frequency of such fears according to the observations and reports of parents.

Many children have fears or apprehensions in which there is an element of fear of punishment or a feeling of guilt or remorse for past misdeeds. In a study of fifth- and sixth-grade children in which a list of "worries" was presented, it was found that a large proportion of children checked items having to do with punishment, being scolded, "making parents sad," telling lies, doing wrong, and the like. The view that fears may represent underlying conflicts, guilt feelings, and concealed anxieties is brought out in psychoanalytic writings (8, 31). Klein (31) cites the case of a child who was afraid of being left alone or abandoned by her mother; according to Klein, this fear arose as a result of the child's desire to injure her mother (because her mother was pregnant).

A tendency to be apprehensive, even though no specific fear that can be named or identified is involved, often occurs as a feature of shyness and various forms of "withdrawing" behavior. In a study by Pritchard and Ojemann of children who were rated by their teachers as being "insecure" (39), it was found that such children, along with other symptoms, exhibited a greater tendency to be apprehensive than did children rated as emotionally "secure."

CHILDREN'S FEARS AS COMPARED WITH "WORST HAPPENINGS"

The extent to which children's fears, as reported by the children themselves, are formulated in terms different from prosaic day-to-day hurts and vicissitudes is illustrated by a comparison between accounts given by school-age children of their fears and of the "worst thing that ever happened" to them. Such a comparison is shown in Table XVIII. In describing "worst happenings," the children predominantly mentioned definite misfortunes, illnesses, and other unpleasant experiences that had actually befallen them. Their fears, by contrast, were predominantly described in terms

TABLE XVIII

FREQUENCY OF MENTION OF VARIOUS CATEGORIES IN CHILDREN'S OWN DESCRIPTIONS OF THEIR FEARS AND OF THE WORST THINGS THAT EVER HAPPENED TO THEM [4]

[Abridged results, based upon interviews with 398 children aged 5 to 12 years.]

	Percentage of Children Naming Event	
Event Described	In Describing Actual "Worst Happenings"	In Describing Fears
Bodily injury, falling, illness, traffic accident, operations, hurts and pains, *etc.*	72.7	12.8
Attack or danger of attack by animals	1.8	13.7
Contacts with, or activities of, criminals, kidnappers, burglars, bad characters, *etc.*	1.3	8.0
Being alone, in dark, in strange place, being lost, and dangers associated with being alone, darkness, *etc.*	2.3	14.6
Death, loss, removal of relatives, being abandoned by relatives	5.0	1.4
Contacts with, or activities of, or dangers from supernatural agents, ghosts, witches, corpses, mysterious agents or events	0.0	19.2
Scolding, embarrassment, being teased, ridiculed, *etc.*	4.5	3.4
Remaining categories	12.4	26.9

[4] From Jersild, A. T., Markey, F. V., and Jersild, C. L.: *Children's Fears, Dreams, Wishes, Daydreams, Likes, Dislikes, Pleasant and Unpleasant Memories*, Child Development Monographs (New York: Teachers College, Columbia University, 1933), No. 12, 172 pp. Reproduced by permission.

of somewhat vague calamities that might occur. Actual harrowing experiences with animals, for example, constituted less than two per cent of the "worst happenings," but fear of animals (mainly remote animals such as wolves, lions, gorillas, and so forth) represented about fourteen per cent of reported fears.

The fears of children (and the same tends to hold true for adults) tend, in many areas, to go far beyond the statistical probabilities that the feared disasters actually will occur. In one study it was noted that in a school system in which the percentage of failure or nonpromotion was less than two, the percentage of children who said they "worried" about the possibility of not being promoted was about fifty (18). However, even such an apparently irrational fear may have a certain logic of its own. Until the final report is made there is a mathematical chance (in the given example) that a child *might* fail and this uncertainty may be aggravated by the child's own feeling that he perhaps is not as diligent as he might be.

PERSISTING FEARS

Although many fears wane and even seem to disappear, a large proportion of childhood fears persist in one form or another into adult years. Fears most likely to wane or to be modified with time are those that have reference to relatively concrete situations—such as specific objects, steam shovels, a hole in the sidewalk, lights and shadows, strange or unfamiliar persons, and objects or places to which the child becomes accustomed in the normal course of his experience—and fears arising from a harrowing experience which does not happen to recur or to be reinforced by other experiences. Even though many such fears seem to vanish, many others may persist, either in their original or in a modified form.

In a study of childhood fears as recalled by adults (19), it was found that in the case of 804 fears concerning which information as to the subsequent outcomes was reported, over forty per cent still persisted into adult years. This percentage cannot, of course,

TABLE XIX

"WORRIES" OF FIFTH- AND SIXTH-GRADE CHILDREN AS REVEALED BY THEIR RESPONSES TO A "WHAT DO YOU WORRY ABOUT?" TEST [5]

Responses	Boys N = 287 % responding				Girls N = 282 % responding			
	Often	Sometimes	Often or Sometimes	Never	Often	Sometimes	Often or Sometimes	Never
Items Relating to School								
Failing a test	15	73	87	13	17	76	93	7
Being late for school	15	47	62	38	15	54	69	31
Being scolded by teacher	6	63	69	31	9	59	68	32
Being left back in school	17	41	58	42	15	39	54	46
Being poor in spelling	19	41	60	40	13	38	51	49
Being called on by teacher to answer questions	11	39	50	50	4	45	49	51
Being poor in reading	7	37	44	56	7	36	43	57
Having a poor report card	16	58	74	26	23	56	79	21
Being told you are wrong by other pupils	5	44	49	51	5	37	42	58
Not doing as well as other children	12	57	69	31	10	56	66	34
Giving a report in class	10	35	45	55	13	31	44	56
Being poor in arithmetic	18	49	67	33	14	53	67	33
Not being good at drawing or printing	12	33	45	55	9	37	46	54
Nonschool Items								
The dreams you have	7	29	36	64	4	30	34	66
Being scolded by father or mother	13	67	80	20	13	66	79	21
Falling or being in a high place	10	32	42	58	7	46	53	47
Dying or being killed	9	19	28	72	11	21	32	68
Being made fun of by other children	5	28	33	67	4	29	33	67
Being bitten by a dog	6	28	34	66	6	31	37	63
Ghosts, spooks	3	16	19	81	4	14	18	82
Being kidnapped	5	16	21	79	9	23	32	68
Strange people following you	5	28	33	67	21	34	55	45
Being alone in the dark	8	33	41	59	11	32	43	57
Losing your friends	7	38	45	55	9	44	53	47
Being hit by rough children	3	42	45	55	9	32	41	59
Average of all items relating to school	13	47	60	40	11	47	58	42
Average of all items not relating to school	7	31	38	62	9	34	43	57

[5] Adapted from Jersild, A. T., Goldman, B., and Loftus, J. J., "A Comparative Study of the Worries of Children in Two School Situations," *Journal of Experimental Education* (1941), 9:323-326. Reproduced by permission.

be accepted without reservation, since adults would be likely to recall the fears that still persisted and to forget many passing fears that had waned, and fears reported to have vanished might have influenced later fears in a manner not recognized by the adults. At any rate, results such as these, as well as snatches of information that one can gain through informal observation and conversation with adults, indicate that there is a large carry-over of childhood fear into later years. Of the fears described in this particular study as "still persisting," about twenty-seven per cent were also described as being the "most intense" fears recalled from childhood, and twenty-eight per cent were described as being the "earliest recalled" fears.

Among the fears that show the largest carry-over into later years are fears of animals, of bodily harm through such dangers as fire, illness, drowning, and the like, and of dangers associated with the supernatural, with the dark, and with being alone. Many such continuing fears undoubtedly are a reflection of anxiety or areas of conflict or insecurity in a person's life.

FACTORS CONTRIBUTING TO SUSCEPTIBILITY TO FEAR

From an early age there are differences in the extent to which children are frightened or startled, although the nature of these differences has not been well explored.

Since actual weakness and incompetence in the face of a situation that demands an adjustment is an obvious factor in the occurrence of fear, anything that weakens the child may render him more susceptible.

Again, anything that lowers the child's confidence in himself is likely to increase his tendency to be afraid.

Apart from fears that arise in a relatively "straightforward" manner through a harrowing experience—as in the case of the child mentioned above who feared a dog after having been knocked over and bitten—there are fears that are influenced to a large degree by underlying tensions, due to a variety of factors in the child's daily life, and fears that are aggravated by vicarious stimulation. Frequently in children, as in adults, the particular event or condition that is feared is relatively incidental. Just as an adult who is tense, fatigued, harassed, or lacking in confidence may now worry about his health, now be apprehensive concerning his ability to do his job, now reflect anxiously upon his past misdeeds, so a child may fasten now upon this, now upon that, as the focus of his fears. The factors underlying fear involve all the complex and diverse influences that have been involved in an individual's life history.

It appears that many of the fears that children describe serve as an image or projection of forebodings and anxieties which the child is unable fully to define. When a child, for example, reports that he is afraid of lions, or of "a corpse, like a dead person I saw once, I can still see him before my eyes," or of "an old man with a black beard and small, hard eyes," the imagery of his fear may be quite vivid; but this image may represent underlying apprehensions that are far from clear, just as the images and events that occur in a nightmare do not explicitly represent the fatigue, illness, emotional turmoil, or other disturbances that played a part in precipitating the nightmare.

Threats and intimidation. Among influences that aggravate a child's fears are threats by parents, teachers, and playmates. Lurid stories about accidents, deaths, ghosts, criminals, and catastrophes may also function as implied threats. In the study cited above (19), numerous instances were reported of appeals to fear by parents, as a means of discipline and intimidation. Following are a few illustrations, as reported by the subjects themselves:

By way of reprimanding a six-year-old boy for striking his sister, the boy's mother told him that because of what he had done a time would come when he would not be able to move the hand that had struck his sister. The mother then described what happened to a neighbor's child. When this child died, the mother said, his hand was outside the coffin, and no one could put it inside, so that the lid of the coffin could not be closed until a parson had struck the hand, when it slipped back into the coffin; in the meantime, "everybody talked about this child, and laughed and laughed, *and this may also happen to you.*" A child's fear that his mother might die (his mother actually was sickly) was aggravated by taunts from other members of his family, who told him that the mother would leave this earth because the boy was so mischievous. Numerous accounts were given of similar techniques, such as threatening that the child would be put into a "big, black hole," threatening him with abandonment, with being locked in the cellar, attic, or closet, and with specific objects that had been described to the child as being sinister (such as a broken doll's head which a maid kept in a closet, a menacing picture hanging on the wall, and a teddy bear that was kept in a dark room).

In many instances in which such techniques are used, the specific form that the threat or intimidation takes is less important than the hostility and rejection that underlie the threats.

It is hard to conceive of anything more brutal than a policy of using terror as a means of controlling a child. But it is not merely older children or a child's elders who thus play on a child's fears. The whole of society conspires and contrives to use fear for ulterior ends. So it is that the main support of morality, the incentive to thrift, honesty, and sobriety and all the virtues so often lies not in a bent for what is good but in fear of consequences of doing wrong. The point that anxiety, involving fear of punishment and fear of loss of social approval, is an important factor in bringing a person into conformity with standards has been emphasized by Davis (3).

In passing, it may be noted that, at the present time, children are apparently being exposed to more vicarious fear stimulation than was the case in earlier generations in the form of sensational newspapers, the speedy communication of catastrophe, exciting movies and radio programs, and so on. Although, as noted above, children's fears are influenced to a considerable degree by these factors, it does not appear that the fears of children today, as reported by themselves, differ substantially from the fears of children of a generation ago, as reported by adults in recollections of their childhood fears. More important than this or that specific form of excitement that may prevail at one time and not at another, it seems, is the undertow of factors leading to insecurity, and the threats and other forms of intimidation that carry on from one generation to the next.

Influence of example. Apart from deliberate attempts to frighten, adults may have a distinct influence on a child's fears through the example set by their own fears. By obvious or subtle manifestations of their fears, adults may not only suggest to the child the presence of danger but also weaken the child's conviction of security in their protection. In a study by Hagman (15), a correlation of 0.667 was found between the gross number of children's fears and the gross number of mothers' fears, as reported by the mothers. A study by John (26) of children's reactions to wartime events, such as an air raid, likewise emphasizes the influence of adult example.

Ulterior uses of assumed fears. In passing, it should be noted that a child's display of fear may come to serve an ulterior purpose, as when he proclaims his fear of the dark in order to have company at bedtime or, at a later age, uses a plea of fear of going out alone to the woodshed, with the result that he gets help in carrying in the wood. There are countless ways in which such factors, both deliberate and unwitting, may play a role in motivating expressions of fear. A person may even appeal to his own fears as a means of condoning his actions, as when he uses this device to excuse his lack of ambition and industry.

VALUES OF FEAR

Any condition that mobilizes an individual's energies and puts him on the alert in the face of danger is obviously of tremendous value as a protection against possible harm. Even anxieties and apprehensions concerning dangers that are never likely to befall him may have a salutary effect. Yet, it may be observed that fear often produces commotion and consumes energy without helping much to solve the underlying problem. The bodily changes accompanying fright presumably help a person to face an emergency and give him greater strength and endurance for fight or for flight (2). However, often in modern life an issue which one fears cannot be solved by using one's fists or taking to one's heels. If a worried student could pass a hard examination by outrunning his instructor or by throwing him out of the window, the energies mobilized within him would be well suited to the occasion. But civilized life being what it is, the student must sit down and write with a trembling hand, even though he may be better prepared to push stiff uppercuts than to push ideas through a pen. Most of the emergencies in modern life call for quick wits rather than for strong fists.

Even though the child may have unwarranted fears, many of his fears may still provide a motive for prudence and caution. They may lead him to avoid some dangers and to prepare himself for those that might occur. Also, the fears that the child experiences in daily life are often mild in character and change the direction of his conduct, without producing the severe internal upset that takes place when a person is in terror. However, the point may still be maintained that many fears are in excess of what is needed for prudent living and that a number of the effects produced by intense fear inhibit rather than promote effective action.

OVERCOMING FEAR

As already noted, many fears are overcome in the normal process of growth. As a child lives and learns he comes to take more and more things in his stride. In adult accounts of childhood fears that since have been overcome, there are many such statements as: "I outgrew it," "I learned how to take care of myself," "After a while I knew how to handle it." Sometimes also, of course, a fear vanishes or recedes when the apparent cause of it has been removed, as when a child who fears bigger boys in a certain locality moves to a new neighborhood.

Many apprehensions wane as the individual has a chance gradually to face and to cope with the feared situation. An interesting account of some of the signs of fear or uneasiness shown by children when facing a new situation and of the decline in such signs as the children become accustomed to the situation is shown in the summary below. This summary (adapted from a study by Slater, 44) is based upon observations of forty children, aged two years to three years and four months.

TABLE XX

CHANGES WITH THE PASSAGE OF TIME IN CHILDREN'S RESPONSES TO A NEW SITUATION[6]

Responses	\multicolumn{4}{c}{Number of Children Who Showed These Responses During the First and Subsequent Weeks of Nursery School Attendance}
	First week	Second week	Third week	Fourth week
Postural tensions (hunching shoulders, twisting head or body, tense method of locomotion, *etc.*)..	20	12	9	4
Tics (grimacing, twitching, nail biting, handling various parts of the body, *etc.*)................	31	15	8	3
Anxious expressions.............................	27	10	5	3
Long periods of dreamy watching................	23	11	6	3
Rejection of group activities.....................	17	9	5	2
Calls for mother; asks to go home...............	16	7	3	1

The preceding table, in Slater's report, shows the frequency of these responses during the first four days. It appears that there was a marked decline in these evidences of uneasiness after the very first day, and outstanding emotional disturbances did not appear after the first visit, except in the case of the very young chil-

---

[6] Adapted from Slater, E.: *II. Types, Levels, and Irregularities of Response to a Nursery School Situation of Forty Children Observed with Special Reference to the Home Environment,* The Center for Research in Child Health and Development, School of Public Health, Harvard University, Society for Research in Child Development Monographs (1939), Vol. 4, No. 2, 148 pp. Reproduced by permission.

dren. In passing, Slater points out that the observers in this study gained the impression that a child's apparent degree of concern or unconcern on his first visit did not indicate how well or how soon the child would adjust to the new situation: ". . . children who cried loudest on their first morning might often be the happiest later on, whereas some who were tearless on their first morning sometimes continued for days to be rather solemn and none too happy."

Attention to underlying causes. A first principle in dealing with fear is that one should look not simply at the specific symptoms but at the circumstances and conditions surrounding the fear. If a child's fear has emerged from a setting of insecurity, uncertainty, demands that go beyond his powers, inconsistency or confusion in the discipline to which he is exposed, threats, severe punishments, and various means of intimidation, it obviously is more important to look for ways in which such conditions can be remedied than to deal directly with the child's symptoms of distress. As long as there are underlying difficulties that press upon the child from many sides, the elimination of one particular expression of fear may shortly be followed by other fears of a slightly different cast. For example, a child's apparent fear of being abandoned, exhibited whenever his mother leaves the house on a brief errand, may be associated with other symptoms of distress that first appeared when a new baby came into the household. This particular expression of fear may abate, only to be followed by other expressions of fear—such as fear of sleeping alone in a dark room—if the underlying uncertainties still persist. Frequently, before definite help can be given along this line, it is necessary to have opportunity for becoming acquainted with the child and his circumstances over a period of time, although sometimes the mere fact that the child has a friend in court and a chance to receive some kindly attention and recognition may help him to gain insight into his troubles and to find strength to meet them.

Practical techniques. Numerous studies have been made of the overcoming of fear in experimental situations and of methods used by parents in dealing with their children's fears (15, 16, 20, 29).

In studies by Hagman and by Jersild and Holmes, it was found that the method used most frequently by parents is to try to talk the child out of his fears, to explain matters to him, and to endeavor to convince him that there is no danger. It was noted that this procedure alone seldom helps much, although it may help in some cases, especially if the child has confidence in the adult (the child's confidence in the adult is more important than the truth of what the adult says) or if, by his statements, an adult substantially disposes of the matter that is feared (as when a child who fears punishment or the assignment of a task from which he shrinks is convincingly informed that the feared event will not happen). A verbal explanation may be useless if phrased in terms that the child does not comprehend (as when a father gives an exposition of thermodynamics to a child who is afraid of the noise made by a steaming tea kettle), or it may not touch upon the aspects of a situation which frighten the child.

One method that has been found helpful is to set an example of fearlessness. Such an example, among other things, may bolster the child's assurance in the protection of another person, at least for the time being; carry the suggestion that there is nothing to be afraid of; illustrate techniques for handling the feared situation; and set a standard of courage for the child to emulate. The example of fearlessness is not so likely to succeed, however, if it involves the use of abilities and techniques that are beyond the child's capacities. Nor does an example of courage help if it merely strengthens the child's conviction or fear that he himself is a coward.

In many situations the example of fearlessness set by other children may have a good effect. A child will frequently follow other children into activities that he would be afraid to undertake if he were alone (as when he goes through a pasture in which there are cattle that he fears, or climbs a tree, or enters an isolated barn, or approaches a strange dog). Sometimes children as a group will venture into situations that each would fear if he were alone (such as entering an abandoned barn that may be "haunted"). Sometimes the mere fact of watching the example set by another child will have a salutary effect, as when a child permits himself to be tossed into the air by an adult after having observed that another child laughingly accepts such treatment. It often happens that a child subsequently shows no fear after thus having been initiated into a situation and having discovered that it is harmless (or, better yet, after having discovered that he has the power to cope with the situation).

Another procedure that has been found to work in some situations is to try to effect "positive reconditioning" by presenting the feared stimulus with an attractive or benign stimulus. This method is likely to work best if the unfeared stimulus is not simply presented side by side with the feared event but if the latter can be incorporated into a larger setting that is reassuring.

Apart from efforts to alleviate tensions and pressures in the situation that surrounds a child's fear, the most effective method of dealing with fear is to help him, by degrees, to come actively and directly to grips with the situation that scares him, to aid him in acquiring experience and acquaintanceship with it, to aid him in acquiring skills that are of value in coping with the feared event. Although skill alone may fail to root out fear, in general it may be said that, other things being equal, the child who has acquired the widest range of competence and the best array of skills is likely to have the fewest fears. Such competence and skills include not simply proficiency in the motor activities that are involved in everyday play—such as opening doors and switching on lights— but also competence in ways of dealing with other persons—meeting and greeting and fraternizing with them—and intellectual skills in the form of information and knowing how to proceed.

Frequently a child will exert himself to improve upon his competence in coping with a feared situation. Indeed, some children are almost pathetically eager to "practice" activities that will help them to overcome fear. An example of this appears in the case of a child who was afraid of heights, and who repeatedly was seen to arrange boards and boxes so that he could climb to higher and higher altitudes on more and more precarious footing. On one occasion, when he had succeeded in going up and down the whole length of an unstable inclined board, he gave a shout of triumph. Another example is the case of a child who was afraid of being alone in a room; while "practicing" to overcome this fear, he first asked his nurse to stand at the end of the hallway as he went into the room alone, then to stand out of sight in another room, then to go to a remote part of the house. However, frequently when a child is afraid he will not have the ingenuity to devise such techniques without adult help, and the techniques he does devise may not help him to master the underlying difficulty.

In a study in which parents described their methods of dealing with children's fears (20), it was found that the most active procedures, those that help the child to face and deal with the feared situation, were reported by parents to be most helpful. The parents reported many futile efforts to talk a child out of his fears. Procedures such as ridicule, ignoring the fear, or forcibly compelling the child to face the feared situation were of little help.

The principle of dealing with fear by helping the child to cope directly with the feared event was used in an experimental study by Holmes (16). In one series of observations, Holmes found that of twenty children in a nursery-school group, fourteen were initially afraid to enter a strange, dark room to recover a ball which the experimenter had thrown into the room, seemingly by inadvertence, while playing with them in an adjoining large room. The children were then familiarized with the place, and after relatively few sessions, thirteen of these fourteen children went into the room without hesitation, turned on the light, and recovered the ball.

Another series of experiments dealt with two children who were afraid of walking the length of a plank that was raised above the ground. After eight brief sessions, over a period of about a month, one child, who at first had clung to the experimenter when placed at even a low altitude and had whined and protested that she would fall and get hurt, happily walked back and forth the length of a board raised six feet above the ground. Previous to the experiment, the child had been described by nursery-school teachers as one who exhibited poor motor coördination and fear of climbing on the playground. After the experiment proper, a high board, with a ladder leading to it, was installed on the playground. On the first occasion, the child walked across the board, at a height of six feet, though somewhat slowly and hesitatingly; at the third exposure, she walked promptly from one end to the other, with no signs of apprehension. Even the sight of another child who had tried to climb the ladder and had fallen and cried did not seem to deter her.

Another child also made progress, but less rapidly, and after having shown some improvement he relapsed. This relapse occurred at a time when his nurse left the household and his mother was in the hospital having a baby. The whining and infantile responses which he showed in the fear experiment were similar to behavior that also was prominent at home, and it appeared that, far from having any strong desire to overcome his fear, he used the fear situation as a means of getting attention and of having contacts with an adult. The procedure of simply helping the child to acquire competence in dealing directly with a specific feared situation did not suffice to overcome a fear that seemingly had a certain amount of utility in his scheme of living and that was deeply interwoven with other emotional difficulties.

It has been noted that an active approach may be helpful even in overcoming fears of imaginary dangers. One child in the study cited above of parental experiences with children's fears, was afraid of an imaginary dog, which hounded him, troubled him when he was alone, and haunted him in dark places. When his resourceful mother observed this, she set out to help him. She first watched the child in his make-believe play. Gradually she entered into this play herself and joined the child in games of "let's pretend"; gradually, also, she began to introduce the imaginary dog into the make-believe play. In time, the child took the dog with him into closets and elsewhere, all as part of the play pattern, and eventually he no longer appeared to be bothered by the dog.

Much of the value of the technique of helping the child to cope directly with his fears no doubt lies in the fact that in the process the child benefits from the companionship and participation of the adult. His burden of fear is being shared. He is being told, in effect, that he need not be ashamed of being afraid and that he is not, at least for the time being, defenseless and alone.

Many of the techniques that can be used in overcoming fear may likewise be adapted to the prevention of fear. In addition, steps frequently can be taken to forewarn or forearm the child, so that he may be prepared against a sudden or abrupt happening that might cause fear and, by degrees, be prepared for a new situation (such as having a trusted adult at hand on his first exposure, letting him make his way into a new play group at his own pace, letting him become accustomed to the doctor as a kindly person before a painful treatment is begun, and so forth).

Because many events are unpredictable and a child's reactions to new situations are likewise unpredictable, it would of course be impossible to undertake a thoroughgoing program of forewarning and forearming the child. Furthermore, the very steps taken to prepare a child for a situation that might frighten him might even have effects just the opposite of those intended. In the observational studies of fears mentioned above, one of the most acute instances of terror—involving an outcry, hasty flight, and prolonged crying, followed by moaning and trembling—occurred when a child first met a badly crippled neighbor, after the parents had previously taken some pains to prepare the child for the event. What a child is told in preparation for an event, and the very fact that his elders go out of their way to forewarn him may, under some conditions, endow an event with terrifying qualities and thus aggravate rather than forestall a child's fear.

It may be pointed out that every passing sign of fear in a child need not be looked upon as a signal of distress. Apart from fears that induce wholesome caution and serve a useful purpose, and fears that are likely to wane if the child is simply given enough time to accustom himself to the situation, many mild apprehensions arise through the child's own choosing, as when he courts danger and "plays" with fear by taking chances in play or by seeking vicarious thrills through exciting stories.

ANGER, HOSTILITY, AND AGGRESSIVE BEHAVIOR

In the usual child, anger is displayed more frequently than fear. Many happenings in the ordinary home routine provoke anger, whereas fear stimuli tend to be less frequent since they usually involve something novel, intense, or out of the ordinary. Also, a child can take measures to avoid many of the situations that he fears, such as high places or the neighbor's dog; but it is difficult to avoid irritating conditions in his everyday environment. Moreover, many children soon learn to make use of a display of anger as a means of getting attention or of having their way.

In a child's early relations with other children, under the eye of parents or teachers, occasions leading to irritation and aggression are likely to occur more often than are occasions leading to fear, especially after children have become accustomed to one another. In a study of a group of preschool children aged three to five years, Felder (6) found that the number of anger outbreaks were many times as frequent as the number of manifestations of fear. However, this difference in public manifestation does not mean that there is a similar difference in the actual frequency or role of anger and fear, since many children who express their anger overtly may be quite subdued in manifestations of fear or may even seek to disguise their fear.

Causes of anger. Anger can be aroused in young children by forcible restraint, interference with movement, blocking of activities that are in progress, and thwarting of wishes. Frequently anger occurs as a response to cumulative irritations. The younger the child, the more his anger will turn upon an interference with his physical activities. As he grows older, the conditions that cause anger include not only actual bodily restraint but also interference with his possessions, frustration, thwarting of plans, purposes, expectations, and criticism of his ideas or faults.

Anger, like fear, is influenced by factors of both learning and maturation. As was noted in Chapter I, during the first few days of life such interferences as having his arms pinned momentarily to his sides or having his nostrils closed, so that breathing is prevented for a few moments, do not usually seem to arouse the ire of an infant. When the infant does protest, his movements are likely to be uncoördinated and to display no uniform or characteristic pattern of rage. As he grows older and matures organically, he becomes more responsive to interference and exhibits more specific reactions of a defensive or offensive sort. After the child's capacities have improved through growth, learning plays an increasingly important role in determining the manner in which he will express his rage and the conditions that excite him. Throughout childhood, however, there are individual differences in the irascibility and violence of children that seem due in part to inborn factors. Moreover, at all stages of growth, an individual may, when acutely enraged, "go to pieces," strike out blindly, and revert to diffuse, uncoördinated reactions.

The infant's anger, like that of an older person, often occurs as the result of his own ineptitude. He may seek, for example, to put a spoon in his mouth but, failing because he makes a broadside approach, become angry in the attempt. He may be able to pull himself to his feet before he has acquired the ability to ease himself back into a sitting position, and as he grows tired his rage may become quite violent. Even though the child is not provoked or obstructed by others, he is likely to meet many provocations to anger in connection with his own activities.

In children, as in adults, anger due to the person's own foibles or mistakes may be ascribed to something external. An example of this is offered by a seven-year-old child who was very fond of candy and who had had cavities in her teeth. On one occasion she heard adults discuss some findings which seemed to show that sweets helped the growth of bacteria that cause tooth decay. That evening after she had gone to bed when a request for candy was refused by her father, her temper flared more than was usual when something was denied. It appeared that her anger at her father was in part a projection of anger with herself for wanting candy in spite of its harmful effects.

Changes with age in the expression of anger. A description of conditions which promote anger and of changes in the child's anger behavior as he grows older is given by Goodenough (12), who studied children between the ages of seven months and eight years. Among other things, Goodenough noted that as the infant grows older his expressions of anger become less random and more directly aimed at something or someone. Before the age of one year, his outbursts are chiefly explosive expressions, not well designed to remove obstacles or to attack an enemy. But by the age of four, almost half of his expressions are aimed at the object of his wrath. With this change there comes an increase in retaliative behavior of a kind apparently aimed to secure revenge for an injury. The most frequent single expression of anger in early childhood is crying, but this diminishes with age. Threats make their appearance between the ages of two and three and increase in frequency thereafter.

Indirect forms of retaliation and attack observed in Goodenough's study took the form of such activities as the overturning of furniture and the doing of acts previously forbidden, although distinct from the immediate cause of anger. One child of three, when angry, sucked his thumb in a conspicuous manner, although thumb sucking was not his usual habit. Other indirect forms of aggression were raucous laughter and the refusal to speak. One child voiced her resentment toward her mother by such remarks as: "I wish I had a mother like Mary's." In some cases, children expressed their anger by attacks upon themselves; for example, a child was observed to bite himself when angry. Aftereffects of anger were almost twice as frequent and prolonged in children over the age of four as in children under four.

Individual children may go to quite extreme lengths in showing anger, such as holding their breath or vomiting. At the age of about four some children resort to threats, such as threatening to run away, or to chop off the offender's head, or to chop his house to pieces. Many youngsters go through a period of threatening to kill when angered. In expressing anger, a child will frequently vary the nature of his outburst under different circumstances. He is more likely, for example, to cry at home than at school (41) and to hit and kick when angered by another child than when angered by an adult.

Factors contributing to susceptibility to anger. In the study above there was evidence that children were slightly more disposed to anger after a restless night, especially following nights when the subjects had wet their beds. They were more irascible also on days when regular bowel movements had not occurred. Anger outbursts were especially frequent just before meals. Children who had records of illness tended to exhibit slightly more anger outbursts than children who had not been ill. The number of anger outbursts increased somewhat, on the average, when there were adult visitors, and they increased to a greater degree when there were child visitors in the home. Also, there was a tendency toward a greater frequency of anger in children who had more than two adults in the household. The more adults in the home the more occasion for everyone to get into everybody else's hair.

Parents whose children gave vent to many outbursts of anger more frequently attempted to calm them by granting their desires, by removing the sources of trouble, and by coaxing and soothing them than did parents whose children experienced fewer outbursts of anger. The difference gives a clew to the cause of many anger outbursts. When a child gets what he wants, his anger is successful; but if he fails to get what he wants, his anger is abortive and he will have less reason to resort to anger as a means of solving a problem another time. Threatening was more often reported as a device for meeting the anger of the more irascible children, whereas spanking was more often resorted to by parents whose children had few outbursts. The difference here is suggestive, but it is too small to permit the conclusion which one might draw.

At all ages after two years boys displayed anger outbursts more frequently than girls, but the number of children included in the study is somewhat too small to support final conclusions concerning this difference. The difference is accounted for in part, no doubt, by the fact that parents ignored the girls more often than the boys when they were angry and more often used bribery, spanking, threatening, and isolation as a means of coping with the boys' anger.

Anger is more likely to occur in homes where parents are overanxious and concerned with whether the child's behavior is "good" or "bad" than in homes where parents are tolerant and capable of looking upon the child objectively (Goodenough, 12). Anger is more likely to occur also where there is worry and anxiety or lack of a sense of humor. Furthermore, anger is often provoked by the critical attitude of parents who tend to nag and recriminate rather than to view each anger episode as a thing of the past when the event is over. Consistency in methods of discipline appeared to be a more important factor than the strictness or lenience of the disciplinary procedures that were used. Some methods, such as bribery and letting the child have his own way, may bring an outburst to an end but pave the way for future outbursts.

Even though, on the whole, the provocations leading to anger are usually more obvious and predictable than those producing fear in the young child, it is often difficult to trace the cause of a particular resentment or animosity which the child carries with him for a long time. As in the case of fears, chance remarks, fortuitous unpleasant contacts with a person or situation, and suggestions obtained from stories and readings may contribute to lasting prejudices or resentments. In the case of older people and adults, anger in a mild form is likely to extend to those who are associated with anything that stands in the way of one's designs. Even the staid scientist may develop a prejudice against colleagues who fail to support one of his favorite theories.

Conditions influencing susceptibility to thwarting and frustration. As has already been suggested, the circumstances in which thwarting and frustration occur depend upon the external stimulus as well as upon the inner state of the person who is being exposed to the stimulus. This fact has been emphasized in the foregoing statements about change in the child's susceptibility to anger as he matures. At any given level of maturity, likewise, a variety of factors within the organism itself will play an important role.

The effect of the child's physical and physiological condition on his susceptibility to anger has been noted. The hungry infant may be enraged if his bottle is withdrawn, but the same child, when sated, will himself push the bottle away. Moreover, the reaction of the hungry child is likely to be the more prompt the hungrier he is (4). Similarly, a remainder of chores yet undone is likely to be more annoying to the child when physically tired than when he is well rested. In like manner, the extent to which something in the child's path represents a thwarting obstacle depends in part upon the child's own strength and endurance.

At later age levels, as at earlier levels, the individual's irascibility is likely to be greater when he is hungry or tired. Accordingly, it is a good rule not to start an argument before mealtime. A few mouthfuls of food may do more to settle a dispute than the best of logic emanating from an empty stomach. Late afternoon, before dinner, is a time when many adults are especially disposed to be angry, although others favor the time between getting out of bed and breakfast as a period when a little irritant can provoke a big rage. It would help if such persons would realize that a soft-boiled breakfast egg, like a soft answer, will turn away wrath.

Thwarting and frustration depend also to an important degree on what the child has at stake—his plans, desires, hopes, the level of his aspirations, his notions as to what others expect of him, and his ideas of what he might properly expect of himself. Many factors influence the mental set or attitude which determine whether or not the child will regard a circumstance as a challenge. The fact that a slight obstacle may serve as an incentive rather than a frustration is demonstrated in a study by Wright (50) in which adults selecting dessert tended to pick out the rather more remote but actually no bigger dish of sweets. Such incentives are recognized in the folk saying, "The grass is greener on the other side of the fence."

The level of the child's abilities and, in time, his ideas as to the level of his abilities, will have an important bearing on whether or not a happening is potentially frustrating. When he is able, or thinks he is able, to walk by himself on rough ground, he may be angry if someone tries to take his hand, whereas earlier, when this feat was beyond what he expected of himself, he was glad to take a hand or to be carried (and later, when the rough terrain is no longer a challenge, he again may be quite glad to hold a hand or to get a lift). Similarly, at a certain stage, failure to put on a jacket or to put on a shoe may be very frustrating, whereas earlier the child was quite nonchalant when he half-heartedly tried and failed.

What constitutes a challenge and a potential frustration not only varies as the child matures but also varies from child to child, and it varies for the same child in different circumstances. The frustration may be much more severe when a child fails to hoist himself into a sitting position on a trapeze while other children are performing the same feat without difficulty, than when he fails repeatedly while practicing the performance alone. Again, the child may be frustrated by failure to perform in the presence of others of about his own age, but he may be quite complacent if he tries and fails in a feat that has been performed by someone older than he.

In countless ways, in different aspects of his life, the child may thus exhibit more or less vaguely defined boundaries within which he is put on his mettle and within which he can have the gratifying experience of success or feel thwarted and frustrated by failure. Within broad limits he exhibits what might be called a margin within which he is sensitive, an upper and lower threshold, so to speak, within which he holds himself on trial. If he fails, is blocked or thwarted within this range, he may variously feel remorse, guilt, and anger, and, when angry, experience various aggressive impulses toward himself or other persons and things.[7]

Suppression of overt signs of rage. As a rule, the young child has no sooner acquired the ability to stage a good performance of rage than he must begin to learn how to suppress it. Through social restraints and partly through his own discovery as to what is the best policy, he must learn not to cry, bite, pinch, kick, hit, destroy, tear, and attack by physical means when his ire is aroused. During a period of one year, at the preschool age, a notable decline can be observed in the relative frequency of crying and in hitting and other forms of physical attack, and an increase in the use of language, scolding, and fussing (22, 41). Studies of anger in adults by Richardson (40), Gates (9), and Meltzer (36) show how

---

[7] The reader is referred to Lewin (32) for a very instructive account of the play of psychological forces in the "life space" of the individual.

far this learning has gone by the time a person reaches maturity. In several hundred occasions of anger described by adult subjects, there were only a few good fights. The adult has learned to smother most of his violent expressions, even though he may still have a strong impulse to do physical injury to the offender or to scream or swear and make a scene (36). Of course, this does not mean that the anger is disposed of.

In his efforts to suppress anger an older person may go so far as to display just the opposite sentiments. Instead of showing hostility toward a person whom he basically dislikes he may show solicitude and appear to be anxious about the welfare of this person.

Devious manifestations of anger. As a person grows older he learns to use many devices as a substitute for overt attack. A frequent substitute is the use of language in the form of sneers, innuendoes, or violent and abusive phrases. The angry person may resort to roundabout methods of overcoming the object of his rage. He may try to belittle his opponent in the eyes of others, to overcome him in competition; he may rejoice in tragedies that befall his adversary, lay plans for overcoming him, imagine himself superior, resort to ridicule and irony and barbed witticism, or imagine situations that will bring sorrow upon his foe. The latter expression occurs when children imagine themselves as dead and in the process of being buried while secretly relishing the tears of remorse that wet the cheeks of those who have abused them.

In extreme cases, anger may be expressed in the form of cruelty, active revolt, vandalism, thievery, and other antisocial acts. Likewise, as noted, a child may discover that he can "get another's goat" by using "bad" words, by using ungrammatical speech, or by mannerisms and little acts which in themselves are relatively harmless but which cause irritation. A whisper behind the offending person's back may take the place of a blow on his chin, or the attack upon the object of one's anger may be cloaked in humor or take the form of satire. The angry person may claim that his indirect attack upon someone else is not due to personal feelings but is to uphold a cause or a principle. Expressions of aggressive impulses may range from violent attack to a demeanor of calm and frigid politeness. They may range from direct cruelty to a show of kindness, as when a child's generosity toward a playmate is calculated to make another playmate feel badly.

Finding a scapegoat. Sometimes when the situation does not permit a person to direct his aggressive impulses toward the person or circumstance that provoked him, he will direct them toward someone or something else. He may try to find a scapegoat. In a study by Lewin, Lippitt, and White (33), referred to in Chapter VI, it was noted that children who hesitated to attack an autocratic adult leader diverted their aggressive feelings toward a member of their own gang. If a study could be made, it undoubtedly would be found that similar conditions prevail in many homes: the child who has been angered by his parents, but who does not dare to strike back at his parents, no doubt often "takes out" his anger on a brother or sister.[8]

Change in quality of performance. A child may respond to a thwarting situation by changing the quality of his performance. One response may be to show restless and aimless forms of behavior. Another response may be to leave the situation: the child walks away, if free to do so. Even when confined, in the flesh, to the annoying situation he may try to absent himself psychologically, as when he finds the arithmetic too difficult and sits through a class period without paying attention to what is going on. Similarly, the child may remain bodily in the situation but leave the field of operation. An instance of this occurred in a study of frustration by Seashore and Bavelas (42). One at a time the children were asked to draw a man, but as soon as a child had completed a drawing the experimenter, without taking further notice of it,

---

[8] In passing it may be noted that a child who sometimes vents his anger upon his parents is not necessarily a more hostile or poorly reared child than one who does not. The latter child may not only be angry at his parents but also afraid of them.

gave the child another piece of paper and asked him to draw another man, and so on, one drawing after the other. One child, after many such trials, bent over his paper for a time and when he displayed it he had not drawn a man but had written the name "Dick," and he maintained, "There, that's a man! That's writing."

Yet another response is to remain in the situation but to give less effort to it and to do an inferior job. Illustrations of this appear in the "Draw a man" study, just cited. As one trial followed another, many of the children gave less and less time to the drawing. A child who devoted seven or eight minutes to his first drawing or two might, several trials later, dash off a drawing in a few seconds. Again, the drawings of some of the children deteriorated as one trial followed the next.[9] The change in quality of performance in response to frustration may also take the form of regression—the child backslides and behaves in a more childish or infantile manner.[10]

THE PREVENTION OF ANGER

Although much of the anger that occurs in everyday life solves no problem, complete eradication of anger would not be wise or possible. As noted earlier, occasions for anger frequently arise by reason of the child's lack of strength or his ineptitude in his own play and work. Furthermore, owing to the child's lack of understanding, it is inevitable that the discipline he must undergo will often strike him as a form of opposition rather than of kindness. The business of getting along with others requires that some restraints be put upon the child, and even when his elders try to impose such restraints in ways best calculated to win coöperation, they are likely to fail at times.

---

[9] A scale by Goodenough (13) makes it possible to rate the drawing of a man in terms of the mental age.

[10] For accounts of loss of constructiveness, regression, and other forms of lowered quality of performance in frustrating situations see Barker, Dembo, and Lewin (1), Keister (30), and Updegraff and Keister (46).

When a child is reprimanded for a line of conduct which he has deliberately chosen with an understanding of the issues involved, he may feel ashamed, or angry, or vengeful, even if he realizes the reasons for the disapproval of others. But if the relationship between the child and the disciplinarian is generally one of friendship and mutual respect, such effects are likely to be short-lived. The child who is overindulged and never reprimanded may come to feel just as insecure as a child whose elders are unduly strict, especially since such overindulgence may be a symptom of uncertainty in his elders. The normal child appreciates a certain amount of moral arbitration and even a certain amount of arbitrariness in his elders.

It should also be noted that anger in adult-child relationships may sometimes be of value as an antidote to parental tendencies to overindulge and "spoil" a child. Their impulse to protect the child may be so strong that they grant his wishes and tolerate his vagaries to such an extent that the child establishes habits that become a handicap. As against this impulse, parents also have a human propensity for being annoyed when a child gets too far out of hand, and this annoyance may serve as the starting point for wiser ways of dealing with the youngster. To be sure, if a child's behavior becomes aggravating because his parents, as a matter of self-indulgence, have encouraged habits which seem cute or amusing, their subsequent annoyance when things get out of hand should be directed against themselves.

The foregoing does not, of course, condone periodic outbursts of rage in an adult's dealings with a child. Such outbursts, whether directed against a child or another adult, are usually a symptom of weakness. Under most circumstances they simply indicate that the individual not only is at a loss as to how to solve a problem that confronts him but also has lost control of himself. Disciplinary measures taken under such conditions may serve merely as a means of projecting one's rage upon someone else and as an outlet for rage rather than as a means of remedying the underlying problem.

A parent's anger will be influenced by his own foibles. A child's acts are likely to be particularly annoying if they touch upon something about which the parent is sensitive in his own life. If a parent, for example, tends to dawdle or has difficulty in making up his mind, he may be especially angered when his child dawdles or is indecisive, asking now, let us say, for more meat and then a moment later declaring he doesn't want any more meat. Again, a child's behavior is likely to be very annoying if it injures a parent's vanity. A parent who likes to think of himself as someone worthy of great respect may feel more enraged when his child contradicts him than a parent who has less pretentious ideas about himself. The degree of annoyance felt by a parent when his child disobeys depends not simply upon the act of disobedience but upon the extent to which the parent considers it his right to demand unquestioning obedience. The fact that the parent's attitudes, his desires, and his pride often are involved when anger arises in relations with a child means that the parent, in seeking to understand his child's anger, should also try to understand his own.

In deploring such tactics, one should not, however, go so far as to rule that anger should never be shown. A parent or teacher, and certainly a long-suffering neighbor, has the right to be angry on occasion. Part of a child's education is to become familiar with the fact that other human beings, being what they are, are subject to anger, just as he himself is. For that matter, an occasional display of asperity by a child's elders is likely to have a much less harmful effect on his "sense of security," if it has any effect at all, than may be induced by the tactics of adults who really are annoyed and go to exhausting lengths in trying to outmaneuver a child, or, as often happens, try to find an outlet by picking at the child, nagging him, ignoring him, pointedly praising others in his presence, and badgering him in countless little ways.

One factor that makes it difficult to deal wisely with an angry child is that a display of anger is likely to provoke resentment in the person against whom it is directed. If an adult is thus angered too readily he not only will be less reasonable in finding a solution for the initial cause of rage but his own show of anger will give added provocation to the child. This circumstance often leads to unnecessarily bitter, mutual animosities. Another difficulty is that anger includes a tendency to place the blame on other persons or things when the angry person himself actually may be responsible for the occasion of his wrath. Thus a vicious circle of recrimination may be established.

Anger, as noted above, is a response to a problem. If a child learns that outbursts of rage will dispose of a problem, his anger or the behavior initially associated with anger is likely to become habitual. A person so habituated is doubly unfortunate; not only is the tendency toward anger encouraged by frequent exercise, but the necessity for anger also grows greater, for he is not driven to acquire competence in other methods of solving his difficulties.

An important factor in the prevention of anger consists in the avoidance of needless provocation. For one thing, a child should not be compelled constantly to meet difficulties for which he has no adequate solution. Such problems may involve a variety of conditions, such as continual teasing and nagging, constant irritation in the form of unnecessary interference, undue difficulties in competition for affection and recognition, and the imposition of tasks or standards which are beyond the child's ability but from which there is no escape.

Sometimes a child can be helped to acquire skills that will enable him to cope with his environment by methods other than anger. The acquisition of skill and ability as a means of obviating anger will be especially helpful in situations in which the child is thwarted by reason of lack of abilities which he actually can acquire. An account of the effectiveness of graded training in overcoming immature behavior patterns, including destructiveness and other symptoms of anger, is presented in studies by Updegraff and Keister (30, 46).

Many children resent school in its entirety, or a particular subject or teacher, because of constant frustration through inability to meet the school's demands. A child who is weak in a certain project may come to resent the project and his teacher as well, especially if he is constantly reminded of the superior work of his schoolmates. If the child's incompetence is due to disabilities that cannot be overcome, the evident remedy is to revise what is required of him. If the task which the child now resents actually is one that he could master in time, his reaction may be remedied if better ways of instruction are used, if he is helped by degrees to master first the easier and then the more difficult features of the work, and if matters are so arranged that he can experience a measure of success and the satisfaction that success brings.

Frequently a person's anger over one issue may be mitigated or even overcome by a feeling of satisfaction over something else. Thus a child's resentment arising from being thwarted in one field may be assuaged by success and recognition in some other field. A word of praise, a small favor, a little compliment or act of deference—such as asking the child for information or for an expression of opinion, or letting him have a voice in decisions that are unrelated to the matter at issue—often will divert wrath where reasoning and argumentation, however calm, merely provoke more rage. Somewhat related to this is the rule that the farther one can go in "giving in" or yielding to another without sacrificing the main point at issue, the greater is the likelihood of an amicable solution. By this means, the area of friction is reduced. In dealing with a recalcitrant person it may be worth while to go out of one's way to find extraneous issues on which the angry person may score a victory. Usually what happens is that once hostilities between two persons are under way each of them looks for more, rather than fewer, grounds for offense.

JEALOUSY

Jealousy may be expressed in countless ways, ranging from direct attack to subtle and indirect manifestations. Even more variable and complicated are the "inner" or subjective characteristics of jealousy. The term "jealousy" actually covers not one emotional state or type of response but a variety of conditions. The situation in which jealousy is aroused usually is one in which other persons, objects, or conditions possess or share, or threaten to possess or share, affection, honor, or esteem which one desires for oneself. The reaction, in varying ways, may be directed not only against the real or imagined usurper, but also against the person or group whose affection one seeks.

The response may take the form of an obsession which, for a time, takes complete possession of the victim's thoughts, or it may be sporadic, appearing only when the individual is directly confronted by the conditions which produce jealousy. Issues and conditions that provoke jealousy may be relatively definite, as when an individual is jealous of a certain person in circumstances which he could describe and define, or the underlying conditions may be vague and only dimly recognized by the jealous person. The issues involved in jealousy, as they represent themselves to the sufferer, may concern actual issues that are at stake or they may involve rationalizations and many disguises. In any event, whether the condition of jealousy is chronic or fleeting, localized or vaguely defined, relatively straightforward or highly disguised, it will be influenced by factors in the immediate situation and by factors in the past history of the individual, many of which the individual himself may be unable to formulate or recall.

Quite as complex and difficult to define are the feelings and impulses involved in jealousy. In most instances, jealousy will involve emotional experiences akin to anger, an impulse to attack, or a disposition toward vengefulness or toward sulking and surliness. Implicit in jealousy, likewise, are elements similar to those that are found in fear, for jealousy involves a tacit admission of weakness in the face of an issue which the individual regards as crucial to his own desires or welfare. The fear aspects may involve forebodings or acute anxiety concerning the final turn of events, or experiences of self-deprecation, "feelings of inferiority," and kindred conditions.

To probe the feelings involved in jealousy in childhood would at best be a difficult matter, since the child's experiences are not likely to be differentiated into distinct feelings; and even if they were, a child would not be able to give a well-formulated introspective account of them. An account of feelings described by adults in introspective accounts of jealousy has been offered by Gesell (10). The item most frequently mentioned was anger, and many persons described feelings of hatred and vengeful thoughts; self-pity was also mentioned by many persons, and sulking; and there was frequent mention also of grief, sadness and dejection, mortification, fear, and anxiety. The most frequent combination was anger, self-pity, and grief.

Expressions of jealousy. Many specific examples of the behavior of jealous children have been described in studies of the subject.[11] A four-year-old boy, at first well-disposed toward his baby sister, became aroused when a blanket which had been his was used to cover her; thereafter, he would hit her if the two were left alone together. An extreme case was that of a five-year-old child who had the whooping cough. The doctor told him that if he coughed near his baby sister she might become sick, and "then you won't have a baby sister any more." Thereafter, he was caught several times in the act of coughing into his sister's face.

Sometimes children will express their jealousy through their make-believe and will wreak vengeance by proxy. In a study by

---

[11] See Foster (7), Sewall (43), and Smalley (45).

Markey, which is discussed in the chapter on imagination, a "housekeeping game" was used to investigate children's make-believe (35). One three-year-old child promptly took the "baby" doll, placed it on the "stove," and earnestly told the baby that it would have to sit there and burn and burn. On further inquiry it was found that this child was acutely jealous of a younger sibling.

It sometimes happens that a child who is jealous of a sibling but is subdued in his competition with the sibling in the home will be all the more explosive and rebellious in his relationships outside the home. However, this turn of events is not at all invariable, for no two children are likely to react in the same way and the same child may exhibit quite different types of behavior in different situations. Moreover, although competition for affection and attention within the family may take many forms, one should be careful not to attribute all forms of behavior, including "problem" behavior, to jealousy or insecurity in the child's relationships with members of his family.

A jealous child will sometimes revert to earlier infantile habits. For example, a child who for some time has achieved bladder control at night may revert to bed-wetting or may call frequently to his parents at night to come and take him to the toilet. Likewise, he may seek more help and attention than at an earlier time in connection with eating, dressing, and other activities. Also, apparently as a bid for attention, he may exhibit fears which did not appear at an earlier time and which, in effect, represent a plea for sympathy and attention (although it should be said that such subtle manifestations can easily be misinterpreted). Again, he may become more affectionate than was his wont. As the child grows older, his expressions of jealousy become quite varied. The jealous child may take to gossip, tattling, and lying. Again, the symptoms may take the form of swaggering, strutting, assuming a conspicuous attitude of nonchalance, and consciously ignoring others. Vindictive plans and fantasies of self-glorification or of misfortunes for others may occur. The child may assume a martyr's role and brood upon the unfairness of his plight. Again, the child may imagine himself in a future conquering-hero role.

Sometimes parents unwittingly discriminate against one child by showing greater admiration for another child in the family. It is only human for parents to prefer some traits and characteristics to others, and, in the process, one child may vaguely realize that he does not rank as high in their estimation, in this particular regard, as does his brother or sister. One often sees children whose behavior seems influenced by such discrimination. Even though the child who plays second fiddle may not express himself aggressively against his sibling, he is likely to find some means of giving vent to his condition. He may become somewhat loud of speech, in an effort to attract attention, or he may become meek and submissive and, by being helpful, silently strive to win good will. He may even go so far as to show an uncommon degree of solicitude for his sibling rival. The frantic activities of a child who is thus striving for a place but is barred from direct attack upon his rival often appear, at first glance, to mark the youngster as a loud show-off or as an unusually "good" child, while, as a matter of fact, such activities may merely betoken the child's uneasiness and helplessness.

Related factors. It is likely that all siblings near each other in age will exhibit symptoms of jealousy at some time or other, in one situation or another. When notably jealous children are singled out as a class for special study and compared with children who are not notably jealous, the findings do not lead to any sweeping generalization that would account for the difference in all cases. It has been found, however, that jealousy is often entangled with other symptoms of emotional difficulty. Among the characteristics observed more frequently among jealous than among nonjealous children in a study by Foster (7) were selfishness, pugnacity, a special attachment to one parent, and neurotic fears. A higher proportion of jealous children exhibited sleep disturbances, enuresis, habits of nail biting and thumb sucking, hyperactivity, destructiveness, and excessive demands for attention. Where one finds many disorders of this kind, the aggressive expressions of jealousy that occur may be simply a feature of a bundle of disorders that spring from a common cause. However, a cluster of other unfavorable characteristics such as those listed above will not invariably accompany jealousy.

Studies of jealous children indicate that jealousy may occur both among the bright and the dull. In one investigation, there was evidence that the duller of two siblings was more likely to be jealous, especially if he was the older of the two (45). However, it is not the mere fact of a difference in ability but the parental attitudes associated with the difference that will be most influential.

It has been observed that jealousy is likely to be less frequent when the age difference between two siblings is less than eighteen months or more than forty-two months (43). The behavior and qualities of a sibling who is considerably older or younger may be outside the child's competitive range, so to speak. Jealousy has been found to be associated to a marked degree with evidences of oversolicitude on the part of the mother, inconsistency in discipline, and discord in the marital relations of the parents.

The coming of a new baby into the home often marks the beginning of symptoms of jealousy; but in many cases, the child who becomes jealous does not show this attitude until the new arrival is above a year or two in age. Many parents often take great pains to "prepare" an older child for the advent of a new baby by informing the child of its coming, trying to enlist the child's interest in planning for the new member of the family, and trying to plant the suggestion, by one means or another, that the newcomer is not to be regarded as a rival. Frequently, plans of this kind fail to forestall jealousy. The very steps taken by the parents may betray their own uncertainties and may throw the spotlight on the new baby to such an extent that the older child senses the coming of a rival even before the new baby is born. This is all the more likely to occur if the child, for any reason, already is ill at ease with his parents.

The mere academic fact of informing the child that a new baby is expected is not likely to have much effect in forestalling jealousy (43). The success of efforts to forestall jealousy will depend not only upon the subtlety and naturalness of the methods that are used but even more on relationships that exist between the child and his parents. In homes where there already are several children whom the parents treat with the proper balance of affection and matter-of-factness, a child may be quite without forewarning as to the coming of a new baby and yet show neither surprise nor consternation when he learns of the blessed event. The question as to whether parents should make a special effort to inform a child that another baby is coming might even be debated. In recent years, there has been much emphasis on the importance of giving heed to every possible subtle sentiment that a child may have in relation to his parents. This solicitude often defeats its own purpose, for it singles out and makes an issue of matters which the child might otherwise take in his stride. There may be as much danger in taking pains to talk everything over with the child as in taking the opposite course.

Competitive relations between siblings sometimes are stimulated by visitors who call attention to the fact, say, that George, although a year younger, is just as tall as his brother, Jim, or who gush over Mildred's curls in the presence of sister Janet, whose hair is straight. It often happens that an older child who used to be noticed by callers is especially neglected and slighted when visitors come to see a newly arrived baby. It would be a good rule if visitors who come bearing gifts at such a time would bring their gifts to the older child rather than to the newborn child (especially since the presents mean nothing to the newcomer). One complication in the matter of trying to forestall jealousy is the fact that parents themselves cannot anticipate the effect that a new arrival in the family will have upon them. Sometimes the very child who was "unwanted" becomes the apple of his mother's eye. Moreover, parents, who after all are human beings, cannot possibly achieve a thorough and perfectly rational balance in the handling of their children. An effort to "think out" and to weigh the merits of every practice used in the rearing of children might only confuse matters. A genuine affection on the parents' part for each member of the family will cover a multitude of practices, which, if evaluated singly, might be labeled as "bad." Certainly, there is no simple, practical rule of thumb that will solve all difficulties.

Sometimes parents, in an effort to achieve at least the outward forms of fairness, will adopt the policy of "two of everything" if there are two children in the family. Such a policy may not only do an injustice to the children (each of whom may have abilities or interests which would justify special consideration and privileges) but may also, in a practical way, fail to forestall rivalry between the children (34). At best, a policy of supplying two tricycles, two sandboxes, two pairs of similar galoshes, and so forth, might not even begin to touch upon the real areas of friction and rivalry. This is all the more true by virtue of the fact that the tricycle or wagon or swing may be the battleground but not the cause of combat.

Jealousy is not, of course, confined to relationships between siblings in the same family, for frequently a child will be jealous of one or both of his parents, as manifested by protests when the parents display affection for each other or share conversations or activities in which the child cannot join. Again, older children frequently suffer from jealousy in their relations with teachers and other adults outside the home and with their associates.

The link between jealousy in early childhood and a jealous disposition in later years has not been traced adequately in scientific studies. Children normally lose their more obvious symptoms of jealousy as they become older and more absorbed in interests outside the family. On the other hand, some children maintain a jealous attitude into mature years, not only toward members of their own family, but sometimes even more toward their associates in daily life. Among adults, the degree of jealousy a person exhibits frequently bears little relationship to his relative status or power as compared with others. The person who has "arrived" and has achieved the outward semblance of success will sometimes begrudge the recognition bestowed upon an underling, much as a big hound bristles when his master pets a forlorn poodle.

It seems reasonable to believe that jealous attitudes in children are influenced by competitive attitudes in parents. A parent's own zeal to surpass, to excel, to prove himself as an able, successful person is likely in many ways to permeate his relationships with his child. The competitive attitude may appear in small details: the parent may feel triumphant if his baby walks a month or two before the average or says his first word while neighboring children of the same age are still babbling. Later such competitive attitudes may appear in efforts to get the child to learn to read precociously or to excel in other ways. If now a child fails to meet the parent's desire to outdo others, the parent is tempted to become angry, to complain, to make unfavorable comparisons between one child and another. This in turn may lead the child who is rebuffed to feel that he is being discriminated against. It is likely that competitive pressures such as these in the lives of the parents contribute more to the development of jealous attitudes in children than the more spontaneous expressions of affection, enthusiasm, admiration, or sympathy which a parent now displays toward one child, now toward another.

OTHER EMOTIONAL ASPECTS OF PARENT-CHILD RELATIONSHIPS

The relationships between parents and children involve many feelings and emotions in addition to affection, anger, and jealousy. Until recently the problems and headaches involved in having children have received much more attention in research than the

TABLE XXI

COMPARATIVE FREQUENCY OF VARIOUS CATEGORIES OF SATISFACTIONS AND PRESENT PROBLEMS AS REPORTED BY PARENTS REPRESENTING 544 FAMILIES AND 1,137 CHILDREN[12]

	Satisfactions			Problems		
	% of Children[a]	% of Families[b]	% of Items[c]	% of Children	% of Families	% of Items[c]
I. Fact of Having; Presence or Absence of Companionship; Congeniality; Pride or Otherwise in Role as Parent:						
Fact of having; having or not having children of desired number or sex; children give meaning to life, etc.	30.9	31.8	3.0	7.5	8.1	1.3
Reflection of self in child; child has or has not favorable or unfavorable parental traits	8.5	15.5	.73	5.2	9.9	.85
Companionship; affectionate relationships, affinities with parents or the opposite	65.3	72.3	8.1	8.7	12.1	1.4
Satisfaction, pride, self-congratulation or the opposite in practices and policies of being a child rearer	59.2	63.7	7.3	23.7	29.3	4.8
Perplexities regarding specific practical problems in rearing and discipline	—	—	—	6.9	9.2	1.2
(Total)			(19.13)			(9.56)
II. Phenomena of Development, Differences Between Children, etc.:						
Growth was natural, normal, or otherwise; fact of growth, change	22.0	31.5	1.7	5.1	8.7	.81
Fact of difference in qualities, traits, behavior of separate offspring[d]	—	16.9	—	—	—	—
(Total)			(1.7)			(.81)

(a) Per cent of children mentioned in connection with a report of one or more items in each general category.
(b) Per cent of families in which there was mention of one or more items in each category mentioned in the account of one or more children.
(c) Per cent of all items classified respectively as satisfactions or problems. Total satisfaction items: 18, 121; total problem items: 7, 760.
(d) Computed on the basis of the number of families (356 of the 544) that contained two or more children.

[12] From Jersild, A. T., Woodyard, E. W., and Fehlman, C.: *Joys and Problems in Child Rearing*, unpublished manuscript, 1945. To be published under the auspices of the Horace Mann-Lincoln Institute of School Experimentation by the Teachers College Bureau of Publications, New York. Reproduced by permission. The original monograph includes tabulations of the results according to age, sex, socio-economic status, urban and suburban residence, Negro and white populations.

TABLE XXI (Continued)

	Satisfactions			Problems		
	% of Children	% of Families	% of Items	% of Children	% of Families	% of Items
III. Factors in Child Relating to Parental Convenience, Bother, Ease, or Difficulty in Everyday Care:						
Favorable or unfavorable progress or response to training in routines (eating, sleeping, grooming, etc.)	48.3	58.3	5.6	26.2	41.8	5.9
Performance or nonperformance of chores, help in practical household affairs	42.3	47.8	3.4	10.1	14.2	1.7
Child is or is not easy to manage; causes or does not cause inconvenience, labor, drudgery	17.7	28.3	1.2	18.7	19.9	3.5
Satisfaction or apprehension concerning child's coping with or susceptibility to hazards, dangers (fire, traffic, etc.)	13.0	16.2	.88	15.0	17.9	3.0
Accidents, injuries, actual occurrence of difficulties in connection with traffic, water, fire, etc.[a]	—	—	—	1.9	4.1	.37
Negativism, disrespect, obstinacy, impertinence, naughtiness, disobedience, etc.	—	—	—	17.5	28.3	3.1
(Total)			(11.08)			(17.57)
IV. Features in General Social and Physical Environment:						
Physical environment, living quarters (size, space, convenience, ventilation, etc.)	—	25.9	2.4	—	31.3	7.0
Social, moral environment, satisfactory or unsatisfactory influence of group, customs	9.2	15.6	.62	1.8	3.7	.34
Resources or lack of resources in community; availability of playmates; congenial or uncongenial neighbors	32.7	35.0	2.8	24.9	24.8	4.7
Favorable or unfavorable influence of playmates, unfavorable standards of other people in community	1.1	2.0	.07	17.5	19.5	3.8
Family finances, means	15.2	14.7	1.3	22.0	20.6	3.9
Qualities of child's relations with maids, household help	8.1	11.4	.61	5.1	6.3	.97
Qualities of doctors, nurses, medical aids	7.4	12.1	.52	2.8	3.5	.41
School facilities, program, personnel	17.7	25.0	1.4	11.7	16.9	2.2
Values or defects of books, articles, expert advice on child rearing	4.1	5.3	.27	1.8	2.9	.30
(Total)			(9.99)			(23.62)

[a] There was no separate category for this in the analysis of satisfactions.

TABLE XXI (Continued)

	Satisfactions			Problems		
	% of Children	% of Families	% of Items	% of Children	% of Families	% of Items
V. Child's School Progress and Adjustments:						
Progress and achievement in school subjects, projects	24.1	32.6	1.6	5.6	9.9	.83
Deportment, adjustment to school's demands	10.4	14.4	.67	2.6	4.6	.46
Social adjustments in school	7.7	13.3	.55	2.6	4.8	.47
Attitudes, industry, liking for or dislike of school	14.9	25.8	1.1	5.2	9.4	.86
(Total: All categories dealing with school)	(46.3)	62.4	5.3	22.4	33.7	5.4)
VI. Qualities, Assets, or Liabilities of Child's Personality, Adjustments, and Relations with Other People:						
Personality traits, temperament, character, disposition	63.9	81.7	9.0	32.5	57.0	8.1
Miscellaneous pleasing or displeasing propensities; moral faults or virtues (thrift, lying, stealing, etc.)	27.7	33.9	2.2	11.0	16.0	1.9
Pleasing or distasteful mannerisms, habits, cute and not so cute ways	14.3	21.7	1.0	10.9	20.2	1.9
Desirable or undesirable emotional tendencies, crying, tantrums, etc.	10.6	17.1	.73	16.5	30.2	3.3
Social relationships with peers and other people; gregariousness, ability to lead; manners, poise	47.5	64.0	5.1	15.0	25.6	2.9
(f, g) Relationships with siblings; presence or absence of jealousy, etc.	41.5	55.6	2.4	30.9	41.6	5.4
Adjustment to sex, sex development, interests, heterosexual attitudes	28.5	35.1	2.3	10.2	15.3	1.8
Health, good or bad, robustness or frailty; illness and recovery	20.7	25.8	1.5	18.5	28.7	3.9
Physical appearance	13.0	19.3	1.0	2.4	5.0	.36
Intellectual ability, mental traits, reasoning, judgment	45.0	67.3	5.7	9.5	18.0	1.6
Motor abilities, skills, coördination, or motor lacks or deficiencies	25.5	39.9	1.8	4.7	8.3	.80
Ability, appreciation, interest or lack thereof in art, music, aesthetic matters	24.4	52.1	3.5	5.3	9.9	.93
Miscellaneous interests, hobbies, preferences (incl. radio, movies, etc.)	46.8	55.9	5.7	14.1	18.8	3.2
(Total)			(41.93)			(36.09)

(f) "Per cent of items" computed on the basis of all items reported by families with one or more children; "per cent of children" computed on the basis of number of children who had siblings (949 of the 1,137).

(g) "Per cent of items" in category 18 computed on basis of all items reported for children who had siblings and those who had not.

312

TABLE XXI (*Continued*)

	Satisfactions			Problems		
	% of Children	% of Families	% of Items	% of Children	% of Families	% of Items
VII. Miscellaneous:						
Qualities of child's relations with other parent and with relatives	50.7	53.7	6.2	23.7	29.6	6.5
Religious attitudes, practices (incl. availability and quality of church facilities)	24.2	21.5	2.3	4.3	5.2	.73
Reaction to the war	33.5	34.2	3.7	14.3	17.9	2.5
(Total)			(12.20)			(9.73)

313

fun and satisfaction that parenthood entails. This neglect of the happy side of the ledger of child rearing is rather curious in view of the conventional notions about the blessings of parenthood.

An indication of some of the joys and problems involved in being a parent is shown in Table XXI, which is based on results obtained when parents, in private interviews, were asked to describe the joys and satisfactions and the problems and difficulties that they had experienced in rearing their children. The children ranged from a few months to over twenty years of age. The percentages shown in the table should be considered on a comparative basis. No doubt many of these percentages would be much higher if the parents had been specifically questioned on this point or that. For example, it is likely that a considerably larger percentage of parents would have reported at least minor problems in connection with "routine" training (eating, sleeping, elimination) if questions bearing upon these particulars had been asked. So, also, in a number of other categories.

One of the most prominent satisfactions of parenthood, according to the parents represented in Table XXI, is the companionship a child affords—the child's friendliness, his manifest affection for his parents, the fact that he and his parents can have interests in common and can enjoy things together. Enjoyment of children's personality traits and characteristics of their disposition or temperament represented another prominent source of satisfaction to parents. Many of the satisfactions in this and related categories represented an interest in the development of the child, pleasure in watching the phenomena of growth and the emergence of a distinct personality. This interest in development of the child's unique qualities as a person led many parents to report that they obtained pleasure from observing the child's personality development even when this involved characteristics which are not usually, *per se,* regarded as assets, such as a quick temper or a tendency to be very sensitive. Another important source of pleasure and pride, perhaps of a somewhat self-congratulatory nature, comes from what might be called the *vocational* aspects of parenthood, the job of caring for children, carrying out small and large duties, plans, and policies in child rearing, successfully coping with problems, and the like.

The problems and dissatisfactions involved in child rearing are not consistently the counterpart of the satisfactions, according to the parents represented in Table XXI. Some features stand relatively high in both satisfactions and problems, such as children's favorable or unfavorable personality traits, good or bad relationships between siblings, good or poor response in "routines." However, many of the things that are noted as "problems" when conditions are bad tend to be taken for granted when conditions are good. Examples of this appear in categories relating to family finances and goodness or badness of living quarters and also, to a lesser degree, in the category of health.[13] An interesting feature is that parents tend to a greater extent to take credit to themselves in describing satisfying features of child rearing than to blame themselves in describing their problems (note especially the large number of "problems" under the heading "Features in the General Social and Physical Environment").

A comparison between the findings in Table XXI, which are based primarily on the testimony of mothers, with preliminary findings in a study of fathers by Tasch,* indicates that the two parents show, in general, a high degree of agreement, but also some differences. Enjoyment of companionship provided by children, of children's personality traits, and of children's intellectual qualities similarly occurred among the three top categories in the reports by fathers and by mothers. In accounts of "problems," a large percentage of both the fathers and the mothers mentioned "routines" and matters relating to health. In accounts of satisfactions, fathers mentioned physical appearance and a category

---

[13] In assessing the relative weight given on the positive and negative side it should be noted that fewer problems than satisfactions were reported.

* Tasch, Ruth J.: *The Role of the Father in the Family,* unpublished.

including "cute and cunning ways, mannerisms, bright sayings, and the like" considerably more than did the mothers. On the other hand, in accounts of problems, fathers also more often than mothers mentioned the inconveniences and minor annoyances caused by the child, such as leaving a toy about that someone might trip over, getting into things, and the like.

Table XXII

FREQUENCY OF VARIOUS SATISFACTIONS AND PLEASING QUALITIES (IN SELECTED CATEGORIES) ASSOCIATED WITH 36 CHILDREN AS DESCRIBED BY PARENTS AND AS DESCRIBED BY THE TEACHERS OF THE SAME CHILDREN [14]

Quality or Characteristics	Number of Children So Described By Parents	By Teachers
Miscellaneous personality traits and temperamental qualities:		
Amenable, considerate, coöperative, affectionate, kind	28	17
Honor, integrity, dependability, truthfulness	19	2
Inner strength, fortitude, independence, self-sufficiency	16	7
Good sense of humor, full of fun, jolly, laughs easily	13	9
Enterprising, ambitious, full of initiative	11	13
Vigorous, lively, busy, decisive, plays hard	9	12
Pertinacious, persistent, finishes things, slow but sure	7	7
Even tempered, good disposition, passively happy	4	7
Intellectual qualities:		
Amount, quality, taste in reading	14	13
Good mind, bright, intelligent	11	16
Good imagination, fanciful, constructive	7	11
Good capacity for concentration	4	8
"Social" qualities:		
Gets along well with other children	13	18
Good manners, courteous, gracious	13	2
Leadership, is leader in his group	6	6
Artistic interest, ability, appreciation:		
Music	16	2
Painting	10	8
"Sensitive to beauty," artistic nature	6	0
Companionship, shared interests	28	1
Pleasure, pride in duties in bringing up, in educating child	16	1
Friendly sibling relationships	16	0
Response to routine habit training	14	0
Motor abilities, good coördination	13	3
Miscellaneous hobbies, interests	10	3

[14] Adapted, in much abridged form, from Fehlman, C.: *Parents and Teachers View the Child*. Unpublished Ph.D. dissertation, Teachers College, Columbia University, 1946. To be published under the auspices of the Horace Mann-Lincoln Institute of School Experimentation. Reproduced by permission.

As one might expect, it has been found that a parent is likely to derive many satisfactions from a child that are not experienced to the same extent by the child's teacher. Table XXII gives illustrations of this from a study of thirty-six children. The fact that the parent has a greater emotional stake in the child is indicated, for example, by the finding that enjoyment of the child as a companion was spontaneously mentioned in parents' accounts of twenty-eight of the children and by teachers in only one instance. Parents also revealed much more identification with the child's nonacademic hobbies, habits, skills (including both motor and artistic), his manners and his morals. Teachers and parents showed most agreement in mention of intellectual qualities and of the child's ability to get along with other children outside the home.

BIBLIOGRAPHY

1. Barker, R., Dembo, T., and Lewin, K.: *Studies in Topological and Vector Psychology: II. Frustration and Regression,* University of Iowa Studies in Child Welfare (1941), 18, No. 1, 314 pp.
2. Cannon, W. B.: *Bodily Changes in Pain, Hunger, Fear and Rage,* second edition (New York: Appleton-Century, 1929), 404 pp.
3. Davis, A.: "Socialization and Adolescent Personality," *Forty-Third Yearbook of the National Society for the Study of Education* (Bloomington, Illinois: Public School Publishing Company, 1944), Pt. 1, *Adolescence,* Ch. XI, pp. 198-216.
4. Dollard, J., Doob, L., Miller, N., Mowrer, O., Sears, R., et al.: *Frustration and Aggression* (New Haven: Yale University Press, 1939), 209 pp.
5. English, H. B.: "Three Cases of the Conditioned Fear Response," *Journal of Abnormal and Social Psychology* (1929), 24:221-225.
6. Felder, J. G.: "Some Factors Determining the Nature and Frequency of Anger and Fear Outbreaks in Preschool Children," *Journal of Juvenile Research* (1932), 16:278-290.
7. Foster, S.: "A Study of Personality Make-Up and Social Setting of Fifty Jealous Children," *Mental Hygiene* (1927), 11:53-77.
8. Freud, S.: *The Problem of Anxiety* (New York: Norton, 1936), 165 pp.
9. Gates, G. S.: "An Observational Study of Anger," *Journal of Experimental Psychology* (1926), 9:325-336.

10. Gesell, A. L.: "Jealousy," *American Journal of Psychology* (1906), 17:437-496.
11. ———: "The Individual in Infancy," *The Foundations of Experimental Psychology,* edited by C. Murchison (Worcester: Clark University Press, 1929), pp. 628-660.
12. Goodenough, F. L.: *Anger in Young Children,* Institute of Child Welfare Monograph Series (Minneapolis: University of Minnesota Press, 1931), 278 pp.
13. ———: *The Measurement of Intelligence by Drawings* (Yonkers-on-Hudson, New York: World Book Co., 1926), 177 pp.
14. Green, G. H.: *Daydream, a Study in Development* (London: University of London Press, 1923), 303 pp.
15. Hagman, R. R.: "A Study of Fears of Children of Preschool Age," *Journal of Experimental Education* (1932), 1:110-130.
16. Holmes, F. B.: "An Experimental Investigation of a Method of Overcoming Children's Fears," *Child Development* (1936), Vol. 7, 1:6-30.
17. ———: "An Experimental Study of the Fears of Young Children," in Jersild, A. T. and Holmes, F. B.: *Children's Fears,* Child Development Monographs (New York: Teachers College, Columbia University, 1935), No. 20, Pt. 3, pp. 167-296.
18. Jersild, A. T., Goldman, B., and Loftus, J.: "A Comparative Study of the Worries of Children in Two School Situations," *Journal of Experimental Education* (1941), 9:323-326.
19. Jersild, A. T. and Holmes, F. B.: *Children's Fears,* Child Development Monographs (New York: Teachers College, Columbia University, 1935), No. 20, 356 pp.
20. ———: "Methods of Overcoming Children's Fears," *Journal of Psychology* (1935), 1:75-104.
21. ———: "Some Factors in the Development of Children's Fears," *Journal of Experimental Education* (1935), 4:133-141.
22. Jersild, A. T. and Markey, F. V.: *Conflicts Between Preschool Children,* Child Development Monographs (New York: Teachers College, Columbia University, 1935), No. 21, 181 pp.
23. Jersild, A. T., Markey, F. V., and Jersild, C. L.: *Children's Fears, Dreams, Wishes, Daydreams, Likes, Dislikes, Pleasant and Unpleasant Memories,* Child Development Monographs (New York: Teachers College, Columbia University, 1933), No. 12, 172 pp.
24. Jersild, A. T. and Thomas, W. S.: "The Influence of Adrenal Extract on Behavior and Mental Efficiency," *American Journal of Psychology* (1931), 43:447-456.
25. Jersild, A. T., Woodyard, E., and Fehlman, C. in collaboration with Osborne, E. G. and Challman, R. C.: *Joys and Problems of Child*

Rearing, unpublished (New York: Teachers College, Columbia University).
26. John, E.: "A Study of the Effects of Evacuation and Air Raids on Children of Preschool Age," *British Journal of Educational Psychology* (1941), 11:173-182.
27. Jones, H. E. and Jones, M. C.: "Fear," *Childhood Education* (1928), 5:136-143.
28. Jones, M. C.: "Emotional Development," *A Handbook of Child Psychology,* edited by C. Murchison (Worcester: Clark University Press, 1933), Ch. VI, pp. 271-302.
29. ———: "The Elimination of Children's Fears," *Journal of Experimental Psychology* (1924), 7:383-390.
30. Keister, M. E.: *The Behavior of Young Children in Failure: An Experimental Attempt to Discover and to Modify Undesirable Responses of Preschool Children to Failure,* University of Iowa Studies in Child Welfare (1937), 14:26-82.
31. Klein, M.: *The Psycho-Analysis of Children* (New York: Norton, 1932), 393 pp.
32. Lewin, K.: "Behavior and Development as a Function of the Total Situation," *Manual of Child Psychology,* edited by L. Carmichael (New York: John Wiley, 1946), Ch. XVI, pp. 791-844.
33. Lewin, K., Lippitt, R., and White, R.: "Patterns of Aggressive Behavior in Experimentally Created 'Social Climates,'" *Journal of Social Psychology* (1939), 10:271-299.
34. McFarland, M. B.: *Relationships Between Young Sisters as Revealed in Their Overt Responses,* Child Development Monographs (New York: Teachers College, Columbia University, 1938), No. 23, 230 pp.
35. Markey, F. V.: *Imaginative Behavior in Preschool Children,* Child Development Monographs (New York: Teachers College, Columbia University, 1935), No. 18, 138 pp.
36. Meltzer, H.: "Students' Adjustments in Anger," *Journal of Social Psychology* (1933), 4:285-309.
37. Pintner, R. and Lev, J.: "Worries of School Children," *Journal of Genetic Psychology* (1940), 56:67-76.
38. Pratt, K. C.: "A Study of the 'Fears' of Rural Children," *Journal of Genetic Psychology* (1945), 67:179-194.
39. Pritchard, E. and Ojemann, R.: "An Approach to the Measurement of Insecurity," *Journal of Experimental Education* (1941), 10:114-118.
40. Richardson, R. F.: *The Psychology and Pedagogy of Anger,* Educational Psychology Monographs, No. 19 (1918), 100 pp.
41. Ricketts, A. F.: "A Study of the Behavior of Young Children in

Anger," Jack, Manwell, Mengert, et al.: *Behavior of the Preschool Child,* University of Iowa Studies in Child Welfare (1934), Vol. 9, 3:159-171.
42. Seashore, H. G. and Bavelas, A.: "A Study of Frustration in Children," *Journal of Genetic Psychology* (1942), 61:279-314.
43. Sewall, S.: *Two Studies in Sibling Rivalry,* Pt. I: *Some Causes of Jealousy in Young Children,* Smith College Studies in Social Work (1930), 1:6-22.
44. Slater, E.: *II. Types, Levels, and Irregularities of Response to a Nursery School Situation of Forty Children Observed with Special Reference to the Home Environment,* Studies from the Center for Research in Child Health and Development, School of Public Health, Harvard University, Society for Research in Child Development Monographs (1939), Vol. 4, No. 2, 148 pp.
45. Smalley, R. E.: *Two Studies in Sibling Rivalry,* Pt. II: *The Influence of Differences in Age, Sex, and Intelligence in Determining the Attitudes of Siblings Toward Each Other,* Smith College Studies in Social Work (1930), 1:23-40.
46. Updegraff, R. and Keister, M. E.: "A Study of Children's Reactions to Failure and an Experimental Attempt to Modify Them," *Child Development* (1937) 8:241-248.
47. Valentine, C. W.: "The Innate Bases of Fear," *Journal of Genetic Psychology* (1930), 37:394-420.
48. Watson, J. B.: *Behaviorism* (New York: People's Institute, Inc., 1924), 251 pp.
49. ———: *Psychology from the Standpoint of a Behaviorist* (Philadelphia: Lippincott, 1924), 448 pp.
50. Wright, H. F.: *The Influence of Barriers Upon Strength of Motivation,* Duke University Series, Contributions to Psychological Theory (1937), 1, No. 3, 143 pp.

CHAPTER IX

LANGUAGE DEVELOPMENT

This chapter will be confined mainly to structural aspects of language formation, since the functions of language in a child's life and the interplay of language on other aspects of development are considered throughout the book.[1]

The development of language manifests many trends and principles that are characteristic of other aspects of development. It demonstrates the roles of both learning and growth. It involves the emergence of new responses as well as a differentiation and refinement of older forms. It involves both a process of adding on and a process of casting away. It demonstrates the principle that with the development of a capacity there is associated an impulse to put the capacity to use. In addition, a study of language formation emphasizes the fact that what happens in any aspect of a child's development has a profound influence on and is profoundly influenced by other developments in the organism as a whole.

EARLY VOCALIZATIONS

The healthy child begins life as quite a vocal creature. During the first two or three weeks of life his vocalizations include cries that vary from time to time in pitch, quality, and loudness. He produces also a number of other sounds, such as grunts, yawns, sighs, an "inspirational crow," and, of course, sounds connected with coughing, sneezing, and belching.

During the first days of life it is questionable whether the child's crying and other vocalizations are differentiated into sounds char-

---

[1] When we call a child an "infant" we testify to the importance of language since "infancy" is from the negative *in* and *fans*, the present participle form of *fari, to speak*. For an account of language basied on a review of several hundred studies see McCarthy (39).

acteristic, say, of hunger, pain, anger, or fright. However, according to one study, such differentiation is achieved by the age of one month, so that a child will give different cries for hunger, pain, and discomfort (17). One feature of early development is increased differentiation.

The child's earliest vocalizations do not include many sounds which later will appear. In other words, another feature of development is the emergence of new sounds, the enlargement of the repertory of vowels and consonant sounds that the child can produce.

Vowel sounds predominate in the child's earliest vocalizations (25, 34, 50). Moreover, "front" vowels far outnumber "middle" and "back" vowels. Examples of sounds involving front vowels are: *See, it, at.* Middle: *Calm, bird, butter.* Back: *Moon, good, hope, saw, song.*

During the first days of life certain consonant sounds appear while others occur seldom, if at all, until later in the child's development.[2]

The changes that occur in vocalization do not consist solely, however, of additions to the repertory of sounds. A baby produces many sounds that are not elements of the particular language he will learn, and many such sounds may, accordingly, drop out as he grows older. Thus, a child destined to speak English may produce sounds corresponding to the German *ü* or the Danish *ö* or the French guttural *r*. Many of the sounds he produces may not correspond precisely to any known alphabet or system of phonetic recording. From ordinary observation it appears that a person may find it difficult when he is older to reproduce some of these same sounds.[3]

Early forms of communication. A child's utterances serve as a means of social communication long before he has acquired the

---

[2] For a review of findings with respect to early vocalizations see Irwin (26).

[3] It appears that a child who is later going to learn one or more "foreign" languages would profit if sound elements from these languages could be incorporated into his speech from an early age.

ability to articulate precise words or phrases. The babies in Shirley's study (50) babbled to examiners at a median age of twenty-five weeks, and many of the mothers reported babbling as a social reaction at a considerably earlier age (the median child was credited with his "first word" in the examiner's presence at sixty weeks). Inflections and intonations resembling those found in adult speech were also noted in advance of the "first word." Among these early inflections, intonations, and expressive utterances were "squeals of delight, strong grunts of pain or disgust, grunts with the rising inflection of a question, guttural barking growls that reminded the examiner of a dog worrying a bone, shouting and calling to attract attention, and calling in scolding or warning tones. . . ."

The child usually understands many words spoken to him by others before he himself can use the words. In his early response to the language of others he reacts to inflections and intonations before he seems to be responsive to precise pronunciation. If he has learned to wave in response to "bye-bye," he may similarly respond to "my-my" or even "pooh-pooh," if these words are spoken in the same tone of voice. An incidental feature of the child's recognition of intonations is the development of ability to distinguish between emotional qualities which an adult endeavors to convey by means of his voice. According to Bühler (8), the average child reacts to a change in the tone of the adult's voice at two months (as when an adult, hidden behind the child, first speaks in a normal tone and "then suddenly begins to growl" or begins to emit falsetto tones), and distinguishes between angry and friendly talking at six months.

Gesture language, often accompanied by unintelligible vocalizations and taking such forms as pointing, reaching, and movements indicating efforts to reject, avert, or accept, also frequently serves as a means of communication long before the child can express himself in so many words.

The "first word." As can be seen, much language development has taken place before the baby speaks his "first word." It is rather difficult to spot the first word. A child may have used a certain sound to convey a definite meaning even though that sound may not be found in any known dictionary. For example, one child used the expression "oi-yoi" to ask for water and for no other purpose. The expression functioned as a word even though it might take a visiting observer some time to recognize it as such. On the other hand, a child might use an utterance that sounds like a word but it may not be clear that this sound functions as a word or is used by the child in a meaningful way. By reason of ambiguities of this sort, one mother may credit her child with a "first word" where another would not. As is only to be expected, mothers are likely to detect discriminating use of one or more words earlier than will an examiner who sees the child only on occasion.

In view of differences in interpretation as to what constitutes a first word, and in view of large differences among individual children, any statement as to age at which the normal child uses his first word or words must be taken with a good deal of caution. In the study of Shirley, cited above (in which the children represented a selection somewhat above the average of children in the general population), the median age at which the first comprehensible word was spoken in the examiner's presence was sixty weeks, while most of the mothers reported that the babies had a vocabulary of two or three words at fifty-two weeks (50). Twenty-five per cent of the children spoke their first comprehensible words in the presence of the examiner by the age of forty-seven weeks, and twenty-five per cent had not yet reached this accomplishment by the age of sixty-six weeks. In the case of individual children, the age at which the first word appears varies from eight months or less to well over two years (4).

Content of child's early vocabulary. Nouns are likely to be most numerous among children's "first words," but there is also a sprinkling of verbs, adverbs, and adjectives. Pronouns usually appear later.

The appearance of the first well-defined word in the child's utterances does not usually denote a sharp break in the course of his language development, with an immediate large increase in new words during the ensuing weeks or months. For a long time to come the child continues to babble and to use a good deal of incomprehensible speech, and, during the months immediately following the appearance of articulate words, additional new words may be rather slow in coming to the fore.

In a study of size of vocabularies at different ages, Smith (54) found an average vocabulary of three words at twelve months, nineteen words at fifteen months, and twenty-two words at eighteen months. As can be seen, the increase in the averages from twelve to eighteen months is enormous in terms of percentages, but in absolute terms and in comparison with the tremendous number of words yet to be acquired, the increase is not large. At twenty-one months, the average was 118 words, which represents quite a jump over the earlier performance. The fact that children do not necessarily forthwith make large strides in their vocabularies immediately after they begin to "talk" is of practical interest, for some parents, fascinated by the advent of language, seem to become impatient when large gains do not immediately ensue.

At two years the average number of words spoken by children in the study above was 272, again a substantial increase in terms of actual numbers. The averages at later levels follow: 896 words at three years; 1,540 words at four; 2,072 at five; and 2,562 at six (based on only nine subjects).

Decline in incomprehensible speech. As the child adds more and more words to his repertoire, there is a decline also in his use of unrecognizable or incomprehensible utterances. In a study by McCarthy (38), it was found that only 26 per cent of the utterances made by children in response to the investigator were comprehensible at the age of eighteen months, while nearly all that the child said (99.8 per cent) was comprehensible to the investigator at fifty-four months. An indication of the child's progress in more or less precise pronunciation is given in a study by Wellman and her associates (62), in which it was found that children at the age of three years (with an average I.Q. of 115.9) correctly pronounced 82.5 per cent of the diphthongs, 75.2 per cent of the vowels, 68.4 per cent of the consonant elements, and 51.8 per cent of consonant blends covered in the investigation. The ability to pronounce words so clearly that any intelligent person can understand them may lag considerably behind the development of a rather large vocabulary. Frequently a child will continue for a time to use a large number of words that can be understood by an older brother or sister, or by the child's mother, while remaining incomprehensible to outsiders or even to the child's father.

Spontaneous revision of language habits. The development of language usage provides almost countless illustrations of the principle of developmental revision of habits, as set forth in an earlier chapter. In his own good time, if provided with a correct model, the child corrects his earlier mispronunciations even though no adult is hounding him. Most of the children who for a time say "free," because that is the best they can do, eventually say "three," and so in countless other examples that might be given.

However, in spite of a great amount of self-correction, many children show faulty articulation of some speech sounds in the elementary grades. When such faults are not due to an organic condition (such as defective hearing), they represent habits that perhaps might have been avoided. Available evidence does not give a good answer to the question as to when it is timely, and by what means, to help the child's own process of self-correction.

Misunderstanding due to faulty articulation. While a child's articulation is still childish, there must be many times when his elders strike him as hopelessly stupid people. Often he repeats himself over and over, and yet they do not understand. An example of slow comprehension by a parent follows:

A father noticed that there was a dog in the nursery school attended by his three-year-old daughter, and on their way home the following conversation occurred:

Father: What is the name of the dog at your school?
Child: Way.
Father: Way?
Child: No, Way.
Father: Did you say Way?
Child: No. (Angrily) You stupid, I said WAY!
Father: Oh, you mean Ray?
Child: Yes, that's what I said.

In a similar vein:

Mother (to two- and three-year-old Peggy and Marian): Oh, look, there's a monkey wearing a red coat!
Peggy: Oh, yook!
Marian: Don't say yook, say wook.

Development of phrases and sentences. When a child first begins to "talk," single words are likely to predominate (although a string of sounds with varying inflection and resembling sentences may be noted before that time). The single words frequently function as sentences. As McCarthy has pointed out (37), the single word "mama," with varying inflections and gestures, may variously be tantamount to "mama give me," "mama look," or "there is mama."

Even the single words thus used are likely to be short ones. Up to the age of two years, one-syllable words constituted about seventy per cent of all the comprehensible words spoken by all the babies in the study by Shirley cited earlier. For several years many youngsters continue to shorten words by dropping a syllable or two so that "inspect" is " 'spect," "conductor" is " 'ductor," and a neighboring "Missus" may continue for several years, in the child's nomenclature, to be a maiden "Miss." Some of the children in Shirley's study began to use phrases and sentences shortly before the age of eighteen months, but such combinations of words were relatively infrequent before the age of two years. When sentence formation did appear it was noted that children frequently tended to repeat a sentence over and over. One child, for example, at sixty-six weeks, repeated "Wha's dat?" seventeen times during an examination and used only two other sentences.

The increase with age in number of words per remark has been measured with considerable care in several studies (9, 14, 38, 39, 50). The averages in different studies agree quite closely when based upon a substantially normal or representative selection of children. The average length per remark is considerably higher, however, in the case of bright children. In one of the studies (38), in which an analysis was made of fifty consecutive remarks made by each of twenty children at each half-yearly age level from eighteen to fifty-four months (the children were selected from various socio-economic groups; the average I.Q.'s at the various half-yearly age levels ranged from 103 to 112), it was found that the average number of words per remark increased from 1.2 at eighteen months to 4.6 at fifty-four months. In another study of brighter children, observed mainly on the nursery-school playground and primarily when conversing with one another, the corresponding averages at eighteen months and fifty-four months were 3.7 and 9.5.

Quite as significant as the increase in the length of sentences is the change that comes with age in other characteristics of the sentence. Among other things, there is an increase in the use of sentences that are structurally complete with nouns, verbs, and other parts of speech. There is also an increase in the use of complex and compound sentences, although, throughout the preschool period, simple sentences by far predominate over sentences containing dependent or coördinate clauses. Of the sentences used by the older preschool children in a study by Fisher (14), representing children above average in intelligence, only five per cent were complex and only two per cent were compound. Coincident with the development of complete sentences is an increase also in the number of verbs as compared with nouns and in the number of conjunctions and prepositions. During this period of development, the increase in the child's language repertory is, of course, associated with development of his mental abilities in general. Among other things, there is an increased use of inflections and verbs, and an increase in the use of the past tense (which is infrequent at the age of two years) and in the use of the future tense.

Increases in loquacity. One notable feature of the child's progress in language is the tremendous amount of exercise he undertakes on his own accord, as noted earlier. The gains that children show in volume of talking may be considerably greater than the gains they show in their vocabularies. Results obtained in a study by the writer and an associate (28), in which tallies were made of the total number of words uttered by children during a forenoon in the nursery school (from the time they arrived in the morning until after lunch, a period of a little more than three hours), are summarized below. The total-number-of-words-spoken tally al-

Table XX

NUMBER OF WORDS SPOKEN AND NUMBER OF DIFFERENT WORDS USED PER THREE HOURS (APPROXIMATELY) BY NURSERY-SCHOOL CHILDREN[4]

Age in Months	Number of Children	Total Number of Words Spoken Range	Total Number of Words Spoken Mean	Total Number of Different Words Used Range	Total Number of Different Words Used Mean
24–29	11	236– 729	402	60–142	94
30–35	20	99–1,967	763	32–298	153
36–41	22	396–1,990	1,296	111–394	254
42–47	26	332–3,084	1,772	117–552	309

[4] Adapted from Jersild, A. T. and Ritzman, R.: "Aspects of Language Development: The Growth of Loquacity and Vocabulary," *Child Development* (1938), 9, 3:243-259. Reproduced by permission.

lowed a count of one for each word or each repetition of a word (for example, a count of ten for the word "swing" if the child used this word ten times during the forenoon). The total-number-of-different-words-used tally, on the other hand, allowed a count of only one for each separate word, whether the word was used once or many times (for example, only one tally for "swing" in the above illustration). The figures would, of course, be much larger if the children were observed throughout the day.

LATER LANGUAGE DEVELOPMENT

Beyond the nursery-school level, the child's language activities become increasingly complex and they assume increasing importance in connection with the child's schooling. Sometime between the ages of four and eight years, the child must learn to deal with language by eye, in his reading, as well as by ear; and he must learn to express himself by way of the hand, in writing, as well as by word of mouth. In his reading, and to a lesser extent in his writing, he eventually utilizes an enormous number of words which he seldom or never uses in speech, and his language activities become saddled with the need for many associated learnings—such as spelling, grammar, punctuation, sentence formation, paragraphing, and so on.

Increase in vocabulary. One of the more obvious changes as a child grows older is a gain in vocabulary. As noted at an earlier point, Smith's findings, based on a limited number of six-year-old children (54), indicated that at this age a child will have a vocabulary of about 2,600 words. Horn (24) has estimated that the beginner at school is likely to have a vocabulary of about 2,500 words. To obtain an exact measure of vocabulary at this as well as at later ages is difficult. One method of measuring vocabulary, devised by Seashore and Echerson (49), involves a procedure for estimating total vocabulary from words correctly identified on a list comprising a systematically derived random sampling from the Funk and Wagnall's Unabridged Dictionary. Smith,[5] using a modification of the technique developed by Seashore and Echerson and designed to elicit the maximum response from children, found vocabularies much larger than past estimates had suggested. The forty-four children she tested in the first grade in three schools had recognition vocabularies ranging from 6,000 to 48,000 words. At the twelfth grade the range was found to be from 36,700 to 136,500 words, with an average of 80,300. Another investigator (Hartmann, 20) estimates that the average undergraduate in normal schools can identify the meaning of over 200,000 words and that his reading vocabulary is probably larger.

The above estimates pertain to the number of words children are able to recognize the meaning of. The child's vocabulary is much smaller when measured in terms of the number of words he actually uses. In a large sampling of children's writings, Rinsland (46) found only a little more than 5,000 different words used in the first grade, and 2,000 of these represented ninety-eight per cent of all the words used in a sample of over 350,000 words. At the eighth grade children used about 18,000 different words in their compositions.

Changes in understanding of the connotation of words. A child's mastery of language develops not only by adding "new" words but also, to a significant degree, through the increased understanding of the connotations of "old" words. In theory, it should be possible for teachers and textbook writers to introduce new words gradually, so that a child may continually incorporate new terms into a familiar context. But this policy is difficult to work out in practice, especially with older children. In the reading matter of the average child and in the conversations and discussions in which he participates, a large number of the words

---

[5] Smith, M. K.: *Measurement of the Size of General English Vocabulary Through the Elementary Grades and High School,* Genetic Psychology Monographs (1941), 24:311-345.

he meets will be unfamiliar to him, and the meanings of many others are likely to be vague. The child himself may use many terms that have relatively little meaning to him, as compared with the meaning intended by the writer or the teacher.

In much of what is presented to the child, the problem is not so much one of complete mastery as opposed to complete ignorance as it is one of varying degrees of understanding. As soon as the child's status in school gets him into the study of such matters as history and geography, for example, it becomes a difficult, if not impossible, task to map out a list of terms that can be mastered and "laid by," much as a child might lay by one row after another as he hoes the potato patch. Many of the terms he meets can be understood only by means of other terms that may be just as unfamiliar.

Examples of vague meanings. In a study by Scott and Myers (48), children in the fifth through the eighth grades were tested on a list of terms taken from history and geography. It was found that the meanings of many terms which they met frequently in their reading and classwork were quite vague to them. Less than forty per cent of the children below the eighth grade were able to give "reasonably correct" definitions of such terms as "colonists," "taxation," "minister" (ambassador), and "constitution." In a seventh-grade class, some of the children were under the impression that, since Benjamin Franklin was a foreign *minister,* he must have been a clergyman. The subject of children's understanding of various concepts is further treated in Chapters X and XI.

Illustrations of varying levels or degrees of understanding appeared in an unpublished study by the writer in which children were asked, among other things, to tell what is meant by a *strike*. To some children, the term had no other meanings than those connected with the verb *to hit*. Most of the subjects who were questioned in the fourth through the sixth grades had other associations with the term. At one extreme were children who could offer little more than answers such as the following: "It's when people break windows and throw stones at the police"; or "It's when people walk outside a shop with signs on their backs with words like 'unfair' on them." Answers such as these, it can be observed, phrased in terms of visual images drawn from pictures or actual observation, indicate that the child has a notion that a strike involves conflict of some sort. Still more comprehension of the term was revealed in an answer such as: "It's when the workers and the bosses have an argument and the workers stop working," which indicates that the child knows there is a dispute between employers and employees, even though he may not be able to define things further. At a higher level of understanding, the child may not only mention the fact of a dispute and describe the parties to the dispute but he may also describe the issues involved, such as demands for more pay or shorter hours, and so forth. At a still higher level of comprehension were a few children who not only described what happened in a strike and the issues that might be involved but also went so far as to elaborate upon steps that might be taken to terminate a strike and the possible effects on the employer's business or on the workers' buying power if the strikers won.

MENTAL AND SOCIAL ORIENTATION OF THE YOUNG CHILD AS REVEALED BY HIS LANGUAGE

Once a child has begun to talk, his language development becomes increasingly interesting as a means of studying his mental processes, his interests, and his orientation to the material and social world in which he lives. A study of these aspects of development, as revealed by language, would carry us into fields covered by other chapters in this volume, but certain trends in the child's language from two to five years may be listed briefly.

"I" and "you." The child's use of pronouns shows interesting trends. When pronouns appear, various forms of "I" predominate. In a study by Smith (52) of children aged two to five years,

"I" had a frequency of 2,543, as compared with a score of 955 for "you." "I" is especially frequent as compared with other pronouns at the earlier age levels, and it continues to show a high frequency of use throughout the preschool period (and from that point onward, too); but as children advance in age during preschool years, there also is an increase in other forms, such as "we," "you," "she," and "it." Table XXIV summarizes the number of times these pronouns were used at half-yearly age levels in the spontaneous speech of two- and three-year-old children (above average in I.Q.), as recorded during observation of the children on the nursery-school playground.

TABLE XXIV

FREQUENCY OF VARIOUS PRONOUNS IN CHILDREN'S CONVERSATIONS[6]

Age in Months	24–29	30–35	36–41	42–47
Number of Children	11	11	11	11
Total Number of Words Spoken During Period of Recording	13,124	22,016	46,624	64,352
Pronouns Used:				
I (*my, me, etc.*)	1,442	2,991	5,692	5,753
you (*your, -self*)	94	468	1,770	2,372
we (*our, us, etc.*)	28	177	406	881
he, she (*him, her, etc.*)	33	187	437	698
it (*it's, -self, etc.*)	155	567	1,206	1,485
they (*their, them, etc.*)	24	58	139	266

The relatively high frequency of the first-person pronoun in the speech of young children is of some interest, although it is difficult to see how one could expect anything else. A child's own impulses and desires, activities, pleasures, and pains are more vivid and closer to him than is his comprehension of the personalities and concerns of other people. That the child's private and personal concerns stand uppermost in his first reactions to the world about him, in so far as these are revealed by his language, appears not only through his frequent use of "I" but also through the con-

---

[6] Adapted from Jersild, A. T. and Ritzman, R.: "Aspects of Language Development: The Growth of Loquacity and Vocabulary," *Child Development* (1938), 9:243-259. Reproduced by permission.

tent and tone of his remarks, questions, and demands. However, from the time he begins to talk, the very fact that he expresses himself at all bespeaks a certain degree of sociability and adaptation to other persons. This point has been emphasized in a study by Fisher (14) of the content of children's spontaneous speech on the playground. When comprehensible remarks were analyzed according to three categories—*self* as subject: "I want to be first"; *other person* as subject: "Mary is coming along"; and *thing* as subject: "The carriage goes there"—it was found that slightly over one-third of the remarks were of the first-named type. However, while a child's remarks are heavily studded with "I's," there also is a vein of sociability running through them, for they at least are usually addressed to another person.

This tendency to refer to oneself is not, of course, confined to children, for adults, in their conversation, are likewise likely to deliver a large proportion of remarks about themselves (21).

Egocentric and socialized speech. The fact that a large proportion of the remarks of a young child deal with himself, his activities, interests, and personal concerns raises the question as to the extent to which he is capable of conversation of the adult type. To what degree is his talk so one-sided as to amount to little more than a monologue, as contrasted with an effort really to communicate with others and to exchange ideas on a give-and-take basis?

One investigator (Piaget, 44), working with French-speaking children in Europe, distinguishes (among other things) between "egocentric" and "socialized" speech. "Egocentric" speech involves no endeavor to interchange ideas, to consider the other person's point of view; it represents, rather, a form of "collective monologue" or "pseudo-conversation." In "socialized" speech, on the other hand, the talker really addresses the listener, considers the other person's viewpoint, and tries to communicate ideas and to share meanings. According to Piaget, up to a certain age children think and act more egocentrically and share one another's intellectual life much less than do adults; and there is little in the nature of a meeting of minds or real social life (of an intellectual sort) below the age of seven or eight years. Not until this age, he says, are children really able to enter into genuine arguments in which each is aware of the other's point of view and joins issue with it.

This egocentricity, according to Piaget, springs from intellectual limitations which appear also in the child's own private thoughts, for according to Piaget, the young child is not conscious of his own thought processes and does not enter into genuine arguments with himself (in the sense that he weighs and checks his own private reasoning and conclusions).

Several studies of young children made by other investigators, however, do not confirm these theories of Piaget's. In these studies the percentage of egocentric remarks has been found to be decidedly lower than the proportion claimed by Piaget (11, 30, 36, 38), and many observers have noted "socialized" language in children as young as three or four. However, even though the weight of available evidence goes counter to Piaget's conclusions as to the extent of egocentrism in the language of young children and his conclusions as to the young child's lack of ability to share his thoughts and to enter into a genuine conversation, it remains true, as everyone can recognize, and as will be noted more particularly in the next chapter, that the less mature a child is the more limited will be the extent to which he can understand or join in another's point of view.

FACTORS IN THE DEVELOPMENT AND ACQUISITION OF LANGUAGE

We have noted many of the processes involved in the child's progress from the cries, grunts, and other vocalizations of the first days of life to his highly organized speech during the late preschool years. It is instructive, partly by way of review, partly by way of further elaboration, to note factors that play a part in this progress.

Learning and growth. Much of the raw material that goes into the structure of speech, as we have seen, is present from the time of birth, for the child is capable of many sounds. However, all of the raw material is not there, for new sound elements progressively emerge, a product, at least in part, of maturation. In the process of physical maturing, for example, there are changes that influence vocalization. The acquiring of teeth, for example, and the changes in the structure and form of various parts of the vocal apparatus in the process of growth have an influence on the sounds that a child can produce.

That changes associated with maturation, as distinguished from special stimulation, play an important role in early language development is indicated by the findings in a study by Strayer (57) that have been referred to in an earlier chapter.

While a child's progress is thus influenced by growth there remains, of course, not only the fact that learning is essential to language development but also the fact that conditions or opportunities for learning influence the amount and kind of learning that takes place. Practice is required as the child progresses from the relatively diffuse and undefined vocalizations of early life to precise and well-defined usage. Similarly, learning is involved in the mastery of shades and refinements of meaning.

Language as related to socio-economic status, and age of associates. In studies at the preschool level it has been found that there is a relationship between children's language and the socio-economic status of their homes (11, 14, 38). Children of higher socio-economic status surpass those of lower status in such matters as length of sentences used, frequency of questions, proportion of remarks involving adapted information, and vocabulary. A part of this difference is no doubt due to the fact that children of higher socio-economic status also tend to be brighter than children of lower status, but it is likely that children living in a superior environment would have some advantage even if the factor of intelligence were equalized (61, 64).

To what extent the superiority of children of higher socioeconomic status may arise simply from the fact that they live in an environment that affords the stimulus of a richer vocabulary and greater literacy, the data do not tell. It may be conjectured, however, that the advantage of children in families of higher socioeconomic and educational status may in part be due to the fact that their parents are able to spend more time with them. It may also be noted that there is evidence indicating that children who associate primarily with adults are more precocious in their language development than are children who associate mainly with children (10, 38).

Language of twins and "singletons." It has also been found that twins tend to progress less rapidly in their language development during the age from two to five years than do "singletons." In one study of twenty pairs of twins at each yearly age level from two to five years it was found that the twins began to talk one month later, on the average, than their older brothers and sisters (11, 12). In another study that included children up to the age of nine and a half years (10), it likewise was found that twins lagged behind singletons; by the age of nine and a half, twins from upper occupational groups had practically overcome their handicap, but twins from the lower occupational groups were still inferior in language.

Apart from any hereditary or congenital factors that might exert an influence, the phenomenon is no doubt due in part to environmental factors. Among other things, the type of companionship which twins afford each other may mean that there is less occasion and less motivation for using language to communicate with others. It appears in some cases that twins can communicate with each other by means of fewer words than would be required to communicate the same meanings to someone else. Facial expressions, gestures, and other subtle signs, as well as grunts, single words, cryptic murmurings, and the like, which each has learned to understand through close companionship with the other, may take the place of the conventional flow of words and sentences.

It has also been found that only children tend to surpass "singletons" who have brothers and sisters (10).

Sex differences. In several investigations girls have been found to surpass boys in many aspects of early language development, such as in amount of talking, number of different words used, and use of sentences. Findings to the effect that girls are superior during early childhood and preschool years have been quite consistent, but the amount of the difference has varied in different studies (10, 14, 28, 38, 39, 64).

Language and intelligence. A positive relationship is usually found between language ability, as measured by various means, and mental ability, as measured by standard intelligence tests. Since the understanding and use of words play so large a role in many intelligence tests it is difficult to determine just what this relationship means. Does the child earn a good score on a verbal intelligence test because he has a good command of language or does he have a good command of language because he has good intelligence? A straight yes or no answer cannot be given to either of these queries.

Among other things, it has been found that children who in time turn out to be "feeble-minded," as measured by mental tests or other criteria, begin to talk at a later age than do children of normal intelligence (41, 59). On the other side, in a Terman study of gifted children (58), the data indicate that children who score high on intelligence tests (I.Q. 130 or more) when old enough to be tested are likely to begin talking at an earlier age than children of normal intelligence.

Findings on this subject are reported by Shirley (50), who correlated various measures of language development with intelligence, as measured by the Minnesota Preschool Scale (the computations represent seventeen subjects). Between *cumulative vocabulary* and the score on the mental test there was a correlation of .63 at eighteen months and of .76 at two years. The corresponding respective coefficients of correlation between mental test scores and *number of different words* spoken by the child per examination period were .63 and .74; and in the case of vocalization developmental score, the respective coefficients were .15 and .69. It will be noted that all coefficients were higher at two years than at eighteen months.

The relationship is not so high that early language development can be used to predict later intelligence, except within broad limits. If a child is quite precocious in his language development, this may be taken as a pretty good sign that he is at least normal in intelligence and probably is somewhat superior. On the other hand, if he does not begin to talk until beyond the average age, this does not preclude the possibility that he may turn out to be bright. A delay of many months, as compared with the average, is not at all a certain indication that he is likely to turn out to be somewhat dull.

Bilingualism. Throughout our own country and in the world at large many children are called upon to adjust to two different languages. The problem of bilingualism is interesting not only from the point of view of children who live in homes that use a foreign or unofficial language, but also, to a lesser extent, from the point of view of the educational problem as to when instruction in foreign languages might best be introduced in the curriculum.

A systematic inquiry into the subject would require, of course, attention to many factors. For one thing, the ways in which a child is called upon to adjust to two different languages may vary decidedly. In one situation, he may meet one language almost exclusively until he reaches school age and then be called upon to acquire a new language. In another situation, he may be confronted with two languages from the start. Here again there may be many variations. The two languages may be on an almost equal basis, or one may predominate over the other in varying degrees, or one child may be called upon to use both languages, while another, under other circumstances, may be reared to speak in only one language but to understand when spoken to in another language. His progress in each language, as well as his adjustment to the bilingual environment, may also be complicated by ridicule, prejudices, feelings of inferiority, and other tensions in the social and emotional sphere. These latter matters have received relatively little systematic attention.

Theoretically, if a child is called upon to acquire two different languages, he should make slower progress in each than he would make if he were learning only one. That children might possibly be handicapped in this way has been suggested by findings based upon studies of a limited number of children (52). From observations of a family of eight children (53) who made frequent moves between China and America and who were exposed to the two languages for varying periods and from different sources, Smith concludes that a bilingual environment is not likely to delay the first use of words; if a handicap occurs, it is likely to appear later. It should be recognized that a child might be below standard in the use of each of two languages and still make a good showing if a scheme could be found for crediting him with his proficiency in both languages combined.

Whatever may be the effect of being confronted with two languages during the early stages of vocabulary and sentence formation or at a later time, the available data certainly do not indicate that this circumstance in itself has a damaging effect on otherwise normal children. The necessity of adjusting to two languages does not at all mean that the child's mental processes will be thrown out of gear. Although some children may be at a disadvantage, especially if a social handicap is involved, it is not unlikely that, in some cases, the advantages of having to learn to deal with two languages quite outweighs the disadvantages. That a child's mental growth and ability to cope with the work at school are not seriously affected is indicated in a study by Arsenian (1) in which comparisons were made between a group of monoglot children and a group of bilingual children, matched person for person on the basis of race, sex, socio-economic status, and age in months. Among the subjects in this study were over a thousand American-born children of Italian parentage, over a thousand American-born Jewish children, and smaller samplings of foreign-born Italians, foreign-born Jews, and children of mixed parentage. The children ranged in age from nine to fourteen years. No reliable differences were found between the two groups in average intelligence or in age-grade status. In a study of matched children at the preschool level Darcy (9) found that bilingual children did relatively much better on a "performance" test of intelligence (Adkins Object-Fitting Test) than on a test which involves greater use of language (the Stanford-Binet).

Somewhat more difficult to probe than the effect on mental growth of the necessity for adjusting to two languages at an early age are the possible effects that bilingualism may have on a child's social and emotional adjustments. A child from a foreign-language background may, in some situations, be subject to teasing and ostracism. Even when no such unpleasantnesses arise, the child himself may be self-conscious with regard to his background and language, and may be timid (or sometimes overassertive) when called upon to express himself, especially if he is in the process of transition from one tongue to another, still uses accents and speech forms from the foreign language, or still "thinks" in a foreign language. In a study by Spoerl (55) at the college level it was found that students from bilingual backgrounds showed poorer emotional adjustment than did control subjects.

Such effects as ostracism, teasing, and feelings of inferiority by reason of bilinguality are, undoubtedly, less likely to arise if the child is a member of a rather large community in which the majority of the children are of the same national origins and have much the same home background, as far as language is concerned, than if the child is a member of a small minority or stands alone. However, the effects will vary in different communities and with different children. In one situation, a child with a foreign-language background may meet persecution from his associates, especially if strong prejudices prevail among the children's elders; in other situations, his condition may provoke little or no notice, or he may even win admiration by reason of his knowledge of another language.

ACADEMIC ASPECTS OF LANGUAGE DEVELOPMENT

We shall take space in this chapter to touch only briefly upon a few considerations, from the developmental point of view, that have a bearing upon the learning of the language arts in school.

As noted in Chapter II, there is a need for examining the time and effort devoted to various academic skills at different maturity levels. Much time may be spent, without yielding commensurate return, in teaching certain matters (such as spelling), at a certain grade level, which the child himself will learn incidentally and without special teaching in his own good time.

One problem, among others, in the teaching of good language usage in writing is that as a child matures his thought processes and his mode of expression tend to become more complex, with the result that certain errors in grammar and punctuation which he had mastered at a simpler level recur on a more complex level. An even more pervasive problem is the problem of adjusting what is taught and what is expected to the capabilities of individual children. In the matter of reading, for example, children at a certain age differ considerably in the extent to which they are ready. Two children may eventually achieve equal competence even though one begins to read a year or two in advance of another. Children differ not only in their apparent readiness at a certain age but they differ also in the speed and pattern of their progress. As a result, it is important not simply to know what a child's achievement is at a given moment but also to know the rate at which he is progressing (42).

BIBLIOGRAPHY

1. Arsenian, S.: *Bilingualism and Mental Development,* Teachers College Contributions to Education (New York: Teachers College, Columbia University, 1937), No. 712, 164 pp.
2. Baker, H. V.: *A Study of Children's Contributions in General Discussion and Their Implications for the Curriculum,* unpublished Ph.D. dissertation (New York: Teachers College, Columbia University, 1940).
3. Barker, C.: *A Study of the Development of Children's Concepts,* unpublished (New York: Teachers College, Columbia University).
4. Bateman, W. G.: "Papers on Language Development: I. The First Word," *Pedagogical Seminary* (1917), 24:391-398.
5. Bean, C. H.: "An Unusual Opportunity to Investigate the Psychology of Language," *Journal of Genetic Psychology* (1932), 40:181-202.
6. Blanton, M. G.: "The Behavior of the Human Infant During the First Thirty Days of Life," *Psychological Review* (1917), 24:456-483.
7. Brandenburg, G. C.: "Psychological Aspects of Language," *Journal of Educational Psychology* (1918), 9:313-332.
8. Bühler, C.: *The First Year of Life* (New York: John Day, 1930), 281 pp.
9. Darcy, N. T.: "The Effect of Bilingualism Upon the Measurement of the Intelligence of Children of Preschool Age," *Journal of Educational Psychology* (1946), 37:21-44.
10. Davis, E. A.: *The Development of Linguistic Skills in Twins, Singletons with Siblings, and Only Children from Age Five to Ten Years,* Institute of Child Welfare Monograph Series (Minneapolis: University of Minnesota, 1937), No. 14, 165 pp.
11. Day, E. J.: "The Development of Language in Twins: I. A Comparison of Twins and Single Children," *Child Development* (1932), 3:179-199.
12. ———: "The Development of Language in Twins: II. The Development of Twins: Their Resemblances and Differences," *Child Development* (1932), 3:298-316.
13. Fenton, J. C.: *A Practical Psychology of Babyhood* (Boston: Houghton Mifflin, 1925), 348 pp.
14. Fisher, M. S.: *Language Patterns of Preschool Children,* Child Development Monographs (New York: Bureau of Publications, Teachers College, Columbia University, 1934), No. 15, 88 pp.
15. Fitzgerald, J. A.: *Letters Written Outside the School by Children of the Fourth, Fifth, and Sixth Grades: A Study of Vocabulary, Spelling Errors and Situations,* University of Iowa Studies in Education (1934), IX, 1:7-50.

16. Gesell, A.: *The Mental Growth of the Preschool Child* (New York: Macmillan, 1925), 447 pp.
17. ———: *Infancy and Human Growth* (New York: Macmillan, 1928), 418 pp.
18. Goodman, J. H.: "Growth in Punctuation and Capitalization Abilities," *Journal of Educational Research* (1934-1935), 28:195-202.
19. Guiler, W.: *The Ohio Survey of English Usage* (Columbus: State Department of Education, 1931), 35 pp.
20. Hartmann, G. W.: "A Critique of the Common Method of Estimating Vocabulary Size, Together with Some Data on the Absolute Word Knowledge of Educated Adults," *Journal of Educational Psychology* (1941), 32:351-364.
21. Henle, M. and Hubbell, M. B.: "'Egocentricity' in Adult Conversation," *Journal of Social Psychology* (1938), 9:227-234.
22. Hoppes, W. C.: "Considerations in the Development of Children's Language," *Elementary English Review* (1934), 11:66-70.
23. ———: "Some Aspects of Growth in Written Expression," *Elementary English Review* (1933), 10:67-70.
24. International Kindergarten Union (M. D. Horn, chairman), *A Study of the Vocabulary of Children Before Entering the First Grade* (Baltimore: Williams and Wilkins, 1928), 36 pp.
25. Irwin, O. C.: "Research on Speech Sounds for the First Six Months of Life," *Psychological Bulletin* (1941), 38:277-285.
26. Irwin, O. C. and Curry, T.: "Vowel Elements in the Crying Vocalization of Infants Under Ten Days of Age," *Child Development* (1941) 12:99-109.
27. Jersild, A. T., Meigs, M. F., and Brown, L. S.: *A Study of Elementary Classes in Action,* unpublished (New York: Teachers College, Columbia University, 1939).
28. Jersild, A. T. and Ritzman, R.: "Aspects of Language Development: I. The Growth of Loquacity and Vocabulary," *Child Development* (1938), 9, 3:243-259.
29. ———: *Aspects of Language Development: II. Words Used Most Frequently,* unpublished (New York: Teachers College, Columbia University, 1939).
30. Johnson, E. C. and Josey, C. C.: "A Note on the Development of the Thought Forms of Children as Described by Piaget," *Journal of Abnormal and Social Psychology* (1931), 26:338-339.
31. Kelley, T. L. and Krey, A. C.: *Tests and Measurements in the Social Sciences,* Report of the Commission on the Social Studies (New York: Scribner's, 1934), Pt. IV, 635 pp.
32. Kelty, M. G. and Moore, N. E.: "The Kelty-Moore Test of Concepts

in the Social Studies," in Kelley and Krey: *Tests and Measurements in the Social Sciences* (1934), pp. 227-233.
33. LaBrant, L.: *A Study of Certain Language Developments of Children in Grades Four to Twelve Inclusive,* Genetic Psychology Monographs (1933), 14:387-491.
34. Lewis, M. M.: *Infant Speech; A Study of the Beginnings of Language* (New York: Harcourt, Brace, 1936), 325 pp.
35. Lyman, R. L.: *Summary of Investigations Relating to Grammar, Language and Composition,* Supplementary Education Monographs (Chicago: University of Chicago, 1929), No. 36, 302 pp.
36. McCarthy, D.: "A Comparison of Children's Language in Different Situations and Its Relation to Personality Traits," *Journal of Genetic Psychology* (1929), 36:583-591.
37. ———: "Language Development," *A Handbook of Child Psychology,* revised edition, edited by C. Murchison (Worcester: Clark University Press, 1933), Ch. VIII, pp. 329-373.
38. ———: *The Language Development of the Preschool Child,* Institute of Child Welfare Monograph Series (Minneapolis: University of Minnesota Press, 1930), No. 4, 174 pp.
39. ———: "Language Development in Children," *Manual of Child Psychology,* edited by L. Carmichael (New York: Wiley, 1946), Ch. X, 476-581.
40. Mabie, E.: "A Study of the Conversation of First Grade Pupils During Free Play Periods," *Journal of Educational Research* (1931), 24:135-139.
41. Mead, C. D.: "The Age of Walking and Talking in Relation to General Intelligence," *Pedagogical Seminary* (1913), 20:460-484.
42. Millard, C. V.: "The Nature and Character of Pre-Adolescent Growth in Reading Achievement," *Child Development* (1940), 11, 71-105.
43. Nice, M. M.: "A Child Who Would Not Talk," *Pedagogical Seminary* (1925), 32:105-142.
44. Piaget, J.: *The Language and Thought of the Child* (New York: Harcourt, Brace, 1926), 246 pp.
45. Pressey, L. C.: "A Study in the Learning of the Fundamental Special Vocabulary of History from the Fourth Through the Twelfth Grades," Kelley, T. L. and Krey, A. C.: *Tests and Measurements in the Social Sciences,* Report of the Commission on the Social Sciences (New York: Scribner's, 1934), Pt. IV, pp. 115-218.
46. Rinsland, H. D.: *A Basic Vocabulary of Elementary School Children* (New York: Macmillan, 1946), 636 pp.
47. Rugg, H., Krueger, L., and Sondergaard, A.: "A Study of the Language of Kindergarten Children," *Journal of Educational Psychology* (1929), 20:1-18.

48. Scott, F. and Myers, G. C.: "Children's Empty and Erroneous Concepts of the Commonplace," *Journal of Educational Research* (1923), 8:327-335.
49. Seashore, R. H. and Echerson, L. D.: "The Measurement of Individual Differences in General English Vocabularies," *Journal of Educational Psychology* (1940), 31:14-38.
50. Shirley, M. M.: The *First Two Years: A Study of Twenty-Five Babies,* Vol. II: *Intellectual Development,* Institute of Child Welfare Monograph Series (Minneapolis: University of Minnesota Press, 1933), 513 pp.
51. Smith, M. E.: *An Investigation of the Development of the Sentence and the Extent of Vocabulary in Young Children,* University of Iowa Studies in Child Welfare (1926), III, No. 5, 92 pp.
52. ———: "A Study of Five Bilingual Children from the Same Family," *Child Development* (1931), 2:184-187.
53. ———: "A Study of the Speech of Eight Bilingual Children of the Same Family," *Child Development* (1935), 6:19-25.
54. Smith, M. K.: *Measurement of the Size of General English Vocabulary Through the Elementary Grades and High School,* Genetic Psychology Monographs (1941), 24:311-345.
55. Spoerl, D. T.: "The Academic and Verbal Adjustment of College Age Bilingual Students," *Journal of Genetic Psychology* (1944), 64:139-157.
56. ———: "Bilinguality and Emotional Adjustment," *Journal of Abnormal Social Psychology* (1943), 38:37-57.
57. Strayer, L. C.: *Language and Growth: The Relative Efficacy of Early and Deferred Vocabulary Training, Studied by the Method of Co-Twin Control,* Genetic Psychology Monographs (1930), 8:209-319.
58. Terman, L. M., et al.: *Genetic Studies of Genius,* Vol. I: *Mental and Physical Traits of a Thousand Gifted Children* (Stanford, California: Stanford University Press, 1925), 648 pp.
59. Town, C. H.: "Language Development in 285 Idiots and Imbeciles," *Psychological Clinic* (1913), 6:229-235.
60. Tracy, F.: "The Language of Childhood," *American Journal of Psychology* (1893), 6:107-138.
61. Van Alstyne, D.: *The Environment of Three-Year-Old Children: Factors Related to Intelligence and Vocabulary Tests,* Teachers College Contributions to Education (New York: Teachers College, Columbia University, 1929), No. 366, 109 pp.
62. Wellman, B., Case, I. M., Mengert, I. G., and Bradbury, D. E.: *Speech Sounds of Young Children,* University of Iowa Studies in Child Welfare (1931), V, 82 pp.

63. Wesley, E. B.: *Teaching the Social Studies: Theory and Practice* (Boston: D. C. Heath, 1937), 635 pp.
64. Williams, H. M., McFarland, M. L., and Little, M. F.: *Development of Language and Vocabulary in Young Children,* University of Iowa Studies in Child Welfare (1937), XIII, No. 2, 94 pp.
65. Zyve, C.: "Conversation Among Children," *Teachers College Record* (New York: Teachers College, Columbia University, 1927), 29:46-61.

CHAPTER X

THE GROWTH OF UNDERSTANDING

EARLY MENTAL DEVELOPMENT

It would be fascinating if we could know the nature of an infant's awareness of happenings in the world about him. Unfortunately, we cannot look upon the world from an infant's point of view; what we see is too much influenced by ways of perceiving and thinking that have developed through the years of our own experience. In the first chapter it was noted that the newborn child has quite a range of responses but that just how his experiences are organized we do not know. When, however, we see that his overt responses are diffuse and lacking in coördination, it seems reasonable to assume that his "mental" experiences, whatever they may be, similarly are not as clearly defined or as well differentiated as are an older person's. Apart from this, it is obvious that the special meanings that come to be associated, as time passes, with the happenings of everyday life are also lacking in the child's first experiences.[1]

SIGNS OF INCREASING AWARENESS AND ALERTNESS

A glance at Table XXV, which is drawn from a study by Bayley of the mental growth of young children, will show many landmarks in the development of the child's ability to discriminate and to react adaptively to more and more events in the world about him. In Bayley's summary, we see, for example, the child giving momentary heed to a dangling ring at about two weeks, more pro-

---

[1] The discussion in this chapter is confined mainly to the preschool years and the chapter which follows deals mainly with older children. The subject of mental development is treated also in chapters dealing with imaginative behavior (Chapter XII), language development (Chapter IX), morals and religion (Chapter XIII), and intelligence (Chapter XIV).

Table XXV

MENTAL DEVELOPMENT TEST ITEMS DURING THE FIRST THREE YEARS[2]

Name of Test	Age-Placement Value (months)	Name of Test	Age-Placement Value (months)
1. Postural adjustment when lifted	.5	40. Regards pellet	5.35
2. Lateral head movements, prone	.6	41. Recovers rattle	5.35
3. Momentary regard of ring	.6	42. Discriminates strangers	5.55
4. Responds to sound	.6	43. Vocalizes eagerness	5.6
5. Prolonged regard of ring	1.2	44. Simultaneous flexion and thumb opposition	5.75
6. Horizontal eye coördination	1.2	45. Lifts cup	5.8
7. Responds to voice	1.3	46. Paper play	5.8
8. Arm and leg thrusts in play	1.3	47. Accepts second cube	5.85
9. Vertical eye coördination	1.4	48. Vocalizes pleasure	5.9
10. Circular eye coördination	1.45	49. Vocalizes displeasure	5.95
11. Social smile	1.45	50. Reaches persistently	6.05
12. Vocalizations	1.55	51. Turns after spoon	6.1
13. Turns eyes to light	1.9	52. Mirror-image approach	6.1
14. Free inspection	2.2	53. Picks cube deftly	6.2
15. Eyes follow pencil	2.3	54. Several syllables	6.3
16. Anticipatory excitement	2.4	55. Bangs in play	6.35
17. Manipulates ring	2.9	56. Sustained inspection of ring	6.4
18. Reaches for ring	3.0	57. Unilateral reaching	6.45
19. Blinks at shadow	3.1	58. Vocalizes satisfaction	6.5
20. Vocalizes to social stimulus	3.1	59. Lifts cup by handle	6.6
21. Fingers hand in play	3.2	60. Exploitive string play	6.7
22. Reacts to paper on face	3.2	61. Rotates wrist	6.7
23. Carries ring to mouth	3.3	62. Scoops pellet	6.8
24. Aware of strange situation	3.3	63. Smiles at image	7.2
25. Follows vanishing object	3.35	64. Interest in bell details	7.2
26. Anticipatory adjustment to lifting	3.4	65. Looks for spoon	7.25
27. Regards cube	3.45	66. Frolic play	7.3
28. Play with rattle	3.5	67. Pulls string: secures ring	7.35
29. Manipulates table edge	3.6	68. Vocal recognition	7.4
30. Inspects hand	3.65	69. Sound production, interest	7.6
31. Closes on dangling ring	3.95	70. Complete thumb opposition	7.65
32. Turns to sound	4.0	71. Partial finger prehension	7.8
33. Beginning thumb opposition	4.1	72. Retains two or three cubes	8.0
34. Active table manipulation	4.4	73. Vocalizes interjections	8.1
35. Reaches for cube	4.5	74. Attends scribbling	8.1
36. Eye coöperation in reaching	4.8	75. Coöperates in games	8.45
37. Partial thumb opposition	5.1	76. Exploits formboard and block	8.5
38. Picks up cube	5.2	77. Listens to familiar words	8.5
39. Retains two cubes	5.3	78. Says "da-da" or equivalent	8.55
		79. Explores formboard holes	8.6

[2] Adapted from Bayley, N.: *Mental Growth During the First Three Years,* Genetic Psychology Monographs (1933), XIV, No. 1, pp. 26-30. Reproduced by permission. In addition to age-placement values, in months, the original table also shows the score value of each item. The full test contains 185 items and extends to the age of thirty-seven months.

TABLE XXV (Cont.)

Name of Test	Age-Placement Value (months)	Name of Test	Age-Placement Value (months)
80. Attempt to secure three cubes	8.7	90. Unwraps cube	10.6
81. Interest in throwing	8.9	91. Holds crayon adaptively	11.2
82. Fine prehension	9.3	92. Inhibits on command	11.5
83. Pulls string adaptively	9.5	93. Repeats: laughed at	11.6
84. Uses handle; secures cube	9.6	94. Strikes doll imitatively	11.6
85. Play to mirror	9.7	95. Imitates words	11.7
86. Differentiates words	9.8	96. Spoon imitation	12.1
87. Rings bell purposively	9.9	97. Holds cup to drink	12.2
88. Puts cube in cup	10.4	98. Adjusts round block	12.6
89. Scribble imitation attempt	10.4	99. Says two words	12.9
		100. Dangles ring by string	13.1

longed regard at a month, and regard with manipulation at about three months. An expansion in his reaction to events that do not directly confront him can later be seen when he turns his head toward the direction of a sound, or keeps his attention fixed upon an object that has been covered or hidden. The summary likewise illustrates the development of discrimination, perception of form, evidences of memory, and increasing ability to understand and to use symbols, as in language. Some illustrations of changes with age in the child's discrimination and awareness in his social responses are presented in Chapter V.

MEMORY

Signs of memory appear early in life when the child ceases crying at the sound of someone's approach or adjusts himself to being lifted. Later come evidences such as signs of discriminating between a familiar and an unfamiliar face.

The development of ability to retain impressions and to act in terms of past impressions even though the objective stimulus is absent represents an important feature of the child's widening mental world. We see signs of this when a child keeps his attention fixed upon an object that has disappeared from sight, as when he proceeds directly to get hold of a spoon that has been covered with a napkin, or keeps his eyes fixed on the door through which a person has disappeared, or redirects his attention to an object from which it has been distracted for some moments.[3] An example of this ability to retain and to act upon an impression follows: At the age of 10½ months, while visiting her grandparents, a child watched as her father hid a cookie under the cushion of a sofa. The child then was taken from the room for three minutes. At the end of the time she immediately crept to the sofa and procured the cookie. Two and a half months later the child again was taken to the grandparents' house in the late afternoon. She went to the sofa, lifted the cushion, and whimpered, apparently disappointed at finding no food.

As might be expected, children improve as they grow older in their ability to remember. In a study of the latent memory span of two- to four-year-old children, Mallay (35) measured the extent to which children could remember over a period of time the technique involved in opening a series of boxes. In the case of the easiest problem, involving a relatively simple movement of pushing, pulling, or lifting the lid, the number of days during which the children remembered the correct technique, without fumbling or redirection, ranged (according to the nature of the original directions and amount of experience) from about three to eight days in the case of two-year-olds, from about nine to fifteen days in the case of three-year-olds, and from about seven to twenty days at four years. At the two-year level it was found that verbal directions accompanying a demonstration were especially helpful in directing the child's attention to the operation and in helping him to grasp the solution of the problem.

Early memories. From an early age, children show many evidences of memory of snatches of happenings in their everyday

---

[3] Studies of the ability to act upon impressions after a delay or lapse of time have been reported by Hetzer and Wislitzky (30), Hunter (32), and Skalet (44).

GROWTH OF UNDERSTANDING

lives.[4] But even though there is a great amount of remembering from day to day at the age of one, two, and three years, the recollections from these early years that are carried into later life are very few. When adults report their earliest memories many are unable to recall anything earlier than the third year although there are some who describe memories extending back into the second and first years. In several studies the findings indicate that the earliest event that can be recalled by persons of adolescent or adult years is likely to have occurred at an average age of three years or more (3, 16, 17, 18, 24, 27, 28, 36).

In one study in which an effort was made to verify the occurrences reported as early recollections, it was found that the average age of the earliest reported memory of college students was three years and seven months.[5] In the literature there have been claims to the effect that individual persons have recollected happenings that occurred during the first year of life, extending as far back as even to the day of birth. However, it would be necessary to have further verification before such claims, especially those relating to the first few months of life, can be accepted as true.

As is apparent, a vast number of discrete experiences, during early childhood and later, lose their identity in the general process of habit formation. We cannot recall when we first were able to distinguish between the voices of different members of the family, or grew wary of a swinging door, or resisted the approach of a person who handled us roughly.

It is reasonable to assume that experiences occurring during the early months and years of life while learning and growth proceed at a rapid pace, while habits are being formed, and modes of behavior are being established, will have a bearing on the individual's

---

[4] For a review of records of early evidences of memory, based upon biographical records of children, see Hurlock and Schwartz (33). A study by Bryan (8) deals with the organization of memory in children.

[5] Dudycha and Dudycha (18) have published a review of thirty-five studies dealing with the subject of early memories.

ways of thinking and feeling and on his social and emotional adjustments in later life. Yet this vast array of happenings and this vast body of experiences which help to determine a person's destiny are lost in oblivion. If it were possible to recapture or to reconstruct these early happenings, much that later is mysterious or baffling to the individual himself and to others would no doubt be made clear.

For this reason, no doubt, some of the first systematic studies in genetic psychology dealt with the subject of early memories. Experiences of infancy and early childhood have also received preeminent attention in psychoanalytic theory. One psychoanalytic theory is to the effect that mental disorders and various peculiarities and quirks of behavior that appear in later life may stem from unrecalled disturbing experiences during early childhood. Such a theory is provocative, to say the least. Obviously, anything that would offer scientific verification with respect to this theory or any other interpretation of the later psychological consequences of early experiences, whether remembered or forgotten, would be of great importance for the understanding of human behavior. It is difficult to obtain good scientific evidence in this area.

From a theoretical point of view, there is reason to doubt that the child's earliest experiences are of such character that they could be retained in such a manner as to make it possible for a person to recollect them when he is mature. When we consider the lack of coördination in the infant's early behavior, a lack so great that even many simple reflex patterns are imperfectly formed, it seems unlikely that clearly demarcated impressions take place within him. He needs to grow and to learn before he acquires the capacity on the one hand, and the experience on the other, to enable him to perceive and to catalog events in the same manner as an older person. Moreover, until he has acquired the ability to use language, he lacks an important means of formulating the experiences in terms of symbols that he can communicate.

Experiences may, however, leave a residue whether or not they are well defined or clearly understood. An example of the manner in which impressions can leave their mark on a child is shown in an interesting study by Burtt (9, 10, 11). Passages from Sophocles in the original Greek were read to a child (who had no other contact with Greek) when he was no more than fifteen months old; twenty lines were read to him daily for a period of three months, and at the end of each period a new selection was read. This reading was continued until the child was three years old. When he was eight and a half years old, the same passages, as well as new ones, were read to him; but he was now required to memorize the lines. To commit to memory new passages that never before had been read to him required an average of 435 repetitions, while an average of only 317 repetitions were needed for passages that had been read to him when he was a baby. Thus he showed the effect of past impressions, even of material that had been read to him between the ages of fifteen and eighteen months.

Again, when this child was fourteen years old, he undertook to memorize Greek passages, some of which had been read to him before the age of three and some of which were new (10). This time, the difference between the effort required to learn "old" and "new" material was appreciable but much decreased. A final check was made when the child was eighteen years old (11). At this age no difference was apparent in the number of repetitions required to master new and old passages.

PERCEPTION

During the first three years of life a child advances rapidly in his ability to discriminate between sizes and shapes, to judge distances and dimensions, and to recognize meanings associated with impressions that come to him by way of his eyes and ears and other senses. Examples of the development of a child's perception of sounds can be observed in many of his early social responses, as when he reacts differently for a time to angry and friendly tones and distinguishes between the voice of his mother and that of a stranger. In his response to sounds and to all other sensory stimuli, a child has much to learn before he can detect meanings that adults take for granted. A cracking sound from the ice underfoot means danger to the adult, while a child of two or three may be interested but recognizes no danger. The adult recognizes with alarm the sound of a tear in his clothes and steps aside at the sound of an approaching vehicle; if blindfolded, he judges by creaking sounds whether his footing on a plank is secure; he can judge, with some degree of accuracy, when a container into which liquid is being poured is nearly full; and so on.

Each such response is the fruit of many concrete experiences of the past. Sounds previously occurring as part of a total situation are now effective as reduced cues.[6] As learning proceeds, an individual may hear in sounds a character common to many different situations. In time, he will be able to tell blindfolded whether an object that was struck is metal or solid earth; and he becomes able to estimate, with some degree of accuracy, the relative size of the object from which the sound proceeds. A particular cue is met so often or is learned so well that it produces an appropriate response, even though some details associated with it have not been met before.

In this development, as in other departments of his mental development, the child's progress depends upon first-hand experience and the capacity to learn. In the latter capacity, children differ widely.

It appears that many of the cues involved in the perception of distance and size are learned at a relatively early age. In one of a series of experiments of visual perception of distance, two discs of equal size were used. One was kept at a standard, the other at a variable distance from the eye, and tests were made to find how small a difference in the distances of the two the subject was able to judge correctly. In another series, one of the stimuli was made

---

[6] For a systematic account of ways in which a part of a past total stimulus comes to function for the whole, see Hollingworth (31).

GROWTH OF UNDERSTANDING

larger than the other. As it proved, four-year-old children were more variable than adults in the acuity of perception of the relative distances of objects, but the difference in accuracy was not great (48). Tests of younger children would perhaps show greater differences, but it is difficult to devise adequate tests of space discrimination for young infants.

The degree to which visual orientation depends upon past training is shown by observation of children's "space-order reaction." In one investigation, children between the ages of two and a half and five and a half were asked to point out and to name each of sixteen pictures that were arranged in four rows on a card (50). Adults, when asked to do this, name the pictures from left to right, one line at a time, using the same order as in reading. Only one of the twenty-three children used the reading order; twenty-one used no regular order. The children also were asked to put a check in each of sixteen circles, arranged in four rows; and in this performance, fourteen children used no regular order.[7]

The child of two or less appears to be a good deal less sensitive to color differences than an adult. His ability to distinguish colors develops more rapidly, however, than his ability to name them. In a study of color discrimination, children were called upon to match colored squares (13). Two-year-old children were correct less than half of the time in matching colors; they named the colors correctly only twenty-five per cent of the time. Six-year-old children, when tested with the same material, made an almost perfect score (ninety-seven per cent correct).

CAPACITY FOR ATTENTION AND CONCENTRATION

One important accompaniment of mental development is an increase in the child's "staying power," in his ability to keep his attention concentrated upon a stimulus or project. This ability has variously been called "duration of attention," "interest span,"

---

[7] Some studies dealing in detail with the development of perception of form and other aspects of visual perception are listed in the bibliography (20, 26, 34, 38, 39, 40, 45).

and "persistence." Except in response to urgent physical demands, the young child's concentration span tends to be brief. When he fixates an object with his eyes, his regard is likely to be fleeting at first and to lengthen with time. Of course, the span of concentration is no unitary ability, for it will vary in different situations and it depends not simply on the child's energies but upon his interests and motives. For this reason, an exact measure of increase with age would be difficult to obtain; the results would vary with different children and in different situations. It is possible, however, to trace the rise in duration of attention in some situations.

In one study in this area, Miles (37) measured the length of time children would continue to give sustained attention to a delayed happening. Each child was presented with a jack-in-the-box and asked to watch it until it was opened. The experimenter timed the child until he looked away. The average duration of sustained attention, according to this criterion, as exhibited by the children in this study was eight seconds at three and four years, about seventeen seconds at five years, and about twenty-eight seconds at six years. In a somewhat different approach, Shacter (43) timed children to see how long they would persist, without further persuasion, at little tasks such as taking colored paper disks out of a box and laying them in rows across a table. On the simplest task used in the study, the average duration of attention ranged from a little over eight minutes at three years to a little over nine minutes at five years (the differences between three-, four-, and five-year-olds was not significant, and there were large individual differences).

Another approach to this problem has been through observation of the amount of time children will spend upon a project, without interruption or turning to something else, during their free play. Table XXVI summarizes results from three studies (4, 25, 49). It will be noted that the averages differ considerably, due in part to differences in the situations in which the children were observed

TABLE XXVI

AVERAGE DURATION IN MINUTES OF SUSTAINED ATTENTION DURING CHILDREN'S FREE PLAY AS SHOWN IN STUDIES IN THREE DIFFERENT SITUATIONS[8]

Age in Years	Average Duration of Sustained Attention		
	According to Van Alstyne[a]	According to Bott[b]	According to Gutteridge[c]
2	6.9	2.5	9.4
3	8.9	4.7	13.4
4	11.4	5.6	18.97
5	12.6	...	23.82

[a] Van Alstyne, D.: *Play Behavior and Choice of Play Materials of Preschool Children* (Chicago: University of Chicago Press, 1932), 104 pp.
[b] Bott, H.: *Observation of Play Activities in a Nursery School*, Genetic Psychology Monographs (1928), IV: 44-88.
[c] Gutteridge, M. V.: *The Duration of Attention in Young Children*, Australian Council for Educational Research (Melbourne: Melbourne University Press, 1935), 52 pp.

and also to differences in the criteria as to what constituted an "interruption" or abandonment of an activity. That the duration of a child's interest will vary in connection with different activities has been shown in the studies reviewed in Table XXVI and in other studies (29).

In spite of these variations, the findings in the three studies represented in Table XXVI agree on some general points. First, it is apparent that the average span is relatively short throughout the age range included in the studies. Second, there is an increase in the averages from year to year.

In all three of the studies cited, this increase is quite large in relative terms; but in no year do the averages show a marked and sudden rise in terms of actual minutes of time. The tables do not reproduce the large individual differences among different children; nor do they reproduce the large variations that can be found in the behavior of the same child at different times. In the study by Gutteridge, for example, it was found that a child might devote himself uninterruptedly to a given project for an hour or longer

---
[8] See accompanying text.

and then, on several other occasions, spend only a few minutes at a time on various projects. It has also been observed that the amount of persistence on the first occasion of dealing with a given project does not give an accurate prediction of the length of time the same project might appeal to a child when he meets it again. For example, it was noted by Wolf (51) that the median amount of time spent by kindergarten children in working with a peg board was 5.7 minutes on first presentation but that on the second presentation the median was 7.1 minutes. A tinker toy, on the other hand, held the children for 22.5 minutes for the first time, 15.5 minutes the second time, and 9.5 minutes the third time it was offered.

The length of time children persist in a performance varies also under different conditions of motivation. On five tasks in the study cited above the average duration was 7.2 minutes when no special incentive was offered; when the children were praised, the average rose to 10.9 minutes; and in a competitive situation the average rose still further to 17.2 minutes. The responsiveness of individual children to these different incentives also varied.

The ability to stay with a problem or project represents an important feature of effective use of one's mental abilities. As a child grows older, he acquires the ability increasingly to organize and control his behavior in terms of interests and purposes as distinguished from the appeal of a passing, external event.

CHILDREN'S QUESTIONS

From early infancy the child is an explorer and his curiosity takes many turns. Once he has learned to talk, his curiosity expresses itself through a vast number of questions. The child's questions may serve many motives in addition to curiosity, for sometimes the purpose of a question is to establish social contact, or to receive attention, or to gain reassurance, solace, or help. Children may even use persistent questioning as a form of resistance or as a means of expressing resentment. Again, questioning sometimes seems to represent a general outflow of language spoken for its own sake without apparent expectation of an answer. As noted elsewhere, a young child "practices" his language a good deal and part of this "practice" may take the form of raising questions.

In one study (22) it was found that the proportion of questions in children's language during the nursery-school day rose with age from two per cent at eighteen to twenty-four months to fifteen per cent at three years. At the age range from thirty-six to fifty-four months, the proportion was about eleven per cent. A study of children's language at the kindergarten level showed that about a tenth of children's remarks were questions (41). A larger proportion of questioning would no doubt have been found had these children been studied exclusively in the company of older children and adults, rather than in the company of their peers (21).

In a study of one child in the home environment it was found that questions occurred at the rate of thirty-one per hour when the child was thirty-eight months old; this constituted eighteen per cent of her conversation. At fifty-two months the rate was thirty-three per hour, and twenty per cent of her conversation was questioning (6). An even higher rate of questioning was shown by another girl whose language was recorded for a time at yearly intervals from her second to her eighth year. Her questions rose from two per cent of all her conversation at two years to twenty-eight per cent at three years. In the interval from four to eight years, questions constituted about a fifth of her total conversation (5).

In a study of the questions asked by eight two- to four-year-old nursery-school children (12) it was found that the questions were about equally divided between inquiries that seemed designed primarily as a means of social interchange and questions that seemed definitely designed to elicit information. Children differed considerably in the relative frequency of the two types of questioning. The investigator noted, in passing, that the technique of turning a question back upon a child, as a means of getting him to think things out for himself, did not work well with some children, for the children would proceed to address the same question to others. Also, after having questions thrown back at them, they tended to ask fewer questions.

The questions raised by children vary with their changing abilities and interests. Thus, when a child is in the "naming stage" in his language development he is likely to ask many "what" questions to learn what things are and to acquire names for them. The youngster may likewise go through a "Who is that?" period during which he wants to know the names of all people who pass by. Such questions usually precede "why" questions, dealing with causal relations in everyday happenings or with reasons for another's behavior.

Davis (15) gives an analysis of 3,650 questions asked by seventy-three children aged three to twelve years. The questions were recorded by parents and relatives at the time they were asked. Of these questions, 87.8 per cent seemed to arise from something in the immediate situation, as distinguished from questions about remembered or remote events (which constituted 10.8 per cent; 1.4 per cent could not be accounted for). A novel occurrence was more likely to provoke a long series of logically related questions, but frequently ordinary situations also provoked such a series of questions. Boys asked more questions involving causal explanation than did girls, while girls exceeded boys in questions regarding social relations.

The following illustrations of questions asked by preschool children (above average in intelligence) are from data collected by Rust (42) in a study of the growth of children's concepts.[9]

The following conversation began after the child (who was four and a half years old) had been told a story about a six-year-old girl:

---

[9] Rust, M. M., *The Growth of Children's Concepts of Time, Space, and Magnitude*, unpublished (Teachers College, Columbia University). Reproduced by permission.

Child: I'm four, aren't I?
Mother: Yes, four years.
Child: What's a year?
Mother: (*Explains.*)
Child: Is that a long time?
Mother: Quite a long time.
Child: How long?
Mother: It's hard to explain, but it is a lot of days, 365, and that's many.
Child: Well, but how long?
Mother: Well, well, you know when it was Christmas.
Child: Oh, yes, and I had a tree, and once I had the tree in the corner and once I had it on the table.
Mother: Well, that was twice, and it takes a year to have a Christmas. You see we have Christmas, then the time between that Christmas and the time between the next is a year.
Child: Well, that's a very long, long time. When I was very small we had a Christmas. Is a year a birthday?
Mother: Well, you have one birthday, then the time between is called a year, then you have the next birthday.
Child: Yes, three then four—then five— Say, how old are you?
Mother: Thirty.
Child: How did you stretch up?

This turn in the conversation appeared to suggest another line of questions to the child. She immediately continued:

Child: When I'm thirty will I be a mother?
Mother: If you have a baby you will.
Child: Do all womans have babies?
Mother: No.
Child: Why?
Mother: Some are not strong enough, some are too busy doing other things—some . . .
Child: Well, in three or six weeks when I'm thirty, I shall have a baby— Where do babies come from?
Mother: Seeds.
Child: Where do the seeds come from?
Mother: The father and the mother.

Child: Where does the father keep his?
Mother: They're in his body.
Child: Oh, is he keeping them warm same as the mother does the baby?
Mother: He doesn't have them there to keep them warm, but because they belong there.
Child: Well, when I'm six weeks I'll marry you because you're so cute.
Mother: But— (*Father comes in.*)
Child: Hello, Daddy. Did you buy me something? (*No further questioning.*)

The following questions and comments of a four-year-old child deal in part with concepts of time:

Child: Is this today?
Teacher: Yes, why?
Child: Well, is tomorrow tomorrow?
Teacher: Yes.
Child: Well, Sunday is my birthday.
Teacher: Do you know what date this is?
Child: Yes, it's March 5 and I will be four years old. That's this many (*counts down four buttons on his coat*).
Teacher: That is right, Frank.
Child: Some day I will be this old (*stretches out his arms at full length*).

The problem of time was the subject of the questions of another child, aged four and a half.

Child: What time is it?
Mother: 6:30.
Child: What means that?
Mother: What do you mean?
Child: What means 6:30?
Mother: Well, when it's evening it means time for you to think of bed and time for me to get dinner.
Child: How long is 6:30?
Mother: Just one minute, then it is 6:31.

Child: Is a minute big?
Mother: No, very short.
Child: Just a little bit like this? (*Demonstrates with finger and thumb and a tiny pinch.*)
Mother: I'll show you with my watch.
Child: (*Watches watch for a minute or two, then speaks.*) Do you like me mummy? (*Dismisses subject of time.*)

The same child, at another time, ended a series of questions concerning the days of the week with the query, "Where does time go?"

Most of the questions raised by young children are difficult if not impossible to answer. Sometimes an adequate answer would go beyond the child's comprehension or willingness to listen (e.g., an answer to the question by a three-year-old, "Where is the people in the radio?" or "What makes the subway run?"). Sometimes the adult is at a loss how to put his answer (e.g., "Who made God?").

As indicated above, children's questions may spring from motives more pressing than intellectual curiosity. There may be fear, worry, or uneasiness. A child who has been frightened by an animal may ask about any new thing that he sees, "Has it got a mouf? Does it bite?" The child of a mother who works away from home a good deal may ask, repeatedly, on seeing an unaccompanied adult or a child, "Where is his mamma?" A three-year-old boy raised many questions after the slaughter, at his home, of two pigs that had been reared there since they were little. "Why did you butcher Blackie and Whitie?" (the pigs). When told (as he had been told repeatedly beforehand) that pigs are butchered for meat when they are big and fat, he asked, "Will me and—(naming his sister) be butchered when we are big?" On later days he asked questions such as, "Do people close their eyes when they are dead?" After one such question, he asserted firmly, "When I be dead I won't close my eyes and I'm going to run around." (In this remark he seems to show resistance to the idea of death.) Apparently it was the idea of death rather than the demise of the two particular pigs that bothered him, for he later identified parts of the pigs at table and ate with great relish.

The following (from Rust, 42) is another example of a child who was puzzled about death:

Child (four and a half years old): Mummy, what means a dead mother?
Mother: A woman that has died and does not walk or talk any more.
Child: But what will the children do?
Mother: Well, if a mother should die, the father would take care of them and maybe an aunt.
Child: Will you be a dead mother some day?
Mother: Why yes, though I don't expect to be for a long time.
Child: A *very* long time?
Mother: Yes.
Child: But I don't want you to die; I want you here like this.
Mother: Well you will probably be quite grown-up before that happens.
Child: A *long* time?
Mother: Yes.
Child: But what *means* dead, mummy?
Mother: Well, your heart stops beating and you lie still without breathing.
Child: And what do you do with the talking part—you know, the inside talk?
Mother: I'm not sure, but some people think you live in another world and of course some don't.
Child: I guess we do (excitedly). Yes! And then you die in a *long,* long time—a *very* long time, and then I die and we both hug each other and then you won't have any wrinkles— Oh, look at that cute pussy? Isn't she darling? (*Runs off.*)

It often happens that a child will continue to repeat a question after an adult has given an answer. Such repetition may function as a technique for getting attention, but it may also mean that the child is still puzzled or troubled. To answer a child's question it is, of course, first necessary to understand the question. Sometimes the meaning of a question is not so obvious. If an adult would understand the more elusive questions he must prepare to be sympathetic and patient. It is also helpful if he is genuinely interested. Moreover, some questions cannot be understood without some knowledge of what has gone before in the child's life. A child might, for example, ask again and again during an afternoon, "Are you going to put the car in the garage?" This repetition becomes more understandable when the parent realizes that the question really means, "Are you going to stay home or are you going out this evening?"

In trying to fathom the meaning of a child's question it is well, on the other hand, not to read too much into his inquiry. An example of this occurred in a home in which there was a two-and-a-half-year-old girl who had just received a new rubber doll. She held it up for both father and mother to see, saying, "See my baby?" When she added, "Where baby come from?" the father at first thought the child was asking her first question about the origin of babies, but before he could collect himself for an answer worthy of this occasion the mother simply said, "Woolworth's." This answer suited the child perfectly, for all she apparently wanted to know was whether the doll had been bought by one of the parents in the store or had been mailed to her as a gift.[10]

In trying to satisfy the questioning child it is important, of course, to try to answer the question he has in mind even though the inquiry may not be too clearly put.

BIBLIOGRAPHY

1. Baker, E.: *Children's Questions and Their Implications for Planning the Curriculum* (New York: Bureau of Publications, Teachers College, Columbia University, 1945), 172 pp.

---

[10] For additional findings concerning children's questions see Storm (46) and Baker, E. (1).

2. Bestor, M. F.: "A Study of Attention in Young Children," *Child Development* (1934), 5:368-380.
3. Blonsky, P. P.: "The Problem of Earliest Childhood Memories and Their Significance" (translated title), *Arch. für die Gesamte Psychologie* (1929), 71:369-390.
4. Bott, H.: *Observation of Play Activities in a Nursery School,* Genetic Psychology Monographs (1928), 4:44-88.
5. Boyd, W.: "Development of Sentence Structure in Childhood," *British Journal of Psychology* (1926-1927), 17:181-191.
6. Brandenburg, G. C.: "The Language of a Three Year Old Child," *Pedagogical Seminary* (1915), 22:89-120.
7. Brandenburg, G. C. and J.: "Language Development During the Fourth Year. The Conversation." *Pedagogical Seminary* (1919), 26:27-40.
8. Bryan, A. L.: *Organization of Memory in Young Children,* Archives of Psychology (1934), No. 162, 56 pp.
9. Burtt, H. E.: "A Further Study of Early Childhood Memory," *Journal of Genetic Psychology* (1937), 50:187-192.
10. ———: "An Experimental Study of Early Childhood Memory," *Journal of Genetic Psychology* (1932), 40:287-295.
11. ———: "An Experimental Study of Early Childhood Memory: Final Report," *Journal of Genetic Psychology* (1941), 58:435-439.
12. Coan, L.: *Children's Questions,* unpublished (New York: Teachers College, Columbia University, 1939).
13. Cook, W. M.: "Ability of Children in Color Discrimination," *Child Development* (1931), 2:303-320.
14. Curti, M. W.: *Child Psychology,* second edition (New York: Longmans, Green, 1938), 458 pp.
15. Davis, E. A.: "The Form and Function of Children's Questions," *Child Development* (1932), 3:57-74.
16. Dudycha, G. J. and Dudycha, M. M.: "Adolescents' Memories of Preschool Experiences," *Journal of Genetic Psychology* (1933), 42:468-480.
17. ———: "Some Factors and Characteristics of Childhood Memories," *Child Development* (1933), 4:265-278.
18. ———: "Childhood Memories: A Review of the Literature," *Psychological Bulletin* (October, 1941), 38: No. 8:669-681.
19. Dunford, R. E.: "The Genetic Development of Cutaneous Localization," *Journal of Genetic Psychology* (1930), 37:499-513.
20. Emerson, L. L.: "The Effect of Bodily Orientation Upon the Young Child's Memory for Position of Objects," *Child Development* (1931), 2:125-142.

21. Fahey, G. L.: "The Questioning Activity of Children," *Pedagogical Seminary* (1942), 60:337-357.
22. Fisher, M. S.: *Language Patterns of Preschool Children*, Child Development Monographs (New York: Teachers College, Columbia University, 1934), No. 15, 88 pp.
23. Friedmann, P.: "The Cutaneous Spatial Threshold in Children" (translated title), *Zeitschrift für Psychologie* (1927), 103:185-202.
24. Gordon, K.: "A Study of Early Memories," *Journal of Delinquency* (1928), 12:129-132.
25. Gutteridge, M. V.: *The Duration of Attention in Young Children*, Australian Council for Educational Research (Melbourne: Melbourne University Press, 1935), 52 pp.
26. Hartmann, G. W. and Triche, A.: "Differential Susceptibility of Children and Adults to Standard Illusions," *Journal of Genetic Psychology* (1933), 42:493-498.
27. Henri, V. and Henri, C.: "Enquete sur les premiers souvenirs de l'enfance," Annee Psychol. (1896), 3:184-198.
28. ———: "Earliest Recollections," *Popular Science Monthly* (1898), 108-115.
29. Herring, A. and Koch, H. L.: "A Study of Some Factors Influencing the Interest Span of Preschool Children," *Journal of Genetic Psychology* (1930), 38:249-279.
30. Hetzer, H. and Wislitzky, S.: "Experimente über Erwartung und Erinnerung beim Kleinkind," *Zeitschrift für Psychologie* (1930), 118:128-141.
31. Hollingworth, H. L.: *Psychology: Its Facts and Principles* (New York: Appleton-Century, 1928), 539 pp.
32. Hunter, W. S.: "The Delayed Reaction in a Child," *Psychological Review* (1917), 24:73-87.
33. Hurlock, E. B. and Schwartz, R.: "Biographical Records of Memory in Preschool Children," *Child Development* (1932), 3:230-239.
34. Line, W.: *The Growth of Visual Perception in Children,* British Journal of Psychology Monograph Supplement (1931), No. 15, 148 pp.
35. Mallay, H.: "The Latent Memory Span of the Preschool Child," *Child Development* (1935), 6:110-119.
36. Miles, C.: "A Study of Individual Psychology," *American Journal of Psychology* (1893), 6:534-558.
37. Miles, K. A.: "Sustained Visual Fixation of Preschool Children to a Delayed Stimulus," *Child Development* (1933), 4:1-5.
38. Miller, N. E.: "The Perception of Children: A Genetic Study Employing the Critical Choice Delayed Reaction," *Pedagogical Seminary and Journal of Genetic Psychology* (1934), 44:321-339.

39. Munn, N. L.: "Learning in Children," *Manual of Child Psychology,* edited by L. Carmichael (New York: Wiley, 1946), Ch. VIII, 370-449.
40. Munn, N. L. and Stenig, B. R.: "The Relative Efficacy of Form and Background in a Child's Discrimination of Visual Patterns," *Journal of Genetic Psychology* (1931), 39:73-90.
41. Rugg, H., Krueger, L., and Sondergaard, A.: "A Study of the Language of Kindergarten Children," *Journal of Educational Psychology* (1929), Vol. 20, 1:1-18.
42. Rust, M. M.: *The Growth of Children's Concepts of Time, Space, and Magnitude,* unpublished (New York: Teachers College, Columbia University).
43. Shacter, H. S.: "A Method for Measuring the Sustained Attention of Preschool Children," *Journal of Genetic Psychology* (1933), 42:339-371.
44. Skalet, M.: *The Significance of Delayed Reactions in Young Children,* Comparative Psychology Monographs (1931), 7: 82 pp.
45. Skeels, H. M.: "A Study of Some Factors Influencing Form-Board Accomplishments of Two- and Three-Year-Old Children," *Journal of Genetic Psychology* (1932), 40:375-395.
46. Storm, H. C.: "Who Can Ask the Better Questions—Teachers or Pupils?," *Elementary School Journal* (1928), 28:610-615.
47. Trettien, A. W.: "Language Interests of Children," *Pedagogical Seminary* (1904), 11:113-177.
48. Updegraff, R.: *The Visual Perception of Distance in Young Children and Adults: A Comparative Study,* University of Iowa Studies in Child Welfare (1930), 4, No. 4: 102 pp.
49. Van Alstyne, D.: *Play Behavior and Choice of Play Materials of Preschool Children* (Chicago: University of Chicago Press, 1932), 104 pp.
50. White, R.: "The Space Order Reaction of Young Children," *Child Development* (1931), 2: p. 75.
51. Wolf, T. H.: *The Effect of Praise and Competition on the Persisting Behavior of Kindergarten Children,* University of Minnesota Institute of Child Welfare Monograph Series (Minneapolis: University of Minnesota Press, 1938), 138 pp.

Chapter XI

THE GROWTH OF UNDERSTANDING
(*Continued*)

MENTAL DEVELOPMENT IN LATER CHILDHOOD

By the time a child has reached elementary-school age, he is capable of most, if not all, of the kinds of intellectual operations that are found in the mental life of an adult. He can recollect the past and plan for the future. Within the limits of his experience and information, he is capable of both inductive and deductive reasoning. He is able to imagine, to daydream, and to give play to fantasy. He is able to deal with some problems on a level of ideas as distinguished from dealings with tangible and concrete things. He can manipulate countless symbols without actually having to handle the physical material or do the physical acts these symbols represent.

On reaching the age conventionally regarded as the time for the beginning of formal education, the child is already a highly trained and very versatile person. However, he still has a long way to go in his intellectual development.

Some broad developmental objectives. During the elementary-school years he will show marked increases in his knowledge and general information, as one would expect. He will show increased ability to deal with the abstract. He will acquire an increasing interest in and ability to deal with affairs in the world at large that do not directly touch his everyday life. He will show an increasing capacity for intellectual teamwork, for understanding and discussing the ideas and viewpoints of others, and for joining with others in the give and take of group discussion. He will be able to deal with problems and plans of increasing complexity.

He will show an increase in his ability to concentrate his attention on intellectual tasks.

EXPANSION OF INTELLECTUAL HORIZONS

By the age of six the world of happenings and things in which the child dwells has expanded far beyond the cradle and the nursery which confined him at birth. Even so, at the beginning of the elementary-school period a child's intellectual enterprises—his thoughts, plans, and interests—tend to be restricted mainly to things that are near in time and space. During the ensuing years there is a great expansion.

Awareness of people. This expansion manifests itself in many ways. It appears in the child's awareness of and interest in people in the world at large. An illustration of this is found in one study in which the children were asked to name persons whom they regarded as their heroes or ideals. A summary of changes from the age of six through later ages appears in Table XXXIII in Chapter XIII from a study by Hill (28). In the age range from six to eight, fifty-eight per cent of the characters named by the children were characters who belonged in the immediate everyday environment of the children. At the age of twelve, only thirty per cent of the characters belonged in this category. At the age range from six to eight only about one-third of the persons named by the children were historical or public characters—characters in the world at large apart from the child's immediate environment; at the age of twelve almost two-thirds of the characters were in this category. Findings such as these are, of course, in line with what one might expect. Yet they show graphically one of the aspects of growing up intellectually—a process which includes increasing awareness and appreciation of people beyond, away from the confines of the home.

Widened range of response to world at large. The extension of the child's intellectual life takes place also through an increased responsiveness to happenings in the world outside his own immediate sphere of everyday activity. An example of this appeared in a study in which a record was made of what children said during free discussion periods in the classroom. Some of the findings are reproduced in Table XXVII from a study by Baker (4).

TABLE XXVII

SUBJECT MATTER, CONTENT, AND SOURCE OF EXPERIENCES REPRESENTED IN TOPICS CONTRIBUTED DURING CLASS DISCUSSION IN GRADES II, IV, AND VI[1]

Grade	II	IV	VI
Number of pupils	62	54	45
Subject Matter Content			
Personal Activity	61%	41%	18%
Animals	10	7	8
Books, Radio, Movies	7	13	6
Current Happenings in World at Large	18	29	60
Miscellaneous	4	10	9
Medium of Acquisition			
Personal Presence	83	52	25
Reflection	1	15	18
Other Media (books, magazines, radio, theater, personal conversation)	16	31	56
Unknown	0	2	1

One conspicuous change, as can be seen in Table XXVII, is a decided drop from the second to the sixth grade in discussion of topics relating to a child's own personal activities and experiences. At the second grade, sixty-one per cent of all contributions dealt with personal activities and experiences as contrasted with eighteen per cent at the sixth grade.

Paralleling the foregoing, there was a corresponding increase from the second to the sixth grade in contributions dealing with world and domestic news, and with activities of people other than the child himself.

---

[1] This and the following table are adapted from Baker, H. V.: *Children's Contributions in Elementary School General Discussion*, Child Development Monographs (New York: Teachers College, Columbia University, 1942), No. 29, pp. 32-33. Reproduced by permission.

In keeping with the foregoing, a change also appeared in the extent to which children were preoccupied with events they had directly witnessed, whether or not they themselves were the main actors in an event. At the second grade most of the topics or items of information discussed by the children dealt with matters that had actually happened in their lives or in their presence—eighty-three per cent of contributions fell in this category. At the sixth grade, however, only about one-fourth of the contributions dealt with matters concerning which the children had become aware through personal experience or direct contact.

Increase in intellectual teamwork. A very notable feature of intellectual development during the years following the beginning of the elementary-school period is an increasing ability to understand, appreciate, and share the intellectual interests of other persons. There is an increased ability to join in an exchange of ideas and to achieve a meeting of minds with other persons. This line of development is illustrated by the findings represented in Table XXVIII. This table, like Table XXVII, is based upon a study of

TABLE XXVIII

PERCENTAGE OF CONTRIBUTIONS IN CHILDREN'S DISCUSSIONS IN GRADES II, IV, AND VI THAT REPRESENTED A LOGICAL CONTINUATION OF PREVIOUSLY DISCUSSED TOPICS OR NEW AND INDEPENDENT SUBJECT MATTER

Grade	II	IV	VI
Number of Pupils	62	54	45
New Topic, not obviously related to what earlier speaker had said	87%	33%	23%
New Topic, but apparently suggested by something said by a previous contributor	8	24	33
Logical Continuation of a topic previously introduced	4	43	44

children's contributions during free discussion periods. It may be noted that at the second grade only twelve per cent of the contributions made by the children during class discussion represented a continuation of a theme or topic that had been discussed or suggested by a previous speaker, whether immediately preceding or earlier during the period. At the sixth grade, in contrast, well over two-thirds (seventy-seven per cent) of the contributions carried on the elaboration or development of an idea that someone else had introduced during the discussion period. Conversely, most of the contributions at the second-grade level represented "new topics"—that is, the child was simply giving voice to something that happened to be interesting or something that happened to occur to him, and he made no effort to link what he was saying to what had been said before or to merge his contribution into the treatment of a common topic.

Changes such as these in the child's intellectual orientation are paralleled by developments in other aspects of the child's life. As noted in another chapter, the youngster as he moves through the elementary-school years becomes increasingly able to throw himself into group activities, to enter into teamwork. The changes that thus are taking place in overt social behavior are paralleled by an increased capacity for social interchange on an intellectual level.

The fact that children acquire this increased capacity for sharing the thoughts of others does not mean, of course, that they are no longer occupied with their own private desires and concerns. The child's own thoughts and feelings, his problems and desires as a person distinct from others, continue to be matters of primary concern to him as was true during earlier years and as will be true throughout life. The process of becoming socialized does not mean that the child surrenders his individuality. Rather the process of socialization means an extension of the child's individuality, so that his mental life encompasses thoughts and concerns that have reference to others and also includes concerns arising within his own immediate, personal experience.

Increased capacity for generalizing. Another feature of mental development during the elementary-school years and beyond is an increased understanding and use of general and inclusive categories of thought. A child at the age of six tends to a much greater extent than a child aged ten or twelve or older to think in specific terms. As time goes on, a child is able increasingly to encompass larger classes or categories as distinguished from the specific item or event.

This ability to think in terms of the more inclusive category or class is illustrated by the responses given by children when they are asked to express their wishes. In one such study, in which children aged five to twelve were asked to give three wishes, the responses were tabulated under a number of headings including one heading that represented wishes for specific material objects and another that included wishes for general benefits for self and others. The percentage of wishes falling in these two categories are shown in Table XXIX (32).

A younger child might wish, for example, for a football, a football helmet, a football suit, while an older child instead of devoting three wishes to different objects might wish for money to buy a football outfit and still have two wishes left.

TABLE XXIX

PERCENTAGE OF CHILDREN WHOSE FIRST WISH WAS FOR SPECIFIC THINGS OR FOR MORE GENERAL BENEFITS IN THE AGE RANGE FROM FIVE TO TWELVE[2]

(Other categories not reproduced bring the total at each level to 100 per cent.)

Type of Wish	All Subj.	Age Groups				IQ Groups		
		5–6	7–8	9–10	11–12	120 and above	100–119	80–99
I. Specific material objects and possessions............	35.8	55.	48.	26.	14.	23.3	38.3	47.9
II. General benefits for self and others....	17.9	8.0	14.	22.	27.	25.6	17.1	8.3

[2] Adapted from Jersild, A. T., Markey, F. V., and Jersild, C. L.: *Children's Fears, Dreams, Wishes, Daydreams, Likes, Dislikes, Pleasant and Unpleasant Memories,* Child Development Monographs (New York: Teachers College, Columbia University, 1933), No. 12, 172 pp. Reproduced by permission. This version omits comparisons between boys and girls and between school groups that are included in the original table.

Capacity for self-understanding. As we have noted elsewhere in the section on children's language development, and in the section of this chapter dealing with mental development during preschool years, children are very much preoccupied with themselves. This tendency to be preoccupied with his personal affairs and concerns continues in a child even though, as he grows older, he becomes more capable of appreciating the point of view and the thoughts and feelings of others. "I-mindedness" is not limited, of course, to children, for it is true also of the behavior of adults.

An illustration of the extent to which this preoccupation with self prevails at the adult level is offered by a study by Henle and Hubbell (26) in which an analysis was made of over three thousand remarks which the investigators had surreptitiously recorded from the conversations of graduate students and other adults. These remarks were classified under five general headings, one of which was entitled "ego-related sentences" and included statements concerning the activities of the speaker, his feelings, emotions, desires, and interests, as well as statements of opinion, attitude, criticism, and other evaluative remarks. Other categories included "social sentences" (such as statements or questions about other people); "sentences containing mixed reference"; "objective sentences"; and "yes and no and equivalent phrases." It was found that for all subjects combined, remarks of the "ego-related" type constituted 40.7 per cent of sample conversations that were recorded.[3]

A child's tendency to be preoccupied with his own personal concerns is not accompanied, however, by a corresponding tendency to be introspective or to analyze himself. In thinking about their own concerns children do not as a rule reveal that they have insight into their own characteristics, powers, and limitations. This

---

[3] It was noted also that "ego-related" remarks were more frequent in the case of women than of men, but the difference was relatively small (less than four per cent); "objective sentences" were relatively more frequent in the case of men (constituting 17.8 per cent of the remarks of an unselected group of men as compared with 7.8 per cent of the remarks of an unselected group of women).

is illustrated by children's wishes. In the study of the wishes of children of elementary-school age cited above it was found that children's wishes were directed mainly toward accomplished objective facts, rather than toward the possession of powers within themselves which would enable them to win the things they desired. The child will wish for a good grade in school rather than for the ability within himself to get good marks. Few children wished for higher mental ability, and among those who did, the wish was expressed as frequently by children who already had superior intelligence as by children who were below average. Wishes dealing with improvement in personal ability, strength, size, or appearance constituted only about eleven per cent of the children's wishes (even with the liberal inclusion of wishes for specific accomplishments, such as the ability to ride horseback or to play the piano).

In answering questions as to what changes they would like in themselves if they could be different the children likewise thought mainly in terms of the external environment rather than of factors within themselves that would give them power to cope with the environment. Only about a third of the children in the study saw in this question an opportunity to wish for an improvement in their personal qualifications by asking for greater intelligence, strength, and ability.

Findings such as these, indicating a lack of critical self-appraisal, do not mean, of course, that children are completely unaware of their own qualifications. A child may, for example, savor the fact that he is popular with the other children. But even so, it is likely to be the objective fact of being popular that he thinks about and appreciates rather than the qualities within himself that are responsible for his popularity.

This tendency to think in terms of the objective or accomplished fact rather than psychological processes appears also in a child's outlook upon people and conditions in the world at large. In the above-mentioned study of children's wishes it was found that many of the children who expressed altruistic wishes asked, for example, for new hospitals, better housing, money to endow charities, and organizations to promote peace rather than for alleviation of conditions that cause poverty and strife. Behavior such as this is also frequently shown by adults.

One thing that has been regarded as a mark of intellectual maturity is a capacity for self-appraisal, at least to the extent that a person has some awareness of his limitations and his strength, some capacity to formulate his goals and aspirations, and a certain amount of self-understanding with respect to his motives. Presumably the person who is able to achieve a certain amount of insight with respect to himself would be in a better position to cope with his frustrations and his fears and should be more immune to the emotional turmoil that arises from unresolved conflicts than the person who is unaware of his own mental life. Unfortunately, the research data with respect to the development of a capacity for insight into self are very limited.

CHILDREN'S REASONING

The quality of a child's reasoning is likely to vary in connection with different problems. In arriving at explanations, generalizations, and conclusions a child who is quite logical in pursuing one problem may be very naïve in dealing with another.

Many investigations have shown that children are capable at an early age of many reasoning processes such as are shown by adults (8, 11, 22, 24, 29, 40, 42). However, as one would expect, there are certain limitations when children are called upon to deal with problems that go beyond their understanding and experience. Some of these characteristics also appear in the reasoning of adults when adults are on unfamiliar ground. Children's ability to reason is a matter of interest not only from a psychological point of view but also from the practical standpoint of education and mental hygiene. Moreover, there have been conflicting theories and findings with reference to this question.

Piaget (52), as noted earlier, has described stages in children's thinking and has maintained that up to about the age of seven or eight years a child tends to reason only in terms of isolated or particular cases, is incapable of a genuine argument, feels no need for verification or logical justification, has difficulty in making generalizations or deductions or in reasoning from the point of view of another person or from the point of view of a general proposition.[4]

It has also been maintained that not until about the age of eleven or twelve years is a child able sufficiently to adopt another's point of view, to reason correctly from another's beliefs, or to carry on formal thought or arrive at pure deductions, and, likewise, that it is not until about this age that the ability to give a logical explanation of causal relationships has completely evolved (53).

The findings in many studies, however, go counter to the view that there are distinct stages in the development of children's reasoning. To be sure, as a child increases in knowledge and experience, there is an increase in his ability to solve problems of greater number, variety, and complexity, in his ability to formulate answers and to give reasons, and in his ability to reorganize experience and to arrive at generalizations. But these gains are not of such a character that the child's reasoning processes at the age of six are essentially different from his reasoning processes at the age of twelve or eighteen.

It is also true that children's explanations and solutions often are naïve, inconsistent, and self-contradictory. But when adults are called upon to deal with wholly unfamiliar material, they tend to give some of the same types of answers as do children (1, 24, 51). In one such study (51), the subjects were thirty-five members of the faculty in a liberal arts college. A number of experi-

---

[4] See also the discussion on pages 335-336, in the chapter on language, McCarthy's account of findings in studies of egocentricity in children (41) and Curti's account of concept formation (8a).

ments, demonstrating primarily certain principles of physics, were performed in the presence of these adults and the adults were asked to make a prediction as to what would happen or to give an explanation of what would happen. The variety of explanations that were offered included even some statements—twenty-three comments by eighteen different adults—that bordered on the mystical or magical (e.g., "It is a long time since I studied any science. Maybe nature has changed a little," or "That means the air is misbehaving," or "It seems a bit unfair that the iron doesn't get there first").

The possibility has been suggested that there might be a prelogical stage in the development of reasoning but that children have already passed through this stage by the time they reach the age attained by children represented in the studies cited above. Findings on this point have been reported by Dennis (9), who asked questions designed to throw light upon his daughter's conception of the world and of the nature and cause of various happenings. At the age of six years and two months this child gave much the same kind of answers as do adults to a variety of questions about the nature and cause of things. However, many of the answers that she gave before the age of three were of a different character. For example, at the earlier age she would give certain explanations that were more on the side of magic than of physical cause and effect. She said, for example, "I move the sun when I go up and down." Also she seemed to believe that she could make the auto run by blowing the horn.

This child also, at first, had notions such as: Dreams are not something that are produced and occur within the dreamer, but are external happenings. Things originate through human construction (such as, a daddy-man makes daddies, candy is made by a candy-man). Observations such as these are interesting in that they suggest the possibility that there may be a stage during which children think in prelogical, magical, or animistic terms. However, more evidence than is now at hand would be needed to substantiate this point. Moreover, various observations indicate that nonlogical or logical thinking is not an either-or phenomenon. The same child, at a given time, may exhibit both varieties. In the Dennis study, while the child was answering to the effect that a moon-man made the moon, she answered that milk came from a cow.

It has been observed by the writer that children similarly may give a naïve answer to one question and a sophisticated answer to another. One three-year-old, for example, when asked, "What makes the wind blow?" answered, "It blows itself." When asked, "What makes a car run?" she answered, "The motor." It is quite likely that the second answer, which was the more acceptable from an adult point of view, meant little more to her than did the first. In any event, the two answers do not seem to represent two different kinds of thinking but, rather, the best explanation or verbal response the child was able to supply, out of his experience, at the moment.[5]

Tests of children's reasoning. Several investigations dealing with children of kindergarten age and upward have indicated that children are capable at an early age of the kind of reasoning involved in explaining cause-and-effect relationships. In one such study (12), a number of experiments were performed in the children's presence, such as covering a jar in which was a lighted candle and then asking the child to explain why the light went out, placing pebbles in a beaker of water and asking why the water rose, and the like. When the answers were rated and quantified, there was an increase in the children's scores from year to year. The various types of answers were found over a wide range, and at no age did the children's answers fall into any single type. It was found that causal thinking develops, not by stages, but by a gradual process. Moreover, the answers given by individual chil-

---

[5] Various studies suggest the possibility that there may be differences between children at a given age in different cultures and also at different socio-economic levels in the frequency of explanations of a seemingly "prelogical" sort (10, 17, 22, 30, 49).

dren did not fall into a single class; a child might handle quite effectively a problem that touched upon matters on which he was informed and then give a naïve answer to another problem. Children's ability to solve the problems was more closely related to their school experience than to chronological or mental age.

Another study by Burt (8) deals with the ability of English children at various age levels to reason inductively—that is, from the particular to the general—and their ability to handle arguments that proceed by eliminating in succession each of a number of alternative hypotheses except the right one.

In this study it was found that there were differences between the ability of older and younger children to handle problems of varying degrees of difficulty and complexity but that there was no evidence that the reasoning processes of the younger children of elementary-school age differed in kind from the reasoning processes of older children.

At seven years, for example, the children could solve this problem:

Tom runs faster than Jim; Jack runs slower than Jim: who is the slowest, Jim or Jack or Tom?

Seven-year-olds also found the correct answer to the following puzzle:

It is Sunday, and on a Sunday afternoon Ada usually takes the baby out, or goes by herself to the pictures, or walks over to see her aunt, or else goes by train to the cemetery. Today she has no money with her and the baby is asleep upstairs. Where do you think she has probably gone?

At eight years, the children solved a problem such as this, which likewise called for elimination of untenable hypotheses:

I don't like sea voyages, and I don't like the seaside. I must spend Easter either in France, or among the Scottish Hills, or on the South Coast. Which shall it be?

It was not until a later age, near the end of the elementary-school period, however, that the children were able to solve a problem calling for the discovery of a general rule from a number of particular instances, such as:

> One pound of meat should roast for half an hour; two pounds three-quarters of an hour; three pounds one hour; eight pounds two-and-a-quarter hours; nine pounds two-and-a-half hours. From this, can you discover a simple rule by which you can tell from the weight of a joint how long it should roast?

Children at a given age level are likely, of course, to differ in their ability to solve problems such as the foregoing.

Ability to reason from the standpoint of an abstract proposition. As indicated earlier, children show an increase with age in knowledge of and ability to deal with the abstract. This appears in their ability to apply a general proposition to a specific case, as in an earlier illustration. It also appears in the eventual development of ability not only to apply a general proposition which they know or believe to be true but also the ability to reason in terms of an hypothesis which for the time being is supposed to be true. Eventually, also, a large proportion of people are able to reason from the standpoint of a proposition that is contrary to fact (e.g., If Alfred Landon had been elected President instead of Franklin Roosevelt in 1936, it is likely that . . . .). Some persons also eventually achieve, with varying degrees of success, the ability to reason in terms of a proposition that is contrary to their own desires. This ability to reason in terms of hypotheses contrary both to fact and to desire represents a decided advance beyond thinking in concrete and wishful terms.

Observation of children indicates that they vary greatly in ability to reason from the point of view of an abstract proposition that goes counter to their wishes. The writer observed an example of this in a fifth-grade class. The children were reporting current events. One boy reported his current event in the form of a question or riddle: "There will be no war if the President of what country gives in to Hitler's demands?" At the time, Hitler was making demands on Czechoslovakia and the idea behind the boy's question was that if the head of the Czechoslovakian government acceded to these demands Hitler would not start a war. When no one else could answer, the boy himself answered that if the President of Czechoslovakia yielded to Hitler there would be no war. But many children protested that this answer was wrong. The teacher let the children debate the issue. It was apparent that most members of the class were arguing the merits of Hitler's demands and not the merits of the boy's answer. The argument was: What right has Hitler to ask for this territory? How would you like it if you were a Czechoslovakian? and so on. The boy who first raised the issue tried to maintain that he was not arguing the merits of the demands, he was simply arguing that *if* the Czechoslovakians yielded there would be no war between Czechoslovakia and Germany. When a vote was taken almost every pupil in the class voted that the boy who had presented the proposition had lost the debate.

This episode is cited as an illustration of failure to grasp an abstract proposition. It is not presented with the suggestion that this kind of failure is characteristic of children alone, for adults also often, of course, make their verdicts on the basis of what they desire to be true rather than on the basis of logic.

Other differences between the reasoning of older and younger persons. In keeping with the fact that an older person usually has more experience and information on which to draw, one would expect certain differences between the ways in which older and younger persons approach a given problem. In various studies it has been found that when older and younger persons are confronted with a similar problem some, if not all, of the older ones will tend to be more deliberate in their procedure, to turn the matter over in their minds, so to speak, whereas a child is more likely to forge ahead in overt trial and error.[6] Also, as one would expect, adults are likely to reach a conclusion or correct answer more quickly and to see the point more readily. Moreover, adults are likely to have more patience and to show more persistence in dealing with a difficult problem. On all these points there are, of course, large individual differences both among children and adults.

Another difference between an older person and a young child is that the older person is likely to be more resigned to the inevitable and to accept the objective fact. At the age of two and a half a child may ask, for example, for more prunes and then reply, when told that there are no more prunes, "Yes there are, because I want some." At the age of five or six, when confronting a similar situation, the child's reaction if he desires prunes is less likely to take the form of arguing or insisting that there actually are some prunes in the kitchen. Instead, he is likely to accept this fact and then express his disappointment or desire by complaining that he still is hungry or scolding his mother for not providing a large enough supply.

Another difference appears in the fact that the younger child tends to express himself more frankly and freely than does an older person. A young child, to borrow a phrase from Piaget, "has no verbal continence" (54). The greater tendency on the part of the child to speak what is on his mind does not, however, mean that there is a corresponding tendency to inquire whether the other person is interested and following the line of talk. To what extent this tendency in older children and adults to keep their thoughts more to themselves is something that normally develops in the nature of things, and to what extent it is a result of pressure that is mainly cultural in origin, would be difficult to determine.

---

[6] For studies bearing upon this point see Gould and Perrin (16), Hamilton (20), Heidbreder (25), Hicks and Carr (27).

In any event, in our culture the person regarded as mentally mature tends to be silent about his feelings and to keep many of his thoughts to himself. There is the ideal of the "strong, silent" character. It is possible, of course, that this ideal has developed as a result of natural necessity. Presumably the older a person becomes the more he has on his mind, and an impasse would occur if everyone tried to tell everything to everybody else. On the other hand, this reticence in an older person may amount to a kind of deceit. Moreover, an adult's image of himself as a "strong, silent" character may be false, for in many situations it takes more strength of character to reveal one's feelings than to remain silent. In addition, this ideal often puts a needless burden upon people whose problems could be solved if shared with someone else. Simply the act of formulating a problem in terms that others can understand may add to the person's own understanding of the problem and his ability to deal with it.

Examples of children's misconceptions. Practically all adults can recall from childhood many erroneous impressions, false beliefs, and misinterpretations of words and phrases. Such misconceptions throw some light upon the difficulties which children have in formulating their ideas and in grasping the meaning of what they hear and see. It would be more revealing if somehow it were possible to obtain cumulative reports from children themselves, for an adult will have forgotten many temporary misconceptions that he entertained as a child and he is especially likely to forget the ways in which his ideas constantly were being revised, supplemented, and clarified. (It may be added that misconceptions are not, of course, limited to children.)

Among children's misconceptions are many that take the form of mistaken beliefs, frequently arising quite by chance or through the solemn testimony of a playmate. Unless a child, through somewhat bitter experience, has learned to distrust others, he is prone to accept as true anything that is told to him and that is not contradicted by his own experience or by some higher authority.

Such beliefs may also influence his actions. Following are examples from one child: He accepted the superstition that a swallowed hair turns into a worm once it gets into the stomach; that a swallowed apple seed would sprout in the stomach; that a withered spot on the lawn or in the pasture meant that the ground was hollow underneath and that, if one landed on such a spot hard enough, he might sink all the way to China; that the devil came when people whistled.

A child's ideas concerning sex are especially likely to involve many mistaken notions if they are obtained from the back alley or if his elders deliberately try to frighten or mislead him with falsehoods. Numerous misconceptions may likewise arise through deliberate or half-joking remarks which adults make concerning individuals against whom the adults are prejudiced. Such falsehoods are often elaborated by children and passed on to others. Thus a boy of nine believed that members of a certain small Protestant sect could spit blood whenever they wanted to and that one would catch a bad disease if one went to a toilet that had been used by members of another sect.

It should be recognized, of course, that adults also are quite gullible, especially in matters that concern their own desires. Also, many childish misconceptions persevere into adult years; and even when erroneous ideas that were entertained during childhood have undergone correction, there still may be residual effects of the earlier images and beliefs. One of the arts of the demagogue is to appeal to such childish images and attitudes.

Many of the more obvious misconceptions simply concern misinterpretation or lack of understanding of words and phrases. Thus a child was overheard to give this version of the oath of allegiance to the flag: "I pledge a legion to the flag and to the Republic of Richard Sands; one nation and a vegetable with liberty and justice to all." Another sang: "Long train run over us (Long to reign over us)"; and another patriotically intoned: "I love thy rots and chills (rocks and rills)." After a moment's hesitation on a line in "The Night Before Christmas," a child came forth with: "I rushed to the window and vomited (threw up) the sash." One youngster for several years quite contentedly sang, "The grandpas we watched were so gallantly screaming."

Faulty perception of a word may lead to confusion, as in the case of the child who defined a pioneer as "one who moves father (farther) west." At two years, a boy at table folded his hands and assumed a devotional attitude when his mother asked him whether he would like some pears ("pears" sounded the same as the word he used for "prayers").

Even a written symbol may be puzzling because of its associations, as in the case of the child who answered during class recitation that the abbreviation of Illinois is "Sick," and another who reported that "Copra is a dried snake." In a study referred to earlier in this chapter, a child decorously tried to avoid the use of what he regarded as a slang term and reported that a baby goat is called a "child"; when questioned further, he said he knew some people called it a "kid."

CHILDREN'S INFORMATION AND CONCEPTS

As one might expect, all studies show gains in children's information from year to year and from grade to grade. However, the information that children possess, the extent to which they grasp the concepts that are involved in their lessons at school, in what they meet through the newspaper, the radio, adult conversation, and the like, tends to be quite spotty. Also, in connection with many topics children may possess a great deal of seeming information and yet may lack any real understanding. They may know the words by which to give the right answers without knowing the meanings of the words.

Children's knowledge and understanding are influenced profoundly by a factor which we might call "seasoning." In many areas it appears that in order to grasp certain meanings it is necessary for the child to have an accumulation of impressions and experiences distributed over a period of development as distinguished from lessons or impressions concentrated within a limited period of time. It has been found that impressions concentrated within a short period of time, even when quite dramatic and charged with emotion, are not likely to produce the same grasp of the subject as a child will obtain through a gradual accumulation of impressions and information over a longer period of time.

Findings in two studies dealing with children's information in certain limited areas are shown in Tables XXX and XXXI. Table XXX represents one hundred children about to enter the first grade of school (57); they ranged in age from five years and four months to six years, and they were carefully selected to represent a cross-section of the population in the city where the study was made. It is interesting to note that certain items registered on the minds of children while many other items that were available for them to overhear or to see seemed to have made little impression.

A large percentage of the children knew the names of certain comic-strip characters. On the other hand, they had formed no impressions about certain public characters that were prominent in the news. The study was made during the heat of the presidential campaign in the fall of 1928, but not a single child recognized the name of one of the major candidates (Herbert Hoover) and only one child recognized the name of the other (Alfred E. Smith). Although this campaign must have aroused a good deal of interest among the children's elders, it apparently had no significance to children near beginning school age. The mere fact of being exposed to a topic that is receiving a good deal of attention from adults does not mean that children are going to form clear impressions or acquire information or learning relating to that topic. This point will be elaborated further in the discussion of the information and understanding about war exhibited by children at different levels while World War II was in progress.

The child's store of information is influenced not only by his ability to grasp meanings, but also by his first-hand opportunities

TABLE XXX

RESULTS OF INFORMATION TEST ADMINISTERED TO 100 CHILDREN, AGED 5 YEARS AND 4 MONTHS TO 6 YEARS[7]

(The values show the percentage of children who answered each question correctly. Some of the items and questions have been abbreviated in the present table.)

Test Items	Percentage of Children Who Answered Correctly
Local Points of Interest:	
Tell me the name of a Minneapolis newspaper.	85
What is the name of a lake in Minneapolis?.	27
What is the Mississippi?.	78
What is Hennepin Avenue?.	52
What is the Great Northern?.	39
What is WCCO? (local radio station).	56
What is Dayton's? (large department store).	92
What large city is closest to Minneapolis?.	29
What do they make in the Ford plant?.	51
What do people go to look at in the Art Gallery?.	5
In what city is Minnehaha Falls?.	44
Tell me the name of a hotel in Minneapolis.	16
Time and Number:	
How many pennies in a dime?.	22
What time of year do flowers grow outdoors?.	99
What time of year is the weather cold?.	92
How many eggs in half a dozen?.	12
What day comes after Sunday?.	75
What time or what o'clock is it at noon?.	30
How many pennies in a nickel?.	37
How many hands has a clock?.	94
What time of the year is the weather hot?.	89
How many eggs in a dozen?.	12
What day comes after Saturday?.	86
What time or what o'clock is it at midnight?.	22
Current Topics and History:	
Who is Andy Gump?.	74
What did Lindbergh do?.	87
Who was the first President?.	55
Who is Dempsey?.	63
Who is Jackie Coogan?.	22
Who is Herbert Hoover?.	0
Who is Skeezix?.	81
What are the colors in the flag?.	95
What people lived in America before the white men did?.	22
Who is Joesting? (local football hero).	8
Who is Coolidge?.	38
Who is Al Smith?.	1
Natural Phenomena:	
What shape is the sun?.	85
Of what is snow made?.	75
Where do you sometimes see a rainbow?.	71
What makes it warm in the summertime?.	91

[7] Adapted from Probst, C. A.: "A General Information Test for Kindergarten Children," *Child Development* (1931), 2:81-95. Reproduced by permission. The original tables report separate scores for boys and girls and for different occupational groups. For an earlier study of children's information see Hall (18, 19).

TABLE XXX (Continued)

Test Items	Percentage of Children Who Answered Correctly
Natural Phenomena (*Continued*):	
Where does the sun set in the evening?	12
What are clouds made of?	34
Where are the clouds?	99
Of what is ice made?	89
What makes it light in the daytime?	82
What shape are snowflakes?	8
Where does the sun rise in the morning?	33
What is lightning made of?	5
Literature and Music:	
What colors are the keys on a piano?	84
Whom was Red Riding Hood going to see?	58
What did Cinderella lose at the ball?	38
On what part of the violin do you play?	46
Who was Hiawatha?	7
How do you play a cornet?	24
What did Jack and Jill do?	94
With what do you play a drum?	94
When the three bears came home, whom did they find in bed?	85
What was the name of the boy who climbed the bean stalk?	44
What was Cinderella's coach or carriage made of?	11
How do you play a saxophone?	49
Animals, Birds, and Insects:	
How many legs has a horse?	100
What does a cat scratch with?	97
From what are little chickens hatched?	63
What do bees make that we eat?	59
A baby dog is called a puppy; what is a baby cow called?	26
What do we call a butterfly before it becomes a butterfly?	19
What do we drink that we get from a cow?	99
What color is a crow?	33
A bird flies in the air; what does a fish do in the water?	87
How many horns has a cow?	87
A baby cow is called a calf; what is a baby horse called?	12
How many wings has a butterfly?	9
Plants and Flowers:	
What do apples grow on?	97
What color are buttercups?	30
What color is wheat when it is ripe?	35
How many stones in a peach?	72
What do we call the part of the plant underground?	32
What do we eat that grows on vines?	29
What must we plant to have flowers?	95
What color are dandelions?	70
What do we call a flower before it opens?	36
What color is an apple before it is ripe?	66
What is the outside of a tree called?	26
What do we eat that grows under the ground?	59
Occupations and Industries:	
Who makes money by cutting hair?	96
To whose office do we go to get a tooth pulled?	95

GROWTH OF UNDERSTANDING

Table XXX (*Continued*)

Test Items	Percentage of Children Who Answered Correctly
Occupations and Industries (*Continued*):	
What does a plumber do?	60
What is butter made from?	40
What is a shoe made of?	79
Where does coal come from?	32
Who brings letters to the house?	98
Who takes people's tonsils out?	91
What do we call a man who raises corn and wheat?	57
What does a carpenter do?	60
Where does wood come from?	69
What is paper made from?	25
Household Arts:	
What do we use to cut cloth?	100
From what animal do we get bacon?	25
What is the outside of an egg called?	70
What is a vacuum cleaner used for?	94
From what does leather come?	17
From what do we get wool?	44
What do you use to cut meat?	100
What do you put with the lemon juice to make lemonade?	82
How do we get water out of clothes before hanging them up to dry?	90
For what is baking powder used?	84
What is the yellow part of an egg called?	30
From what do we get cotton?	11
Simple Mechanics:	
What do you use to put a screw into wood?	75
What do you see on the ground that trains run on?	98
What is the brake on an automobile for?	55
How are trees made into boards?	19
What is a thermometer for?	50
Gas or gasoline makes an automobile go; what makes a street car go?	12
What do you use to put a nail into wood?	98
What do you use a saw for?	100
What is sandpaper for?	45
How can you get to the top floor of a building without walking?	54
What makes a sailboat go?	45
What do we put in the radiators of automobiles?	53
Games and Amusements:	
How do you play leapfrog?	21
What do people fish with?	96
What must you not do in tin-tin?	1
On what do people play hockey in the winter time?	60
In what game do you have a king-row?	10
In what game do you have a touchdown?	28
What do we use to play croquet?	33
What are skis made of?	92
What must you have to play anty-over?	7
What do people play bridge with?	39
In what game do you use a racket?	26
In what game do you have a home run?	26

for observation and learning. In Table XXX, under the general heading of household arts, it can be noted that all of the children knew what is used to cut cloth. Only twenty-five per cent of the children, on the other hand, knew from what animal we get bacon. It is probable that this percentage would have been larger if this question had been asked of farm children who had had experience with the home butchering and processing of pigs.

The replies given by the children in this study when they did not know the correct answer to an item frequently were quite interesting. One boy could not give the name of any newspaper, but he gave a vivid description of a recent sensational murder, ending with the confident assertion: "That's the paper we take." "Clang" (sound) associations appeared in some answers, such as: a carpenter fixes carpet sweepers or repairs cars; energine is put in the radiator of cars; the Great Northern is the North Star; butter is made from buttermilk or butterflies make it; plants, seeds, and flowers are manufactured in the Ford plant; a plumber plumbs, pulls out plums, or sells plumbers; beans grow in gardens but bees make them. The effect of juvenile literature appeared in answers such as: "Clouds are made of animals"—the result of hearing a verse in which children see animals in the clouds, and "Butter is made from tigers" after *Little Black Sambo*. The source of many incorrect answers was somewhat obscure: one child, for example, asserted that a man who raises corn or wheat is called a "bachelor."

A further brief sampling of children's information concerning certain topics is shown in Table XXXI. This table is based upon results obtained by the writer in a study of about five hundred children, aged eight to twelve years, most of whom were pupils in public schools in New York City. The younger children were interviewed; the older ones wrote their answers on individual test blanks.

On many of the items in Table XXXI the percentage of children who answered correctly would no doubt be considerably lower if guesses were eliminated. On some items, the percentage

TABLE XXXI

PERCENTAGE OF CHILDREN IN GREATER NEW YORK CHOOSING THE
CORRECT ALTERNATIVE ANSWER OR SUPPLYING THE CORRECT
ANSWER TO VARIOUS ITEMS OF AN INFORMATION TEST

(Abridged and adapted from an unpublished study by the writer.)

Test Item	\multicolumn{5}{c}{Percentage of Children Giving Correct Answer}
	Aged 8	Aged 9	Aged 10	Aged 11	Aged 12[a]
The sun rises in the: (a) east; (b) north; (c) west; (d) south..............	54	51	63	66	71
The moon sets in the: (a) east; (b) north; (c) west; (d) south..............	29	40	35	50	49
Up the Hudson River is: (a) east; (b) north; (c) west; (d) south.........	29	50	59	54	65
To the Rocky Mountains is: (a) east; (b) north; (c) west; (d) south......	10	34	53	59	70
A boy walks a mile in about: (a) 1 hour; (b) 2 hours; (c) 25 minutes; (d) 5 minutes.......................	27	44	58	52	47
A soldier can march in a day about: (a) 5 miles; (b) 100 miles; (c) 200 miles; (d) 30 miles......................	42	53	60	64	52
A ton of coal would: (a) fill this classroom; (b) almost fill this classroom; (c) not nearly fill this classroom....	22	36	55	54	61
Which is bigger, a corn plant or a wheat plant?...........................	54	58	66	77	77
Which is bigger, a tiger or a cow?......	67	72	73	78	79
Which is bigger, a duck or a goose?....	92	84	91	89	79
Which of the following is known as: (a) a President; (b) an actor; (c) a prizefighter; (d) a Senator:					
Copeland?............................	8	10	25	29	40
Wagner?.............................	8	18	25	32	37
Coolidge?............................	37	38	46	54	58
Hoover?.............................	45	66	76	84	95
Roosevelt?..........................	93	97	96	99	100
Jack Dempsey?......................	62	65	82	82	86
Joe Louis?...........................	79	92	96	98	95
Clark Gable?........................	87	96	98	98	100
From what animal do we get:					
Caviar?.............................	6	7	9	9	6
Venison?............................	14	18	19	31	—
Mutton?............................	6	12	30	45	39
Bacon?..............................	41	51	67	63	65
Beef?...............................	48	48	62	74	78
Pork?...............................	32	65	84	92	91
Does a mother ...... have milk for her baby?[b]					
Elephant?...........................	18	16	23	18	20
Wolf?...............................	19	19	28	32	20
Goat?...............................	69	81	90	91	93

[a] The twelve-year olds were not as representative as the younger children, since they included no pupil above the sixth grade.

[b] Introductory item: A mother cow has milk for her baby, but a mother hen does not. Does a mother .... have milk for her baby?

TABLE XXXI (*Continued*)

Test Item	Percentage of Children Giving Correct Answer				
	Aged 8	Aged 9	Aged 10	Aged 11	Aged 12 [a]
Do the following grow: (*a*) on vines; (*b*) in the ground; (*c*) on trees; (*d*) on bushes:					
Peanuts?	20	39	29	36	33
Watermelons?	10	17	45	48	45
Carrots?	65	80	73	91	93
Oranges?	87	86	95	91	91
Apples?	98	96	99	99	98
Potatoes?	78	90	92	95	98
Which of the following comes from: (*a*) an animal; (*b*) a mine; (*c*) a plant; (*d*) the air:					
Linen?	29	50	69	68	83
Salt?	30	44	74	82	85
Sugar?	44	58	75	82	80
Cotton?	42	75	87	90	92
Leather?	63	68	82	92	80
Coal?	64	82	94	96	92
Wool?	89	93	95	93	94
Meat?	92	100	91	99	100

of correct answers is not much larger than could be expected of chance.

Among other things, it can be noted that relatively few children recognized the names of Senators of their own state (even though both of them were prominently in the newspapers at the time); that relatively few were well informed concerning points of the compass (some children were quite ready with the information that Columbus had sailed *west* when he discovered America and that Byrd went to the *South* Pole, but seemed to have no notion at all as to the meaning of directions when translated into terms of local geography). A large percentage of children believed that only one animal, the cow, has milk for its young, although some also included the goat.

Certain comparisons, not reproduced in the table, show large differences between brighter and duller children. In one public school, the children in two bright classes were correct on sixty-seven per cent of the questions concerning the points of the compass, as compared with a score of only twenty-eight per cent in the case of older children in four dull classes. The difference between the bright and dull children was not so large, however, in the case of questions which they could not so readily answer on the basis of everyday observation or experience (such as the questions as to where peanuts grow, how far a man can walk in a day, and the like).

Frequently in the course of this study, it was noted—as has been noted by other investigators—that a child's answer to a question may not at all represent what the child actually thinks. He may give an answer with tongue in cheek, or bluff, or give the first answer that comes to mind, even though it is inconsistent with earlier replies, rather than frankly say he doesn't know. An unwary investigator of children's thought processes might easily be misled and, after collecting a number of answers of this sort, reach erroneous conclusions concerning the naïveté of children's thinking. A child may appear to be quite uninformed and may seemingly be lacking both in logic and consistency when approached with adult problems, and yet be quite realistic and hard-headed in dealing with matters of concern in his own world.

In the present study, among other tongue-in-cheek guesses, were the answers that bacon comes from a tiger (or a zebra), because both are striped. A child may even go to some lengths in maintaining a position when it appears that he actually is in doubt. Thus, a ten-year-old boy answered that only cows have milk for their young. When asked how a puppy gets its food, he answered that since a puppy must have milk you have to have a cow. To the question, "What about a baby horse?" he again answered, "You have to have a cow"; and the same to, "What about a baby camel?" By this time, he seemed to feel that he had got into difficulties, so when asked, "What about a baby elephant?" he replied, "Oh, let him eat hay!"

It should be emphasized that a child may possess vast stores of information that are meaningful and useful to him in his everyday life, even though he may be lacking in information on many items of knowledge that adults take more or less for granted.

Children's understanding of academic terms and concepts. It usually is quite difficult for an adult to approach a topic from a child's point of view and to fathom how much or how little the child actually understands. Several factors contribute to this difficulty. For one thing, a child's grasp of a topic, term, or idea usually involves partial knowledge rather than complete knowledge or complete ignorance, and so he may use words in proper context even though he may not fully understand their meanings. The same child may be well informed along some lines and be quite lacking in understanding on other matters. Again, even though they are similar in intelligence and academic status, children may vary considerably in the degree of their understanding of a specific subject. Also, children often are quite cagey about revealing their lack of understanding, and sometimes it is only by virtue of an inadvertent remark that a child betrays his ignorance.

A failure on the part of adults to appreciate a child's viewpoint or lack of understanding can often be observed in connection with the teaching of the social studies in the elementary grades. In recent years, many schools have given much emphasis to the social studies in the intermediate and early elementary grades, by way of consideration of topics such as conservation, technological developments, monopoly, government control, problems of production and consumption, democratic as against other forms of government, and so forth. What often seems to happen is that these topics are treated in a manner that is just as unrealistic, from the point of view of the child's interest and understanding, as were some of the old-fashioned drills in history and grammar.

What often happens is that children are called upon to use a number of terms and ideas in large relationships when they have little understanding of the underlying meanings of the individual terms and ideas. Illustrations of this can be seen in a study by

Scott and Myers (62). Children were first asked, for example, to give an example under a certain category (e.g., give the name of a colony, of an explorer, and so on). Many children were able to name two explorers or to give the names of colonies but then were unable to make a clear statement as to what *is* an explorer or a colony. To be sure, a child's difficulty with such questions may not be due so much to a lack of recognition of the meaning as to an inability to find the right words to express the meaning; but this hiatus is interesting nonetheless.[8] It should be recognized, of course, that some vagueness on the child's part as he studies a given subject is unavoidable, for it is only by using terms and concepts in various contexts and relationships that they come to be defined and to have more and more meaning. Although this truth is recognized, it still may be said that, where there is a choice, it would be better to approach a topic by way of conditions known to the child in his own experience than by way of abstract and remote terms or propositions.[9]

Instructive findings concerning children's knowledge of terms and concepts used in the social studies have been presented by Kelley and Krey (35). Among other things, these investigators found an increase from grade to grade in the percentage of children who were able to recognize the meanings of the various terms that were included in the tests. There was little evidence that any particular subject is inherently more difficult than others, with the possible exception of the analytical social sciences. Children's advance in knowledge of social affairs was found to take place by a process of accumulation and integration, varying greatly according to the individual. One pupil may be operating on a con-

---

[8] For a review of studies of children's understanding of terms and concepts involved in school subjects, including investigations by Lacey (37) and Mathews (45), see Jensen (31).

[9] For example, a child may fail for a long time to see any relationship between the taxes he reads about in his study of history and the extra penny he pays as a sales tax in making a small purchase.

siderably higher or lower level of understanding than his classmates. Again a child may be able to comprehend a given term in one context and not in another.

Difficulty in understanding economic and political concepts is not, of course, limited to children of elementary-school age. At the high-school and the freshman and sophomore college levels, many students have difficulty in dealing with a number of economic concepts (43). Indeed, Thorndike has found a high degree of ignorance and gullibility among adults who are much above average in both education and intelligence (65).

In a study by Shaffer (61), ten newspaper cartoons were presented to approximately 150 children in each grade from four through twelve and the children were asked to write an answer to the questions, "What does this cartoon mean?" [10] It was noted that a large proportion of responses in grades four and five were in the nature of a description of the cartoon, without interpretation. At the later grade levels interpretations which recognized the symbolic nature of the picture predominated. There was an increase in the merit of the interpretations from grade four through grade twelve, although the increase was not entirely uniform.

The findings indicate that the average pupil at the junior-high-school level and beyond is able to interpret cartoons abstractly even though such cartoons are presented without contextual material, discussion, or previous training. It was noted that the ability to give an abstract as distinguished from a concrete interpretation of cartoons was more closely associated with mental maturity than with other factors. The average age at which abstract interpretations occurred was 12.83.

Ability to solve problems in logic. Various studies have indicated that children, by the time they reach school age, if not considerably before, are able to deal with problems that call for in-

---

[10] The cartoons dealt with topics such as the progress of transportation, profiteers, war, unemployment, and so on.

ductive or deductive reasoning. In one study children were presented with various propositions to ascertain whether they could correctly apply a generalization to a specific event or could detect illogical generalizations. In a study by Moore (47), two hundred children, ranging in age from five to twelve years, were tested. Several reasoning tests, such as the following, were used: "If all fish in the world have gills, can I be sure that fish in Alaska have gills? Why?" Some of the youngest children were able to give a satisfactory answer to such a question as this, which called for a specific conclusion based upon a general proposition. Another set of statements consisted of "autistic" fallacies, such as the following: "If one washes, he cleanses himself from dirt; if one sins, he is dirty; if one washes, he cleanses himself of sin. Why?" Children below seven-and-a-half years seemingly were unable to understand and to refute this type of proposition. A third test included logical fallacies such as the following: "All automobiles have four wheels. This vehicle has four wheels; therefore it is an automobile. Why?" Some children between five and a half and six and a half were able to analyze a fallacy of this kind and to tell why the conclusion was false. On the various tests, there was a fairly steady increase in score with age.

Concepts of time, space, and magnitude. Through concrete experience in the day's routine,[11] a child has an opportunity gradually to form a notion as to what is meant by a minute or a day, although much confusion often prevails, partly because of vagueness in adult usage (such as the indefinite "Just a minute"). As is the case with adults, a child's experience of the passage of time will be influenced by what happens to fill the time; time spent in waiting is long, and a twenty-minute lesson may seem almost interminable, whereas a similar recess period spent in play may seem short.

In a study of the time concepts of young children it was found

---

[11] An incidental effect of radio programs is to accelerate some children's learning to tell time by the clock in order that they may follow the radio schedule.

that children referred to the present before they referred to the future, and that they dealt with the future before they expressed ideas involving the past. The word "today" was used at about 24 months, "tomorrow" at 30 months and "yesterday" at 36 months (2).

Children's ideas of historical time, in terms of decades, centuries, or epochs are likely to be quite hazy until they are well along in school.[12] Youngsters in high school have difficulty in grasping duration and sequence in connection with historical events and movements. In a study by Oakden and Sturt (50) children's ideas of degrees of antiquity were measured by such means as having them arrange the names of well-known historical personages in order of their remoteness in the past and having them respond to pictures denoting customs and costumes representing different historical periods. They found that concepts of historical time were rather hazy until about the age of eleven years. In a study of Polish children, Rebello (59) found that children aged seven to nine years had no clear conception of the historical past, of the length of a year, or of the length of human life. Time evaluations were found to be made in terms of association with concrete experiences.[13] Also difficult for children is the concept of time in relation to space (see, for example, the large number of children who had no approximate notion of how long it would take a boy of ten years or more to walk a mile or how far a man could walk in a day, as summarized in Table XXVII).

The foregoing statements no doubt must be accepted with some reservation, for some children will acquire ideas of time considerably earlier than others; likewise, a given child may have a good grasp on some time relations and not on others.

---

[12] For studies of children's time concepts, see Bandura (5), Harrison (21), Oakden and Sturt (50), Rebello (59), and Schaeffer (60).

[13] Note that children for many years are quite content with "once upon a time" or "once a long time ago" in the stories they hear. Everyday examples of a child's lack of orientation in time can frequently be found. Thus, a seven-year-old, after hearing from her mother the story of Noah's Ark, asked, "Did you get very wet, Mummy?"

Undoubtedly, much that a child is exposed to in history lessons, or in units on Ancient Egypt or on the Early American Indian (not to mention units in geology dealing with the age of the earth!),[14] is lost upon him as far as time relations are concerned.[15]

Children's concepts and understanding in relation to amount of instruction. Studies such as the foregoing indicate that children's information tends to be spotty in many areas and that a large proportion of children below the junior-high-school age show relatively little understanding of many topics relative to historical or contemporary social, economic, and political affairs. The findings raise certain practical issues. It appears that in many schools what the educators had hoped to achieve and had expected children to understand through the social studies has been quite out of line with reality. It appears that a large proportion of children have either failed to understand or have acquired no more than a superficial familiarity with certain words.

We might ask: What is the reason? Have expectations been too high? Have methods of teaching been poor? Available evidence does not give a complete answer to these questions. However, there is evidence to indicate that the reason for the discrepancy between what has been expected and what children have achieved resides both in a failure to scale what is taught to the mental maturity of the child and in a failure to present what is being taught in such a manner that the child can learn it and interpret it in the light of his own everyday experience.

First a word with respect to scaling to maturity level. Findings from various studies indicate that children's information and un-

---

[14] In a fifth-grade class observed by Professor Gerald Craig, the children were discussing the Appalachian Mountains, and the teacher took this opportunity to question them on what they had retained from previous discussions of the age of the earth. The question, "How old do you think those mountains are?" stumped the group, until a hardy youngster answered, "I think those mountains came there at about the same time as the Pilgrim Fathers."

[15] For illustrative studies of children's understanding of geographic terms and relationships, see, for example, Eskridge (14) and Anderson (3).

derstanding concerning contemporary and historical, social, economic, and political affairs is not dependent simply upon the amount that is taught, or the method of teaching, or the concentrated or dramatic manner in which information is presented, for what is grasped depends in part upon a process of maturing and upon experiences associated with the fact of growing older.

One series of studies bearing indirectly on this point relates to children's understanding of wartime happenings. During a period of wartime, and notably during a period such as that of World War II, children's opportunities to gain impressions and obtain information concerning happenings in the world at large are sharply augmented. War news, news about historical events in the making, and information relating to geographical locations, military, economic, diplomatic, and governmental matters are provided through screaming headlines, through the movies and radio, and through adult conversation which children overhear. The happenings that take place are likely to have a stronger emotional bearing on the child's life than would be true of happenings in the world at large during times of peace. The child hears about the possibility of destruction and injury on the home front. He may be concerned about relatives or friends who are on the fighting fronts. He cannot escape the impact of rationing and scarcities. In countless different ways he is exposed to happenings in his everyday life that are signs and effects of war conditions.

In other words, wartime should, if anything, provide more of stimulus to learning about events in society at large than prevail in times of peace. Accordingly, one might expect that during time of war children at a certain age would show more sophistication in their knowledge and understanding of happenings in the world of affairs than is true during peacetime. Actually, findings from a number of studies indicate that children's information concerning wartime happenings are substantially of a sort that might have been predicted from studies of children's information an understanding with respect to peacetime affairs.[16] To be sure, observers have noted that some children show interests that were distinctly influenced by the war, including greater acquaintanceship with military and political leaders, or an increase in information about geographical locations and perhaps greater interest in maps than normally is exhibited during times of peace. Also, certain aspects of the war situation have affected children's emotional lives. However, along with effects such as these the findings also indicate that children exhibit much the same kind of information and degree of understanding in connection with wartime events as in connection with peacetime events. For example, in one study children at beginning elementary-school age were found to respond to wartime happenings largely in specific terms (36). In discussing an air raid, for example, they are likely to deal with happenings and the specific local effects, much as their discussions during peace deal with the concrete and near at home. In keeping with this, younger children were found in one study to respond to the war situations on a perceptual rather than a conceptual level (7). With advanced age, on the other hand, children showed increased understanding of larger military and social implications. In another study (56), conducted with children in the New York City area in 1940, it was found that sixty-two per cent of children aged nine and ten did not know that the British Navy was larger than the German Navy, and fifty-two per cent did not know that the German Air Force was stronger—at the time—than the British Air Force. Both of these facts were crucial to an understanding of the war situation and both facts were constantly being stressed in news and comments about the progress of the war. At ages thirteen and fourteen thirty-five per cent of the children did not know that the German Air Force was the

---

[16] For findings and observations of children's response to wartime events see Bender and Frosch (7), Geddie and Hildreth (15), Kimmins (36), Preston (56). A review of studies in this area appears in reference (33).

stronger, and only eighteen per cent did not know that the British Navy was the stronger.

Various other lines of evidence indicate that the understanding of certain concepts depends not upon concentrated study of vivid experiences alone but upon impressions that accumulate in the process of becoming older. One study in this area (by Pistor, 55) deals with the development of time concepts. A time-concept test was given for two groups of sixth-grade pupils, aged ten, eleven, and twelve years. One group had previously received, in the fourth and fifth grades, systematic training both in history and geography. The children of the other group had received training primarily in geography alone, with only incidental attention to historical matters. Included in the test were items dealing with Time-Order Relationships (groups of five historical events were presented for ranking in chronological order). A comparison of the two groups of children showed that there was no significant difference between the scores of children who had systematically been exposed to history during the two preceding grades and the scores of children who had been exposed to history only in an incidental way.

The same children were again tested after they had completed the work in the sixth grade. Again the one group received instruction in history and chronology, including extensive use of time charts, time lines, and other devices for the teaching of time relationships, with an effort, as far as possible, to show the relationship between historical events and present-day affairs. The second group again received only incidental instruction in history and chronology. When tested early in the seventh grade, both groups showed a substantial gain over the scores earned before they began their work in the sixth grade. Again, however, the average scores of the two groups of children were practically equal. Special emphasis on time concepts in one case, and absence of special attention to such concepts in the other, had not produced any significant differences.

A result such as this is highly interesting. Needless to say, both groups were exposed to many experiences through their voluntary reading, through moving pictures, radio programs, and other media, that might influence their understanding of historical time relationships. In other words, the gains showed by the children who received no systematic instruction could not be attributed to maturation alone, for while the children were growing they also had many opportunities to learn. It does appear, however, that the changes in interest and mental capacity that come with advancing mental age, plus such opportunities to learn as arise in the course of the children's everyday experience, were more influential in promoting the development of time concepts than the special training afforded through emphasis on historical matters in the classroom.

In connection with a study such as this, it might be argued that the development of the concepts of children in the first group might have been accelerated if the teachers had been more resourceful and if the study projects had been more interesting. However, this remains to be proved, and in the absence of such proof findings such as these should receive practical consideration in planning units of study in the school.

In keeping with the foregoing are other findings which indicate that the amount of understanding and information which children have with respect to matters commonly considered in the social studies at school is not directly related to the amount of time devoted to such topics in the school program (13). Unfortunately we do not have enough systematic evidence to answer the many practical questions that findings such as these raise. It does seem safe to state, however, on the basis of present evidence, that a good deal of time and effort has been wasted in trying in the early grades to teach concepts which require not direct teaching alone but the opportunity for learning that is incidental to the child's everyday living and learning over an extended period of time.

Moreover, the consequence of such a practice may be more than just a waste of time. When children are called upon to study and discuss ideas that are beyond their grasp, the result is not simply that they fail to learn. They may learn a good deal, but not what was intended by the teacher. They may learn, for example, to bandy certain empty words. Again, they may accept certain conclusions uncritically. Even when they do not understand they may still catch emotional undertones, and thus acquire prejudices.

It is conceivable, of course, that many concepts which now are vague and confused because they have been taught in terms that are abstract and remote from the child's everyday experience might become meaningful, in a much more limited setting, if the learning could come by way of practical circumstances in the child's experience.

Children can undertake many things that involve the practical counterparts of abstract concepts. A sixth-grade group, for example, had a class newspaper that was sold for a few cents. On one occasion the children were discussing editorial and business policies. This discussion overlapped many conventional school subjects, even though the children perhaps were not aware of this fact, and the teacher, no doubt wisely, made no special effort to point it out. An itemized account of receipts and expenses was on the blackboard. The paper was barely meeting expenses. What should be done? One proposal: raise the selling cost one cent. This should leave a nice profit. Against this: some persons might not wish to spend an extra penny and so the circulation might drop. How much would the traffic bear? How much circulation could be lost at a higher price and still leave a slight margin of receipts above expenses? Another proposal: raise the price and at the same time raise the quality; people will pay more for a better article, so let the editor and the reporters do everything possible to improve the content and news coverage of the paper throughout the school. Another suggestion: the cost of typing, of stencils and ink was high in proportion to the cost of the paper. An extra fifty or hundred copies would cost very little compared with the original cost of a few copies. Accordingly, increased sales would bring greater receipts without a similar increase in expenses. Without putting it into so many words the youngsters here raised issues and considered practical implications of important principles of economics. (Projects such as this are not set forth as models but merely as illustrations.)

CULTURAL INFLUENCES ON THE LEARNING OF CONCEPTS

Children's information and concepts will be influenced not only by factors such as those mentioned above but also by the incentive to learn which they gain through the example of others. The extent of a child's knowledge and his interest in a topic that he has the capacity to understand will be influenced by the knowledge and interest exhibited by his elders. To the extent that this is true it is not surprising that studies have revealed that a large proportion of children in the upper elementary grades as well as in the lower and in the upper high-school grades show a great deal of ignorance with respect to many topics that are important in the everyday affairs of the world. Surveys at the adult level have indicated that a large proportion of adults are like children in their lack of knowledge about important events and people prominently connected with important events.

At all intellectual and educational levels it appears that a large proportion of adults in a country such as ours have, at least until recently, permitted themselves the luxury of ignorance about important national and world affairs. This ignorance is reflected in their children, and it seems reasonable to assume that the average adult, instead of aiding and abetting his child's acquisition of information and concepts about the world in which he lives, has, if anything, through his example hindered what the school has tried to achieve. It may be noted in passing that such ignorance and nonchalance not only have psychological but social consequences. The greater the ignorance of the populace, the greater is the likelihood of being misled by false leaders, of being caught by surprise by international and economic calamities which wise people might in part have foreseen and perhaps in part forestalled.

EMOTIONAL AND INTELLECTUAL ELEMENTS IN CHILDREN'S THINKING

The relationship between intellectual grasp and emotional response is varied and complex. By reason of lack of understanding a child may be relatively unaffected by a happening that is exciting or disturbing to an adult. Observations during wartime indicate, for example, that an air raid might have much more sinister meaning for and therefore arouse more profound fear and anxiety in an adult than in a child. To the extent that the adult responds to the raid not only as a temporary danger but also as an omen of similar or even greater danger to come, his fears will be more profound than the fears of a child who responds only to the immediate happening as such. On the other hand, lack of understanding may render the child more susceptible. He may, for example, be frightened by threats of harm or disaster which a better informed person would immediately be able to discount.

As indicated earlier, thinking usually involves factors other than pure intellectual activity. The process and the outcome of thinking will be influenced not simply by objective facts that are in keeping with reality and that can be communicated to others; the process of thinking also is affected by feelings and emotions which vary in quality and intensity. A person may pursue a line of thought primarily because he is curious to know, or his thoughts and his conclusions may be influenced primarily by his desires (39) or his fears.

A person's past habits, modes of thought that have become habitual even though they may not originally have been strongly charged with emotion, will also influence his thoughts and his conclusions.

The tendency of old forms and images to persevere is shown by the resistance that usually is made to any radical departure from the accustomed. Habitual modes of thought to a greater extent than problems in engineering have been responsible for the fact that it took decades for the automobile to change drastically from the appearance of a horse-drawn carriage. Similarly, ideas about geography drawn from maps constructed when the emphasis was on transportation by land and sea have a limiting effect on a person's ability to re-think his own mental picture of the globe. Many persons acquired the habit, for example, of looking upon Hawaii as lying upon the sea lanes to Japan, even though in terms of air travel the mind's eye should instead follow a route more by way of Alaska than by way of Hawaii.

Ordinarily a person, whether child or adult, is not well aware of these restricting and limiting factors, whether the restrictions are due to intense emotion or to habit. He may be quite unaware that his conclusion is dictated by fear, or that the truth he now so confidently accepts is a rationalization of his desires, or that the generalization he has reached simply is a reassertion of an habitual way of thinking. He may be able to marshal strong arguments to support beliefs that are founded on emotion or that are accepted because they fit comfortably with his past habits.

Factors other than purely intellectual or logical considerations may appear to varying degrees in the thinking of the same person on different topics. So it is that one individual may let his mind operate without restraint and let his imagination flow without hindrance when he studies the evolution of animal life, but his mind may be completely incapable of disinterested speculation when he thinks about economic problems. Another person may be objective and original in his thinking on economic issues and very conventional and opinionated in his views on the discipline of children. One writer (48) has stated that "the towering genius of the great scientist often lapses into childish babbling as he turns to problems in which his personal desires give structure to his thought."

Obstructions to free intellectual inquiry operate, of course, not only in the thinking of private individuals but also in the thoughts people share with one another. People of one country may have stereotyped ideas of their own virtues and of the peculiar ways and vices of people in another country. The problems of achieving international understanding and accord is complicated not simply by issues that can be directly defined and arbitrated but by viewpoints, reservations, and emotional currents concerning which the actors are completely unaware and which therefore are beyond reach of negotiation. The fact that thinking is directed and influenced by feeling does not, of course, operate solely to the disadvantage of the individual or society. There are good loyalties just as there are bad prejudices. But this makes it all the more important for the research psychologist to try to understand and for the educator to try to promote the processes of thinking and feeling that are involved in effective use of the human mind.

BIBLIOGRAPHY

1. Abel, T. M.: "Unsynthetic Modes of Thinking Among Adults: A Discussion of Piaget's Concepts," *American Journal of Psychology* (1932), 44:123-132.
2. Ames, L. B.: "The Development of the Sense of Time in the Young Child," *Journal of Genetic Psychology* (1946), 68:97-125.
3. Anderson, H. R.: "Testing Basic Skills in the Social Studies," *Elementary School Journal* (1936), 36:424-435.
4. Baker, H.: *Children's Contributions in Elementary School General Discussion,* Child Development Monographs (New York: Teachers College, Columbia University, 1942), No. 29, 150 pp.
5. Bandura, L.: "The Concept of Time Among Children Seven to Nine Years Old," *Kwart. Psychol.* (1936), 8:151-184.
6. Barlow, M. C.: "Transfer of Training in Reasoning," *Journal of Educational Psychology* (1937), 28:122-128.
7. Bender, L. and Frosch, J.: "Children's Reactions to the War," *American Journal of Orthopsychiatry* (1942), 12:571-586.
8. Burt, C.: "The Development of Reasoning in Children," *Journal of Experimental Pedagogy* (1919), 5:68-77, 121-127.
8a. Curti, M. W.: *Child Psychology,* second edition (New York: Longmans, Green, 1938), 458 pp.

9. Dennis, W.: "Piaget's Questions Applied to a Child of Known Environment," *Journal of Genetic Psychology* (1942), 60:307-320.
10. Dennis, W. and Russell, R. W.: "Piaget's Questions Applied to Zuni Children," *Child Development* (1940), 11:181-187.
11. Deshaies, L.: "La Notion de Relation Chez L'Enfant," *Journal de Psychologie* (1937), 33:112-133.
12. Deutsche, J. M.: *The Development of Children's Concepts of Causal Relations* (Minneapolis: University of Minnesota Press, 1937), 104 pp.
13. Eaton, M. T.: "A Survey of the Achievement in Social Studies of 10,220 Sixth Grade Pupils in 464 Schools in Indiana," *Bulletin of the School of Education, Indiana University* (1944), 20:5-64.
14. Eskridge, T. J., Jr.: *Growth in Understanding of Geographic Terms in Grades IV to VII,* Duke University Research Studies in Education (1939), No. 4, 68 pp.
15. Geddie, L. and Hildreth, G.: "Children's Ideas about the War," *Journal of Experimental Education* (1944), 13:92-97.
16. Gould, M. C. and Perrin, F. A. C.: "A Comparison of Factors Involved in the Maze Learning of Human Adults and Children," *Journal of Experimental Psychology* (1916), 1:122-154.
17. Granich, L.: *A Qualitative Analysis of Concepts in Mentally Deficient School Boys,* Archives of Psychology (1940), No. 251, 47 pp.
18. Hall, G. S.: "The Contents of Children's Minds On Entering School," *Pedagogical Seminary* (1891), 1:139-173.
19. Hall, G. S. and Browne, C. E.: "Children's Ideas of Fire, Heat, Frost and Cold," *Pedagogical Seminary* (1903), 10:27-85.
20. Hamilton, G. V.: "A Study of Trial and Error Reactions in Mammals," *Journal of Animal Behavior* (1911), 1:33-66.
21. Harrison, M. L.: "Nature and Development of Concepts of Time Among Young Children," *Elementary School Journal* (1934), 34:507-514.
22. Harrower, M. R.: "Social Status and the Moral Development of the Child," *British Journal of Educational Psychology* (1934), 1:75-95.
23. Hartmann, G. W. and Triche, A.: "Differential Susceptibility of Children and Adults to Standard Illusions," *Journal of Genetic Psychology* (1933), 42:493-498.
24. Hazlitt, V.: "Children's Thinking," *British Journal of Psychology* (1929), 20:354-361.
25. Heidbreder, E. F.: "Problem Solving in Children and Adults," *Journal of Genetic Psychology* (1928), 35:522-545.
26. Henle, M. and Hubbell, M. B.: "Egocentricity in Adult Conversation," *Journal of Social Psychology* (1938), 9:227-234.

27. Hicks, V. C. and Carr, H. A.: "Human Reactions in a Maze," *Journal of Animal Behavior* (1912), 2:98-125.
28. Hill, D. S.: "Personification of Ideals by Urban Children," *Journal of Social Psychology* (1930), 1:379-392.
29. Huang, I.: "Children's Conception of Physical Causality: A Critical Summary," *Journal of Genetic Psychology* (1943), 63:71-121.
30. Huang, I. and Lee, H. W.: "Experimental Analysis of Child Animism," *Journal of Genetic Psychology* (1945), 66:69-74.
31. Jensen, K.: "The Social Studies," *Thirty-Eighth Yearbook of the National Society for the Study of Education* (Bloomington, Illinois: Public School Publishing Company, 1939), Ch. XVII, pp. 325-360.
32. Jersild, A. T., Markey, F. V., and Jersild, C. L.: *Children's Fears, Dreams, Wishes, Daydreams, Likes, Dislikes, Pleasant and Unpleasant Memories,* Child Development Monographs (New York: Teachers College, Columbia University, 1933), No. 12, 172 pp.
33. Jersild, A. T. and Meigs, M.: "Children and War," *Psychological Bulletin* (1943), 40:541-573.
34. Jersild, A. T., Thorndike, R. L., Goldman, B., and Loftus, J. J.: "An Evaluation of Aspects of the Activity Program in the New York City Public Elementary Schools," *Journal of Experimental Education* (1939), 8, 2:166-207.
35. Kelley, T. L. and Krey, A. C.: *Tests and Measurements in the Social Sciences* (New York: Scribner's, 1934), 635 pp.
36. Kimmins, C. W.: "The Special Interests of Children in the War at Different Ages," *Journal of Experimental Pedagogy* (1915-1916), 3:225-236.
37. Lacey, J. M.: *Social Studies Concepts of Children in the First Three Grades,* Teachers College Contributions to Education (New York: Teachers College, Columbia University, 1932), No. 548, 90 pp.
38. Lacey, J. I. and Dallenbach, K. M.: "Acquisition by Children of the Cause-Effect Relationship," *American Journal of Psychology* (1939), 52:103-110.
39. Lund, F. H.: "The Psychology of Belief," *Journal of Abnormal and Social Psychology* (1925), 20:63-81, 174-196.
40. McAndrew, M. B.: "An Experimental Investigation of Young Children's Ideas of Causality," *Studies in Psychology and Psychiatry* (Washington, D. C.: Catholic University of America, 1943), 6, No. 2:66 pp.
41. McCarthy, D.: "Language Development in Children," *Manual of Child Psychology,* edited by L. Carmichael (New York: Wiley, 1946), Ch. X, 476-581.
42. McHugh, G.: "Autistic Thinking as a Transitory Phenomenon of Childhood," *Child Development* (1944), 15:89-98.

43. Macomber, F. G.: "A Placement Study in Secondary-School Economics," *Journal of Experimental Education* (1936), 4:353-358.
44. Maier, N. R. F.: "Reasoning in Children," *Journal of Comparative Psychology* (1936), 21:357-366.
45. Mathews, C. O.: *Grade Placement of Curriculum Materials in the Social Studies,* Teachers College Contributions to Education (New York: Teachers College, Columbia University, 1926), No. 241, 152 pp.
46. Meltzer, H.: *Children's Social Concepts: A Study of Their Nature and Development* (New York: Teachers College, Columbia University, 1925), 91 pp.
47. Moore, T. V.: *The Reasoning Ability of Children in the First Years of School Life,* Studies in Psychology and Psychiatry (Baltimore: Williams and Wilkins, 1929), 2, 2:34 pp.
48. Murphy, G.: "The Freeing of Intelligence," *Psychological Bulletin* (1945), 42:1-19.
49. Nowell, J. F. and Arrington, M. G.: "The Explanations of Physical Phenomena Given by White and Negro Children," *Comparative Psychology Monograph* (1945), 18:1-43.
50. Oakden, E. C. and Sturt, M.: "Development of the Knowledge of Time in Children," *British Journal of Psychology* (1922), 12:309-336.
51. Oakes, M. E.: *Children's Explanations of Natural Phenomena,* Teachers College Contributions to Education (New York: Teachers College, Columbia University, 1946).
52. Piaget, J.: *Judgment and Reasoning in the Child* (New York: Harcourt, Brace, 1928), 260 pp.
53. ———: *The Child's Conception of Physical Causality,* translated by M. Gabain (New York: Harcourt, Brace, 1930), 309 pp.
54. ———: *The Language and Thought of the Child,* translated by M. Gabain (New York: Harcourt, Brace, 1932), 246 pp.
55. Pistor, F.: "How Time Concepts Are Acquired by Children," *Educational Method* (1940), 20:107-112.
56. Preston, R. C.: *Children's Reactions to a Contemporary War Situation,* Child Development Monographs (New York: Teachers College, Columbia University, 1942), No. 29, 96 pp.
57. Probst, C. A.: "A General Information Test for Kindergarten Children," *Child Development* (1931), 2:81-95.
58. Pyle, W. H.: "An Experimental Study of the Development of Certain Aspects of Reasoning," *Journal of Educational Psychology* (1935), 26:539-546.
59. Rebello, S.: "Pesquiza Sobra a Noçao de Tempo" ("Study of the Notion of Time"), *Bol. Educ.* (Pernambuco, 1934), 4:134-182.

60. Schaeffer, G. C.: "An Informational Unit on Time," *Elementary School Journal* (1937), 38:114-117.
61. Shaffer, L. F.: *Children's Interpretation of Cartoons,* Teachers College Contributions to Education (New York: Teachers College, Columbia University, 1930), No. 429, 73 pp.
62. Scott, F. and Myers, G. C.: "Children's Empty and Erroneous Concepts of the Commonplace," *Journal of Educational Research* (1923), 8:327-335.
63. Smith, L. Z.: "An Experimental Investigation of Young Children's Interest and Expressive Behavior Responses to Single Statement, Verbal Repetition, and Ideational Repetition of Content in Animal Stories," *Child Development* (1930), 1, 3:232-247.
64. Thiele, C. L.: *The Contribution of Generalization to the Learning of Addition Facts,* Teachers College Contributions to Education (New York: Teachers College, Columbia University, 1938), No. 763, 84 pp.
65. Thorndike, E. L.: "Increasing Knowledge and Rationality About Economics and Business," *Proceedings of the Seventh Conference on Educational Policies* (New York: Teachers College, Columbia University, 1939), pp. 15-22.
66. Wilson, F. T.: "Expressed Wishes of Elderly Persons, College Men, and Birthday Wishes of First Grade Children," *Journal of Genetic Psychology* (1939), 55:81-101.
67. ———: "Verbally Expressed Wishes of Children and College Women Students," *Journal of Psychology* (1938), 5:91-105.

CHAPTER XII

CHILDREN'S MAKE-BELIEVE, DREAMS, AND OTHER IMAGINATIVE ACTIVITIES

Make-believe, daydreams, and other imaginative activities occupy an important place in the child's mental life. Through his imagination the child is able to transcend the boundaries of time and space. He can deal with happenings, persons, and things that lie beyond his ordinary reach and he can perform feats beyond the limits of his actual strength.

A child's imaginative activities also play an important role in his emotional life. Through his imagination the child can give play to his wants and desires, his hopes and fears, without facing all the risks and hardships of reality. Imaginative behavior also serves as an important vehicle for the child's social development, for much of his play with other children takes place in make-believe settings. There is interaction even between a child's imaginative activity and his motor development: many important motor skills are acquired or are practiced in connection with enterprises that have a high imaginative content such as doll play and housekeeping, and make-believe often supplies the plot or purpose in settings in which the child practices motor activities such as climbing, swinging, or riding a coaster or a bicycle.

EARLY MANIFESTATIONS

Just when a child becomes capable of responding in imaginative terms is difficult to tell, but it would seem that this development appears at least as early as the ability to talk. There is reason to believe that at least some children are capable of quite complicated imaginative activity before they are able to talk.

An example of such early imaginative behavior was shown by

a child of eleven months who was observed by the author. This child in the course of her creepings about the house had discovered the garbage pail and had also discovered that she was not supposed to explore its contents. Once she started to creep across the kitchen floor toward the pail while her mother was watching. When the mother gave a warning sound the child stopped for a moment, then crept a short distance, then looked up at her mother, laughing heartily. Again she made a false start and again she looked up, laughing merrily. She obviously was getting great sport out of this game of *pretending* to go to the garbage pail while the mother looked on. This episode occurred several months in advance of the time when this child combined two or more words in her speech.

Other early signs of imaginative activities are shown by some children when they imitate, in pantomime, activities of older persons. At ten months, for example, a child was seen to go through the motions of "telephoning" with a toy telephone belonging to an older sister. Similarly, a child at about the age of a year may go through motions such as "feeding" a doll, putting on Daddy's hat, and dragging his brief case toward the door.

Manifestations of make-believe become more obvious and frequent once a child has learned to talk. Comments of an imaginative sort often appear in children's language when they are at play with one another. Findings at the preschool level indicate that imaginative play activity increases in the age range of about two to four years. In one study in which records were made of children's language it was found that 1.5 per cent of children's remarks at twenty-four to twenty-nine months of age were imaginative in character; at forty-two to forty-seven months the percentage of imaginative remarks was 8.7 (4). In another study, in which language as well as overt behavior was recorded, there was a sixfold increase in frequency of imaginative episodes from two and a half years to four years (18).

Apart from changes with age in amount of make-believe language and activity, there are some changes also in the themes with which children deal. In a study by Markey it was found that a large proportion of the imaginative activity of children under the age of three fell into three large categories including: (1) activity involving personification, such as talking to dogs and talking to inanimate objects; (2) activity involving make-believe use of materials, such as calling a slide a train, drinking out of an empty cup; and (3) participation in make-believe situations, such as in a game of putting out a fire or taking a bath. At the age of three years and over, make-believe uses of materials were among the most typical imaginative activities; but after the age of three years and six months, make-believe situations, making and naming constructions with blocks, crayons, and the like, and dramatic play became quite common. Markey also found that younger children most frequently engage in imaginative activity revolving around specific materials which are actually there before them and which they can handle, whereas the older preschool child frequently engages in complicated make-believe that involves relations and themes (18).

FUNCTIONS OF MAKE-BELIEVE

As we have indicated above, make-believe activities serve many functions in the child's mental life. By virtue of being able to transcend his actual limitations and to go beyond the restrictions imposed by reality, the child is able to deal with the world in a freer manner. He is able to reason on a lower level of concentration. He is not held to all the rules of logic and consistency. He can combine fragments of ideas. A wagon with which he plays is now a car, now a train, now a ship, now a lunch counter in a restaurant. He can manipulate ideas which he only partly grasps. He may, for example, know the names of certain cities where relatives live or through which his parents have recently traveled; then, in connection with imaginary boat play he may visit these cities, going by boat from one city that is located on a seacoast to another city that is situated far inland. A trip between two cities five hundred miles apart may require less time than a trip between adjacent towns. Moreover, even though the voyage is by water, there is nothing to prevent him from stepping off and making little side trips on foot, for when he steps off, the water accommodatingly becomes dry land.

Through his imagination the child is able to deal with situations and to solve problems that he could not so easily handle when dealing with reality. He can manipulate his environment with greater ease; he is able to solve problems without having to keep all relevant things in mind.

Through make-believe the child is able to mold the world nearer to his heart's desire. Make-believe enables the child not only to realize his wishes vicariously but also provides a means for him to cope with his fears. Frequently children will deal on an imaginative level with things that in reality they fear. An example of this appeared in the behavior of a two-and-a-half-year-old child who showed signs of fear whenever she saw a dog on the street. At home she repeatedly went through a game in which she would get down on all fours, bark, growl, and head toward her mother saying, "I'm going to bite you." When she came close to her mother, she would say in a comforting tone, "I'm a good dog. I'm not going to bite you, Mama, I will kiss you." Then she would proceed to lick her mother's stockings with a great show of affection. It was as though she were acting the way she wished a feared dog would behave.[1]

Such an opportunity to deal with a feared situation on an imaginative level not only seems sometimes to have the effect of comforting a child but it also sometimes seems to give him greater facility and strength with which to meet a real danger. In the example above it was observed that after several episodes in which the child had played the part of a dangerous dog suddenly turned friendly, the youngster took to using similar verbal expressions on

[1] From observations reported by Margaret F. Meigs, unpublished.

the street. While holding her mother's hand, she would say about a dog very much in the same tone as she had used in her play, "Mama, he's a good dog. He doesn't bite me." She still stayed with her mother, but there was now much less manifestation of fear in the manner in which she held her mother's hand and in the manner in which she spoke than was the case when the fear of dogs was first observed.

Children are also sometimes able by way of make-believe to be rid of irritations, to remove or overcome conditions that annoy and thwart them in real life. Their disposition of such problems may be rather drastic. In a study by Markey, cited above, children were provided with small pieces of kitchen equipment and a "family" in the form of dolls. They were permitted to play a housekeeping game. One boy proceeded at once to lay hands on the dolls. He called them bad babies, put them on the toy stove, and said, "You've got to be dead. You've got to stay on there for three weeks." Then he proceeded imaginatively to break the house down and to beat the dolls, talking while he did so and calling attention to the burning of the bad babies in the imaginary fire. The school records of this child revealed that he was very jealous of a baby brother and, at home, had shown delight at the baby's squirming and crying when his nose was being cleaned, just as now, in the imaginary situation, he seemed to relish the thought of watching the baby burn.

Another child, aged about three years, began to "make supper for the little girls"; she opened the icebox and said: "Dolly dear, we *always* leave the icebox door open." Here again the child's behavior was related to actual circumstances; the child's mother revealed that, to keep the youngster from raiding the icebox at home, it had finally become necessary to tie a heavy wire around the box, and one night the mother had discovered the child trying unsuccessfully, to the accompaniment of angry mutterings, to open the icebox. The child's remark to the doll seemed to describe a state of affairs that she hoped might prevail at home.

Escape by way of the imagination from a situation which to the child was unpleasant appeared also in the case of a child of four-and-a-half years who announced to her mother: "I'm inventing a new paint for the bathtub. It will take twelve years to dry, and you can't use the bathtub for twelve years."

Degrees of vividness. The usefulness of imaginary projects as a means of learning to cope with the real is enhanced by the fact that the imagined may be intensely vivid in the child's experience. An example of this appears in the behavior of a four-year-old child (observed by the writer) who had acquired a fear of a bogey man. She sometimes faced this fear on an imaginary level by prevailing on her two-year-old brother to play the role of a bogey man; she would put a white towel over his head and he would sit by as she called him a bogey man. As part of the game the four-year-old then would take to her heels to escape from the bogey man. However, it was noted on several occasions that the fleeing which began in fancy ended in earnest—she seemed to become genuinely afraid of the bogey man whom she had created. One can imagine that there are many gradations between a situation such as this in which the imagined almost if not entirely takes on the frightening aspects of reality and situations at the other extreme in which the imagined is regarded as fanciful in character and yet can provide a mild taste of the real thing.

Make-believe as a form of logic. Make-believe not only enables the child to avoid the necessity for complete rationality but it also provides him with a means of making things seem rational. Examples of the way in which make-believe enables the child to give a good reason or explanation appear when children are in the beginning stages of drawing. Frequently it appears that the thing a drawing is meant to represent is thought of after the drawing is completed. Certain lines and colors that had been put together without plan may slightly resemble a flower and so now it is called a flower.

Moreover, the child may be able through make-believe to substitute one rationale for another. An example of this is supplied by a five-year-old girl who had visited her grandmother in the city and was inspired on her return home to make a colored drawing of her grandmother's apartment house. She first made a good representation of an eight-story apartment building. Then, in the process of putting a street into the drawing, she happened to run the lines of the street through the fourth floor so that the lower floors appeared to be buried under the street level. This apparently went counter to the original theory of the drawing and so, it being impossible to erase the crayoned street, the youngster changed the theory of her drawing. She shaded all the portion below the fourth-floor level. She added little insectlike creatures, both in the stories under the ground and above the ground. Then she proudly displayed the drawing and said that this was a drawing of the "home of the ant-killers." (The little insectlike creatures were "ants.") She now made it appear that she had intended from the beginning to have part of the building below the surface of the ground.

Some consequences of the ability to imagine. In addition to the foregoing accomplishments, an important feature of imaginative activity is the ability to anticipate an event before it actually occurs. The child becomes able to project himself into occurrences that are yet to transpire. This ability to anticipate the future, to borrow what is yet to be, not only augments the child's powers, but also exposes him to difficulties. Just as he can savor future pleasure and success he also, in anticipation, can taste fear and trouble. The toddler may feel delight at the prospect of taking a walk when he sees his mother bring his wraps from the closet, but his delight may be diminished when similarly in anticipation he dreads a ride on the elevator which he fears. When he is in the park he may feel depressed when he sees that his mother is preparing to take him home, for now, still eager to taste the excitement of the outside world, he can anticipate the horrible prospect of having to go home just as earlier he anticipated the pleasant prospect of getting out of the place.

As a child becomes older, this ability to anticipate both the good and the ill appears in more complicated forms. One characteristic of the mental life of the older child is that it is lived with considerable reference to the future. The expectation of what lies in store may, for example, sustain some children through long periods when they practice the playing of a musical instrument, or try to perfect their ability to swim or to play ball or to dive or to ride a bicycle without touching the handle bars, or later to build a dam or to assemble materials for the building of a raft.

This capacity to work for deferred goals is, of course, prominent in the later high-school years and at the college level when the student goes through years of preparation for entering a profession and accepts the academic chores that are assigned even though he may have difficulty in seeing the value of what he is learning in relation to the vocation for which he is preparing.

FUNCTIONS OF MAKE-BELIEVE IN SOCIAL DEVELOPMENT

As indicated above, make-believe activity provides an important vehicle for the learning of social behavior. In a large proportion of instances in which two or more children of preschool years play together they are held together by a make-believe activity. Make-believe not only provides a basis for children of similar age level to play together but also makes it possible to supply themes that will hold children together at play even though they may be several years apart. Thus two sisters or brothers, a six-year-old and a three-year-old, might play at a game of being parent and child, doctor and patient, captain and engineer on a boat, although there are few if any activities of a more prosaic character that would keep the two together (unless an adult entered into the activity with them). Make-believe is thus one of mother's greatest helpers.

Besides supplying the basis of activities that bring children together, make-believe activities provide a setting in which children are better able to tolerate and enjoy one another than would be true in a realistic setting. A six-year-old may be annoyed when in real life her two-year-old sister cries easily, or needs help with her clothes, or spills her food. Now, in a make-believe setting, in which she is the mother and the two-year-old is the baby, the same six-year-old not only accepts but she may even encourage babyish behavior of this sort. Likewise, the younger child who resents the bossing of an older sibling may, in a make-believe role as a pupil or a baby, cheerfully obey orders and even accept punishment from the older sibling. In a make-believe setting with other children, a child often will accept restraints and deprivations which he would protest vigorously if they were imposed by a very well liked adult. Thus, when told by an older child who is the "teacher" that he must sit very still, a young child may remain quiet for a relatively long time; and when at a "birthday party" he may be Spartanlike in waiting until all imaginary guests are served before he begins to eat.

Often, of course, reality intrudes upon such idyllic scenes, especially if one child or the other begins to take advantage or if the demands within the imaginary setting become too taxing. For example, a four- or five-year-old in a cops and robbers game with an older child will rebel if required to be "dead" for an unendurable period of time. Even so, it appears that it is often in a make-believe setting, in play with other children, that children for the first time achieve feats of self-restraint, patience, perseverance at a task, good manners, and the like, which adults constantly are trying to promote.

By way of the imagination children also are able to practice social techniques even though no one else is at hand. Thus a child who fancies himself wronged is able verbally to scold the absent wrongdoer just as the adult in a similar situation subjects others to subvocal castigation. Likewise a youngster can go through the motions of dressing, trying on various costumes, and assuming polite manners before an imaginary audience.

Other consequences of imaginative behavior. The fact that a child is able through his imagination to anticipate a future event adds greatly to undercurrents in his behavior that are difficult for others to understand. Sometimes when the child seems to be unduly unreasonable, or when he gives what appears to be an exaggerated emotional response, the reason may be that in his fancy he has built vivid expectations which now are thwarted. So, for example, a four-year-old who has looked forward to going on a shopping trip with his mother may show extreme anger and disappointment when, for one reason or another, it becomes impossible for the mother to go on the shopping trip. In his fancy he may not only have made the trip several times but he may also have built elaborate plans and experiences around what he expected his mother to buy. The fact that the trip simply had to be postponed does not minimize the child's disappointment.

An older child may similarly react to deprivations in a manner that, from an adult point of view, seems quite unreasonable. An example of this appeared in the case of an eight-year-old boy who sometimes had been permitted to stay up late enough at night to listen to a certain exciting radio program. One evening the father announced that it would not be possible for the boy to listen that night and the father gave what he thought was a good reason. But the boy became violently angry. He scolded and accused his father of rank injustice and made it seem that he was a victim of great unfairness and persecution. Later the father learned that the announcement that the boy could not listen did not simply mean that he would be deprived of the pleasure of following a program for fifteen minutes; instead it meant that what amounted to a little plan of life had been broken. All during the day the child had been pointing toward the program in his make-believe play. He had taken the part of one of the characters. He was counting on living with this character and with the other characters on the program that evening. He was counting on this listening experience as an especially enjoyable feature in a make-believe enterprise that could be continued after the program was over.

In this example the father happened to discover how much the deprivation meant, and thus was enabled better to understand the behavior of his child. No doubt situations analogous to this, many of them perhaps less violent in nature, are repeatedly occurring without being detected in the everyday lives of children.

As can be seen, the play of a child's imagination provides one clew among many to childhood behavior which frequently in the eyes of adults seems unreasonable and perverse. In both of the examples above the adults acted according to what to them were good and sufficient reasons. The children, on their part, responded in terms of what to them were powerful and all-important reasons. In many situations such as these the issue does not involve the position of one who is right opposed to someone else who is wrong. Rather each may be right in the light of his own experience and wishes. Much friction, opposition, and suffering in the lives of individual persons and in society at large could be avoided if somehow people could better learn to understand that the solution of many problems cannot be attained simply by showing one party to a dispute that he is wrong. In many disputes both parties may be equally right or equally wrong, depending upon the viewpoint from which the dispute is considered. The issue then is not one of determining who is right or wrong but of discovering the most reasonable way of reconciling positions which clash because they are different.

DAYDREAMS AND FANTASIES

Toward the end of the preschool period and throughout later years, more and more of a child's imaginary activities take the form of private fantasies and daydreams. These private fantasies, like the earlier more overtly expressed forms of make-believe, may variously serve as a means of riddance, escape, compensation, fulfillment of desire, vicarious adventure, and excitement, and they may provide a means for the exercise of many interests and ideas. In most of such daydreams, the child plays a dramatic and heroic role and utilizes powers, abilities, privileges, and opportunities that normally lie beyond his reach. In many of these fantasies the child projects himself into roles and scenes that are more remote from everyday happenings than the make-believe activities of an earlier age.

Daydreams of one sort or another are likely to continue throughout life. The themes involved and the extent to which the individual indulges may vary from time to time as different life situations arise, and at different times the daydream may range from the abandonment of sheer fancy to an ordered procession of ideas. Whatever may be the degree of unreality involved, such enterprises will be related in some way to the individual's everyday problems and desires. Even though the imaginings of an older child are not bound by the facts of experience, it is likely as a child becomes older that his make-believe will have more logical coherence than it had at an earlier age. In the process of achieving semblance of plausibility and logic, an undertaking that begins as a fanciful daydream may end as a form of businesslike problem solving. Thus, an eight-year-old boy rides, in his fancies, jauntily over the Western range on a fine horse, ready for combat with horse thieves, coyotes, or other adventures. As the plot unfolds his activities become increasingly complex. He has a trusty rifle and a belt of ammunition at the start; but when he stops to camp he needs materials for making a fire, cooking utensils, and what not, so he finds it is necessary to pretend that he had an extra pack horse with him from the beginning. As the tale goes on, he may find himself so burdened with equipment, horses, and other paraphernalia that the job of planning and ordering things in the day dream becomes somewhat strenuous. This tendency for a daydream to bog down under its own weight as it calls for more and more ingenuity and "thinking" frequently occurs in adults and spoils what might otherwise have been a fine time.[2]

IMAGINARY COMPANIONS

An especially interesting form of imagery occurs when a child has what is called an "imaginary companion."[3] This phenomenon, if it appears at all in the life of an individual child, is likely to appear some time between the approximate ages of three and ten years, although the occurrence is more probable during the earlier than during the later years within this range. It is difficult to formulate a precise definition of what constitutes an imaginary companion since the difference between this phenomenon and an ordinary play of imagery apparently is a difference mainly in degree. The label "imaginary companion" is commonly applied to an imagined creature or thing that is unusually vivid and that tends to have quite stable characteristics as long as it lasts.

The character may be a person, an animal or an object. In some cases it appears to be almost as vivid as an hallucination. Although it is a figment of the child's mind, yet it may assume for a time what seems to be an independent reality. An example of such vividness appears in the following: A girl of four screamed a warning to her father as he was in the act of sitting down on a sofa. When questioned she reported that her imaginary playmate (a monkey) was having a sick spell and had just soiled the cushion on which her father was about to sit.

The imaginary companion may appear in many forms, with varying degrees of vividness, and, like other imaginative enter-

---

[2] A study by Griffiths (10) deals in an illuminating way with the imaginative activities of children of preschool age. A book by Green (9) discusses the make-believe activities of older children.

[3] For studies of imaginary companions see Hurlock and Burstein (12) and Svendsen (24).

prises, it may serve a variety of purposes in the life of an individual child. One obvious purpose it may serve, as the name of the phenomenon implies, is to provide the child with a companion. Through this imaginative device the child can possess a playmate who is always at hand. Moreover, the playmate can be endowed with characteristics which the youngster desires but does not find in his associates in real life. However, the phenomenon cannot be explained simply on the theory that it is a child's means of meeting a need for agreeable companionship. For one thing, the companions described by some children seem to be rather disagreeable characters. Again, a child may describe several companions varying in congeniality. Moreover, whether or not a child will have an imaginary companion does not depend solely upon the extent to which he is alone or has much company in real life. Available evidence indicates that a bright child is more likely to have an imaginary companion than is a dull child, whether or not he happens to be an isolated child. One bright child who was a member of a large family with several children near him in age, and who lived in a community where there were many neighboring children at his age level, had not one but four imaginary companions: a husband, a wife, and two children. Perhaps in thus concocting a small family the child was expressing a desire for more attention from his parents.

Many motives other than a desire for companionship may be served by the imaginary character. The character may possess powers and virtues which the child lacks. He may have many privileges the child himself is denied. He may have the courage or the boldness to do things which the child himself would like to do but does not do. Again, the companion may serve as a basis for excusing or defending the child's conduct or his demands; the child with the imaginary family described above would try to excuse himself from various tasks by claiming that his husband, wife, or one of his children had a stomach-ache. Another boy had an imaginary uncle who always allowed children to do what they wanted; this boy also threatened to call upon the imaginary uncle to come and hit people who did not do what the boy wanted. These items illustrate only a few of the ways in which the imaginary character, like other forms of make-believe, may serve a variety of purposes.

In a study by the interview method (13), four hundred children, aged five to twelve, were asked to describe their daydreams and imaginary companions. Over thirty per cent of the daydreams reported dealt with amusements, play, or some form of diversion. Specific mention of some form of self-glorification—of prestige or playing a superior or heroic role—was made in nineteen per cent of the cases; many children also reported daydreams about specific objects which they wished to possess.

In this study, it was found that inability to describe any make-believe activity occurred more frequently among younger than among older children and more frequently among the less intelligent than among the more intelligent. Also, younger children and less intelligent children of all ages reported a larger proportion of daydreams dealing with specific objects and amusements than did the older and the more intelligent. The brighter the child, the more likely he is to entertain daydreams with a plot.

When asked about their imagined playmates, only about a third of the children observed in this study described creatures that seemed to have fairly definite and stable characteristics. (It must be recognized, however, that the interview method is not as well suited to a study of imaginary companions as is direct and more intimate observation.) The number of boys who reported companionships with special objects—such as a particular piece of furniture, a block, a toy, and so forth—corresponded closely to the number of girls who described companionships with dolls. Girls reported imaginary boy companions more often than boys reported girl companions, but the number in each case was small. The companions were more often of the same sex as the child himself or consisted of animals and objects.

OTHER FORMS OF VIVID IMAGERY AND ASSOCIATION OF IMAGES

In addition to ordinary make-believe, special forms of imagery may be observed in some children. People differ in the vividness of their images; at one extreme are those who have difficulty in forming a clear image of an absent event, while at the other are individuals who report images almost as vivid as the impression derived if the event were actually before them.

A phenomenon known as *synaesthesia* also may occur in children of school age (and perhaps at an earlier time), as well as among adults.[4] A sensation from one sense modality has associated with it images from another modality. In "colored hearing," the individual reports, for example, that bass tones look blue and high soprano tones look pink. Or the synaesthesia may take the form of colors associated with certain names, as when a child of six reports that Mildred, her friend, is blue and Margaret is yellow, the number "17" is pink, and the word "rush" is gray. Tones likewise may accompany words, according to the testimony of those who report this phenomenon; thus, "paper" brings an association of soprano tones, "piazza" carries a tinkling sound, and so on.

The origin of the phenomenon is difficult to trace. Undoubtedly, experiences in the past have resulted in a more than usually vivid association between different sense impressions, so that the recurrence of one now revives the other; yet this conjecture leaves still unanswered the question as to why some individuals seem more susceptible than others.

CHILDREN'S DREAMS

Children's dreams, like their waking fancies, consist of material drawn from actual experience. Even more than in waking

---

[4] For an interesting account of a case of synaesthesia persisting over a period of years, see Hollingworth and Weischer (11).

fancies, however, the events and emotional elements in a dream may be so diverse and confused that it is difficult to trace them to their source.

Early signs of dreaming. Little systematic information is available as to the age at which the average child begins to dream. Undoubtedly, much in the nature of dreaming takes place before the child is able to give a clear description. The first sign of dreaming may occur when a child makes outcries in his sleep or awakens in apparent fright. For example, a child aged two-and-a-half years woke up during the night, cried, and said that a cat was under the bed, and an hour later again awakened his parents and complained about a cat. The age at which the first signs of dreaming appear, as reported by parents, varies considerably with different children. A few children, as well as adults, according to their own reports, never have the experience of dreaming.

Some children when they first begin to dream seem to confuse the dream with reality not only while still asleep and dreaming, but also, at least momentarily, on awakening. Thus a child as he emerges from sleep may look around searchingly and perhaps say, "There was a pony here, where did he go?" It appears that children vary in their tendency to be carried away in this manner.

Factors influencing dreams. The following dream of an adolescent boy illustrates some of the interplay of sensory impressions, past recollections, and emotional complications that may occur in a dream: The door of the sleeper's room opened with a slight click and in stepped a large, spectral figure, clad in black. It approached the bed, and there was a grinding sound as it laid hands upon the sleeper's heart and slowly compressed it. Then, the next moment, the terrified sleeper found himself awake, standing against the farther wall of his bedroom.

When he had composed himself, the dreamer was able to reconstruct the following situation: In the dream, he had felt that he was dying because his heartbeats were being forcibly stopped; on awakening, he found that one arm was slightly numb—in his sleep, he had rested upon the arm in such a way as to cut off circulation. He noted next that two weeks earlier he had attended the funeral of his father, who had died suddenly of heart disease—another item that apparently turned his dream toward the malfunctioning of the heart. He further observed that a breeze was moving the door of his room, causing a slight clicking of the latch; here, apparently, was the cue to the opening of the door as the specter entered the room. And he noticed also that a sound came from the water pipes of an adjoining room; here, apparently, was the cue to the sound in his dream. Finally, on the floor of his bedroom was an open umbrella, which he had stretched to dry after he had taken a walk in the rain, and this black object lay in the line of vision from the head of the bed to a window which admitted a dim light; the image of this black, dimly defined object might have been the cue to the black-clad specter that had attacked him. Thus, recollections from the past, a previous waking reminder of heart disease, undoubtedly many unidentified emotional associations connected with the dead father, and stimuli actually affecting his sense organs contributed to the content of his dream.

Dreams are puzzling in the sense that all mental activity is baffling; the dream seems more mysterious at times than some of our waking activities because the events that it includes are difficult to untangle. The dream may be influenced by external stimuli, by stimuli occurring within the body, by desires and fears and other emotional conditions that may be clearly defined or only vaguely understood during the person's waking moments. The elements of imagery and emotion in the dream may be highly distorted and the logic of the happenings may be highly obscure.

In the interview study mentioned previously in this chapter, four hundred children between the ages of five and twelve were questioned about their dreams. They were first asked simply to tell what they dreamed about and then to describe the dreams in detail. They were then asked to tell about their recurrent dreams and their pleasant and unpleasant dreams. At the end of the interview, each child was asked what kind of dreams he had most frequently, dreams he liked or dreams he did not like; and he was also asked whether he wished he would have no more dreams of any kind.

In the replies of the children, it appeared that a child's dreams are likely to reflect any kind of event, whether real or imagined, that occurs during his waking life. The similarities in the general content of dreams of children of the age of five and six, as compared with those of children aged eleven and twelve, were more outstanding than the differences. Exceptions to this general rule appeared in a few minor categories.

The unpleasant dreams reported by the children somewhat more closely resembled their fears, as described in response to other questions, than the unpleasant events that actually had befallen them.[5] The children named dreams that appeared to be unpleasant somewhat more frequently than pleasant dreams. When asked whether they wished never to dream any more, less than half of the children expressed a definite desire to continue to dream.

Terror dreams. Unpleasant dreams, nightmares, and night terrors are a frequent source of distress in children and often cause parental concern. A large percentage of children have rather intensely unpleasant dreams. The extent to which unpleasant dreams occur and some of the symptoms and conditions associated with unpleasant dreams have been described in a study by Foster and Anderson (6), in coöperation with a large number of parents who kept records of their children's dreams for a seven-day period. The parents and children in this study represented all socio-economic levels but included a larger percentage in the upper socio-

---

[5] The study by Griffiths, referred to above, describes ways in which children's dreams are related to their emotional problems.

economic strata than is found in a normal sampling of the population. Some of the findings, as revealed through classification of the reports submitted by parents, are summarized in Table XXXII.

Table XXXII

EVIDENCES AND FREQUENCIES OF UNPLEASANT DREAMS EXHIBITED BY 519 CHILDREN, AS REPORTED BY PARENTS WHO KEPT RECORDS FOR A SEVEN-DAY PERIOD[6]

	1–4	5–8	9–12
Age in Years			
Number of Children	81	215	223
A. Average Frequency Per Week of Various Evidences of Unpleasant Dreams:			
Moans during the night	.81	.57	.17
Comes to adult	.18	.16	.05
Reports bad dream in the morning	.21	.42	.26
Any evidence of bad dreaming	.93	.71	.39
B. Percentage of Children Having Some Unpleasant Dreams During the Week	43.0	39.2	22.2
C. Subject Matter of Bad Dreams (Percentages):			
Personal difficulties	26.7	33.3	54.5
Difficulties of friends, pets	13.3	6.3	18.2
Animals (probably strange or fearful)	40.0	15.9	9.1
Strange or bad people	6.7	20.6	13.6
The unknown, dark, etc.	6.7	7.9	.0
Loss of property	.0	4.6	.0
Impersonal dangers	6.7	9.5	.0
Miscellaneous	.0	1.6	4.5

The first entry shows the average frequency per week of various evidences of unpleasant dreams. From the frequencies shown for moaning and coming to an adult during the night, it can be inferred that a rather large number of the dreams recorded by the parents must have been quite disturbing to the children. The second entry shows that over forty per cent of the children at the one- to four-year level exhibited at least one unpleasant dream during the seven-day period; the percentage drops to twenty-two at the nine-to-twelve level. Section C of the table indicates, among other things, that there is an increase with age in the percentage of dreams involving personal difficulties and a decline in dreams in which the unpleasantness is represented by animals and the dark and the unknown.

[6] Adapted from Foster, J. C. and Anderson, J. E.: "Unpleasant Dreams in Childhood," *Child Development* (1936), 7: 77-84. Reproduced by permission.

PROJECTIVE METHODS

The fact that children reveal their thoughts and feelings by way of imaginary situations has provided the basis for a number of interesting methods of studying children.[7] The label "projective methods" has been used more or less loosely to identify techniques in which imaginative productions are used. The individual is presented with a task or situation so arranged as to give him freedom to interpret or to improvise in his own way. He may be asked, for example, to complete an unfinished story, to tell a story about a picture, or to do something with a "family" of dolls. The purpose is to provide him with a means by which he indirectly and perhaps unwittingly reveals something about himself. One feature of many projective methods is that the person who is being studied may have no notion whatever concerning the psychological inferences that will be drawn from what he says and does.

The brief account of projective methods which follows is intended to round out the present discussion of imagination and is not meant to supply a set of adequate directions. The descriptions will perhaps be sufficient to enable a reader to apply some of the methods in an informal manner in his dealings with children, but a more complete account of the method involved and of the scientific safeguards required would be necessary in order to use these methods for scientific purposes. As a matter of fact, much additional research is needed in order to establish the validity of most of the procedures described below and to demonstrate the kinds of interpretations that can safely be drawn from the data which they yield.

Play techniques. The use of a play situation for the study of children is illustrated by the reference to the doll family on an earlier page. It is possible to use a great variety of situations and

---

[7] For descriptions of techniques that involve an interpretation of imaginative productions see Frank (7), Lerner and others (16), Murphy and Horowitz (19), Sargent (22), and White (26). MacFarlane (17) has written an interesting critique of projective techniques.

equipment and to choose the materials quite deliberately to suit a certain purpose, such as dolls that represent members of different races, or fragile things which the child can destroy. It is possible also to use various kinds of equipment, furniture, miniature toys, and the like. The play technique has been used both with children and adults. The technique has been used in the practice of mental hygiene both to obtain information about the child and also as a help in the course of his treatment.[8]

Drawing and painting. Drawing or painting under free or quasi-controlled conditions provides the child with an opportunity to express his fantasies and, as such, comprises a graphic play situation (1). The child's choice of a theme for his drawing may reveal something about his interests, and in many studies it has also been assumed that various themes and particular aspects of a drawing symbolize particular desires and conflicts of various kinds. One variation of this procedure is finger painting, which has been described by Shaw (23). Claims concerning the extent to which a child (or an adult) unknowingly reveals himself through his drawings and paintings go beyond what has been proved through conclusive scientific study; but a study of children's art work still has large promise as a means of studying children. Sometimes, also, a drawing that the child has made may serve as a point of departure for discussion of his interests and problems.

Response to pictures. The way in which a child describes, interprets, or tells a story about pictures that he sees may provide a good deal of information about him as a person. In the use of this procedure it is assumed that what a child sees in a picture or reads into it might reveal something about his own attitudes, his desires, his hopes, and his fears. One application of the use of pictures which has developed from studies of adults is the Murray Thematic Apperception test (20). The test material consists of a series of pictures. On being shown a picture the individual is asked to

---

[8] Interesting accounts of children's play have been given by Bach (2) and Erikson (5).

make up a story about the scene that is pictured, how it came about, what is going on, what the characters are feeling, and what the outcome will be. The theory underlying this procedure is that while in the process of being absorbed in an attempt to explain the objective occurrence the individual may become less conscious of himself, less conscious of the presence of others, and while thus off guard, so to speak, he may disclose inner tendencies, fears, wishes, and traces of past experience. Pictures have been used by Temple and Amen to study children's anxieties (25).

Story completion. Here again the assumption is that the way in which a child (or adult) completes a story might reveal something about his own inner life. An adaptation of this technique was used in a study, cited in an earlier chapter, dealing with delinquent and nondelinquent children. Various unfinished stories were presented which enabled the boys to complete a narrative in a manner that would be favorable to their parents or favorable to someone else. The assumption was that the more the youngster was attached to his parents the more he would tend to favor them when given an opportunity; for example, to help them rather than a friend when, according to the uncompleted story, the parents and a friend had been in an accident.

The Rorschach Test. The Rorschach test material consists of a set of cards each one of which contains an enlarged "ink blot"; the ink blots vary in contour and include some that are in black and white and others that are multicolored. On being shown each ink blot the person is asked to tell what it might be or what it looks like. There are standard directions for administering the test and very elaborate directions for interpreting the results.[9]

The theory underlying the Rorschach test is that the responses a person gives do not merely throw light on the way he perceives things or is able to imagine things but also represent an expression of an individual's personality. Various features are noted in the responses, such as an individual's tendency to see the thing as a

---
[9] For discussions of the Rorschach test see (3, 14, 15, 21).

whole or to notice each portion or a small detail, the attention he gives to form, color, shading, and movement, the total number of things he sees, the proportion of various types of response, and so on.

Other techniques. Other techniques have also been used more or less systematically to study children by way of their imaginative behavior, including the use of dramatics and puppetry. Various forms of "free association" and "word association" have also been used; the individual may be given a certain word and asked to respond with the first word he thinks of, or he may be asked to give a chain of such associations. The assumption is that such associations do not just happen in a casual fashion but that they may in the aggregate reveal something about the individual's emotional life.

Apart from projective procedures such as the foregoing in which the individual is studied indirectly, the procedure has also been used of directly asking an individual to tell about his fantasies and daydreams or to relate his dreams. Here again it is possible to go beyond the literal account into an attempt to interpret what the content of the daydream or of the dream might mean.

Most prominent among the theories with respect to the meaning and interpretation of dreams are those proposed by Freud (8). There is need for research in the area, but this much is certain: dreams do not just happen. They are caused or elicited by stimuli that impinge upon the organism and they are influenced by conditions that prevail within the organism.

The same may be said also with respect to all other forms of imagery and imaginative activities. Even though all of the approaches described above stand in need of further research to validate the underlying theories and to define the possibilities inherent in each method, each approach is sound in the assumption that the imaginative life of an individual does not occur simply by chance.

BIBLIOGRAPHY

1. Alschuler, R. H. and Hattwick, L. A.: "Easel Painting as an Index of Personality in Preschool Children," *American Journal of Orthopsychiatry* (1943), 13:616-626.
2. Bach, G. R.: *Young Children's Play Fantasies*, Psychological Monographs (American Psychological Association, Inc., 1945), 59, No. 2, 69 pp.
3. Beck, S. J.: "Introduction to the Rorschach Method: a Manual of Personality Study," *Research Monograph of the American Orthopsychiatric Association* (1937), No. 1.
4. Burnham, M. P.: *Imaginative Behavior of Young Children as Revealed in Their Language*, unpublished Ph.D. dissertation (New York: Teachers College, Columbia University, 1940).
5. Erikson, E. H.: "Studies in the Interpretation of Play," *Genetic Psychology Monographs* (1940), 22:557-671.
6. Foster, J. C. and Anderson, J. E.: "Unpleasant Dreams in Childhood," *Child Development* (1936), 7:77-84.
7. Frank, L. K.: "Projective Methods for the Study of Personality," *Journal of Psychology* (1939), 8:389-413.
8. Freud, S.: "Interpretation of Dreams," 1900 (translated by A. A. Brill), in *The Basic Writings of Sigmund Freud* (New York: Modern Library, 1938).
9. Green, G. H.: *The Daydream* (London: University of London Press, 1923), 303 pp.
10. Griffiths, R.: *Imagination in Early Childhood* (London: Kegan, Paul, 1934), 367 pp.
11. Hollingworth, H. L. and Weischer, V.: "Persistent Alphabetical Synesthesis," *American Journal of Psychology* (1939), 52:361-366.
12. Hurlock, E. B. and Burstein, W.: "The Imaginary Playmate: A Questionnaire Study," *Journal of Genetic Psychology* (1932), 41:380-392.
13. Jersild, A. T., Markey, F. V., and Jersild, C. L.: *Children's Fears, Dreams, Wishes, Daydreams, Likes, Dislikes, Pleasant and Unpleasant Memories*, Child Development Monographs (New York: Teachers College, Columbia University, 1933), No. 12, 172 pp.
14. Klopfer, B.: "The Technique of the Rorschach Performance," *Rorschach Research Exchange* (1937), 2:1-14.
15. Krugman, M.: "Out of the Inkwell: the Rorschach Method," *Character and Personality* (1940), 9:91-110.
16. Lerner, E., Murphy, L. B., Stone, J. L., Beyer, E., and Brown, E. W.: *Methods for the Study of Personality in Young Children*, Mono-

graphs of the Society for Research in Child Development (1941), VI, 30, 298 pp.
17. MacFarlane, J.: "Problems of Validation Inherent in Projective Methods," *American Journal of Orthopsychiatry* (1942), 12:405-410.
18. Markey, F. V.: *Imaginative Behavior of Preschool Children,* Child Development Monographs (New York: Teachers College, Columbia University, 1935), No. 18, 139 pp.
19. Murphy, L. B. and Horowitz, R.: "Projective Methods in the Psychological Study of Children," *Journal of Experimental Education* (1938), 7, 2:133-140.
20. Murray, H. A.: *Explorations in Personality* (New York: Oxford University Press, 1938).
21. Rorschach, H.: *Psychodiagnostik. Methodik und Ergebnisse eines wahrnehmungsdiagnostischen Experiments* (Berlin: Huber, 1937, third edition).
22. Sargent, H.: "Projective Methods: Their Origins, Theory, and Application in Personality Research," *Psychological Bulletin* (1945), 42: 257-293.
23. Shaw, R. F.: *Finger Painting* (Boston: Little, Brown, 1934).
24. Svendsen, M.: "Children's Imaginary Companions," *Archives of Neurology and Psychiatry* (1934), 32, 5:985-999.
25. Temple, R. and Amen, E. W.: "A Study of Anxiety in Young Children by Means of a Projective Technique," *Genetic Psychology Monographs* (1944), 30:59-113.
26. White, R. W.: "Interpretation of Imaginative Productions" in *Personality and the Behavior Disorders,* edited by J. McV. Hunt (New York: Ronald Press, 1945), 1, 6:214-251.

Chapter XIII

CHILDREN'S IDEALS, MORALS, AND RELIGION

This chapter deals briefly with aspects of the moral development of children, the development of standards of conduct, children's attitudes, their heroes and ideals, and some factors in the development of religious concepts.

FACTORS IN THE MORAL TRAINING OF CHILDREN

From an early age, children are exhorted by adults (often rather half-heartedly) to be peaceable in their dealings with others, generous, helpful, and virtuous. Children learn, at an early age, more or less clearly to recognize the good things they should do and the bad things they should not do.

The development of an individual's moral standards and moral conduct is influenced by factors as complex and varied as those which influence all aspects of a child's development. On the intellectual side, moral conduct requires knowledge of standards and the ability to perceive the situations to which they apply. On the social and emotional sides, moral conduct is influenced by emotional factors in the individual's private life and all the innate and acquired dispositions that determine his relations with his fellows. An individual's motor ability may have a bearing even on moral behavior (the abler the child is at games involving motor skill, for example, the less occasion he will have to cheat in order to win). Physiological factors also come into play in determining the strength of the temptation when there is a conflict between a person's physical appetites and his moral scruples.

Development of moral concepts.[1] A child's earliest formulation of what is right or wrong, good or bad, is in terms of rules laid down by his elders with regard to specific acts and situations. In time he learns more and more to formulate standards of conduct in general terms and to judge a specific situation in terms of the general rule, although this type of generalization seldom is complete, even in mature years. In time, likewise, he learns to formulate (or to rationalize) standards of conduct in his own terms and to give reasons for them, rather than simply to state that a thing is right because his mother and father have told him so and wrong because they say it is bad and punishable. At first he may regard the act of grabbing another's toy as wrong because his mother has told him it is bad, but later he may say: "It isn't fair or honest," or "It would make him feel bad," or "I wouldn't want him to do that to me, so why should I do it to him?" or some such statement. The advance from authoritarian standards to acceptance and formulation of abstract concepts of equality, fairness, and justice is seldom thoroughgoing, however. Even in mature years, a person's conformity to rules of conduct may to a large extent be dictated by social pressures and fear of the consequences of nonconformity.

Some children are able at an early age to phrase some of their ideas of right and wrong in rather mature terms. This is illustrated in a study by Harrower (14), who questioned children aged about six to eleven years concerning their ideas of cheating, as follows: "Why must you not copy from your neighbor? What do you think about cheating?" As noted in an earlier reference to this study, children from homes of relatively high educational and socio-economic status most frequently answered to the effect that: "It doesn't do any good," or "One can't learn that way." Children from a poorer environment more frequently gave an answer such as: "Cheating is forbidden," "It is naughty," "It is a

---

[1] An extensive review of literature dealing with morals and character development has been prepared by Jones (21).

lie." At eight to eleven years, the type of answer most frequently given by the group of lower economic status was to the effect that cheating is unfair: "It is not fair play."

In this study, Harrower (14) also questioned children concerning their ideas of punishment. They were told a little tale about two boys, Peter and Tommy, who were playing together. Peter had a lovely new engine and Tommy had a boat. Naughty Tommy suddenly kicked Peter's engine and smashed it. Now, what should be done with naughty Tommy? Should he be "smacked" (appeal to authority and a retaliatory concept of punishment), should his own boat be broken up (the idea of reciprocation, an eye for an eye), or should he be made to save up his pocket money until he can buy Peter a new engine (the idea of equity, restitution, or making amends)? Again in response to these questions, a majority of the poorer children, in the age range from six to eight years, gave the authoritarian answer: "Smack him." At eight to eleven years, a majority of the poorer children gave the third type of answer: "He should make up for the damage." On the other hand, a large majority of children from more privileged homes, both at the age range from six to eight and from eight to eleven, gave the answer that Tommy should replace the toy that he had broken. (The factor of intelligence and the factor of difficulty in obtaining pocket money, quite apart from notions of justice or punishment, perhaps had some influence with the poorer children.) In both groups and at both age ranges, the "eye-for-an-eye" (break his toy) type of answer occurred relatively infrequently.

Other examples of moral concepts are given in Chapter VI in connection with a discussion of differences in the moral ideas of children of high and low socio-economic status.

In appraising a child's moral concepts, as in appraising his concepts on any topic, the answer a child gives to a direct question may fail to reveal the extent of his understanding. This is especially likely to be true if he is being called to account for a misdeed or if a question, in one way or another, puts him on the defensive. He may answer evasively, giving any reply that seems to be expedient, and sometimes his replies will be inconsistent,[2] as is also likely to be the case with adults.

Correspondence of children's ideas of right and wrong to the ideas of adults. In a study by Lockhart (24), school children in the fourth grade and above were compared with graduate students and lawyers in their attitudes toward certain laws. Twenty laws were selected, and various circumstances were described which provided motives for disobeying them, such as the saving of a human life when to do so would violate a law. It was found that as children grow older they learn more and more to regard the law much as adults do. In the group as a whole there were not, however, significant differences between the responses of elementary-school children and those of adult students and lawyers.

In passing, it is interesting to note that although there is generally much agreement between boys and girls with regard to moral standards, there also is a tendency with time to accept the view that these standards should be somewhat more rigorously applied to girls than to boys. In a study of 1,500 college students by Katz and Allport (22), only half the men and sixty-nine per cent of the women reported the view that there should be equal or similar standards for men and women. Furthermore, a large percentage of persons regarded certain acts—such as drinking, illicit sex behavior, cursing, smoking, and gambling—as being more serious if committed by women than if committed by men.

Problems in the moral training of children. Many factors complicate the moral training of children. For one thing, moral injunctions are likely to clash with practical pressures in everyday life. Fite (10) has shown, for example, that a child of three or four years may be strongly admonished by his parents never to hit or fight; but in the play group of which he is a member there

---

[2] See, for example, a study by Carmichael of the behavior of children when called to account for past irregularities (5).

IDEALS, MORALS, AND RELIGION

is a good deal of fighting, so that there is a conflict between what parents have impressed upon him and the habits of the group to which he belongs. Moreover, if the child is a sociable creature, occasions are bound to arise when he is practically forced to defend his interests and his rights. If the child does not rise to his own defense he practically is denied the freedom to share and enjoy the social contacts and opportunities afforded by the group situation. On the other hand, when occasionally his moral fiber is put to too strong a test and he does take the aggressive, his response may lack spontaneity and he may, even at an early age, experience feelings of guilt. Such an impasse might be avoided, to some extent, if training were scaled to a child's maturity level. An adult's abstract moral stand against aggression may be splendid as a general rule of conduct and yet may be artificial and needlessly rigid when brought to bear against the normal tussles which arise in the social relations of young children. Training in morals and good conduct should proceed with due regard for the abilities and problems of children at different stages of their growth.

Confusing and conflicting pressures. The moral training of a child at any age level is complicated by the fact that many confusing influences are being brought to bear upon him. For one thing, the moral admonitions of his parents and teachers often will be incompatible with the examples set by them. He is urged by his teacher to be friendly in his dealings with others, and yet he may notice that the teacher is carrying on a feud with another teacher and perhaps is showing favoritism toward individual pupils in the class. He is admonished against anger and vindictiveness and yet witnesses many examples of such behavior in the daily conduct of his preceptors. One of the most serious problems in the moral training of a child arises from the inconsistency of those who try to teach him. A discrepancy between what is professed and practiced by his elders may arise, in part, from the fact that his elders themselves are struggling with the difficulty that the spirit is willing but the flesh is weak, or they are genuinely uncertain as to what is the proper thing to do. Examples of discrepancies between what is preached and what is practiced by those who set up to be his moral guides could be multiplied indefinitely. Since adults are only human beings, some discrepancies are inevitable, but this does not solve the child's problem.

Apart from the fact that adults frequently are confused and take divided counsel within themselves is the further fact that different adults, whose influence is brought directly or indirectly to bear upon the child, may differ in the stand they take with regard to a given form of conduct. Adults in authority in the home may set different standards from adults in authority outside the home, and within the same family conflicting pressures may be brought to bear by the father and mother. In addition, the standards of conduct in reading matter, comics, movies, and radio programs may be at variance with the ideals fostered by home and school. This point is brought out in the discussions of these media in Chapter XIV.

A further element of confusion arises from the child's difficulty in distinguishing between general rules of conduct and more specific rules of the game. Under some circumstances, a lie—whether white, black or gray—is regarded as reprehensible by his elders; under other circumstances, a similar lie may not only be tolerated but encouraged. Again, depending upon the prejudices of the parent, a charitable attitude is required with regard to one group, while the same parent tolerates uncharitable attitudes toward other persons or groups.

Discrepancy of words and deeds. Inconsistencies such as those shown by adults between expressed ideas as to what is the proper conduct and what is actually practiced are exhibited by children at an early age. Most children, for example, will profess that cheating is bad, and yet a large percentage of them will cheat when an occasion arises. When one visits elementary-school classrooms one can readily see many illustrations of the divorcement of verbal patterns and actual conduct. In a class observed by the writer, the children exhibited a high moral tone and laid down many fine moral precepts when discussing standards of behavior and the responsibilities of the individual to his group; but within a few minutes after this discussion, the very pupils who had contributed most to the discussion violated all the precepts that they had just endorsed. Again, children may extol in the abstract principles of fair dealing and sharing, and then violate these very principles even while discussing them (as when some children insist on holding the floor, refuse to give an equal hearing to others, and seek to dictate the course of events).

Such discrepancies can be found at all age levels, extending down into the preschool years. In the study by Fite, referred to above, it was noted that a child might maintain during an interview that hitting is bad and then, in his actual behavior on the playground, exhibit a good deal of hitting. Another child might, during an interview, express the view that hitting is not particularly bad, but in his actual conduct he may exhibit less hitting than a youngster who verbally expressed a strong stand against hitting.

There may be a discrepancy even on a purely verbal level between acceptance of what the children have come to understand as "good" and their translation of this into something concrete. In connection with a study by the writer and his associates (20), a number of children were asked, among other things, what they would do if they had a lot of money. In one of the schools in the study, a large percentage of the children stated that they would do good for others, and many of them described large philanthropic ventures. When, at a later time, the interviewer casually asked each of a number of such children what he would do if he found a quarter on the way home, it did not occur to any child that he might begin the good work on a small scale with a small sum. Here the children responded in terms of their own immediate interests. Obviously, responses such as the foregoing can readily be matched in the behavior of adults.

Observations such as these do not constitute an argument against moral training, but they do emphasize the problem that is involved in getting precepts into line with practice. They suggest, among other things, that there is a need for presenting precepts in such a way that they are intelligible, concrete, are reinforced by the example set by others, and show the way toward specific skills and practices. They also suggest the need for scaling the instruction to the child's level of growth. To be sure, it would be impossible to achieve an exact balance here, and it may be recognized that the moral instruction a child receives may exert an influence on his behavior in the long run, even if it has no apparent immediate effects.

The greatest need in the moral training of children is that we as adults should set our own moral house in order. But to say this is simply to rename and not to solve the problem. For the moral inconsistency exhibited by our adult society represents a continuing unsolved problem. As of old so of late the spirit is willing but the flesh is weak. Moreover, in addition to the shortcomings which an adult sees and confesses, there may be inconsistent currents in his moral life which he does not see but which none the less confuse the moral training of his children. He may, for example, have very strong feelings of hostility toward certain people and yet succeed in justifying his hostility to himself to such an extent that he does not see that the hostile feelings belie his profession of brotherly love.

In the morals of the child's adult preceptors there not only are inconsistencies between what is practiced and what is preached but there are inconsistencies even within the scope of what is preached. The morals of the adult world tend to be quite selective, just as they tend, as suggested earlier, to be quite varied. So a person may regard smoking as wrong on the theory that it is physically harmful, but not, on the same theory, condemn overeating. He may insist on strict observance of one commandment but not of another. He may even be selective in his notion as to the way in which a given precept should apply, as when he preaches honesty but condones some sharp practices.

Emotional adjustment and moral conduct. A child's ability to do the "right thing" depends not merely upon his ability to perceive the issue at stake and his knowledge of specific ways of conducting himself but also upon his emotional stability. Feelings of resentment or fear may block the expression of friendly social impulses. His own inner hurts may impel him to hurt others. The play between morals and emotion also goes in the other direction, for many conflicts may arise by virtue of conduct that goes counter to moral scruples.[2a]

HONESTY

Deceit in one form or another can be noticed in children at an early age. The child of three or younger may hide a toy that he has broken or assume an innocent expression and feign ignorance when confronted with his misdeeds. At an even earlier age he may pretend to be in great distress, by means of exaggerated cries or expressions of pain, to gain attention. And when he learns to talk, "I can't" frequently is far from the truth, meaning simply "I won't." He may also use definite falsehoods to gain his ends. Occasionally, however, what appears to be untruthfulness may mean that the child misunderstands or is unable to distinguish between the fancied and the real. A child will sometimes tell a tale spun out of his own fantasies. Fabrications of this kind may be a bid for attention, although many of the untruths spoken by the imaginative child are merely playful and can hardly be classed as deceit. It is dishonesty of the sort that is used for some practical end, either to escape discomfort or to gain something desired, that is most significant in the study of character, especially if an advantage is thus gained at the expense of others.

[2a] Karen Horney, in *The Neurotic Personality of Our Time* (W. W. Norton, 1937), 299 pp., has described pressures and contradictory ideals in our society that contribute to emotional conflict and self-deception.

Many studies of children's lying and deceit have been made, outstanding among which is an extensive study by Hartshorne and May (15). This study included nearly 11,000 school children of varying cultural, socio-economic backgrounds and intelligence; and numerous ingenious tests, designed to provide an objective test of honesty, were used. These tests included opportunities to cheat in classroom work, in athletic contests, in games, and in schoolwork done at home; they included also opportunities to give false answers in reply to questions concerning personal conduct and to steal coins (under conditions which appeared entirely safe to the child). Some of the general findings of this study, based upon statistical treatment which isolated each of several factors for separate study, are summarized below.

Older pupils were slightly more deceptive than younger children.

On particular tests, some sex differences appear; but in general, there was no outstanding difference in the deceptiveness of boys and girls.

There was a positive relationship between honesty and intelligence; children of higher levels of intelligence deceived definitely less than the children of lower intelligence.

The tests revealed, however, no significant relationship between honesty and physical condition, although children who showed symptoms of emotional instability (as measured independently by a standard test) showed a greater tendency toward deceptiveness than those who were better adjusted emotionally.

The relationship between deceptiveness and the socio-economic status of parents parallels the relationship found between honesty and intelligence. When children were classified into four occupational levels, according to socio-economic status, those at the highest level deceived the least, those at the second and third highest levels, progressively more, and those at the lowest level, the most.

Children belonging to the same family resembled each other more in honesty and deceptiveness than children matched at random. But the authors believe it is possible that children would vary in deceptiveness even if all were brought up under similar conditions.

There was a positive relationship between cheating and low marks in school deportment.

Among still other relationships that appeared were the following: Children who were friends, even though not members of the same class, showed more than a chance resemblance in the amount of cheating. Children who cheated less tended to be less suggestible. Children who were in charge of a teacher who was able to stimulate coöperation and good will cheated less than those who were taught under a more conventional and rigid routine; children who were members of organizations purporting, as one of their aims, to teach honesty, cheated about as much as nonmembers.

The findings in this study indicate that no generalized, uniform trait that can be labeled "honesty" characterizes the child in all situations. The child who lies, steals, or cheats in one situation may be quite without guile in another; he may be a brazen cheater when given a chance to copy in a test and be completely honorable in an athletic contest.

However, the fact that cheating is quite specific cannot be interpreted to mean that it occurs by chance. When a child cheats there is a motive underlying his behavior—he has something at stake, a desire or purpose. One situation may elicit a desire to win or to succeed by hook or by crook and another may not. If Tom is a rival of Jim he may cheat in an arithmetic test which Jim is also taking, but he may not have the same desire to succeed and the same incentive to cheat if Jim is absent. It may be very important for a child, from the standpoint of his own desires and aspirations, to win in a spelling contest but not very important to win in a game of marbles. So he may cheat in one situation and not in the other. Again, he may undertake one activity with a desire to learn and to correct his mistakes (and in keeping with this, let his errors be known so that he can get help in learning), whereas, in another situation in which he desires only to "get by," he may cheat if that shortens or eases the task. Accordingly, a child may seem inconsistent in his tendency to cheat when his behavior is viewed from the standpoint of the external situation, and yet his tendency to cheat or to be honest may be consistent when viewed in the light of his own motives.

The chief motives for deception set forth in the study above may be listed under such general headings as: revenge, jealousy and envy, self-defense, desire to compensate oneself for loss or for a handicap, loyalty to friends or a cause, and aggressive greed for property, approval, or prestige.

These findings with regard to honesty illustrate the fact that both nature and nurture play a role in determining how individuals will behave. One is not born honest or dishonest; nor does it follow that because one has a lower than average I.Q. he will be dishonest in his behavior. Inasmuch as deceit offers a means of meeting a difficulty, the person who is poor in wit is more likely to need methods which are classed as dishonest in solving certain problems. A person of high intelligence is likely to be more able to make certain adjustments without being deceptive. (But he may also be cleverer at cheating.)

GENEROSITY

In an extensive investigation, Hartshorne and May (16) used objective methods to study generosity and the readiness to serve others. Willingness to give up ice cream for the sake of helping someone else, to vote money (which each child actually received) to charity, to surrender attractive objects (in a kit which each child received as a present), to prepare materials for children in a hospital, and to work as hard for the group as for oneself were among the items that were tested. In this study, as in the study of deceit, it was found that the intercorrelations between the various tests were positive but low. Although it is probable that a child who is generous in one situation will show the same tendency, rather than the opposite, in another situation, one cannot with any degree of confidence predict from a single episode just what his behavior in general will be.

No consistent changes in the readiness to serve others were observed with relation to age. Bright children were somewhat more coöperative than normal and dull children; but the relationship between generosity and intelligence was low, as compared with the correlation between honesty and intelligence. This suggests that the greater honesty of the bright may not be due so much to greater virtue as to practical expediency, since the abler person can solve more problems without cheating. Another factor, however, is that the more intelligent person may be relatively more honest than generous because he recognizes the relative value placed upon these virtues by others. In one study of high-school children (40) it was found that, in rating various virtues, a much higher rank was assigned to honesty than to charity. In the culture in which our children are being reared it seems that George Washington and his hatchet is a symbol of higher virtue than is the Good Samaritan.

In the study by Hartshorne and May, girls were found to be somewhat more coöperative than boys. There was only a slight association between coöperativeness and physical condition or emotional stability. Children from the higher occupational levels were somewhat more coöperative than those from the lower levels, but the relationship was small. There was some resemblance between children from the same family, and friends resembled each other more than classmates chosen at random, although less than children within the same family. Again, those who attended Sunday School were somewhat more coöperative than those who did not, but the difference was slight. Children who were more suggestible (as measured by a test of suggestibility) were somewhat less coöperative than the average, while those who were less suggestible were more coöperative. Also, children who were more sociable than the average did not tend to be more coöperative than the average.

These statements suggest some of the facts associated with generosity, but here, as in the measurement of other forms of behavior, much remains unsolved. It is significant, of course, that children from the same family resembled each other a good deal; yet it seems that the effect of home training varies. The resemblance between siblings, when measured with respect to generosity, was not as high on the whole as the resemblance found in measurements of their intelligence.

CHILDREN'S HEROES AND IDEALS

Some insight into a child's values and his ideas as to what constitutes model conduct can be gained from his choice of heroes and ideals. To be sure, when a child names a given character as his hero or ideal, one cannot be certain how genuine his attachment may be. One child may name someone whom he himself sincerely admires and tries to emulate, while another may simply mention a character whose name he knows only through popular hearsay.

In various studies, several thousand children have been asked questions such as: "Of all the persons you have heard or read about or seen, whom would you most care to be like?" or: "Whom do you admire most?"[3]

Table XXXIII summarizes the results obtained in one study; here the children's replies have been classified under a number of general headings. The percentages of heroes in the various categories is likely to vary somewhat with different groups and may vary also over a period of time. In an unpublished study in 1945 by Ray and Stoughton, the results showed, for the particular population, a considerably lower percentage of choices in the "Historic-and-public-characters" category and a larger percentage of choices

---

[3] Among investigations dealing with this topic are studies by Bateman (3), Barnes (1), Hill (17, 18), Gilbertson (11), Goddard (12), and Macaulay (25).

in the "Characters-from-fiction" category (with numerous mentions of comic book characters) than in Hill's study.

Table XXXIII

SOURCES OF IDEALS CHOSEN BY URBAN CHILDREN FROM THREE CITIES[4]
(Showing the distribution, in percentages, of various classes of ideals at successive age levels.)

Sources of Ideals	Distribution in Percentages								
	Age 6-8	Age 9	Age 10	Age 11	Age 12	Age 13	Age 14	Age 15	Age 16	Age 17-20
Characters from the immediate environment....	58.2	44.5	37.9	35.1	30.0	29.8	28.5	27.5	29.8	27.4
Historic and public characters..................	32.3	44.9	53.0	54.7	61.3	61.3	64.5	64.2	60.5	61.3
Characters from fiction....	2.2	3.7	3.5	3.9	2.4	3.3	1.4	2.5	2.5	2.8
Characters from religion[a]..	3.0	2.4	1.7	1.7	2.6	1.9	1.5	1.3	1.8	2.4

[a] A class labeled "miscellany," which brings the total to 100 per cent in each column, is not reproduced.

It will be noted in Table XXXIII that there is a marked decline with age in ideals chosen from the immediate environment and an increase with age (from six to twelve years) in ideals chosen from history or from current public affairs. Characters from fiction and from religion are mentioned by only a few children at each age level and show only small changes with age. Comparisons between boys and girls, which are not reproduced in the table above, show that girls choose ideals from immediate environment considerably more frequently than do boys, a difference that appears at each age level. When results from all ages are convened, 46.5 per cent of the ideals chosen by girls are from their immediate environment, as compared with only 19.9 per cent in the case of boys. From the age of eleven to the age of twenty, 40 per cent or more of the girls chose characters from the immediate environment, while similar choices by the boys dropped from 26 to 11 per cent. On the other hand, boys consistently selected historical or public characters more often than did the girls.

[4] Adapted from Hill, D. S.: "Personification of Ideals by Urban Children," *Journal of Social Psychology* (1930), I: 379-392. Reproduced by permission.

The age trends shown in Table XXXIII appear even more impressive in another child population studied by Macaulay (25). The children in this study, 1,600 in number, wrote answers to the question: "What person whom you have ever known, or of whom you have ever heard or read, would you most wish to be like?" Following is the percentage of children at successive age levels who chose acquaintances as their ideals:

Age	7	8	9	10	11	12	13	14	15
Percentage	65	59	40	32	24	17	8	2	3

In this study, likewise, girls chose more characters from their immediate circle of relatives, acquaintances, and friends than did boys. Girls also chose male characters more often than boys chose female characters.

The fact that the range of characters whom children admire widens more and more beyond the immediate home environment as children grow older is not surprising, but it still gives a striking indication of the widening with age of the ranges of a child's interests and values. An earlier study by Hill (16) shows changes with age in the tendency of children to regard their parents as their heroes and ideals. At seven years, thirty per cent of the children who were questioned named fathers or mothers as their ideals. At ten years, this percentage had dropped to nine, and it showed a further drop to zero by the age of fifteen. This change reflects the child's widened interests. It cannot be concluded, however, that the influence of the parents had waned to a corresponding degree, and no doubt a different result would be obtained if children were asked, for example, whom they cared for most.

Whatever may be the motives or the sincerity underlying each child's choice, the ideal he chooses symbolizes to some degree the values that have been stressed in the culture in which he lives and the values within that culture that appeal to him. In individual cases, a child's choice of an ideal may tell much concerning his attitudes toward home, school, and society at large. In informal studies, it has been found, for example, that individual maladjusted children in the upper elementary grades may carry their revolt so far that they defy tradition, refuse even to pay lip service to conventional morals, and name a celebrated criminal as their hero and ideal.

RELIGION

All children in a culture such as ours are influenced to some degree by religious practices, ideas, and beliefs, whether or not parents give them religious instruction in the home or send them to church. As Conklin has pointed out (7), religion plays a large part in the lives of most people in one way or another. The tendency of children is to accept, rather than to reject, what they hear and read, especially if it ties in with their own desires and interests, and as long as they meet with no direct contradictions. Parents who do not provide religious instruction sometimes discover that a child through his conversation with others and his reading has accepted many religious beliefs, and occasionally a child whose parents disavow religion may even acquire the habit of praying quite regularly for a time. This interest in religious matters varies considerably, however, with different children.

Factors influencing the meaning of religious teachings. A child's religious ideas and images will, of necessity, be influenced by his experiences in everyday life, and this fact presents a practical issue to parents and teachers who endeavor to give religious instruction. If the instruction is to be genuine, it must not merely come by way of verbal precepts but must be interpreted also by the practical example set by the child's elders. A child's image of God the Father may include a blend of details from pictures he has seen and Bible stories he has heard. The image may vary from time to time, including now a kindly expression, now a wrathful countenance. His conception of the attributes of a fatherly God will be influenced, perhaps imperceptibly, by his experience of the attributes of his own father or of others in a paternal role. His ideas of sin will be influenced by his experiences of grief or remorse through having caused distress to other persons and by experiences of regret flowing from hostility or fear aroused by the treatment he has received as a consequence of having disobeyed someone in authority. His ideas of forgiveness will be influenced by his own experience of being forgiven by his elders and the idea of forgiveness may be a difficult one for him to grasp if in his own relations with his elders he finds it impossible to confide or confess his troubles and must bottle up his feelings of guilt and fears of retribution. On the other hand, lack of anyone in the everyday environment in whom to confide may, under some circumstances, impel a person toward religion. The child's response to any aspect of religious instruction will be influenced by parental examples and evidences of parental sincerity.

The younger the child, the more his ideas in matters of religion, as in other matters, will be built upon his own concrete experiences. These are likely to be elaborated by fantasies. His ideas may be influenced by a multitude of conditions, such as the physical appearance, atmosphere, and facilities of the church; the odors and echoes of the church building; the confinement of movement imposed upon him if he must sit quietly longer than is agreeable to his limited attention span; the kindliness or austerity of his teachers; and so forth.

From early childhood through the elementary-school years, numerous religious concepts will have relatively little meaning to him in the abstract, and a problem in religious education is how to translate religious concepts into terms that are meaningful.[5] Misconceptions through failure to understand the terms that are used can be seen when the child, for example, comes home and tells his mother about Jesus' twelve bicycles (disciples), or sings: "A wonderful guy (guide) is He," or is puzzled by "the consecrated cross-eyed bear" (the consecrated Cross, I'd bear). Chil-

---

[5] For an account of children's understanding of religious terms and concepts, see Bose (4), Tanner (36), Barnes (2), Case (6), and Harms (13).

dren also are confused at times by denominational differences, and frequently they have difficulty in distinguishing between the form and intended substance of religious observances.

In a brief passage, Murphy (30) has tried to construct a picture, from the child's point of view, of the way Jesus is sometimes presented. Children are likely to learn of Him, "not as an ideal grown-up who helped people, but as a little baby whose mother put him in a straw thing in a barn instead of a crib, and to whom queer-looking men in striped gowns brought presents no baby could use. They learn, too, that there was a bad king, with a ferocious face, of whom the baby's mother was afraid, so that she had to take him a long way from home, riding on an animal that is not seen in the city, nor even in the zoo."

One problem which many children who receive religious instruction face at an early age is that their own innocent and even genuine interpretations and versions of religious events and relations are rebuked by their parents and religious teachers. Sometimes the statements made by children represent, from an adult point of view, vulgarity or even sacrilege; but the manner of correcting such statements makes a great deal of difference.

Interest in the Bible. Children's interest in Biblical characters and scenes and in different portions of the Bible have been studied by Dawson (9) in an investigation conducted many years ago in a New England community. Since results of such a study are likely to be influenced by the religious background and affiliations of the children involved and might also vary over a period of time, the findings cannot be regarded as typical for all children who have had religious training, but the general trends noted are interesting.

Age trends appear in preferences for various books of the Bible. Up to eight or nine years the children expressed most interest in accounts of the birth and childhood of Jesus and in stories concerning the childhood of characters such as Moses, Samuel, Joseph, and David. From nine to thirteen or fourteen years, portions of the Old Testament, especially the historical books, had greatest appeal. At about the age of fourteen, and from then until twenty years (the upper age level in the study), interest in the historical sections receded and there was a distinctly preponderant interest in the Gospels. Dawson also shows "age curves" for other portions of the Bible. From the age of about ten through adolescence, poetic sections of the Bible appeal to numerous children, although the number who chose these sections was considerably smaller than the number who selected the historical books and the Gospels. Books of prophecy received a few votes from the age of twelve and onward. The Proverbs and doctrinal sections received relatively little mention until about the adolescent period and then were preferred by relatively few children. At all ages, children expressed more interest in persons than in other elements of the Bible.

Children's prayers. One of the many aspects of childhood religion that adults have difficulty in understanding from the child's point of view is prayer. The approach that is made in teaching the child to pray often involves parents in many pitfalls, as when they teach the child to approach God as though He were an absent-minded magician, given to granting any reckless or thoughtless petition that might be addressed to Him. The idea of praying to a higher power is usually accepted quite readily by children, who, in their experiences, frequently have occasion to be reminded of their own limitations and unfulfilled desires. The desires that lie back of the child's frequent "I wish" or "If only I had" and which he realizes vicariously in his own make-believe can readily be translated into the petition: "Please give." It is considerably easier, of course, to lead a child to petition that his passing desires be granted than to petition that he be helped to have desires and aspirations of the kind that should be granted and the determination to carry out these aspirations. The same, to be sure, holds true also of adults.

Although the "pennies-from-heaven" type of prayer is easier to learn—and also readily leads to some perplexity when the pennies are not forthcoming—it has been observed that children who receive religious instruction can, at a relatively early age, learn to voice prayers more in keeping with theological interpretations of the purpose of prayer. Frequently a child will recite prayers that he has been taught without understanding what they mean and then proceed to express prayers of his own in less conventional language. In a study by MacLean (26), it was found that a large proportion of children in primary Sunday-school classes described prayer in terms of "talking to God," with emphasis more frequently upon such factors as help in doing right, avoiding wrong, help in "trying harder to get the things we want," and thanksgiving than upon requests for concrete gifts. Children in the junior and intermediate classes likewise carried out this emphasis. In response to a questionnaire, ninety-five per cent of the children expressed agreement with the statement: "When I talk to God, I often find out what is right for me to do"; ninety per cent expressed agreement with the statement: "God answers prayers mostly when we do our best to answer them ourselves"; and eighty-five per cent agreed: "God won't give us anything we ask for, but He knows what is best for us and gives us that." In this group of Sunday-school children, six per cent expressed agreement with the statement: "It doesn't do a fellow any good to pray."

Sherrill (35) cites the case of a five-year-old child (who must have been somewhat precocious) who was overheard to pray: "Father in Heaven, help me to be kind and good, . . . to know what's what; help me to know what is good and what is bad, and what is poison and what is not poison, and what is right and what is wrong. Amen." [6]

A child may also be moved to voice thanksgiving, as in the case of an eight-year-old boy who, while walking homeward after having delivered milk to a neighbor on Christmas Eve, with snow under foot and a clear sky above, and with keen anticipation of a

---

[6] Adapted from Sherrill, L. J.: *The Opening Doors of Childhood* (New York: Macmillan, 1939), 193 pp. Reproduced by permission.

good dinner and gifts to come, turned his eyes skyward and exclaimed: "Gosh, God, you're good—and help everybody to be happy like me!"

Effects of religious training. The influence of religious training on children has not been studied at all in a systematic manner. In the general literature of psychology there are miscellaneous findings dealing, for example, with such points as the honesty of children who have attended Sunday School and of children who have not (as measured by tests that give the children an opportunity to cheat), the generosity of such children (again as measured by limited test situations), the degree of "liberal-mindedness" (as defined by the investigator) of members of various religious denominations and of nonmembers, the religious affiliations of delinquents, and so forth. Such studies, while instructive as far as they go, have dealt with the problem in a manner that is limited and inconclusive.

This problem is one that is difficult to explore in a scientific way, especially since many ends sought by religious instruction are designed to reside in the subjective realm of faith and hope, and since the good works that religion fosters are supposed to be done with a minimum of fanfare. Even if measurement of such outcomes were possible, it would be difficult to find a "control" group with which to compare the religiously trained individual, since religious influences are deeply imbedded in the culture and there is a large degree of overlapping between the morals and virtues that are promoted under religious and nonreligious auspices. By reason of this large overlap between the kind of training and influence brought to bear upon technically religious and nonreligious individuals, it is difficult adequately to measure the effects of religious training on the more commonplace expressions of moral conduct.

Apart from this overlap on many points between those who have formal religious affiliations and those who do not, there also are large variations in the religious influences brought to bear upon children who technically receive religious instruction. One child may be sent to church by parents who never themselves attend; another attends with his entire family. In one case the religious practices of the child's elders may be quite perfunctory, while in another case they occupy an important place in the family's everyday activities. In one case the child's attention may be centered only upon some of the externals of religion, and in another, his training may be under the auspices of parents and teachers whose religion is a matter of deep feeling and concern. Thus there may be a decided psychological difference between the experiences of two individuals whose training, as measured only by the criterion of church attendance, appears to be similar.

Even more difficult to measure are the subtle and indirect influences. In her study of sympathy, Murphy (30) reports an incidental observation concerning the relation of the behavior of young children to the religious background of the children's parents. The influences of the church were difficult "to detach from the deepest personality characteristics of the parents who had been identified with it [the church]." Among the children in the Murphy study, there were eight whose parents had been or who were then identified with the church. With one exception, the children were less aggressive than the median child in the group as a whole. In some of these children, the observers noted manifestations of gentleness and considerateness that seemed to indicate that patterns of kindness had become deeply assimilated by the families to which the children belonged. These observations, obviously, are not presented as conclusive; other children in other groups might not conform at all to this trend. But the observations are suggestive in pointing the way toward a line of study to discover some of the subtler ways in which a religious background in the home might be reflected in the everyday behavior of children.

A study of the effects of religious instruction would not only have to cover ground such as the foregoing but it would have to appraise the more subjective phenomena denoted by such terms as peace of mind, relief from guilt feelings, hopefulness, the disposition to be forgiving and patient, and the like.

ALTRUISM

Partly through increased realization of what is expected of them and partly perhaps through an increase in genuine concern for others, children tend increasingly with age to take account of others and their welfare in their own private thoughts. An indication of this trend is shown by studies of children's wishes. In a study earlier referred to, it was found that the percentage of wishes concerning "benefits for relatives" rose from about three to fifteen per cent from the age of five and six years to the age of eleven and twelve years. The same comparison shows a rise in general philanthropic wishes from three to thirteen per cent of the total (20). A study by Washburne (38) shows a rise in wishes for the welfare of others in the age range from ten to seventeen years. The rise was larger in the case of girls (twenty-two per cent) than in the case of boys (eleven per cent).[7]

That altruistic impulsions may be impermanent and superficial is indicated in a study by Moore (28) of high-school children. Sixty-six per cent of the children in this study answered "yes" when asked whether, prior to the present year, they had ever felt, for a period of several days, a strong impulse to give their lives to helping certain classes of people who are suffering from poverty, ignorance, disease, or some other misfortune, or in helping to prevent these evils.[8] Those who answered "yes" were then asked to

---

[7] This upswing in expressions of altruism apparently is halted sometime in late adolescence. Wilson (39) found that only about eight per cent of the wishes of college students dealt with philanthropies and general benefits for others. It is likely, however, that results will vary with different populations, and it is also possible that altruistic preoccupations express themselves more in the form of action than in the form of wishes at the older levels.

[8] It may be noted here that when children are specifically questioned concerning altruistic impulses a larger percentage will report such impulses than when they are asked (as in the other studies here reviewed) simply to mention their wishes, whatever these might be.

report specifically what they had hoped to do; sixty-nine per cent gave concrete replies and thirty-one per cent gave vague replies or failed to answer. About a third of the children reported that they had abandoned these ambitions, and of those who reported they still had the ambition, about two-thirds gave vague or general replies when asked how they proposed to carry out or to prepare themselves for carrying out their altruistic ambitions.

PREJUDICES

A child begins his career with no prejudices, but after a few years he is likely to have many. These may range all the way from strong and organized antipathies to relatively mild disposition to avoid or to look with indifference upon certain persons or groups.[9]

Prejudices acquired through direct experience. Some prejudices rise through unpleasant events in the child's own direct experience, as when he is hurt or frightened by someone and retains a feeling of suspicion or ill will. This disposition may be confined to a specific individual or it may be generalized, as when he reacts unfavorably toward all members of a certain group—say, toward all people with whiskers, or all people with a certain skin color, or all people with prominent cheekbones. Prejudice which thus arises through first-hand experience is likely, of course, to vary considerably from person to person. Countless occasions for the development of an unfavorable attitude toward others arise in the give-and-take of everyday social contacts, sometimes by virtue of real grievances, sometimes by virtue of imagined affronts. Again, feelings of distrust or lack of fellow feeling may arise out of fear or uneasiness in response to persons who are strange, who differ in physiognomy or manner from the persons within the child's accustomed circle.

Varying degrees of liking and disliking for other individuals or

---

[9] Studies by Zeligs and Hendrickson deal with the social attitudes of children who were first studied at the sixth grade and again in adolescence (41, 42, 43, 44).

groups inevitably arise in the experience of the individual child. Even when no distinct antipathies develop, some degree of discrimination in favor of certain persons will arise by virtue of the fact that a child cannot have equally strong ties with everybody. There is a limit to the range of his active loyalties. The very fact that he is affiliated with one group will leave him with less opportunity to fraternize with another group.

There may be, therefore, "social distance" between a child and others even if no active prejudices come into play. However, awareness of social distance is likely to be increased and may even give rise to a certain amount of suspiciousness and distrust if he discovers that he is viewed as an outsider by members of other groups such as the children on the other side of the track, or the children belonging to a certain school, camp, or church. The very loyalties that exist within one circle may serve as a barrier to members outside the circle and may lead to antagonism, especially if the outsider would like very much to join.

The influence of the child's elders and of culture patterns. However, the natural antipathies that arise in the normal flow of everyday experience with other persons and the friction that may arise in direct encounters between different groups of children represent only a small factor in the development of prejudices between groups. More important are the influences that come at second hand, the prejudices passed on to the child by his elders, the attitudes that he comes to adopt through precept and example in the culture that surrounds him. He may be exposed to traditional antipathies that persist as a hangover from an earlier period. He may, through his reading and through what he hears, acquire legendary prejudices against peoples with whom he has had no direct contact. Eventually he may even join in the indoor sport of trying to enhance his pride in his group, and thereby his own self-esteem, by belittling and defaming people of other races, classes, or nationalities.

Among the factors that influence prejudice the home is very

prominent. In countless situations the child has an opportunity to absorb the prejudices of his father and his mother. The younger he is, the more ready he is to believe all that he hears and to adopt the parents' point of view. Frequently prejudice thus has its inception in the home, even though neither of the two parents openly displays any antipathy for another group. The child may acquire an attitude of distrust simply by being exposed to family and cultural traditions which set the child and his people off from others.

Many of the impressions that a child gains from adults and that may add up to at least a passive form of prejudice occur by way of words and acts which an adult may not even regard as biased. Many parents, for example, who teach their children to be "correct" in all things, do not stop to think that when they teach a child the formula, "Eenie, meenie, minie moe . . ." they may, in effect, be encouraging an attitude of belittlement of Negroes by using the term "nigger."

Countless influences may also operate outside the home to produce prejudice. An example of this appears in a study of the effect of motion pictures by Peterson and Thurstone (32). In this study, children's attitudes on various subjects were tested before and after the showing of motion-picture films. It was found that children were less friendly toward Negroes after seeing the picture *The Birth of a Nation* than before. Likewise, one group of children showed a more friendly attitude toward the Chinese after seeing a picture that was favorable to the Chinese, while another group showed a less friendly attitude toward the Chinese after seeing a film that pictured Chinese people in an unfavorable light.

A study of racial cleavage. Racial cleavage as related to age has been studied by Criswell (8). Criswell used the sociometric technique of having each pupil in various classes in a number of schools list the pupil whom he would like most to have as a seat mate and the pupil whom he would like next best as seat mate. The classes ranged from nine to ninety-five per cent Negro. In the lower grades it was found that there was considerably more selection of members of another race than appeared in the higher grades. White children restricted their choices to their own race to a larger extent than did Negro children. Even in the primary grades, however, race and color preferences were observed in the intersexual choices. In the first two grades, colored boys preferred white girls and then shifted their choice to light (slightly less colored) girls. Colored girls preferred light boys until Grade IV, then medium boys. White boys and girls preferred their own race, but choices of Negroes occurred as late as Grade VI or VII. By the eighth grade, choices of boys by girls and girls by boys had almost completely ceased to cross racial lines. In other words, as children approach sexual maturity and come nearer to the age of courtship and marriage the pressures that make for social cleavage become more marked.

The rationalization of prejudice. Whatever may be the starting point of an unfavorable attitude toward a given group, a prejudice once begun is likely to find plenty of nourishment as time goes on. Even when there is only a mild degree of antipathy, it is easy to find support and confirmation for this antipathy. Acts that may be ever so innocent, or mild unpleasantnesses which normally would be ignored, are interpreted in the light of the prejudice that already prevails. If a member of one's own group cheats or is rude or boisterous, we hold this against the individual; but let a member of a group against which we are prejudiced commit the same acts, and we charge them not only against him as a person but also against the group to which he belongs. Such prejudices are likely to become all the more acute if complicated by rivalry and competition in the affairs of daily life. Frequently, of course, prejudices against other groups are merely a form of rationalization and a case of "sour grapes" and are often, as history shows, played upon for political and selfish purposes. Dispassionate teaching and, as far as possible, avoidance by parents and teachers of the practice of passing their ready-made resentments down to their children, would, of course, go far to minimize prejudices. *Mutual recrimination.* One factor that helps to perpetuate and to intensify prejudice is the mutual recrimination that usually develops. In adult prejudices we see a parallel to many of the problems connected with the elimination and treatment of anger in young children. Whoever may be at fault at the beginning, a vicious circle of self-defense and counterattack is started. The measures which an innocent person takes to protect himself against the unjust anger of another may simply convince the angry one that he has a just grievance. Each antagonist finds it difficult to take stock of himself. In the case of prejudices between groups, it would be helpful if members of opposing camps would be as zealous in inquiring into the reasons for their prejudice and in seeking friendly means by which it might be dispelled as they are in deploring the folly and unfairness of their opponents. The average human being will not readily, however, subject himself to such dispassionate self-examination, and sometimes the odds of prejudice are so great that the individual has no other recourse than to fight back as best he can.[10]

BIBLIOGRAPHY

1. Barnes, E.: "Children's Ideals," *Pedagogical Seminary* (1900), 7:3-12.
2. ———: "Theological Notions of California Children," *Studies in Education* (1902), 2:283-320.
3. Bateman, W. G.: "The Ideals of Some Western Children," *Educational Review* (1916), 52:21-39.
4. Bose, R. G.: "Religious Concepts of Children," *Religious Education* (1929), 24:831-837.
5. Carmichael, A. M.: "The Behavior of Six-Year-Old Children When Called Upon to Account for Past Irregularities," *Journal of Genetic Psychology* (1930), 38:352-360.

---

[10] For studies of the development of racial attitudes, see, for example, Lasker (23), Horowitz (19), Meltzer (27), the studies by Zeligs referred to on p. 000, and a review of many studies by Murphy, Murphy, and Newcomb (29). A review by Nelson (31) deals with the general subject of attitudes, and numerous recent studies by Remmers and his associates, in Bulletins of Purdue University, have dealt with factors influencing changes in attitudes (33, 34, 37).

6. Case, A.: "Children's Ideas of God," *Religious Education* (1921), 16:143-146.
7. Conklin, E. S.: *Principles of Adolescent Psychology* (New York: Henry Holt, 1935), 437 pp.
8. Criswell, J. H.: *A Sociometric Study of Race Cleavage in the Classroom,* Archives of Psychology (1939), No. 235, 82 pp.
9. Dawson, G. E.: "Children's Interest in the Bible," *Pedagogical Seminary* (1900), 7:151-178.
10. Fite, M. D.: *Aggressive Behavior in Young Children and Children's Attitudes Toward Aggression,* Genetic Psychology Monographs (1940), 22:151-319.
11. Gilbertson, A. N.: "A Swedish Study in Children's Ideals," *Pedagogical Seminary* (1913), 20:100-106.
12. Goddard, H. H.: "Ideals of a Group of German Children," *Pedagogical Seminary* (1906), 13:208-220.
13. Harms, E.: "The Development of Religious Experience in Children," *American Journal of Sociology* (1944), 50:112-122.
14. Harrower, M. R.: "Social Status and the Moral Development of the Child," *British Journal of Educational Psychology* (1934), 1, 1:75-95.
15. Hartshorne, H. and May, M. A.: *Studies in the Nature of Character,* Vol. I: *Studies in Deceit* (New York: Macmillan, 1928), 414 pp.; 306 pp.
16. ———: *Studies in the Nature of Character,* Vol. II: *Studies in Service and Self-Control* (New York: Macmillan, 1929), 559 pp.
17. Hill, D. S.: "Comparative Study of Children's Ideals," *Pedagogical Seminary* (1911), 18:219-231.
18. ———: "Personification of Ideals by Urban Children," *Journal of Social Psychology* (1930), 1:379-392.
19. Horowitz, R. E.: "Racial Aspects of Self Identification in Nursery School Children," *Journal of Psychology* (1939), 7:91-99.
20. Jersild, A. T., Markey, F. V., and Jersild, C. L.: *Children's Fears, Dreams, Wishes, Daydreams, Likes, Dislikes, Pleasant and Unpleasant Memories,* Child Development Monographs (New York: Teachers College, Columbia University, 1933), No. 12, 172 pp.
21. Jones, V.: "Character Development in Children: An Objective Approval," in Carmichael, L.: *Manual of Child Psychology* (New York: John Wiley and Sons, 1946), Ch. 14, 707-751.
22. Katz, D. and Allport, F. H.: *Students' Attitudes: A Report of the Syracuse University Reaction Study* (Syracuse: The Craftsman Press, 1931), 408 pp.
23. Lasker, B.: *Race Attitudes in Children* (New York: Henry Holt, 1929), 394 pp.

24. Lockhart, E. G.: "The Attitude of Children Towards Certain Laws," *Religious Education* (1930), 25:144-149.
25. Macaulay, E.: "Some Social, Age and Sex Differences Shown in Children's Choice of Ideals," *Forum Education* (1925), 3:105-114.
26. MacLean, A. H.: *The Idea of God in Protestant Religious Education,* Teachers College Contributions to Education (New York: Teachers College, Columbia University, 1930), No. 410, 150 pp.
27. Meltzer, H.: "Nationality Preferences and Stereotypes of Colored Children," *Journal of Genetic Psychology* (1939), 54:403-424.
28. Moore, H. H.: "The Social Impulses of Youth," *School and Society* (1935), 42:657-664.
29. Murphy, G., Murphy, L. B., and Newcomb, T. M.: *Experimental Social Psychology* (New York: Harper, 1937), 1,121 pp.
30. Murphy, L. B.: *Social Behavior and Child Personality* (New York: Columbia University Press, 1937), 344 pp.
31. Nelson, E.: "Attitudes: I. Their Nature and Development," *Journal of General Psychology* (1939), 21:367-399; "Attitudes: II. Social Attitudes" (1939), 401-416; "Attitudes: III. Their Measurement" (1939), 417-436.
32. Peterson, R. C. and Thurstone, L. L.: *Motion Pictures and the Social Attitudes of Children,* Payne Fund Studies (New York: Macmillan, 1933), 75 pp.
33. Peterson, T. D.: "The Relationship Between Certain Attitudes of Parents and Children," *Further Studies in Attitudes,* Purdue University Studies in Higher Education, second series, edited by H. H. Remmers (1936), 37:127-144.
34. Remmers, H. H. (editor): *Further Studies in Attitudes, Series II. Studies in Higher Education* (Lafayette: Purdue University, 1936), 37:298 pp.
35. Sherrill, L. J.: *The Opening Doors of Childhood* (New York: Macmillan, 1939), 193 pp.
36. Tanner, A. E.: "Children's Religious Ideas," *Pedagogical Seminary* (1906), 13:511-513.
37. Taylor, C. T.: "A Study of Certain Attitudes of Negro Junior High School Pupils," *Further Studies in Attitudes,* Purdue University Studies in Higher Education, second series, edited by H. H. Remmers (1936), 37:192-202.
38. Washburne, J. N.: "The Impulsions of Adolescents as Revealed by Their Written Wishes," *Journal of Juvenile Research* (1932), 16:193-212.
39. Wilson, F. T.: "Birthday Wishes of First Grade Children," *Journal of Genetic Psychology* (1939), 55:319-352.

40. Mitchell, C.: "Do Virtues and Vices Change?" *School and Society* (1943), 57:111-112.
41. Zeligs, R. and Hendrickson, G.: "Racial Attitudes of 200 Sixth-Grade Children," *Sociology and Social Research* (1933), 18:26-36.
42. ———: "Factors Regarded by Children as the Basis for Racial Attitude," *Sociology and Social Research* (1935), 19:225-233.
43. Zeligs, R.: "Racial Attitudes in Children Expressed by Their Concepts of Races," *Sociology and Social Research* (1937), 21:361-371.
44. ———: "Tracing Racial Attitudes through Adolescence," *Sociology and Social Research* (1938), 23:45-54.

Chapter XIV

CHILDREN'S INTERESTS

This chapter will deal only with selected aspects of the topic of children's interests, since practically all of the foregoing and succeeding chapters deal, in one way or another, with the activities children undertake on their own accord.

In an earlier section, we have noted how the young child seeks to exercise and put to use his growing abilities and powers. Just as "fish gotta swim, birds gotta fly," so the young child exercises his voice, his limbs, his mental machinery, and all his equipment as best he can. His early interests are a feature of the larger dynamic pattern of his growing capacities and powers.

Throughout the period of growth, a child's interests are closely related to his abilities. However, after the basic coördinations involved in the use of hands and legs have been established, and after language has become established and the child has acquired some ability to plan and to weigh alternatives, the scope of his abilities is so wide that the choices open to him become increasingly numerous and complex. As time passes, the channels through which he chooses to exercise his abilities are influenced to an increasing degree by opportunities that happen to come his way and by the conditioning effects of past experience.

Generally speaking, the younger the child is, the more will the things he *chooses* to do give an indication of what he *can* do or can *learn to like* to do. (There are exceptions to this, of course.) Thus, while still too immature to walk, the child does not show an interest in walking, and efforts to coach him or force his progress are of little avail. A further illustration is provided in a study in which it was found that two-year-old children showed little spontaneous interest in the process of dressing themselves, handling buttons, and so forth (58). In another study, it was found that children at this age made relatively little progress when adults endeavored to coach and train them in buttoning (39).

On the other hand, at the age of eight, a child's lack of an active interest in riding a bicycle gives little indication as to whether he can learn to ride one or how much he would enjoy the riding once he has had a chance to learn.

DISPARITY BETWEEN EXPRESSED AND POTENTIAL INTERESTS

There is much variation in the appeal of things children choose to do in their day-to-day lives. Thus, a young child may return again and again to his crayons or his work in a sand pile. An older child may plunge into music, practice on his own accord, and study the works of favorite composers through reading, radio programs, attendance at concerts, and so forth. Frequently, however, children are more desultory in their interests and simply float with the tide of play activities engaged in by children of their own age or fall in with projects engineered for them by parents and teachers. When this is the case, the interests that such children report or exhibit in their overt conduct at any given time may fail to reflect the fruitful enterprises that they might enjoy if given the proper opportunity.

Even the activities mentioned when children are questioned about their interests likewise are likely to vary in their appeal.

A method that frequently has been used to study the interests of children who are old enough to read has been to supply them with a long list of activities, with instructions to check those that they have recently undertaken on their own accord or that they like best. Such data are informative as far as they go but they may fail to tell the whole story. This is indicated by Osborne in a study of children in summer camps (77). In checking the items of an "interest-finder" when they first arrived in camp, the children gave a high vote to baseball and other conventional pastimes;

but these votes gave little indication of the interests that could be developed during the course of the camp season. For example, many of the children, when free to follow their own inclinations, developed an interest in sand play, even though they were of an age when children tend to regard such play as "baby stuff." From watching a resourceful camp counselor, they saw possibilities of architecture and design in sand play that were quite above the level of the mounds, holes, and furrows made by small children. Likewise, by virtue of the example set by an adult, many of them acquired a strong interest and much competence in handicrafts of various sorts, again in a manner that could not be predicted from their original testimony. The behavior of these children revealed, as often is shown in the conduct of both children and adults in everyday life, that one's interests of the moment, or one's neutral or negative attitude toward an activity, give little indication of the potential appeal of untried activities.

The role of learning. As indicated above, children's interests are influenced both by the factor of instruction and the factor of learning. The child's interests will be limited by his capacities, but at any level of maturity his capacities are such as to allow for a vast array of particular interests. Accordingly, the particular interests a child has are determined to that extent by the opportunity and incentive he has for learning to acquire an interest in this or that thing. His interests will be determined by the equipment and facilities that are available, the enterprises that are open to him, the opportunity he has to get a taste of this or that activity or experience. Moreover, the incentives that are provided—including the example of other children and adults—will play an important role. These factors in the environment not only have an important bearing on the specific interests acquired by individual children but also upon general trends in the interests of children at a given maturity level. In other words, interests are to a large degree *culturally* determined.

The bearing of learning on interests has not always been properly recognized by educators who maintain that what children are taught at school should be based on children's interests. Actually, as pointed out above, children's interests do not grow as separate entities that can be plucked like apples from a tree. Most interests are learned. Accordingly, an educational policy of utilizing children's interests should be aimed to help children to cultivate and to acquire the most rewarding interests and should not be bound by the particular interests that children happen to have acquired.

As suggested above, the resourcefulness of the adult who is in charge is an important factor in helping children get a taste of various undertakings. The influence of the teacher is illustrated by the fact that a subject which is most popular in one school may be the least popular in another.

LIMITING FACTORS IN CHILDREN'S INTERESTS

Although the interests of children beyond the early preschool years are decidedly influenced by environmental conditions, they are, of course, subject to many limiting factors. Foremost among these is the child's underlying ability. The normal child who acquires an interest in long division and adapts it to his own purposes at the age of eleven would probably be unable to do so at the age of six, regardless of his background or the ingenuity of his tutors. In like manner, while the bodily mechanics involved in catching and throwing a ball are still in process of development, a child will not acquire an interest in playing baseball as it is played by older children. Again, during early school years, he will not so readily learn and use the complex rules of play that an older child is able to grasp and enjoy.

Apart from limitations of maturity, there will be controlling factors within the child's own make-up. Thus, one child may have more of a knack for music or art than another, and his interests may be influenced accordingly. Similarly, native or acquired differences in motility, in sociability, or in a tendency to be cautious or afraid may express themselves in widely different patterns of interest at any given age. Countless factors other than sheer ability in the child's "personality" determine his style of life and the organization of his interests. One thing, among others, that can be noted is the fact that an individual's apparent interest in specific enterprises may be subordinate to more persuasive motives; thus one child may be moved by envy or feelings of inferiority to exert himself in an enterprise which another child light-heartedly undertakes as something that carries its own appeal.

INTEREST AS RELATED TO SKILL

Many projects which a child at first undertook because of pressure or in the service of more comprehensive motives become interesting in their own right as the youngster gains competence. His first venture in skating, for example, may be due less to a desire for skating than to a desire to follow the crowd. But once he has acquired some mastery of the skill, it is likely to acquire an appeal of its own, so that he engages in it even if the original pressures no longer prevail. At a later age, he may undertake algebra and geometry as jobs that must be done, then become increasingly absorbed as he gains competence, and perhaps go on to do his life's work in the field of applied mathematics. This phenomenon of interest rising with rising competence can be seen in countless situations in everyday life in the case of both children and adults. The reverse of this phenomenon also can frequently be seen. A child who is being pushed beyond his ability or who has got off to a bad start in reading, arithmetic, spelling, or any other project may acquire an increasing dislike for such a project as time goes on.

AREAS OF INTEREST

Children are likely to give a variety of answers concerning their interests, depending upon the way in which the question is phrased. If asked specifically to tell about his interests in radio programs, the child may reply at length; but the same child may make no mention of radio at all if asked in more general terms, "What are you interested in?" Accordingly information concerning children's interests should be interpreted in the light of the setting in which the information was obtained.

CHILDREN'S PREFERENCES IN GAMES

Surveys of favorite play activities reveal certain general age trends and certain differences between boys and girls, even though the order of popularity of different play activities varies somewhat according to locality, season, socio-economic background, and intelligence. Children's play activities parallel trends in motor, social, and mental development as described in earlier chapters.[1]

Findings regarding specific preferred activities and materials. Findings regarding children's play preferences have varied somewhat in different studies, largely, no doubt, because no two play situations duplicate each other or provide the same range of choice.[2]

Among the toys that appeared to be most popular with a group of nursery-school children studied by Bott were "pattern toys" (beads, puzzles, peg boards, tinker builders), although the younger children used these toys chiefly as materials to manipulate and carry. Next in order of preference were "raw materials" (beans, blocks, color cubes, a blackboard and chalk, spools), and these were followed by locomotor toys (trains, wagons, tricycles). According to the group results, small, mechanical toys were the least preferred, although everyday observation indicates that individual children show intense interest in such toys.

In a study of kindergarten and first- and second-grade school

---

[1] For an interesting account of changes with increased maturity in a child's activities and preoccupations, see Furfey (29).

[2] For representative studies of the play activities of preschool children, see Benjamin (4), Bott (7), Bridges (8), Farwell (26), Hostler (42), Hulson (43), Johnson (56), Manwell and Mengert (72), Shallit (89), Van Alstyne (102), and Vance and McCall (103).

children's choices of indoor play materials by Farwell (26), it was found that building materials, especially blocks, were most popular with boys, and painting and modeling materials ranked next; drawing and cardboard construction material were not very popular, and paper construction and sewing materials were least popular. Girls spent the most time with water-color painting and clay-modeling materials, and sewing came next in their preferences; they showed less preference for building blocks than boys. With added age there was a decline of interest in blocks. Girls' interest in paper construction material increased somewhat from the kindergarten to the second-grade levels. Girls were found to be somewhat more interested than boys in other human beings and in furniture, while boys showed more interest in vehicles than did girls. This tendency on the part of girls to show relatively more interest in persons, and, on the part of boys, to show relatively more interest in things, has been noted also in other studies and has been commented on in Chapter VI.

The reactions of over a hundred children to twenty-five play materials in nursery schools and kindergartens have been studied by Van Alstyne (102). From the ages of two to five years, a gradual change of interest in play materials was observed; but some materials, such as blocks, clay, and doll corners (including dolls, doll equipment, and furniture), appealed strongly to children of all age levels. Three-year-olds showed more interest than two-year-olds in wagons and books; four-year-olds showed an increased interest in balls, beads, small cars, and scissors; five-year-olds showed an increased interest in crayons. The youngest children tended to play more with active than with sedentary materials, but at the five-year level, there was about an equal interest in active and sedentary occupations. Boys showed more interest than girls in blocks, trucks, wagons, and small cars; girls showed more interest than boys in dolls, crayons, scissors, clay, colored cubes, and books. Boys tended to select materials that called for active play somewhat more than did girls. These differences between boys and girls were not, however, as prominent as the similarities between the play interests of the two groups.

Table XXXIV illustrates some of the play preferences of children aged seven to eleven; it is based upon reports by Minneapolis children who were asked to name their favorite activities. The table shows the five activities that were mentioned most frequently at each age level.

As noted later, results of different studies in this field vary somewhat as to the order of popularity of various games.[3] Such differences may be due not only to actual differences in game preference and opportunities at different levels but also to the season of the year when the study is made and the method of study that is employed. The data in Table XXXIV were obtained by asking children to name their favorite activities; they had no check list to serve as a reminder. A considerably larger number of activities would be listed if the children were supplied with a long check list. Again, as a study by Osborne shows (77), the use of the method of direct observation to watch and record just what children do in their play may reveal many things that the children themselves fail to mention in their own reports.

Without somewhat detailed description or supplementary observation, it is difficult to tell just what a child means when he reports a given item; thus, two children may say that they like hiking, but one may be absorbed in hiking for its own sake, while the other likes hiking only because it enables him to be in the company of others.[4]

When children check the number of activities in which they engage, there is a tendency toward a decrease with age in the number of different activities that are named (Lehman and Witty, 63, 65). Older children also tend to engage in more solitary

---

[3] For other representative studies of children's play interests see Lehman and Witty (63, 64, 65), Schwendener (88), Croswell (18), Osburn (78), Hurlock (45), Roberts (85), Sheldon (90), Lehman (62), Johnson (55), Ellis and Hall (25), and (84).

[4] For findings concerning factors that make for inconsistency and unreliability in children's reports, see a study by Fitzpatrick of children's science interests (27).

TABLE XXXIV

FAVORITE GAMES OF CHILDREN OF DIFFERENT AGES, IN ORDER OF PREFERENCE[5]

(A *t* means that the two games in question were tied for the same place.)

| Outdoor Games || Indoor Games ||
Boys	Girls	Boys	Girls
Age 7			
Hide and seek	Hide and seek	Hide the thimble	Hide the thimble
Washington poke	Tag	Checkers	Rig-a-jig-jig
Baseball	Stillwater	Cat and rat	*t* Checkers
t Tag	Stoop tag	*t* Brownies and fairies	*t* House
t Stoop tag	Jacks	*t* Farmer in the dell	*t* London Bridge
		t Pop goes the weasel	
		t Button button	
Age 8			
Hide and seek	Hide and seek	Checkers	Hide the thimble
Tag	Tag	Hide the thimble	Checkers
Baseball	Jacks	Dominoes	House
Washington poke	Washington poke	Brownies and fairies	School
Stillwater	Jump rope	Cat and rat	Dominoes
Age 9			
Tag	Tag	Checkers	Hide the thimble
Hide and seek	Jacks	Hide the thimble	Checkers
Baseball	Hide and seek	Dominoes	House
Washington poke	Washington poke	*t* Old maid	School
Stillwater	Jump rope	*t* Basketball	Jacks
Age 10			
Baseball	Jacks	Checkers	Hide the thimble
Tag	Tag	Hide the thimble	Checkers
Hide and seek	Hide and seek	Basketball	*t* Uncle Wiggly
t Football	Washington poke	*t* Volleyball	*t* Jacks
t Washington poke	Baseball	*t* Uncle Wiggly	*t* School
Age 11			
Baseball	Jacks	Checkers	Checkers
Football	Tag	Basketball	Jacks
Tag	Hide and seek	Cards	Hide the thimble
Hide and seek	Baseball	Hide the thimble	Cards
Run sheep run	Run sheep run	Volleyball	School

[5] Adapted from Foster, J.: "Play Activities of Children in the First Six Grades," *Child Development* (1930), I:248–254. Reproduced by permission.

games. One study (64) indicated that educationally retarded and accelerated children engage in about the same number of play activities as do children who are making normal progress in school, but there appeared to be a marked tendency among pupils who had low progress quotients to turn to social play activities, as compared with children who made normal school progress.

Among the games that are dropped with advancing age are many that consist to a large degree of gross muscular coördination (such as tag, dodging, pom-pom-pull-away, run sheep run). Many of the movements involved in these activities are incorporated into the more complex games that appear at later levels. Another form of play that diminishes sharply with increasing age is play of a make-believe sort, including playing cowboys, Indians, cops and robbers, house, and playing with dolls.

The decline with age is not limited, however, to make-believe games and relatively simple physical enterprises, for there is a high degree of mortality among games that require considerable skill and coördination. As children advance toward adolescence many of them tend to become spectators rather than participants. Much of the activity stressed in their own games and many of the activities stressed in directed play periods at school fall into disuse. One of the activities most widely emphasized in recreational and physical-education programs, for example, is baseball; yet, after the elementary years, large numbers of children seldom find occasion to play baseball.

It might be maintained that play activities and games have served their purpose if they are sufficient to the time and age level at which they flourish. But much of children's play is not influenced solely by their own spontaneous interests, for the environment in which their interests are learned is to a large extent controlled by adults. To the extent that this is true, the adult-controlled environment should encourage activities and interests that not only will be valuable during childhood but that also can be carried over into adult years.

An incidental problem in making practical arrangements for children's play arises in connection with the provision of play space and recreation centers. It appears that this problem is not solved simply by giving the children a large amount of space and equipment, for many children, while making use at times of available space, will also be interested in playing on the streets and congregating where adults are going about their affairs. An interesting indication of this is provided in a study by Reeves (81), based on a survey of street play in a large number of cities. It was found that a large proportion of the children (boys more than girls) were simply "hanging around" on the streets during their free time; on the average, less than half of the children who were in the streets were actively playing, and only a small proportion played organized games. The percentage of children on the streets bore little relationship to the amount of open play space available in the city.

The extent to which children frequent the streets when play space is available will vary, however, with the attractions afforded by the playgrounds. In some instances it has been observed that children are more likely to go to a playground if there is an able adult supervisor in charge. In the case of younger children, it has been found that children who for a long time have attended nursery school and kindergarten frequently become bored with repetitious play activities and look to adults for ideas and stimulation. As noted above, a child's ability to master and enjoy a performance may exceed his ability to invent or improvise a performance that will serve as a proper challenge to his powers. This is all the more reason for giving children the benefit of the stimulation that a resourceful adult can supply.

Tables XXXV, XXXVI, XXXVII, and XXXVIII present some of the results obtained in a series of studies in which children were asked, among other matters, to tell what they "liked best" and "disliked most" in and out of school and to identify one of the "happiest days" of their lives. The first two tables show certain

TABLE XXXV

RESPONSES OF PUBLIC SCHOOL CHILDREN WHEN ASKED TO IDENTIFY ONE OF THE "HAPPIEST DAYS" OF THEIR LIVES. THE VALUES SHOW PER CENT OF CHILDREN NAMING ONE OR MORE EXPERIENCES IN A GIVEN CATEGORY[6]

Grade	1 2 3	4 5 6	7 8 9	10 11 12
Age	6, 7, 8, 9	9, 10, 11, 12	12, 13, 14, 15	15, 16, 17, 18
No. of Children	544	452	372	230
I. Receipt or use of material objects, toys, food, clothes, money, shelter	9.6	9.1	4.6	3.9
II. Games, play, sports, recreation, holidays	42.3	40.3	16.1	12.6
1. Games, sports, gym, outdoor activities	8.5	5.7	5.9	6.5
2. Drive car, learn to drive	0	.4	.5	2.6
3. Spectator sports, going to stadium, pool hall, etc.	0	.7	.8	.4
4. Holidays, festive occasions	32.0	34.5	8.3	3.0
a. Birthday	5.1	9.7	3.0	.9
b. Christmas	19.9	20.6	4.6	.4
c. Easter	4.2	5.5	0	.4
d. Thanksgiving	0	.4	0	0
e. Fourth of July	.2	.7	0	0
f. Other	2.9	3.1	.8	1.7
5. Other	1.9	.4	.5	.4
III. Going to places of recreation, diversion, travel	10.7	11.9	9.9	3.9
1. Parks, beaches, picnics, circus, etc.	4.8	2.9	.5	1.7
2. Going to country, camp, resort	2.9	2.7	2.2	.4
3. Travel, trips to distant places	2.4	6.9	7.3	1.7
4. Going about in city, shopping	.6	0	0	0
IV. Going to movies	1.3	.2	.3	.9
V. Going to parties, dances, hangouts	4.4	2.9	2.7	3.0
VI. "Go and see," sights, zoo, etc.	1.7	1.5	.5	.9
VII. Gaining information, reading, etc.	.7	.2	0	0
VIII. Artistic activities	.9	2.2	.8	2.2
IX. Mechanical or domestic arts, hobbies	0	.2	.3	0
X. Self-improvement, vocational, moral, or religious happenings	3.3	2.4	3.8	12.6
1. Intellectual, educational	.2	1.1	1.1	5.7
2. Religious experiences	2.8	.9	1.3	3.5
3. Vocational, work experience	.2	.4	1.1	2.2
4. Other	.2	.2	.3	1.3
XI. Special successes (won contest)	.9	.7	2.2	2.6
XII. School: first day, admitted to certain school, privileges in school	5.7	4.2	16.9	8.7

TABLE XXXV (*Continued*)

Grade	1 2 3	4 5 6	7 8 9	10 11 12
Age	6, 7, 8, 9	9, 10, 11, 12	12, 13, 14, 15	15, 16, 17, 18
No. of Children	544	452	372	230
XIII. Relations with people, companionship	12.7	15.9	17.5	13.5
1. With parents, relatives	10.5	13.3	11.0	9.6
2. Return of parent or relative from war	1.9	7.7	7.8	7.8
3. Companionship with friends	2.2	1.1	1.1	.4
4. Boy-girl relations	0	1.1	4.0	3.0
5. Other	0	.2	0	0
XIV. Good fortune befalling relatives (recovery from illness)	.2	.4	1.9	.9
XV. General benefits, self (health)	0	.7	.8	1.7
XVI. Benefits for mankind (end of war)	.9	3.8	3.5	8.3
XVII. Living in certain city, place	1.3	2.4	2.4	3.5
XVIII. Miscellaneous	2.1	3.5	5.6	7.8
XIX. No response, unintelligible	7.4	5.3	17.7	33.0

[6] From an unpublished study of children's interests. Reproduced by permission of the Horace Mann-Lincoln Institute of School Experimentation, Teachers College, Columbia University. Since a child received a tally of one for one or several items in a given category or subcategory the cumulative total in the subcategories may exceed the value shown for the main category.

prominent age trends. A rather large percentage of junior and senior high-school pupils preferred not to describe a "happiest day" (when given the blank containing this and other questions they were pointedly told that they did not have to answer any item which they preferred to omit). It can be noted that as children become older they less often mention days on which they had an especially happy time at play, or holidays or festive occasions, and more often refer to happenings under such headings as "self-improvement," "special successes," and happenings such as the end of war.

In describing what they liked best at school, pupils of junior and senior high-school age less often mentioned academic subjects than did the younger children; on the other hand, the older pupils

TABLE XXXVI

RESPONSE OF PUPILS TO THE ITEM, "WHAT I LIKE BEST IN SCHOOL." THE VALUES REPRESENT PER CENT OF PUPILS GIVING ONE OR MORE ANSWERS IN EACH CATEGORY[7]

Grade	1, 2, 3	4, 5, 6	7, 8, 9	10, 11, 12	1–6 6–12		7–12 12–18	
Age	6, 7, 8, 9	9, 10, 11, 12	12, 13, 14, 15	15, 16, 17, 18	Boys	Girls	Boys	Girls
No. of Pupils	544	452 Boys and Girls	372 Boys and Girls	230	497	499	281	321
I. School plant and facilities	.6	0	.3	0	.6	0	.4	0
II. Games, sport, gym, recess, etc.	7.0	2.9	30.6	33.9	6.0	4.2	27.4	35.8
1. Games, play, playground sports	6.4	.7	2.4	7.4	4.0	3.6	6.8	2.2
2. Gym, physical education	.2	.9	27.2	26.1	.4	.6	19.6	33.0
3. Recess, lunch, "free time"	.7	1.3	1.1	1.7	1.6	.4	2.5	.3
4. Other	0	0	.3	0	0	0	.4	0
III. Parties, dances, etc.	0	1.3	1.1	.9	0	1.2	1.1	.9
IV. Academic subjects, information on various topics	77.8	85.3	57.3	45.7	78.5	84.4	49.5	55.8
1. Numbers, arithmetic, math.	27.2	33.0	26.1	13.5	30.2	29.4	25.6	17.4
2. Spelling	8.4	23.0	9.1	0	13.1	17.0	5.3	5.9
3. Reading, language arts, writing	41.7	29.2	18.0	19.1	33.2	38.9	11.0	24.9
4. Nature study, science	1.1	4.2	5.6	13.9	1.4	3.6	11.7	6.2
5. Health	0	.4	0	0	.4	0	0	0
6. Social studies, community, world affairs, peoples, industry, biography, conservation, etc.	1.1	10.6	6.4	8.7	5.0	5.8	7.1	7.5
7. Miscellaneous	.2	0	5.1	2.2	.2	0	1.1	6.5
V. Arts, fine and dramatic	12.5	10.4	9.4	12.2	10.9	12.2	10.3	10.6
1. Graphic and plastic	11.8	7.5	3.8	.4	9.8	9.8	2.8	2.2
2. Music	.7	3.1	5.1	12.2	1.0	2.6	7.1	8.4
3. Dramatics	0	.9	1.1	.9	.4	.4	1.1	.9
VI. Mechanical and industrial arts, shopwork, etc.	0	0	9.4	7.4	0	0	18.1	.3

TABLE XXXVI (Continued)

Grade	1,2,3	4,5,6	7,8,9	10,11,12	1–6		7–12	
Age	6,7,8,9	9,10,11,12	12,13,14,15	15,16,17,18	6–12		12–18	
No. of Pupils	544	452 Boys and Girls	372 Boys and Girls	230	497 Boys	499 Girls	281 Boys	321 Girls
VII. Domestic arts	0	0	3.8	4.8	0	0	.4	7.5
VIII. Personal self-improvement, vocational, self-understanding:								
1. Intellectual, improve mind	0	0	0	4.3	0	0	.4	2.8
2. Knowledge of human nature	0	0	0	1.7	0	0	.7	.6
3. Religious, moral improvement	.4	.4	.3	0	.2	.6	0	.3
4. "Commercial," typing, etc	0	0	0	3.9	0	0	.4	2.5
IX. Special successes, awards	0	0	0	.9	0	0	.4	.3
X. Self-government, forums, discussion	0	1.3	.8	.9	.6	.6	.7	.9
XI. Monitor duties	.6	.2	0	0	.2	.6	0	0
XII. School privileges, requirements, discipline, management	.9	.2	1.1	.9	.4	.8	1.1	.9
XIII. People	2.4	6.0	3.5	8.3	3.0	5.0	3.2	7.2
1. Pupils (other than 3)	.9	1.1	1.3	8.3	1.0	1.0	1.8	5.9
2. Teachers	1.5	5.1	1.1	0	2.0	4.2	.4	.9
3. Boy-girl friendships	0	.4	1.1	1.3	0	0	1.1	.3
XIV. Miscellaneous	0	.4	.8	1.3	.2	.2	1.1	.9
XV. No response, unintelligible	1.3	2.6	3.0	2.2	2.4	1.4	3.9	1.6

[7] From an unpublished study of children's interests. Reproduced by permission of the Horace Mann-Lincoln Institute of School Experimentation, Teachers College, Columbia University. Since a child received a tally of one for one or several items in a given category or subcategory the cumulative total in the subcategories may exceed the value shown for the main category. This table *illustrates* children's interests at school, but it is not presented as *typical*. See wide variations between groups in Table XXXVIII.

489

more often mentioned sports, industrial and mechanical arts, intellectual self-improvement, vocational preparation and relations with other persons of their own age. The fact that children's responses are determined to a large degree by what the school offers is shown in Table XXXVIII. School *D* was equipped with a variety of gymnasium facilities, a swimming pool, good facilities in the fine arts, and opportunities for shop work. It is no doubt largely by virtue of this fact that the children in this school mentioned activities so provided relatively more often, and academic subjects relatively less often, than did children in some of the other schools. The influence of unfavorable neighborhood conditions is reflected in the responses of children in School *C,* which was situated in a community in which people lived in crowded circumstances and in which there was a good deal of violence and crime. The children in this school, it can be noted, were much more preoccupied with *people* and characteristics of people in naming what they disliked most than were children in the other schools. (This preoccupation with "bad" people was even more pronounced in reports concerning what the youngsters disliked most in their lives outside of school.)

READING INTERESTS

The beginnings of reading interests appear in the young child's manipulation of books and pictures, his interest in looking at and identifying pictures, and his desire for storytelling and being read to. Many children are interested in being "read to" even before they can understand the words—apparently the flow of sound, the changes in facial expression and vocal inflection, attract their attention (and the "reading" is no doubt all the more attractive if they are cozily nestled in the lap of the one who reads). Children may thus show an interest in one feature or another of the total reading situation before the age of two years and even before they are a year old. Reading interests emerge out of experiences that go back to early infancy.

CHILDREN'S INTERESTS

Table XXXVII

PER CENT OF CHILDREN GIVING RESPONSES IN VARIOUS LIMITED SELECTED CATEGORIES, WHEN REPORTING WHAT THEY LIKED BEST AND WHAT THEY DISLIKED MOST AT SCHOOL[8]

	Like Best	Dislike Most	Like Best	Dislike Most
Grade	1–6	1–6	7–12	7–12
Age	6–12	6–12	12–18	12–18
No. of Pupils	996	996	602	602
Games, sport, gym, recess, etc.	5.1	5.4	31.9	2.8
Academic information, subjects	81.4	42.7	52.8	46.2
Art	11.5	4.8	10.5	3.2
Mechanics, shop, domestic art	0	.2	12.8	3.7
People	4.0	4.6	5.3	15.1
Pupils	1.0	4.1	4.0	7.0
Teachers	3.1	.2	.7	8.0
Other	0	.2	.7	.8

Table XXXVIII

PER CENT OF CHILDREN IN GRADES 4, 5, AND 6 IN VARIOUS SCHOOLS GIVING RESPONSES IN SELECTED, LIMITED CATEGORIES WHEN INDICATING WHAT THEY LIKED BEST AND DISLIKED MOST IN SCHOOL[9]

	Like Best				Dislike Most			
School*	A	B	C	D	A	B	C	D
No. of Pupils	176	368	200	176	176	368	200	176
Games, play, sports, recess, gym	3.5	2.6	19.0	51.1	1.4	6.8	4.5	2.3
Academic information	79.0	89.0	50.0	34.1	60.1	48.9	39.0	41.5
Art	10.5	10.4	15.0	21.0	6.3	4.9	5.0	11.9
Mechanics, shop, domestic arts	0	0	1.0	8.0	0	0	1.0	1.7
People	7.0	5.5	6.0	4.5	2.1	8.7	23.0	8.5
Pupils	.7	1.3	0	1.7	1.4	7.8	14.5	4.0
Teachers	7.0	4.2	6.0	2.8	0	.3	9.0	6.2
Other	0	0	0	0	.7	.6	0	0
Unintelligible, no response	3.5	2.3	3.5	2.3	23.8	27.8	15.5	15.9

* A and B are public schools located, respectively, in a middle-western and a southern city; C is a public school located in one of the most congested and unfavorable neighborhoods in New York City; D is a private school in New York City.

[8] Adapted from an unpublished study. Reproduced by permission of the Horace Mann-Lincoln Institute of School Experimentation, Teachers College, Columbia University.

[9] Adapted from an unpublished study. Reproduced by permission of the Horace Mann-Lincoln Institute of School Experimentation, Teachers College, Columbia University.

When the child himself has learned to read, his reading activities and interests show certain age trends, both in the amount read and in the range of topics read. There are large individual differences within each age level, however, and frequently it is difficult to tell to what extent children's interests have been influenced by custom and what happens to be available.[10] Among trends that have been noted are the following:

Prior to the age of five many children show a fondness for simple factual stories about happenings in the everyday environment, animal stories, nature stories, rhymes and jingles, and stories illustrated by pictures that can be discussed with an older person.[11] Many children, as early as the age of three or four, are strongly attracted to "comic" books and ask to have them read to them even when it is obvious that they cannot understand the words or have a clear conception of the flow of the action.

At the school-age level, there is an increase with age in the percentage of children who read books of their own volition. A review of the literature on this subject by Gray (34) indicates that this trend continues into the junior high-school level, when divergent trends appear. In some schools, children continue to read widely, while in other groups there is a slackening in amount of independent reading.

The reading interests of individual children during the primary- and elementary-school period differ widely, depending in part on such factors as differences in intelligence, available materials, and the stimulus supplied by the child's associates and his elders. That interests at the primary-school level are not highly specialized is shown in a study by Dunn (22). The children liked surprise and plot; stories about animals had a good deal of appeal to boys, and

---

[10] The literature dealing with children's reading interests is huge. For representative reports of original findings or reviews of findings see Gates (30), Gray (32, 33, 34), Terman and Lima (95), Dunn (22), Washburne and Vogel (105), and Hunnicutt (44).

[11] Note how such interests in stories parallel characteristics of the children's own imaginative play. As described in Chapter XII, the make-believe themes of preschool children deal to a large extent with household affairs and other everyday activities.

stories about children and familiar experiences had considerable appeal to girls. There was no evidence that children at the primary-school level were in an "age of pure fancy" or that legends and folk tales, as a class, were the most interesting materials.

With increasing age comes an increased interest in robust adventure, especially in the case of the boys. Realistic stories about animals likewise have much appeal. During the elementary years, girls tend to show more interest than do boys in stories of home life and domestic happenings, and girls show an earlier interest than do boys in romance. From a study of children in the fourth, fifth, and sixth grades, Lazar (60) found that the following elements had considerable appeal: adventure, action, excitement, thrills, mystery, realism, suspense, child life, humor-mischief, animal life and nature, sportsmanship and bravery, sports, airplanes, and other inventions. Toward the junior high-school and the high-school age, an increasing number of children show an interest in history, biography, and in books and magazine articles dealing with the social and natural environment. Girls show more interest in sentimental fiction of the adult type than do boys, but both boys and girls are likely cheerfully to digest fictional materials that distort realities and deal with impossible situations. In addition to such trends, there is an increased taste for humor, and there is likely also to be some reading in connection with hobbies, how to make things, and the like (Gray, 32).

In a study by R. L. Thorndike (100) children's reading interests were investigated by means of a list of fictitious (but very plausible) titles, accompanied by brief annotations such as:

Bowser the Hound. Bowser went hunting rabbits with his master. What happened when they met Jimmy Skunk instead?
King of the Gangs. How Slick McCoy made himself king of the underworld. A story of gangs and gang warfare.
The Ghost Ranger of Lonesome Valley. Why were cattle always disappearing from Lonesome Valley? Who was the shadow that carried them away?

Me and My Job. What different jobs are really like. What to think about in picking out your job.
Cupid Takes a Holiday. Joan and Fred had always been good friends —just good friends and nothing more. Then Fred went away to college. When he came back he found a different Joan.
History of the Lutheran Church. The story of the Lutheran church, from the time of its beginning up to the present.

The list included both fiction and nonfiction with topics such as adventure and mystery involving boys and girls, animals and fairies, romance, sports and hobbies, self-improvement, history, travel, and so forth. Boys and girls showed more differences in their preferences than did old or young or bright or dull children of the same sex (within the age range from 10 to 15 years). There were, however, differences between bright and dull children. The brighter children (with a median I.Q. of about 125) had interests resembling those of mentally slower children (median I.Q. about 92) who were two or three years older. This greater maturity of the reading interests of the brighter children appeared not simply (or even predominantly) in connection with scholarly or bookish topics but in connection with other topics, such as mystery and adventure. Within the same sex there were some titles that differed widely in popularity at different age levels, but there were many titles that appealed both to the youngest and the oldest children in the study. Of the ten titles that had the highest appeal for average ten-year-old boys, five were still among the top ten titles at the fifteen-year-old level.

Interest in fact and fancy. In their reading, children are both romanticists and realists. They will read fictional books that deal with situations that are not only impossible but absurd, but the same children may also read solid discussions or travel, biography, descriptions of other lands and people, and similar topics. Although children are thus quite catholic in their tastes, they are likely to exercise some critical powers in going from one kind of reading matter to another. If they have sought out a book that deals with actual happenings, they like to have a truthful and informative account, although they may prefer treatment of the dramatic and unusual to a systematic treatment of all phases of a topic.

That children prefer straightforward, factual material in books dealing with science and that adults may be quite mistaken in their judgment as to the probable appeal of a book has been shown by Williams (107). Among other things, children in his study were not much influenced by the color and design of a book's cover or by general features of format. The content is what interested them most and they wanted informative content—new information, explanations of how animals live and how things work—rather than rhapsodies about the glories of nature and the wonders of the subject under treatment. Many objected strenuously to devices that some authors inject to appeal to children, such as personification, glowing introductory essays that reflect the author's enthusiasm but tell no facts, or the device of having an indulgent adult enter into conversation with a child as a means of injecting both a human and an informative quality. Also it was noted that children would read books representing a wide range of "reading difficulty." If interested in the topic, a reader of eighth-grade ability would dip into a book of fourth-grade difficulty, and a poorer reader would delve into books that were above his reading level as measured by an achievement test. The important consideration was the child's interest in the subject and his ability to get the general flow of ideas from the context and the pictures, even if he failed to understand a large number of individual words.

In this study, adults were also asked to rate the books that the children had used and commented on. First, they were told to rate them in terms of their own reactions, on a scale ranging from most liked to least liked; then they were asked to rate the same books in terms of their judgment as to how well the *children* would like them. The interesting finding was that there was more correspondence between *adults' preferences* and children's preferences than between *adults' judgment* as to what the children would like and what the children actually did like. Broadly speaking, it would appear that one good guide for adults to follow in selecting books in the field of science for a child, assuming that they are choosing from a general area that appeals to the child and that they show some regard for his reading ability, is to select books which they themselves find most interesting. On the other hand, a study by Rankin (80) of children's interest in fiction shows that some children's books selected by adult reviewing committees as being especially outstanding have been not at all popular with children. Among factors that seem to lower a book's popularity are: a large proportion of descriptive matter, whimsy, and scenes and customs foreign to a child's background. The children reported that their choices of books for leisure-time reading were influenced more by librarians than by teachers but, far more, by recommendations of other children.

RADIO INTERESTS

The average child of school age spends many hours a week in listening to radio programs. In some studies, the estimate runs as high as two or more hours per day, but the time varies with different children and in different localities.[12] In one study it was found that children of high intelligence in a private school spent only about half as much time at the radio as did less privileged children in the same city (47).

In the case of certain types of radio programs, there are definite age trends in children's interests and differences between the preferences of boys and girls. Many programs, however, have a high degree of popularity with children differing in age, sex, socioeconomic status, and intelligence.

Table XXXIX briefly identifies the twenty programs that were

---

[12] For reports of findings in this field and reviews of other studies, see Tyler (101), Jersild (51), Clark (15, 16), Lewis (66), Eisenberg (24), Lazarsfeld and Stanton (61), and Herzog (38).

TABLE XXXIX

THE TWENTY RADIO PROGRAMS REPORTED AS "LISTENED TO" MOST FREQUENTLY BY CHILDREN IN THE METROPOLITAN NEW YORK AREA IN 1935, 1936, AND 1937, INCLUDING COMPARISONS BETWEEN BOYS AND GIRLS, AND, IN THE 1935 RESULTS, COMPARISONS BETWEEN CHILDREN AGED 6 TO 8 AND 10 TO 12 YEARS[13]

(Values show where each program ranked in frequency of mention as compared with all other programs that were named. Programs designed primarily for children (juvenile) and for adults are so labelled. Absence of a value for a program at a given season means either that the program was not on the air at the time or that it received a rank below 60.)

Radio Programs	Fall 1935 Boys and Girls 6 to 14 years	Fall 1935 Boys and Girls 6 to 8 years	Fall 1936 Boys and Girls 10 to 12 years	Fall 1936 All Boys	Fall 1936 All Girls	Spring 1936 All Boys and Girls, 6 to 14 years	Spring 1936 All Boys	Spring 1936 All Girls	Fall 1937 Boys and Girls in Grades IV to VI	Fall 1937 All Boys	Fall 1937 All Girls
Number of Children	1,344	355	649	726	618	1,059	497	562	715	341	374
Program Identification:											
Adventures of a boy and company, cowboy setting, but varied locale; considerable humor and horse-play (juvenile)	1	3	1	2	1	4	$3\frac{1}{2}$	4	4	4	6
Interplanetary adventures in a future setting; rocket ships; etc. (juvenile)	2	2	2	1	3	3	5	3	28	25	29
Comic-strip detective hero (juvenile)	3	1	3	3	2	2	1	2	2	3	2
"Western" drama of an earlier generation (juvenile)	4	9	4	4	$6\frac{1}{2}$	5	$3\frac{1}{2}$	5	3	2	$3\frac{1}{2}$
Adult comedian; songs; jokes; variety (adult)	5	$7\frac{1}{2}$	5	$5\frac{1}{2}$	$4\frac{1}{2}$	1	2	1	1	1	1
Melodramatic adventures of a high-school boy and company (juvenile)	6	$7\frac{1}{2}$	6	$5\frac{1}{2}$	$8\frac{1}{2}$	9	7	13	10	7	15
Adult comedian; relatively subtle humor, variety (adult)	7	16	10	7	$6\frac{1}{2}$	14	$15\frac{1}{2}$	16	5	6	$3\frac{1}{2}$
Melodramatic adventures of a girl and company (juvenile)	8	5	8	13	$4\frac{1}{2}$	12	21	10	12	19	9

497

TABLE XXXIX (*Continued*)

Radio Programs	Fall 1936					Spring 1936				Fall 1937		
	Boys and Girls 6 to 14 years	Boys and Girls 6 to 8 years	Boys and Girls 10 to 12 years	All Boys	All Girls	All Boys and Girls, 6 to 14 years	All Boys	All Girls	Boys and Girls in Grades IV to VI	All Boys	All Girls
Number of Children	1,344	355	649	726	618	1,059	497	562	715	341	374
Mystery and crime (adult)	9	14	7	10	8½	16	17	18	30	29	31½
Comic-opera strong man, with music; phantasy in contemporary setting (juvenile and adult)	10	6	11	10	11	23	22	23	7	5	13
Homely drama of two black-faced characters (adult)	11	11	12	12	11	20	19	19	19	18	22½
Melodramatic adventure and crook-thwarting by a juvenile character and company (juvenile)	12	18	9	10	15	25	23	30	59	47½	72
Adult male and female comedy team (adult)	13	12	13	15	11	10	12	7	8	12	8
Adventures of a boy and company in prehistoric times (juvenile)	14	17	14	8	28	55	38	66	……	……	……
Drama of two women characters and company (adult)	15	13½	16	19	13	17	27	15	……	……	……
Amateur hour (adult)	16	23½	17	16	16	13	15½	14	17	21	14
Crime and crime detection (adult)	17	32	15	14	21½	29	24	36½	……	……	……
Chitchat, story, and song for young folk (juvenile)	18	4	25	17	17	24	28	21	24	26½	18½
Everyday and unusual adventures of two everyday children, and company (juvenile)	19	19	18	19	18½	8	11	8	11	16½	7
Amateur hour of juvenile performers (juvenile)	20	15	19	29	14	27	43	17	21	41	12

498

TABLE XXXIX (*Continued*)

Radio Programs	Fall 1936						Spring 1936			Fall 1937		
	Boys and Girls 6 to 14 years	Boys and Girls 6 to 8 years	Boys and Girls 10 to 12 years	All Boys	All Girls		All Boys and Girls, 6 to 14 years	All Boys	All Girls	Boys and Girls in Grades IV to VI	All Boys	All Girls
Number of Children	1,344	355	649	726	618		1,059	497	562	715	341	374
Other programs among the top 20 in the spring of 1936:												
Adventure involving mystery, magic, and villainy (juvenile)	23	21	24	22	23		6	6	6	47	47½	43½
Adventures of two boys and company (juvenile)	44	20	47½	41½	37½		7	8	9	...	...	...
Comedian and cast (adult)	24	32	23	21	25		11	9	12	6	8½	5
Weekly dramatized stage or screen play (adult)	22	32	20	35	18½		15	23	11	16	23	10
Canadian Mounted Police adventures (juvenile)	...	25½	47½	33½	45		18	10	29	14	10	22½
Dramatizations (adult)	39						19	13	22	20	16½	27½
Other programs among the top 20 in the fall of 1937:												
Adult funny man (juvenile and adult)	...	...	...	...	...		...	...	...	9	13	11
Cowboy and Western serial (juvenile)	21	27½	21	16	30½		42	30	61½	13	8½	18½
Crime and detective (juvenile)	...	...	...	...	...		...	...	...	15	11	17
News dramatization (juvenile)	...	...	...	...	...		21	14	25	18	14	25½

[13] From Jersild, A. T.: *Children's Interests in Radio Programs*, unpublished (New York: Teachers College, Columbia University, 1937). Reproduced by permission.

mentioned most often when children reported the programs they "listened to" during three successive surveys. In these surveys, the children were simply asked to write down or report orally the programs they had listened to recently; they were not aided by check lists or other forms of prompting. In the same surveys, each child also named the three programs he liked best. The standing of the program was about the same, whether based on a count of the number of children who listened to it or of the number who named it as liked best, but there were some notable exceptions. A popular program that recently has been put on the air is likely to have a higher rank when in the "liked best" count. An "old" program is likely to be recalled and mentioned by a large number of children, even if they were not especially fond of it.

As indicated in Table XXXIX there were several programs that ranked among the top twenty in all three of the successive surveys. No survey of this sort is definitive, however, for the popularity of programs varies from time to time and successive surveys will show new crops of popular programs. Popularity depends also upon the particular programs that happen to be available in a given locality, the extent to which two or more popular programs compete with each other at the same period, shifts in the radio schedule, and other similar factors. Surveys more recent than those represented in Table XXXIX show a larger proportion of adult programs among children's favorites, partly because there has been some decline in the number of "blood-and-thunder" children's programs in recent years.

Sex and age differences. Among programs that decline in popularity as children grow older are dramatizations of fairy tales and other programs of a frankly make-believe sort, programs involving chitchat and brief stories and songs, and programs dealing with the antics of everyday children (as distinguished from melodramatic juvenile adventures). Certain adult comedians who supply a relatively broad type of humor, supplemented by "funny" noises or slapstick, have a strong appeal at all age levels (partly, perhaps, because many adults select such programs, and children thus get a taste), while comedians whose humor is of a more subtle variety are likely to rank relatively lower at the early age levels and then gain in popularity with advancing age. In the survey represented in Table XXXIX one such program moved from no mention at six years to a rank of fifteen at ten years and a rank of seven at fourteen years. Dance music and romantic serials gain an increasing audience in the teens, and there is a rising trend with age in the popularity of sports broadcasts, quiz programs, general news broadcasts, programs dealing with hobbies, historical dramas and other "quality" dramas. A program that deals realistically with the activities and foibles of genuine children is likely to appeal more to younger children and to adults than to children in the intermediate range.

In general, boys show a higher preference than do girls for programs involving crime and violence, but some such programs also stand high in favor with girls. Girls show a higher preference than do boys for domestic drama, "crooners" and movie stars, and for programs in which a girl or a child character plays a prominent role. Both boys and girls, however, tend to prefer a cast of characters that includes older children or adults rather than child characters only.

Although trends such as the foregoing may be noted, the appeal of a program of any type depends to a large extent on the ingenuity of the script writer and the skill that goes into the production of the show. It has amply been shown that a fairly well-produced melodramatic serial of the cops-and-robbers or blood-and-thunder variety, involving impossible situations and a good deal of distortion of realities, can attract a large child audience. It requires more ingenuity and skill to win a similar audience for a more authentic type of dramatization.

Surveys of children's interests at any given time do not reveal to what extent these interests have been determined by their past radio fare and by the taste of older children and adults, or to what extent such interests could be modified if radio offerings were substantially changed. In the field of radio programs, as in other areas, children's interests are, of course, influenced to a large extent by learning and past experience. Some program materials are, to be sure, more likely to gain an immediate hearing than are other materials (e.g., a melodramatic crime or detective dramatization is more likely, other things being equal, to win a hearing than an authentic dramatization of actual crime). However, once a child has had a taste of the more authentic treatment, he may prefer it. One difficulty is that a program which embodies a certain amount of truth and integrity and which, as judged by adults, is of high quality from a literary and dramatic standpoint, must compete for a hearing with melodramas which children already have formed the habit of listening to, and therefore it does not have much chance to get a hearing. In other words, there may be interests that go by default. Interests such as those revealed in a survey of children's program preferences are culturally determined and as such do not reflect the extent to which it might be possible to cultivate other interests.

Some children, when they first begin to listen to the radio, tend to regard the action and the characters as real (11). This is not a universal phenomenon, however. A child may regard the characters in one program as real after he has come to regard characters in other programs as fictional.

The effect that radio programs may have on children's fears and dreams has been touched upon in earlier chapters. Many children are frightened while listening to an exciting program and many report that programs have influenced their fears and dreams. When such fears are reported, they sometimes are related quite specifically to radio programs; but sometimes the radio may have had only an incidental influence on fears and anxieties that spring primarily from other factors in the child's life. When children are asked specifically whether they have ever been frightened by a radio program, a large percentage will answer that they have. When they are asked simply to tell about their fears and unpleasant dreams, radio programs likewise will be mentioned, but by a smaller number of children, and then only as one of a large number of influences that contribute to fear. But it often seems to happen that a child who is afraid and who has a disturbed sleep would not have been troubled on that particular night if he had not listened to the radio.

Adult reactions to children's radio interests. In many homes there is a discrepancy between the radio tastes of children and their parents, just as there sometimes was a clash between children and parents of an earlier generation on the subject of the dime novel. The programs children like best are the ones some parents dislike most (14, 24, 67). When children in large numbers prefer programs that adults deplore, there may be right and wrong on both sides. Adults are prone to judge a program in terms of their own adult point of view. A program that seems trashy to an erudite adult may still be suitable for a child, just as a child's pants may fit him well even though they don't fit his father. There is another aspect to this, however: the fact that a child is interested in a program does not necessarily mean that the program fills a "need." Moreover, the critical adult has grounds for complaint, not against the child but against the broadcaster, if a children's program simply takes advantage of a child's lack of knowledge and discrimination and plies him with distortions and humbug, when a more competent script writer and dramatist, working in the same field, might meet the child on his own ground with a more genuine treatment.

Practical considerations. In seeking vicarious excitement and thrills, children are not, of course, showing a form of behavior that has been brought about by the radio. They seek similar thrills in much of their reading, and for generations before the radio was born, children have found vicarious adventure in their own make-believe. Frequently adults, in judging a program they themselves do not happen to enjoy, will deplore its excitement and suspense, even though the child can take it in his stride and show no harmful effects. In this matter, again, the program maker has an obvious responsibility, for the fact that children enjoy exciting happenings does not justify him in supplying materials that are overexciting to many children. As a practical matter, this problem of overexcitement seldom comes alone, for if a program depends for its effectiveness on terrifying suspense, it usually has other objectionable features. The better the underlying quality of the program, the more ably its characters are drawn, and the more competently it deals with genuine dramatic situations, the less need there is for trying to inflame the child in order to hold his interest.

The underlying quality of the radio program likewise is the important consideration in dealing with another feature on which parents and children sometimes are at odds, namely, children's interest in stories that involve conflict. An easy way to meet this interest is to ply the child with radio programs dealing with crime. Although a child does not himself acquire a motive for committing crime simply from hearing about crime, it is difficult to justify a children's serial that is built primarily upon crime, especially in view of the fact that the standard "crime" program is rather false. It is likely to dramatize exciting fragments of the criminal's career and heroic highlights of the detective's operations, omitting the very unheroic and unappetizing features of the life of the criminal.

More pressing, often, than the problem as to whether the child should listen to this or that program is the problem as to how much of a child's time the radio should take, regardless of what he may be listening to. When a child tunes in to the extent of two or more hours per day, he is giving more than a third as much time to the radio as he spends at school. (Many children, to be sure, do other things while the radio is operating.)

Actually it appears that much of the time children listen to the radio as a matter of second choice, for lack of better things to do. When spring comes with long hours of daylight a great many children who have been listening upward to two hours or more now leave the radio to spend as much time as possible in outdoor play. Other interests likewise can cut down the time a child devotes to the radio. Even when other competing interests are lacking, it appears that children are not nearly as passionately devoted to this form of entertainment as might be indicated by the amount of time they devote to it. In a companion to the study represented in Table XXXIX it was found that scarcely any of the children named radio listening when describing what they "liked best" to do outside of school, yet most of them spent a lot of time at the radio.

Even more pressing at times than the question of the total amount of time to be spent at the radio is the problem of when the listening should take place without causing too much inconvenience to other members of the household, disrupting the schedule of meals, bedtime, and other daily routines. Frequently the radio causes friction and irritation on this score. The practical fact, of course, is that radio, like all other modern conveniences and appliances, complicates the everyday management of children (and adults) and to manage its use requires some regimentation and a certain amount of courtesy and mutual give-and-take, just as do other features of modern life.[14]

MOTION-PICTURE INTERESTS

Motion pictures occupy an important place in the leisure-time activities of children, but largely for practical reasons they usually take less of a child's time than do radio programs. In a study by Dale (20), conducted in Ohio, it was found that at the age range

---

[14] For a discussion of some of the practical aspects of the management of radio programs, see Gruenberg (36), Washburne, Milligan, Gruenberg, *et al.* (104), Jersild (48, 51), and Rowland and associates (86, 87). Educational uses have been discussed by Tyler (101), and Woelfel (109, 110). An excellent bibliography on educational uses has been published by Cooper (17).

from five to eight years the average child attended the movies about once every two weeks, but about twenty per cent of the children in this age range attended the movies two or more times per week.

Children's movie interests roughly parallel their reading and radio interests, as described earlier in this section, although there are exceptions.[15] For example, "comedy" seems to figure more in movie than in reading interests (unless comic strips are so classed). Reports of movie interests at any given time must be taken with a good deal of reservation, just as is the case with radio programs, for the choices depend to a large degree upon what happens to have been available recently and upon the tastes that have been cultivated by the kind of fare offered in the past. A child's vote for a bizarre "Western thriller" does not mean, for example, that he might not be quite interested in a more authentic film. In a study by Dale (19), several thousand children were asked to name books or stories they would like to see in motion pictures. A large proportion of the votes were cast for books judged by adults to be acceptable or of high quality as literature for children, as distinguished from books that most teachers or librarians would rate as trash. In a study of a limited number of children, Blumer (6) noted some changes with age: at the fourth-grade level, children tended to be quite frank in expressing their enthusiasm for certain serial "thrillers"; at the sixth-grade level, children admitted interest but showed awareness of "childish" characteristics in flimsy films; and at the eighth-grade level, there were expressions of frank disapproval.

As in the case of radio programs, a large proportion of films that children see are not specifically designed for children and many are not highly regarded by educated adult critics. A report by Holy (41) illustrates this. Of the movies seen by children in

---

[15] For accounts of children's movie interests, see Holy (41), Jones and Conrad (57), and Miller (75).

one city, thirty per cent were judged by a reviewing committee to be of poor quality, twenty-nine per cent to be of good quality, and the rest to be of average quality. To be sure, in judging what is proper fare for children, educated adults will be influenced to a large extent by their own tastes, and they may tend to disparage harmless interests that they themselves have outgrown. In the case of motion pictures, as in the case of radio programs, there are, however, broad distinctions—on which most reasonable persons would agree—between productions that appeal to certain interests in an artistic and authentic way and productions that take advantage of a child's ignorance and credulity.

A study by Holaday and Stoddard (40) deals with the impressions retained by children after seeing a motion picture. Objective tests were administered to children the day after they had attended a given movie, and such tests were administered at later periods to matched groups who also had seen the movies involved in the experiment. Children in Grades II and III answered an average of fifty-two per cent of the items correctly; the corresponding percentages for Grades V and VI were sixty-six and fifty-six, and for Grades IX and X, eighty-one and sixty-five. Apart from leaving impressions concerning the plot and action, a movie may influence children's attitudes (79) and ideas concerning customs, dress, manners, and morals (5).

The influence that motion pictures may have on children's fears and dreams has been discussed in an earlier chapter. When children are asked outright whether they ever have been frightened by what they hear or see, most of them will answer in the affirmative (23). When asked to tell about their fears, without the use of any leading questions, fears attributed to the movies will constitute only a relatively small, though still quite impressive, proportion of all the fears described. At times, a motion picture, like a radio program, may so excite a child who might otherwise have had a calm night that he may be frightened and suffer from disturbed sleep. In other instances, the motion picture may precipitate and give an image and a focus to fears that arise out of other tensions and disturbances in the child's life.[16]

Studies of the educational uses of motion pictures indicate that under proper management such pictures may help to inject vitality and interest into a topic, stimulate children's imagination, help them to grasp concepts concerning abstract or remote conditions, and vastly extend the range of their observations.[17]

COMICS

Most children from an early age are interested in "comics" in the form of comic strips, "comic" books, and serial "comic" magazines. Studies by Witty (108) show the wide scope and variety of children's interests.

A study by R. L. Thorndike (99) indicates that the volume of reading matter represented by twelve monthly issues of a popular comic serial was equivalent approximately to the contents of two standard-sized fourth-grade readers. In other words, while the pictures no doubt provide the lure, the comic book provides the child with a good deal of opportunity to obtain practice in reading. (Just how much of the printed matter the average child at various age levels actually reads was not ascertained in this study.) According to reports given by children in a study by Strang (94), comics sometimes serve as a transition stimulus to more mature reading.

In an investigation of children's reading of comic books in the primary grades, Young (111) found that only eleven per cent of the children in Grade I, thirty-three per cent in Grade II, and

---

[16] Some of the studies mentioned above belong to a series conducted under the auspices of the Payne Fund. Other studies in this series are listed in the bibliography (6, 12, 83). The results in these studies have been discussed by Adler (1). For a succinct, practical discussion of the topic of motion pictures see Stoddard (93).

[17] For a review of studies dealing with educational uses of motion pictures and many practical suggestions as to selection and procedure, see Dale, Dunn, Hoban, and Schneider (21).

sixty-seven per cent in Grade III read the comics to themselves; the others reported that they either merely followed the pictures or had someone read the comics to them.

In an investigation by Meigs (74) of teachers' reactions to comic books, fifty-eight per cent of a group of 120 teachers explained that when they last had looked at a comic book they did so in order to keep up with children's interests or to evaluate the educational possibilities of the comics. Only twenty-three of the 120 said they had never read a comic book.

It is obvious from the fact that most children (and a large proportion of adults) are drawn to the comics that there is something in the comic strip format that has a strong appeal. This fact should be taken into account for practical purposes. The comics have been used by some workers in connection with the teaching of reading and the format has been put to use for various other educational purposes. No doubt even more use will be made of it in the future. A number of ways in which comics can be used in the classroom have been described by Sones (92).

Many of the questions with respect to standards, good taste, and possible good or harmful effects that arise in connection with the comics are much the same as the questions that arise in connection with radio programs and the movies, and these will not be further elaborated at this point.

One additional point may be mentioned, however. Through these media of entertainment the child (and the adult) is permitted vicariously to do many things he would not be allowed to do in fact. While parents and teachers are trying to teach the child to be kind, these media sometimes condone cruelty (as when the hero is allowed to knock down his helpless victim or the hapless wolf in the animated cartoon is systematically tortured). While parents and teachers are trying to teach the child not to solve his problems by violence, these media sometimes portray heroes who proceed with brute force. While the school is seeking to promote good human relationships, these media sometimes have portrayed members of a minority group as being characteristically menial or subservient, or stupid or crafty people. While the home and school have been trying to promote respect for law and order, these media have sometimes glorified crime by portraying criminals and criminal escapades in a glamorous light. The same issues also arise in connection with the movie, radio, comic-strip, and reading interests of adults.

In passing it may be pointed out that one viewpoint which has been advanced is that crime, physical violence, and various other forms of aggressiveness in children's radio programs, movies, and comics might actually have a good psychological effect. According to this viewpoint, the child, as he identifies himself with the action, may give play to his aggressive impulses, or wield power which he would like to possess in real life, or satisfy other unfulfilled desires. In a make-believe or vicarious setting, according to this view, he thus gives vent to feelings that have arisen in response to actual conditions in his everyday life and he thus is relieved from tension and strain.

It would be pleasant, indeed, if these media of entertainment thus enabled a child safely and comfortably to "let off steam," to get things "off his chest," and thus enabled him to resume the prosaic business of life in a more serene and relaxed frame of mind.[18] The view that comics help children solve their emotional problems has been set forth by Bender and Lourie (3).[19] This theory is a very inviting one. Unfortunately, there is a lack of convincing scientific evidence as to whether or to what extent the average child derives benefit from the movies, radio programs, and comics in keeping with the theory.

---

[18] This notion that the vicarious experiences children have by way of radio, movies, and the comics might somehow purge their troubled spirits is derived from a theory of the drama that was expounded by Aristotle.

[19] The December, 1944, number of the *Journal of Educational Sociology* (Vol. 18, No. 4), under the editorship of H. W. Zorbaugh, carries several articles dealing with the comics (112).

INTERESTS AND INCENTIVES AS RELATED TO LEARNING

It is axiomatic that a child learns best when what he undertakes is tied in with his own purposes, when he recognizes at least some of the meanings and goals involved and finds himself absorbed in the process of learning rather than simply in the end point of mastering a particular problem. To be sure, in the case both of children and adults, a vast amount of learning takes place apart from consciously formulated goals. Furthermore, both children and adults learn to adjust to a good deal of regimentation and countless regulations pretty much as a matter of course, without stopping to inquire into the underlying purposes or reasons. This, of course, is fortunate, for if adults stopped to explain or if children tried to formulate the significance and purpose of all everyday acts, it is likely that everyone would go crazy.

A primary consideration in helping children to utilize and cultivate their interests is to take account of their abilities, to scale the program of opportunities and requirements to their growing capacities. Another important consideration noted previously is that interests thrive on successful effort. This principle, in turn, implies that, in *teaching* children, it is important to be ready to *learn from* the children who are being taught, so that there may be a degree of give-and-take and adjustment by the teacher to the child's concerns and problems. In the case of very young children, the teacher is perforce a learner. The teacher, while thus participating in the learner's problem, will also better be able to make effective use of other incentives and aids. It has been found, for example, that judicious praise usually is more effective than reproof.[20]

It likewise has been noted in experimental studies, as is known from everyday practice, that a suggestion or a bit of help at a

---

[20] For studies on the subject of praise and reproof and of success and failure as incentives, see Chase (13), Anderson and Smith (2), Hurlock (45), Lorge (69, 70, 71), and Thorndike (96, 97, 98).

strategic juncture may decidedly expedite a child's progress and help him to detect errors and to achieve techniques and insights that would require needless expenditure of time if he were left to explore for himself.[21]

An interesting illustration of an informal approach to the understanding of children's own preoccupations as related to subjects taught at school is provided in a study by Wahlstrom (103a). The third-grade children in this study talked to teachers concerning their own everyday experiences involving arithmetical computations. It was found that over sixty per cent of the problems reported by the children dealt with the use of money, primarily in connection with purchases. Of the problems that were analyzed, about half involved addition, about two-fifths subtraction, only about a tenth multiplication, and only about two per cent division.[22]

One area, among many, in which an endeavor to gauge the child's own abilities and interests would be helpful is in music and art. A child's first artistic ventures occur as spontaneous features of his play and general activity.[23] As time passes, many children lose this spontaneity. This shift toward greater self-consciousness and conventionality is no doubt due in part to formal requirements at school. A part of the shift, however, seems to arise from within the child himself, for as a child gains in ability to draw or dance or sing, he also becomes more able to look critically upon his performance. Not only does the child come to realize the discrepancy between his conception and his execution, but he is further reminded of his shortcomings by the example set by a fortunate classmate who happens to have a special knack. His interest is especially likely to wane if he falls into the hands of a teacher who

---

[21] See, for example, Goodenough and Brian (31).
[22] For other studies in this field see Brueckner (10), Reid (82), Brownell (9), Grossnickle (35), Harap and Barrett (37), and Willey (106).
[23] Sequences in the early development of children's drawings and block buildings have been noted briefly in an earlier chapter. The changing characteristics of children's interests and performances in the graphic arts have been described by Meier (73).

feels it to be his duty to convert his pupils into professional artists, along conventional lines, and who sets "art" off as something apart from the countless workaday projects of everyday life.

In the field of music, likewise, a child's potential abilities and interests often bog down under the weight of stereotyped requirements. As noted in an earlier chapter, children at an early age can profit from practice in singing and, at the same time, acquire an increase in interest and enjoyment. However, the conventional requirements go hard with many children. The tremendous resources for enjoyment that reside in the use of the voice are realized by only a small proportion of individuals. One difficulty, among others, seems to be that the course of study frequently is planned more in terms of the preoccupations of finished musicians than in terms of the developing abilities of children. In a study by Kwalwasser (59) it was found that musical concepts and skills recommended in a course of study that had the endorsement of authorities in musical education were far out of line with what the children actually learned to accomplish during the time allotted to musical instruction at school.

Another factor that creates difficulty for many children as well as adults is that they are called upon to sing in a higher key than seems to be congenial to their voices (witness the contortions and strains exhibited by a large proportion of males when singing the national anthem or Christmas carols). Even in the case of preschool children, it has been observed that children are able to sing lower tones than those recommended in musical manuals (53). In a study of children at the elementary- and high-school levels, Sherman found that a large number of children prefer lower tones (91) than the key in which the songs are published.[24]

BIBLIOGRAPHY

1. Adler, M. J.: *Art and Prudence* (New York: Longmans Green, 1937), 686 pp.

---

[24] For a review of studies dealing with the development of musical abilities and with factors in musical training, see Mursell (76).

2. Anderson, H. E. and Smith, R. S.: "Motivation of Young Children: The Constancy of Certain Behavior Patterns," *Journal of Experimental Education* (1933), 2:138-160.
3. Bender, L. and Lourie, R. S.: "The Effect of Comic Books on the Ideology of Children," *American Journal of Orthopsychiatry* (1941), 11:540-551.
4. Benjamin, H.: "Age and Sex Differences in the Toy Preferences of Young Children," *Pedagogical Seminary and Journal of Genetic Psychology* (1932), 41:417-429.
5. Blumer, H.: *Movies and Conduct,* Payne Fund Studies (New York: Macmillan, 1933), 257 pp.
6. Blumer, H. and Hauser, P. M.: *Movies, Delinquency and Crime,* Payne Fund Studies (New York: Macmillan, 1933), 233 pp.
7. Bott, H.: *Observation of Play Activities in a Nursery School,* Genetic Psychology Monographs (1928), 4:44-88.
8. Bridges, K. M. B.: "Occupational Interests of Three-Year-Old Children," *Pedagogical Seminary* (1927), 34:415-423.
9. Brownell, W. A.: *The Development of Children's Number Ideas in the Primary Grades,* Supplementary Educational Monograph (Chicago: University of Chicago Press, 1928), No. 35, 241 pp.
10. Brueckner, L. J.: "The Development of Ability in Arithmetic," *Thirty-Eighth Yearbook of the National Society for the Study of Education* (Bloomington, Illinois: Public School Publishing Company, 1939), Pt. I, Ch. XV, pp. 275-298.
11. Cantril, H. and Allport, G. W.: *The Psychology of Radio* (New York: Harper and Brothers, 1935), 276 pp.
12. Charters, W. W.: *Motion Pictures and Youth,* Payne Fund Studies (New York: Macmillan, 1933), 66 pp.
13. Chase, L.: *Motivation of Young Children: An Experimental Study of the Influence of Certain Types of External Incentives Upon the Performance of a Task,* University of Iowa Studies in Child Welfare (1932), No. 3, 119 pp.
14. Child Study Association: "Radio for Children—Parents Listen In," *Child Study* (April, 1933), 10:193-198; 214.
15. Clark, W. R.: "Radio Listening Activities of Children," *Journal of Experimental Education* (1939), 8:44-48.
16. ———: "Radio Listening Habits of Children," *Journal of Social Psychology* (1940), 12:131-149.
17. Cooper, I. M.: *Bibliography on Educational Broadcasting* (Chicago: University of Chicago Press, 1942).
18. Croswell, T. R.: "Amusements of Worcester School Children," *Pedagogical Seminary* (1899), 6:314-371.

19. Dale, E.: "Books Which Children Like to See Pictured," *Educational Research Bulletin* (1931), 10:423-429.
20. ———: *Children's Attendance at Motion Pictures,* Payne Fund Studies (New York: Macmillan, 1935), 81 pp.
21. Dale, E., Dunn, F. W., Hoban, C. F., Jr., and Schneider, E.: *Motion Pictures in Education: A Summary of the Literature* (New York: Wilson, 1937), 472 pp.
22. Dunn, F. W.: *Interest Factors in Primary Reading Material,* Teachers College Contributions to Education (New York: Teachers College, Columbia University, 1921), No. 113, 70 pp.
23. Dysinger, W. S. and Ruckmick, C. A.: *The Emotional Responses of Children to the Motion Picture Situation,* Payne Fund Studies (New York: Macmillan, 1933), 122 pp.
24. Eisenberg, A. L.: *Children and Radio Programs* (New York: Columbia University Press, 1936), 240 pp.
25. Ellis, A. C. and Hall, G. S.: "A Study of Dolls," *Pedagogical Seminary* (1896), 4:129-175.
26. Farwell, L.: *Reactions of Kindergarten, First, and Second Grade Children to Constructive Play Materials,* Genetic Psychology Monographs (1930), 8:431-562.
27. Fitzpatrick, F. L.: *Science Interests* (New York: Teachers College, Columbia University, 1936), 72 pp.
28. Foster, J. C.: "Play Activities of Children in the First Six Grades," *Child Development* (1930), 1:248-254.
29. Furfey, P. H.: *The Growing Boy,* Case Studies of Developmental Age (New York, Macmillan, 1930), 192 pp.
30. Gates, A. I.: *Interest and Ability in Reading* (New York: Macmillan, 1930), 264 pp.
31. Goodenough, F. L. and Brian, C. R.: "Certain Factors Underlying the Acquisition of Motor Skill by Preschool Children," *Journal of Experimental Psychology* (1929), 12:127-155.
32. Gray, W. S.: "Reading," *Thirty-Eighth Yearbook of the National Society for the Study of Education* (Bloomington, Illinois: Public School Publishing Company, 1939), Pt. I, Ch. IX, pp. 185-209.
33. ———: "Summary of Reading Investigations, July 1, 1942, to June 30, 1943," *Journal of Educational Research* (1944), 37:401-440.
34. ———: *Summary of Investigations Relating to Reading,* University of Chicago Supplementary Educational Monographs (1925), No. 28, 275 pp.
35. Grossnickle, F. E.: "Concepts in Social Arithmetic for the Eighth Grade Level," *Journal of Educational Research* (1937), 30, 7:475-488.

36. Gruenberg, S. M.: *Radio and Children* (New York: Radio Institute of the Audible Arts, 1935), 23 pp.
37. Harap, H. and Barrett, U.: "Experimenting with Real Situations in Third Grade Arithmetic," *Educational Method* (1937), 16:188-192.
38. Herzog, Herta: *Children and Their Leisure Time Listening to the Radio,* A Survey of the Literature in the Field (New York: Radio Council on Children's Programs, 1941).
39. Hilgard, J. R.: "Learning and Maturation in Preschool Children," *Journal of Genetic Psychology* (1932), 41:36-56.
40. Holaday, P. W. and Stoddard, G. D.: *Getting Ideas from the Movies,* Payne Fund Studies (New York: Macmillan, 1933), 102 pp.
41. Holy, T. C.: *Survey of the Schools of Euclid, Ohio,* Bureau of Educational Research Monographs (1936), 177 pp.
42. Hostler, A. M.: "Learning Through Play," *Parents Magazine* (January, 1933), 8:18-20.
43. Hulson, E. L.: "An Analysis of the Free Play of Ten Four-Year-Old Children Through Consecutive Observations," *Journal of Juvenile Research* (1930), 14:188-208.
44. Hunnicutt, C. W.: "Reading of Children in Activity and Regular Schools in New York City," *Elementary School Journal* (1943), 43:530-538.
45. Hurlock, E. B.: "Experimental Investigations of Childhood Play," *Psychological Bulletin* (1934), 31, 1:47-67.
46. ———: *Value of Praise and Reproof as Incentives for Children,* Archives of Psychology, 1924-1925, No. 71, 78 pp.
47. Jersild, A. T.: *Children's Interests in Radio Programs,* unpublished (New York: Teachers College, Columbia University, 1937).
48. ———: "Children's Radio Programs," *Talks* (April, 1938), 3:41-45.
49. ———: "Music," *Thirty-Eighth Yearbook of the National Society for the Study of Education* (Bloomington, Illinois: Public School Publishing Company, 1939), Pt. I, Ch. VI, pp. 135-151.
50. ———: "Radio and Motion Pictures," *Thirty-Eighth Yearbook of the National Society for the Study of Education* (Bloomington, Illinois: Public School Publishing Company, 1939), Pt. I, Ch. VII, pp. 153-173.
51. ———: "Radio and Motion Pictures," *Encyclopedia of Child Guidance* (New York: Philosophical Library, 1943), 851-857.
52. ———: *The Effects of Radio Programs on Children as Revealed by Interviews with Mothers,* unpublished (New York: Teachers College, Columbia University, 1938).
53. Jersild, A. T. and Bienstock, S. F.: "The Influence of Training on the Vocal Ability of Three-Year-Old Children," *Child Development* (December, 1931), 4:272-291.

54. Jersild, A. T. and Holmes, F. B.: *Characteristics of Teachers Who Are "Liked Best" and "Disliked Most,"* unpublished (New York: Teachers College, Columbia University, 1939).
55. Johnson, G. E.: *Education by Plays and Games* (New York: Ginn, 1907), 234 pp.
56. Johnson, M. W.: "The Effect on Behavior of Variation in the Amount of Play Equipment," *Child Development* (1935), 6:56-68.
57. Jones, H. E. and Conrad, H. S.: "Rural Preferences in Motion Pictures," *Journal of Social Psychology* (1930), 1:419-423.
58. Key, C. B., White, M. R., Honzik, M. P., Heiney, A. B., and Erwin, D.: *The Process of Learning to Dress Among Nursery School Children,* Genetic Psychology Monographs (1936), 18:67-163.
59. Kwalwasser, J.: *Problems in Public School Music* (New York: M. Witmark and Sons, 1932), 159 pp.
60. Lazar, M.: *Reading Interests, Activities and Opportunities of Bright, Average, and Dull Children,* Teachers College Contributions to Education (New York: Teachers College, Columbia University, 1937), No. 707, 127 pp.
61. Lazarsfeld, P. F. and Stanton, F. N., editors: *Radio Research (1942-1943)* (New York: Duell, Sloan, and Pearce, 1943), 599 pp.
62. Lehman, H. C.: "A Study of Doll Play in Relation to the Onset of Pubescence," *Pedagogical Seminary and Journal of Genetic Psychology* (1927), 34:72-76.
63. Lehman, H. C. and Witty, P. A.: "A Study of Play in Relation to Pubescence," *Journal of Social Psychology* (1930), 1:510-523.
64. ———: "Play Activity and School Progress," *Journal of Educational Psychology* (1927), 18:318-326.
65. ———: *The Psychology of Play Activities* (New York: Barnes, 1927), 242 pp.
66. Lewis, D.: *Broadcasting to the Youth of America* (A Report on Present Day Activities in the Field of Children's Radio Programs), Washington National Association of Broadcasters (1941).
67. Longstaff, H. P.: "Preliminary Results of a Study of Mothers' Opinions of Children's Radio Programs," *Journal of Applied Psychology* (1936), 20:416-419.
68. ———: "Mothers' Opinions of Children's Radio Programs," *Journal of Applied Psychology* (1937), 265-279.
69. Lorge, I.: "Is Punishment Necessary for Discipline?" *Understanding the Child* (June, 1933), pp. 7-9.
70. ———: "The Efficacy of Intensified Reward and of Intensified Punishment," *Journal of Experimental Psychology* (1933), 16, 2:177-207.
71. Lorge, I. and Thorndike, E. L.: "The Comparative Strengthening of

a Connection by One or More Occurrences of It in Cases Where the Connection Was Punished and Was Neither Punished Nor Rewarded," *Journal of Experimental Psychology* (1933), 16:374-382.
72. Manwell, E. M. and Mengert, I. G.: "A Study of the Development of Two- and Three-Year-Old Children with Respect to Play Activities," Jack, Manwell, Mengert, *et al.: Behavior of the Preschool Child,* University of Iowa Studies in Child Welfare (1934), 9, 3:67-111.
73. Meier, N. C.: "The Graphic and Allied Arts," *Thirty-Eighth Yearbook of the National Society for the Study of Education* (Bloomington, Illinois: Public School Publishing Company, 1939), Pt. I, Ch. VIII, pp. 175-184.
74. Meigs, M. F.: *Teachers' Reactions to Comic Books,* unpublished (New York: Teachers College, Columbia University, 1946).
75. Miller, E.: "What Children Like," *Sight and Sound* (1936), 5:131-132.
76. Mursell, J. L.: *The Psychology of Music* (New York: W. W. Norton, 1937), 389 pp.
77. Osborne, E. G.: *Camping and Guidance* (New York: Association Press, 1937), 260 pp.
78. Osburn, W. J.: *A Study of Children's Interests,* mimeographed (Madison: Wisconsin Department of Public Education, 1926), 23 pp.
79. Peterson, R. C. and Thurstone, L. L.: *Motion Pictures and the Social Attitudes of Children,* Payne Fund Studies (New York: Macmillan, 1933), 75 pp.
80. Rankin, M.: *Children's Interests in Library Books of Fiction* (New York: Teachers College, Columbia University, 1944), 146 pp.
81. Reeves, W. R.: "Report of Committee on Street Play," *Journal of Educational Sociology* (1931), 4:607-618.
82. Reid, F. E.: "Incidental Number Situations in the First Grade," *Journal of Educational Research* (1936-1937), 30:36-43.
83. Renshaw, S., Miller, V. L., and Marquis, D.: *Children's Sleep,* Payne Fund Studies (New York: Macmillan, 1933), 242 pp.
84. "Research Projects in Play," *Recreation* (1930), 24:277-282.
85. Roberts, M. P.: *When Children Play at Home,* University of Iowa Extension Bulletin, Child Welfare Pamphlets (December, 1936), No. 52, 16 pp.
86. Rowland, H.: *Radio Crime Dramas,* Educational Research Bulletin, Vol. 23 from Radio Service, U. S. Office of Education (Washington, D. C.: Government Printing Office, 1944), pp. 210-217.
87. Rowland, H., Tyler, I. K., and Woelfel, N.: *Criteria for Children's*

CHILDREN'S INTERESTS

Radio Programs (Washington, D. C.: Federal Radio Education Committee, 1942).
88. Schwendener, N.: *Game Preferences of 10,000 Fourth-Grade Children* (New York: Teachers College, Columbia University, 1932), 49 pp.
89. Shallit, R.: "The Dramatic Play of Ten Nursery School Children," *Child Development* (1932), 3:359-362.
90. Sheldon, D. R.: "Children's Interests," *Elementary School Journal* (1939), 33:205-214.
91. Sherman, A. H.: *A Study of the Pitch Preferences of Children*, unpublished Master's thesis (Syracuse: Syracuse University, 1935).
92. Sones, W. W. D.: "Comics in the Classroom," *School Executive* (1943), 63:31-32, 82.
93. Stoddard, G. D.: *What Motion Pictures Mean to the Child*, University of Iowa Bulletin, new series, Child Welfare Pamphlet (1933), No. 31, 8 pp.
94. Strang, R.: "Why Children Read the Comics," *Elementary School Journal* (1942-1943), 43:336-342.
95. Terman, L. M. and Lima, M.: *Children's Reading* (New York: Appleton-Century, 1931), 422 pp.
96. Thorndike, E. L.: *An Experimental Study of Rewards*, Teachers College Contributions to Education (New York: Teachers College, Columbia University, 1933), No. 580, 72 pp.
97. ———: *Human Learning* (New York: Appleton-Century, 1931), 206 pp.
98. Thorndike, E. L., et al.: *Fundamentals of Learning* (New York: Teachers College, Columbia University, 1932), 638 pp.
99. Thorndike, R. L.: "Comic Magazines as an Aid to Vocabulary Building," (New York: Juvenile Group Foundation).
100. Thorndike, R. L.: *Children's Reading Interests* (New York Teachers College, Columbia University, 1941), 48 pp.
101. Tyler, I. K.: "Factors in the Evaluation of School Broadcasts," *Educational Broadcasting*, Proceedings of the First National Conference on Educational Broadcasting (Chicago: University of Chicago Press, 1937), 220-226.
102. Van Alstyne, D.: *Play Behavior and Choice of Play Materials of Preschool Children* (Chicago: University of Chicago Press, 1932), 104 pp.
103. Vance, T. F. and McCall, L. T.: "Children's Preferences Among Play Materials as Determined by the Method of Paired Comparisons of Pictures," *Child Development* (1934), 5:267-277.
103a. Wahlstrom, E. L.: "The Computational Arithmetic of Social Experiences of Third Grade Children," *Journal of Educational Research* (1936-1937), 30:124-129.

104. Washburne, C., Milligan, H. V., Gruenberg, S., Jersild, A., and Langworthy, B.: "Radio and the Child's Education," *Educational Broadcasting,* edited by C. S. Marsh (Chicago: University of Chicago Press, 1937), pp. 258-282.
105. Washburne, C. and Vogel, M., *What Children Like to Read, Winnetka Graded Book List* (Chicago: Rand, McNally, 1926), 286 pp.
106. Willey, R. DeV.: "Social Situations Which Lead the Elementary School Child to Natural Arithmetical Experiences," *California Elementary School Principals' Yearbook* (1940), 12:70-79.
107. Williams, A. M.: *Children's Choices in Science Books,* Child Development Monographs (New York: Teachers College, Columbia University, 1939), No. 27, 163 pp.
108. Witty, P.: "Children's Interest in Reading the Comics," *Journal of Experimental Education* (1941), 10:100-104.
109. Woelfel, N. and Tyler, I.: *Radio and the School* (New York: World Book Company, 1945), 358 pp.
110. Woelfel, N. and Wiles, K.: "How Teachers Use School Broadcasts," *Educational Research Bulletin,* 23:227-232 (December, 1944).
111. Young, I.: *A Preliminary Survey of Interests and Preferences of Primary Children in Motion Pictures, Comic Strips, and Radio Programs as Related to Grade, Sex, and Intelligence Differences,* Kansas State Teachers College, Emporia, Bulletin of Information (1942), 22; No. 9, 40 pp.
112. Zorbaugh, H. W., editor: "The Comics as an Educational Medium," December issue of the *Journal of Educational Sociology* (1944), 18:193-255.

CHAPTER XV

THE GROWTH AND PREDICTION OF INTELLIGENCE

This chapter deals with the development of mental abilities that are measured by intelligence tests. In perhaps no branch of psychology has more progress been made than in the measurement of verbal intelligence. This holds true even though the instruments for measuring intelligence, especially at the lower age levels, are still imperfect and many issues remain unsettled.

The intelligence test is designed to measure an individual's ability to cope with situations that call for the exercise of mental processes, his ability to act in accordance with the demands of the situation that confronts him, to comprehend the situation and solve the problems it involves, to learn and to apply past learnings.

Numerous definitions have been made of intelligence, including varying emphasis upon the ability to learn, to apply past learnings, to carry on abstract thinking. Among the operations listed by Thorndike (93) under the heading of intelligence are "a wide variety of operations such as we may call attention, retention, recall, recognition, selective and relational thinking, abstraction, generalization, organization, inductive and deductive reasoning, together with learning and knowledge in general." Other things being equal, according to Thorndike, the more intelligent person is one who not only can master a *greater number* of tasks and solve problems with greater *speed* but also is able to perform *harder* tasks, such as solving a mathematical problem which a lesser intellect never could master or reaching an effective solution to an economic problem that would bewilder a less able person with as much good will and access to pertinent information.

According to a definition by Stoddard (84), "Intelligence is the ability to undertake activities that are characterized by (1) difficulty, (2) complexity, (3) abstractness, (4) economy, (5) adaptiveness to a goal, (6) social value, and (7) the emergence of originals, and to maintain such activities under conditions that demand a concentration of energy and a resistance to emotional forces."

The usual intelligence test includes a number of concrete intellectual tasks yielding, in the aggregate, a total score. In tests of children, an important consideration is to select items suited and scaled to children's capacities at various maturity levels. Thus a young child may be asked to fit blocks of various shapes into holes of the same shape in a board, to repeat numbers that are spoken to him, to name objects or identify pictures of objects, and so forth. Items used with older children include tests of vocabulary, ability to solve problems of various kinds, immediate memory, speed of learning, ability to understand and interpret the meanings of written passages, to make deductions or inductions from observed facts, and so forth.

The Stanford-Binet scale. A number of considerations that enter into the testing of children can be illustrated by one test which has been widely used, an instrument originated by Binet and subsequently revised and perfected by Terman and by Terman and Merrill (87). This scale consists of tests that are graded in difficulty from the age of two and upward and can be scored as passed or failed.[1] There are six test items at each half-yearly level from two years through four years, and six tests at each yearly age level thereafter up through age fourteen, after which follow tests for the "average adult" and "superior adult" levels. The test items at any given age level represent tasks that the normal child of that age has been able to perform successfully. Accordingly, a child's score on the test indicates his status as compared with that of other children.

---

[1] This statement refers to the 1937 revision. An earlier revision included tests from the age of three upward, with six tests at each age level.

INTELLIGENCE

A child's performance on the scale can be scored in terms of *mental age*. Thus, if he passes all the tests up to and including the third year and fails all tests beyond that point, he has a mental age of three years. If he succeeds on tests beyond the three-year level, he receives credit for each such success. Each of the twelve tests at the two-, three-, and four-year levels counts as one month of mental age; and each of the six tests at later yearly levels counts as two months of mental age. Thus, if a child passes all tests up to and including three years, plus four of the twelve tests at four years, he is credited with a mental age of three years, four months, which means that his mentality is equal to that of the average child of three years and four months.

Intelligence quotient. To obtain an index of the child's brightness it is necessary to consider his mental age in relation to his chronological age. With the Stanford-Binet scale the procedure is to divide the child's *mental age* by his *chronological age* and multiply the result by 100 to yield a value known as the *intelligence quotient*. Thus a normal or average three-year-old child will have a mental age of three, a chronological age of three, and an I.Q. of 100. If the same child earns a mental score of four years, his I.Q. is 133; if he does no better than the normal two-year-old, his I.Q. is only 67. As can be seen, the I.Q. provides a convenient means of comparing the brightness of children at different age levels.[2]

Other types of intelligence tests. The test described above is administered to one child at a time. There are other individual tests and there also are tests applicable to older children and adults that can be administered to several persons in a group. Some tests depend entirely upon spoken or written answers; others do not call for verbal answers, but the person who is being tested gives

---

[2] When the test is used with adults the value representing chronological age does not become higher as the person becomes older; instead, an upper limit of fifteen years is set. Thus, a man of thirty with a mental age of twelve has an I.Q. of 80.

his answer by way of some performance—such as completing a picture or design, solving mazes and puzzles, fitting geometrical forms together.

Tests of infants and preschool children. Intelligence scales designed for children below the age of three have been developed more recently and are less reliable than tests for older children, but much work has been done in this field in recent years. As can well be understood, many difficulties beset mental testing at the level of infancy, before a child has learned to talk and to understand spoken language, as well as all the other symbols, gestures, and facial expressions that come into play in a verbal interchange between two persons. Moreover, it is more difficult than will be the case later to segregate the more strictly mental from the motor, social, and even emotional forms of response. The young child's response is also likely to be more variable.

Early developmental norms. Partly by reason of the difficulty of obtaining a measurement of more or less strictly "mental" performances in early infancy, the scales applied to infants are usually not referred to as "intelligence tests" but as measurements of developmental age, or mental growth, or maturity level, without the restrictive label of "intelligence."

Items from an inventory of early mental growth are shown in Table XXV in Chapter X. This table reproduces a portion of the findings obtained in a three-year study by Bayley (4) of infants who were selected to provide, as far as possible, a representative sampling of the population at large, and who were first seen within three days after birth and examined systematically during the ensuing weeks and months. Some of the items are self-explanatory; others are not. The reader should consult Bayley's monograph for a full description of the tests and the scoring procedures. Studies by Gesell have provided detailed inventories of developments during infancy (23, 24, 25).

Mental growth proceeds rapidly during infancy and early years. However, since a child's progress consists not simply in greater efficiency in doing what he has done before but in an increase in the number, scope, and variety of his performances, it is not possible to compute the rate of increase in precise, quantitative terms, as can be done in measurements of a child's height or weight from month to month or year to year.

Predictive value of infant tests. Infant tests, in their present form, do not give a very accurate prediction of what a child's future intelligence is likely to be. Generally speaking, the younger the child at the time he is tested, the smaller will be the predictive value of his score as an indication of the child's probable I.Q. in later years, although even in early infancy a markedly subnormal or a markedly superior rating may have significance for the future.

A child's ratings on *consecutive* tests, near in time, are likely to show a good deal of resemblance, but the longer the interval between two tests, the lower the resemblance is likely to be. Bayley found, for example, a positive correlation[3] of .57 between average scores at one to three months and at four to six months, and a correlation of .42 between scores at one to three and seven to nine months. As the interval increased, the correlations decreased, so that there was practically a zero correlation between scores at one to three months and scores beyond the age of twelve months. There was, however, a tendency for the scores to become more stable as the children grew older; thus, average scores at thirteen to fifteen months showed a correlation of .70 with a child's average ratings at eighteen to twenty-four months, and a correlation of .54 with average ratings at twenty-seven, thirty, and thirty-six months.

---

[3] To illustrate what is meant by a correlation coefficient two examples are given below. One example shows the correlation between I.Q. ratings based on two separate tests; the other, the correlation between I.Q. and strength of grip. In these examples, one of the simplest methods of correlation, known as the "rank-difference method," is used. It can be applied when there are only a small number of cases. The examples below include only seven cases, a number which is large enough for illustrative purposes but too small for ordinary statistical work.

The rank difference correlation coefficient is expressed by the symbol ρ. The formula used in the present case is:

$$\rho = 1 - \frac{6 \times \text{sum of } D^2}{n(n^2 - 1)}$$

Many factors contribute to this lack of consistency: different rates of growth; irregularities in rate of growth; changes in adjustment to the test situation; and the possibility that the test measures different functions, maturing at different rates, at different age levels.

Differences between children become greater with advancing age according to Bayley's findings. With increasing age there also was a greater spread in the performance of individual children on a given examination (as when a child of eighteen months

---

The illustrations show that the subjects' scores must first be ranked. D represents the difference between the same subject's rank in the two tests; N, the number of cases.

Individuals Tested	I.Q. Test I	Rank	I.Q. Test II	Rank	D	D^2	I.Q. Test I Rank	Strength of Grip in Kgm.	Rank	D	D^2
Albert	80	7	79	7	0	0	7	22	6	1	1
Henry	90	6	95	4	2	4	6	28	3	3	9
John	104	3	110	3	0	0	3	20	7	4	16
Peter	95	5	92	6	1	1	5	30	2	3	9
Palmer	140	1	135	1	0	0	1	26	4	3	9
Robert	120	2	125	2	0	0	2	34	1	1	1
Walter	100	4	94	5	1	1	4	24	5	1	1

$N = 7$
$N^2 - 1 = 48$
$N(N^2 - 1) = 336$

Sum of $D^2 = 6$
$6 \times$ sum of $D^2 = 36$

Sum of $D^2 = 46$
$6 \times$ sum of $D^2 = 276$

$\rho = 1 - \dfrac{6 \times \text{sum of } D^2}{N(N^2 - 1)}$

$= 1 - 36/336$

$= +.89$ (between the first and second test of I.Q.)

$\rho = 1 - 276/336$

$= +.18$ (between the first test of I.Q. and scores on strength of grip)

According to the examples given, there is a high degree of correspondence between the children's I.Q.'s on Tests I and II. Each child maintains about the same rank on both tests. If each child kept exactly the same rank on both tests, there would be a perfect correlation of $+1.00$. If there were no consistency at all between scores on the first and second tests, the correlation would be 0. If there were a complete reversal of ranks, the correlation would be -1.00. For practical purposes, we would be able to make a fairly accurate estimate of what a child's rating on Test I would be if we knew his relative standing on Test I. In the second example, we find a positive but low correlation between I.Q. and strength of grip. On the basis of the figures in this example, there is a likelihood that a child with a high I.Q. will also tend to be above rather than below average in strength of grip. But the correspondence is so small that, if we tried to estimate his score in one test on the basis of our knowledge of his score on the other, our estimate would be little more than a guess.

TABLE XL

COMPOSITE OF TEST-RETEST CORRELATIONS FROM SEVERAL STUDIES OF INFANT AND PRESCHOOL GROUPS[4]

Age at Earlier Test	Less than 4 months	4 to 9 months	10 to 15 months	16 to 21 months	22 to 29 months	30 to 41 months	42 to 53 months	Over 53 months
Under 4 months	.57	.33	.10	−.03	−.09			
4–9 months	.77	.53	.49	.23	.16	.46	.00	
10–15 months	.78	.66	.50	.45	.33			.55
16–21 months	.76	.68	.51	.44	.38	.41	.25	.33
22–29 months	.82	.74	.68					.43
30–41 months	.87	.68	.66	.49	.57	.57	.56	.66
42–53 months	.81	.65	.72	.71	.66	.63	.63	.41
54–65 months			.76		.73			

performs at a level several months beyond that on some parts of the scale and no better than the average child of eighteen months on other parts).

It was also noted that there was a positive relation between children's scores and the education of the children's parents after about the age of two years, but not before that time.

The findings also suggest that a series of tests from which can be determined the speed or rate of a child's growth over a period of time gives a more trustworthy prediction of his probable standing in the future than does a single measurement.

Consistency and predictive value of intelligence ratings at the preschool level. Beyond the age of two, there is a good deal more resemblance between intelligence-test scores from month to month and from year to year than is the case in measurements of mental growth at an earlier age. Even so, a child's score at the age of three or four does not give a very accurate prophecy of what the child's I.Q. will be at the age of six or seven and thereafter. The score may fluctuate considerably, up or down. But if the tests have been properly administered and if no unusual changes in cir-

---

[4] From Thorndike, R. L.: "'Constancy' of the I.Q.," *Psychological Bulletin* (1940), 37, p. 173. Reproduced by permission of the American Psychological Association.

cumstances have intervened, the chances are that in the average case a child's I.Q. at six or seven years will remain within the general neighborhood of his I.Q. as determined at the age of three or four. If there is a change, it is more likely that he will move, say, from an "average" to a "superior" classification, or the reverse, than from an "average" to a "very superior" classification, or the reverse; it is still less likely that he will move from an "average" to a "genius" or a "feeble-minded" rating, although shifts ranging as large as forty points or more have been found.

Several groups of children in one investigation (15) were tested first between the ages of two and four years, on two scales designed for preschool children (the Kuhlmann-Binet and the Merrill-Palmer scales), and then, in later years, on the Stanford-Binet scale. There was a correlation of .66 between I.Q.'s of children tested between the ages of two and three on the Kuhlmann-Binet scale and the children's I.Q.'s when tested at the age of five on the Stanford-Binet scale. A slightly higher correlation (.71) was found between ratings on tests between the ages of three and four and tests given after the age of five. The corresponding correlations between ratings on the other preschool test (the Merrill-Palmer) and those on the Stanford-Binet test after the age of five were .61 and .41.

At the preschool level, as at the infancy level, the general finding has been that the longer the interval between testings, the smaller becomes the correspondence between scores made by the same child at one period as compared with another. The same holds true, but to a lesser extent, at the school-age level.[5]

Factors influencing test results in early childhood. The findings reviewed above and in Table XLI show that the intelligence

---

[5] For a discussion of the correlations between tests and retests as related to the interval of time between the tests, see R. L. Thorndike (95).

Table XLI gives a summary, adapted from Anderson and based upon three studies, one by Honzik (44) of children who were tested periodically for several years from the age of two and onward, and separate studies of older children by Hirsch (36) and by Dearborn, Rothney, and Shuttleworth (14).

quotient as determined by standardized tests during the infancy and preschool years, while showing a much higher degree of constancy than could be expected by chance, does not give as reliable a forecast of a child's intelligence some years later as do tests applied at the school-age level or later. Why is this? Is the child actually more changeable and are his abilities, as compared with other children of his own age, less constant during the earlier years, or is it possibly the fault of the tests that are used and the way in which they are administered? A definitive answer to this ques-

Table XLI

CORRELATIONS BETWEEN INTELLIGENCE RATINGS OF THE SAME CHILDREN AT VARIOUS AGE LEVELS, INCLUDING CORRELATIONS BETWEEN SCORES ON INITIAL TESTS AND TESTS DURING LATER YEARS, AND CORRELATIONS BETWEEN TERMINAL TESTS AND TESTS DURING EARLIER YEARS[6]

Correlations with Initial Status

With 1.9 years		With 7 years			With 6–8 years	
Age		Age	Boys	Girls	Age	
2 yrs.	.68	8 yrs.	.735	.651	7– 9 yrs.	.868
3 yrs.	.47	9 yrs.	.697	.604	8–10 yrs.	.824
4 yrs.	.46	10 yrs.	.726	.719	9–11 yrs.	.787
5 yrs.	.32	11 yrs.	.670	.668	10–12 yrs.	.839
6 yrs.	.30	12 yrs.	.642	.655	11–13 yrs.	.800

Correlations with Terminal Status

With 7 years		With 16 years			With 11–13 years	
Age		Age	Boys	Girls	Age	
2 yrs.	.46	11 yrs.	.752	.728	6– 8 yrs.	.800
3 yrs.	.56	12 yrs.	.790	.776	7– 9 yrs.	.770
4 yrs.	.66	13 yrs.	.778	.812	8–10 yrs.	.773
5 yrs.	.73	14 yrs.	.829	.822	9–11 yrs.	.828
6 yrs.	.81	15 yrs.	.901	.906	10–12 yrs.	.902

[6] Adapted from Anderson, J. E.: "The Limitations of Infant and Preschool Tests in the Measurement of Intelligence," *Journal of Psychology* (1939), 8: 351-379. Reproduced by permission. For a full description, see Anderson's article. The tables reported by Anderson consist in part of reproductions of tabular materials from the underlying studies, in part of new computations based upon individual scores reported in the underlying studies.

tion cannot be supplied, but many pertinent observations can be offered. On theoretical grounds, one might reasonably expect that there would be less constancy in rate of mental growth during earlier years. The child is progressing rapidly; new abilities are emerging and are being consolidated. A slight temporary acceleration or retardation may produce larger upward or downward swings in the intelligence quotient than would be the case if the prevailing rate were slow. The child of six or seven years also is still maturing quite rapidly, to be sure, but the farther along a child is in the process of maturing, the more his improvement takes on the form of greater power, sagacity, and scope in the use of capacities that can be remeasured from time to time, as distinguished from the emergence of relatively new abilities.

The development of language serves as an example. Although language development is a continuous process, the change that takes place over a period of a few months during early childhood (from the period before the "first word" and the first sentences) is more striking and could have a more variable effect on an estimate of a child's ability than the changes that normally take place over a similar period of months after the age of six. One child may speak his "first words" quite clearly and then add new words to his vocabulary at a relatively slow rate; another may begin to talk later but then advance rapidly and catch up with the child who started to talk at an earlier time. To the extent that language facility enters into tests of these children, the first child would score higher on an earlier test but not on a later test. The shift in the relative standing of the two children would be due to somewhat different patterns of development and could not be attributed to errors in the tests.

It is possible that an intensive and detailed study of the mental growth of younger children would show that even under optimum conditions there would be more irregularity in individual growth curves at the earlier ages than at later ages.

However, the lower predictive value of tests at the preschool than at the school-age level cannot be attributed entirely to irregularities in the growth pattern or to imperfections in the measuring instruments. As in infancy, so to a lesser but important degree at the preschool level, the reliability of test results depends upon the tester's success in winning the child's full coöperation and in enlisting the child's best effort. Resistance or fear on the child's part may interfere with the test. Even if there is no resistance or fear, the young child may fail to make a serious effort. To many young children a mental-test situation and its demands are quite different from anything that they meet in their everyday lives. Among other things, the child may fail to recognize the importance of doing things according to the letter of the tester's instructions; thus it has been observed, for example, that a child who some time ago may have mastered a certain form board (putting blocks of different shapes into holes of the same shape) in his everyday play and who has lost interest in the performance may fail through lack of trying on a task of this sort in the testing situation. Again, a child who has learned to conform to directions and routines in a nursery-school situation may have an advantage, when tested on the nursery-school grounds by a familiar person, over a child who is new to this situation.

Effects of resistance and adjustment to the test situation. A careful study by Rust (76) shows how a child's resistance may affect his score, even when the test is administered by a person who is experienced and highly competent as a mental tester.[7]

On the initial presentation of one of the two scales, seventy-five per cent of the children resisted one or more items of the Kuhlmann-Binet scale; but on a later presentation, ninety-six per cent of the children accepted every test. Sixty-eight per cent of the children initially refused one or more items of the other scale, but after subsequent presentations, all but one child accepted all the tests. *Fifty-eight per cent* of the initially refused items were later

---
[7] The procedure in this study is described in an earlier section dealing with resistance as an aspect of social behavior (Chapter V).

successfully answered when presented to the children again within a few days, and this without coaching or help.

Of the children who initially refused and finally accepted every test item of the Kuhlmann-Binet scale, seven per cent made gains of from twenty-five to thirty-five points of I.Q.; eighteen per cent made gains ranging from fifteen to twenty-four points; twenty-six per cent made gains ranging from five to fourteen points; and fourteen per cent of the children made gains of from one to four points. On the Merrill-Palmer scale (which required more overt performance and less verbal response than did the Kuhlmann-Binet), the gains were not as numerous or as large.

These findings show impressively the extent to which a child's coöperation in the test situation may influence his score. By virtue of two or three added opportunities for becoming acquainted and for establishing rapport, and the chance therewith provided for attempting test items that previously were refused, some children gained as much as from twenty-five to thirty-five points. Obviously, the child's I.Q. had not expanded by thirty-five points during the two to four days involved in the experiments. Equally obviously, a difference as great or even greater might appear if the same child had been tested at intervals separated by one or several years and on one occasion had coöperated perfectly while on another had shown a good deal of resistance. Large variations might also occur by virtue of differences in the extent to which different examiners are able to elicit his best effort.

That the child's adjustment to the environment in which the test is given may influence the consistency of his scores is shown in a study by Updegraff (98), in which children in one group were tested during the week preceding the opening of the fall term of the nursery school, and children in another group were tested after they had attended the school not less than two weeks; in the spring, both groups were tested again. There was considerably less correspondence between the fall and spring scores of the children who had their first test before entering school than in the case of children who were first tested after they had attended school at least two weeks. The respective correlations were .535 and .837. In both groups, there were more children whose I.Q.'s increased than children whose I.Q.'s decreased during the school year.

It appears that test results were affected by the fact that children who were tested before the school term had to face a strange examiner in a strange place whereas children who were tested after their entrance into the school had a previous opportunity to become acquainted with the personnel, the grounds, and the nursery-school environment (and with the general tendency toward conformity with adult directions which characterizes the usual nursery-school group).

Although the intelligence ratings of preschool children, based on tests which have been used most frequently until the present time, are likely to be less trustworthy as a prophecy for the future than the scores of children of school age, it still is apparent from the findings reviewed earlier that there is a substantial correlation between ratings obtained after the age of three years and ratings obtained beyond the age of five.

Constancy of mental test scores beyond the preschool level. As already indicated above, there is a relatively high degree of consistency in intelligence-test ratings from year to year at the school age and beyond. Individuals tend to keep about the same rank or relative position from age to age. As shown in Table XLI, the correlations between intelligence-test ratings separated by an interval of one or more years are far from perfect, however.[8] Fluctuations are likely to occur, but if the tests have been well administered and no outstanding changes in the child's circumstances have intervened (such as illness, emotional maladjustment, or transfer to a different environment), the upward or downward shift is likely to be relatively small in a majority of cases.[9]

---

[8] For a review of findings concerning the constancy of the I.Q. see Thorndike (94).

[9] Studies dealing with changes in I.Q. through environmental influences are discussed in a section that follows.

It should be emphasized in passing that when psychologists speak of the "constancy" of the I.Q. they do not at all imply that the I.Q. will remain precisely the same from year to year. The concept implies, rather, that there is a high degree of probability (not certainty) that fluctuations will be relatively small in a majority of cases. Indeed, because of the variables involved in measuring the complex operations that constitute "intelligence," it is improbable that a child would obtain precisely the same score on two equivalent forms of the same test, even if they were administered on successive days. In discussing results obtained with the best known of all individual tests for children (the Stanford-Binet scale), Terman (86) several years ago pointed out that the chances were one in two that the I.Q. might increase as much as six points or decrease as much as four points; the chances of an increase of twelve points or a decrease of eight points were one in five; the chances of shifts larger than twelve points were considerably smaller but still impressive.

In tests and retests of large numbers of children, it is recognized not only that individual cases may show larger shifts but that such shifts are to be expected. In other words, a child's I.Q. as determined by a test at a given time should not be taken as a final verdict. In discussing this topic, Goodenough (28) points out that when one or more of the modern revisions of the Binet scale are administered under standard conditions and by competent examiners, it can be expected that fifty per cent of elementary-school children will not change their standing by more than five points of I.Q. in either direction, whereas the remaining fifty per cent will show somewhat greater variation. Goodenough estimates that in tests of a group of five hundred children under the best conditions, at least a hundred may be expected, on retests, to show changes in I.Q. of as much as ten points; changes of as much as fifteen points may be expected in about twenty-five cases, and four or five cases may shift as much as twenty points. Goodenough points out that even greater fluctuations may be expected if the tests are not administered by workers of equal competence or if comparisons are based upon results of different types of tests.

Errors in practice obviously will occur if a child's I.Q., as determined by a given test, is regarded as a fixed value that can be used once and for all in classifying a pupil or in guiding his work at school. Again, misconceptions of another sort occur when it is concluded, upon discovery of a shift of many points in I.Q. on two different tests, that such shifts completely discredit the theory and practice of mental testing. Actually, those who have played the most responsible role in the development and use of mental tests are the ones who have emphasized variational tendencies, have acknowledged that the instruments are not infallible, and have stressed the fact that while the I.Q. tends to show a relatively high degree of constancy as measured by standard tests, changes of a few points are likely to occur in a large number of cases, and relatively large changes may be expected in many other instances.

Fluctuation and error in test results. Although tests are designed as far as possible to rule out the effects of practice, it is difficult to do this is a thoroughgoing way. In the case of group tests, for example, a veteran examinee, accustomed to many types of examinations, may have an advantage through knowing what is expected; and if the directions and sample tests are on the same page as the main test, he can begin to study the first questions while the others are still looking at the directions. Although previous experience with tests may thus make a difference, the errors in rating through this factor alone seem to be relatively small by and large.

An incorrect estimate of a child's intelligence may arise if the child by reason of unique circumstances in his environment is at a disadvantage on certain test items. Thus a child who lives in an environment in which he seldom has a chance to use money may fail, less through lack of ability than through lack of opportunity to learn, on a problem that calls for knowledge of the names and values of coins. To the extent that a test involves items that are better suited to the experience of one group than another (as, for example, urban as compared with rural, or isolated mountaineer, or Indian reservation groups), it may yield misleading results (47, 50, 77). Also, if a child moves from a highly restricted to a more stimulating environment, he may exhibit a rise in intelligence, not so much by virtue of a change in his underlying ability as by virtue of the fact that his ability in dealing with the particular kinds of information and problems involved in a test is now better in line with his potentialities than it was at an earlier time. Furthermore, a child's I.Q. may change from one test to a later one if he is definitely malnourished on the first occasion and has overcome the effects of malnutrition when tested at a later time (72), and fluctuations in I.Q. have also been found to be associated with emotional maladjustment (26). However, a change for the better in a child's physical condition does not invariably produce a change in his score (75).

LIMITS OF INTELLECTUAL GROWTH

When tests of various mental operations are repeated, an increase in ability is usually found from year to year. The question may be raised: "At what age does this 'upward extension' or 'vertical' increase in intelligence come to an end?" Obviously, it would be impossible to distinguish precisely between changes in underlying abilities and changes brought about through the use or application of such abilities. The evidence on the question as to when growth has reached its maximum is conflicting. Not only are there differences between individuals with respect to the age at which an increase in capacity appears to taper off, but it also appears that there are differences, within the same individual, in the age at which various intellectual processes reach their maximum development. There likewise is a difference in the pattern of the "growth curve" of different operations.[10]

---

[10] For illustrative "growth curves" of general intelligence and of different operations included in intelligence tests see, for example, Thorndike, *et al.* (93), Freeman and Flory (20), and Conrad and Jones (11).

INTELLIGENCE

The age at which individuals cease to grow in intellectual ability has been set all the way from thirteen and a half years to some time in the twenties. The increase in ability that occurs after the time when intellectual growth has come to an end presumably consists chiefly in an increase in skill and knowledge—a "horizontal" extension, so to speak—rather than an increase in underlying capacity. The question as to when mental growth reaches its maximum has many practical implications. Among other things, the more variation there is between individuals in the age of continuing intellectual growth, the less adequately will a test administered during childhood serve to give an accurate indication of a person's intelligence at maturity. If, for example, two children have the same score at fifteen years and one of them tapers off from that time on, showing little growth beyond the age of about sixteen, while the other is still showing significant gains at that age, the latter will of course outstrip the former.

The question as to the rate and duration of mental growth during adolescence and beyond is interesting also from the point of view of prognosis of the future abilities of bright and dull children. If, for example, dull children continue their mental growth longer than bright children, they would tend to overcome some of the advantage of the former as they grow older; if the reverse were true, added years would bring an increase in the relative superiority of the bright. On this question the evidence is conflicting. In a study which dealt in part with this problem, Freeman and Flory (20) found that children of average ability continued to advance intellectually during the period of later adolescence in the same proportion as did the bright children and that they continued to advance to at least as late an age. According to their findings, "children or youth of lesser promise may profit by continued education as much if not more than their precocious and brighter comrades." These findings concern children of about average intelligence as compared with bright children and do not give data concerning distinctly dull children as compared with the bright.

There is some evidence to indicate that distinctly dull persons reach their maximum growth at an earlier age than do average or superior children (107). On the question as to whether children who are bright are likely to show a loss or a gain during a period of years, the evidence is somewhat divided. In remeasurements of gifted children by Burks, Jensen, and Terman (8), there was evidence of some loss in I.Q. as the children grew older, but the gifted children were found to maintain or almost maintain their relative superiority, at least through the period of adolescence. Of course, even if a gifted child should lose several points of I.Q. he would still be ahead of a majority of his fellows. One problem in this connection is that of finding tests which adequately measure the same functions over a period of years. In a study by Cattell (10), children with I.Q.'s of 120 and above showed a gain in I.Q. over an interval of five years or more between the first and final tests. In a study by Hollingworth and Kaunitz (43), children who originally showed I.Q.'s of 130 or more were retested after the lapse of ten years at a median age of eighteen and a half years. Eighty-two per cent of the children who were among the top one per cent of the population on the first test were again found to be in the top one per cent when tested ten years later; no individual regressed to normal or nearly to normal. A later study of the same group of children by Lorge and Hollingworth (59) indicates that children who were found to be superior at the age of seven to nine also retained their status at or near maturity.

THE INFLUENCE OF NATURE AND NURTURE ON INDIVIDUAL DIFFERENCES IN MENTAL ABILITY

In the foregoing discussion we have noted that there are wide differences in the intelligence of children as measured by available tests and that these differences generally tend to remain relatively constant from the school age and onward. To what extent are these differences due to inborn factors and to what extent are they a product of the environment? This question can be raised as a practical issue, even though no precise distinction can be made between hereditary and environmental factors. Some of the angles from which this problem has been approached are described below.

Resemblances between members of the same family. Physical evidences of the influence of heredity appear in the obvious fact that animals of a given species beget their own kind and in the resemblances between parents and children in such features as skin color, color and texture of hair, physiognomy, and other physical features. The resemblance may be so great that a child may turn out to be almost the image of one of his parents, although such close resemblance, even in anatomical characteristics, is infrequent. Actually, the physical basis of heredity is highly complicated. The general "recipe" for an individual's physical development is present in the fertilized egg in the forms of biochemical substances known as *genes*. These genes do not, however, constitute a preformed mosaic of structural elements that simply multiply and produce an enlarged pattern as the individual grows. Moreover, even if hereditary influences were as simple as a fixed mosaic, they would still be highly complicated, for each individual is "double" with respect to his genes (in the fertilized egg there is one set of genes from each parent). As a result, a person may possess in his germ plasm the basis for characteristics that are not manifest in his make-up but are latent within him and may be transmitted to his offspring. A child may thus inherit a physical characteristic which neither of his parents displays. Even more difficult to trace directly are hereditary influences on complex functional characteristics, especially on anything so complicated as the operations involved in what we call intelligence.

One of many indirect approaches to the study of the influence of heredity on intelligence has been to measure resemblances between parents and children. In an early study in this field by Pearson (68, 69, 70), parents and children were compared with respect to certain physical characteristics, and the resulting correlations were about .50. About the same correlation was found when parents and children were compared with respect to certain mental characteristics. Pearson concluded that physical and mental characteristics in man are inherited "within broad lines in the same manner and with the same intensity." Subsequent studies, using standardized mental tests, have likewise found a correlation between the intelligence of parents and children. One such study deals with 997 cases in 269 family groups, constituting a cross section of a New England rural and small-town community (Conrad and Jones, 11). Mother-son, mother-daughter, father-son, and father-daughter comparisons were made. The parent-child correlations were all closely alike, averaging about .50. Other studies have likewise found correlations ranging in the neighborhood of from .35 to .50.

Positive correlations ranging upward to above .50 and tending to vary around .50 have likewise been found between the intelligence of siblings who live in the same home environment.[11]

Of special interest has been the study of resemblances between twins. Twins have been classified into two groups, the *identical* (also called *uniovular* and *monozygotic*) and the *nonidentical* (also called *biovular* and *dizygotic*). Identical twins presumably develop from a single fertilized egg and therefore they have the same heredity, while nonidentical twins develop from two separate fertilized eggs and so, as far as their germ plasm is concerned, should correspond to the same degree as brothers and sisters who are born some time apart. It is difficult to determine precisely whether twins are identical or nonidentical, especially at an early age, but many criteria can be applied in making the judgment.[12]

To the extent that heredity counts and uniovularity can be established, one should expect greater intellectual resemblances between identical than between nonidentical twins. Actually, this is what

---

[11] For other references see Hildreth (34), Thorndike (90, 93), Pintner (71), and an earlier report by Jones of the above-mentioned study in a New England community (45).

[12] For a discussion of biological aspects of twinning, see early chapters in a volume by Newman, Freeman, and Holzinger (65).

has been found. In several studies, correlations from .80 to .90 have been found between the intelligence of twins who are judged to be identical on the basis of their physical characteristics and who share the same environment. On the other hand, the correlations in the case of twins judged to be nonidentical (including twins of the same sex who definitely are dissimilar in physical appearance and "fraternal" twins—that is, pairs including a boy and a girl) range considerably lower, from about .50 to .70.[13] High resemblances have also been found between identical twins reared apart, but the findings vary as to the magnitude of this resemblance (36, 62, 65), and large differences between separated identical twins have been observed. It appears, however, that the resemblance between "identical" twins who have been reared apart is likely to be higher than that between ordinary brothers and sisters reared in the same home.

Studies of foster children. Since a foster child shares the same environment but not the immediate biological heredity of the family or the group with which he is raised, the resemblances between foster children and foster parents, as compared with resemblances between blood relatives in the same home, tell something about the effect of a common environment on the similarities normally found between the latter.

Two important early investigations of foster children as compared with children in their own homes, one by Burks (7) and the other by Freeman and his associates (21), disagreed as to the extent of the effect of the foster-home environment. Burks found that the correlations between parents and their own children were considerably higher than correlations between children and foster parents. Her findings led to the conclusion that heredity contributes far more to the child's mental status than does environment. Burks placed the estimate of the total effect of heredity as high as from seventy-five to eighty per cent.

---
[13] For studies in this field see Thorndike (89), Wingfield and Sandiford (108), Hirsch (36), Merriman (63), and Newman, Freeman, and Holzinger (65). Carter (9), and more recently Jones (45), have reviewed studies in this area.

A higher estimate of the effect of the environment was given by Freeman, Holzinger, and their associates (21). These investigators found that children improved in intelligence after being placed in foster homes, the improvements being greater among children who were placed in the better homes. The correlation between the intelligence of children and that of their foster parents was .37, and correlations between unrelated children reared in the same house ranged from .25 to .37. To estimate what these figures mean, it is necessary only to bear in mind that if children and adults were paired quite at random the correlation to be expected would be zero. Siblings separated before the age of six and reared in different homes showed a correlation of .25 as compared with the correlation upward to .50 among siblings reared in the same home. Although the authors in this study do not venture to estimate by means of statistical devices just what percentage of influence heredity exerts on a person's intelligence, their correlations indicate that if such an estimate were made it would be much lower than the estimate given by Burks.

That it is necessary to be cautious in interpreting the resemblance between parents and foster children has been emphasized in findings obtained by Leahy (55). Because of the efforts of placement agencies to "fit the child to the home," a child may resemble his adopted parents quite apart from any influence which they have had upon him. Leahy correlated such factors as the education and the occupation of foster parents with factors in the family background of the true parents of the adopted children. Leahy's figures indicate that, as a result of selective placement, some resemblance between adopted children and their foster parents may be expected quite apart from the influence of living in the same home.

Subsequent studies of foster children have also disagreed as to the probable effect of the home environment on the child's intelligence. In a study by Leahy (56), in which care was taken to consider factors such as selective placement, it was found that the correlation between "own" parents and children ranged considerably higher (clustering around .50) than correlations between foster parents and children (clustering around .20). After weighing factors involved in the original placement of the children, Leahy's estimate of the influence of the home environment is smaller even than Burks'.

A higher estimate of the influence of the environment is given in findings reported by Skeels (78) and Skodak (80, 81). Skodak (80) studied foster children whose true parents were low in occupational status; many of them were also very low in educational status, although the median mother had a tenth-grade education according to such information as could be obtained. Some children whose true parents appeared to be incompetent and intellectually inferior exhibited I.Q.'s that were well above average. Furthermore, the average child in a group of 154 children who were placed in foster homes in early infancy showed a higher level of development than would be expected on the basis of such information as could be obtained concerning the intellectual status of their parents. The findings also indicate, however, that environmental factors are not solely responsible. Intelligence ratings were available in the case of eighty of the true mothers of the children who were placed in foster homes in early infancy; the correlation between the I.Q.'s of these mothers and the I.Q.'s of their children when first tested was practically zero (.06), but when the children were tested a second time, it was .24.

As can be seen, the testimony from studies of foster children varies, but certain generalizations can be made. The studies indicate that there will be a considerably higher than chance resemblance between foster children and their true parents, even though they have lived in different environments since the children's birth. Most of the studies likewise indicate that the environmental factor will have an effect on differences in intelligence. The estimate as to the influence of the environment varies. In individual cases, there may be a large discrepancy between the intelligence of a foster child and the intelligence of his true parents; such discrepancies may be quite noticeable if, for example, the foster child lives in an optimum environment while his true parents, by reason of unfavorable circumstances, have lacked the opportunity and stimulus fully to develop and utilize their intellectual powers. It may also be noted, however, that by reason of complex hereditary and environmental factors, marked differences sometimes also appear in the case of parents and one of their own offspring living in the same home.[14]

Findings with respect to the intelligence of foster children are of interest to people who are thinking of adoption. Unfortunately for such persons, the findings are not definitive or conclusive. On the one hand, the findings show that at least in individual cases a child whose family background seems to be very unpromising may turn out to be a bright child. It is only reasonable to assume that the better a home is the more it should call forth the best there is in a child. On the other hand, the quantitative findings, considered in their totality, certainly do not indicate that a bright husband and wife could adopt any child, chosen quite at random, and count on the home environment to produce a child with the same level of intelligence as theirs. (But neither can such parents be sure that a child of their own will be as intelligent as they.) In the writer's judgment, a prospective foster parent who thinks it is very important that his adopted child should be a *bright* child should think twice, for if he is genuinely interested in adoption, it is a *child* he should want, not an I.Q. However, if there is a good reason to believe, from a practical point of view, that a bright child would fit more comfortably into a certain family circle in a certain community, it obviously would be wise to select a child (if there is room for choice) whose true parents give evidence of being

---

[14] Many questions with regard to test procedures, selection of children, age at placement, statistical procedures, and interpretation of statistical results have been raised with respect to the studies of foster children reviewed above. Students who are interested should see Jones (45a) and the *Thirty-ninth Yearbook of the National Society for the Study of Education,* Parts I and II (1940).

above average in intelligence (this does not mean, necessarily, that they should be above average in education or occupational status). It should also be remembered that the kind of mental ability measured by intelligence tests represents only a small feature of a child's total personality and this ability constitutes only one factor among a great many that will determine whether a foster child and a foster parent will be good companions.

EFFECT OF SCHOOLING ON INTELLECTUAL DEVELOPMENT

The question as to whether and to what extent a child's intelligence will be influenced by the amount, kind, and timing of the schooling he receives has important implications.

If a child's intelligence test scores vary according to the schooling he has received, several questions arise. Does this mean that intelligence tests are, to a large extent, a measure of the skills and performances a child has learned? Or does it mean that through his schooling the child not only has learned specific things but is now equipped with a mind that possesses more power and incisiveness in dealing with new or different intellectual tasks than it would have possessed if the youngster had gone to a different school or had not gone to school at all? If such a gain in power is produced, would it be possible through education to produce a race of adults with minds superior on the average to those of present human beings, just as the average human being now is superior to the average moron or (to put it in even more high-falutin terms) just as the average moron is intellectually superior to the average ape? These are heady questions, which the research findings do not answer conclusively but which show the kind of speculation to which findings in this area might lead.

Many studies have dealt with the effect of nursery-school experience on the I.Q. Controlled studies at this level are especially timely and have been somewhat easier to conduct than studies at later age levels, since it is possible to match children who go to nursery school with children who do not, whereas all children are required by law to go to school at the elementary level. The findings in these studies do not add up to one answer but to several generalizations, and most of these generalizations do not answer yes or no, but maybe.

In several studies, most prominent among which are studies conducted by Wellman and her associates at the University of Iowa, children who have attended nursery school have shown gains in I.Q. In several other studies the findings have shown little or no change in I.Q.[15] The reported average gains following a year in nursery school, in studies in which gains have appeared, have not been large as compared with the differences between the I.Q.'s of children in the population at large. In one of Wellman's studies average gains of about six to eight points were noted between fall and spring tests (104).

In the Iowa studies it was found that the gains were not shared alike by children of high and low mental ability. Children of average ability gained most; children somewhat above average gained less; and very bright children gained little or nothing.[16]

In a study by McCandless, reported by Wellman (102), an experiment was performed with six superior five-year-old children (I.Q.'s ranging from 125 to 165), who were given "an especially enriched curriculum" in the nursery school. For several months the children worked on special projects for about an hour a day. They were compared with a control group of children of similar age and initial ability who shared the same nursery-school environment, with the exception of periods of time spent on special projects. Such projects included a trip to a farm, building and equip-

---

[15] For an account of many studies dealing with this problem see references numbered 2, 6, 19, 31, 46, 53, 66, 83, 96, 99. A more recent study has been reported by McHugh (60a).

[16] When a complex function such as intelligence is tested by means of measurements that are subject to error, it is likely, of course, that there will be some shift in individual score on a second test, regardless of any actual change in intellectual ability that may have taken place. Moreover, if a change in scores does occur the chances are greater that those who earned the lowest scores on the first test will score somewhat higher and that those who earned the highest scores will show a downward rather than an upward shift on a second test.

INTELLIGENCE

ping of a miniature farm, various other constructional enterprises, expeditions, stories, and efforts on the teachers' part to answer all questions fully and to make suggestions leading to higher levels of thinking. The special projects did not produce statistically reliable gains, but at the end of the project, the experimental children were found to stand "slightly higher than the control group intellectually."

One of the most interesting studies of the effects of the nursery-school environment (79) was undertaken in a large orphanage. The orphanage children came from poor homes and from parents who, in the main, would be considered below normal. The orphanage itself provided meager stimulation, it offered limited opportunities, involved a good deal of mass treatment of the younger children, and was crowded and understaffed. From a large group of residents, matched experimental and control groups were selected. Both groups were kept in the orphanage environment, but for certain hours of the day the experimental group attended a nursery school that was established in the institution.

The usual preschool procedures had to be modified considerably at the start by virtue of the handicaps of these children as compared with the usual child who comes to nursery school from his own home. The orphanage children were lacking in their background of routine habits, in imaginativeness and enterprise in using materials, and in other respects. They showed an attitude of distrust that had grown out of their previous habit of shifting for themselves without the reassurance of parental protection. They were notably deficient in language development; their vocabularies, at most ages, were only one-fourth to one-half the size of those of children of average intelligence at the same age.[17]

Large changes in intelligence during the course of the experiment were noted in individual cases. Children who attended

---
[17] The opportunity which the nursery school gave to these children to overcome these and other effects of deprivation and psychological poverty in their customary environment will no doubt strike many readers as being far more important than the fact that they might also in the process gain in average I.Q.

nursery school during a period of about twenty months showed an average gain of 4.6 points in I.Q. as measured by the Kuhlmann or Stanford revisions of the Binet scale, while the control children during this time showed an average loss of 4.6 points. The direction of the change, especially in comparisons between subgroups, is noteworthy. During the period of the study, children in the higher classifications of intelligence, as compared with the general level of the group as a whole (I.Q. averaging 90 to 99 and 80 to 89), in the control group were heading toward lower levels, but the trend in the preschool group was not so uniform. Those who initially were about average tended to remain so, while those at lower levels moved upward. Children of the higher levels who were transferred to foster homes made gains in intelligence following placement, but such children from the control groups did not, within the time limits of the later observations, reach the level of children who had attended the nursery school.

Other studies in the Iowa series likewise emphasize the possible effects of environmental conditions. In one study it was found that preschool children who moved on to certain elementary schools maintained or continued to increase their I.Q.'s, while other preschool children who went on to certain other schools did not make further gains (101). Another study (82) indicated that three different schools differed in their "mental stimulation value."

The possibility that the mental level of the group with which a child associates may have an important effect on his intellectual growth is indicated by findings in a study of institutional children by Crissey (12). Children of border-line or moron levels tended to hold their own or to make slight gains when in company with children of normal or dull-normal intelligence; but in the same company, children of normal or superior intelligence showed losses. Again border-line children showed losses when transferred to a feeble-minded group. According to Wellman (102), there is "no really satisfactory substitute for association with other children of high ability. Children set goals for themselves in terms of what other children do."[18]

The results noted above are arresting. However, numerous questions have been raised concerning the findings reviewed above,[19] and in several other studies it has been found that nursery-school attendance has no significant effect on the I.Q., especially in the case of children who come from normal or relatively superior homes. Among these is a study by Goodenough and Maurer (31) which gives a number of comparisons after one, two, and three years of nursery-school training, as well as comparisons between the initial scores of matched groups and the scores of the same children at the age of six and a half years. Comparisons are shown for the groups as a whole and for subgroups corresponding to the occupations of the children's parents. In none of the comparisons do the children who have had nursery-school experience exhibit significant gains or changes as compared with the non-nursery-school children. The findings indicate, among other things, that the children who were sent to nursery school were superior from the start, on the average, to the general run of children in their occupational groupings. The findings also show that children of both nursery-school and control groups made gains on retestings, but the gains thus exhibited were about the same for the two groups.

Many of the studies of the effects of nursery-school experience

---

[18] This statement pertaining to the general subject of intellectual growth is borne out more specifically by studies reviewed in Chapter IX which indicate the influence a child's associates may have on his language development.

[19] Problems of methodology and interpretation that arise in studies in this area—including the difficulty of obtaining valid intelligence ratings at the preschool level, problems of sampling and matching, the problem as to whether gains in I.Q. represent a true improvement in intellectual capacity as distinguished from increased skill in dealing with the practical details of the test situation, and the possibility that changes and leveling tendencies might represent, in part, the phenomenon of regression toward the mean which frequently appears in remeasurements of a complex function by means of a fallible instrument—have been discussed in a review by McNemar (61), a reply by Wellman, Skeels, and Skodak (105), and in articles by Goodenough (28, 29), J. E. Anderson (1), and R. L. Thorndike (94).

have dealt with children from homes that were average or, if anything, superior to homes in the general population. It might be that with such children the cards are loaded against findings to the effect that nursery school might raise the intellectual level. If the child already enjoys a "good" environment there is less that the nursery school could add to it than would be the case if the child suffered from neglect and deprivation at home. This is shown by Olson and Hughes (66) who found that nursery-school children from privileged backgrounds did not differ significantly in their intellectual growth from non-nursery-school children of similar backgrounds; and children who attended nursery school an average of over two hundred days did not differ significantly from children who, on the average, had attended only about half as many days. The investigators point out, however, that it might be argued that the home nurture of these children was already of such character that the nursery school could add little to it. They suggest also that different results might possibly be obtained if studies were made of children who suffer from deprivation in the home environment and for whom the nursery school might provide intellectual nurture more in keeping with their potential achievement.

Because of the many as yet unsolved problems in connection with the measurement of intelligence, especially at the early age levels, it is not possible at the present time to give a definitive appraisal of the nature-nurture problem in the light of recent studies of preschool children. It is possible to hazard some generalizations, however. The findings mentioned above do not, by and large, promise that a child from a good home environment will be likely to show a substantial rise in I.Q. if sent to nursery school. (He may, of course, gain in many other ways, as has been shown in studies of the effects of nursery-school experience on children's social adjustments, habits, and skills.) The evidence cannot, however, be weighed simply by counting the investigations that show gains as against those that do not. By virtue of differences in educational programs and teacher personnel, it is possible that nursery schools vary in the extent to which they stimulate the child's intellectual development. It is likewise possible that even if programs were similar they might have a different effect on children who enjoy few advantages in their everyday lives than upon children who have many advantages.

Effect of schooling on I.Q.'s at the elementary-school level. In studies of older children gains in intelligence have been reported after children have been transferred from institutions to foster homes or from one community to another offering better educational opportunities (51, 52, 57). One study (mentioned above) suggests that different schools may vary in the intellectual stimulus they afford (82). On the latter point, however, it appears that no large changes can be expected simply by sending children, who already have average educational opportunities, to relatively superior elementary schools or by transferring children from regular classes in a reasonably good school system to special "opportunity" classes.

Pritchard, Horan, and Hollingworth (73) report a study of 111 children of below average intelligence and socio-economic status who were transferred from their regular classrooms in the New York public-school system to special classes in a school that was designed to provide an optimal educational environment.[20] The curriculum for the slow-learning group was elastic; the work centered around units of work selected by pupils and teachers. There was extensive use of trips to museums, motion pictures, and other visual devices. The children had the use of class libraries and a large college library, and were guided in their use of these by teachers and librarians. Many of the children received special "remedial" instruction; special teachers gave them instruction in numerous fields, such as general science, music, nutrition, and physical education. Classes were considerably smaller than those previously attended by the pupils, and the children received much

---

[20] For a description of this school see Featherstone (16).

individual attention. The children were tested when they were transferred to this school and again after two or more years of attendance. At the time of the first test, the children ranged in age from about six years to twelve years and three months. The average I.Q.'s on the first tests and on the tests administered after two or more years were substantially the same. There was an average gain of 1.11 points. Gains in I.Q. occurred primarily in the case of the youngest children (the largest gain, 5.33 points, was shown by eight-year-old children who had been in the school an average of two and a half years), while the older children showed losses (thirteen-year-olds and fourteen-year-olds who had been in the school an average of about three years showed respective average losses of 0.72 and 3.40 points). The children seemed to derive many benefits from the school's program, but these benefits did not consist in a gain in scores on intelligence tests. The program did not significantly alter the pattern of their mental growth as measured by standardized intelligence tests.[21] The likelihood that an elementary-school program of a sort generally regarded as superior will not induce consistent or substantial gains in average I.Q. is indicated in a study by R. L. Thorndike and others (96).

A question can be raised, of course, as to what constitutes a superior educational environment. But on this question, as on the question as to why some schools seem to produce gains while others do not, we have no definite information. Apart from these considerations, it may be added that the results in studies such as those cited immediately above might have been different if children had been transferred from conditions of extreme deprivation to a good school environment. At the elementary and high-school level it might make little difference as far as I.Q. is concerned whether a child attended a "good" school or a school rated

---

[21] The authors add that the results might be quite different if measurements were made of factors other than changes in I.Q., such as changes in degree of personal satisfaction and adjustment. A preliminary report by Featherstone bears out and amplifies this conjecture (17).

not so good, and yet it might make a great deal of difference if he did not attend school at all. Findings in a study by Lorge (58) support this view. A number of boys who were first tested in 1921-1922 when they were in the eighth grade were retested, twenty years later, in 1941. During the intervening twenty years the young people had continued their schooling for varying lengths of time; some had gone no farther than to the end of the eighth grade while others had gone beyond high school. The youngsters were now grouped in terms of highest grade completed by 1941 and in terms of scores earned in 1921. In a large number of comparisons that could be made on the basis of this two-dimensional grouping it was found that higher scores were earned by those who had gone on to complete higher grades in school. The farther persons went in their schooling (as measured by *highest grade completed,* not number of years of school attended)[22] the higher their scores tended to be as compared with their original ratings in 1921.[23]

Such findings show that "schooling makes a difference," but what is this "difference"?[24] Does this ability to earn a higher score on an intelligence test mean a difference in "basic" intelligence? The answer is that "basic" intelligence, if we assume that such exists, can be measured only indirectly by means of a person's ability in dealing with intellectual tasks and intelligence tests have been found to provide a good measure of such ability.

Findings such as these do not, of course, mean that intelligence rises in proportion to amount of schooling or that people with

---
[22] That this distinction must be made is shown in a study by E. L. Thorndike (91) of the ablest and least able children in a group of seven hundred. Many of the least able spent years in school repeating the same grade without gaining in intelligence.

[23] In a study by McConnell (60) it was found that college students showed gains in scores when tested in the freshman year and again in the senior year. In a study by Finch (18) it was found that the average score on a test of mental ability earned by the high-school population of an entire city in 1942 was slightly higher than the average score in the same high school in 1923 when the enrollment was much smaller, by reason, largely, of the fact that a smaller and presumably more "select" proportion of the children attended high school.

[24] Problems of interpretation in dealing with findings such as these are discussed by Garrett (22).

equal schooling will have equal intelligence. In spite of gains in scores of many (but not all) individuals who continued their school progress in Lorge's study, there was a high degree of correspondence between scores obtained twenty years apart (correlations of .62 and .64 respectively on the two instruments that were used at the time of the final test). Gains were relative to initial scores. A few children whose scores were among the highest on the first test and who went no farther than the eighth grade earned decidedly higher scores twenty years later than did children initially in the lowest brackets who successfully completed two, three, or four grades in high school.

The studies by Wellman and her associates and a study such as the one by Lorge suggest that the potentialities that might be realized through nurture are greater than has commonly been supposed. The implications of these findings for human betterment are obvious. If further studies confirm and extend the results so far obtained, it will be a matter for rejoicing; if they modify or contradict the results, that too will be valuable, for in the process, more will be learned concerning the development of intellectual ability and factors that influence it.

In passing, it may be re-emphasized that the foregoing discussion does not imply that the stimulus value of nursery-school education or of later educational provisions can be measured simply by "before-and-after" mental tests. Such educational provisions are usually not designed primarily to accelerate the development of abstract intelligence. As noted earlier, the opportunities so afforded may have an effect on the child's everyday habits and skills, his motor development, and his social and emotional adjustments, quite apart from any gains in I.Q. There may be gains also in the child's "functioning intelligence," in the effectiveness and the ways in which he puts his intelligence to use, even if there are no demonstrable gains in his intelligence quotient as measured by mental tests.

From everyday observation we can note that two children may

have the same I.Q. yet differ decidedly in the way they use their abilities. Children may differ so much in their everyday behavior and adjustment that the fact of their similarity in intelligence seems to be a minor detail. Moreover, the manner in which intelligence functions in the life of an individual child will not simply depend upon environmental stimuli but will be influenced also by the constellation of factors that constitute what we call an individual's "personality." Much of the research on intellectual ability has dealt with intelligence as a thing apart; relatively little systematic study, from a developmental point of view, has been made of the way in which mental ability functions in the child's "all-round" development.

Implications of changes in I.Q. for future use and development of mental tests. The values of mental tests are by no means negated by findings that show changes in I.Q. or by the observation that there are many aspects of mental activity that are not measured by intelligence tests. If a stimulating educational environment can produce gains in intellectual capacity, it becomes all the more vital to apply mental tests to find what changes are being accomplished. On the other hand, if there is no change in the child's intellectual capacities, mental tests remain quite as useful and important as they have been in the past as a practical aid in understanding and guiding the child.

GIFTED CHILDREN

Children with high intelligence tend also to be above, rather than below, average in many other characteristics, but by virtue of the fact that human abilities are uneven a child may have a very high I.Q. and still be rather mediocre in art or mechanics, or ability to get along with others. Indeed, the fact that a person has very high abstract intelligence is no guarantee that he will surpass others in insight into himself, in understanding of other people, in practical shrewdness, in "common sense" or ordinary "horse sense."

In studies conducted by Terman and his associates and by L. S. Hollingworth (37), children of high intelligence have been observed over a period of years. The original investigation by Terman (85) included 1,000 children, all with I.Q.'s above 130, who were compared with unselected children. Many tests and ratings were applied.

In the majority of cases, the mental superiority of the gifted child appeared at a very early age in such forms as precocity in learning to talk, greater intellectual curiosity, greater wealth of information, and a desire to learn to read. Even when the children had similar educational opportunities in public schools, the gifted children were more rapidly promoted and stood decidedly higher in educational achievement tests.

The reading of gifted children surpassed that of their unselected peers in both quantity and quality. Gifted children had a larger fund of play interests and of play information than had unselected children. They also surpassed in tests of honesty, trustworthiness, and similar moral traits.

The gifted children, as a group, were somewhat superior to their less intelligent peers in physical status and health.

The above statements review some of the many points of superiority shown by highly intelligent children as compared with children whose average intelligence is lower. It must be remembered that these statements describe the characteristics of gifted children as a group, rather than those of any one particular child.

These gifted children were once more studied after a period of six years, and among the many findings obtained are the following: As in the original study, intellectually gifted children as a group are found to be slightly superior to unselected children in health and physique; they average better than the general school population in character traits, emotional stability, and social adaptability; gifted children excel in school progress as measured by promotion to higher grades, but they excel even more in mastery of school subjects; as a rule, gifted boys maintain or almost maintain their superiority from childhood through adolescence, while girls somewhat more frequently show a drop in I.Q. at the time of adolescence or soon thereafter.

The interesting feature in this study was that after the passage of six years the children, as a group, exhibited much the same all-round superiority as they had displayed when studied at an earlier age. Individual children, of course, varied from the general trend, and some showed changes in I.Q. as they grew older.

In the year 1938, new information was obtained in the case of over 1,300 gifted children who, earlier, had been studied during elementary- or high-school years.[25] It was found that nearly ninety per cent of the boys and eighty-five per cent of the girls had gone to college. Although the gifted children were on the average nearly two years younger than their classmates, they were about three times as likely to graduate with honors. About two-fifths of the boys and one-fifth of the girls had earned half or more than half of their expenses as undergraduates. The gifted group received more than its proportionate share of class and student-body honors, except in athletics.

Although a large majority of the individuals made superior records in college, some did not. Of those who did not do well, the poor college record was not due to lack of ability, but to various other factors—such as lack of interest, maladjustments of various kinds, or deliberate neglect of college studies in favor of private pursuits or extracurricular activities. It appeared that many of those who did not do well in college had underestimated the amount of effort necessary to make a good record by virtue of the small amount of study required to earn good grades prior to college. Of those who had completed their training and could be classed as employable, less than one per cent were unemployed in 1936, even though this was a period of widespread unemployment. The moral record of the group was found to be "well above that of the generality." At least half of the boys were launched upon

---

[25] For a full account of the findings, see Terman and Oden (88).

promising careers, and several of them were already nationally or internationally known.

In summarizing general accomplishments of the group, Terman and Oden state that although a considerable proportion of the subjects had not lived up to their ability, the accomplishment of the group as a whole was as good as could reasonably be expected, in view of the fact that most of the young people were still under thirty years of age and that the economic depression had prevented many from going to college and, in many other cases, had interfered with post-graduate professional training or occupational placement.

A very interesting conclusion is that, for children brought up under present-day educational regimes, the possession of an I.Q. in excess of 140 or 150 adds little to one's achievement in the early adult years. Above this level, adult success is largely determined by social adjustment, emotional stability, and the drive to accomplish. This does not mean, the investigators state, that the potentiality for achievement is the same for individuals with an I.Q. of 150 as for persons with higher I.Q.'s. Rather, they state, the more probable interpretation is that we have not learned how to bring the highest gifts to fruition and how best to guide the personality development of those who are extremely bright.

In a review of literature in this field, Hollingworth (38) also notes that as a group gifted children maintain themselves in superior fashion in their later academic work and in their adult adjustments. However, there are individuals who do not do so well at maturity, indicating the important role played by factors other than intelligence. Intelligence alone is not enough for "success."

The fact that level of achievement and general excellence as a person do not necessarily rise with rise in intelligence appears in an account by Hollingworth of exceedingly bright persons with I.Q.'s of 180 or more (42). A person of such towering intelligence may perform spectacular feats and yet, for lack of well-balanced personal qualities, his achievements as an individual or his contribution to society may be quite mediocre.

In passing it may be noted that the label "genius" is sometimes applied to children of high I.Q. Actually a person is not a genius simply by virtue of having an I.Q. of 130 or 140 or more; he is not a genius even by virtue of having an I.Q. of 200, although he may be something of a freak.

Education of the gifted. Gifted children represent a valuable social asset. According to Hollingworth, "There is no more serious question than this in education: How shall a democracy educate the most educable." (41, p. 318.) Although such children are quite resourceful in finding ways of putting their abilities to work, they cannot themselves create an environment that would bring out their full potentialities (39, 40, 41, 42). What often happens is that these gifted children are held back rather than helped. If they are made to slacken their pace to that of classmates of the same age, they have time on their hands. Hollingworth estimates that in the ordinary elementary-school situation children of 140 I.Q. waste half of their time and those above 170 I.Q. waste practically all of their time!

In one case, one of the most tangible results of a child's brightness was an increase in the amount of laundering that the mother had to do because of the amount of cleaning of blackboards and erasers this child engaged in while her classmates were working at their lessons. Frequently a bright child becomes a strain upon the teacher, especially if the teacher resents pupils who know more than he or if the child not only knows much but shows no hesitation in parading his knowledge and correcting others."[26]

If a gifted child is promoted in keeping with his academic abili-

---

[26] The late Professor Leta S. Hollingworth made outstanding contributions in the field of education of gifted children. During the last years of her life, she directed an educational program for bright public-school children. Some of her observations and findings have been compiled in a posthumous volume prepared for publication by H. L. Hollingworth (42).

ties, he may have difficulty because he has been placed with older and bigger children. Rules and regulations and customs and restraints of various kinds conspire to prevent him from realizing his potentialities, especially if his parents do not have the means or the desire to help; and it would be "an impossibly shrewd and strong child" who could work out his own education. Should he want to use some of his spare time to earn money for his own needs, he would not only encounter difficulties in getting employment but would also run afoul of truancy laws and child-labor restrictions.

Following are a few illustrations from Hollingworth (41) of the problems of bright children in school. A ten-year-old boy with an I.Q. of 165 was referred as a problem: "Not interested in schoolwork. Very impudent. A liar." His trouble was by no means lack of interest. The teacher had resented the boy's superior knowledge and had given him a "raking-over" before the whole class. A friendly counselor to whom he was telling his troubles suggested that he should learn to be more tolerant. But the child was so filled with resentment that when told: "One of the first things to learn in the world is to suffer fools *gladly*," he heard only the word "suffer" and replied: "Yes, that's it. That's what *I* say! Make 'em suffer. Roll a rock on 'em." As the conversation proceeded, however, he was "straightened out on the subject of who was to do the suffering. He agreed to do it himself." The epithet, "Perfesser," was thrown at another ten-year-old child, of I.Q. 175, when he tried to discuss events of medieval history; when he persisted, his schoolmates pulled his hair, tore his shirt from his back, and hit him with a beer bottle. Two other bright children came to the new school followed by reports that they were hard of hearing. Actually, they had good hearing; but in self-defense, "they learned not to hear the insupportable drill on things they had known for years," so that their teachers thought them deaf. When transferred to classes for bright children, their hearing turned out to be good, "almost too good!"

The children in Hollingworth's experiment were able to cover the regular elementary-school course requirements in less than half their time and were able to push far ahead into projects with which the average child and even the average adult, usually does not become familiar. Hollingworth has emphasized that a program of intellectual training represents only a part, however, of the bright child's needs. Quite as much does he need training and opportunities for the development of wholesome attitudes toward other persons and competence as a social being. Hollingworth lists five special problems of general conduct faced by bright children: to find enough hard and interesting work to do at school, to learn gladly to accept and be tolerant of others who are less able, to keep from becoming negativistic, to keep from becoming hermits, and to avoid the formation of habits of extreme chicanery.

MENTAL DEFICIENCY

What constitutes "feeble-mindedness" is largely a matter of definition. A frequent procedure is to class as feeble-minded those individuals who have an I.Q. below 70. Children with low intelligence can roughly be classified into various groups, with idiots representing the lowest group, then imbeciles, then morons. Next above the moron is the "borderline" group with I.Q.'s between 70 and 80, then come those with a rank of "dull" (80-90 I.Q.), and then the "average" (I.Q. 90-110). In some educational writings children with lower than average intelligence who are unable to keep the pace with youngsters of their own age have been called "slow learners." These names of classifications are quite arbitrary; the individual's underlying ability, rather than the label, is the important thing to consider.

Mental deficiency is usually a condition which characterizes a child throughout his development. In the usual case, the defect is continuous rather than a condition which either suddenly or gradually sets in after a period of normal growth.

By reason of the fact that children at the lower end of the intellectual scale usually require special care and protection, considerably more attention has been devoted to them than to children at the upper end of the scale. Children who are feeble-minded or who have border-line or dull-normal intelligence have produced many problems in the elementary school. A large proportion of pupil "troublemakers" are youngsters with low intelligence. The "troublesomeness" of such children does not arise, however, primarily because a child of low intelligence has a special bent for getting into difficulties. The trouble lies more in the kinds of demands that are placed upon him. Pressure is put upon him to keep pace with others in the conventional curriculum. The less able he is in the usual school subjects, the less opportunity there is for him to enjoy the satisfaction that comes with achievement. Sometimes, to be sure, special remedial work can go far to help him gain satisfaction through mastery and thus provide more of an incentive for academic work. Also, as has been suggested in studies reviewed earlier in this chapter, many children of apparently low intelligence may have latent potentialities and may considerably improve their status under proper environmental stimulation. However, even the most optimistic interpretation of available evidence concerning environmental effects on intelligence does not suggest that mental deficiency can be eliminated by a program designed to raise the level of abstract intelligence of children who are below normal.

More important is the adjustment of educational demands and opportunities to the child's abilities, a policy which, in effect, might raise the level of the children's functioning or practical intelligence, whether or not gains were shown in the I.Q. The problem of adapting educational procedures to children of lower mentality has been sharpened in recent years by the fact that children who, in the past, would drop out somewhere along in the grades when they reached the age of fourteen or thereabout are now compelled to remain in school. Some years ago, the high-school population tended to represent a somewhat select group of children; but now, in many school systems, it represents practically a normal distribution of intelligence, including a large proportion of children whose minds are not especially receptive to classical high-school requirements, such as algebra and Latin. It has been necessary to change offerings in the direction of a program that more realistically meets the abilities and needs of such children. Much of what is introduced for the slow learner is also of value to children of higher intelligence.

An important aspect of the education of dull children is to cultivate and utilize qualities that are most educable, rather than to badger them into being mathematicians or historians. Although good traits tend to be positively correlated, the bright children by no means have a corner on the market. The child who is less bright has much the same potentialities for acquiring good habits of everyday social behavior. Furthermore, as noted in an earlier chapter, there is relatively little correlation between mental and motor abilities, and there are many everyday skills (except those that require a good deal of inventiveness and problem solving) that the less intelligent child can master practically as well as the bright child. Indeed, such skills may be quite as remunerative as the more learned occupations (for example, the mechanic who makes a dental appliance may be getting a higher average rate of pay than the dentist).

One complication here is the pressure of conventions and parental ambitions, and of traditions concerning "high-brow" and "low-brow" occupations. Children get the notion, quite early, that it is more honorable to head their ambitions toward the learned professions. As a result, the occupational preferences voiced by many children are out of line with what the child eventually will be able to achieve or would find most satisfying. It is possible that as the school program is brought more into line with children's capabilities and as the influence of legislation that affects wages and working conditions takes effect there will be greater appeal in the kinds of work that a large majority of the children will ultimately have to do.

FAMILY AND SOCIO-ECONOMIC STATUS AND
INTELLIGENCE

Children's intelligence and parents' occupational status. Intelligence tests of men drafted into the United States Army during the World Wars and numerous other studies of adults have shown that there is a wide difference between the average intelligence of individuals belonging to different occupational groups. The intelligence of men employed as unskilled laborers is lower on the average than that of people occupied in the professions or engaged as business executives. Similar differences appear when the children of parents in different occupational groups are compared. Children of unskilled laborers, to much the same degree as their parents, stand relatively low in intelligence as compared with children in the professional classes. In tests given by Haggerty and Nash (32), the median I.Q. among grade-school children of parents engaged in the professions was found to be 116; children of skilled laborers had a median I.Q. of 98, while that of children of unskilled laborers was 89.

In Terman's study of 1,000 gifted children, who were selected at random without regard to family background, it was found that parents who were engaged in the professions and who constituted a very small percentage of the population of the state provided a greater number of gifted children than did industrial workers, who constituted 57.7 per cent of the population (85).

These differences in intelligence as related to occupational status also appear when measurements are taken of children between the ages of two and four years. Goodenough (30) made a sixfold classification of the occupations of parents of two- to four-year-old children who were given intelligence tests; they were arranged in terms of rough hierarchy, ranging from the professions (medicine, law, journalism, and so forth) in the first group to unskilled labor in the sixth group. When two-, three-, and four-year-old children were thus classified, the average I.Q. of the children of the professional group on the first two tests was 116.1, while that of children of unskilled laborers was 96. When the children were tested a second time, the respective averages were 125 and 95.8. The children of each succeeding occupational group, going upward from the unskilled laboring class to the professional class, showed a progressively higher average score.

Needless to say, individual differences within each occupational group are a good deal larger than the differences between the average scores of different groups.

The question arises: To what extent is the higher average intelligence of children of the "upper" occupational levels due to a better environment, and to what extent is it due to heredity? A precise answer cannot be given to this question. A child's environment obviously may have an important bearing, as is indicated by findings such as those reviewed earlier in this chapter. It is also possible that the native abilities of a child's parents played a part in determining their occupational status. Both factors, no doubt, are at work, but perhaps not to the same degree or in the same manner in the case of individual children. The fact that the average intelligence score varies with socio-economic status is obviously not an argument for discriminating against one group or another in the kind of education that is provided. Rather, educational opportunity should be equalized in terms of the merit of the individual, whatever his origin, rather than in terms of the prestige, financial means, and customs of his parents.

Intelligence and family size. Repeated investigations bring out the fact that parents of high intelligence have a smaller average number of children than parents of low intelligence. This trend has been accelerated during recent generations. In Terman's study of gifted children, it appeared that the average number of offspring per individual in the intelligence level represented by gifted children was fifty per cent lower than that found for the same families in the preceding generation. According to these findings, the average person representing the stratum from which the gifted children were drawn produces 0.72 of a child. While this general trend appears in the population as a whole, it will not necessarily hold true within a given segment of the population. One study (67) indicates, for example, that the ablest men among the graduates in selected Princeton classes from 1891 to 1921, as measured by various criteria of success in and out of college, show a higher birth rate than the least able, even though the group as a whole had a birth rate below replacement.

This finding that there is, on the average, an inverse relation between family size and intelligence is sometimes misinterpreted in popular discussions. It does not mean that if parents have many children the family as a whole will therefore have a low I.Q.; nor does it mean that if a family is small its members will therefore have a high I.Q. The relationship indicates that parents with high intelligence seem to limit the number of their offspring more, on the average, than do parents with lower intelligence. It is obvious that this trend, if it were to continue over a long period of time, would have important social implications.

Birth order and intelligence. Much study has centered upon the question as to whether the first-born child has advantages or disadvantages in his development as compared with children born later.[27] First-born children are more likely to be still-born, to suffer from abnormal delivery, to die during early infancy. On the whole, the evidence does not indicate that birth order as such is an outstanding factor in causing individual differences in mentality.

BIBLIOGRAPHY

1. Anderson, J. E.: "The Limitations of Infant and Preschool Tests in the Measurement of Intelligence," *Journal of Psychology* (1939), 8:351-379.
2. Anderson, L. D.: "A Longitudinal Study of the Effects of Nursery-School Training on Successive Intelligence-Test Ratings," *Thirty-Ninth Yearbook of the National Society for the Study of Education*

---

[27] Studies in this field have been reviewed by Thurstone and Jenkins (97) and by Jones (45a).

(Bloomington, Illinois: Public School Publishing Company, 1940), Pt. II, Ch. I, pp. 3-10.
3. Barrett, H. E. and Koch, H. L.: "The Effect of Nursery-School Training Upon the Mental-Test Performance of a Group of Orphanage Children," *Pedagogical Seminary and Journal of Genetic Psychology* (1930), 37:102-122.
4. Bayley, N.: *Mental Growth During the First Three Years,* Genetic Psychology Monographs (1933), Vol. 14, No. 1, 92 pp.
5. ———: "Mental Growth in Young Children," *Thirty-Ninth Yearbook of the National Society for the Study of Education* (1940), Pt. II, Ch. II, pp. 11-48.
6. Bird, G. E.: "The Effect of Nursery-School Attendance Upon Mental Growth of Children," *Thirty-Ninth Yearbook of the National Society for the Study of Education* (1940), Pt. II, Ch. IV, pp. 81-84.
7. Burks, B. S.: "The Relative Influence of Nature and Nurture Upon Mental Development: A Comparative Study of the Foster Parent-Foster Child Resemblance and True Parent-True Child Resemblance," *Twenty-Seventh Yearbook of the National Society for the Study of Education* (1928), Pt. I, Ch. X, pp. 219-316.
8. Burks, B. S., Jensen, D. W., and Terman, L. M.: *Genetic Studies of Genius. III. The Promise of Youth* (Stanford University: Stanford University Press, 1930), 508 pp.
9. Carter, H. D.: "Ten Years of Research on Twins: Contributions to the Nature-Nurture Problem," *Thirty-Ninth Yearbook of the National Society for the Study of Education* (1940), Pt. I, Ch. VIII, pp. 235-255.
10. Cattell, P.: "Do the Stanford-Binet I.Q.'s of Superior Boys and Girls Tend to Decrease or Increase with Age?" *Journal of Educational Research* (1932-1933), 26:668-673.
11. Conrad, H. S. and Jones, H. E.: "A Second Study of Familial Resemblance in Intelligence: Environmental and Genetic Implications of Parent-Child and Sibling Correlations in the Total Sample." *Thirty-Ninth Yearbook of the National Society for the Study of Education* (1940), Pt. II, Ch. VI, pp. 97-141.
12. Crissey, O. L.: *Mental Development as Related to Institutional Residence and Educational Achievement,* University of Iowa Studies in Child Welfare (1937), Vol. 13, No. 1, 81 pp.
13. Davis, R. A.: *Mentality of Orphans* (Boston: Richard G. Badger, 1930), 182 pp.
14. Dearborn, W. F., Rothney, J. W. M., and Shuttleworth, F. K.: *Data on the Growth of Public School Children (From the Materials of the Harvard Growth Study),* Monographs of the Society for Research in Child Development (1938), Vol. 3, No. 1, 136 pp.

15. Driscoll, G. P.: *The Developmental Status of the Preschool Child as a Prognosis of Future Development,* Child Development Monographs (New York: Teachers College, Columbia University, 1933), No. 13, 111 pp.
16. Featherstone, W. B.: "An 'Experience-Curriculum' for Slow Learners at Public School 500: Speyer School," *Teachers College Record* (1938), 39:287-295.
17. ———: "Teaching Slow Learners in Speyer School—A Report of Progress," paper delivered at the meeting of the American Educational Research Association (February 26, 1940).
18. Finch, F. H.: "Are High School Pupils of the Present Day Inferior to Those of an Earlier Period?" *School Review* (1944), 52:84-91.
19. Frandsen, A. and Barlow, F. P.: "Influence of the Nursery School on Mental Growth," *Thirty-Ninth Yearbook of the National Society for the Study of Education* (1940), Pt. II, Ch. VII, pp. 143-148.
20. Freeman, F. N. and Flory, C. D.: *Growth in Intellectual Ability as Measured by Repeated Tests,* Monographs of the Society for Research in Child Development (1937), Vol. 2, No. 2, 116 pp.
21. Freeman, F. N., Holzinger, K. J., and Mitchell, B. C., assisted by H. R. Bobo and C. H. Lorenzen: "The Influence of Environment on the Intelligence, School Achievement, and Conduct of Foster Children," *Twenty-Seventh Yearbook of the National Society for the Study of Education* (1928), Pt. I, Ch. IX, pp. 103-217.
22. Garrett, H. E.: "The Effects of Schooling on I.Q.," *Psychological Bulletin* (1946), 43:72-76.
23. Gesell, A.: *Infancy and Human Growth* (New York: Macmillan, 1928), 418 pp.
24. ———: *The Mental Growth of the Pre-school Child* (New York: Macmillan, 1925), 447 pp.
25. Gesell, A. and Thompson, H.: *The Psychology of Early Growth* (New York: Macmillan, 1938), 290 pp.
26. Gildea, H. and Macoubrey, C.: *Factors Affecting the Constancy of the Intelligence Quotients of Problem Children,* Smith College Studies in Social Work (1932-1933), 3:229-248.
27. Goodenough, F. L.: "A Preliminary Report on the Effect of Nursery-School Training Upon the Intelligence Test Scores of Young Children," *Twenty-Seventh Yearbook of the National Society for the Study of Education* (1928), Pt. I, Ch. XVI, pp. 361-369.
28. ———: "New Evidence on Environmental Influence on Intelligence," *Thirty-Ninth Yearbook of the National Society for the Study of Education* (1940), Pt. I, Ch. XI: 307-365.
29. ———: "Some Special Problems of Nature-Nurture Research,"

Thirty-Ninth Yearbook of the National Society for the Study of Education (1940), Pt. I, Ch. XII, pp. 367-384.

30. ———: "The Relation of the Intelligence of Preschool Children to the Occupation of Their Fathers," *American Journal of Psychology* (1928), 40:284-294.
31. Goodenough, F. L. and Maurer, K. M.: "The Mental Development of Nursery-School Children Compared with that of Non-Nursery-School Children," *Thirty-Ninth Yearbook of the National Society for the Study of Education* (1940), Pt. II, Ch. IX, pp. 161-178.
32. Haggerty, M. E. and Nash, H. B.: "Mental Capacity of Children and Paternal Occupation," *Journal of Educational Psychology* (1924), 15:559-572.
33. Hildreth, G.: "The Effect of School Environment Upon Stanford-Binet Tests of Young Children," *Twenty-Seventh Yearbook of the National Society for the Study of Education* (1928), Pt. I, Ch. XV, pp. 355-359.
34. ———: *The Resemblance of Siblings in Intelligence and Achievement,* Teachers College Contributions to Education (New York: Teachers College, Columbia University, 1925), No. 186, 65 pp.
35. Hirsch, N. D. M.: *An Experimental Study Upon Three Hundred School Children Over a Six-Year Period,* Genetic Psychology Monographs (1930), 7:487-548.
36. ———: *Twins: Heredity and Environment* (Cambridge: Harvard University Press, 1930), 159 pp.
37. Hollingworth, L. S.: *Gifted Children: Their Nature and Nurture* (New York: Macmillan, 1926), 374 pp.
38. ———: "Review of Research," Hollingworth, L. S., Terman, L. M., and Oden, M. "The Significance of Deviates," *Thirty-Ninth Yearbook of the National Society for the Study of Education* (1940), Pt. I, Ch. III, pp. 43-66.
39. ———: "The Founding of Public School 500: Speyer School," *Teachers College Record* (November, 1936), 38:119-128.
40. ———: "The Child of Very Superior Intelligence as a Special Problem in Social Adjustment," *Proceedings of the First International Congress on Mental Hygiene* (New York: The Informational Committee for Mental Hygiene, Inc., 1932), II: 47-69.
41. ———: "What We Know About the Early Selection and Training of Leaders," *Teachers College Record* (April, 1939), 40:575-592.
42. ———: *Children Above 180 I.Q.* (New York: World Book Company, 1942), 332 pp.
43. Hollingworth, L. S. and Kaunitz, R. M.: "The Centile Status of Gifted Children at Maturity," *Journal of Genetic Psychology* (1934), 45:106-120.

44. Honzik, M. P., "The Constancy of Mental Test Performance During the Preschool Period," *Journal of Genetic Psychology* (1938), 52:285-302.
45. Jones, H. E.: "A First Study of Parent-Child Resemblance in Intelligence," *Twenty-Seventh Yearbook of the National Society for the Study of Education* (1928), Pt. I, Ch. V, pp. 61-72.
45a. ———: "Environmental Influences on Mental Development," Chapter XI, p. 582-632 in Carmichael, L. (Editor) *Manual of Child Psychology* (New York: John Wiley and Son, 1946).
46. Jones, H. E. and Jorgensen, A. P.: "Mental Growth as Related to Nursery-School Attendance," *Thirty-Ninth Yearbook of the National Society for the Study of Education* (1940), Pt. II, Ch. XII, pp. 207-222.
47. Jones, H. E., Conrad, H. S., and Blanchard, M. B.: *Environmental Handicap in Mental Test Performance* (Berkeley: University of California Press, 1932), 99 pp.
48. Kawin, E. and Hoefer, C.: *A Comparative Study of a Nursery-School Versus a Non-Nursery-School Group* (Chicago: University of Chicago Press, 1931), 52 pp.
49. Klineberg, O.: "An Investigation of Psychological Differences Between Racial and Environmental Groups in Europe," *Ninth International Congress in Psychology, Proceedings and Papers* (1930), pp. 261-263.
50. ———: "Racial Differences in Speed and Accuracy," *Journal of Abnormal and Social Psychology* (1927), 22:273-277.
51. ———: *Negro Intelligence and Selective Migration* (New York: Columbia University Press, 1935), 66 pp.
52. ———: "The Intelligence of Migrants," *American Sociological Review* (1938), 3:218-224.
53. Lamson, E. E.: "A Follow-Up Study of a Group of Nursery-School Children," *Thirty-Ninth Yearbook of the National Society for the Study of Education* (1940), Pt. II, Ch. XIV, pp. 231-236.
54. Lawrence, E. M.: *An Investigation Into the Relation Between Intelligence and Inheritance,* British Journal of Psychology Monograph Supplement (1931), Vol. 16, No. 5, 80 pp.
55. Leahy, A. M.: "A Study of Certain Selective Factors Influencing Prediction of the Mental Status of Adopted Children," *Journal of Genetic Psychology* (1932), 41:294-329.
56. ———: *Nature-Nurture and Intelligence,* Genetic Psychology Monographs (1935), Vol. 17, No. 4:236-308.
57. Lithauer, D. B. and Klineberg, O.: "A Study of the Variation in I.Q. of a Group of Dependent Children in Institution and Foster Home," *Journal of Genetic Psychology* (1933), 42:236-242.

58. Lorge, I.: "Schooling Makes a Difference," *Teachers Record* (1945), pp. 483-492.
59. Lorge, I. and Hollingworth, L. S.: "Adult Status of Highly Intelligent Children," *Journal of Genetic Psychology* (1936), 49:215-226.
60. McConnell, T. R.: "Change in Scores on the Psychological Examination of the American Council on Education from Freshman to Senior Year," *Journal of Educational Psychology* (1934), 25:66-69.
60a. McHugh, G.: *Changes in I.Q. at the Public School Kindergarten Level,* Psychological Monographs (1943), Vol. 55, No. 2, 34 pp.
61. McNemar, Q.: "A Critical Examination of the University of Iowa Studies of Environmental Influences Upon the I.Q.," *Psychological Bulletin* (1940), 37:63-92.
62. ———: "Special Review: Newman, Freeman and Holzinger's Twins: A Study of Heredity and Environment," *Psychological Bulletin* (1938), 35:237-249.
63. Merriman, C.: *The Intellectual Resemblance of Twins,* Psychological Review Monographs (1924), Vol. 33, No. 152, 58 pp.
64. Miles, W. R.: "Psychological Aspects of Ageing," Cowdry, E. V., *Problems of Ageing: Biological and Medical Aspects* (Baltimore: Williams and Wilkins, 1939), pp. 535-571.
65. Newman, H. H., Freeman, F. N., and Holzinger, K. J.: *Twins: A Study of Heredity and Environment* (Chicago: University of Chicago Press, 1937), 369 pp.
66. Olson, W. C. and Hughes, B. O.: "Subsequent Growth of Children With and Without Nursery-School Experience," *Thirty-Ninth Yearbook of the National Society for the Study of Education* (1940), Pt. II, Ch. XV, pp. 237-244.
67. Osborn, J. J.: "Fertility Differentials Among Princeton Alumni," *Journal of Heredity* (1939), pp. 565-567; *Eugenic News* (1939) 24:78-81.
68. Pearson, K.: "On the Inheritance of the Mental and Moral Characters in Man, and Its Comparison with the Inheritance of the Physical Character," *Journal of the Anthropological Institute* (1903), 33:179-237.
69. ———: "On the Laws of Inheritance in Man," *Biometrika* (1904), 3:131-190.
70. ———: "I. Inheritance of Physical Characters," *Biometrika* (1919), 12:367-372.
71. Pintner, R.: "The Mental Indices of Siblings," *Psychological Review* (1918), 25:252-255.
72. Poull, L. E.: "The Effect of Improvement in Nutrition on the Mental Capacity of Young Children," *Child Development* (1938), 9:123-126.

73. Pritchard, M. C., Horan, K. M., and Hollingworth, L. S.: "The Course of Mental Development in Slow Learners Under an 'Experience Curriculum,' " *Thirty-Ninth Yearbook of the National Society for the Study of Education* (1940), Pt. II, Ch. XVI, pp. 245-254.
74. Proctor, W. M.: *Psychological Tests and Guidance of High School Pupils,* Journal of Educational Research Monographs (1923), No. 1, 125 pp.
75. Richey, A.: "The Effects of Diseased Tonsils and Adenoids on Intelligence Quotients of 204 Children," *Journal of Juvenile Research* (1934), 18:1-4.
76. Rust, M. M.: *The Effect of Resistance on Intelligence Test Scores of Young Children,* Child Development Monographs (New York: Teachers College, Columbia University, 1931), No. 6, 80 pp.
77. Sherman, M. and Key, C. B.: "The Intelligence of Isolated Mountain Children," *Child Development* (1932), 3:279-290.
78. Skeels, H. M.: "Mental Development of Children in Foster Homes," *Journal of Consulting Psychology* (1938), 2:33-43.
79. Skeels, H. M., Updegraff, R., Wellman, B. L., and Williams, H. M.: *A Study of Environmental Stimulation: An Orphanage Preschool Project,* University of Iowa Studies in Child Welfare (1938), No. 4, 191 pp.
80. Skodak, M.: *Children in Foster Homes: A Study of Mental Development,* University of Iowa Studies in Child Welfare (1939), Vol. 16, No. 1, 156 pp.
81. Skodak, M. and Skeels, H. M.: "A Follow-up Study of Children in Adoptive Homes," *Journal of Genetic Psychology* (1945), 66:21-58.
82. Starkweather, E. K.: *I.Q. Changes Over a Long Interval in Relation to Sex and Group Mental Level,* unpublished Master's thesis, reviewed by Wellman (101) (State University of Iowa, 1938), 79 pp.
83. Starkweather, E. K. and Roberts, K. E.: "I.Q. Changes Occurring During Nursery-School Attendance at the Merrill-Palmer School," *Thirty-Ninth Yearbook of the National Society for the Study of Education* (1940), Pt. II, Ch. XXII, pp. 315-335.
84. Stoddard, G. D.: *The Meaning of Intelligence* (New York: Macmillan, 1943), 504 pp.
85. Terman, L. M.: *Genetic Studies of Genius,* Vol. I: *Mental and Physical Traits of a Thousand Gifted Children* (Stanford University: Stanford University Press, 1925), 628 pp.
86. ———: *The Intelligence of School Children* (New York: Houghton-Mifflin, 1919), 317 pp.
87. Terman, L. M. and Merrill, M. A.: *Measuring Intelligence* (New York: Houghton-Mifflin, 1937), 461 pp.

88. Terman, L. M. and Oden, M.: "Status of the California Gifted Group at the End of Sixteen Years," *Thirty-Ninth Yearbook of the National Society for the Study of Education* (1940), Pt. I, Ch. II, pp. 67-89.
89. Thorndike, E. L.: "Measurement of Twins," *Journal of Philosophy, Psychology, and Scientific Methods* (1905), 2:547-553.
90. ———: "The Resemblance of Siblings in Intelligence," *Twenty-Seventh Yearbook of the National Society for the Study of Education* (1928), Pt. I, Ch. III, pp. 41-53.
91. ———: "The Distribution of Education," *The School Review* (1932), 40:335-345.
92. ———, et al.: *Adult Learning* (New York: Macmillan, 1928), 335 pp.
93. Thorndike, E. L., Bregman, E. O., Cobb, M. V., Woodyard, E., et al.: *The Measurement of Intelligence* (New York: Teachers College, Columbia University, 1927), 616 pp.
94. Thorndike, R. L.: "'Constancy' of the I.Q.," *Psychological Bulletin* (1940), 37:167-186.
95. ———: "The Effect of the Interval Between Test and Re-Test on the Constancy of the I.Q.," *Journal of Educational Psychology* (1933), 24:543-549.
96. Thorndike, R. L., Flemming, C. W., Hildreth, G., and Stanger, M.: "Retest Changes in the I.Q. in Certain Superior Schools," *Thirty-Ninth Yearbook of the National Society for the Study of Education* (1940), Pt. II, Ch. XXIV, pp. 351-361.
97. Thurstone, L. L. and Jenkins, R. L.: *Order of Birth, Parent-Age, and Intelligence* (Chicago: University of Chicago Press, 1931), 135 pp.
98. Updegraff, R.: "The Determination of a Reliable Intelligence Quotient for the Young Child," *Journal of Genetic Psychology* (1932), 41:152-166.
99. Voas, W. H.: "Does Attendance at the Winnetka Nursery School Tend to Raise the I.Q.?" *Thirty-Ninth Yearbook of the National Society for the Study of Education* (1940), Pt. II, Ch. XXV, pp. 363-376.
100. Waring, E. B.: "A Report of the Psychological Examinations of Preschool Children in the Nursery School Over a Period of Eight Years," *Ten-Year Report of Studies in Child Development and Parent Education,* Cornell University Agricultural Experimental Station Contributions from Studies in Home Economics Bulletin (1935), No. 638, pp. 42-43.
101. Wellman, B. L.: "Growth in Intelligence Under Differing School Environments," *Journal of Experimental Education* (1934), 3:59-83.

102. ———: "Guiding Mental Development," *Childhood Education* (1938), 15:108-112.
103. ———: "Mental Growth from Preschool to College," *Journal of Experimental Education* (1937), 6:127-138.
104. ———: "The Effect of Preschool Attendance Upon the I.Q.," *Journal of Experimental Education* (1932), 1:48-69.
105. Wellman, B. L., Skeels, H. M., and Skodak, M.: "Review of McNemar's Critical Examination of Iowa Studies," *Psychological Bulletin* (1940), 37:93-111.
106. Wellman, B. and Pegram, E. L.: "Binet I.Q. Changes of Orphanage Preschool Children: A Re-Analysis," *Journal of Genetic Psychology* (1944), 65:239-263.
107. Wheeler, L. R.: "The Mental Growth of Dull Italian Children," *Journal of Applied Psychology* (1932), 16, 6:650-667.
108. Wingfield, A. H. and Sandiford, P.: "Twins and Orphans," *Journal of Educational Psychology* (1928), 19:410-423.

Chapter XVI

PERSONALITY AND PROBLEMS OF ADJUSTMENT

When we speak of an individual's personality we refer to the quality of his total behavior, the organization and integration of his behavior as a whole. Many definitions of personality have been offered, stressing now the totality of an individual's behavior as manifested in his overt conduct, now the inner organization of his drives and purposes. To define a concept so big and inclusive as "personality" requires mouth-filling words, for the term includes everything a person has that can be seen and a good deal more that cannot be seen, and also the way in which everything expresses itself and hangs together.[1]

APPROACHES TO THE STUDY OF PERSONALITY

Human nature is so diverse and the factors underlying human conduct are so numerous that it is necessary to make a many-sided approach in order to study personality. This statement seems rather innocent and obvious, yet it touches upon a major problem. Students of human nature are often tempted, as are scientists in other fields, to go "all out" for this or that theory or principle of explanation.

The need for an approach that recognizes the play of many fac-

---

[1] For discussions of personality see Allport (2), Stagner (79), Woodworth (96), Murphy and Jensen (62), Lewin (53), Horney (43), and Plant (67). The theories of Freud (32), Adler (1), and Jung (50) stress motivation in human behavior and thus directly or indirectly deal with the topic of personality. Writings by Murray (64) and Symonds (85) also lay emphasis upon motives and needs. Studies in which one or two or several children have been studied "longitudinally" over periods ranging from several months to several years include works by Shirley (74, 75), Gesell (35), H. E. Jones (48), and Sanford, et al. (72). Two important volumes on personality and behavior disorders, edited by Hunt (44), include chapters by a number of authorities in psychology and psychiatry.

tors becomes apparent as soon as we begin to describe personality in particular terms. All aspects of behavior and development are more or less interrelated and interact upon one another. A child's motor ability, for example, has an important bearing upon his social behavior and thus may have an important influence on his behavior as a whole. Again, the role of any factor will be relative to other factors: to be tall or short may have quite a different consequence at one age level as compared with another and in one setting (such as the playground) as compared with another (such as the classroom).

"EXTERNAL" ASPECTS OF PERSONALITY

In spite of such interrelationships, it is possible to single out certain factors or components for separate study. Among the many features that may be noted in an account of personality are an individual's physical characteristics, his bodily size and physique, and factors in the mechanics and chemistry of his body that influence the energy and speed of his movements and the nature and strength of his drives. These physical features have a far-reaching influence not only upon the "external" person whom others can see but also upon the "internal" person. An individual's concept of himself is strongly influenced by the physical properties of his body. Again, a trait such as "masculinity" may have a physical basis as indicated, for example, by a positive relation between the tendency of a young male to show "masculine" interests and the production of male hormones (82a).

Also among the features that enter into an account of personality are an individual's abilities and talents, his level of intelligence, his manual dexterity, artistic skill, imaginative capacity, and his competence in countless enterprises that are involved in what an individual can do in serving himself and in dealing with others.

In addition, the features of personality that meet the eye include an almost endless list of qualities, "traits," habits, behavior patterns, modes of action that denote what is characteristic of an individual's behavior. So we may note that he is vigorous or the opposite, gregarious or the opposite, that he tends to be irascible or domineering, and so forth.

The meaning of such "traits," and of physical features and abilities, depends in part upon cultural standards. The impact on the individual as a whole of an ability to run fast or a tendency to be gregarious will depend partly upon the extent to which others regard such qualities as valuable or important. The factor of age or maturity level also has an important bearing upon the manner in which such social standards are applied, since behavior that is acceptable to others at one age is disapproved as a form of "infantilism" or as a sign of "immaturity" at a later age.

"INTERNAL" ASPECTS OF PERSONALITY

To understand personality it is necessary also to take account of less observable "internal" facts: the individual's motives, aspirations, and feelings; his ideas about himself, about his outward appearance, and inner worth; and the manner in which his "inner life" is organized. It is only, of course, by observing and interpreting his behavior that we can discover what these "inner" circumstances might be.

In interpreting such signs it is necessary to bear in mind a number of features of child psychology that have been noted in preceding chapters.

One such feature is that from an early age a child begins to learn ways of keeping his thoughts and feelings to himself. So it is, in adult years, that the laughter of one person may mean that he is happy, another's laughter may be a sign of embarrassment, still another laughs that he may not cry. One person smiles and his smiles mean friendliness; another smiles and is a villain. The following statements summarize and supplement what has been said in earlier chapters with regard to factors that should be taken into account in interpreting the meaning of a person's overt behavior.

One observation is that different forms of behavior may be used to express the same feeling or motive. A child who is afraid may retreat, or cringe, or cry; or he may be passive and silent; or he may be seemingly angry and aggressive in his efforts to avoid something he fears.

Another observation is that similar behavior may serve different functions. An illustration of this was given in an earlier chapter in which it was noted that fighting may be a symptom of poor social adjustment in the case of one child and it may be a sign of improving social adjustment in the case of another differently situated child.

Behavior that seems outwardly similar may also represent motives that vary greatly in their strength or intensity. Behavior also differs in the extent to which it represents a means or an end. Behavior that is outwardly similar may vary in the extent to which it is undertaken for its own sake or the extent to which it serves an ulterior purpose.

Behavior that is outwardly similar also varies in the complexity of the factors that lie behind it. One child's poor performance in reading may be due to eye trouble which can be quite simply corrected with glasses; another child's difficulty in reading may be due to faulty habits that can be remedied; another child's difficulty may be an outcome of jealousy between him and his brother.

The circumstances that lead a child (or an adult) to camouflage or conceal his private thoughts and feelings are many. In an earlier chapter we noted how children from an early age are under social pressure to conceal their fears. In like manner they discover that it is well not to be openly aggressive. By virtue of pressures in their moral training they learn to conform, but there may be a decided discrepancy between the good behavior they display in public and their own private impulses and feelings. Externally they may be virtuous while internally they may nourish illicit thoughts and struggle with many temptations. The kind of behavior they display may be a façade.

The foregoing represents only a few considerations that must be taken into account in interpreting a child's overt behavior.

A disparity between what a person openly says or does and his "inner" feelings and motives may occur as something quite deliberate—a person may be fully aware of what is happening. The disparity between overt behavior and inner feelings and motives may, on the other hand, stem from motives and desires which he himself does not fully recognize or understand. This lack of self-understanding may appear in many ways and it may occur in varying degrees.[2]

Some of the factors that may contribute to a person's lack of understanding of his own mental processes are described in Chapter XI. We noted there, for example, that the child is not at a later age able to remember experiences during early years which may have had an important bearing upon his habits and attitudes. It was noted also in Chapter XI that the thought processes of children as well as adults may be colored with feeling and may be influenced by past habits in a manner that is not recognized by the person himself. His beliefs will be influenced by his desires. His thinking will often conform to his wishes. His reasoning may be a form of rationalization in which he seeks to excuse or defend or bolster a position to which he is committed on emotional grounds. The emotions that influence his thoughts and his actions may have an origin which he does not clearly perceive. Many of the dreads and fears that trouble children have their roots in experiences which the child has forgotten or which he never fully understood. The outlines of thwarting and frustration that produce aggressive behavior likewise may be very dim. There

---

[2] The fact that a person's thoughts and actions may be influenced by factors he does not consciously recognize has been emphasized in the Freudian concept of *the unconscious*. Psychologists have not generally accepted Freud's theories about the unconscious as scientifically established facts. Freud's own followers disagree with respect to the "instinctual" forces that are involved in "unconscious" behavior. However, all careful students of human behavior recognize that a person may lack insight into the nature and origin of many of his acts and impulses and may fail to see that the behavior he presents as rational may be governed by emotion.

are things about him which the child himself does not understand, but which an adult may be able to surmise by studying what the child says and does.

Early manifestations. Many investigators have noted that babies at a very early age show differences in "personality." Each has his own ways (17). Each presents his distinctive characteristics. Findings bearing on this point from studies by Shirley, Gesell, Fries, and others are reviewed in Chapter I.

CONSISTENCY AND CHANGE

Not only do children from an early age exhibit differences but also it has been found that the characteristics that distinguish one child from another tend to show a good deal of consistency. In reporting evidence concerning this, Shirley gives the example of two infants, one of whom remained consistently the most irritable and the other consistently the least irritable in her group of subjects even though both of the children during the course of the study showed a decrease in irritability in common with children in the group as a whole. Shirley noted also that as infants matured a given form of behavior "waned and lapsed, only to be supplanted by another that apparently was its consistent outgrowth." For example, one baby was distinctive at an early age for his "timorous crying"; this crying waned, but then he exhibited "apprehensive watching" and, at a later age, showed a similarly timorous trend by hiding apprehensively behind his mother and by reluctance to play and talk in the presence of a visitor. Shirley also noted that there was a considerable degree of consistency in the general pattern of a child's behavior. When "profile charts" showing ratings and scores for each baby on a number of characteristics were prepared, the profiles of the different babies were so unlike in contour that the examiner could identify them without names; and although the pattern changed with age, there were always "identifying earmarks." Usually one or two items were conspicuous for each baby.

Similarities were also observed between the babies and other members of their families. For example, social reticence was noted in the baby and all members of one family, sociability in another. Shirley points out that, in some instances, "specific training by the mother seemed to have little effect in counteracting a strongly established trait or developing one in which the child was weak." She adds, however, that it is possible that "a more subtle and pervasive influence in the environment was encouraging the very trait that the mother was trying to discourage." At any rate, during the first two years, many of the babies manifested personality traits that corresponded to those of their families.

This tendency on the part of the growing child to show himself as a certain kind of person and then to be true to this pattern as time goes on has also been noted by other investigators, Washburn (91), Bayley (15), Gesell and Thompson (35), and McKinnon (56). (This fact, of course, is an important one although it does not imply that a person's ways are set once and for all at an early age.) Twins in a study by Gesell were under observation until they were about fourteen years old. At the age of fourteen these children showed a high degree of similarity, as was true when they were infants, but they also showed some differences which confirmed differences that had appeared in early infancy. One of the twins (identified as twin *C*) is described by Gesell and Thompson as showing more "sociality" than the other (twin *T*) at the infancy level and also at adolescence. In discussing this the authors point out that the mother stated that she had shown more affection for *C* than for *T* and then they ask whether this factor of mother love might be responsible for *C's* greater sociality. The explanation, however, did not appear to be so simple. Actually, the mother was a stepmother and the children did not come under her care until they were two years old. It appeared that the stepmother's greater affection for *C* was a consequence rather than a cause. By virtue of her own nature, according to Gesell, *C* possessed a greater fund of sociality. *C* was the more amiable. She had "a tithe more of the quality or state of being *lovable"* and as a consequence she attracted more of her mother's love than did her sister. According to Gesell, this characteristic of twin *C* was not created by the environment but deflected the environment.

The last-mentioned point to the effect that a quality within a child may be a factor in determining the child's environment can be verified now and then in everyday life. In keeping with the example above, it can be observed how a child who happens to be friendly tends to win friends and thus to build and to preserve a friendly environment. The child who, for one reason or another, is irritable and peevish tends to arouse impatience and annoyance in others, and by so doing he helps to produce an environment that fosters his peevish ways. The young child who shows an interest in mechanical things may receive a hammer and wrench and much other equipment that would further his interest in mechanics. The same tendency for reputation to confirm itself appears at the adult level. The person who happens to make a good speech may be asked again and again to speak and with practice become an increasingly proficient speaker as compared with another person who might, if afforded the same chances, have become just as good.

While children tend to be consistent in their individuality it does not mean, of course, that no change occurs. As noted above the youngster may be conspicuously high or low in a certain characteristic and yet move along with developmental trends. The youngster who is more aggressive than others at the age of three may also be more aggressive at the age of six, yet at the latter age show much less overt aggressiveness, in common with other children.

Again, as the child grows older there will be a change in the style of his behavior, but this change may be an outgrowth of something nascent or latent that could have been observed at an earlier time. Evidence of this appears in a study by McKinnon (56) in which children were first studied when they were in a nursery school and then were followed through the first two grades of school. At the nursery-school age the youngsters were classified into four groups on the basis of their most conspicuous or prominent characteristic. (These four groups were described as "conforming," "invasive," "withdrawn," and "cautious.") Ten of the sixteen children continued from the age of three to the age of eight or nine to be in the same classification. (The changes that occurred were in the direction of "conformity.") When changes did occur they were anticipated, according to McKinnon, by earlier characteristics. Changes consisted primarily in a building upon characteristics that already had appeared rather than in an about-face or in the tacking on of something strange or new. One child, for example, changed from predominantly "invasive" at three to "conforming" behavior at eight, but at both ages he was a youngster who was very eager to be noticed and accepted by other children. At three his techniques were crude and produced many conflicts, but at eight he had learned better techniques and was better able to enter into companionable give and take.

The tendency of a child to be true to his own pattern, as described above, has been emphasized in a study by Shirley of two boys who were handled quite differently by their mothers and who yet retained their individuality. Shirley maintains that her observations support the hypothesis that "within every newborn infant there is a core or nucleus of temperamental qualities of some degree of toughness that, coupled with the dynamic forces of growth, prevent his ever becoming a puppet of the forces that play upon him." One child in the study had a mother who seemed to try to keep him a baby, who sought to prolong his attachment to her and who in various ways seemed to be rather anxious about practical details of his everyday care. Yet by the age of six this boy had grown into "an independent, objective little boy, . . . a person in his own right . . . who had laid the cornerstone for adequacy in adulthood." His mother, according to Shirley, had shown lack of firmness and inability to pursue a consistent course of action, "leaving her baby to grow up on the shifting sands of insecurity," and the boy "therefore had to build his own foundation of security." He did this by means of different techniques at different times. He gained attention at first by crying, later by refusing to eat, and then as time passed his methods changed so that at the age of six he appeared to be a well adjusted and quite self-sufficient person.

The studies that have dealt with the question of ways in which a child tends to show constant characteristics in his personality development are limited in number and have involved relatively few children. Moreover, it would require more than two case studies, as in the study by Shirley, cited above, to confirm and amplify the concept that each child is born with "a core or nucleus" of temperamental qualities. Yet there is evidence to indicate that this concept (among others) is a valuable one for the understanding of human behavior. Moreover, the theory that there are inborn factors in personality development does not rule out the importance of environmental factors.

IMPACT OF THE ENVIRONMENT

The development of a child's personality is influenced in countless ways by the environment in which he lives. This section will not give a systematic statement of the role of the environment. This topic has been discussed directly or by implication in all preceding chapters of this book. We shall confine our account to a few points that confirm or elaborate findings that have earlier been discussed.

There are, of course, a great many components in the environment in which a child lives (7, 31). The effect of the environment will be determined not simply by what happens in the world about him but also by the factors within the child himself. The child's own physical condition, his weakness and his strength, what he himself aspires to achieve or seeks to be, determine to a great extent whether something will frighten or anger him, tempt him or disgust him, arouse elation or disappointment. As noted in the preceding section, also, the child's own qualities and characteristics will influence the kind of treatment which the environment offers.

Among features of the external environment that are likely to have a very important influence on a child's personality development are the attitudes and practices of his elders. These attitudes and practices are likely to have a more pronounced influence on him than the physical circumstances of his home. Whether or not his mother is fond of him is likely to have more weight than whether or not the family is rich or poor; whether or not the mother is anxious or relaxed in her handling of him is likely to be a more important factor than whether or not he lives in the slums or the suburbs. This does not mean that physical environment, including financial circumstances, is not important.

Evidence regarding the influence the parents have on the child's personality development is especially impressive in the case of children who suffer from severe difficulties and maladjustments. A larger proportion of delinquent than of nondelinquent children come from poor home environments, including broken homes, homes in which there is dissension, in which one or both parents exhibit emotional maladjustment, and the like. Many children who have difficulty in adjusting to life at school also exhibit evidence of unwholesome parental influences (12, 13, 41).

There are, of course, many other influences in addition to the influence of his parents, such as the influence of his companions on his habits and values, the effect of an impoverished environment on his social and intellectual development, the influence of socioeconomic status, and the like. The important influence that a child's associates may have is indicated by the fact that a large proportion of delinquents come from poor neighborhoods in which there are many human derelicts. However, even the effect of living in a home within such a neighborhood is likely to be influenced by the character of the home itself. In one study (97) in which children who had become delinquent were compared with other children, in the same neighborhood, who had not become delinquent, the evidence indicated that the nondelinquent children had more affectionate relationships with their parents, and, apparently as a consequence, were more receptive to the moral instruction given by their parents.

The acts of a parent that influence the child are of great variety and almost countless in number, yet it is likely that they will show a certain amount of consistency, a tendency toward a common quality. If a parent is anxious and uncertain of himself, this disposition may appear in the way in which he feeds the infant and in the way in which he disciplines the same child at four or six. If a parent tends to be rather peremptory and arbitrary, this characteristic may appear in the way in which he forcibly removes the baby's thumb from his mouth at four months and in the way in which the same parent later insists that the child at four years must always eat all of his potatoes before he has another spoonful of peas. Similarly, the parent who is "easygoing," or the parent who tends to be very methodical, or the parent who has high ambitions for his family, is likely to exhibit his characteristic in the practical details of child rearing.

The parent's attitude toward himself, his adjustment toward life in general, his attitude with respect to his role as a parent and the rights of his child, are likely to be revealed in specific practices. This does not mean, of course, that every act betrays the parental attitude. The parent who is ambitious may be much concerned about "success" in one area but not in another; a parent who is anxious to conform to public opinion may be much more of a conformist on some issues than on others. Accordingly it is necessary to obtain information concerning the parent's behavior in a variety of situations before one can make a reliable judgment.

A study by Lafore (52) shows in an interesting manner the way in which parents differ in their approach and in their specific practices. Parents were observed in the home while in contact with children of preschool age. Lafore classified the parents into four groups as follows:

"Dictators." Parents who characteristically used a dictatorial approach with emphasis on authority and obedience.

"Coöperaters." Parents who were predominantly friendly, who seemed to deal with the child on a basis of mutual respect and who appeared to hold a view that if things could be explained, and if there could be joint action, it would not be necessary to require unquestioning obedience.

"Temporizers." Parents placed in this category by Lafore were those whose approach seemed to be preponderantly "situational." These parents followed no consistent pattern of behavior but they more or less fell into one situation after another so that if the situation was pleasant the parent was pleasant, if the situation got out of hand the parent became confused, without seeming to know what he should do, what he had done, or what he would do.

"Appeasers." Parents whose approach was predominantly conciliatory and who seemed to be somewhat afraid of the child, as though he had gained control. Such parents tended to avoid issues and tried to circumvent problems that arose. Their apparent aim was to prevent trouble rather than to face an issue.

A classification such as the foregoing is of course quite arbitrary; it is very improbable that all of any one parent's actions would fall in any one of the four categories, yet it appeared that the practices used by the parents in a variety of different contacts tended to fall preponderantly in one of these classifications. An illustration of two different approaches is offered below in an account of Michael, an enterprising child of three years who had a mother who tended to be a "coöperater" and a father who tended to be a "dictator." Following are extracts from the record of a time when Michael and his father were together.

Michael and a friend are playing happily, sitting at a small table talking about eggs. Michael says, "Eggs are pink." Tom, the friend, adds, "Eggs are purple." Michael continues, "Eggs are green." Michael's father interrupts. "Since when is an egg green? Michael, what is the color of an egg?" Tom says, "Eggs are green, blue, and red." Michael's father says, "No. Michael, what is the color of an egg?" At this point the father notes Michael's face and interrupts himself to say, "Did you get paint on your lips? Come here and let me see. Stand up. Did you put this in your mouth. Open your mouth." Michael says, "No," but allows his father to pull him to his feet and wash out his mouth. When he is released the situation is changed. Michael begins to nag and to ask plaintive questions, and after he and his friend have sat down to painting again they are again interrupted by the father with instructions not to use so much water, not to get the paper wet, not to use a cup but a jar, not to take so much water, not to use a certain brush but another. When Michael calls attention to a painting the father scolds him for the "mess" he has made. . . . The record continues to show repeated interruption, interference, and commands, and after a time the two boys begin to throw clay at each other and the father orders the visiting boy to go home. Michael cries. Michael and his father argue, first about putting some blocks away, then about closing a door, and then about Father's order that Michael should play with blocks. Following this the father tried to undress Michael who kicked and scratched, and then the cat approached the bed on which they were sitting and the father pushed it away. Michael said to his father, "I don't like you any more." His father replied, "I don't like *you* any more."

Another record shows Michael with his mother who gives few commands, offers no interference, and instead enters into a good deal of give and take. Michael several times wants to do things his own way but at no time does he say, "No, I won't." An example of how the two work things out together appears in the following excerpt: "His mother then said, 'Now let's see. How are the hands? I would wash them.' Michael (who insists on doing many things for himself) said, 'I want to wash.' His mother replied, 'All right and try not to soil your clothes. Just wash the hands and that's all.' Michael said, 'I can do it myself.' His mother said, 'Of course you can. Now rinse them off. That's a very good job.'"

The following is an abbreviated version of a summary presented by Lafore to illustrate the differences between the two parents in terms of certain specific practices. During the period when the father and child were together the father *interfered* with the boy thirteen times; during the interval when the mother was with the boy she *interfered* three times. The father *dictated* fourteen times; the mother once. The father *praised* twice; the mother six times. The father *hurried* the child three times; the mother had no instance of hurrying. The father *blamed* three times; the mother had no instance of blaming. The father *offered a reason* four times; the mother seven times. Both father and mother showed a number of other practices in which they were more alike. Another summary shows that when the child was with the parent who tended to be a "dictator" he showed more instances of resistance, hostility, and crying.

The likelihood that the specific acts and practices of a parent will be colored by the parent's attitudes has been emphasized in an interesting study by Shirley (75), cited above, in which two boys were observed from the time of early infancy until they reached the age of six. On the basis of this study Shirley maintains that a mother's attitude and personality characteristics are likely to be revealed in every aspect of her care for her baby. The impact of the mother's attitudes and personality occurs not only by way of the warmth of affection which the mother shows, or the extent to which she is tense or relaxed in handling the child, or is strict or lax in her training methods, but it may even appear in her choice of clothes and in the equipment she uses to meet the child's needs from the time of birth, or the way in which she gives the child his bath.[3]

---

[3] The tendency to show certain predominant characteristics in dealing with others is not, of course, limited to parents. This fact is interestingly brought out in studies by H. H. Anderson of "dominative" and "integrative" behavior (5).

The tendency on the part of parents to show certain dominant characteristics quite consistently in their practical dealings with children was found also in a study by Baldwin and Kelhorn (11). Among other matters these investigators used an instrument for studying parental practices that had been prepared by Champney (20). It was found that the parents showed certain "syndromes" or clusters of behavior. These are described somewhat differently from Lafore's account above, although there are parallels between the two. For example, there was a cluster of practices and patterns of behavior that belonged to a syndrome of "democracy." There was also a syndrome representing "indulgence." This study is very interesting in view of the discussion earlier in this chapter of the tendency on the part of children to show a good deal of constancy or consistency in their characteristics with the passage of time. It was found that there was in many respects a high degree of continuity in the practices used by parents as time passed. When homes were rated with respect to the use of "democratic" policies at one time and then again were rated over two years later there was a correlation of .72 between the two sets of ratings. Some policies showed a higher degree of consistency than did others. The parents in the study were more consistent in their tendency to justify the discipline they employed than in their tendency to baby the child or to use severe penalties. The tendency toward consistency in parental behavior parallels the tendency toward consistency in the child's behavior.

The findings cited above with respect to the manner in which specific practices used by a parent may be symptoms or expressions of general attitudes and behavior tendencies are based upon very limited samplings of parents and children and they leave many questions unanswered. It would require additional research to show how much and in what ways individuals differ with respect to this tendency and to show how happenings in the parent's own life and in his relations with the child confirm or modify his attitudes as the years pass.

Certainly the fact that a parent shows a characteristic attitude does not mean that he inevitably will always show it. The assumption underlying adult education and the practice of mental hygiene is that a person is more or less educable as long as he lives. Moreover, available evidence suggests that some attitudes that influence an adult's dealings with a child may be much less deep-seated than others. Some attitudes may be little influenced by giving the adult the chance to obtain more information or to learn different techniques. This does not mean, however, that such opportunities to learn will have no effect on an adult's practices. Findings such as those reported by Bavelas (14) are suggestive in this connection. In this study playground directors who had been quite autocratic in their handling of children in a recreation center were given a chance to become acquainted with the theory and techniques of more democratic ways of dealing with youngsters and it was found that it was possible to arouse the interest and win the coöperation of the playground directors to such an extent that there was a marked shift toward the use of democratic practices.

The changes that occur in the process of a child's development may also sometimes bring about a change in parental standards and behavior. A parent who is reconciled to the fact, for example, that an infant is incapable of self-help may be less reconciled to the limitations of the same child at six or eight years and, as a result, judge the child by a more severe standard at the later ages.

PROBLEMS OF ADJUSTMENT

The question as to what are the forces in the environment that help or hinder the child becomes especially significant when viewed against the fact that a large proportion of children sooner or later in the course of their development will suffer from varying degrees of maladjustment. The subject of maladjustment and of mental hygiene goes beyond the reach of this book, but there are certain aspects of the problem which will here be discussed briefly.[4]

The maladjusted child is a child whose life is seriously troubled by one or more unsolved problems. However, what constitutes a problem must be defined at least in part from the child's point of view. "Problems" which the parents see or which the school sees may not be problems so far as the child himself is immediately concerned.

Problems of adjustment in children can be classified under certain general headings, such as problems arising out of relationships with parents and with other members of the family; problems arising out of a child's relationships with other children outside the home; problems relating to the work of the school, including pupil-teacher relationships as well as the business of meeting the school's demands. Problems might also be classified in terms of the individual's needs or goals. The extent to which a problem as seen by others will be a problem to the child himself will depend upon what he has at stake, the intensity of the emotions that are aroused, the degree to which he is thwarted or threatened. Accordingly, a certain misfortune, such as not being promoted at school, may be a calamity to one child while to another child the same happening causes relatively little concern.

In addition, it may be noted that many of the "problems" exhibited by children, as judged by parents, are "developmental" in nature: they persist for a time and then disappear in the process of development. Behavior which is characteristic of a certain level of growth and then wanes or disappears should not, of course, be regarded as a "problem" except from the point of view of the practi-

---

[4] This section deals briefly with certain aspects of difficulties of adjustment; a full treatment would, of course, require a separate volume. For discussions of problems of adjustment and mental hygiene, see, for example, Louttit (54), Shaffer (73), Symonds (83), Kanner (51), Hollingworth (42), Witty and Skinner (94), Rogers (69, 70), and Fenton (29). English and Pearson (27) deal with problems of adjustment from a psychoanalytic point of view. Horney (43) also uses a psychoanalytic approach but with many significant modifications of Freudian theory. A book by Preston (67a) gives a brief, succinct, and very readable account of factors influencing mental health.

cal convenience of the parents.[5] However, if in the judgment of a parent a child has a problem, even though this problem will pass and does not signify that anything is fundamentally wrong, a real problem may result by virtue of the attitude of the parent and the methods used to discipline and reform the child.

Varying adult standards. Apart from the fact that the child's level of maturity must be taken into account when gauging whether a certain form of behavior represents a "problem," there is the further fact that the standards by which a child's behavior will be judged are likely to vary. A study by Fehlman (28) on this subject, cited in Chapter VI, shows differences between the values which parents and teachers see in a child and differences in judgment with respect to a child's weak points. In a study by Wickman (93) it was found that teachers and clinical psychologists differed considerably in their rating of the seriousness of various problems. A summary of some of the findings is shown in Table XLII. The clinicians tended to rate various forms of transgression against authority as less serious, and evidences of insecurity, suspiciousness, unhappiness, and fear as more serious, than did the teachers. The findings here do not mean that the clinical psychologists were right and the teachers wrong. The teachers and the clinical psychologists were looking at the behavior of children from somewhat different points of view. The practical consequences of some forms of behavior are more serious to the teacher than to the clinical psychologist. Many of the forms of behavior that stand high on the teachers' list are forms of behavior which the teacher, as an agent of the community, is not allowed to tolerate. If he allowed children to destroy school property he might even lose his job. It is likely that if the teacher and the clinical psychologist were to change places the difference be-

---

[5] MacFarlane (58) shows that some problems show a decreasing incidence with age, including thumb sucking and failure to control the bladder. Certain conditions such as food finickiness, timidity, and speech problems reach a peak at about thirty-six months and then subside. Other studies of behavior problems include 21, 30, 45, 66, 78, 80, 81.

TABLE XLII

THE SERIOUSNESS OF CHILDREN'S BEHAVIOR PROBLEMS, AS RATED BY 511 TEACHERS AND BY 30 CLINICAL PSYCHOLOGISTS[6]

(The table shows the ten problems of a larger list that were rated as most serious, and the ten that were rated as least serious, by the two groups.)

Teachers	Average Rating Teachers	Average Rating Clinicians	Clinicians	Average Rating Clinicians	Average Rating Teachers
Upper Ten:			**Upper Ten:**		
Heterosexual activity	17.3	9.9	Unsocialness	17.3	8.3
Stealing	17.0	12.5	Suspiciousness	16.4	9.1
Masturbation	16.7	6.4	Unhappy, depressed	16.2	11.5
Obscene notes, talk	16.6	8.8	Resentfulness	14.1	10.8
Untruthfulness	15.8	10.3	Fearfulness	14.0	9.7
Truancy	15.6	10.3	Cruelty, bullying	13.5	14.8
Impertinence, defiance	15.0	7.1	Easily discouraged	13.4	11.5
Cruelty, bullying	14.8	13.5	Suggestible	13.3	11.0
Cheating	14.7	10.3	Overcritical of others	13.2	7.9
Destroying school materials	14.3	5.1	Sensitiveness	13.1	7.0
Lower Ten:			**Lower Ten:**		
Dreaminess, unsocialness	8.3	11.3	Masturbation	6.4	16.7
Imaginative lying	8.1	7.5	Disobedience	6.4	14.1
Interrupting	8.0	2.8	Tardiness	5.6	10.5
Inquisitiveness	8.0	5.3	Inquisitiveness	5.3	8.0
Overcritical of others	7.9	13.2	Destroying school materials	5.1	14.3
Tattling	7.5	8.8	Disorderliness in class	3.4	11.7
Whispering	7.5	0.8	Profanity	2.9	12.3
Sensitiveness	7.0	13.1	Interrupting	2.8	8.0
Restlessness	6.9	6.4	Smoking	2.3	12.0
Shyness	5.4	12.5	Whispering	0.8	7.5

tween their practical judgment would be less than seems to be indicated in the table.

In a study of teachers in 1934 by Bain (10) and in another study of teachers in 1943 by Mitchell (61) it was found that there was a considerably higher resemblance between mental hygienists' and teachers' ratings than in 1928, although some differences still appeared. The change in teachers' ratings may be due to greater

---

[6] Adapted from Wickman, E. K.: *Children's Behavior and Teachers' Attitudes* (New York: The Commonwealth Fund Division of Publications, 1928), pp. 124-126. Reproduced by permission of The Commonwealth Fund.

knowledge of how to answer according to the book or it might mean a change in attitude, or both. Whatever the reason, it would require a study of actual practice to determine to what extent both the mental hygienists and the teachers put their beliefs into practice in their ordinary contacts with children. A study of parents by Stodghill (82) and a study of nurses by Bowles (18) indicate that the ratings given by parents and nurses correspond more with teachers' than with mental hygienists' ratings.

Incidence of problems. The fact that a large proportion of children have unsolved problems of greater or lesser severity is indicated in studies cited in earlier chapters on the subject of fear, jealousy, anger, and other emotional states. Similar testimony comes when children have been questioned directly with respect to a variety of symptoms, with inquiries such as: "Are you usually happy?" "Do people find fault with you too much?" "Are you afraid of crossing a bridge?" "Do you have a habit of twitching your head, neck, and shoulders?" "Do you feel that no one loves you?" Questions also have included items with regard to compulsions, such as a compulsion to steal, or to set fire to things, or to hurt others, and inquiries concerning feelings of guilt, of being abused, falling, being tired all the time, being different from others, and so forth. In one study, an instrument devised by Woodworth (95) was adapted by Matthews (60) for use with children and applied to over a thousand youngsters. At the age of ten, seventy-five per cent of the children confessed to six or more of the symptoms on the list (the list contained seventy items). The median ten-year-old boy reported eighteen symptoms; girls at this age had a median score of 11.5. Thus, according to his own ratings, the usual child of ten or more is likely to have several complaints or quirks of one sort or another. He is, in other words, a somewhat troubled creature.

Difficulties such as those described above are likely to be even more numerous and considerably more severe in children who have definitely been singled out as delinquents or as "behavior problems" (76, 86). It is only by being somewhat arbitrary that we can say that a certain child's problems are of such magnitude and are so severe that the child may be called a "maladjusted" child. For this reason it is not possible to say how many children in the population at large are maladjusted. The estimates that have been given have varied considerably. Depending upon the criterion that one uses one might diagnose about half the child population as maladjusted or one might reserve this diagnosis for only a small percentage. Whatever criterion is used, it is clear from statistics that a large proportion of children become psychological casualties somewhere along the course of their development.

It has been estimated by Griffin and Line (38a) that a teacher facing a class of forty children may anticipate that before these youngsters have completed their life span seventeen to twenty-six of them will have suffered from conditions ranging from unhappiness and a sense of futility to criminal behavior and insanity.

A study by Rogers (71) gives an indication of the extent to which children of elementary-school age are maladjusted as measured by objective criteria such as not having been promoted, being an academic or intellectual or chronological "misfit" by virtue of deviation from the group in reading ability, mental ability, or age; being a truant; being rated by classmates, teachers, or visiting observers or on the basis of results of an inventory of adjustment as having unfavorable characteristics of various kinds. A child was judged to be "seriously maladjusted" if, according to the criteria used in the study, he fell in the "maladjusted" category according to four or more of the procedures used in the study. *Twelve* per cent of the 1,524 elementary-school pupils in the study were seriously maladjusted according to this standard. In addition, thirty per cent gave evidence of being poorly adjusted, although not to a degree that would place them in the seriously maladjusted category.

Some implications of the developmental approach. The problems exhibited by children to some extent hold up a mirror to the kind of culture in which they live. When a large proportion of children (and adults) show symptoms of poor mental health the question arises as to whether it is the individual who is out of hand or whether social customs and standards and the rigors of modern life are demanding too much of human nature. As against this, it might be argued that conflicts and insecurities are not only inescapable but are valuable for the sake of human progress. We shall not argue this issue other than to express certain generalizations which, in the writer's opinion, emerge again and again as one studies the course of a child's development.

One generalization is that much of the strain of child-rearing would be relieved if adults would approach the child more consistently from a developmental point of view. It seems to be hard for grown-ups to realize the simple but inexorable fact that it takes time for a child to grow. The two-year-old now behaves like a child of two. His behavior may be trying, but at four he will behave differently, and the process of change will go on from year to year. There are changes that come by virtue of training, it is true, but many significant changes come not as a result of rules laid down by a child's elders but as a consequence of laws of his own nature.

The career of a child and of his elders would be smoother if adults would be more willing to accept a child at a given age level for what he is. This does not mean that the adult will avoid taking a hand in the child's education. As a matter of fact, the opportunities for education scaled to the child's capacities at any level of growth are almost infinite. The more an adult can accept the child's level of maturity the more time and energy there would be for education appropriate to that level.

It would also be helpful if there could be more acceptance of the principle that a child has not only a right to be a child of a certain age but also the right to be the kind of child he is. In the nature of things, children are different. Certainly it is not his own doing that made a child stocky or slim, or gave him the color of his skin, or determined whether he would be bright or dull.

A developmental approach, coupled with a proper regard for the fact that individuals differ, can do much to minimize one great source of hardship for children (and adults)—the tendency of adults to judge a child from a *moral* point of view when no moral issue whatsoever is involved. From all sides children are hounded by misguided applications of the idea of right and wrong and false conceptions of what is to be blamed or praised. The fact that a young child does not have the capacity to control his bladder tells us something about the stage of his development but nothing about the condition of his morals. The same may be said about the child who does not have the mental capacity to read a certain line or word even though he and his exasperated teacher have gone over it a dozen times.

It would be helpful also if adults could learn not only to accept a child for what he is but also to respect him for what he is. Such respect means that adults try to realize that the concerns of a child are as important to him at his level as are the concerns of adults at their level. It means also recognition of the fact that the child is one who, in the main, is trying at all stages of his growth to do the best he can with what he has.

Many other considerations pertaining to the mental health of children have been discussed earlier in this book. We have noted that a child thrives best in an atmosphere of affection and friendliness. Associated with this is the fact, as indicated in Chapter VIII, that one of the primary satisfactions adults derive from children is the companionship children afford, the opportunity they provide for sharing common interests and mutual affection. We cannot, of course, simply by stating facts such as these produce an affectionate relationship between all parents and their children. But what is spoken to the intellect may eventually affect the emotions. In the long run, it would, no doubt, have a profound effect upon the mental health of new generations of children if somehow we could incorporate more fully into our philosophy of child rearing the concept that a child is a person who, at each level of his growth, can be interesting and enjoyable in his own right.

The more this concept takes hold the more likely it is that adults will feel free to allow constructive forces within the child himself to go to work. In earlier sections we have noted many such constructive forces. There resides in the child a powerful impulse to grow. He strives to make use of his growing powers. During the course of development he himself revises many of his ways of behaving. Again, we have seen how children have a strong disposition to be friendly; how they tend to respond in kind if treated in a courteous, democratic manner; how, in a school situation that allows some freedom of choice and initiative, they show more capacity for assuming responsibility for their own conduct than has been assumed in the theory underlying traditional methods of discipline. To recognize these characteristics does not mean a denial of characteristics of a negative character: the child who is friendly can also be exasperating; the child who strives to use his growing powers may also, in other respects, show a tendency to shirk; he may develop bad habits as well as good ones. Nor does a policy of trying to make greater use of positive forces in a child's make-up mean that we turn the task of child rearing over to children themselves. No matter how much we try to draw upon the child's own impulse to grow, the youngster will need adult direction, guidance, and protection. The responsibilities of the adult are, if anything, increased rather than diminished.

It also would contribute to mental health if children somehow could be spared some of the extra burdens that fall upon them by reason of tensions and maladjustments in the lives of their elders. In the foregoing chapters we have noted how a child's life may be complicated by difficulties growing out of adult fears, feelings of hostility, unfulfilled ambitions that stem from harsh competitive urges, and unrequited needs for affection. Here again, it must be said that simply to tell adults not to impose their emotional difficulties on their children can neither cure the parent nor spare the child.

But even in this matter there are grounds for hope. An adult still has the ability to learn and to modify his behavior, even though old habits raise strong barriers. The more an adult seeks to enjoy his relations with children, the more important it becomes for him to examine and to try to solve emotional problems that impel him to use a child as a rod upon which to lean, a scapegoat for his anger, a protection against his fears.

BIBLIOGRAPHY

1. Adler, A.: *The Practice and Theory of Individual Psychology* (New York: Harcourt, Brace, 1929), 352 pp.
2. Allport, G. W.: *Personality* (New York: Henry Holt, 1937), 588 pp.
3. Anderson, H. H.: *Domination and Integration in the Social Behavior of Young Children in an Experimental Play Situation,* Genetic Psychology Monographs (1937), 19:343-408.
4. ———: "Domination and Social Integration in the Behavior of Kindergarten Children in an Experimental Play Situation," *Journal of Experimental Education* (1939), 8:123-131.
5. Anderson, H. H. and Brewer, H. M.: *Studies of Teachers' Classroom Personalities, I. Dominative and Socially Integrative Behavior of Kindergarten Teachers,* Applied Psychology Monographs (1945), No. 6, 157 pp.
6. Anderson, J. E.: "The Methods of Child Psychology," *A Handbook of Child Psychology,* second revised edition, edited by C. Murchison (Worcester: Clark University Press, 1933), pp. 3-28.
7. ———, chairman: *The Young Child in the Home,* White House Conference Series (New York: Appleton-Century, 1936), 415 pp.
8. Anon.: "One Child in Nine in a Broken Family," *Statistical Bulletin of the Metropolitan Life Insurance* (1944), 25, No. 3:3-6.
9. Arrington, R. E.: *Interrelations in the Behavior of Young Children,* Child Development Monographs (New York: Teachers College, Columbia University, 1932), No. 8, 156 pp.
10. Bain, W. E.: "A Study of the Attitudes of Teachers Toward Behavior Problems," *Child Development* (1934), 5:19-35.

11. Baldwin, A. L., Kalhorn, J., and Breese, F. H.: *Patterns of Parent Behavior,* Psychological Monographs (1945), 58, No. 3, 75 pp.
12. Baruch, D. W.: "A Study of Reported Tension in Interparental Relationships as Co-Existent with Behavior Adjustment in Young Children," *Journal of Experimental Education* (1937), 6:187-204.
13. Baruch, D. W. and Wilcox, J. A.: "A Study of Sex Differences in Preschool Children's Adjustment Coëxistent with Inter-Parental Tensions," *Journal of Genetic Psychology* (1944), 64:281-303.
14. Bavelas, A. and Lewin, K.: "Training in Democratic Leadership," *Journal of Abnormal and Social Psychology* (1942), 37:115-119.
15. Bayley, N.: "A Study of the Crying of Infants During Mental and Physical Tests," *Journal of Genetic Psychology* (1932), 40:306-329.
16. Bernreuter, R. G.: *The Personality Inventory* (Stanford University: Stanford University Press, 1931).
17. Blatz, W. E., Chant, N., *et al.*: *Collected Studies on the Dionne Quintuplets* (Toronto: University of Toronto Press, 1937).
18. Bowles, H.: "A Study of Nurses' Attitudes Toward the Behavior Problems of Children Under Hospital Care," *Child Development* (1937), 8:282-288.
19. Challman, R. C.: "Experiments Concerning Level of Aspiration," *Advanced School Digest* (New York: Teachers College, Columbia University, 1940), 5:61-63.
20. Champney, H.: "The Measurement of Parent Behavior," *Child Development* (1941), 12:131-166.
21. Christianson, E., Gates, M., and Goleman, F.: *A Survey of the Intake of a Mental Hygiene Clinic, with Special Reference to the Outcome of Treatment,* Smith College Studies in Social Work (1934), 5:211-212.
22. Conrad, H. S.: "The Validity of Personality Ratings of Preschool Children," *Journal of Educational Psychology* (1932), 23:671-680.
23. Dashiell, J. F.: *Fundamentals of General Psychology* (New York: Houghton Mifflin, 1937), 655 pp.
24. Dembo, T.: "Der Ärger als dynamisches Problem," *Psychologische Forschung* (1931), 15:1-144.
25. Dollard, J., *et al.*: *Frustration and Aggression* (New Haven: Yale University Press, 1939), 209 pp.
26. Driscoll, G. P.: *The Development Status of the Preschool Child as a Prognosis of Future Development,* Child Development Monographs (New York: Teachers College, Columbia University, 1933), No. 13, 111 pp.
27. English, O. S. and Pearson, G. H. J.: *Emotional Problems of Living; Avoiding the Neurotic Pattern* (New York: Norton, 1945), 438 pp.

28. Fehlman, C.: *Parents and Teachers View the Child: A Comparative Study of Parents' and Teachers' Appraisals of Children,* unpublished Ph.D. dissertation (New York: Teachers College, Columbia University, 1946), 159 pp. typewritten.
29. Fenton, N.: *Mental Hygiene in School Practice* (Stanford University: Stanford University Press, 1943), 455 pp.
30. Foster, J. C. and Anderson, J. E.: *The Young Child and His Parents,* The Institute of Child Welfare Monograph Series (Minneapolis: University of Minnesota Press, 1930), No. 1, 247 pp.
31. Francis, K. V. and Fillmore, E. A.: *The Influence of Environment upon the Personality of Children,* University of Iowa Studies in Child Welfare (1934), No. 9, 71 pp.
32. Freud, S.: *The Basic Writings of Sigmund Freud,* edited by A. A. Brill (New York: Modern Library, 1938), 1001 pp.
33. Gesell, A.: *Infancy and Human Growth* (New York: Macmillan, 1928), 418 pp.
34. Gesell, A., et al.: *Biographies of Child Development* (New York: P. B. Hoeber, 1939), 328 pp.
35. Gesell, A. and Thompson, H.: *Twins T and C from Infancy to Adolescence: A Biogenetic Study of Individual Differences by the Method of Co-Twin Control,* Genetic Psychology Monographs (1941), 24:256 pp.
36. Goodenough, F. L.: "Inter-relationships in the Behavior of Young Children," *Child Development* (1930), 1:29-47.
37. ———: "Measuring Behavior Traits by Means of Repeated Short Samples," *Journal of Juvenile Research* (1928), 12:230-235.
38. Goodenough, F. L. and Anderson, J. E.: *Experimental Child Study* (New York: Appleton-Century, 1931), 546 pp.
38a. Griffin, J. D. and Line, W.: *Mental Hygiene; A Manual for Teachers* (New York: American Book Co., 1940), 291 pp.
39. Guilford, J. P.: "Introversion-Extroversion," *Psychological Bulletin* (1934), 31:331-354.
40. Hartshorne, H. and May, M. A.: *Studies in Deceit* (New York: Macmillan, 1928), 414 pp.; 306 pp.
41. Hattwick, B. W. and Stowell, M.: "Relation of Parental Over-Attentiveness to Children's Work Habits and Social Adjustments," *Journal of Educational Research* (1936), 30, 3:169-176.
42. Hollingworth, H. L.: *Educational Psychology* (New York: Appleton-Century, 1933), 540 pp.
42a. Hoppe, F.: "Erfolg und Misserfolg," *Psychologische Forschung* (1930), 14:1-62.
43. Horney, K. *The Neurotic Personality of Our Time* (New York: W. W. Norton, 1937), 299 pp.

44. Hunt, J. McV., Editor: *Personality and the Behavior Disorders* (New York: Ronald Press, 1944), I:618 pp.; II:621-1242 pp.
45. Hurlock, E. B. and McDonald, L. C.: "Undesirable Behavior Traits in Junior High School Students," *Child Development* (1934), 5, 3:278-290.
46. Jersild, A. T.: "The Constancy of Certain Behavior Patterns in Young Children," *American Journal of Psychology* (1933), 45:125-129.
47. Jersild, A. T. and Meigs, M. F.: "Direct Observation as a Research Method," *Review of Educational Research* (December, 1939), 9:472-482.
48. Jones, H. E.: *Development in Adolescence. Approaches to the Study of the Individual* (New York: Appleton-Century, 1943), 166 pp.
49. Jones, M. C. and Burks, B. S.: *Personality Development in Childhood,* Society for Research in Child Development Monographs (1936), 4, 205 pp.
50. Jung, C. G.: *Collected Papers on Analytical Psychology* (London: Baillière, Tindall and Cox, 1922), 492 pp.
51. Kanner, L.: *Child Psychiatry* (Springfield: Thomas, 1935), 527 pp.
52. Lafore, G. G.: *Practices of Parents in Dealing with Preschool Children,* Child Development Monographs (New York: Teachers College, Columbia University, 1945), No. 31, 149 pp.
53. Lewin, K.: *A Dynamic Theory of Personality* (New York: McGraw-Hill, 1935), 286 pp.
54. Louttit, C. K.: *Clinical Psychology* (New York: Harper and Brothers, 1936), 695 pp.
55. McGraw, M. B.: "Later Development of Children Specially Trained During Infancy, Jimmy and Johnny at School Age." *Child Development* (1939), 1:1-19.
56. McKinnon, K.: *Consistency and Change in Personality and Behavior Manifestations—as Observed in a Group of 16 Children During a Five Year Period,* Child Development Monographs (New York: Teachers College, Columbia University, 1942), 30:144 pp.
57. McLaughlin, Sister M. A.: *The Genesis and Constancy of Ascendance and Submission as Personality Traits,* University of Iowa Studies in Education (Iowa City: University of Iowa Press, 1931), No. 6, 95 pp.
58. MacFarlane, J. W.: *Studies in Child Guidance. I. Methodology of Data Collection and Organization,* Monographs of the Society for Research in Child Development (1938), III:254 pp.
59. Marston, L. R.: *The Emotions of Young Children,* University of Iowa Studies in Child Welfare (1925), 3, 99 pp.
60. Mathews, E.: "A Study of Emotional Stability in Children by Means of a Questionnaire," *Journal of Delinquency* (1923), 8:1-40.

61. Mitchell, J. C.: "A Study of Teachers' and Mental Hygienists' Ratings of Certain Behavior Problems of Children," *Journal of Educational Research* (1943), 36:292-307.
62. Murphy, G. and Jensen, F.: *Approaches to Personality* (New York: Coward-McCann, 1932), 427 pp.
63. Murphy, L. B. and Murphy, G.: "The Influence of Social Situations upon the Behavior of Children," *A Handbook of Social Psychology*, edited by C. Murchison (Worcester: Clark University Press, 1935), pp. 1034-1096.
64. Murray, H. A., and workers at the Harvard Psychological Clinic: *Explorations in Personality: A Clinical and Experimental Study of Fifty Men of College Age* (New York: Oxford University Press, 1938), 761 pp.
65. Olson, W. C.: "A Study of Classroom Behavior," *Journal of Educational Psychology* (1931), 22:449-454.
66. ———: *The Measurement of Nervous Habits in Normal Children*, University of Minnesota Institute of Child Welfare Monographs (1929), No. 3, 97 pp.
67. Plant, J. S.: *Personality and the Cultural Pattern* (New York: Commonwealth Fund, 1937), 432 pp.
67a. Preston, George H.: *The Substance of Mental Health* (New York: Farrar and Rinehart, 1943), 147 pp.
68. Preston, R. C.: *Children's Reactions to a Contemporary War Situation*, Child Development Monographs (New York: Teachers College, Columbia University, 1942), No. 28, 96 pp.
69. Rogers, C. R.: *The Clinical Treatment of the Problem Child* (New York: Houghton Mifflin, 1939), 393 pp.
70. ———: *Counseling and Psychotherapy; Newer Concepts in Practice* (New York: Houghton Mifflin, 1942), 450 pp.
71. ———: "A Study of the Mental Health Problems in Three Representative Elementary Schools," *A Study of Health and Physical Education in Columbus Public Schools*, Bureau of Educational Research Monograph (Columbus, Ohio: Ohio State University, 1942), No. 25, pp. 130-161.
72. Sanford, R. N., Adkens, M. M., Miller, R. B., Cobb, E. A., et al.: *Physique, Personality and Scholarship: A Cooperative Study of School Children*, Monograph of the Society for Research in Child Development (1943), 8, No. 1, 705 pp.
73. Shaffer, L. F.: *The Psychology of Adjustment* (New York: Houghton Mifflin, 1936), 600 pp.
74. Shirley, M. M.: *The First Two Years*, Vol. III: *Personality Manifestations* (Minneapolis: University of Minnesota Press, 1933), 228 pp.

75. ———: "Impact of Mother's Personality on the Young Child," *Smith College Studies in Social Work* (1941), 12:15-64.
76. Slawson, J.: *The Delinquent Boy* (Boston: Richard G. Badger, 1926), 477 pp.
77. Smith, R. B.: *The Development of An Inventory for the Measurement of Inferiority Feelings at the High-School Level,* Archives of Psychology (1932), No. 144, 118 pp.
78. Smith College Studies in Social Work, edited by H. L. Witmer and E. Kimball (Northampton: Smith College School for Social Work).
79. Stagner, R.: *Psychology of Personality* (New York: McGraw-Hill, 1937), 465 pp.
80. Steinbach, A. A.: "A Survey of Adjustment Difficulties in Children and Youth Drawn from the Normal Population," *Elementary School Journal* (1933), 34:122-129.
81. Stemsrud, A. L. and Wardwell, S.: *A Comparative Study of Fourteen Socially Well-Adjusted Children with Their Maladjusted Siblings,* Smith College Studies in Social Work (1933-1934), pp. 165-166.
82. Stodghill, R. M.: "Parental Attitudes and Mental Hygiene Standards," *Mental Hygiene* (1931), 15:813-827.
82a. Sollenberger, R. T.: "Some Relationships Between the Urinary Excretion of Male Hormones by Maturing Boys and Girls and Their Expressed Interests and Attitudes," *Journal of Psychology* (1940), 9:179-189.
83. Symonds, P. M.: *Mental Hygiene of the School Child* (New York: Macmillan, 1934), 321 pp.
84. ———: *The Psychology of Parent-Child Relationships* (New York: Appleton-Century, 1939), 228 pp.
85. ———: *The Dynamics of Human Adjustment* (New York: Appleton-Century, 1946), 666 pp.
86. Tenenbaum, S.: "Attitudes of Elementary School Children to School Teachers and Classmates," *Journal of Applied Psychology* (1944), 28:134-141.
87. Terman, L. M.: *Genetic Studies of Genius,* Vol. I: *Mental and Physical Traits of a Thousand Gifted Children* (Stanford University: Stanford University Press, 1925), 648 pp.
88. Thomas, D. S., et al.: *Some New Techniques for Studying Social Behavior,* Child Development Monographs (New York: Teachers College, Columbia University, 1929), No. 1, 203 pp.
89. Tucker, C.: *A Study of the Mother's Practices and Activities of the Children in a Cooperative Nursery School* (New York: Teachers College, Columbia University).
90. Tucker, L. E.: *A Study of Problem Pupils,* Teachers College Contri-

butions to Education (New York: Teachers College, Columbia University, 1937), No. 720, 172 pp.
91. Washburn, R. W.: *A Study of the Smiling and Laughing of Infants in the First Year of Life,* Genetic Psychology Monographs (1929), No. 6:397-539.
92. Watson, G. B.: "Happiness Among Adult Students of Education," *Journal of Educational Psychology* (1930), 21:79-109.
93. Wickman, E. K.: *Children's Behavior and Teachers' Attitudes* (New York: The Commonwealth Fund Division of Publications, 1928), 247 pp.
94. Witty, P. A. and Skinner, C. E. (editors): *Mental Hygiene in Modern Education* (New York: Farrar and Rinehart, 1939), 539 pp.
95. Woodworth, R. S.: "Personal Data Sheet," described in S. D. House, *A Mental Hygiene Inventory,* Archives of Psychology (1927), No. 88, 112 pp.
96. ———: *Psychology,* fourth edition (New York: Henry Holt, 1940), 546 pp.
97. Zucker, H. J.: *Affectional Identification and Delinquency,* Archives of Psychology (1943), No. 286, 60 pp.

AUTHOR INDEX [1]

A

Abel, T. M., 380, 412
Abernethy, E. M., 120, 127
Adkens, M. M., 575, 605
Adler, A., 575, 600
Adler, M. J., 508, 513
Aldrich, C. A., 27, 28, 33, 88, 98
Aldrich, M. M., 88, 98
Allin, K. D., 250, 255
Allport, F. H., 446, 472
Allport, G. W., 502, 514, 574, 600
Alschuler, R. H., 438, 441
Amatruda, C. S., 16-18, 34
Amen, E. W., 439, 442
Ames, L. B., 42, 56, 401-402, 412
Ames, V. C., 101, 127
Anderson, H. E., 511, 514
Anderson, H. H., 149-150, 169, 210, 218, 589, 600
Anderson, H. R., 403, 412
Anderson, J. E., 3, 33, 81, 88, 99, 193, 218, 435-436, 441, 528, 529, 549, 566, 584, 593, 601, 602
Anderson, L. D., 546, 566
Appel, M. H., 147-148, 151, 152, 169
Arrington, M. G., 382, 415
Arrington, R. E., 601
Arsenian, S., 341, 344

B

Bach, G. R., 438, 441
Bain, W. E., 594, 601
Baker, E., 367
Baker, H. V., 344, 373-375, 412
Baldwin, A. L., 590, 601
Baldwin, B. T., 101, 113, 127
Bandura, L., 402, 412
Barker, C., 344
Barker, R., 297, 317
Barlow, F. P., 546, 568
Barlow, M. C., 412
Barnes, E., 456, 460, 471
Barrett, H. E., 567

Barrett, U., 512, 516
Bartelme, P. F., 18, 35
Baruch, D. W., 585, 601
Bateman, W. G., 324, 344, 456, 471
Baum, M., 130
Bavelas, A., 216, 218, 296-297, 320, 591, 601
Bayley, N., 56, 106, 108, 109, 121, 127, 246-247, 255, 349, 351, 525-526, 567, 581, 601
Bean, C. H., 344
Beasley, W. C., 13-14, 33
Beaver, A. P., 173, 218
Beck, S. J., 439, 441
Bell, J., 247, 255
Bender, L., 405, 412, 510, 514
Benezet, L. P., 46, 57
Benjamin, H., 480, 514
Benton, A. L., 16, 17, 18, 19
Bernreuter, R. G., 601
Bestor, M. F., 368
Beyer, E., 437, 441
Biber, B., 115, 127
Bienstock, S. F., 48, 58, 513, 516
Binet, A., 522
Bird, G. E., 546, 567
Bissell, V., 124, 128
Blanchard, M. B., 570
Blanton, M. G., 344
Blatz, W. E., 16, 33, 88, 91, 98, 235, 247, 250, 580, 601
Blonsky, P. P., 353, 367
Blumer, H., 506, 507, 514
Bobo, H. R., 541, 542, 568
Bolles, M. M., 251, 253, 257
Bonham, M. A., 25, 33
Bonney, M. E., 180, 181, 182, 219
Borgeson, G. M., 76, 98
Bose, R. G., 460, 471
Bott, E. A., 91, 98
Bott, H., 88, 91, 98, 358-359, 368, 480, 514
Bowles, H., 595, 601
Boyd, E., 101, 127, 361, 367

[1] Numbers denote pages on which an author's work is cited, whether by name or by reference number or both.

AUTHOR INDEX

Bradbury, D. E., 326, 347
Brandenburg, G. C., 344, 361, 368
Brandenburg, J., 361, 368
Breese, F. H., 590, 601
Bregman, E. O., 521, 536, 540, 573
Brewer, H. M., 169, 210, 218, 589, 600
Brian, C. R., 240, 257, 512, 515
Bridges, K. M., 480, 514
Bridgman, C. S., 9, 33
Brodbeck, A. J., 235, 255
Brown, E. D., 437, 441
Brown, L. S., 345
Brown, S. C., 235, 257
Browne, C. E., 413
Brownell, W. A., 512, 514
Brueckner, L. J., 512, 514
Brumbaugh, F. N., 251, 255, 256
Bryan, A. L., 353, 368
Bühler, C., 66, 98, 133, 135, 136, 137, 140, 169, 170, 256, 323, 344
Burk, F. L., 146, 170
Burks, B. S., 538, 541, 542, 567, 603
Burnham, M. P., 418, 441
Burstein, E. B., 429, 441
Burt, C., 98, 235, 256, 379, 383-384, 412
Burtt, H. E., 355, 368
Busby, L. M., 127

C

Caille, R. K., 146, 170, 199, 200, 219
Caldwell, O. W., 183, 219
Calkins, L. A., 5, 36
Campbell, E. H., 76, 98, 190, 219
Cannon, W. B., 279, 317
Cantril, H., 197, 219, 502, 514
Carlson, A. J., 10, 33
Carmichael, A. M., 446, 471
Carmichael, L., 4, 9, 33, 34, 40, 57
Carpenter, A., 127
Carr, H. A., 382, 414
Carter, H. D., 541, 567
Case, A., 460, 472
Case, I. M., 326, 347
Cattell, P., 538, 567
Cattell, R. B., 192, 219
Challman, R. C., 173, 189, 219, 230, 256, 310-314, 318, 601
Champney, H., 590, 601
Chaney, L. B., 13, 34
Chant, L., 580, 601
Chant, N., 91, 98, 247, 255

Charters, W. W., 508, 514
Chase, L., 511, 514
Chayer, M., 50, 58
Child Study Association, 503, 514
Chittenden, G. E., 153, 170
Christiansen, H., 48, 57
Christianson, E., 601
Clark, K. B., 196, 219
Clark, M. K., 196, 219
Clark, W. R., 496, 514
Coan, L., 361-362, 368
Cobb, E. A., 575, 605
Cobb, M. V., 521, 536, 540, 573
Coghill, G. E., 8-9, 34
Conklin, E. S., 459, 472
Conn, J. H., 97, 98, 252, 256
Conrad, H. W., 506, 517, 536, 540, 567, 570, 601
Cook, W. M., 357, 368
Cooper, I. M., 505, 514
Courtis, A., 46, 53, 57
Coy, G. L., 199, 223
Craig, G., 403
Crissey, O. L., 548, 567
Criswell, J. H., 219, 469-470, 472
Cromwell, H., 122, 127
Croswell, T. R., 482, 514
Curry, T., 322, 345
Cushing, H. M., 199, 220

D

Dale, E., 505, 506, 508, 515
Dallenbach, K. M., 414
Damann, V. T., 107, 127
Darcy, N. T., 328, 342, 344
Dashiell, J. F., 602
Davidson, M. A., 235, 256
Davis, A., 192, 193, 220, 277, 317
Davis, C. M., 69, 70, 71, 98
Davis, E. A., 337, 338-339, 344, 362, 368
Davis, R. A., 567
Dawe, H. C., 146, 170
Dawson, G. E., 461-462, 472
Dawson, H. L., 101, 127
Day, E. J., 336, 337, 338, 344
Dearborn, G. V., 240, 256
Dearborn, W. F., 528, 567
Dembo, T., 229, 258, 297, 317, 602
Dennis, M. G., 42-43, 57
Dennis, W., 23, 34, 42-43, 57, 140, 170, 381-382, 413
Deshaies, L., 379, 413

AUTHOR INDEX

Deutsche, J. M., 382, 413
Dewey, E., 13, 34
Dillon, M. S., 93-97, 98
Ding, G. F., 246, 256
Dolger, L., 195, 220
Dollard, J., 192, 220, 292, 317, 602
Doob, L., 292, 317
Doroschenko, O., 136, 170
Driscoll, G. P., 180, 220, 528, 568, 602
Drought, N., 239, 259
Dudycha, G. J., 353, 368
Dudycha, M. M., 353, 368
Duke, D., 124, 128
Dunbar, H. F., 226, 256
Dunford, R. E., 368
Dunn, F. W., 492, 508, 515
Dysinger, W. S., 507, 515

E

Eaton, M. T., 46, 57, 407, 413
Eberhart, J. C., 153, 170
Echerson, L. D., 330, 331, 347
Eckhardt, B. C., 204, 222
Eisenberg, A. L., 496, 503, 515
Ellis, A. C., 482, 515
Emerson, L. L., 357, 368
English, H. B., 261, 317
English, O. S., 592, 602
Erikson, E. H., 438, 441
Erwin, D., 476, 517
Eskridge, T. J., Jr., 403, 413
Eurich, A. C., 215, 222
Ezekiel, L. F., 199, 200, 220

F

Faegre, M. L., 88, 99
Fahey, G. L., 361, 369
Fallgatter, R., 6, 36
Farwell, L., 480, 481, 515
Fauquier, W., 180, 181, 220
Featherstone, W. B., 551, 552, 568
Fehlman, C., 50, 58, 77, 99, 310-314, 316-317, 318, 593, 602
Felder, J. G., 287, 317
Feldman, W. M., 61, 62, 99
Fenton, J. C., 127, 344
Fenton, N., 592, 602
Festinger, L., 229, 230, 256, 258
Fillmore, E. A., 584, 602
Finch, F. H., 553, 568
Fisher, M. S., 328-329, 335, 337, 339, 344, 361, 369

Fite, M. D., 146, 152, 168, 170, 171, 173, 201, 202, 209, 220, 221, 446, 472
Fitzgerald, J. A., 344
Fitzpatrick, F. L., 482, 515
Fitz-Simons, M. J., 236-237, 256
Flemming, C. W., 546, 552, 573
Flory, C. D., 13, 19, 25, 37, 536, 537, 568
Forbes, H. B., 6, 34
Forbes, H. W., 6, 34
Foster, J. C., 81, 99, 435-436, 441, 483, 515, 593, 602
Foster, S., 303, 305, 317
Francis, K. V., 584, 602
Frandsen, A., 546, 568
Frank, G. G., 199, 223
Frank, J. D., 230, 256
Frank, L. K., 437, 441
Freeman, F. N., 536, 537, 540, 541, 542, 568, 571
Freud, S., 19, 34, 251-252, 256, 271, 317, 440, 441, 575, 579, 592, 602
Freudenburg, E., 12, 34
Friedmann, P., 369
Fries, M. E., 25-26, 34, 580
Frosch, J., 405, 412
Furfey, P. H., 137, 170, 175, 220, 480, 515

G

Gardner, B. B., 192, 220
Gardner, G. M., 204, 222
Gardner, M. R., 192, 220
Garrett, H. E., 553, 568
Garside, H., 127
Gates, A. I., 44, 45, 57, 120, 121, 127, 492, 515
Gates, G. S., 139, 170, 294-295, 317
Geddie, L., 405, 413
Gesell, A., 10, 11, 16, 17-18, 26, 34, 41, 42, 44, 57, 62-63, 65, 68, 73, 74, 88-89, 99, 170, 226, 256, 261, 303, 318, 322, 345, 524, 568, 575, 580, 581-582, 602
Giesecke, M., 123-124, 127
Gilbertson, A. N., 456, 472
Gilchrist, J., 180, 181, 220
Gildea, H., 536, 568
Ginandes, J., 195, 220
Ginsburg, H., 10, 33
Glasshagle, E. E., 9, 38
Glueck, E., 238, 256
Glueck, S., 238, 256
Goddard, H. H., 456, 472

AUTHOR INDEX

Goldfarb, W., 235, 256
Goldman, B., 180, 215, 216, 217, 221, 223, 273, 274, 318, 414
Goodenough, F. L., 81, 99, 112, 120, 127, 128, 225, 226, 240, 256, 257, 289-292, 297, 318, 512, 515, 534, 549, 564-565, 568, 569, 602
Goodman, J. H., 345
Gordon, K., 353, 369
Gould, M. C., 386, 413
Gould, R., 230, 257
Granich, L., 382, 413
Gray, W. S., 492, 493, 515
Green, E. H., 136, 146, 147, 170, 173, 220
Green, G. H., 318, 429, 441
Greenberg, P. J., 163, 170
Greene, K. B., 199, 220
Greenhill, J. P., 16, 34
Griffin, J. D., 596, 602
Griffiths, R., 429, 435, 441
Grosmickle, F. E., 512, 515
Gruenberg, S. M., 505, 516, 520
Guernesy, M., 34
Guiler, W., 345
Guilford, J. P., 603
Gutteridge, M. V., 113, 120, 128, 358-359, 369

H

Haggerty, M. E., 564, 569
Hagman, E. P., 172, 183, 220
Hagman, R. R., 278, 282, 318
Hall, G. S., 413, 482, 515
Halverson, H. M., 42, 57, 96, 99, 105-106, 128, 252, 257
Hamilton, G. V., 234, 257, 382, 413
Harap, H., 512, 516
Hardy, M. C., 180, 220
Harms, E. E., 257, 460, 472
Harrison, M. L., 382, 402, 413
Harrower, M. R., 195, 379, 413, 444-445, 472
Hartmann, G. W., 331, 345, 357, 369, 413
Hartshorne, H., 452-453, 454-456, 472, 603
Hattendorf, K. W., 254, 257
Hattwick, B. W., 199, 220, 585, 603
Hattwick, L. A., 438, 441
Hauser, P. M., 506, 508, 514
Havighurst, R. J., 192, 193, 194, 220, 224
Hazlitt, V., 379, 380, 413
Heidbreder, E. F., 382, 413
Heiliger, L., 48, 59

Heiney, A. B., 476, 517
Heinlein, J. H., 122, 128
Hendrickson, G., 467, 474
Henle, M., 335, 345, 377, 413
Henri, C., 353, 369
Henri, V., 353, 369
Herbst, E. K., 172, 208, 223
Herring, A., 359, 369
Herzog, Herta, 496, 516
Hetzer, H., 352, 369
Hicks, J. A., 44, 57, 58, 122, 128
Hicks, V. C., 382, 414
Higgins, R. A., 129
Hildreth, G., 50, 58, 403, 413, 540, 546, 552, 569, 573
Hilgard, J. R., 44, 58, 476, 516
Hill, D. S., 372-373, 414, 456-457, 458, 472
Hirsch, N. D., 528, 569
Hoban, C. F., Jr., 508, 515
Hocking, A., 81, 100
Hoefer, C., 199, 221, 570
Hoffman, S. J., 16, 34
Holaday, P. W., 507, 516
Hollingworth, H. L., 51, 58, 356, 369, 432, 441, 559, 592, 603
Hollingworth, L. S., 536, 538, 551, 556, 558-559, 560-561, 569, 571, 572
Holmes, F. B., 133, 171, 213, 262-263, 266-275, 282, 284-286, 318, 517
Holy, T. C., 506, 516
Holzinger, K. J., 540, 541, 542, 568, 571
Honzik, M. P., 476, 517, 528, 570
Hooker, D., 4-5, 34
Hoppes, W. C., 345
Horace Mann-Lincoln Institute of School Experimentation, 485-492
Horan, K. M., 551, 572
Horn, M. D., 330, 345
Horney, K., 167, 171, 451, 575, 592, 603
Horowitz, R. E., 196, 220, 437, 442, 471, 472
Hostler, A. M., 480, 516
Huang, I., 379, 414
Hubbell, M. B., 335, 345, 377, 413
Hughes, B. O., 56, 58, 546, 550, 571
Hulson, E. L., 480, 516
Hunnicutt, C. W., 492, 516
Hunt, J. McV., 575, 603
Hunt, W., 226, 257
Hunter, W. S., 352, 369
Hurlock, E. B., 164, 171, 353, 369, 429, 441, 482, 511, 516, 593, 603

AUTHOR INDEX

I

Ilg, F. L., 10, 11, 34, 62, 63, 65, 68, 73, 74, 88-89, 99
International Kindergarten Union, 345
Irwin, O. C., 10, 12, 15, 24, 34, 35, 235, 255, 322, 345
Isaacs, S., 19, 35, 96, 99, 171, 221, 235, 252, 257

J

Jack, L. M., 205, 206, 221, 320
Jackson, E. B., 69, 99
Jenkins, G. G., 175, 221
Jenkins, L. M., 113, 122, 128
Jenkins, R. L., 566, 573
Jennings, H., 183, 221
Jensen, D. W., 538, 567
Jensen, F., 575, 604
Jensen, K., 10, 35, 399, 414
Jersild, A. T., 48, 58, 99, 128, 133, 146, 150, 168, 171, 180, 199, 202, 216, 221, 246, 262, 270, 282, 294, 318, 329, 339, 345, 376, 414, 431, 466, 472, 497-499, 513, 516
Jersild, C. L., 140, 171, 216, 217, 221, 272, 318, 376, 414, 431, 441, 466, 472
John, E., 235, 257, 278, 319
Johnson, A. D., 180, 221
Johnson, E. C., 336, 345
Johnson, G. E., 482, 517
Johnson, H. M., 115, 128
Johnson, M. W., 210, 221, 480, 517
Johnson, W., 124, 128
Jones, H. E., 58, 120, 122, 128, 257, 262, 319, 506, 517, 536, 540, 541, 544, 546, 566, 567, 570, 575, 603
Jones, M. C., 58, 261, 262, 282, 319, 603
Jones, T. D., 110-112, 113-114, 128
Jones, V., 444, 472
Jorgensen, A. P., 546, 570
Josey, C. C., 336, 345
Jung, C. G., 575, 603
Justin, F., 248-250, 257

K

Kalhorn, J., 590, 601
Kanner, L., 592, 603
Kantrow, R. W., 28-29, 35
Katz, D., 446, 472
Kaunitz, R. M., 538, 569
Kawin, E.. 199, 221, 570
Keister, M. E., 297, 301, 319, 320

Kelley, T. L., 345, 399-400, 414
Kelty, M. G., 345
Kenderdine, M., 248, 250, 257
Kephart, N., 180, 221
Kerstetter, L. M., 180, 221
Key, C. B., 476, 517, 536, 572
Kimball, E., 593, 605
Kimmins, C. W., 405, 414
Klein, M., 19, 35, 271, 319
Klineberg, O., 536, 551, 570
Klopfer, B., 439, 441
Knop, C., 27, 33
Koch, H. L., 96, 99, 173, 190, 221, 252, 257, 359, 369, 567
Kraft, R. M., 68, 100
Krey, A. C., 345, 399-400, 414
Krout, M. H., 221, 257
Krueger, L., 346, 361, 370
Krugman, M., 439, 441
Kuhlen, R. G., 180, 221
Kuo, Z. Y., 9, 35
Kwalwasser, J., 513, 517

L

La Brant, L., 346
Lacey, J. I., 414
Lacey, J. M., 399, 414
Lafore, G. G., 210, 222, 586-589, 603
Laing, A., 250, 257
Lamson, E. E., 546, 570
Landis, A. T., 251, 253, 257
Landis, C., 226, 251, 253, 257
Landreth, C., 204, 222
Langworthy, B., 505, 520
Lasker, B., 471, 472
Lawrence, E. M., 570
Lazar, M., 493, 517
Lazarsfeld, P. T., 496, 517
Leahy, A. M., 542, 543, 570
Learned, J., 48, 59
Lederer, R. K., 122, 128
Lee, B. J., 180, 221
Lee, H. W., 382, 414
Lehman, H. C., 482, 484, 517
Leonard, J. P., 215, 222
Lerner, E., 437, 441
Leuba, C., 162-163, 171
Lev, J., 319
Levy, D. M., 63, 64, 96, 97, 99, 236, 237, 252, 258
Levy, J., 237, 258
Lewi, B., 25-26, 34

AUTHOR INDEX

Lewin, K., 155, 171, 214, 216, 218, 222, 228, 229, 258, 296, 297, 317, 319, 575, 591, 601, 603
Lewis, D., 496, 517
Lewis, M. M., 322, 345
Lewis, S. J., 63, 99
Lima, M., 492, 519
Line, W., 357, 369, 598, 602
Lippitt, R., 155, 171, 173, 190, 210, 214, 222, 296, 319
Lippman, H. S., 123, 128
Lithauer, D. B., 551, 570
Little, M. F., 333, 339, 348
Lockhart, E. G., 446, 473
Loeb, M. B., 192, 224
Loftus, J. J., 180, 215-217, 221, 223, 273, 274, 318, 414
Longstaff, H. P., 503, 517
Lorenzen, C. H., 541, 542, 568
Lorge, I., 511, 517, 518, 538, 553-554, 571
Lourie, R. S., 510, 514
Louttit, C. K., 50, 61, 77, 99, 592, 603
Lowenstein, P., 207, 222
Lund, F. H., 410, 414
Lundeen, E. C., 16, 34
Lunt, P. S., 192, 224
Lyman, R. L., 346

M

McAndrew, M. B., 379, 414
McCall, L. T., 480, 519
McCann, K., 110, 129
McCarthy, D., 76, 99, 321, 325, 327, 328, 336, 337, 338, 339, 346, 380, 414
McCaskill, C. L., 110, 129
McConnell, T. R., 553, 571
McDonald, L. C., 593, 603
McElwee, E. W., 121, 129
McFarland, M. L., 160, 163, 171, 222, 308, 319, 337, 339, 348
MacFarlane, J., 437, 442, 593, 604
McGinnis, J. M., 14, 35
McGraw, M. B., 12, 13, 34, 35, 41, 46-47, 48, 58, 89-90, 99, 120, 129, 603
McHugh, G., 379, 414, 546, 571
McKinnon, K., 171, 581, 582-583, 603
McLaughlin, Sister M. A., 604
MacLean, A. H., 463, 473
McLendon, P. A., 67, 100
McNemar, Q., 541, 549, 571
Mabie, E., 346
Macaulay, E., 456, 458, 473

Macomber, F. G., 400, 415
Macoubrey, C., 536, 568
Maier, N. R., 415
Major, D. R., 122, 129
Mallay, H., 83, 85, 199, 201, 222, 352, 369
Maller, J. B., 164, 171
Manwell, E. M., 480, 518
Markey, F. V., 140, 146, 147, 150, 151, 171, 272, 294, 304, 318, 319, 376, 414, 418-419, 431, 441, 442, 466, 472
Marquis, D. P., 28, 29-32, 35, 508, 518
Marston, L. R., 604
Mathews, E., 399, 415, 595, 604
Mattson, M. L., 58
Maudry, M., 135, 171
Maurer, K. M., 546, 549, 569
May, M., 452-453, 454-456, 472, 603
Mead, C. D., 129, 339, 346
Meek, L. H., 129, 196, 222
Meier, N. C., 512, 518
Meigs, M., 345, 405, 414, 420, 509, 518
Melcher, R., 18, 35
Meltzer, H., 294-295, 319, 415, 471, 473
Mengert, I. G., 168, 171, 326, 347, 480, 518
Meredith, H. V., 101, 129
Merrill, M. A., 522, 572
Merriman, C., 541, 571
Meyers, C. E., 222
Miles, C., 353, 369
Miles, K. A., 358, 369
Miles, W. R., 129, 571
Millard, C. V., 343, 346
Miller, E., 506, 518
Miller, N. E., 292, 317, 357, 369
Miller, R. B., 575, 605
Miller, V. L., 508, 518
Millichamp, D. A., 16, 33, 250, 255
Milligan, H. V., 505, 520
Minkowski, M., 35
Mitchell, B. C., 541, 542, 568
Mitchell, C., 455, 474
Mitchell, J. C., 594, 604
Mohr, G. J., 18, 35
Monroe, R., 237, 258
Montagu, M. F., 258
Moore, H. H., 466, 473
Moore, N. E., 345
Moore, T. V., 401, 415
Moreno, J. L., 177, 222
Moro, E., 12, 35
Mowrer, O., 292, 317

AUTHOR INDEX

Munn, N. L., 357, 370
Murphy, G., 137, 171, 411, 415, 471, 473, 575, 604
Murphy, L. B., 137, 147, 156, 157-160, 171, 172, 199, 222, 245-246, 258, 437, 441, 442, 461, 465, 471, 473, 604
Murray, H. A., 438, 442, 575, 604
Mursell, J. L., 513, 518
Myers, G. C., 13, 36, 332, 346, 399, 416

N

Nash, H. B., 564, 569
Nekula, M., 135, 171
Nelson, A. K., 10, 15, 36
Nelson, E., 471, 473
Nelson, V. L., 7, 36
Nesbitt, M., 204, 222
Nestrick, M. V., 118, 129
Neugarten, B. L., 175, 222
Newbery, H., 6, 7, 36
Newcomb, T. M., 137, 171
Newman, H. H., 540, 541, 571
Nice, M. M., 346
Northway, M. L., 180, 181, 222
Nowell, J. F., 382, 415

O

Oakden, E. C., 402, 415
Oakes, M. E., 380-381, 415
Oden, M., 557-558, 573
O'Donnell, J. E., 9, 38
Ojemann, R. H., 122, 129, 271, 319
Olson, W. C., 56, 58, 546, 550, 571, 593, 604
Omwake, L., 250, 258
Osborn, J. J., 566, 571
Osborne, E. G., 156, 172, 206, 210, 223, 310-314, 318, 476, 481, 518
Osburn, W. J., 482, 518

P

Parten, M. B., 135, 172
Paterson, D. G., 121, 129
Pearson, G. H., 592, 602
Pearson, K., 539, 571
Peatman, J. G., 129
Pegram, E. L., 175, 199, 222, 574
Peiper, A., 15, 36
Perrin, F. A., 386, 413
Peterson, R. C., 469, 473, 507, 518
Peterson, T. D., 471, 473

Piaget, J., 335-336, 346, 380, 386, 415
Pilafian, G. J., 68, 100
Pintner, R., 319, 540, 571
Pistor, F., 45-46, 59, 406, 415
Plant, J. S., 575, 604
Potashin, R., 175, 223
Poull, L. E., 536, 571
Poyntz, L., 130
Pratt, K. C., 10, 11-12, 15, 36, 266, 319
Prescott, D., 180, 223
Pressey, L. C., 346
Preston, G. H., 592, 604
Preston, R. C., 405-406, 415, 604
Preyer, W., 36
Pritchard, E., 271, 319
Pritchard, M. C., 551, 572
Probst, C. A., 390-394, 415
Proctor, W. M., 572
Prugh, A. D., 204, 222
Pyle, W. H., 415

R

Ramsay, G. V., 252, 258
Rank, O., 19, 36
Rankin, M., 496, 518
Ray, A. M., 456-457
Ray, W. S., 7, 36
Rebello, S., 402, 415
Reeves, W. R., 485, 518
Reid, F. E., 518
Reininger, K., 137, 172
Remmers, H. H., 240, 258, 471, 473
Renshaw, S., 508, 518
Research Projects in Play, 518
Reynolds, M. M., 83, 85, 99, 142-143, 172
Ribble, M. A., 234, 258
Richards, T. W., 6, 7, 10, 12, 36
Richardson, R. F., 294-295, 319
Richey, A., 536, 572
Ricketts, A. F., 290, 294, 319
Rife, D. C., 122, 127
Rigney, M. G., 204, 223
Rinsland, H. D., 331, 346
Ritzman, R., 329, 334, 339, 345
Roberts, K. E., 546, 572
Roberts, L. J., 72, 100
Roberts, M. P., 482, 518
Rogers, C. R., 592, 596, 604, 605
Rorschach, H., 439, 442
Rothney, J. W. M., 528, 567
Rowland, H., 505, 518
Ruckmick, C. R., 507, 515

AUTHOR INDEX

Rugg, H., 346, 361, 370
Russell, R. W., 382, 413
Rust, M. M., 144, 172, 362-366, 370, 531-532, 572

S

Salter, M. D., 247, 255
Salusky, A. S., 172, 208, 223
Sandford, R. N., 575, 605
Sandiford, P., 541, 574
Sandin, A. A., 180, 223
Sargent, H., 437, 442
Sargent, J., 180, 221
Sargent, M., 25, 33
Scammon, R. E., 5, 36
Schacter, H. S., 358, 370
Schaeffer, G. C., 402, 416
Schaltenbrand, G., 12, 37
Schneider, E., 508, 515
Schwartz, R., 353, 369
Schwendener, N., 482, 519
Scoe, H. F., 91, 100
Scott, A. W., 120, 121, 127
Scott, F., 332, 347, 399, 416
Seagoe, M. V., 175, 223
Sears, P. S., 229, 230, 258
Sears, R., 251, 258, 292, 317
Seashore, H. G., 296-297, 320
Seashore, R. H., 330, 331, 347
Senn, M. J., 61, 100
Sewall, S., 303, 306, 307, 320
Shaffer, L. F., 400, 416, 592, 605
Shallit, R., 480, 519
Sharpe, E. F., 19, 37
Shaw, R. F., 438, 442
Sheldon, D. R., 519
Sherill, L. J., 463, 473
Sherman, A. H., 513, 519
Sherman, I. C., 13, 19, 25, 37
Sherman, M., 13, 19, 25, 37, 85, 100, 226, 258, 536, 572
Shinn, M. W., 122, 129
Shirley, M. M., 10, 13, 18-19, 26, 37, 42, 50, 59, 101, 103, 121, 129, 133, 134, 141, 172, 322, 323, 324, 327, 328, 339-340, 347, 575, 580-581, 583-584, 589, 605
Shock, N., 101, 130
Shuttleworth, F. K., 101, 130, 528, 567
Simpson, M. S., 239, 258
Simsarian, F. P., 67, 100
Skalet, M., 352, 370

Skeels, H. M., 235, 258, 357, 370, 543, 547-548, 549, 572, 574
Skinner, C. E., 592, 606
Skodak, M., 543, 549, 572, 574
Slade, I. M., 235, 256
Slater, E., 74-75, 100, 115-116, 130, 280-281, 320
Slawson, J., 596, 605
Smalley, R. E., 303, 306, 320
Smart, R. C., 120, 128
Smith College Studies in Social Work, 236, 605
Smith, L. Z., 416
Smith, M. E., 325, 333, 334, 341, 347
Smith, M. K., 330, 331, 341, 347
Smith, R. B., 605
Smith, R. S., 511, 514
Sollenberger, R. T., 576, 605
Sondergaard, A., 346, 361, 370
Sones, W. W., 509, 519
Sontag, L. W., 6, 7, 38
Spock, B., 61, 100
Spoerl, D. T., 342, 347
Stagner, R., 194, 223, 235, 239, 257, 259, 575, 605
Stanford-Binet Scale, 523
Stanger, M., 552, 573
Stanton, F. N., 496, 517
Starkweather, E. K., 546, 548, 551, 572
Steinbach, A. A., 593, 605
Steinig, B. R., 357, 370
Stemsrud, A. L., 593, 605
Stendler, C., 196, 198, 223
Stoddard, G. D., 101, 127, 129, 507, 508, 516, 519, 521, 572
Stodghill, R. M., 595, 605
Stole, L., 192, 224
Stone, J. L., 437, 441
Storm, H. C., 367, 370
Stoughton, M. L., 456-457
Stowell, M., 585, 603
Strang, R., 508, 519
Strayer, L. C., 45, 59, 337, 347
Stubbs, E. M., 15, 35
Sturt, M., 402, 415
Sun, K. H., 10, 15, 36
Sung, C., 27, 33
Svendsen, M., 207, 222, 429, 442
Symonds, P. M., 236, 259, 575, 592, 605

T

Tanner, A. E., 460, 473
Tasch, R. J., 315

AUTHOR INDEX

Taylor, C. T., 471, 473
Taylor, G. A., 44, 57
Taylor, M. W., 199, 223
Tedsten, D., 199, 223
Temple, R., 439, 442
Tenenbaum, S., 596, 605
Terman, L. M., 81, 100, 183, 223, 339, 347, 492, 519, 522, 534, 538, 556-558, 564, 567, 572, 573, 606
Thiele, C. L., 416
Thomas, D. S., 136, 172, 606
Thomas, W. S., 318
Thompson, G. G., 199, 203, 204, 223
Thompson, H., 44, 57, 524, 568, 575, 581-582, 602
Thompson, J., 226, 259
Thompson, L. A., Jr., 240, 258
Thorndike, E. L., 232, 259, 400, 416, 511, 517, 518, 519, 521, 536, 540, 541, 553, 573
Thorndike, R. L., 180, 215, 221, 223, 414, 493-494, 508, 519, 527, 528, 533, 546, 549, 552, 573
Thouless, R. H., 235, 257
Thurstone, L. L., 469, 473, 507, 518, 566, 573
Todd, T. W., 101, 130
Town, C. H., 339, 347
Tracy, F., 347
Trainham, G., 68, 100
Trettien, A. W., 370
Triche, A., 357, 369, 413
Tryon, C. M., 182, 223
Tucker, C., 606
Tucker, L. E., 606
Tuge, H., 73
Tyler, I. K., 46, 53, 59, 496, 505, 518, 519, 520

U

Updegraff, R., 48, 59, 122, 130, 172, 208, 223, 235, 258, 297, 301, 319, 357, 370, 532-533, 547-548, 572, 573

V

Valentine, C. W., 14, 37, 261, 320
Van Alstyne, D., 337, 347, 358-359, 370, 480, 481, 519
Vance, T. F., 480, 519
Vickers, V., 130
Voas, W. H., 546, 573
Vogel, M., 492, 520

W

Wahlstrom, E. L., 512, 519
Wallace, R. F., 6, 7, 37
Walsh, M. E., 199, 224
Wardwell, S., 593, 605
Waring, E. B., 573
Warner, W. L., 192, 224
Washburn, R. W., 247, 259, 581, 606
Washburne, C., 492, 505, 520
Washburne, J. N., 466, 473
Watson, G. B., 606
Watson, J. B., 231, 259, 260, 320
Weischer, V., 432, 441
Weiss, L. A., 15, 35
Wellman, B. L., 109, 110, 120, 130, 172, 175, 183, 199, 219, 224, 235, 258, 326, 347, 546, 547-548, 549, 554, 572, 573, 574
Wenger, M. A., 28, 37
Wesley, E. B., 347
West, J., 192, 224
Wheeler, L. R., 538, 574
White, M. R., 476, 517
White, R. K., 155, 171, 214, 222, 296, 319, 357, 370
White, R. W., 437, 442
Wickens, C., 28, 37
Wickens, D. D., 28, 37
Wickman, E. K., 593, 594, 606
Wilcox, J. A., 585, 601
Wiles, K., 505, 520
Willey, R. De V., 512, 520
Williams, A. M., 495-496, 520
Williams, H. M., 235, 258, 333, 339, 348, 547-548, 572
Willoughby, R. R., 251, 253, 259
Wilson, F. T., 251, 256, 415, 466, 473
Windle, W. F., 9, 38
Wingfield, A. H., 541, 574
Wislitzky, S., 136, 172, 352, 369
Witmer, H. L., 259, 593, 605
Witty, P. A., 482, 484, 508, 517, 520, 592, 606
Woelfel, N., 505, 518, 519, 520
Wolf, T. H., 163, 172, 360, 370
Woodworth, R. S., 595, 606
Woodyard, E., 77, 99, 310-314, 318, 521, 536, 540, 573
Wooley, H. T., 42, 91, 100
Wright, B. A., 169, 172, 224
Wright, H. F., 293, 320

Wright, M. E., 224
Wrightstone, J. W., 180, 215, 224

Y

Young, I., 508, 520
Young, M., 50, 58

Z

Zeligs, R., 467, 474
Zorbaugh, H. W., 510, 520
Zucker, H. J., 585-586, 606
Zyve, C., 348

SUBJECT INDEX

A

Ability in relation to interests, 478
Abstractions, understanding of, 384 ff.
Academic concepts, children's understanding of, 398 ff.
Academic subjects, interest in, 487 ff.
Academic work of gifted children, 557 ff.
Activity, pleasure in, 240-242
Adjustment: as influenced by affection, 234-239; problems of, 591 ff.
Adoption, 544 (*see also* Foster children)
Adult practices in relation to children's fights and quarrels, 151 (*see also* Parent-child and Teacher-child relationships)
Affection: development of, 231 ff.; influence of, on adjustment, 234 ff.; of child for parent, 310-314 (*see also* Parent-child relationship; Sympathy)
Aggressive attitudes in gifted children, 560
Aggressive behavior, 146 ff., 287 ff.; in relation to adult practices, 149, 151-152, 155
Aggressiveness (*see also* Anger, Fighting, Prejudice)
Altruism, 466 ff. (*see also* Coöperation, Friendship, Generosity, Sympathy)
Amblystoma, 8
Anger, 23-24, 287-302; as a component of jealousy, 302; bearing of imagination on, 426; moral pressures against, 447 (*see also* Fighting, Jealousy, Prejudice, Resistant behavior)
Anticipation, phenomenon of, 5, 55, 98
Anxiety, 275 (*see also* Fear)
Appetite (*see* Eating)
Archaic behavior tendencies, persistence of, 54-55, 411
Arithmetic, mastery of, in relation to maturity level, 46
Art, children's activities in, 48-49, 115-117, 491, 512-513 (*see also* Music, Painting, Projective techniques)
Articulation, 323-326
Ascendant behavior, 204, 206
Aspiration: influence of, on emotional susceptibility, 229; level of, 227-228, 229-230
Associates, influence of, on mental growth, 548
Attention span, 357 ff.
Attitudes: influence of movies on, 507 ff. (*see also* Interests, Moral development, Prejudice, Emotion); of parents, 3-4, 586 ff. (*see also* Parent-child relationship); toward motor activity, 107, 118-119; toward sex, 252-253; with regard to genital organs, 95-97; with regard to process of elimination, 93-94
Authoritarianism in early moral development, 444
Authoritarian techniques, effects of, 587 ff.
Autocratic practices, influence of, 210-215; modifiability of, 591
Awareness of people, 372

B

Behavior problems, 77, 592 ff. (*see also* Adjustment)
Beliefs: effects of desires on, 411; religious (*see* Religion)
Belonging, desire for, 131, 185-187
Bible, children's interest in, 461-462
Bilingualism, 340-343
Biography, interest in, 493
Birth, 1; behavior following, 1 ff.; trauma, 2
Birth order and intelligence, 566
Birth rate in relation to intelligence, 564 ff.
Bladder control (*see* Elimination)
Blocks, use of, 115-116
Bodily contacts, in life of newborn, 21 ff.
Bodily size, 100-101
Boredom, 240 ff.
Bowel control (*see* Elimination)
Boy-girl relationship, 189-191
Bullying, 156
Buttoning, effects of early practice on, 44

C

Camp experience, influence of, 207-208, 210, 476-477

SUBJECT INDEX

Cause and effect, children's understanding of, 381 ff.
Cephalo-caudal direction of growth, 5
Cerebral cortex, 12
Character (*see* Moral development, Personality)
Cheating, 444 (*see also* Moral development)
Chewing, 66-67
Cleavage between the sexes, 190-191
Climbing, 44, 47
Combativeness, varying functions of, 149
Comics, children's reactions to, 508 ff.
Communication (*see* Language)
Companions, imaginary, 429 ff.
Companionship between parents and children, 310, 314
Competition, 54, 160-168; unwholesome features of, 167-168 (*see also* Jealousy)
Concepts, 389 ff.; as revealed by children's questions, 363-367; moral, 444 ff. (*see also* Reasoning)
Conditioned response in neonate, 27 ff.
Conflict: emotional, 271; moral, 447 ff.
Conflicts, children's, with one another, 146 ff.
Constancy: of popularity ratings, 181-182; of the I.Q., 527 ff., 533 ff.
Constructiveness, 204
Coöperation, 135, 161, 168 ff., 455
Correlation, illustration of method of, 525-526
Crying, 3, 26-27, 133, 245-246
Cultural factors, influence of: on children's interests, 477 ff.; on concept formation, 409-410; on early childhood experiences, 2-3; on play, 208; on prejudices, 468 ff. (*see also* Social class, Socio-economic status)
Cup, use of, 73-74
Curiosity, evidences of, in gifted children, 556; examples of, 360-367

D

Daydreams (*see* Imagination)
Death, illustrative questions concerning, 365-366
Deceit, studies of, 451 ff.
Deductive reasoning, 382-383
Delayed reaction, 358 (*see also* Memory)
Delinquency as related to attitudes toward parents, 585-586
Democratic behavior, 216-217

Democratic techniques, effects of, 209-216, 587
Dependence, 55, 131
Deprivation, early effects of, 42-43
Desire, influence of, on thinking, 411
Desires, vicarious satisfaction of, 510 (*see also* Make-believe)
Development, general characteristics of, Chapter II, 39 ff.
Developmental objectives in mental growth, 351
Dextrality (*see* Handedness)
Discrimination of strangers and familiars, 133
Discussion, children's contribution to, 372-375
Dislike of people, 140
"Dominative behavior," 149
Draw-a-man test, 296-297
Drawing as a projective technique, 438
Dreams, 432 ff.
Drives, discussion of, 226 ff.
Dynamics of development, 50-51 (*see also* Emotion, Motivation)

E

Early memories, 352 ff.
Eating, 60 ff.
Educational status as factor in moral development, 445 ff.
Education of the gifted child, 559 ff. (*see also* School)
Egocentricity, 380-381
Egocentric speech, 334-336
Elimination, 60, 88 ff.
Emotion, 225-320; concealment of, 578 ff. (*see also* Dreams, Make-believe); effects of, on thinking, 410 ff.; of the newborn child, 19 ff., 225-226
Emotional adjustment: in relation to bilingualism, 342-343; in relation to moral conduct, 451
Emotional behavior in relation to prematurity, 19
Emotional problems, vicarious release of, 510
Emotional stability of gifted children, 556
Environment: at birth, 2-3; influence of, on mental ability, 529, 539 ff.; influence of, on personality development, 582, 584 ff. (*see also* Cultural factors, Parent-child relationship, Social class, Socio-

SUBJECT INDEX

economic status); influence on, of factors in children, 582
Example: as factor in children's fears, 278-282; as factor in moral training, 447-448; influence of, in motor learning, 119
Expressions of emotion: adult judgment of, 225-226; changes with age in, 263 ff.
Expressive reactions, perception of, 139

F

Failure, subjective factors determining, 229
Family, resemblances in I.Q., 539 ff. (*see also* Parent-child relationships, Sibling relationships)
Family size and intelligence, 564 ff.
Father, role of, 315
Fatigue, 85; effect of, on irascibility, 292-293
Fear, 24, 54, 134, 260-287; bearing of ability to imagine on, 426; factors influencing (*see also* Motion pictures, Radio programs); in dreams, 435 ff.; influence of intellectual understanding on, 410-411; in relation to sleep, 86-87
Feeblemindedness (*see* Mental deficiency)
Feeding: behavior, 60 ff.; in relation to early learning, 28-32; problems, 77 ff.; schedule, neonate's response to differences in, 30-32
Feeling and emotion, 225-320
Fetal behavior, relation of condition of mother to, 6
Fetus: behavior of, 5-9; development of, 4-7
Fighting, 146 ff.
Finger sucking, 62-64
Food preferences, 76 ff.
Foster children, mentality of, 540 ff.
Free association, 440
Friendly behavior, 168 ff.
Friends, resemblance of, in honesty, 453
Friendships, children's, 173 ff.
Fringer, 207, 243
Frustration, 296-297 (*see also* Anger)

G

Games, children's preferences in, 480 ff.
Generalized activity, 10
Generalizing, development of capacity for, 375-376
Generosity, studies of, 454 ff. (*see also* Altruism)
Genital organs (*see* Sex)

Gifted children, 555 ff.
God, children's ideas of, 459 ff.
Grasp reflex, 12-13
Group behavior (*see* Social)
Growth and learning, 39 ff.
Growth of understanding, 349-442
Guilt: in connection with moral conflict, 447; in relation to fear, 271

H

Habits: archaic, 54-55; developmental revision of, 52-53; influence of, on ways of thinking, 411; "routine," 60-100
Handedness, 122-126
"Happiest day," children's accounts of, 486 ff.
Hearing, in neonate, 15
Heredity, 2; influence of, on mental ability, 538 ff.
Heroes, children's, 456 ff.
Hierarchies, social, 188-189
Honesty, studies of, 451 ff.
Hopping, 113
Hostility, 287 ff.; devious expressions of, 295 ff.; disguised, 156; rationalization of, 450; theory of vicarious release of, 510 (*see also* Aggressiveness, Anger, Fighting, Prejudice)
Humor, 247-251
Hunger, 19, 27; as a primary drive, 226; effect of, on irascibility, 292-293 (*see also* Feeding behavior)
Hurdles of development, 52

I

"I," use of, 333-334
Ideals, children's, 443 ff., 456 ff.
Imaginary companions, 429 ff.
Imagination, 417-442; some emotional consequences of, 426
Independence, early beginnings of development of, 55
Indigenous motivation, 51-52
Individual differences: in fetal behavior, 7; in pattern of academic progress, 343 (*see also* Intelligence, Personality)
Individualism as complement of socialization, 132
Individuation, 8-10
Inductive reasoning, 382-383
Infantile behavior, 56
Infantile experiences, obliviscence of, 352-355

Information: children's, 389 ff. (*see also* Reasoning); children's interests in, 495

"Insecurity," 271, 275; as indicated by a tendency to tease, 156

"Integrative behavior," 149

Intellectual development, role of make-believe in, 417-422

Intellectual factors in fear, 410

Intelligence: definitions of, 521-522; development of, 521-574; early signs of, 29; in relation to: cheating, 452; generosity, 455; humor, 250; language development, 339-340; play interests, 484; popularity, 182; reading (*see* Reading)

Intelligence tests, resistance to, 144

Interaction between aspects of development, 56, 101, 411 ff.

Interests, 475-520; as revealed by topics of conversation, 375; in sex, 253-254; in the Bible, 461-462; occupational, 563 (*see also* Daydreams); of gifted children, 556

Introspection, limited capacity for, 377, 378

I.Q. (*see* Intelligence)

J

Jealousy, 302-309
Jokes, children's, 250-251
Joy (*see* Pleasure)
Jumping, 107-109, 113

K

Kindergarten, interests shown in, 480 ff.

L

Language: development of, 321-348; effects of early training on, 45

Laughter, 247-251

Leadership, 182-184, 204

Learning: and growth, 39 ff.; as factor in prejudice, 467 ff.; during early days of life, 27 ff.; in language development, 337; in relation to adult preoccupations, 118; of meaningless materials, 355; of social techniques, 153; role of, in development of interests, 477 ff.; role of, in fear, 263 ff., 275-276; role of incentives in, 511 (*see also* Developmental revision of habits, Memory); role of, in overcoming fear, 279 ff.; through integration of specific skills, 113-114

"Liked best" teachers, 211-213
"Liked least" teachers, 211-213

Likes, children's, studies of, 486 ff. (*see also* Desires, Interests, Motivation)

Locomotion, 41 ff., 102 ff.; in relation to maturity level, 46

Logic, 401 (*see also* Reasoning)

Loquacity, 329

Love (*see* Affection)

M

Make-believe, 417 ff.; as means of vicarious release of emotional tension, 510; early manifestations of, 417 ff.; functions of, 419-421; in children's reading interests, 492 ff. (*see also* Comics, Movies, Radio programs)

Masturbation, 97, 252

Maturation: and learning, 39 ff.; in relation to language development, 337; role of, in children's fears, 261-262

Maturity, individual differences in, at birth, 16-19

Meanings, associated with use of language, 331 ff.

Memory, early signs of, 351-353

Mental ability, relation to motor, 120-121

Mental deficiency, 561 ff.

Mental development, 349-442 (*see also* Imagination, Intelligence, Morals)

Mental growth, 521-574; early signs of, 349-351

Mental hygienists, attitudes of, 593 ff.

Misconceptions, examples of, 387-389, 394

Moral concepts in relation to socio-economic status, 195-196

Moral development, 442 ff.; of gifted children, 556

Moro reflex, 12

Mother, impact of personality of, on child, 485 ff. (*see also* Parent-child relationships)

Motion pictures, children's reactions to, 505 ff.

Motivation, 50-51, 226 ff.; and moral behavior, 440 ff., 453; in connection with competition, 164; role of, in personality development, 578 ff. (*see also* Emotions, Interests)

Motor ability, specificity of, 117, 120 ff.

Motor achievement tests, 109, 112, 113, 116

Motor behavior in children's play, 480 ff.

SUBJECT INDEX

Motor development, 101 ff.; interaction with intellectual, 56, with social, 56; role of, in adjustment, 117
Mouthing, 65-66
Movies (*see* Motion pictures)
Music, children's interests in, 512-513

N

Nap (*see* Sleep)
Needs, discussion of, 226 ff.
Negativism, 141 (*see* Resistant behavior)
Nervous habits, 204
Nervous system, immaturity of, at birth, 2, 10, 12, 13, 20 (*see also* Cerebral cortex)
Newborn child, emotional behavior of, 225-226
"Newer" practices, 215-216
Norms, developmental, 524
Nursery school: comparison of two programs in, 203-204; experience, effects of, 189 ff.; experience, effects of, on I.Q., 538 ff., 545 ff.; limitations of, 114
Nutrition (*see* Feeding behavior)

O

Occupational status (*see* Socio-economic status)
Organization of behavior, 7-9
Overprotection, 236 ff.

P

Pain in newborn child, 22
Painting as a projective technique, 438
Parallel behavior, 135
Parental attitudes in relation to prematurely born child, 18-19
Parental influence on food preferences, 76-77
Parent-child relationships, 296-297; as affected by adult methods of discipline, 209 ff.; at birth, 2-4; bearing of nursery school on, 199; role of, in anger, 291 ff.; role of, in children's fears (*see* Fear) (*see also* Affection, Anger, Democratic practices, Jealousy, Overprotection, Rejection); role of, in children's questions, 367; role of, in development of prejudices, 468; role of, in personality development, 585 ff.; role of, in religious training, 459-461; role of, in sex development, 255; various emotional components of, 309-319

Parents: attitudes of, compared with mental hygienists, 595; mention of, as heroes and ideals, 458; practices of, in relation to attitudes, 589 ff.
Peer culture (*see* Social behavior)
Perception, 355 ff.; of social relationships, 139
Persistence of effort (*see* Attention span)
Personality: consistent tendencies in development of, 580 ff.; development of, 575-606; early manifestations of, 25 ff., 580; effects of religious training on, 465; "external" aspects of, 575-576; influence of archaic habits on, 54-55; in relation to interests, 479; "internal" aspects of, 577-579; parent's appreciation of child's, 312; possible fetal influences on, 7; problems of development of, in gifted children, 558 ff.
Physical ability, relation of, to mental ability, 120
Pictures, use of, as a projective technique, 438
Plantar reflex, 11-12
Play (*see also* Games); equipment, influence of, 208; techniques, 437-438
Pleasure, 240 ff. (*see also* "Happiest day," Interests, Likes)
Pleasures in child rearing, 310-314
Popularity, 180-182
Potential interests, 476 ff.
Poverty, 194
Prayer, meaning of, 462-463
Predictive value of mental tests, 525 ff.
Prehension, 41 ff., 104 ff.; table of advances in, 106
Prejudice, 467 ff. (*see also* Hostility)
Premature birth, 16-19
Pressure, response to, by neonate, 16
Prestige in daydream content, 431
Principles of development, 39 ff.
Problems: in behavior, 77, 592; involved in child rearing, 310-312
Projective methods, 437-441
Property rights, understanding of, 153
Propinquity as a factor in determining friendships, 175
Proximo-distal direction of development, 6

Q

Quarreling, 146 ff.
Questions: children's, 360-367; concerning sex, 254

R

Race: attitudes (*see* Prejudice); cleavage, 469-470
Radio: effects of, 503 ff.; listening and sleep, 87; programs, children's interests in, 496 ff.
Rage (*see* Anger)
Rationalization, 55, 450; of prejudice, 470-471 (*see also* Emotional influences on thinking)
Reaction time, 112
Readiness (*see* Maturation, Learning)
Reading, children's interests in, 490 ff. (*see also* Comics)
Reasoning, 379 ff.
Reflex action, 11-13
Regression, 36; in anger, 297; through a show of fear, 285
"Rejection," 236 ff.; by peers, 187 (*see also* Unpopularity)
Religion, 459 ff.
Resistance, effects of, on performance in intelligence tests, 531-532
Resistant behavior, 141 ff.
Rest (*see* Sleep)
Restraint of movement, 23
Reversion to earlier forms of behavior, 55-56
Rhythm, effect of practice on, 48
Rivalry, 161-168 (*see also* Competition, Jealousy)
Roller skating, 47
Rorschach test, 439
Routine behavior, 310-314
Routine habits, 60 ff.

S

Scapegoat, 296
School: bearing of, on anger, 301; boredom in, 243; effects of, on intelligence test scores, 545 ff., 553 ff.; role of, in children's interests, 487 ff.; subjects (*see* Arithmetic, Art, Maturation, Learning, Reading, Spelling)
Self: awareness and appraisal of, 138, 198, 228-229, 377-379; effects of ideas about, on emotional reactions, 299; factors limiting understanding of, 376-378, 577 ff. (*see also* Personality, "Internal aspects" of)
Self-assertive behavior, 217
Self-demand: feeding behavior, 66 ff.; sleep, 83
Self-help in eating, 73 ff.
Self-improvement as feature in children's interests, 487
Sex: aspects of development of, 251-255; behavior in early childhood, 95-98; cleavage, 175; differences, anatomical, children's awareness of, 97-98; differences in combativeness, 150 ff.; differences in language development, 339; in radio interests, 500-501; questions concerning, 254 ff.
Shyness, 207 (*see also* Fear)
Sibling relationships, 3, 312 (*see also* Affection, Jealousy, Parent-child relationships, Sympathy)
Siblings, resemblance of: in honesty, 453; in intelligence, 539 ff.
Sight during first days of life, 14-15
Singing, 48, 513
Skill as related to interest, 479
Skills: bearing of anger on, 300; influence of, on social behavior, 204-206 (*see also* Motor development)
Sleep, 60, 80 ff.; disturbance of, by radio and movies, 507 (*see also* Dreams)
"Slow learners," 561 ff.
Smiling, 133, 140
Social adjustment in relation to bilingualism, 341-342
Social behavior, 130-224
Social class, 192 ff.; and child rearing, 193-194; moral training in relation to, 195-196, 445 ff., 452
Social development, interaction with: intellectual development, 134; motor development, 56
"Social distance," 190, 468
Socialization as revealed by language usage, 326
Social pressures in relation to fear, 264
Social status, children's awareness of, 196-197
Social studies: children's understanding of concepts in, 398 ff.; learning of, 46
Socio-economic status: children's awareness of, 192 ff.; in relation to child training, 193-194; in relation to gains in I.Q., 547 ff.; in relation to intelligence, 564 ff.; in relation to language development, 337-338; relation of, to moral concepts and conduct, 445 ff., 452
Sociometric techniques, 177 ff.
Space, concepts of, 401 ff.

SUBJECT INDEX

Special senses, 13 ff.
Spelling, learning of, 46, 53
"Spoiling," 298 (*see also* Overprotection)
Spontaneity, changes in, 511-512
Spontaneous: food demands, 66 ff.; practice, 87; use of growing ability, 50-51
Standards set for self, 229-230 (*see also* Competition)
Stanford-Binet Scale, 522
Status, social, 185-187; awareness of, 138, 192-193; striving for, 305
Stealing, 453
Story completion, use of, as a projective technique, 439
Strangers, fear of, 134
Strength, 112-113
Stubbornness (*see* Resistant behavior)
Success, subjective factors in, 229 ff.
Sucking, 10, 11, 61-64
Symbols: of social class, 198; use of, 356
Sympathy, 157-160, 244-245
Synaesthesia, 432
Syndromes in behavior of parents, 590

T

Tabooed language, 94
Talents and abilities in relation to social behavior, 207
Taste, response to, by neonate, 15
Teacher-child relationships, 316-317, 453
Teachers, characteristics of, 211-213
Teamwork, 138; intellectual, 374-375
Teasing, 156
Temperature, response to, by neonate, 15
Terror dreams, 435 ff.
Thinking, 379 ff.
Threats, role of, in fear, 276 ff.

Throwing, 113
Thumb sucking, 62-64; use of (*see* Prehension)
Time, children's questions concerning, 363-365; concept of, 45, 401 ff.
Tricycling, 47
Tumescence, 96-97
Twins: intellectual resemblances of, 540 ff.; language development of, 338; personality resemblances of, 581

U

Unconscious tendencies, 579 (*see also* Emotional influences on thinking, Rationalization, Self-awareness)
Unpopularity, 174
Urination (*see* Elimination)

V

Vanity, role of, in parental anger, 299
Vicarious experience through comics, 509 (*see also* Imagination, Make-believe)
Vision as a feature of total bodily movement, 9
Vocabulary, 330 ff. (*see also* Language)
Vocalizations, early, 321-322

W

Walking, impact of, 104
War, intellectual reaction to, 404-405
Wheel toys, use of, 110-112
"Wholeheartedness," 51-52
Wishes: altruistic, 466; examples of, 376-377, 378
Worry (*see* Fear)
"Worst happenings" as compared with fears, 272